Exploring Health Care Careers

THIRD EDITION

VOLUME 2

Ferguson
An imprint of Infobase Publishing

Exploring Health Care Careers, Third Edition

Ferguson
An imprint of Infobase Publishing
132 West 31st Street
New York NY 10001

ISBN-10: 0-8160-6448-2
ISBN-13: 978-0-8160-6448-9

Exploring health care careers. — 3rd ed.
p. cm.
Includes bibliographical references and index.
ISBN 0-8160-6448-2 (hc : alk. paper)
1. Medicine—Vocational guidance—Juvenile literature.
I. Title: Health care careers.
R690.E97 2006
610.69—dc22 2005018173

Ferguson books are available at special discounts when purchased in bulk quantities for businesses, associations, institutions, or sales promotions. Please call our Special Sales Department in New York at (212) 967-8800 or (800) 322-8755.

You can find Ferguson on the World Wide Web at http://www.fergpubco.com

Text design by Mary Susan Ryan-Flynn
Cover design by Salvatore Luongo

Printed in the United States of America

VB Hermitage 10 9 8 7 6 5 4 3 2

This book is printed on acid-free paper.

CONTENTS

Volume 1

Volume 2

MEDICAL LASER TECHNICIANS

Medical history may be in the making as Adam Palmer adjusts the strength of the laser in the operating room. Adam looks across the length of the patient's body at the surgeon holding the laser and waits for any signal that will indicate he should lower the laser's power. A probe equipped with lights and a camera illuminates tiny glowing areas inside the patient's prostate. All members of the surgical team watch a monitor that captures the probe's image. The glowing areas have been magnified several times; these are cancerous cells. Armed with the laser, the surgeon directs the precise beam of light toward these cells. Adam, the medical laser technician assisting on the surgery, watches the monitor as, one by one, the small glowing areas wink out as they come into the laser's range.

The patient on the operating table suffers from prostate cancer. Two days earlier the patient was injected with a special drug that cancerous cells retain for a long time. When the light from a laser reaches the drug within the cancerous cells, it creates a chemical reaction that in turn produces a toxin, or poison, within the cancerous cell. This toxin destroys the cancerous cell completely and instantly.

This special photodynamic therapy is part of an ongoing research project at the Goldman Laser Institute at the Jewish Hospital in Cincinnati, Ohio. If this therapy is proven successful, Adam will be part of the medical team that developed a new way to treat prostate cancer.

Definition
Medical laser technicians test, service, operate, and install laser systems in medical or research environments.

Alternative Job Titles
Equipment technicians
Biomedical equipment technicians
Minimally invasive surgeons

High School Subjects
Computer science
Technical/shop

Personal Skills
Mechanical/manipulative
Technical/scientific

Salary Range
$30,000 to $40,000 to $53,000+

Educational Requirements
High school diploma, associate's degree

Certification or Licensing
Voluntary

Outlook
About as fast as the average

DOT
078

GOE
14.05.01

NOC
3212

O*NET-SOC
29-2012.00

What Does a Medical Laser Technician Do?

Medical laser technicians help design, test, install, and repair laser systems and fiber-optic equipment. Medical laser technicians work with medical and research equipment and instrumentation. They routinely perform tests and take measurements using lasers and electronic devices. Medical laser technicians gather data, perform calculations, and prepare reports based on the data they have accumulated. In addition, they must be able to read and interpret shop drawings, diagrams, schematics, and sketches. Based on these drawings, medical laser technicians might build parts or direct the assembly of components.

Medical laser technicians follow safety precautions when they use or service lasers, and when they clean and maintain the lasers they use. They may perform regular alignment procedures on optical systems that use lasers, in order to document the reliability of their measurements and to safeguard against inaccuracies in their measurements or testing. Medical laser technicians may also repair lasers and troubleshoot technical problems as they arise during the use of a laser or fiber optics system in a surgery or other medical situation.

Lingo to Learn

Active medium Usually a solid or gas that produces light by stimulated emission.

Coherence Light waves in step.

Directionality Light with little radiation.

Excitation mechanism A laser's source of energy, such as an electric current or flashlamp.

Feedback mechanism In laser, a pair of mirrors aligned to reflect the laser light back and forth through the active medium.

Laser An acronym for Light Amplification by Stimulated Emission of Radiation. This is the scientific description of the process that creates laser light.

Monochromaticity Light that is made up of a single color.

Output coupler A partially transparent mirror that allows some coherent light to leave the laser device in the form of the output beam.

While all medical laser technicians do not necessarily perform every one of the tasks just described, many different jobs require that a medical laser technician be able to perform any number of them. Much depends on where in the medical community the medical laser technician works and what type of position he or she holds. In the past, the use of lasers in the medical world was primarily restricted to the surgical environment. Today, lasers are used in nearly every medical specialty at locations as varied as hospitals, clinics, and the offices of solo medical practitioners. Lasers and fiber optic technology are used in the medical world for surgery, ophthalmology, dermatology, and research.

What Is It Like to Be a Medical Laser Technician?

"We do about a hundred laser surgeries a month," says Adam Palmer, a medical laser technician at the Goldman Laser Institute. "On a typical day, I'm at the hospital by 7:00 A.M. and in surgery by 7:30, where I may be for the rest of the day." Adam is one of two medical laser technicians employed by the hospital. His preparations for surgery include readying the lasers that will be used during the operation. "Some lasers need to heat up, some need to cool down," Adam explains. "While I warm up or cool down the laser, I make sure that all the necessary accessories, attachments, and materials are in the operating room."

Tim Putnam, director of Laser/Advanced Surgery at St. Mary's Medical Center in Evansville, Indiana, underscores the impact lasers have had on the medical field. "Fifteen years ago, if you walked into an operating room it looked more like a carpenter's shop. There was hardly anything high tech in the room, with the exception of the anesthesia machine. The same operating room, today, looks more like people getting ready to launch the space shuttle."

Increasingly, physicians and surgeons are turning to less invasive methods of surgery and other treatments to cure their patients' problems, and lasers are among the most promising solutions. Medical laser technicians provide support to surgeons and other physicians who use lasers and fiber optic equipment. Before getting into the medical field, Tim worked as a laser technician in other areas, including field service and research.

"Working as a field service laser technician is very different from being part of team in an operating room," he says. "Laser technicians are the technical experts during the operation and must respond quickly and efficiently to any problems."

As Tim explains it, the physician or surgeon is the expert on the patient's needs, while the medical laser technician is the expert on the technology being used. So, while the doctor is the only person who actually uses a laser instrument and has direct contact with the patient, the medical laser technician has to be there to make recommendations; to fine-tune the many attachments, instruments, and machines; and to assist the physician in the event that a technical problem occurs.

Just as a golfer uses many different clubs to hit a ball, depending on the situation, a surgeon needs to choose among many different instruments. Not only do lasers have a multitude of functions, but there are many different ways to deliver a laser to a patient's body. A surgeon might use several different methods during one surgery. A surgeon, for example, could choose to deliver lasers through a microscope, through a fiber-optic tube, or through a contact tip that transfers the energy to the patient's tissue in the form of heat. The surgeon knows what cut to make and where to make it. Medical laser technicians advise how to use laser equipment to make the surgery possible. In addition, medical laser technicians help set up reflection devices, similar to mirrors, which are used to aim the laser beam in very hard-to-reach spots.

Once the surgery is in progress, Adam notes, the medical laser technician monitors the laser, sometimes advising the surgeon on a particular power setting or suggesting the best attachment to use to achieve whatever the surgeon wants to do. Frequently, this means helping direct the laser beam to access a hard-to-reach site inside the patient's body. An example of such a surgery is in the case of an enlarged prostate. The surgeon and medical laser technician carefully position the laser to vaporize a portion of the prostate so that urine is allowed to pass through to the bladder.

In addition to helping assist the surgeon with the laser, the technician has a number of other duties. While the laser is in use, the medical laser technician makes certain that everyone in the operating room, including the patient, is protected from the laser by safety goggles. If there are any windows in the operating suite that the laser can penetrate, the windows are covered and "laser in use" signs are posted on all doors and windows of the operating room suite. Finally, the medical laser technician is responsible for filling out special forms that record the lasers used during the surgery, the strength and other settings for the lasers, and any changes made to those settings either by the medical laser technician or the surgeon. Billing notes are also taken down on these forms, including the use of additional materials or surgical drapes. These records then become part of the patient's surgical file. Should there ever be a question about the surgery, the medical laser technician will have a complete record of everything he or she did during the operation.

As the director of a unit, an average day for Tim means checking the operating room schedule first thing in the morning to make certain that a medical laser technician and nurse are covering all of the laser/advanced surgery cases. "If they're not covered," Tim says, laughing, "that's where I am all day—in surgery." Normally, he divides his day between assisting in surgery, working with new instrumentation, handling administrative tasks, and reading up on new techniques and instruments.

Adam's days are divided among his many responsibilities: He might be in the operating room, scheduling cases, making certain equipment is tested and ready to be used, repairing and maintaining laser equipment, taking stock of necessary accessories and ordering them when needed, or working on a research project with a surgeon or research team.

"The research projects vary," explains Adam. "A doctor may see a technique and want to conduct his own study to see if widespread use of the technique is really warranted, or if it's just a lot of hype. For example, I might work on a blind study examining whether or not lasers should be used to treat wrinkles. Half of the participants' upper lips would be treated with dermabrasion, a method commonly used by plastic surgeons to reduce wrinkles, and the other half of the participants' upper lips would be treated with lasers."

The project described at the beginning of this article is another research project Adam is involved in. It combines laser-and-drug therapy for cancer treatment. This process is used to treat many types of cancer, but is now being approved for prostate cancer treatment. "The photodynamic therapy project is at least 15 years old, but it's taken that long for an interesting reason. The FDA has its procedures for approving drugs, and it has its procedures for approving techniques. But this case is one of the first times a drug and a technique [together] have been approved by the FDA," says Adam.

Do I Have What It Takes to Be a Medical Laser Technician?

Having a calm demeanor and good judgment are important qualities for this field. "You definitely have to have a special type of personality to work in the medical field," Adam says. "Doctors can be extremely arrogant. I think they're not used to having their instructions and ideas questioned or challenged by others. They're used to giving orders, no questions asked," he explains. "Sometimes I think they like to test you, to see what your breaking point is. So, in order to work with them, you have to let a certain amount slide off you, but you also need to stand up to doctors to let them know you won't just sit back and take it all the time." Adam gives a short laugh, "You have to know when to stand up for yourself and when to let things slide."

Adam warns prospective medical laser technicians about the communication difficulties inherent in the medical field. "I don't know of any other field or industry that's like this. For example, in industry, if you have an idea, you can just go up to the engineer and tell him your idea. It's strange, but in medicine, you have to really think about how you bring things up. You have to be clever about it. You can't just go up to the surgeon and say, 'I think it could be done better this way.' Unfortunately, things don't work that way. Sometimes it might even come down to letting the surgeon think it was his idea." Adam doesn't believe in kidding people about how tough-skinned you need to be to survive in the field. "If your feelings are easily hurt, this isn't the best place to work."

On the other hand, Adam loves the variety of his job. "Laser techs working in industry often get stuck doing the same thing, day in and day out. Every day is usually different in the operating room. I like that there are always new things to learn, new types of procedures to master."

Medical laser technicians can always expect some degree of stress, pressure, and even danger. Tim clearly states how these three elements combine in his work. "If equipment fails or a physician is using it incorrectly, it is the laser technician who has the responsibility to intercede—even during an operation—if the patient could be in jeopardy."

Laser technicians working in the medical field also need to be able to work efficiently in a variety of circumstances. Tim's job requires him to work with very little discussion while in surgery. Later, however, working with the same doctor on an experimental instrument, Tim may have to voice his opinion without feeling intimidated by the doctor. He agrees that laser technicians working in the medical field need to feel comfortable around surgeons. "A surgical team operates with very little conversation. Familiarity with procedures and with the physicians is necessary to respond to any situation that might occur with the equipment," Tim says. "The laser technician is a liaison between the physicians and the equipment."

To Be a Successful Medical Laser Technician, You Should . . .

- be able to successfully communicate ideas and disagree when necessary
- be able to work with others
- be interested in technology and be willing to learn new systems as they come along
- have good hand-eye coordination

How Do I Become a Medical Laser Technician?

Tim received an associate's degree in lasers and optics from Vincennes University in Vincennes, Indiana. After graduating, he went to work in research at a hospital in Cincinnati, Ohio, where he received a lot of practical, on-the-job experience.

"A lot of the technology involving lasers was just blossoming when I began in research," Tim says. "I was lucky, in that sense, because it was an incredibly dynamic field then. It still is a very dynamic field, but recent pressures to keep the costs down for insurance purposes have made the field tighten up a bit, in terms of spending money on research."

EDUCATION

High School

If you are interested in becoming a medical laser technician, you should start preparing for this highly technical field while still in high school. Important classes to take include four years of English, two years of mathematics (including algebra), and at least one year of physical science (preferably physics) with laboratory instruction. Computer programming and applications, machine shop, basic electronics, and blueprint reading are also useful. Any class that explores systems and the ways in which they work will help you understand lasers.

Postsecondary Training

The best way to become a medical laser technician is to enter a two-year program at a technical school or community college. There are 11 such programs in the country, according to Dave Tyree, professor and chairman of the laser department at Vincennes University in Indiana. Laser training programs have grown in recent years, but there is still room in most

In-depth

What Is a Laser?

An acronym for Light Amplification by Stimulated Emission of Radiation, the laser is a precisely controlled light beam that is narrowly focused and aimed at a minute target. In each laser, various frequencies of light are converted into an intense beam of a single wavelength, or color. Because it is the color that determines how the beam will interact with particular kinds of tissue, different lasers or strengths are used for different types of surgery. Lasers may function continuously or in pulsed bursts. The type of laser determines the number of pulses per second, the duration of the pulses, and whether the light will be used to cut through, vaporize, or seal tissue. Various lasers take their names from the different substances that produce the beam.

The carbon dioxide laser, with a wavelength in the far infrared spectrum, penetrates tissue to a depth of 1 millimeter. It has been used widely to treat some types of cancer, gynecological disorders, and brain tumors.

The argon laser, functioning in the blue-green frequencies, reacts with the color red and will penetrate the skin until it comes in contact with blood. Because it readily coagulates with blood in the area of the incision or operation, the argon laser has been particularly useful in the fields of ophthalmology, plastic surgery, and dermatology.

The YAG laser, with a wavelength in the near infrared spectrum, is used to cook or vaporize tissue that will then be removed from the body. The most invasive of all surgical laser devices, the YAG laser can penetrate 4 to 5 millimeters.

Dye lasers can be tuned to react to different wavelengths of light, simply by adding or diluting the dye. The free-electron laser, also tunable, uses magnets to stimulate pulsed light from a stream of electrons.

The excimer laser breaks up intermolecular bonds and decomposes matter, allowing precise surgery through holes so small no stitches are necessary. When certain gases are stimulated and combined and then returned to a disassociated state, their electrons emit photons of light in ultraviolet wavelengths. For example, patients undergoing excimer laser surgery to repair corneal damage do not experience the thermal effects of shock waves of conventional lasers. Without even touching the cornea, the excimer vaporizes the molecular links that bond the tissue with cool ultraviolet light.

programs for new students. At Vincennes University, the program can accommodate up to 40 students..

"Most programs are relatively small, but that's changing. This year the graduating class has 10 graduates," Dave says. "It's tough to get high school students interested in this area or any area of high tech. It's not as glamorous as law enforcement or other fields. A lot of students tend to see the old stereotype of the computer geek; they don't view it as a cool job."

A laser technician career is attractive because it is a field with a relatively high starting salary for only a few years of schooling. "I'm sure the heavy demand for graduates will generate more interest in the career, leading to larger classes," Dave says.

The average course of study in lasers includes intensive technical and scientific study with more hours in a laboratory or work situation than in the actual classroom. This hands-on experience is combined with other first-year courses in mathematics, physics, drafting or drawing, diagramming and sketching, basic electronics, electronic instrumentation and calibration, introduction to solid-state devices, electromechanical controls, introductory computer programming, and English composition.

The second year of study includes an introduction to lasers, geometrical optics, digital circuits, microwaves, laser and electro-optic components, devices and measurements, vacuum techniques, communication skills, technical report writing, microcomputers, and computer hardware.

Completing special projects is often a requirement of the second year, and this work can help students to narrow the field in which they plan to use their laser technician degree. At other times, a job simply opens up and presents the technician with an opportunity, as in Adam's case. His lab partner in school told him about an opening and, in his words, "I just fell into medicine. My training had zero to do with the medical field. Most laser technician programs have a real slant towards industry because that's where the majority of the jobs are. Basic laser instruction is the same from laser to laser, it's the application that differs, what you use that laser to do—cut skin or cut metal—and that you have to learn on the job."

At his first job, Adam was a bit of a pioneer since he was the first to hold this position. Adam recalls, "I was the first laser tech hired by the hospital where I first worked, so there wasn't anyone to train me or show me the ropes. Learning on the job can be tough, but it's also the best teacher." Adam also recommends taking classes in anatomy and physiology to ease the learning process: "Anything that will help you understand the terms and references to the body."

Further training after employment is almost always required and is usually paid for by the employer. This training helps laser technicians advance their knowledge and expertise.

CERTIFICATION OR LICENSING

Currently, there are no mandatory certification or licensing requirements for medical laser technicians. The National Council on Laser Excellence is working to establish a minimal competency and quality assurance program for Excellence in Laser Service. Candidates with a two-year certificate and/or experience in laser technology would take an examination to be LSE (Laser Service Excellence) certified. The NCLE currently offers voluntary Laser Operator and Medical Laser Safety Officer certification.

You should know, however, that some employers require their medical laser technicians to take and pass qualifying or certifying examinations on a particular machine or program. Requirements also vary by state. For information about specific certification requirements, check with the medical board in the state where you plan to work.

SCHOLARSHIPS AND GRANTS

Scholarships and grants may be available from individual technical schools or community colleges. You should contact these institutions for specific information, such as requirements and deadlines. Currently, the national associations do not offer scholarships specifically for medical laser technicians.

INTERNSHIPS AND VOLUNTEERSHIPS

Summer or part-time work in areas where lasers are used, such as manufacturing plants, hospitals, medical research facilities, and construction sites, can help to give the aspiring laser technician valuable contacts, information, and experience.

Who Will Hire Me?

Many laser technicians now graduating from a two-year technical school or community college will probably obtain their first jobs through interviews on campus. "For our students graduating with a technical degree, we feel that one of the main parts of our job is placement," remarks Dave Tyree of Vincennes University. Fortunately, he says, his job is made that much easier by the fact that companies are coming to him. "The job market has really taken off," he says. "I've got companies calling me who want every single graduate I've got!" He adds, "And head hunters—they usually only search for executives—are calling me for laser technicians."

While it is true that most of the recent interest has been from nonmedical employers, Dave says the medical field is doing just fine. As lasers gain approval for everything from treating kidney stones to cancers, patients are demanding these less invasive treatments and more insurance companies are covering such procedures. Another relatively new avenue of employment for laser technicians is through employers such as LaserVision Centers Inc., which hires laser engineers and operators to install and maintain transportable lasers and assist physicians in laser vision correction procedures. The Laser Institute of America also provides a list of employers.

Many colleges provide students with lists of companies and resume assistance. Colleges often work closely with hospitals and companies involved in medical research, as in the case of Idaho State University's Laser Electro-Optics Program, which involves a Corporate Advisory Committee of six to 12 companies. This advisory committee is active in hiring graduates as well as in giving advice on curriculum.

Former graduates of the college are frequently valuable resources in placement. "Our first graduating class was in 1975, and whenever any of them needs to fill positions, they call us," Dave says.

The U.S. Armed Forces provides another entry for the medical laser technician. Military training is not always compatible with civilian requirements, however, so those entering the civilian field may need additional training.

Where Can I Go from Here?

There are many possibilities for advancement, although the primary ways are through on-the-job experience and by keeping up with technological changes and developments in the field.

Obtaining a supervisor or director position is one way to advance in this field. After more than 10 years of experience as a laser technician, Tim is now a director of other technicians. He still has technical duties in the surgical room, but now he is also responsible for supervising the department's caseload and personnel and for shaping the future of laser surgery at St. Mary's. "It's definitely possible to advance by learning all you can and getting all the experience you can," Tim says.

Many employers designate levels of employment according to experience, education, and job performance. By working through these levels, medical laser technicians can advance to supervisory positions. It is an essential skill for the supervisor or director to be able to balance many responsibilities. Part of what Tim enjoys most about his work is his variety of duties as technician, administrator, and perpetual student of new technology. "New instrumentation develops rapidly in this field. As best I can, I stay up to date."

Some medical laser technicians may advance to become teachers in laser technician education programs. Also, laser technicians who work in the medical field can always pursue work in other fields and industries. "One company called me looking for laser technicians to work on government optical systems,

In-depth

History of the Laser

Originally commissioned by industry leaders in the 1960s to study the effects of lasers and radioactivity on employees who used lasers in their work, Dr. Leon Goldman, a dermatologist, saw untapped potential for the new technology in the field of medicine. Dr. Goldman followed his vision far beyond the scope of his original study, and today he is considered the father of laser surgery.

While at the Jewish Hospital in Cincinnati, Ohio, Dr. Goldman treated hundreds of patients, pioneered countless treatments and procedures involving lasers, and trained doctors from all over the world in his techniques. The Goldman Laser Institute at the Jewish Hospital is named for him and continues to research and introduce new procedures that take advantage of laser technology. For example, the Institute pioneered the use of a flashlamp-pumped dye laser in the treatment of birthmarks and spider veins.

Dr. Goldman's research and resulting procedures have forever altered medical history. Today lasers are used in a variety of specialties, including ophthalmology, otolaryngology, plastic surgery, urology, neurosurgery, vascular surgery, general surgery, dermatology, and gynecology. The Goldman Laser Institute has conducted research in arthritis, bladder cancer, cervical cancer, gastrointestinal cancer, dermatology, orthopedics, lung cancer, head and neck cancer, and vascular welding.

specifically the repair systems for the Hubble spacecraft," Dave says.

Tim agrees about the diversity of the field. "If I got together with the rest of my graduating class and talked about what we were each doing," he comments, "we'd have almost nothing in common."

Another avenue for advancement is to become a consultant. Consultants work closely with clients to define their needs or problems by conducting studies and surveys to obtain data. They analyze data and recommend solutions to the client's problems.

Constant training in the safety and use of lasers is necessary for all types of laser technicians to keep up with the industry. Many companies pay for employee training. There are also several opportunities for continuing education available through the Laser Institute of America.

What Are the Salary Ranges?

Salaries for medical laser technicians vary greatly in different parts of the country and for different educational backgrounds and applications. The job market has taken off and, as a result, salaries have risen dramatically in a few short years. Although the medical field is currently experiencing slower growth than the other fields that utilize the talents of laser technicians, the starting salaries of medical laser technicians have continued to move upward alongside those of nonmedical laser technicians.

In order to remain competitive, hospitals and private clinics have had to continue to match the salaries of nonmedical laser technicians or face losing their technicians to other fields. Medical laser technicians can expect to start at about $30,000 but some graduates have starting salaries as high as $50,000, according to information provided by Vincennes University. Dave Tyree says, "But most can expect to earn $40,000 or better after three to five years of experience." For advanced, supervisory, sales, service, or private consulting positions, medical laser technicians may earn $49,000 to $53,000 or more.

In addition to good salaries, most medical laser technicians can expect a wide array of benefits, including insurance, paid holidays and vacations, and retirement plans. Some positions include a car as part of the benefits package. Many employers offer opportunities for continuing education.

FYI

Lasers have three special light properties: monochromaticity, directionality, and coherence.

- *Monochromaticity* is useful in photochemistry, atomic isotope separation, and spectroscopy.
- *Directionality* gives laser light the ability to travel great distances while remaining intense, which makes the laser helpful with drilling and welding.
- The *coherence* of laser light helps surveyors to accurately measure distances and helps the military to track missiles.

What Is the Job Outlook?

The job growth for laser technicians entering the medical field should remain about average. Vincennes University boasts nearly 100 percent placement for its laser technician graduates entering all fields. "Last year," says Dave, "we had companies who could not fill all of the positions that they had open, so this year they're back to hire our graduates."

The majority of jobs available for laser technicians are in industry and areas other than medicine, but jobs do exist for laser technicians who wish to work in the medical field. "You really have to go to a pretty big laser center, say a hospital with at least eight to 10 lasers," Adam advises. "A hospital with only two or three lasers will just send a nurse through a training program to learn how to operate the lasers. But in a hospital with 10 or 15 lasers, it's just too much for one person to try and keep up with. Then it becomes cost-effective for the hospital to hire a laser technician."

Calvin Christiansen, instructor/coordinator for Idaho State University, also reports a high job placement rate, but says, "Some who don't find jobs are just not willing to go where the jobs are." For the best entry-level jobs, graduates must sometimes relocate to large, urban centers.

Depending on the strength of the economy, laser technicians who want to work in research areas may have a greater challenge locating a position. On the whole, however, the medical field remains a viable option for laser technicians.

How Do I Learn More?

PROFESSIONAL ORGANIZATIONS

The following are organizations that provide information on careers, schools, and possible employers for medical laser technicians:

American Society for Laser Medicine and Surgery
2404 Stewart Avenue
Wausau, WI 54401
715-845-9283
information@aslms.org
http://www.aslms.org

Laser Institute of America
13501 Ingenuity Drive, Suite 128
Orlando, FL 32826
800-345-2737
http://www.laserinstitute.org

National Council on Laser Excellence and Laser Training Institute
PO Box 522379
Marathon Shores, FL 33052
866-252-0880
http://lasercertification.org

BIBLIOGRAPHY

The following is a sampling of materials relating to the professional concerns and development of medical laser technicians:

Arndt, Kenneth M. et al., eds. *Illustrated Cutaneous and Aesthetic Laser Surgery.* 2d ed. New York: McGraw-Hill, 1999.

Keller, Gregory S. et al. *Lasers in Aesthetic Surgery*. New York: Thieme Medical Publishers, 2001.

McGhee, Charles et al, eds. *Excimer Lasers in Ophthalmology, Principles and Practice.* Newton, Mass.: Butterworth-Heinemann Medical, 1997.

Rosen, Arye, and Harel D. Rosen, eds. *New Frontiers in Medical Device Technology.* New York: John Wiley & Sons, 1995.

Sarnoff, Deborah S., and Joan Swirsky. *Beauty and the Beam: Your Complete Guide to Cosmetic Laser Surgery.* New York: Griffin Trade Paperbacks, 1998.

Slade, Stephen G. et al. *The Complete Book of Laser Eye Surgery.* New York: Bantam, 2002.

MEDICAL RECORD TECHNICIANS

Definition
Medical record technicians compile, code, and maintain medical records to document patient diagnoses and treatments. They also tabulate and analyze data from the records to assemble reports.

Alternative Job Titles
Certified coding specialists
Health information technicians
Medical records clerks

High School Subjects
Biology
English

Personal Skills
Following instructions
Technical/scientific

Salary Range
$27,190 to $30,332 to $33,346+

Minimum Educational Level
Some postsecondary training

Certification or Licensing
Recommended

Outlook
Much faster than the average

DOT
079

GOE
09.07.02

NOC
1413

O*NET-SOC
29-2071.00

The intensive care unit of Saint Patrick Hospital is crowded with doctors, nurses, and visitors as Susan Lucchesi examines a patient's medical chart and writes in her notepad every diagnosis, procedure, and comment that has been added since she reviewed the data two days ago. She jots down a few questions that come to mind, points of clarification that she will call to the attention of the attending physicians.

After discussing the chart with one of the nurses, she adds another comment to her notes. Although the patients in intensive care probably have no idea who she is, and she might not recognize their faces, she's familiar with each of them, because she studies their charts regularly. As a record technician she makes sure that the details of their stay at the hospital are documented with impeccable thoroughness and accuracy.

When she returns to her quiet, pleasant office in the medical records department, she enters information from her notes into the hospital's computer system, prints it, keeps a copy for the patient's medical records folder, writes out her questions for the doctors, attaches them to a second copy of the printout, and sends it back to intensive care for the doctors to review. She'll repeat the procedure every two or three days until the patient is moved to another department, where a different medical record technician will take over.

What Does a Medical Record Technician Do?

If you've ever spent time in a hospital, either as a patient or visitor, you may remember the steady parade of nurses and doctors in and out of the patients' rooms for one thing or another. They might check body temperature, blood pressure, heart rate, or frequency of labor pains, give medication, check incisions, or test range of motion in a damaged limb. They're always writing on that little chart at the foot of the bed, generating an amazing amount of data for each patient at every hospital. If you've wondered what happens to all that information when the patient goes home, you have wondered about the job of the *medical record technician.*

An individual's medical record consists of all the information noted by any health care workers who have dealt with the patient. Along with the patient's medical history, it may include admission date, diagnoses, progress notes, surgical procedures, X rays, lab reports, prescribed medications or treatments, and discharge assessment. Medical record technicians assemble and organize records, make sure they're accurate, and prepare them for the use of doctors, insurance companies, or other authorized agencies or individuals. The technician also may compile statistical reports from groups of records. Hospital administrators, public health agencies, health program planners, and others use these reports to analyze trends and patterns or to see if a treatment is effective.

In smaller organizations, with fewer records to manage, the technician may work in all areas of the medical records department. In larger institutions there may be separate departments for each phase of the work, with each technician having very specific responsibilities.

Technicians who specialize in assigning a numerical code to every diagnosis and procedure are called *medical record coders* or *coder/abstractors.* To determine the correct codes, these technicians use specialized computer software, a coding reference guide, medical dictionaries, and the *Physician's Desk Reference.* Most hospitals in the United States use a nationally accepted coding system, which makes the data easier to handle and analyze in the records department and by organizations that pool information from many institutions. A coded record can be cross-referenced and sorted by its various components, such as physician, patient, diagnosis, or treatment. The technician may also assign the patient to a diagnosis-related grouping (DRG), which helps the Medicare system and insurance companies determine the amount to reimburse the hospital for the patient's stay. At some institutions patients are assigned to DRGs by technicians who specialize in using computers to analyze patients' charts.

In larger facilities some records technicians work in a release-of-information department that does nothing but release medical records to doctors, insurance agencies, state and federal organizations, law enforcement agencies, attorneys, and the patients themselves. These technicians prepare and release information for authorized use only. Maintaining confidentiality of patient records is a priority, not only for this department but for all medical record technicians.

Finally, the medical record must be filed away for storage and easy retrieval, either on computer, paper, or microfilm. In some institutions the medical record technicians supervise other personnel, such as *medical records clerks,* who perform the storage and retrieval work.

Lingo to Learn

Abstracting Removing pertinent information from a patient's medical record for use in a larger study or survey.

Coding In medical records, assigning numbers for systematic classification.

CPT (Common Procedural Terminology) The numerical classification system used in the medical records field to code procedures and treatments.

DRG (Diagnosis-Related Grouping) A system used by Medicare and many insurance companies to classify medical patients' care and treatment.

ICD (International Classification of Diseases) The numerical classification system used in the medical records field to code diagnoses.

Source-oriented chart order A system of organizing patient charts by grouping information into sections based on different health care departments, such as nursing, radiology, or attending physician.

Stat Immediately.

Terminal Digit Order A numerical filing method emphasizing the last two digits, which is the most effective use of filing space, as well as the most effective method of insuring patient privacy.

Transcription Making written copies of orally dictated material.

Most medical record technicians have more advanced training than medical records clerks, but not all have passed certification exams. Those who hold an associate's degree and certification are called *accredited records technicians.* They ensure the accuracy of medical records, create disease registries for research, and submit data to insurance companies, which then reimburse the health care facility.

Registered records administrators hold a bachelor's degree and certification. They are managers who also interpret data, do research and statistical reports, and ensure the privacy of health information.

Certified coding specialists have taken seminars or college classes in coding, along with on-the-job experience, and they are certified. The credential, *certified coding specialist physician-based,* is for technicians who specialize in coding for physician services in facilities other than hospitals.

What Is It Like to Be a Medical Record Technician?

As a medical records coder at Saint Patrick Hospital in Missoula, Montana, Susan Lucchesi spends most of the day at her computer in the medical records department assigning a numerical code to each diagnosis and procedure on patients' charts. She works in cooperation with a team of coders, a transcriptionist, and the clerks in the office next door; the clerks maintain an entire room full of records documented on paper, neatly stored in filing cabinets. "We all help each other out. We work together, and no one person gets the credit for anything. We're a very close team," she says.

Like many technicians in her field, Susan used to see little of the doctors, nurses, and other health care professionals who perform the work summarized in the medical charts. Thanks to a new program at the hospital, however, Susan now spends a few hours each day reviewing charts in the intensive care unit. The other coders on her team have different departments to visit; Susan has the option of covering the intensive care unit for one year and then rotating to another department.

She still communicates with doctors by notes, e-mail, and phone calls from the medical records department, but she has enjoyed the chance to see how the intensive care unit operates. "I've made a lot of friends with doctors and nurses on my floor. That's been a learning experience," she says.

By tracking each patient's progress and assigning codes that help identify the main reason the person was admitted for treatment, Susan helps the doctors zero in on the patient's most pressing health problems and possible remedies. "It's almost like you're trying to solve a puzzle," she says. "There's a lot more to it than you'd think."

It's almost like you're trying to solve a puzzle.

Some medical record technicians are more involved in following up after the patient has been discharged and the paperwork has been done. Terri Young works in the release-of-information department in another hospital. She also works as part of a team that processes many requests for medical information every day. One technician mans the special phone line, known as the "stat line," which receives calls mainly from emergency rooms. Information for those calls may be given over the telephone or by fax after the technician has verified the patient's name and birth date; all other requests must be in writing and include either the patient's authorization or a court order.

Requests are logged into the computer and prioritized. Terri's hospital strives to send out the information within two weeks of receiving it, but medical requests always receive priority over insurance requests. For each request, Terri gets the patient's medical record number from the computer, uses it to locate the chart, looks for the requested information in her records, and locates any specialized information in other areas of the hospital, such as the X-ray department. When she has found everything to complete the request, she fills out a worksheet, indicating what items need to be copied, and turns the file over to a medical record clerk.

Other technicians in the medical records department perform other duties. There are coding and abstracting technicians, most of whom have taken special training in coding. They spend their days almost exclusively at computer terminals. "You have to be able to concentrate," says Terri. "You have to be able to sit and sit and keep your mind on what you're doing."

There's a data entry team, the first technicians to work with patient records. They visit each floor of the hospital daily, pick up the charts for patients discharged the day before, assemble each chart in a specific order, and enter the information into the hospital's computer system.

There's a chart analysis team, which puts each patient's diagnoses in the correct time sequence and uses a computer software package to assign the patient to one of hundreds of diagnosis-related groupings. The groupings determine how much the hospital will be reimbursed by Medicare and insurance companies for the patient's stay. Accuracy is essential for the chart analysis team. Terri explains, "Medicare is so picky that if diagnoses aren't sequenced properly, it may make thousands of dollars difference in what they pay."

Because the hospital's records department never closes, some of the technicians work second and third shifts, as well as some weekends and holidays. Terri works Monday through Friday, 7:00 A.M. until 4:00 P.M. The 40-hour workweek is standard for most medical record technicians.

Do I Have What It Takes to Be a Medical Record Technician?

The medical record technician is responsible for keeping accurate records for the benefit of the hospital, the physician, and the patient. Sloppy work could cause serious problems; the hospital might not receive proper payment, and inaccuracies in the records could affect the patient's health care in the future. The technician must develop precise and fastidious work habits to ensure as complete and correct a job as possible. Susan says a medical record technician should be detail oriented, interested in medicine, and adaptable. "It can be stressful sometimes," she adds. "There are so many federal regulations."

The technician needs to handle heavy workloads, pressure to get things done rapidly, and constant interruption. "It's stressful," Terri Young says, "because people want things immediately. They don't take no for an answer." The phone rings constantly, she says, with requests to have records retrieved, prepared, copied, and faxed. It is also important for the technician to be able to deal with sometimes trying personalities. "Doctors get frustrated," Terri says, "and tempers flare at you, even if it's not your fault." She adds that technicians need to react in a professional manner and avoid taking things personally.

What Terri likes most about her job is that it is challenging. She enjoys the detailed work and the opportunity for growth. "I have learned a great deal by working here," she says. She has worked in several different capacities since she started in the medical records department. The department itself has become more computerized and automated. Terri agrees with Susan that being adaptable to change is very important for a technician.

She also thinks it is important to have a strong interest in the medical field. "I think that a lot of people have a desire to work in the medical field, but they don't want to deal with the actual patients," she says. "This job would fulfill that need." Discretion and tact are also a must, Terri cautions. Medical records are confidential, and maintaining a patient's privacy is an important aspect of this job. "If it's in a file, it's confidential, no matter what," says Terri. "You have to remember that you heard it here, not on the street corner."

To Be a Successful Medical Record Technician, You Should . . .

- be extremely thorough and detail oriented
- feel confident in dealing with medical staff, administrators, and insurance agencies
- be able to concentrate for long periods of time
- be able to handle a heavy workload
- feel comfortable working with computers

How Do I Become a Medical Record Technician?

Susan became interested in the medical records profession soon after she left high school. She heard that job openings were plentiful in this occupation, so she enrolled in a two-year medical records program at a vocational school. After earning an associate's degree, she completed several internships, which gave her experience in various aspects of the profession.

To prepare for a career in medical records, Susan recommends taking high school classes in computers, anatomy, physiology, medical terminology, and pharmacology. She didn't take specific preparatory classes in high school, because at that time she hadn't decided what career she wanted to pursue, but her classes in biology, chemistry, and computers proved helpful.

Terri Young became interested in health information management because two of her older cousins were record technicians. "They just loved it," she says. "They were always talking about their jobs."

Terri decided when she was still in high school that she wanted to be a medical record technician. She earned an associate's degree from a junior college that offered an accredited program, then took the test to become accredited. She says her classes were challenging and enjoyable, good preparation for the examination.

EDUCATION

High School

Students contemplating a career in medical records should take as many high school English classes as possible, because technicians need both written and verbal communication skills to prepare reports and communicate with other health care personnel. Basic math or business math is very desirable because statistical skills are important in some job functions. Biology courses help by familiarizing the student with the terminology that medical record technicians use. Other science courses, computer training, typing, and office procedures are also helpful.

Postsecondary Training

Most employers prefer to hire medical record technicians who have completed a two-year associate's degree program accredited by the American Medical Association's Commission on Accreditation of Allied Health Education Programs (CAAEHP) and the American Health Information Management Association (AHIMA). There are approximately 175 of these accredited programs available throughout the United States, mostly offered in junior and community colleges. They usually include classroom instruction in such subjects as anatomy, physiology, medical terminology, medical record science, word processing, medical aspects of record keeping, statistics, computers in health care, personnel supervision, business management, English, and office skills.

In addition to classroom instruction, the student is given supervised clinical experience in the medical records departments of local health care facilities. This provides you with practical experience in performing many of the functions learned in the classroom and with the opportunity to interact with health care professionals.

CERTIFICATION OR LICENSING

Medical record technicians who have completed an accredited training program are eligible to take a national qualifying examination to earn the credential of Registered Health Information Technician (RHIT). Most health care institutions prefer to hire individuals with an RHIT credential as it signifies that they have met the standards established by the AHIMA as the mark of a qualified health professional.

Technicians who have achieved the RHIT credential are required to obtain 20 hours of continuing education credits every two years in order to retain their RHIT status. These credits may be obtained by attending educational programs, participating in further academic study, or pursuing independent study activities approved by the AHIMA.

AHIMA also offers the following certifications for technicians who complete advanced education and pass a national certification examination: Registered Health Information Administrator, Certified Coding Specialist, and Certified Coding Specialist-Physician Based.

SCHOLARSHIPS AND GRANTS

AHIMA has a foundation that offers scholarships and loans to health information management students. Undergraduate applicants may qualify for loans up to $2,000. The foundation also bestows a number of scholarships, ranging in amount from $1,000 to $5,000. For details, contact AHIMA (see "How Do I Learn More?").

Who Will Hire Me?

When Terri Young graduated from her two-year college program, she put together a resume and started looking for a job. She responded to an ad in her hometown newspaper for a medical record technician's position at the local hospital. After two interviews and a nerve-wracking two weeks, she was offered the job. Her first duty was to transfer some of the older records to microfilm for storage. "I worked way in the back," she says, "and never even saw any current records at first."

About 37 percent of medical record technicians in the United States worked in hospitals in 2002, according to the U.S. Department of Labor. Most of the others work in other health care settings, such as nursing homes, group medical practices, health maintenance organizations, outpatient clinics, surgery centers, or veterinary hospitals. There are also technicians who work for insurance companies and accounting and law firms that deal with health care issues. Public health care departments also use medical record technicians to help collect and research data from health care institutions.

If you are graduating from an associate's degree program, your school placement office might help you find a job. You may also want to apply directly to the personnel departments of local hospitals, nursing homes, and outpatient clinics. Checking newspaper classified ads is also a good idea, since they often list medical record technicians' job openings.

Some publications geared specifically to the health information management field carry classified advertising, including job listings. Also, the American Health Information Management Association (AHIMA) offers a resume referral service to its members. The technician can send the AHIMA office a resume, which will be kept on file and faxed to employers who have notified AHIMA of job opportunities (see How Do I Learn More?).

Where Can I Go from Here?

"The jobs are there, everywhere," says Susan. "You can go overseas. You could go to Saudi Arabia for a year, or Hawaii. There's a lot you can do with this degree."

She explains that medical record technicians have the option of working for companies that assign them to temporary jobs almost anywhere in the nation or in other countries, with travel and lodging allowances included. Some technicians work as consultants, teaching other technicians how to do coding and other tasks that require specialized skills. Others are assigned to temporary, contract jobs. Some freelance or work as independent contractors, typically coding records on a hospital's computer system.

Susan has worked at Saint Patrick Hospital for more than a year and says the hospital's progressive medical records department offers her an excellent opportunity to learn the latest technology, a real advantage if she ever wants to make a career move elsewhere. "This is my first real coding job," she comments. "I really like it. I could leave here and get a job almost anywhere."

In contrast, Terri has spent over seven years in the medical records department of her hospital and has worked in almost every phase of the record-keeping process. She feels she may have exhausted the new frontiers available within the department and is currently taking classes in transcription. She plans to run a doctors' transcription service from her home eventually.

For the technician who works in a large health care facility, advancement may mean becoming a *sec-*

Advancement Possibilities

Tumor registrars compile and maintain records of patients who have cancer to provide information to physicians and for research studies.

Medical record administrators plan, develop, and administer health information management systems for health care facilities; develop procedures for documenting, storing, retrieving, and processing patient information; supervise staffs; and analyze patient data.

Utilization-review coordinators analyze patient records to determine legitimacy of treatment and the patient's hospital stay to comply with government and insurance reimbursement policies. They also review applications for patient admission, abstract data from records, maintain statistics, and determine patient review dates.

Medical billing service owners use special software to help doctors and other health care professionals get payment for services. They send bills to patients, private insurance companies, Medicare, and other insurers. Most billers work from their home offices, though some work in the offices of doctors and clinics.

tion supervisor and overseeing the work of the others in the section. Another way to climb the ladder is to specialize in an area such as coding.

Better advancement and higher pay are possible for the technician who goes back to school. Those with a bachelor's degree in medical record administration, along with AHIMA accreditation, can become department directors or assistant department directors. Because of the shortage of medical record administrators, hospitals often make it easy for technicians to get their bachelor's degree by giving them financial aid and time off to go to class.

What Are the Salary Ranges?

According to a 2000 membership survey by the American Health Information Management Association (AHIMA), 67 percent responding earned between $20,000 and $39,000 annually. A little over 11 percent of the respondents earned between $40,000 and $49,000, while 6.7 percent earned between $50,000 and $74,999. The *Occupational Outlook Handbook* reports that health information technicians had median annual earnings of $23,890 in 2002. Those in the middle 50 percent earned between $19,550 and $30,600 annually. The lowest paid 10 percent earned less than $16,460, and the highest paid 10 percent earned more than $38,640. A review of medical record technicians' earnings in 2005 by Salary.com found that the median earnings nationwide were $30,332. The lowest paid earned $27,190, while the highest paid earned $33,346.

Most full-time positions in health information management include a benefits package. Health care insurance, paid vacations and holidays, pension plans, and sick leave are commonly offered.

What Is the Job Outlook?

Employment prospects for medical record technicians are excellent. The U.S. Department of Labor predicts that employment in this field will grow by 44 percent in the next decade. The demand for well-trained medical record technicians will grow rapidly and will continue to exceed the supply. This expectation is related to the health care needs of a population that is both growing and aging and the trend toward more technologically sophisticated medicine and greater use of diagnostic procedures. It is also related to the increased requirements of regulatory bodies that scrutinize both costs and quality of care of health care providers.

Because of the fear of medical malpractice lawsuits, doctors and other health care providers are documenting their diagnoses and treatments in greater detail. Also, because of the high cost of health care, insurance companies, government agencies, and courts are examining medical records with a more critical eye. These factors combine to ensure a healthy job outlook for medical record technicians.

Technicians with associate's degrees and RHIT status will have the best prospects, and the importance of such qualifications is likely to increase.

How Do I Learn More?

PROFESSIONAL ORGANIZATIONS

For information on earnings, careers in health information management, and RHIT accreditation, contact

American Health Information Management Association
233 North Michigan Avenue, Suite 2150
Chicago, IL 60601-5800
312-233-1100
info@ahima.org
http://www.ahima.org

For a list of schools offering accredited programs in health information management, contact

Commission on Accreditation of Allied Health Education Programs
American Medical Association
35 East Wacker Drive, Suite 1970
Chicago, IL 60601-2208
312-553-9355
caahep@caahep.org
http://www.caahep.org

BIBLIOGRAPHY

The following is a sampling of materials relating to the professional concerns and development of medical record technicians:

Careers in Focus: Medical Technicians. 4th ed. New York: Facts On File, 2004.

Goldberg, Jan. *Medical Record Technician (Careers Without College)*. Mankato, Minn.: Capstone Press, 1999.

McMiller, Kathryn. *Being a Medical Records Clerk/Health Information Clerk*, 3d ed. New York: Prentice Hall, 2003.

Rudman, Jack. *AMRA Medical Record Technician National Registration Examination.* Susosett, N.Y.: National Learning Corporation, 1997.

MEDICAL TECHNOLOGISTS

Reflecting on his 52-year career as a medical technologist and the importance of the profession, Patrick Cuviello says, "My personal feeling is that physicians can't practice medicine without the lab. Technologists help physicians either confirm a patient's diagnosis or help make the diagnosis." He continues, "It takes a special person to go into any medical profession, and medical technologist is as much a profession as nursing, pharmacy, or medical doctors."

Definition
Medical technologists are health professionals who perform laboratory tests to help physicians detect, diagnose, and treat diseases in patients.

Alternative Job Titles
Clinical laboratory technologist

High School Subjects
Biology
Chemistry

Personal Skills
Helping/teaching
Technical/scientific

Salary Range
$31,400 to $44,400 to $60,800

Minimum Educational Requirements
Bachelor's degree

Certification or Licensing
Recommended (certification)
Required by some states (licensing)

Outlook
About as fast as the average

DOT
078

GOE
14.05.01

NOC
3219

O*NET-SOC
29-2011.00

What Does a Medical Technologist Do?

Working under the direction of laboratory managers and pathologists, *medical technologists* perform a variety of laboratory tests that help physicians detect, diagnose, and treat diseases in their patients.

Medical technologists typically work in five major areas: blood banking, chemistry, hematology, immunology, and microbiology. Regardless of their area of work, medical technologists ensure the quality of laboratory tests performed for diagnosis of disease. They also may be responsible for interpreting the test data and results and reporting that information to a patient's physician. Many technologists assist physicians when they compare lab test results with clinical data to recommend a proper course of additional tests or series of tests.

Which duties are assigned to medical technologists is usually determined by the setting in which they work. Those employed by small labs usually conduct a large variety of tests, such as blood counts, urinalyses, and chemical analyses of blood and body fluids. Microscopes are used to study body fluids and tissue samples to determine the presence of bacteria, fungi, and other organisms. On occasion technologists prepare slides from tissue samples and body cells to check for the presence of diseases such as cancer.

Depending on the laboratory's needs, a medical technologist also may be responsible for operating sophisticated medical instruments and equipment, conducting research, and performing minor repairs to the instruments and equipment used in testing.

Unlike their counterparts in small labs who perform a range of tests and complete a variety of duties, medical technologists employed by large laboratories typically specialize in just one area of testing.

What Is It Like to Be a Medical Technologist?

Patrick has been a certified medical technologist with the American Medical Technologists (AMT)

Lingo to Learn

Andrology A branch of medicine that studies male diseases, especially those affecting reproduction.

Bacteriology A science that studies bacteria as it relates to medicine, industry, and agriculture.

Embryology The branch of biology that studies embryos and their development.

Hematology A science that studies the blood and blood-forming organs.

Immunohematology The branch of immunology (the study of the immune systems) concerned with the immunologic properties of blood.

Microbiology The branch of biology that studies microscopic life forms.

Virology The study of viruses and viral diseases.

for 52 years. Although he has retired from his work in a hospital laboratory, he remains active in the profession, working as an adjunct professor in the medical laboratory technology department of Navarro College in Corsicana, Texas, where he teaches future medical technicians. He is also chairman of the AMT Education, Qualification, and Standards Committee, and he is president of the AMT Institute for Education.

When he was a practicing medical technologist, Patrick says, "I was a lab director and had an office in the hospital, but I also did bench work. I ran tests in the lab, all of the blood tests, chemical analysis, microbiology to find the type of infection and bacteria causing the problem and the proper antibiotics to treat it, blood matching for transfusions."

As part of his job, Patrick said he had direct contact with patients and physicians. He also worked closely with each department of the hospital, including with nurses and pharmacists.

Patrick says the work was rewarding and gave him a sense of accomplishment knowing he was helping people. "I enjoyed working with patients and doctors, knowing I was part of the team that helped get patients back to health."

The most difficult aspect of the job for Patrick was accepting that there were patients who could not be helped. "The hard part is knowing the [medical] team has done all it can and the patient doesn't recover."

Do I Have What It Takes to Be a Medical Technologist?

Patrick says that a good medical technologist "first must be dedicated. This isn't an 8 to 5 job." You must be willing to work the necessary hours to provide good patient care. "You also must be compassionate and able to relate to the patients," he continues, "and you have to be honest, sincere, able to get along well with people, and be able to work as part of a team."

Because accurate test results are critical to positive outcomes in patient care, a good medical technologist must possess the skills of accuracy, patience, and an ability to work well under pressure. Technologists should be able to communicate with other members of the medical team, including doctors, nurses, and pharmacists. And because technologists' work involves testing tissue, blood, and other body fluids you need to be comfortable handling those things.

The course of study to be a medical technologist can be difficult and demanding, so those planning to pursue a career in this profession should have above average scholastic abilities.

To Be a Successful Medical Technologist, You Should . . .

- be accurate and patient
- be able to work under pressure
- get along with people and work well as part of a team
- have good manual dexterity
- have good eyesight

How Do I Become a Medical Technologist?

"I earned a bachelor's degree in biology with a split minor in chemistry and English," Patrick says, "Then I did two years of additional training after college in a veterans hospital and got a master's degree in biology: zoology and botany."

EDUCATION

High School

If you are interested in a career as a medical technologist you should take college preparatory classes while in high school. Science courses that include laboratory work such as biology and chemistry will be beneficial. Also take algebra, calculus, and other math courses, and computer science classes. Courses in English will help develop your research and writing skills.

Postsecondary Training

A number of colleges and universities offer bachelor's degree programs in medical technology and clinical laboratory science. The first two or three years of a typical program will include studies in chemistry, biology, math, physiology, psychology, English, and statistics. The final year, studies are focused on the specific skills of medical technologists. During this time you will take classes such as immunohematology, clinical chemistry, and virology. You will also complete an internship in a medical center or hospital laboratory affiliated with the program to gain hands-on experience. Courses in management, business, and computer science may be part of the program as well.

A list of schools in the United States offering accredited programs for medical technologists is available from the National Accrediting Agency for Clinical Laboratory Sciences (NAACLS).

CERTIFICATION OR LICENSING

Some states and Puerto Rico require that medical technologists be licensed or registered. Because requirements vary by state and other states may adopt new licensing laws you need to check with your state's department of health or occupational licensing board for information about your area.

In-depth

History

The history of clinical laboratory work and of medicine are intertwined. In the late 19th century, medical specialties such as bacteriology were developing rapidly, creating a need for people to work in laboratories full time. To meet the growing demand for laboratory workers, in the early 20th century physicians began training their assistants to perform some of the more frequently used lab procedures. Because the quality of the work by assistants varied greatly, in the 1930s efforts were made to develop standardized training programs for medical technologists. Since that time, medical laboratory technologists have become an important part of the health care system. It is estimated that approximately 150,000 medical technologists were employed in the United States in 2002 and that number is expected to grow to 178,900 by 2012.

Whether or not the state where you practice requires licensing, certification is highly recommended for those who wish to advance in this profession. Also, some employers will not hire medical technologists who are not certified.

For certification as a medical technologist (MT) candidates must meet educational and experience requirements and pass exams. Organizations that certify medical technologists include the Board of Registry of the American Society for Clinical Pathology (ASCP), the American Medical Technologists (AMT), and the American Association of Bioanalysts (AAB). Certification as a clinical laboratory scientist (CLS) is offered by the National Credentialing Agency for Laboratory Personnel.

SCHOLARSHIPS AND GRANTS

Scholarships are offered by numerous professional organizations for qualified students enrolled in accredited medical technologist or clinical laboratory programs. Among the organizations that offer scholarships are the American Association for Clinical Chemistry (AACC), which awards fifty $1,000 scholarships annually, and the AMT, which grants five $500 scholarships each year. A list of organizations that award scholarships also is available from the American Society for Clinical Laboratory Science (ASCLS) and the NAACLS. Information about federal student assistance programs, including scholarships and loans, is available from the U.S. Department of Health and Human Services at http://bhpr.hrsa.gov/dsa.

Advancement Opportunities

Chemistry or **biochemistry technologists** test samples of blood, urine, gastric juices, and spinal fluid to detect the presence of chemicals, drugs, and poisons. They also check the levels of substances made by the body such as sugar, albumin, and acetone. The information gathered is used to diagnose diabetes and other metabolic diseases.

Microbiology or **bacteriology technologists** test specimens for the presence of microorganism, including viruses, fungi, bacteria, and parasites. The results of the tests help determine the proper treatment of a condition in a patient.

Clinical laboratory directors usually hold an M.D., Ph.D., or D.O. They oversee the laboratory or laboratory department and supervise the staff of medical technologists. Directors also assign job duties, hire and fire staff, and establish the laboratory work rules and standards.

Clinical laboratory and **medical technology supervisors** manage the laboratory staff on a day-to-day basis by assigning work schedules and projects, reviewing staff work and lab results, and may assist in staff training and continuing education.

Chief medical technologists supervise the work of the entire laboratory operations, assigns duties, and reviews reports and analyses.

INTERNSHIPS AND VOLUNTEERSHIPS

Medical technologists are required to complete a one-year internship as part of their education, which are arranged by the schools. Volunteering in a hospital or medical facility, while you may not be in a laboratory analyzing samples, will give you an opportunity to experience what it is like to work in that environment.

Because some people are uncomfortable handling blood and other body fluids as required by the job, Patrick strongly advises anyone considering a career as a medical technologist "to go to a hospital or clinical lab and observe to be sure you want to be in this profession. See first hand what is done and be sure this is for you." He also suggests attending job fairs and talking with people who are working as medical technologists.

Who Will Hire Me?

Although most medical technologists work in hospitals, other employers include clinics, physicians' offices, pharmaceutical laboratories, public health agencies, and research institutions. The federal government hires medical technologists to work in Veterans Affair hospitals or for the U.S. public health service.

Medical technologists also may choose to concentrate in specific areas such as veterinary science, epidemiology study and application, or diagnostic equipment research. Technologists may find work in crime labs, as sales representatives for pharmaceutical companies, and as teachers in colleges.

"With the changes in science and the development of the equipment used, individuals with training can work in many fields. There are many opportunities besides hospitals and clinics," Patrick says.

Most colleges and universities offer placement services for graduates, and professional organizations typically maintain a list of job openings. Trade journals are also a resource for finding employment opportunities.

Patrick says that internships completed by students may lead to jobs as well. "Often internships can lead to positions in that hospital or clinic because they know the student's work and he's trained already."

Where Can I Go from Here?

Medical technologists may advance their careers by obtaining advanced degrees and specializing in one area of expertise. For example, a medical technologist who gains advanced skills and specializes in cell marker technology, biogenetics, or product development will probably receive a higher salary and greater job responsibilities.

Experienced medical technologists with certification and additional training may advance to a supervisory position. Advancement opportunities for supervisory positions such as chief medical technologist are best in large hospitals or large independent laboratories.

What Are the Salary Ranges?

According to the U.S. Department of Labor, in 2003 the median annual salary for medical and clinical laboratory technologists was $44,400, with the middle 50 percent earning between $37,800 and $53,000. The lowest paid 10 percent earned $31,400 annually, and the highest paid earned more than $60,800.

Benefits vary by employer, but most provide paid vacation time, sick leave, and health insurance.

What Is the Job Outlook?

Employment is expected to grow about as fast as the average for all occupations through 2012 despite fewer job openings for medical technologists in hospital laboratories, according to the U.S. Department of Labor. Demand for laboratory tests will increase as new tests are introduced. Employment opportunities are expected to grow in medical and diagnostic laboratories, physicians' offices, ambulatory health care centers, and blood and organ banks.

Patrick Cuviello says that during his long career as a medical technologist "there has always been a shortage of technologists," which concurs with a 2002 survey by the American Society of Clinical Pathologists that reported nearly half of all labs with openings for medical technologists were having difficulty filling the positions.

How Do I Learn More?

PROFESSIONAL ORGANIZATIONS

For information about medical and clinical laboratory technologist careers, employment opportunities, accredited schools, and certification contact the following organizations.

American Association for Clinical Chemistry
2101 L Street, Suite 202
Washington, DC 20037-1558
800-892-1400
info@aacc.org
http://www.aacc.org

American Association of Bioanalysts
906 Olive Street, Suite 1200
St. Louis, MO 63101-1434
314-241-1445
aab@aab.org
http://www.aab.org

American Medical Technologists
710 Higgins Road
Park Ridge, IL 60068
800-275-1268
http://www.amt1.com

American Society for Clinical Laboratory Science
6701 Democracy Boulevard, Suite 300
Bethesda, MD 20817
301-657-2768
http://www.ascls.org

American Society for Clinical Pathology
2100 West Harrison Street
Chicago, IL 60612
312-738-1336
info@ascp.org
http://www.ascp.org

National Accrediting Agency for Clinical Laboratory Sciences
8410 West Bryn Mawr Avenue, Suite 670
Chicago, IL 60631
773-714-8880
info@naacls.org
http://www.naacls.org

National Credentialing Agency for Laboratory Personnel
PO Box 15945-289
Lenexa, KS 66285
913-438-5110, ext. 4647
nca-info@goamp.com
http://www.nca-info.org

BIBLIOGRAPHY

The following is a list of materials with information relevant to the profession of medical technologist:

Chaskey, Cheryl R. et al. *Opportunities in Clinical Laboratory Science Careers*. New York: McGraw-Hill, 2002.

Graves, Linda. *Case Studies in Clinical Laboratory Science*. Paramus, N.J.: Prentice Hall, 2002.

Nicoll, Diana et al. *Pocket Guide to Diagnostic Tests*. 4th ed. New York: McGraw-Hill, 2004.

Polansky, Valerie Dietz. *Medical Laboratory Technology: Pearls of Wisdom*. 2d ed. Lincoln, Neb.: Boston Medical Publishing, 2002.

Springhouse. *Diagnostic Tests: A Prescriber's Guide to Test Selection and Interpretation*. Philadelphia: Lippincott Williams & Wilkins, 2003.

MYOTHERAPISTS

The patient is clearly in agony. He can only hold his head up with support from his hands. Every little movement leaves him wincing in pain. Janice Stroughton, the myotherapist, gently eases her patient down on the worktable and positions him so his neck is exposed.

As she readies her hands for work, she explains the procedure. "Your pain stems from a muscle spasm in your neck," Janice says. "Right now we need to locate these trigger points, the weak spots of your neck muscles. I'm going to press down on several areas, and you tell me, on a scale of one to 10, the pain tolerance of that area. Are you ready?" Janice gently places her thumb on the patient's lower neck.

The patient screams, "10!"

Definition
Myotherapy is a method of relieving muscle pain and spasms and improving overall circulation through applied pressure to trigger points. Pressure is applied using fingers, knuckles, and elbows. Those who practice myotherapy are called myotherapists.

High School Subjects
Biology
Health

Personal Skills
Communication/ideas
Helping/teaching

Salary Range
$25,000 to $52,000 to $78,000+

Educational Requirements
Some postsecondary training needed for certification

Certification or Licensing
Voluntary (certification)
Required by certain states (licensing)

Outlook
Faster than the average

DOT
N/A

GOE
N/A

NOC
N/A

O*NET-SOC
N/A

What Does a Myotherapist Do?

Myotherapy, also called trigger point therapy or neuromuscular massage therapy, is a method of relieving pain, improving circulation, and alleviating muscle spasms. *Myotherapists* identify the source of pain, called a trigger point, and erase it by the use of applied pressure to these tender spots. Bonnie Prudden, a fitness and exercise enthusiast, first developed myotherapy in 1976.

During the 1970s, Bonnie worked for Dr. Janet Travell, the former personal physician to President Kennedy. Together they treated chronic pain using trigger point injection therapy. Bonnie would identify the trigger points on the patient's body with ink; then Dr. Travell would inject the sites with a solution of procaine (a type of local anesthetic) and saline. Afterward, Bonnie would conduct muscle exercises and teach patients stretching exercises to do at home in order to keep the muscle strong and relaxed. By chance, while working on a patient, Bonnie found that by holding the pressure to trigger points for a longer period of time, the same relief was achieved without the use of invasive needles and solutions.

By 1979, the Bonnie Prudden School of Physical Fitness and Myotherapy was established in Tucson, Arizona. Through the school, students are taught the Bonnie Prudden method of myotherapy, in addition to anatomy, physiology, exercise, and physical fitness. Classes such as modern dance, drawing, and live sculpture are also offered to encourage students to analyze how the human body moves. After completion of the program, students are given an exam and are required to undergo recertification at the school every two years.

A first-time consultation begins with a thorough history of the patient. "Many times pain is the result of an old injury or accident," says Janice Stroughton, a practicing myotherapist in Maryland "It could also occur as the result of the patient's background and lifestyle." Janice explains that weakness and muscle injury is accumulated throughout a lifetime.

Lingo to Learn

Acupressure An ancient Chinese technique of massage that can relieve pain by stimulating the meridian points in the body using pressure from fingers and hands.

Neuromuscular therapy Identifies soft-tissue abnormalities and manipulates the soft tissue to normalize its function.

Shiatsu A modern form of acupressure in which the therapist uses palms, thumbs, forearms, elbows, knees, and feet to apply pressure to the meridians.

Trigger points Tender spots in the muscle or other soft tissue; localized areas of decreased circulation, increased muscle contraction, and increased nerve sensitivity.

The average age of patients is between 35 and 55 years—"about the time a person's bucket of accumulated trigger points starts to overflow." Once weak spots are created in the muscle, both physical and emotional stress can cause the spots to go into painful spasms. Myotherapists get rid of spasms by using their fingers, knuckles, or elbows to apply pressure to these trigger points. As muscles relax, the patient is relieved of pain. Afterwards the muscle is 'taught' to remain loose and lengthened through the use of exercises. Myotherapists also teach the patient several corrective exercises to do at home.

Myotherapy works on pain as long as the source is muscular, not systemic. It has shown to be effective for alleviating pain caused by arthritis, bursitis, scoliosis, sciatica, and even pain associated with lupus, AIDS, and muscular dystrophy.

What Is It Like to Be a Myotherapist?

Janice collected her own trigger points from years of playing tennis. Complications from scoliosis gave her more pain than she could endure. "I first learned about myotherapy from a tennis instructor who had undergone treatments and persuaded me to give the method a try." Janice was so convinced of the benefits of myotherapy that she became a myotherapist. Today, Janice is a Bonnie Prudden-certified myotherapist at the Myotherapy Pain Control Center in Maryland.

Patients are referred to the Pain Control Center by a medical physician, osteopath, chiropractor, or acupuncturist. Usually, patients have already undergone the battery of X rays, tests, and procedures to ensure pain is not structural in origin. For new patients, history and assessment is taken. "Many times chronic pain is caused by occupation, disease, past accident, surgeries, or participation in sports," says Janice. Next patients take the Kraus-Weber Minimum Muscular Fitness Test for Key Posture Muscles. Divided into six tests for different muscle masses, it gauges the flexibility and strength of a person's muscles.

Myotherapists use a trigger point pain chart to mark down the sources of a patient's pain. Once a trigger point is found, the patient identifies its intensity by grading it on a scale of one to 10—one being mild, and 10 almost unbearable. Each location is color marked on the paper chart to indicate the type of pain and the date it is erased.

Patients arrive for treatments barefooted and wearing loose clothing. "Patients are encouraged to bring a friend or family member to observe how treatments and exercises are done," explains Janice. "That way, the exercises may be repeated correctly at home. Treatments are 50 percent myotherapy and 50 percent corrective exercises." Using the completed pain chart, trigger points are identified and erased. The location of a trigger point determines the amount and length of pressure applied—on the average 7 seconds for most body areas and 4 to 5 seconds for the face and head. Tools such as the crook (a metal rod shaped like a shepherd's hook) and the bodo (a wooden dowel) are used to give the myotherapist greater extension and also to help fight fatigue. Small bodos are used to work the hands and feet, while larger bodos are helpful in working larger muscle masses such as the quadriceps and gluteus.

Once the muscles are relaxed, they need to be maintained with exercises specially designed for the patient's problem areas. Patients and their helpers are instructed in the proper way to conduct maintenance exercises to help keep the muscles strong and flexible. These exercises also help improve coordination, strength, and posture.

Janice's work schedule varies. Phone consultations with patients take up a large part of the day, as does paperwork. She limits herself to two or three patient treatments a day. Myotherapy is physically taxing on the practitioner. "You always risk injuring yourself," says Janice. "You need to be aware of how you use your own body."

You need to be aware of how you use your own body.

Do I Have What It Takes to Be a Myotherapist?

"Working with people in pain can sometimes be unpleasant," says Janice. "Don't expect cheery faces and pleasant conversation." Patients, many whom have been suffering pain for some time, will be grouchy and in a foul mood. Sometimes a good sense of humor is enough to erase a patient's crankiness. Despite having to deal with bad tempers, Janice finds reward in helping patients with their problems and offering them relief from pain. "The best part of my job is knowing I made a difference in someone's life, in regards to pain. It is like giving someone new hope." Janice quotes her mentor, Bonnie Prudden, when she says, "Pain, not death, is the enemy."

Questions arise during treatment, such as: Should pressure be kept a few seconds longer? Is the patient ready to end his or her sessions? Are these exercises challenging enough? Having good intuition is another important quality myotherapists need in order to answer such questions on the spot. While myotherapists learn the basics in school, they need instincts and intuition to help them in actual practice.

Because of the repetitive movements used in myotherapy, many practitioners often run the risk of self injury. It's important to be aware of your body's limitation and not overuse your own muscles and joints. Sometimes, myotherapists need treatment for their own repetitive stress problems.

To Be a Successful Myotherapist, You Should . . .

- be interested in helping others
- be physically fit
- be able to work with a variety of personalities and pain tolerance levels
- be caring and have a sense of humor
- have strong hands

How Do I Become a Myotherapist?

EDUCATION

High School

Enid Whittaker, a Bonnie Prudden-certified myotherapist and instructor, suggests taking anatomy and physiology classes if you are interested in a career in myotherapy. This will help you understand how the human body works. Also, creative classes such as drawing and sculpture, especially of the human body, will foster good hand coordination skills. Physical fitness classes or dance classes are helpful in developing a strong and flexible body. This is important because myotherapy is physically demanding on the therapist. If you are interested in setting up a private practice, Enid also suggests studying business classes, such as marketing, accounting, and bookkeeping.

Make an appointment to interview a local certified myotherapist. By shadowing someone already in the field, you can get a firsthand view of what it takes to succeed in this business.

CERTIFICATION OR LICENSING

There are other schools offering classes in myotherapy, but the Bonnie Prudden Myotherapy School is considered the most reputable program available. The school offers a nine-and-a-half month certification program for its graduates. A total of 1,300 hours of program work is completed at the school after which you may sit for the board exam. For recertification every two years, you are required to take continuing education classes (about 45 hours total) covering new techniques.

Plans are currently underway to create a shorter three-step program that will allow you to take one trimester a year (as opposed to the former nine-month program). The Bonnie Prudden Myotherapy School is also considering opening satellite schools throughout the United States.

Certification is also available from other massage therapy schools, usually requiring completion of a series of workshops or seminars. In some states, you must also become a licensed massage therapist before practicing myotherapy.

Who Will Hire Me?

As a myotherapist, you may be employed in a number of health care settings. You may work at a physician's clinic, especially one that treats patients with nerve damage or arthritic pain. You may choose to open your own practice. Remember, though, that in addition to giving treatments, you will also be responsible for all duties associated with running a business—tax concerns, office space and supplies, and hiring support staff. The reward is having the freedom to dictate your own workdays and hours.

Another employment choice is to join an established clinic. Because of the growing interest and acceptance in myotherapy, many clinics have found it necessary to hire more therapists.

Combining your myotherapy training with other disciplines, such as acupuncture, chiropractic, or massage therapy is also an option. In this case, employers would include massage clinics, day spas, and alternative medicine practices.

FYI

Myotherapy works to relieve pain that is related to muscle. Surprisingly, 95 percent of all chronic pain is of muscle origin. Here is a partial list of pains and conditions that can be controlled or eased by myotherapy.

- abdominal cramps
- AIDS
- arthritic pain, even rheumatoid
- bursitis
- cancer
- carpal tunnel syndrome
- fibromyalgia
- headaches
- impotence
- lupus
- menstrual cramps
- muscle weakness
- muscular dystrophy
- myofascial pain
- posture anomalies
- rotator cuff injuries
- sciatica
- tennis elbow
- tunnel vision

Where Can I Go from Here?

Career advancement depends on how you choose to practice myotherapy. If you opt to open a private practice, then the obvious advancement would be a larger office, a bigger client base, and perhaps having a staff of myotherapists working for you. If you choose to join an existing practice, then your advancement possibilities would include a larger client base, seniority, or perhaps establishing your own pain clinic. If you decide to join a medical practice, then your advancements could come in the form of more responsibilities, a larger salary, or better benefits. Experienced myotherapists may go on to become instructors in massage therapy schools.

What Are the Salary Ranges?

According to a 2004 survey by the American Massage Therapy Association, massage therapists practicing in large urban areas typically charge $60 to $100 per hour, and those in smaller communities charge $50 to $75 per hour. Most consider 27 hours of massage full-time employment, or an average of 20 billable hours per week. Based on that, a massage therapist making $50 per hour would have an annual income of $52,000. Those charging $75 per hour would have annual earnings of $78,000, and at the highest rate of $100 per hour the annual earnings would be $104,000. A massage therapist working part time, 10 to 20 hours per week, may earn as little as $25,000, annually. As a subspecialty of massage therapy, myotherapists may expect similar salaries.

Enid sees four to seven patients a day. The average patient, depending on the type of pain, needs about four to eight visits, with each treatment costing an average of $75. On the high end, a patient may spend up to $600 to finish pain treatment. Of course, some myotherapists opt to schedule more patients daily and may work with different treatment fees. Because of the physical demands of the job, like massage therapists, myotherapists often work less than 40 hours a week, and a large percentage of practitioners work part time, from 10 to 20 hours a week. Myotherapists in private practice must also be responsible for overhead costs, in addition to acquiring health insurance and other benefits.

A myotherapist employed full time at a hospital or other clinical setting may enjoy benefits such as health insurance and paid vacation and sick time. Though employed myotherapists may have greater job security and better benefits, they do not have the option of setting their own work schedules and hours that independent myotherapists enjoy.

Enid sums it up best when she stresses, "One becomes a myotherapist because of a desire to help others, not to get rich."

What Is the Job Outlook?

Even though there are no official figures, the field of myotherapy has grown. The public, especially in the past few decades, has become more proactive when it comes to their bodies and health. Many people are tired of the dependence on traditional medicine and are looking for alternative methods of pain relief. There is a growing acceptance of myotherapy from the public and the medical field. Many physicians, especially those specializing in neurology and rheumatology, are referring patients for myotherapy treatments more and more. Insurance companies, though slowly, are beginning to cover myotherapy treatments.

About 85 percent of the population experiences some sort of pain, most commonly back pain and headaches. In addition, many of today's jobs have developed movements that are highly repetitive, with little flexibility. A fairly sedentary occupation such as computer programming will usually result in trigger points to the upper and lower back. Construction work, a highly strenuous occupation, will gather trigger points in the back and torso.

Chronic pain can also be sports-related. Beside traditional activities like tennis and golf, some people are fascinated with extreme sports such as mountain and rock climbing and snowboarding. Many athletes turn to the benefits of myotherapy as a form of injury prevention and maintenance.

How Do I Learn More?

PROFESSIONAL ORGANIZATIONS

For information on the Bonnie Prudden School of Myotherapy or the Bonnie Prudden Pain Erasure Inc., contact

Bonnie Prudden Myotherapy Inc.
PO Box 65240
Tucson, AZ 85728-5240
800-221-4634 or 520-529-3979
http://www.bonnieprudden.com

For certification information and a directory of certified myotherapists, contact

International Myotherapy Association
PO Box 65240
Tucson, AZ 85728-5240
800-221-4634 or 520-529-3979
info@myotherapy.org
http://www.myotherapy.org

For a short history of myotherapy, and seminar information, see

http://www.myotherapy1.com

BIBLIOGRAPHY

The following is a sampling of materials relating to the professional concerns and development of myotherapists:

Davies, Claire. *The Trigger Point Therapy Workbook: Your Self-Treatment Guide for Pain Relief.* 2d ed. Oakland, Calif.: New Harbinger Publications, 2004.

Prudden, Bonnie. *Myotherapy.* New York: Doubleday, 1999.

Prudden, Bonnie. *Pain Erasure: The Bonnie Prudden Way.* New York: M. Evans & Co., 2002.

Riggs, Art. *Deep Tissue Massage: A Visual Guide to Techniques.* Berkeley, Calif.: North Atlantic Books, 2002.

NATUROPATHS

Your medicine cabinet is full of prescriptions. You've seen medical doctors and specialists, been through batteries of tests, and have been poked and prodded, but you only feel worse than when you started medical treatment. So you decide to explore alternative health care methods.

On recommendation from your doctor, you seek the help of Dr. Randall Bradley, a naturopathic physician in Omaha, Nebraska. Dr. Bradley's practice may not look much different than the practice of any other doctor. There's a waiting room, a receptionist to take appointments, and offices in which the doctor meets with patients. But once you are seated across from Dr. Bradley you notice many differences in the way he treats you as a patient. He doesn't just listen to your heart rate and your breathing. He asks you questions and listens carefully to your answers. You tell him about your worries and fears, and your state of mind when you first became sick. You were not sleeping well then, you tell him, and you were nervous about going to college. Whereas other doctors only spent a little time with you as you described your symptoms, Dr. Bradley spends an hour and a half. He doesn't just evaluate your illness, he uses his skills as a counselor to evaluate the state of your whole person, both mind and body.

Definition

Naturopaths are health care providers who help patients prevent illness and recover their health through nutrition, herbs, counseling, homeopathy, and other natural treatments. They have completed the basic medical training medical doctors receive, however, they also have training in natural health treatments.

Alternative Job Titles

Doctors of naturopathic medicine (N.D.)
Naturopathic physicians

High School Subjects

Biology
Chemistry
Health

Personal Skills

Helping/teaching
Technical/scientific

Salary Range

$25,000 to $80,000 to $100,000+

Educational Requirements

Bachelor's degree, Doctoral degree, Medical degree

Certification or Licensing

Recommended (certification)
Required by certain states (licensing)

Outlook

Faster than the average

DOT

N/A

GOE

N/A

NOC

3123

O*NET-SOC

N/A

What Does a Naturopath Do?

Did you eat your corn flakes this morning? If you did, then you were taking part in a long tradition of natural health. One hundred years ago, people flocked to spas to exercise, eat vegetarian foods, and soak their tired, aching joints in hot springs. These people took herbs and other natural remedies promoted by John Kellogg and other doctors. Kellogg owned and operated the Battle Creek Sanitarium in Michigan. He also developed such health foods as corn flakes, meat imitations, and coffee substitutes.

Old photos of some of the trendier health sanitariums of the day show men and women looking silly in long underwear and exercising on stationary bikes or sitting in large tubs of water or in primitive saunas. The practice of today's *naturopath*, however, doesn't look much different than that of your family doctor's office—a waiting room, exam rooms, exam tables. Although the study of naturopathic medicine is much different now, with accredited naturopathic medical schools, continuing education requirements, and highly respected doctors, the basis has remained the same as in Kellogg's day: health care that supports the body's self-healing processes.

What does this mean—the body's self-healing processes? Naturopathic physicians recognize that the human body is naturally capable of healing itself, so they use methods of care that will work with these processes. The last time you visited your doctor when you were ill he or she probably prescribed some medication. Naturopathic physicians believe that most medical doctors treat only the illness, not the patient. In treating the patient, naturopathic physicians recommend methods that will have more lasting effects; these physicians recommend changes in a patient's diet, prescribe botanical medicine (herbs), recommend vitamins, and may even offer counseling to help the patient make lifestyle changes.

Naturopathic physicians take a holistic approach to health care, recognizing the connection between the health of the mind and the health of the body. Depression, stress, and fear, all can have an impact on your physical health. When a naturopathic physician first meets with a patient, he or she doesn't just focus on the symptoms of illness, but also listens carefully to the patient. By learning about the patient, the physician can learn about the impact of outside forces, such as a stressful work environment or family situation that may be contributing to the patient's illness.

Naturopathic physicians are currently licensed as primary health care providers in 13 states and the District of Columbia. In addition, Puerto Rico and the U.S. Virgin Islands license naturopathic physicians. Doctors practicing in states that do not offer licensing must restrict the scope of their practice to such areas as homeopathy (a related branch of therapy that emphasizes natural remedies and treatments) and nutrition counseling.

In addition to botanical medicine, homeopathy, nutrition, and psychological counseling, naturopathic physicians also use a variety of other treatments. Some physicians use Asian methods of treatment, like acupuncture. Some use hydrotherapy, treatment involving immersing the patient in water. Natural childbirth and manipulative therapy are also practiced by naturopathic physicians. Patients come to naturopaths with a variety of health problems, including digestive disorders, asthma, depression, infections, colds, and flu.

Lingo to Learn

Acupuncture For centuries the Chinese have practiced this treatment, which involves inserting needles into the skin at certain points to treat pain or illness.

Botanical medicine A drug made from part of a plant.

Holistic medicine A philosophy of medicine that focuses on treating the whole person, both mind and body.

Homeopathy A branch of therapy with natural remedies and treatments; can involve treating a disease with small doses of drugs that, in a healthy person, would produce symptoms similar to those of the disease.

Hydrotherapy With this treatment, a patient's body, or part of a patient's body, is immersed in water. This helps in the movement of the body for exercise, relieving of pain, and healing wounds.

Manipulative therapy The art of touch, massage, physical therapy, and spinal manipulation.

Natural childbirth The philosophy of childbirth that focuses on labor and delivery as a "natural" process. Mothers receive preparatory education so they can remain conscious and assist during delivery. There is little or no use of drugs or anesthetics.

What Is It Like to Be a Naturopath?

Because the state of Nebraska does not license naturopathic physicians, Dr. Randall Bradley is limited to counseling, clinical nutrition, and homeopathy. He is licensed as a naturopathic physician, however, by the state of Washington and may practice as a primary health care provider there if he so chooses. He also holds certification by the Homeopathic Academy of Naturopathic Physicians. In addition to treating patients, Randall works to promote naturopathy and has served as president of the Council on Naturopathic Medical Education (CNME), an organization dedicated to promoting high standards of education for naturopaths.

Randall specializes in treating patients with chronic diseases. Patients come to him after they've been diagnosed by other doctors. Typically, a naturopath will spend an hour with a patient in the first session and one-half hour in follow-up sessions. But, working as a homeopath, Randall schedules an hour and a half for the first session. "I help the patients recover their health by doing detailed interviews and prescribing a homeopathic remedy for them," Randall says. "The idea is to perceive the person not as a constellation of diseases," he says, "but as a whole person whose system is out of balance."

To put the system back in balance, Randall listens carefully to the patient to determine what may be preventing recovery; he listens for psychological and social issues such as stress at work or home. He also tries to determine if these issues may have contributed to the patient's first becoming sick. "You have to ask the questions," he says, "and dig for the information. It's like an Agatha Christie novel. You've got all these mysteries and all these events occurring. How does it all fit together?" This information can help determine the origin of the patient's disease, headaches, allergies, fatigue, and other health problems.

Once he has conducted a detailed interview, he can counsel the patient in lifestyle changes, dietary changes, or exercise routines. He may prescribe vitamins and herbs. "I do get very good results," he says, "sometimes very dramatic results in situations some would call hopeless." Randall spends three days a week in his Omaha office and one day a week in an office in Lincoln.

In a licensing state, a naturopath's practice is somewhat different. Patients come in off the street or are referred to a naturopath by other physicians. The naturopath will diagnose the patient or confirm a diagnosis, then monitor a patient's progress with the usual tools: lab tests, physical exams, and X rays.

The offices, though, may be more comfortable and less clinical than those of general practitioners (some naturopaths set up their practices in a house). Naturopaths may also refer a patient to a specialist, such as a cardiologist. Even if a patient is seeing a specialist, however, the naturopath continues to work with the patient and the patient's self-healing processes.

Typically, a naturopathic physician works 30 to 50 hours per week. Some provide evening and weekend hours for their patients and some even make house calls.

Many medical doctors today are prescribing herbs and vitamins. The naturopath, however, not only works with natural substances, but also helps the body's natural healing powers. "The goal," Randall says, "is to get the body/mind to heal itself."

Do I Have What It Takes to Be a Naturopath?

Because counseling plays such an important role in treatment, a naturopath should have good listening and observation skills. This means being emotionally prepared to deal with a patient's illness and complaints. Randall emphasizes that someone pursuing a career as a naturopath must want to practice medicine. Though some naturopaths go into research or teaching, the majority of them become practitioners. "I advise people to go out and see what it's like," he says. "People will let you shadow them; go with them on rounds. If you get excited by that setting, you've got a good chance of being a good doctor."

Though a naturopathic physician can make a comfortable living, naturopathy isn't as financially rewarding as other branches of medicine. So some idealism is helpful. "You must believe in what you're doing," Randall says. This faith in the profession can also help see you past the skepticism that you're likely to confront. Natural health treatment has become much more respected within the medical profession in recent years, but it is still unaccepted by some doctors.

For Randall, any negative aspects of the job are overshadowed by the positive. As a naturopath, he feels he is capable of helping people no other doctors can help. Randall says, "You can help people recover in ways that would be a miraculous event in a typical medical office. And it's most gratifying when you have a child sick with something—it might be ADD [Attention Deficit Disorder], or it might be rheumatoid arthritis or asthma—and you treat that child and he recovers right before your eyes, so to speak. And

To Be a Successful Naturopath, You Should . . .

- be an exceptional listener
- have excellent observation skills
- be an effective communicator
- enjoy science
- have a great deal of idealism
- have good business skills

you know that that is going to radically change that person's life."

How Do I Become a Naturopath?

When Randall first got involved with naturopathic medicine more than 20 years ago, the field didn't have a lot of support from the medical community. "To get into naturopathic medicine when I got into it," Randall explains, "you almost had to be a fanatic." He first became interested in naturopathy after stumbling upon a natural health magazine that contained an ad for a naturopathic college. After doing some research, he discovered that naturopathy was alive and well. He had already completed premedical studies and received a degree in human biology, so he enrolled in the National College of Naturopathic Medicine in Oregon. He performed his residency at Bastyr University in Washington.

EDUCATION

High School

Because you will be entering a premed program in college, you will want to take high school science courses such as biology, chemistry, and physics. The physical education courses of some high schools offer instruction in health, nutrition, and exercise. Psychology and sociology courses are also helpful in giving you a basis for understanding your patients. Take English classes to improve your communication skills, which are essential for this work. Finally, round out your education by taking mathematics, history, and computer science classes, all of which will help prepare you for college. In addition to taking these classes, there are other ways you can explore this career. For example, even if you're not an athlete, you can get involved with the athletic department as a student assistant; this may allow you to work alongside doctors who specialize in sports medicine. Some sports doctors use natural treatments like hydrotherapy, massage, and nutritional counseling.

Many communities also offer volunteer opportunities to high school students. Spending afternoons in a hospital or nursing home will help you become familiar with a medical setting and give you experience working with patients. Your local YMCA might need volunteers to lead children's health and recreation programs. You could also pursue a part-time job in a health and nutrition store, or a store that specializes in organic fruits and vegetables.

Postsecondary Training

After high school, you must first complete a premed undergraduate program before you can pursue a Doctor of Naturopathic Medicine degree (N.D.). Bastyr University recommends that your undergraduate studies include courses in biology, general chemistry, organic chemistry, physics, mathematics, psychology, and English. In addition, you should take several humanities courses since medical schools typically accept only the best candidates with well-rounded backgrounds.

Following your undergraduate studies, you may enroll in a naturopathic medicine program. Programs leading to the N.D. degree last four years and require courses in anatomy, physiology, biochemistry, and other basic medical sciences. Students are also required to take courses in nutrition, botanical medicine, and homeopathy. In addition to course instruction, students receive extensive clinical training.

When you are searching for a naturopathic medical school, you must be very careful to find one that is accredited and offers the Doctor of Naturopathic Medicine degree. Schools without accreditation may offer a mail-order education consisting only of correspondence work and recommended textbooks. Only a degree from an accredited school will prepare you to become a licensed naturopath. Currently there are only three such schools in the United States: Bastyr University in Washington, the National College of Naturopathic Medicine in Oregon, and Southwest College of Naturopathic Medicine & Health Sciences in Arizona. The College of Naturopathic Medicine in Connecticut has received candidacy status from CNME, which is a step in the accreditation process. CNME can provide additional information on accreditation.

Some people choose to attend naturopathy programs after completing traditional medical training. Reasons for this vary, but they may have become disillusioned with traditional medicine or discovered naturopathy after beginning their traditional studies. Nevertheless, these students typically must fulfill the same requirements as other students in the N.D. program.

In-depth

History of Naturopathic Medicine

The term naturopathy originated in the 19th century but its practice can be traced back to the ancient Greeks. Hippocrates, considered by many to be the father of modern medicine, extolled natural health care by saying, "Let your food be your medicine and your medicine be your food."

The German homeopathic practitioner John H. Scheel is credited with first using the term naturopath in 1895. Naturopathy was introduced in the United States by Dr. Benedict Lust. The American School of Naturopathy, founded by Dr. Lust in New York City, graduated its first class in 1902. It was the first school of its kind in the United States. In 1909 California became the first state to legally regulate the practice of naturopathy.

Naturopathy flourished in the early part of this century. By 1930 there were more than 20 naturopathic schools and 10,000 practitioners nationwide. With the rise of modern pharmaceuticals, naturopathic medicine witnessed a decline beginning in the 1940s. Since the 1970s, however, more and more people have become interested in natural health care philosophies and naturopathic medicine has experienced a revival.

CERTIFICATION OR LICENSING

The Homeopathic Academy of Naturopathic Physicians offers the certification Diplomate of the Homeopathic Academy of Naturopathic Physicians (DHANP). Requirements for certification include graduating from a four-year naturopathic medical school accredited by the American Association of Naturopathic Physicians (AANP) and passing written and oral tests. To keep this certification, naturopaths must fulfill certain requirements, such as engaging in continuing education on homeopathy.

In addition to the District of Columbia and the U.S. territories of Puerto Rico and the U.S. Virgin Islands, licensing for naturopathic doctors is available in 13 states: Alaska, Arizona, California, Connecticut, Hawaii, Kansas, Maine, Montana, New Hampshire, Oregon, Utah, Vermont, and Washington. Licenses are contingent upon passing the Naturopathic Physicians Licensing Exam, a national standardized test administered by the North American Board of Naturopathic Examiners. In addition, a naturopath must fulfill any requirements for licensure in the state where he or she intends to practice. As this field of medicine continues to gain acceptance, the number of licensed states is expected to grow. Naturopathic physicians who practice in unlicensed states are not allowed to function as physicians, but they still use their skills and knowledge to treat patients, usually limiting their practice to homeopathy or nutritional counseling. In order to maintain their licenses in naturopathic medicine, N.D.s are required to take continuing education courses.

SCHOLARSHIPS AND GRANTS

The AANP and the CNME have information on and links to accredited schools on their Web sites. Contact these schools for information on financial aid and grants. (See "How Do I Learn More?")

FYI

Some highlights of the naturopathic philosophy are as follows:

- Do no harm.
- Recognize the healing power of nature.
- Find and eliminate the cause.
- Involve the total person.
- Teach rather than treat.
- Prevent disease.

Who Will Hire Me?

After completing the Doctor of Naturopathic Medicine degree, Randall did his residency at Bastyr University. He then taught for a few years before moving to Nebraska. He currently has his own practice in which he sees patients four days a week.

Most naturopaths go into private or group practice. Due to the small number of accredited doctoral programs, only a very small percentage of naturopaths become teachers. More research opportunities are becoming available, and some naturopaths are pursuing this aspect of the profession. Also, the natural food industry, which has been thriving, is providing more opportunities for naturopaths as consultants.

Where Can I Go from Here?

"In this day and age," Randall says, "naturopathy is at the forefront of change." Randall keeps up with the latest in natural health research by reading journals, attending conferences, and taking courses for his continuing education requirements. Naturopathic research is also finding its way into the mainstream media.

Because most naturopaths work in private or group practice, advancement depends on the physician's dedication to building up a patient base. Naturopaths in private practice must have a general sense of how to run successful businesses. They must promote their practice within the community, develop a network of contacts with medical doctors who can provide patient referrals, and keep up on natural health research.

What Are the Salary Ranges?

Most naturopaths can make a comfortable living in private practice, but naturopathic medicine is not as financially rewarding as other branches of medicine. Financial success as a naturopath requires dedication to building up a practice and promoting natural health treatment. Though a well-established naturopath may possibly make well over $100,000 a year, most earn much less. A naturopath may make anywhere from $25,000 to $80,000 a year; the salary depends on such factors as the size of the city in which the naturopath practices and the geographic location of the practice.

In licensing states such as Arizona and Oregon, where many in the population are highly interested in natural health and herbs, a naturopath will probably have a larger number of patients and, therefore, a higher salary.

What Is the Job Outlook?

As people become more frustrated with the high cost of traditional medical treatment, medications, and managed care, they will likely turn to alternative forms of health care. Naturopathic medicine is one alternative method that is gaining in popularity.

There are several trends that show naturopathic medicine's increasing acceptance, both by traditional medicine and the general public. For example, the College of Naturopathic Medicine became the first naturopathic department to open within a university (Bridgeport University in Connecticut). Favorable articles about naturopathic medicine have begun to appear in medical journals, and more mass-circulation health magazines are being published. Finally, more insurance companies are covering natural health treatment. All these factors point to a growing need for naturopathic health care providers.

How Do I Learn More?

PROFESSIONAL ORGANIZATIONS

The following organizations provide school, career, and licensing information on naturopathic medicine:

American Association of Naturopathic Physicians
3201 New Mexico Avenue NW, Suite 350
Washington, DC 20016
866-538-2267
http://www.naturopathic.org

Council on Naturopathic Medical Education
PO Box 11426
Johnson, VT 05656
802-635-7090
dir@cnme.org
http://www.cnme.org

Homeopathic Academy of Naturopathic Physicians
PO Box 8341
Covington, WA 98042
253-630-3338
http://www.hanp.net

For information on schools and licensing in Canada, contact

Canadian Association of Naturopathic Doctors
1255 Sheppard Avenue East
Toronto, Canada M2K1E2
416-496-8633
info@naturopathicassoc.ca
http://www.naturopathicassoc.ca

BIBLIOGRAPHY

The following is a sampling of materials relating to the professional concerns and development of naturopaths:

Hudson, Tori. *Women's Encyclopedia of Natural Medicine: Alternative Therapies and Integrative Medicine.* Lincolnwood, Ill.: Keats Publishing, 1999.

Murray, Michael, and Joseph Pizzorno. *Encyclopedia of Natural Medicine.* 2d ed. Roseville, Calif.: Prima Publishing, 1997.

Pizzorno, Joseph E., and Michael T. Murray. *Clinician's Handbook of Natural Medicine.* Kent, U.K: Churchill Livingstone, 2002.

Pizzorno, Joseph E., and Michael T. Murray, eds. *Textbook of Natural Medicine.* Kent, U.K.: Churchill Livingstone, 1999.

Steinfeld, Alan. *Careers in Alternative Medicine.* New York: Rosen, 2003.

Weil, Andrew. *Natural Health, Natural Medicine: The Complete Guide to Wellness and Self-Care for Optimum Health.* Boston: Houghton Mifflin, 2004.

Werbach, Melvyn R. *Case Studies in Natural Medicine.* Tarzana, Calif.: Third Line Press, 2002.

Werbach, Melvyn R. et al. *Textbook of Nutritional Medicine.* Tarzana, Calif.: Third Line Press, 1999.

NEUROLOGICAL SURGEONS

Paramedics shout out vital statistics as a crushed and bloody victim is rushed into the emergency room. Dr. Sherry Robertson looks down at the man she's helping wheel into the operating room and quickly assesses his condition. There is a traumatic eye injury, a smashed rib cage, broken arms, and a broken leg. His skull is cracked. Unbelievably, he is still conscious, but quickly drifting into unconsciousness. She whispers some words of assurance to him and quickly goes to scrub for surgery.

Sherry and another neurological surgeon evaluate and treat his head injuries. Surgery is performed to open the skull, stop the bleeding, and relieve the pressure on his brain. Other surgeons assess and repair the damage done to the rest of his body. He will need extensive reconstructive surgery to put his face back together, but he survives, in large part because of Sherry's skills. Her knowledge, quick assessment of the injuries, and her manual dexterity all work together to save his life.

Definition
Neurological surgeons diagnose and treat patients who have disorders or injuries affecting the nervous system, including the brain, spinal cord, and nerves. They may provide surgical and nonsurgical care for their patients.

Alternative Job Title
Neurosurgeons

High School Subjects
Biology
Chemistry
Health

Personal Skills
Helping/teaching
Technical/scientific

Salary Range
$235,510 to $310,433 to $419,769+

Educational Requirements
Bachelor's degree; four-year medical degree; general surgery residency; neurosurgical residency

Certification or Licensing
Recommended (certification)
Required by all states (licensing)

Outlook
About as fast as the average

DOT
070

GOE
14.02.01

NOC
3112

O*NET-SOC
29-1069.99

What Does a Neurological Surgeon Do?

A board-certified *neurological surgeon* diagnoses, evaluates, and treats patients with disorders or injuries affecting the central, peripheral, and autonomic nervous systems—which include the brain, meninges (any of the three membranes that envelope the brain and spinal cord), skull, spinal cord, pituitary gland, and nerves—and their supporting structures and vascular (blood) supply.

This specialist provides both nonsurgical and surgical care, depending on the nature of the injury or illness. Neurological surgery also includes the operative and nonoperative management, diagnosis, evaluation, treatment, critical care, and rehabilitation of patients with disorders of the nervous system.

Neurological surgeons treat a wide variety of illnesses and conditions. Within the broader specialty of neurological surgery, there are three subdivisions, or subspecialties: brain, spine, and peripheral nerves and muscles. An accident that injures the head, spinal cord, or nerves might require neurosurgical treatment. Or a patient who suffers a serious stroke may require neurosurgery to increase the blood supply to areas of the brain and spinal cord. In order to restore normal circulation to the brain, neurological surgeons may remove the arteriosclerotic debris that clogs neck arteries. Children born with a deformed or injured brain or spinal cord or who are suffering from poor spinal fluid circulation may benefit from neurosurgery to correct these problems and to help them live a more normal life.

Perhaps the most common problem neurological surgeons treat is a ruptured disc that causes neck or lower back pain that can spread to the arms and hands. Slipped discs and pinched nerves, on the other hand, may be treated nonsurgically, with bed rest, braces, physical therapy, or a combination of these methods.

Many people often confuse the work of neurologists and neurological surgeons. Of the two professions, however, only neurological surgeons are allowed to perform the complex neural surgeries.

Patients usually see neurological surgeons in two different situations. In the first instance, the patient may be injured through an accident or has suffered a stroke or brain aneurysm. If a patient is admitted to an emergency room with traumatic injuries, the emergency room physician will ask that a neurological surgeon evaluate the patient. Cases such as these are called acute care, because the patient requires immediate attention and might need surgery. In the second instance, neurological surgeons see patients who have been referred to them by neurologists. Generally, a neurologist evaluates all nonacute care patients and refers the patient to a neurological surgeon if surgery is believed to be the best treatment.

Neurological surgeons work with many of the same illnesses and injuries as neurologists, such as epilepsy, peripheral nerve diseases, and tumors. However, the neurological surgeon usually becomes involved with non-acute care patients when nonsurgical treatments, such as medication, have failed or are ineffective. Because of their specialized surgical talents and skills, neurological surgeons spend most of their time in the operating room. Some of their time, however, is devoted to clinic care, hospital rounds, consultations, conferences, and teaching responsibilities.

Lingo to Learn

Computerized tomography (CT or CAT scan) A form of radiology, or X ray, that uses computers to construct two-dimensional pictures of selected body parts. Dye may be injected into a vein to obtain a better picture.

Electroencephalogram (EEG) A procedure that uses electrodes attached to the scalp to record the brain's continuous electrical activity.

Electromyogram (EMG) A test that measures and records electrical activity from the muscles and nerves. It is often used in cases involving pain, numbness, tingling, or weakness.

Magnetic resonance imaging (MRI) A way of imaging internal organs, including the brain. For an MRI of the brain, a patient lies still in a small chamber for approximately 30 minutes while a very strong magnet passes over the head.

Myelogram A test in which dye is injected into the spinal canal, making the structure clearly visible to X rays. The test is often used to diagnose patients with neck or back pain or suspected spinal tumors.

Neurosonogram A test that uses ultra-high-frequency sound waves to analyze blood flow, most often in stroke victims.

What Is It Like to Be a Neurological Surgeon?

Neurological surgeons routinely operate on bundles of nerves the size of hairs. They expertly wield lasers near the fragile stem of the spinal cord, and they systematically cut through the rock-hard skull that protects our brains to remove tumors buried in the delicate gray matter. In short, they work on the most sensitive areas of the human body, areas that are responsible for both our most basic and advanced functions.

Patients often come to the neurological surgeon in bad shape, and it is up to the neurological surgeon to quickly determine the best course of action. "There are some specialties where you make decisions based on lots of information. This isn't one of them," states Dr. Frances Conley, retired Chief of Neurosurgery at the Palo Alto Veterans Administration Medical Center.

In many situations, the emergency room physician brings the neurological surgeon in to evaluate the patient and see if surgery is, in fact, necessary. Based on training and experience, the neurological surgeon must act quickly and decisively, whether that means ordering advanced tests, consulting with a neurologist, or performing emergency surgery.

A typical case may be a patient who is brought to the emergency room with a bruise on his forehead. He's awake, but not talking, and he has a left-sided weakness. The following determinations must be made: Where is the injury? Did he have a fall? Does he have a blood clot as a result of the fall?

Neurological surgeons use several diagnostic procedures to determine if the patient is functioning normally, especially in terms of cranial nerve function. To determine if there are any problems, the patient's balance, reflexes, motor skills, and cognitive abilities are assessed. The results may indicate a problem but not necessarily the source of the problem. Neurological surgeons use simple logic combined with a vast knowledge of neural anatomy and physiology to solve the problem behind a patient's complaint of pain or abnormal function. Based on their conclusions, they may order a number of tests to try to pinpoint the source and location of the problem or to rule out other possibilities.

Tests that may be requested are computerized tomography or computer-assisted tomography (also referred to as a CT or CAT scan), electroencephalogram (EEG), and magnetic resonance imaging (MRI). These tests may help the neurological surgeon determine whether surgery is an option.

Children present specific challenges to neurological surgeons. Dr. Alexa Canady is a pediatric neurological surgeon at Children's Hospital of Michigan and a professor and vice-chair of neurosurgery at Wayne State University in Detroit. Every day she treats infants and children who have a variety of neurological problems and disorders, including brain tumors, traumatic head injuries, congenital spinal problems, abnormal skull development, epilepsy, and hydrocephalus (excessive fluid in the brain). These children may have been born with these problems, or the problems may be a result of injuries. "Basically, I see anyone with a neurological problem with a possible surgical solution," she says.

Alexa enjoys working with children. She explains, "The patients in the adult neurosurgery wing are terrified. It's serious and somber. The children's unit is completely different. Kids don't know enough to be terrified. Their parents might be, but they're not. So, the atmosphere is lighter, more playful." She adds, "I also like the spectrum of diseases in pediatric neurosurgery. I like working with congenital problems versus degenerative problems."

As with any surgery, neurological surgery carries a great deal of risk. There is, however, a great deal of variety in the surgeries. Dr. Frances Conley admits that it would have driven her crazy if she had had to perform the same procedure every day. She loved the wide range of challenges that her work presented. "Backs, necks, carotid arteries, the front and back of the brain—it's all so diverse."

Neurological surgeries often require the surgeon to be innovative in terms of surgical technique or even instrumentation. Sometimes, the creative part of the surgery is how the neurological surgeon accesses the surgical site. Other times the creative part is how the actual repair work is conceived and executed. Still other times, the creative moment of the surgery comes in devising a unique tool that will allow a neurological surgeon to attempt something that has never been done successfully before.

Dr. David Kline, Chairman of the Department of Neurosurgery at the Louisiana State University Medical Center in New Orleans, is one of the world's leading peripheral nerve specialists. "I see patients, take histories, sort through the injuries, and determine what can be surgically repaired," he says. He subdivides his specialty into three areas. Many patients come to him with lacerations, stretches, and lesions on the brachial plexus, the nerves running to the arm, forearm, and hand. Other patients come to him with what are called spontaneous entrapments, where a nerve becomes trapped and compressed, causing a great deal of pain. Carpal tunnel syndrome is the most common nerve compression problem. In a patient with carpal tunnel syndrome, the nerve into the hand thickens and rubs against a ligament in the wrist. The solution is straightforward—make more room for the nerve. The surgical remedy, however, is complex. David first identifies the precise location of the compressed nerve using electrical studies. A segment of the ligament is then cut to decompress the nerve and create more space.

The third category of nerve problems that David treats is tumors. They can grow in or next to nerves, affecting muscles and sensation. David's reputation is well known.

Neurological surgeons spend most of their day in the operating room (OR), and that day begins early. "I would get up at 5:00 A.M. and go for a run for 30 minutes to an hour. I'd be at the hospital by 7:15 and operating by 7:30," says Frances. "I was usually in the OR all day."

Alexa says, "I usually operate four days a week. Mondays I'm in my office seeing patients, other days

I'm teaching or running clinics." Alexa and David teach and work with residents, who usually accompany them on their rounds. They also supervise clinical presentations and conferences.

Do I Have What It Takes to Be a Neurological Surgeon?

Neurological surgery is one of the most demanding of the medical specialties. Those who enter the field will be challenged emotionally, physically, and intellectually. The career involves high levels of stress, long hours, and difficult, complex cases.

Patients are usually quite ill. Often, a surgical procedure is possible, but it may not be successful. "You need to know your limitations," explains Frances as she looks back on her practice. "I frequently had to tell families there was nothing more I could do, or that there wasn't a surgical solution."

"It's harder to help people with this type of surgery than with any other," explains David. "There are limits to what you can do, but the complexity appeals to me." Part of the complexity of the cases comes from the delicate nature of neurological surgery and the sensitive areas of the body on which it is performed.

Neurological surgeons work long hours, and on those days that they have surgeries scheduled they usually spend the entire day on their feet in the operating room. "You need stamina," says Frances. "A surgery can last anywhere from an hour to 15 hours." Alexa says her longest surgery lasted 23 hours. "That's very unusual," she says. "It was a surgery to correct a malformation of a child's brain."

In addition to long days filled with surgeries, neurological surgeons are also on call several nights a week, depending on such factors as the number of neurosurgical cases there are or the number of other neurological surgeons on staff at the hospital or the clinic where they work. David, for example, is on call every fourth weekend, while Alexa is on call every third night during the week. Neurological surgeons are on call 24 hours a day for their own patients.

The instruments and technology used in neurological surgery also add to its complexity. "You have to love using instruments," David stresses. "This is a technology-driven field and you've got to keep up with it." Surgeons routinely use electrodes, recording machines, microscopes, and micro-instruments. Frances lists some of the instruments she used. "When practicing, I used air-driven power tools to remove and cut through bone, special soft-tissue instruments and, if necessary, I created a tool." In addition, neurosurgeons must be able to understand and interpret complex medical and diagnostic tests.

A sense of humor comes in handy in most professions. Surgeons, however, seem to thrive on joking banter, both in and out of the operating room. Prospective neurological surgeons should be aware of this propensity for sharp humor. Those who work with surgeons usually learn to put up with the cutting remarks or decide to work elsewhere. One explanation may be that with the stress, long hours, and emotionally taxing cases, these specialists develop thick skins in order to deal with their work. At the very least, Alexa believes humor keeps her grounded.

How Do I Become a Neurological Surgeon?

Science and the medical field appealed to Sherry even when she was a child. Although she did not originally plan to become a neurological surgeon, the brain seemed to fascinate her from a very early age. "I won a science fair in the second grade for a project on the brain," she says with a chuckle. "So, I guess it was in my future."

Because of the complexity of the nervous system and the advanced techniques that are used in neurosurgical procedures, neurosurgery has one of the longest training periods of any medical specialty.

EDUCATION

High School

If you are interested in pursuing a medical degree, a high school education emphasizing college preparatory classes is a must. Science courses, such as biology, chemistry, and physics, are necessary, as are math courses. These classes will not only provide you with an introduction to basic science and math concepts but also allow you to determine your own aptitude in these areas. Since college will be your next educational step, it is also important to take English courses to develop your research and writing skills. Foreign language and social science classes will also help make you an appealing candidate for college admission as well as prepare you for your future undergraduate and graduate education. Courses in computer science are a must, as well, since the computer is changing the way medicine is communicated and shared by busy medical professionals.

If you are certain you wish to pursue a medical career, you may want to consider entering a college or university that is associated with a medical school and offers an accelerated medical education program. In these accelerated programs, you spend either two or three years completing your undergraduate work and then spend four years at the medical school associated with that college or university. Students in accelerated programs have the advantage of finishing medical school before their peers who take the normal educational route. More information on such programs is available from high school guidance counselors.

Postsecondary Training

Following high school, the next step on your educational path to be a neurological surgeon is to earn a bachelor's degree from an accredited four-year college or university. While you are in college, prepare for medical school by taking science courses, including physics, biology, and organic and inorganic chemistry. Courses in English, mathematics, and the social sciences are also highly recommended.

After receiving an undergraduate degree, you need to apply to, and be accepted by, a medical school. Admission is competitive, and applicants must undergo a fairly extensive and difficult admissions process that takes into consideration grade point averages, scores on the Medical College Admission Test (MCAT), and professor recommendations. Most students apply to several schools early in their senior year of college. Only about one-third of the applicants are accepted.

In order to earn the degree doctor of medicine (M.D.), you must complete four years of medical school. For the first two years of medical school, you attend lectures and classes and spend time in laboratories. Courses include anatomy, biochemistry, physiology, pharmacology, psychology, microbiology, pathology, medical ethics, and laws governing medicine. You learn to take patient histories, perform routine physical examinations, and recognize symptoms.

In your third and fourth years, you are involved in more practical studies. You work in clinics and hospitals supervised by residents and physicians and you learn acute, chronic, preventive, and rehabilitative care. You go through what are known as rotations (brief periods of study) in such areas as internal medicine, obstetrics and gynecology, pediatrics, and surgery. Rotations allow you to gain exposure to many different medical fields.

Upon graduating from an accredited medical school, you must pass a standard examination given by the National Board of Medical Examiners. Most physicians complete an internship, also referred to as a transition year, during which they decide their area of specialization.

Following your internship, you begin what is known as a residency, which is graduate medical education in a specialty and is paid, on-the-job training, usually in a hospital. If you wish to pursue the specialty of neurosurgery you must first complete a residency in general surgery. Per requirements established by the Accreditation Council for Graduate Medical Education and the Royal College of Physicians and Surgeons of Canada, general surgery residents must complete a five-year program that is broad-based and leads to either continued study and training in general surgery or to entering a training program in another surgical specialty.

Throughout the general surgery residency, you are supervised at all levels of training, with the attending surgeon ultimately responsible for the patient's care. You begin your training by first assisting and then performing basic operations such as the removal of an appendix or a hernia repair. As your residency years continue, you gain responsibility through teaching and supervisory duties. Eventually you are allowed to perform complex operations independently.

Neurological surgery residency programs, which follow the general surgery residency, include 60 months (five years) of specialized training, following fundamental clinical skills. As a resident in neurosurgery you study research, the basic neurosciences, neuropathology, neuroradiology, and other related disciplines. During your residency, you are required to maintain a record of the operative procedures you complete. This record will be used later when you seek board certification.

CERTIFICATION OR LICENSING

Licensing is mandatory in the United States. It is required in all states before any doctor can practice medicine. In order to be licensed, doctors must have graduated from medical school, passed the licensing test of the state in which they will practice, and completed their residency. Physicians licensed in one state can usually get licensed to practice in another state without further testing, however, some states may limit reciprocity. Foreign medical school graduates usually must pass an examination and complete a U.S. residency before qualifying for licensure.

Certification is not mandatory but is highly recommended. The American Board of Neurological Surgery (ABNS), formed in 1940, is responsible for certifying neurological surgeons who graduate from accredited programs in the United States.

To be considered for certification, the candidate must successfully complete training, residency, and practice requirements. Other requirements include a valid license to practice medicine, hospital staff privileges, and an endorsement from the program director. Certification by the ABNS is based upon approval of an applicant's education and training qualifications, a review of the physician's professional practice, and the passage of written and oral examinations. This certification process includes a thorough assessment of the surgeon's skill, judgment, and knowledge.

Once all these steps have been met and approved by the ABNS, the candidate is certified as a Diplomate of the ABNS. Once board-certified by the ABNS, a neurosurgeon is eligible to become an active member of the American Association of Neurological Surgeons (AANS). As an AANS member, the surgeon must attend educational seminars, meetings, and classes to keep current in the field.

SCHOLARSHIPS AND GRANTS

Tuition costs vary depending upon the size of the school, whether or not the school is in the state where you reside, and whether the school is privately or publicly funded. The profession you choose will also determine your costs.

There are usually grants, scholarships, and loans available through most colleges. The easiest way to explore the various financial aid possibilities is to write directly to the financial aid offices of schools and request information and application forms.

There are also various loan programs available through the federal government, including Pell Grants, Stafford Student Loans, National Direct Student Loans, Health Education Assistance Loans, and Health Professions Student Loans. Your high school guidance counselor should have information about these programs.

Many students finance their education through the Armed Forces Health Professions Scholarship Program. Each branch of the military participates in this program, paying students' tuitions in exchange for military service. Contact your local recruiting office for more information on this program.

The U.S. Public Health Service also provides financial assistance to students in return for service. Information regarding aid can be found at the Web site: http://nhsc.bhpr.hrsa.gov. Application for this program should be made through your school's financial aid office.

For information about federal funding for education see the Guide to All U.S. Government Grants and Loans Benefiting Students Web site: http://www.fedmoney.org.

Many public and private organizations and businesses offer scholarships as well. Libraries, the Internet, and your school guidance office should be able to provide you with more information. A good starting point for financial aid research is the SmartStudent Guide to Financial Aid Web site. This site has an extensive list of financial assistance information and links: http://www.finaid.org.

Who Will Hire Me?

There are few solo practitioners of neurological surgery. Most neurological surgeons enter into private practice with a partner or a small group. If you are working at a medical school, private clinic, or hospital you will most likely be part of a larger group of neurological surgeons in a large population area that has major medical facilities.

Where Can I Go from Here?

Research and teaching are two options for you as a neurological surgeon. Many neurological surgeons combine the two with a private practice. You may ascend through the ranks of physicians and surgeons to head a department or a hospital. Or, you may aspire to become the Chief of Neurosurgery, but appointment to this position is extremely competitive.

What Are the Salary Ranges?

Physicians have among the highest earnings of any occupation. According to the Association of American Medical Colleges, salaries in 2004 ranged from about $46,722 to $53,607 annually for sixth year residents. Salaries vary depending on the kind of residency, the hospital, and the geographic area.

Self-employed physicians who own or are part owners of their medical practice had higher median incomes than salaried physicians. The U.S. Department of Labor *Occupational Outlook Handbook* states that in 2002 the median income for surgeons after expenses was $255,438 annually. Salary.com, a company specializing in recruitment and salary information, reports annual median earnings for neurological surgeons were $310,433 in 2005. The highest paid surgeons earned $419,769 and the lowest paid earned $235,510. Specialty surgeons can expect to make more than general surgeons. Other factors influencing individual incomes include size of practice, skill, hours worked per week, geographic area, and professional reputation.

What Is the Job Outlook?

The health care industry is thriving, and the *Occupational Outlook Handbook* predicts employment of physicians in almost all fields to grow about as fast as the average for all occupations through 2012. As the population grows and ages, the demand for physician services will increase. In addition, technology continues to improve and procedures are developed that enable physicians to treat more injuries and illnesses.

Additionally, the *Occupational Outlook Handbook* notes that new physicians will be less likely to enter solo practices in the future and are more likely to take salaried jobs in group practices, hospitals or other health networks. However, neurological surgery is so specialized and competitive that there will always be a demand for the special skills and expertise of the neurological surgeon.

How Do I Learn More?

PROFESSIONAL ORGANIZATIONS

The following are organizations that provide information on the profession of neurological surgeon:

American Association of Neurological Surgeons
5550 Meadowbrook Drive
Rolling Meadows, IL 60088
888-566-2267
info@aans.org
http://www.aans.org

American Board of Neurological Surgery
6550 Fannin Street, Suite 2139
Houston, TX 77030
713-441-6015
abns@tmh.tmc.edu
http://www.abns.org

American College of Surgeons
633 North St. Clair Street
Chicago, IL 60611-3211
312-202-5000
http://www.facs.org

The Association of Women Surgeons publishes Pocket Mentor: A Manual for Surgical Interns and Residents, *a guide for women in the surgical specialties. It also provides a video,* Women Are Surgeons, *that can be ordered from the Web site listed below.*

Association of Women Surgeons
414 Plaza Drive, Suite 209
Westmont, IL 60559
630-655-0392
info@womensurgeons.org
http://www.womensurgeons.org

BIBLIOGRAPHY

The following is a sampling of materials relating to the professional concerns and development of neurological surgeons:

American Medical Association. *Neurological & Orthopaedic Surgery.* Chicago: American Medical Association, 1999.

Arriaga, Moises A., and J. Diaz Day, eds. *Neurosurgical Issues in Otolaryngology: Principles and Practice of Collaboration.* Philadelphia: Lippincott Williams & Wilkins, 1999.

Black, Peter M., and Eugene Rossitch. *Neurosurgery: An Introductory Text.* New York: Oxford University Press, 1995.

Connolly, E. Sanders et al. *Fundamentals of Operative Techniques in Neurosurgery.* New York: Thieme Medical Publishing, 2002.

Flitter, Marc. *Judith's Pavilion: The Haunting Memories of a Neurosurgeon.* New York: Warner Books, 1998.

Greenberg, Mark S. *Handbook of Neurosurgery.* 5th ed. New York: Thieme Medical Publishing, 2000.

Greenblatt, Samuel H., T. Forcht Dagi, and Mel H. Epstein. *A History of Neurosurgery.* Park Ridge, Ill.: American Association of Neurological Surgeons, 1997.

Rengachary, Setti, and Richard Ellenbogen. *Principles in Neurosurgery.* 2d ed. St. Louis: C. V. Mosby, 2004.

NEUROLOGISTS

Bad examples sometimes teach important lessons. During her residency training Dr. Janet Jankowiak learned from just such an example. One Monday morning she was with a group of residents on neurological service. The attending physician led the group to the room of a patient who had been brought into the trauma unit over the weekend. Although the trauma physicians and nurses had desperately tried to save the patient's life, only machines now kept the woman technically alive. By law, the neurological service unit had to perform specific tests to determine whether or not the patient was brain dead. The woman's family waited in an area nearby, and as the residents approached they could see the family members huddled together in prayer.

A nurse walked up to the attending physician and said in low tones, "The family has waited all night to speak with the neurologist. I promised I'd let them know when you got here."

Although he nodded, the attending physician made no move toward the area with the family members. Instead, he continued on into the patient's room and began leading the residents through the series of perfunctory tests. When they finished, he signed the patient's chart, indicating the woman was brain dead. Then, without so much as a glance over his shoulder, he silently lead the surprised residents down a back stairway, away from the grieving, confused family.

"I was so appalled by the whole thing, I actually can't believe I experienced it," Janet says. "But it taught me the importance of understanding what people need from me, as a doctor and as a person." Today as a neurologist at a major hospital, Janet works hard to address her patients' individual concerns as well as treat their illnesses.

Definition
Neurologists diagnose and treat patients with diseases and disorders affecting such areas as the brain, spinal cord, peripheral nerves, muscles, and autonomic nervous system.

High School Subjects
Biology
Chemistry
Physics

Personal Skills
Helping/teaching
Technical/scientific

Salary Range
$143,143 to $162,685 to $191,471+

Educational Requirements
Medical degree

Certification or Licensing
Recommended (certification)
Required by all states (licensing)

Outlook
About as fast as the average

DOT
070

GOE
14.02.01

NOC
3112

O*NET-SOC
29-1069.99

What Does a Neurologist Do?

A *neurologist* evaluates, diagnoses, and treats patients with diseases and disorders impairing the function of the brain, spinal cord, peripheral nerves, muscles, and autonomic nervous system, as well as treating the supporting structures and vascular supply to these areas. A neurologist conducts and evaluates specific tests relating to the analysis of the central or peripheral nervous system.

In addition to treating such neurological disorders as epilepsy, neuritis, brain and spinal cord tumors, multiple sclerosis, Parkinson's disease, and stroke, neurologists treat muscle disorders and pain, especially headache. Also, illnesses, injuries, or diseases that can adversely affect the nervous system, such as diabetes, hypertension, and cancers, are treated by neurologists.

Neurologists see patients in two capacities: as a consulting physician or as the patient's principal physician. A neurologist works as a consulting physician when asked by a patient's primary care physician to consult on a case as, for example, when a patient has a stroke or shows signs of mental confusion. As a consulting physician, the neurologist conducts a neurological evaluation and evaluates mental, emotional, and behavioral problems to assess whether these conditions are treatable. The neurologist also works with psychiatrists, psychologists, or other mental health professionals as necessary.

A neurologist is the principal physician for patients with such illnesses as Parkinson's disease or multiple sclerosis. A neurologist working as the principal physician, for example, might evaluate a patient who has suffered several inexplicable seizures. The neurologist might use the results of a CT scan and an encephalogram to diagnose the patient with epilepsy. To manage this disorder, the neurologist might prescribe medications, such as antiepileptic drugs. If the patient tolerates the medications well, the neurologist might see the patient every three to six months, maybe only once a year.

Sometimes, a primary care physician believes a consultation with a neurologist might benefit a patient. In this case the primary care physician would refer the patient to a neurologist for what is called a neurological consultation. A neurological consultation is a review of the patient's medical history, a physical examination, and tests of vision, strength, coordination, reflexes, and sensation. These tests help the neurologist to determine whether the source of the patient's problem is within the nervous system. Further tests may be necessary to confirm the diagnosis and determine specific treatment.

Lingo to Learn

Cerebral spinal fluid analysis Under local anesthesia, fluid is drawn from the spinal column and then analyzed. The test is often crucial in making the diagnosis of a bleeding disorder, tumor, or infection of the brain or spinal cord. Also referred to as a **spinal tap.**

Computerized tomography A form of radiology, or X ray, which uses computers to construct two-dimensional pictures of selected body parts. Dye may be injected into a vein to obtain a better picture. Also referred to as a **CT** or **CAT scan.**

Electroencephalogram (EEG) A procedure that uses electrodes attached to the scalp to record the brain's continuous electrical activity.

Electromyogram (EMG) A test that measures and records electrical activity from the muscles and nerves. It is often used in cases involving pain, numbness, tingling, or weakness.

Evoked potentials A test that records the brain's electrical responses to visual, auditory, and sensory stimuli. They are useful in evaluating and diagnosing symptoms of dizziness, numbness, and tingling, as well as some visual problems.

Magnetic resonance imaging (MRI) An advanced way of making images of body parts. For a brain MRI, a patient lies still in a small chamber for approximately 30 minutes while a very strong magnet passes over the brain.

Myelogram A test in which dye is injected into the spinal canal, making the structure clearly visible on X rays.

Neurosonography A test that uses ultra high frequency sound waves to analyze blood flow, most often in stroke victims.

Seizure A sudden attack often characterized by altered consciousness and convulsions.

What Is It Like to Be a Neurologist?

"The nervous system gives you specific symptoms to let you know what's wrong," says Dr. Jack Whisnant, professor of health services research at the Mayo Clinic College of Medicine and currently working with the Mayo Clinic's stroke epidemiology research facility in Rochester, Minnesota. "In other areas of medicine, discomfort doesn't necessarily indicate the precise problem." It has often been said that neurology is as close as clinical medicine comes to obeying scientific principles of biology. "Symptoms and functions are very closely related in neurology," says Jack. "You have to understand the anatomy and physiology of the brain and the spinal cord."

The close relationship between symptoms and functions signifies the importance of the neurologist's evaluation of the patient. Taking the history and performing a physical examination combine to provide the neurologist with the answers to important questions. "The history helps you determine the process, and the exam tells you where the problem is located," Jack says. As part of the physical examination, the neurologist performs reflex tests; examines the patient's ability to walk, balance on one foot, or other movements; and analyzes the patient's strength, vision, and sensation.

"The distribution of abnormalities throughout the body can tell you where the problem is," explains Jack. "The nervous system tells you what's going on," he emphasizes. "So, it's extremely important to detail the onset and the evolution of the problem—when the symptoms stopped or subsided, for example."

Dr. Janet Jankowiak works at an inner-city hospital in Boston, where she specializes in rehabilitating patients with strokes, geriatric dementia (mental deterioration caused by aging), traumatic brain injuries, and behavioral neurological problems. Almost all of her patient evaluations begin with a mental status examination in which she gauges how alert and attentive her patients are. She runs them through a series of tests, checking such things as their attention span, language skills, and memory. For example, she might ask a patient to show her how to use a hammer or to name in order the days of a week. If the patient has trouble remembering what a hammer is or the names and order of days, it could be an indication of damage to the frontal lobes of the brain.

Diagnostic neurology reveals the patient's condition, but this is only one side of the job; managing the case is the other side. Practicing neurologists often have the responsibility for managing the acute- and long-term care and rehabilitation of their patients.

Since 1994, Janet has been the Director of Brain Injury Rehabilitation at Jewish Memorial Hospital and Rehabilitation Center. "Seventy percent of traumatic brain injuries are to young men in their early twenties—men in the prime of their lives, really—who are victims of motor vehicle accidents, assaults, gun shot wounds." Janet works with her patient's family to get the patient into rehab. "Getting through to these patients and convincing them of the necessity of rehabilitation is often difficult in these circumstances. Most of these patients say they don't need help or rehabilitation," says Janet. "And they usually have a host of other problems that complicate things." These problems range from alcoholism and drug use to poverty to physical abuse. According to Janet, however, if the patient leaves the hospital without help, his or her problems could multiply. "Often, these patients have short-term memory problems. If a patient has a job, he could lose it in the days following his head injury because he just can't remember things. A housewife can't divide her attention between tasks because that part of her brain has suffered some damage."

It's no wonder, then, that part of Janet's job involves identifying the social issues that complicate her patients' lives and then trying to get her patients to agree to some modification of those issues for the betterment of their own health. Sometimes, she can get her patients into group homes, but the odds are usually against her patients scoring triumphant recoveries. Often, they revert to the drugs or alcohol or physical abuse that, in turn, leads them back into situations in which they sustain more damaging injuries. "You just do the best you can," says Janet. "You try and help them modify their behavior."

Jack's specialty is stroke patients. Strokes are caused by abnormalities in the brain's blood vessels. According to Jack, strokes generally occur in one of two manners. Either the force of blood coursing through the arterial wall causes the wall to break and blood leaks (hemorrhages) through the breach or the blood vessel itself is obstructed (occluded) and the tissue dies. The dead tissue is also called an infarction. Strokes occur more frequently in older patients, but younger patients, even children, can experience strokes. Neurologists can usually identify a stroke easily by the patient's complaint of a sudden onset of paralysis on one side. Often, the paralysis is complicated by compromised vision and aphasia (loss of speech and language). Amazingly, for all the damage it has wreaked, the stroke might not alter the patient's consciousness at all.

"A stroke is severe at the outset, but it can subside," Jack says. "It can do its maximum damage in a second." More often, he explains, the stroke evolves for a short period of time, usually several hours. In more rare cases, the stroke may evolve over a period of a few days. In severe cases, the patient typically goes to the hospital or urgent-care center where a neurological surgeon evaluates him or her. With a more mild stroke, the patient often delays the visit to his or her physician or neurologist for up to a week or more. Jack says that although patients usually know something is wrong, if the symptoms seem mild enough to ignore for a bit, patients usually do ignore them. Unfortunately, this can jeopardize their recovery. "It's so important that they be evaluated, because strokes can be prevented," stresses Jack. "We have preventive medications and surgical procedures to prevent strokes. There are drugs to dissolve clots and promote recovery, but they must be administered within the first three hours of the stroke's occurrence."

Among the most common surgical remedies is the carotid endarterectomy. In this procedure an angiogram (a radiographic image of blood vessels) is taken to show exactly where the artery narrows due to the accumulation of plaque. Neurological surgeons then surgically remove the plaque from the arterial wall. Preventive medications carry their own set of risks. For example, thrombolitic drugs (drugs that cause the break up of a blood clot) that have the potential to prevent strokes or reverse paralysis are not appropriate for all patients because they can increase the risk of hemorrhage. These drugs have been through clinical trials and received Federal Drug Administration approval, but their practical application hasn't yet been perfected. "The clinical trials are complete," Jack says, "but they're still evolving." He goes on to explain that using drugs like these requires a team of doctors working together to monitor the application of the drugs.

Jack is at ease discussing the research side of neurology for good reason. Since 1975 he has been the director of the Mayo Clinic's Cerebrovascular Clinical Research Center, dividing his time between practicing neurology and working in neurological research—specifically, population-based epidemiology. He recently retired from diagnostic neurology to devote himself full time, to his research. "The primary goal of my research has been to discover what causes diseases, or chronic disease epidemiology," explains Jack. Epidemiology is the record of the natural history of a disease. His work focuses on the epidemiology of strokes in Rochester County, Minnesota—a comparison of factors that influence the occurrence of strokes in patients within that defined area. "The records for Rochester County begin in 1907, but the most important data begins in the 1950s," Jack says. His duties as director of the clinical research center include planning studies, supervising data collection and abstract writing, and conducting statistical analysis of as many as 1,500 patients in order to determine the outcomes and what influenced those outcomes.

Do I Have What It Takes to Be a Neurologist?

Janet doesn't mince words when describing the rigors and frustrations of her job. "I work in an inner-city hospital," she says, "with the kind of patients Medicaid and Medicare don't want to pay for. I don't get soccer players with mild head injuries, I get patients in comas from gang fights. Many don't make it. Those who do come around generally have a whole host of other problems to complicate their rehabilitation: alcoholism, drug use, abusive behavior."

Each day presents a new challenge, whether it is cutbacks due to managed care, insurance companies refusing to pay for an expensive test for an indigent patient, or patients who refuse to be helped. Granted, not all neurologists practice in the inner city, but most do have a variety of cases. Because they treat patients who have suffered injuries to the head, neurologists need to have a calm and soothing presence with patients who may be experiencing fluctuating emotions, including confusion and anger.

Many of Janet's patients are older and have geriatric dementia. "Very often, I spend a lot of time reassuring them that they're not crazy," she says. "They realize something is wrong, but they don't want to admit it and they don't want to be treated like children. In fact, the closer you get to the areas of their deficits, the more angry and defensive they get. Sometimes, you have to struggle to remember that each person is different, and will require from you something different than the last patient. It can be very difficult. You need the patience of a saint." Janet adds, "You do as much as you can—but you have to realize there are limits. Still, it's not always easy to let go. You need to be able to treat your patients with a great deal of compassion. You have to try and preserve the dignity of each patient. People always seem amazed when I manage to reach through to a patient with dementia. It's like learning another language. You don't always

To Be a Successful Neurologist, You Should . . .

- be a good clinician
- be able to listen and communicate well
- be patient and detail-oriented
- enjoy helping and working with people
- have good hand-eye coordination and manual dexterity

have to know the words to get your point across." She uses a common analogy to illustrate her point. "I like to see the glass as half full, rather than seeing the glass as half empty. I always ask myself, 'what can we do to expand their lives?'"

In addition to compassion, neurologists need a mind capable of sifting through a lot of data for specific details. "You need an interest in relating to people and sorting out diseases," advises Jack. "People who are very compulsive about details are attracted to neurology," he adds. "It's a demanding specialty, and medical students aren't easily attracted to it because it seems too complicated. You do need a broad base of knowledge, but neurology looks to be more complicated than it really is."

People who are very compulsive about details are attracted to neurology.

While Janet acknowledges that neurology is a challenging specialty, she believes young doctors considering a specialty should not be intimidated by the field. "If you like it and have the passion to do it—do it," she says. "You really need the passion. Just don't lose sight of what uniqueness you bring to the job."

Both Jack and Janet agree that the field is incredibly exciting. "Talk about a frontier," says Janet. "Neurology truly is a pioneering field."

How Do I Become a Neurologist?

EDUCATION

High School

If you are interested in pursuing a medical degree, a high school education emphasizing college preparatory classes is a must. Science courses, such as biology, chemistry, and physics, are necessary, as are math courses. These classes will not only provide you with an introduction to basic science and math concepts but also allow you to determine your own aptitude in these areas. Since college will be your next educational step, it is also important to take English courses to develop your researching and writing skills. Foreign language, social science, and computer classes will also help make you an appealing candidate for college admission as well as prepare you for your future undergraduate and graduate education. Some colleges and universities that have medical schools have accelerated programs for students who are certain that they want at attend medical school. High school seniors who are sure of their desire to pursue a medical degree may wish to look carefully at these programs. These programs typically reduce or consolidate the number of years spent as an undergraduate and thereby speed up entrance into medical school. Often, the programs refer to the number of years in their title. For example, a six- or seven-year med student is actually enrolled in two or three years, respectively, of undergraduate school, plus the requisite four years of medical school. Special restrictions and qualifying requirements apply, so students interested in this option should contact the school early on in the application process. High school guidance counselors should also be able to provide you with information and direction.

Postsecondary Training

If you are not entering an accelerated program following high school, the next step on your educational path to be a neurologist is to earn a bachelor's degree from an accredited four-year college or university. Suggested premedical courses include physics, biology, and organic and inorganic chemistry. Courses in English and the humanities, mathematics, and the social sciences are also highly recommended.

After receiving an undergraduate degree, you must then apply and be accepted to medical school. Admission is competitive and applicants must undergo a fairly extensive and difficult admissions process that considers grade point average, score on the Medical College Admission Test (MCAT), and recommendations from professors. Most students apply to several schools early in their senior year of college.

In order to earn the doctor of medicine (M.D.) degree, a student must complete four years of medical school study and training. For the first two years of medical school, students attend lectures and classes and spend time in laboratories. Courses include anatomy, biochemistry, physiology, pharmacology, psychology, microbiology, pathology, medical ethics, and laws governing medicine. Students learn to take

In-depth

Repetitive Head Injuries

Nationally, repetitive head injuries account for a large portion of traumatic brain injury cases, many of which come from sports-related incidents. "Football players, boxers," Dr. Janet Jankowiak ticks them off a mental list, "and, believe it or not, soccer players, who constantly butt the ball with their heads. What used to be considered a mild concussion, may not be so mild after all." She explains, "It used to be that a loss of consciousness was the standard for keeping players from going back into the game. Fortunately, there is a new grading system for checking out players before they return to the field. It's a lot easier to keep players off the field with the new system, and thus prevent further damage to their brains."

Repetitive blows to the brain damage it in subtle ways that have not-so-subtle repercussions down the line. "Strange, violent, and socially inappropriate behavior may be attributable to head injuries. Patients with a history of these sort of injuries tend to have impaired insight and judgment and lose all inhibitions. They get themselves into situations that can only lead to further damage. It's a vicious cycle," says Janet.

As Director of Brain Injury Rehabilitation at Jewish Memorial Hospital and Rehabilitation Center (JMHRC) in Boston, Massachusetts, Janet is all for preventive measures that would safeguard against damage to the brain. "The most prominent injury is to the frontal lobes," she warns. "This is the part of the brain that is responsible for organization, planning, insight—for what makes you a human being," she says forcefully. "So, wear your seat belt at all times, keep infants and small children in the back seat, and when you're riding your bike, wear your helmet." She adds, "I biked all over France without a helmet, and then I did my first rotation in neurology. I never rode a bike without a helmet again." Also, the helmet has to be worn correctly for it to do any good. "It should cover the entire forehead," she instructs. "On most people, the helmet is back too far, leaving the frontal lobes vulnerable to injury."

patient histories, perform routine physical examinations, and recognize symptoms.

In their third and fourth years, students are involved in more practical studies. They work in clinics and hospitals supervised by residents and physicians and learn acute, chronic, preventive, and rehabilitative care. They go through what are known as rotations (brief periods of study) in such areas as internal medicine, obstetrics and gynecology, pediatrics, dermatology, psychiatry, and surgery. Rotations allow students to gain exposure to the many different fields within medicine and to learn firsthand the skills of diagnosing and treating patients.

Janet decided to go to medical school in France and attended the L'Universite Louis Pasteur de Strasbourg, Faculte de Medecine. Taking science courses in French was difficult, she says, but worthwhile. "Science saved me," she admits. "My French wasn't so good, back then."

Upon graduating from an accredited medical school, physicians must pass a standard examination given by the National Board of Medical Examiners. Graduates of non-U.S. medical schools must pass the examinations administered by the Educational Commission for Foreign Medical Graduates.

Most physicians complete an internship, also referred to as a transition year. The internship is usually one year in length, and helps graduates to decide on their area of specialization.

Following the internship, physicians usually begin what is known as a residency. Those physicians who choose to specialize in neurology must first complete a full year of training in internal medicine in a program approved by the Accreditation Council for Graduate Medical Education (ACGME). Then, the physician must enroll in an accredited, three-year neurology residency program. As an alternative to this prescribed training, the physician may complete four years of training in an ACGME-approved neurology program. These residency programs provide supervised neurology experience in both hospital and ambulatory (outpatient) settings. Educational conferences and research training are also part of a neurology residency.

"Look for a mentor to give you feedback and encouragement," Jack suggests. He had already chosen internal medicine as his specialty and entered the residency that would move him one step closer to becoming a neurologist, but he credits a professor with whom he worked as being the real force behind his decision. "One of my mentors, the chair of the department, nurtured me through my rotation in neurology. He was an excellent teacher who gave a lot of attention to me and my learning," explains Jack. "He influenced me by his care of patients, but even more than that, he took the time to nurture me as an individual, rather than treating me as just another resident rotating through."

Often, residents learn quickly what they don't want to do, which helps them narrow down their interests. "I knew I didn't want to be in acute care," says Janet. "I respect and admire those who can withstand all that stress, but I didn't like the emergency room. I didn't want to be on the spot all the time. I like to mull things over, sit back and think about a problem."

CERTIFICATION OR LICENSING

Licensing is a mandatory procedure in the United States. It is required in all states before any doctor can practice medicine. In order to be licensed, doctors must have graduated from medical school, passed the licensing test of the state in which they will practice, and completed their residency.

Upon completion of residency training, neurologists may seek certification from the American Board of Psychiatry and Neurology (ABPN). To be eligible for certification, qualified applicants must have an unrestricted state license to practice medicine; completed the required years of residency training; and successfully passed both a written (Part I) and oral (Part II) examination, as administered by the ABPN.

SCHOLARSHIPS AND GRANTS

Scholarships and grants are often available from individual institutions, state agencies, and special-interest organizations. Many students finance their medical education through the Armed Forces Health Professions Scholarship Program. Each branch of the military participates in this program, paying students' tuitions in exchange for military service. Contact your local recruiting office for more information. The National Health Service Corps Scholarship Program (http://nhsc.bhpr.hrsa.gov) also provides money for students in return for service. Another source for financial aid, scholarship, and grant information is the Association of American Medical Colleges (http://www.aamc.org). Remember to request information early for eligibility, application requirements, and deadlines.

Who Will Hire Me?

Positions are available in general and subspecialty neurology in academic teaching institutions and group practices, the military, health maintenance organizations, and solo practices in urban and rural areas. Subspecialization in new and emerging areas include neuroimmunology, neuromuscular disorders, instrumental brain and nervous system monitoring, neurooncology, rehabilitation, and geriatric neurology.

There are also many opportunities in academic neuroscience and clinical and basic research in neurology for M.D. investigators. Neuroscience is the most rapidly expanding field in all of medical research and, as a result, research and teaching positions should be plentiful in the future.

FYI

According to the American Academy of Neurology, neurological diseases affect approximately 50 million Americans and cost an estimated $400 billion annually in medical and related expenses.

Where Can I Go from Here?

Neurologists can advance in their field by heading departments and chairing committees, by assuming administrative and/or supervisory positions, and by increasing their standing in the field by publishing articles in respected medical journals, such as *JAMA* or *Neurology*.

Research is a vital part of neuroscience, and neurologists who are interested in research can advance their careers by running research projects and neurological studies. Pharmaceutical companies also need trained researchers to head their research in neurological science.

Participating in committees and professional organizations and societies can also help neurologists make valuable connections that may one day lead to other jobs. In addition, Janet recommends getting involved in medical politics. "I believe it's important to be politically involved. You can't just sit back and complain without trying to make a difference." Janet started a faculty and administration organization called Forum for Positive Change to address issues in medicine. She also volunteers for the American Academy of Neurology, helping to publicize the role of the neurologist and the field.

What Are the Salary Ranges?

The average median salaries of medical residents were $40,788 in 2004–05 for those in their first year of residency. For those in their sixth year the median earnings were $50,258, according to the Association of American Medical Colleges.

A 2002 Physician Compensation Survey conducted by Physicians Search reported the average earnings for internal medicine specialists in neurology were $196,563, with the lowest paid earning $130,872 and the highest paid earning $252,765.

According to Salary.com, the annual median base salary nationwide in 2005 for neurologists is expected to be $162,685. Half of the people in this job are expected to earn between $143,143 and $191,471.

Individual salaries vary depending on such factors as type and size of practice, geographic area, and professional reputation.

What Is the Job Outlook?

The health care industry is thriving and the employment of physicians in almost all fields is expected to grow about as fast as the average for all occupations through 2012, according to the U.S. Department of Labor. In particular, the specialty of neurology should increase. In the United States, neurologic illnesses make up 15 to 20 percent of all general medical care. As effective therapies are developed for more neurologic diseases and diseases such as Alzheimer's and Parkinson's disease increase in prevalence, the demand for neurologists will increase.

How Do I Learn More?

PROFESSIONAL ORGANIZATIONS

The following organizations provide information on the certification and profession of neurologist:

American Academy of Neurology
1080 Montreal Avenue
St. Paul, MN 55116
800-879-1960
http://www.aan.com

The American Board of Psychiatry and Neurology Inc.
500 Lake Cook Road, Suite 335
Deerfield, IL 60015-5249
847-945-7900
questions@abpn.com
http://www.abpn.com

BIBLIOGRAPHY

The following is a sampling of materials relating to the professional concerns and development of neurologists:

Aminoff, Michael J. *Neurology and General Medicine.* 3d ed. Kent, U.K.: Churchill Livingstone, 2001.

Emerich, Dwaine F. et al., eds. *Central Nervous System Diseases: Innovative Animal Models from Lab to Clinic.* Totowa, N.J.: Humana Press, 1999.

Gilman, Sid, and Sarah Winans Newman. *Manter and Gatz's Essentials of Clinical Neuroanatomy and Neurophysiology.* 10th ed. Philadelphia: F. A. Davis Company, 2002.

Gilroy, John, ed. *Basic Neurology.* 3d ed. New York: McGraw-Hill, 1999.

Kaufman, David M. *Clinical Neurology for Psychiatrists.* 5th ed. Philadelphia: W. B. Saunders Company, 2001

Kandel, Eric R., ed. *Principles of Neural Science.* 4th ed. New York: McGraw-Hill, 2000.

McLeod, James et. al. *Introductory Neurology.* 3d ed. Cambridge, Mass.: Blackwell Science, 1995.

Mendell, Jerry R. et al. *Diagnosis and Management of Peripheral Nerve Disorders.* New York: Oxford University Press, 2001.

Sacks, Oliver W. *The Man Who Mistook His Wife for a Hat: And Other Clinical Tales.* Beavertown, Colo.: Touchstone Press, 1998.

Weiner, William J. et al., eds. *Neurology for the Non-Neurologist.* 4th ed. Philadelphia: Lippincott Williams & Wilkins, 1999.

Zollikofer, Christoph, and Gustav K. von Schulthess. *Diseases of the Brain, Head and Neck, Spine: Diagnostic Imaging and Interventional Techniques.* New York: Springer, 2004.

NUCLEAR MEDICINE TECHNOLOGISTS

The patient, Mrs. Kelly, had been experiencing a great deal of back pain and fatigue lately. Her doctor had referred her to have a diagnostic test conducted. As the nuclear medicine technologist who runs the test, Tim Dunn takes it upon himself to familiarize himself with each patient's medical history prior to the visit. By the time he introduces himself to Mrs. Kelly, he is already aware that her right breast was removed for cancer three years ago. His concern, and her doctor's, is that the cancer might have spread to her bones now.

When he enters the waiting room, he says, "Good morning, Mrs. Kelly. My name's Tim, and I'll be running your tests. How are you feeling today?" Mrs. Kelly acknowledges that she's been in some pain lately and worries it could be something serious.

Tim nods and says, "These tests are a good way to find out why your back hurts. I'm going to inject a radioactive substance into your bloodstream to see how your bones absorb it. It won't hurt, and it'll only expose you to about the same amount of radiation as an X ray."

He gives her the injection and explains that since it takes the substance some time to be absorbed, he'd like her to come back in two hours for the actual test. When she returns, he greets her and takes her into the room where the test will be conducted. "If you could just take off your watch and earrings, then lie down and relax on the table," he says.

The test, which involves shooting images of her whole body with a gamma scintillation camera, takes about 45 minutes. After the test, Tim prints several images out on film for the nuclear medicine physician to review. But by this time, Tim suspects what the physician will later confirm. Mrs. Kelly's breast cancer has spread into her lower spine. This diagnosis will be relayed to her oncologist (a cancer specialist), who will discuss treatment options with Mrs. Kelly.

Definition
Nuclear medicine technologists work with patients and physicians to diagnose and treat certain conditions with radioactive drugs. They prepare and administer dosages, operate cameras that record images of the drug as it passes through or stays in parts of the body, and keep careful records for review by the supervising physician.

High School Subjects
Biology
Chemistry
Mathematics
Physics

Personal Skills
Helping/teaching
Technical/scientific

Salary Range
$44,234 to $47,472 to $51,038+

Minimum Educational Requirements
Some postsecondary training

Certification or Licensing
Required by certain states; recommended in all other states

Outlook
Faster than the average

DOT
078

GOE
14.05.01

NOC
3215

O*NET-SOC
29-2033.00

What Does a Nuclear Medicine Technologist Do?

Radiation has long been used to diagnose and treat many illnesses. Doctors use radiography (X-ray imaging) to penetrate the soft tissues of the body to reveal on film a crack in a bone, for example, or a mass in an organ. Nuclear medicine technology is also used to diagnose and treat illness and disease, but,

Lingo to Learn

Cancer A general term for many diseases that are characterized by uncontrolled, abnormal growth of cells, which can spread through the bloodstream to other parts of the body.

Gamma camera The equipment used to produce a nuclear medicine image.

Gamma ray Electromagnetic radiation put out by an element going through radioactive decay, having the energy of thousands or even millions of electron volts.

In vitro Procedures done in a test tube.

In vivo Procedures in which trace amounts of pharmaceuticals are given directly to the patient. The majority of nuclear medicine tests are in vivo.

Nuclear medicine The area of medical technology and knowledge based on using radioactive elements to identify and treat certain diseases.

Planar This is a two-dimensional view of the specific organ being imaged by nuclear medicine.

Radiation The energy that is emitted from atomic elements when their nuclei break up.

Radioimmunoassay An in vitro procedure that measures the levels of hormones, vitamins, and drugs in a patient's blood.

Radionuclides Unstable atoms that emit radiation spontaneously. They are used in radiopharmaceuticals to diagnose and treat disease.

Radiopharmaceutical The basic radioactively tagged compound needed to produce nuclear medicine images. Also known as tracer or radionuclide.

unlike radiography, with nuclear technology a patient is given radioactive drugs, either by injection or by drinking liquid or taking a pill. The progress of the radioactive substance through the body is recorded by special cameras or scanners, and the functions of body systems are thus documented.

Nuclear medicine imaging is used to diagnose several types of diseases and disorders of major organs such as the bones, heart, brain, lungs, liver, and kidneys. Sometimes the technology is used on specimens from a patient, such as blood or urine, to detect and measure small amounts of hormones or drugs. At other times, the technology is used for therapy. For example, nuclear medicine can be used to destroy abnormal thyroid tissue that has migrated throughout the body. In some instances, radioactive strontium is administered to ease the pain of terminally ill patients with bone cancer.

Under the direction of physicians, *nuclear medicine technologists* are responsible for patient care. They prepare dosages of radioactive drugs to give to patients, explain procedures to patients and reassure them that the procedures are safe, position patients for imaging, and operate the gamma-ray-detection equipment and scanner. They make sure the images of the target organ are clear and understandable and then process the images. Technologists sometimes have to rescan certain areas to get a better diagnosis. Nuclear medicine technologists also work in the lab, applying radioactive drugs to specimens from patients to detect certain drugs or hormones. In a clinical study, for instance, it is important for researchers to be able to assess the behavior of a radioactive substance inside the body.

Radioactive substances are under the control of either the federal Nuclear Regulatory Commission or a state agency, depending on where the hospital or clinic is located. Because they work with radioactive substances, nuclear medical technologists must follow strict procedures and keep complete and accurate records. Technologists are responsible for the inventory, storage, and use of these substances, and the correct disposal of radioactive waste. The technologists are exposed to very little radiation themselves and use lead shields to reduce their risk. As an added precaution, they also wear badges that measure radiation while they are in a radiation area.

A nuclear medicine technologist must also perform significant administrative duties, which include keeping records of patients and the scanned images, keeping track of the radioactive drugs received into the office and used for patients, and overseeing other staff members. Some technologists are responsible for scheduling and assigning tasks for other colleagues.

What Is It Like to Be a Nuclear Medicine Technologist?

Nuclear medicine technologists usually work in hospitals, although employment in clinics and outpatient facilities is becoming more common. They work closely with other professionals in the field, especially radiologic (X-ray) technicians and nuclear medicine physicians.

Tim Dunn works at Maine Medical Center, the largest hospital in his state. Since most nuclear medicine tests are done during the day, Tim usually works Monday through Friday, from about 8:00 A.M. until 5:00 P.M. At some hospitals and clinics, nuclear medicine technologists are scheduled for night and weekend hours as well. In addition, technologists are often on call for evening and weekend emergencies on a rotating basis with their colleagues.

According to Tim, patients with potential recurrences of cancer make up the majority of his caseload. He also sees a number of people who are referred by cardiologists. These patients need cardiac function tests to determine how their heart muscles are working. In such a test, the patient is asked to walk and run on a treadmill to the point of exhaustion. Tim then asks the patient to lie on a stretcher, and he injects a radioactive substance into the bloodstream. Next, Tim takes sequential pictures of the heart as the substance passes through blood vessels. After 45 minutes, the patient can leave the hospital but is asked to return in three hours so that Tim can take more pictures of the heart in a resting state.

Other common nuclear medicine applications include diagnosis and treatment of hyperthyroidism (Graves' Disease), bone scans for orthopedic injuries, lung scans for blood clots, and liver and gall bladder procedures to diagnose abnormal function or blockages. Nuclear medicine technologists also work with a number of pediatric patients. Children commonly undergo procedures to evaluate bone pain, injuries, infection, and kidney and bladder function.

Tim has been at this job for more than three years. "You set your own schedule," he says. "You need to know how long each test takes, how often the images must be recorded, and so on, so that you can make the most efficient use of your time." Tim is especially careful to allow enough time in his schedule to thoroughly explain the procedures to the patients and answer any questions.

He notes that his job can also be physically demanding at times. "You have to be physically fit. You're on your feet most of the time. Sometimes, if you can't get an orderly, you have to lift patients up onto the table."

Depending upon the size of the hospital or clinic, a nuclear medicine technologist may also handle tasks that are not directly related to patient care. For instance, each morning when Tim arrives at the hospital, he performs a quality-control test on his equipment cameras that takes about 30 minutes. Other aspects of the job include recording pertinent information about each test in the patients' medical records and maintaining a record of the radioactive drugs administered every day. Tim notes that in his particular hospital, nuclear medicine technologists are not required to handle much of this paperwork. "I'm lucky to be in a big hospital, since we have a unit secretary who does the everyday tasks," he says.

A nuclear medicine technologist must be prepared for emergencies as well. "Just last Monday," says Tim, "another technologist came running into my room and said that her heart patient had just arrested [had a heart attack] right after his stress test. I called in a code and started CPR [cardiopulmonary resuscitation]. Someone else gave him the oxygen bag. When the code team got there they said I was doing just fine, so I kept it up until they got the paddles on him. Whew! I don't want to do that every day. The guy's fine, just got out of surgery with a triple bypass. Boy, I'm glad I insisted I learn CPR!"

Do I Have What It Takes to Be a Nuclear Medicine Technologist?

Nuclear medicine technologists must be good with people. "First of all," Tim says, "patients are worried about their diagnosis. Some of them suspect that their cancer may have come back or that their heart is in bad shape. You have to be compassionate about their illness and the pain and fear they are experiencing. Then too, you have the "nuclear" tag. You need to reassure people that they won't be harmed by radioactivity.

"I was a high school hockey player and can't stress enough the importance of being on a team. You have to work together with the doctors and other technologists. You need to be able to communicate clearly. Part of this is keeping up with your paperwork so that every

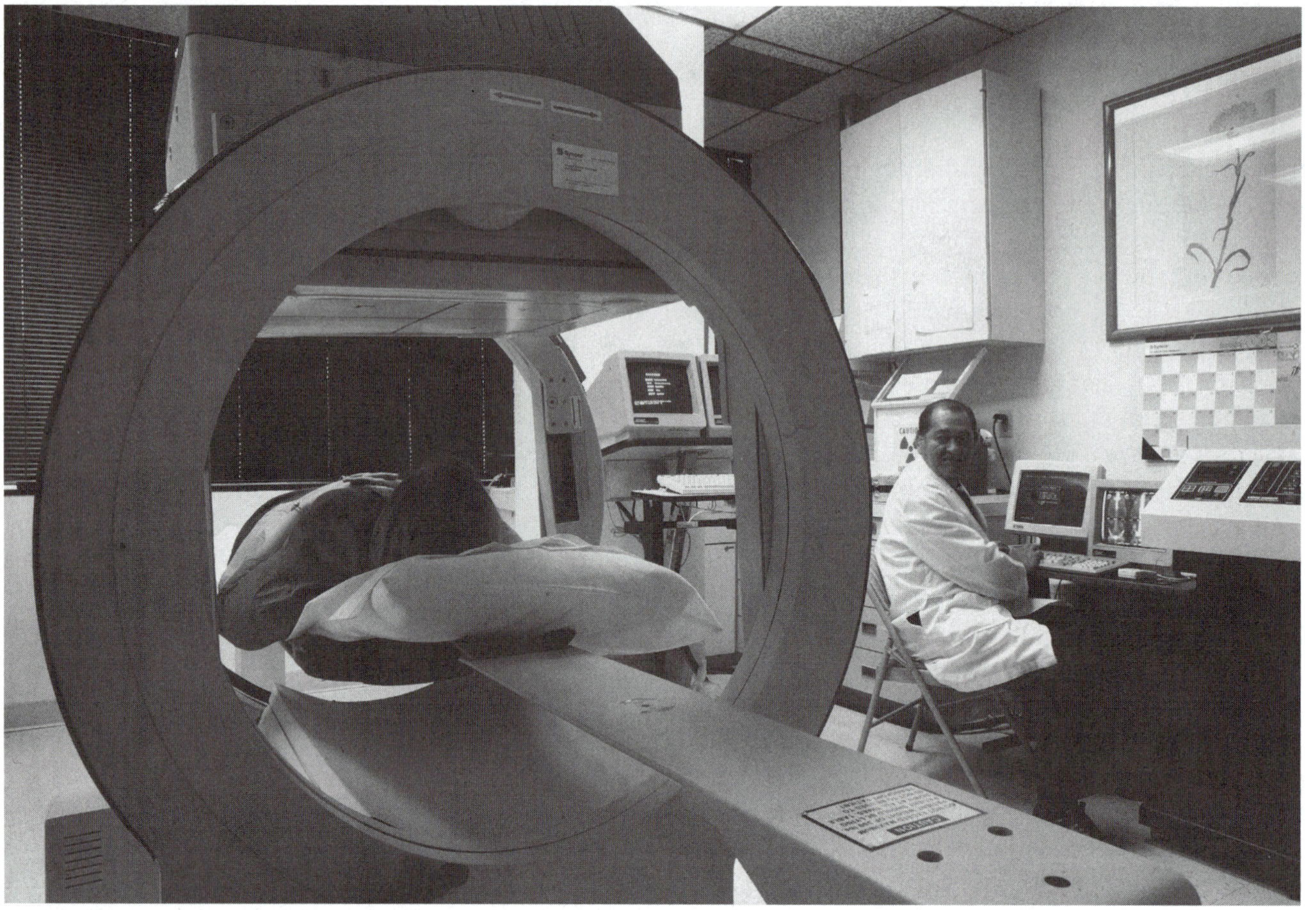

A technician uses a nuclear medicine camera on a patient. *(Spencer Grant / Photo Researchers Inc.)*

member of the team understands what tests the patient had, what the results were, and so forth."

Nuclear medicine technologists must also be able to grasp and explain scientific concepts. In order to work well with other medical professionals, it's especially important to have a solid understanding of biology, physics, anatomy, and physiology.

In some hospitals, nuclear medicine technologists must concoct radioactive drugs out of the raw materials. They need to have good attention to detail, be able to follow procedures, and have math skills adequate enough to understand the relationship of the patient's weight to drug dosage.

A familiarity with computers and an ability to do visual analysis (that is, to see certain patterns) are important as well. "I never thought that the art history course I loved in college would be so useful," states Tim.

To Be a Successful Nuclear Medicine Technologist, You Should . . .

- communicate well with people and be compassionate about their health concerns
- be able to analyze visual material
- understand mathematical concepts
- have the capacity and knowledge to perform CPR
- be organized
- be relatively physically fit

How Do I Become a Nuclear Medicine Technologist?

After earning a bachelor's degree in biology, Tim briefly considered getting his master's degree so that he could work in that field. "Then I heard that a fellow graduate had become a [nuclear medicine] technologist," he explains. "Soon after that, I was waiting tables and found out that the wife of one of the regular customers was a nuclear medicine technologist. On her suggestion I toured a local hospital, liked it, and applied to their program."

EDUCATION

High School

All programs in nuclear medicine technology require a high school diploma. High school courses in biology, physics, chemistry, and algebra will help prepare you for the postsecondary training program. As in Tim Dunn's case, having been involved in a team sport is surprisingly helpful. And, as with many careers, volunteer work (in this case, perhaps in social service) provides valuable learning experiences.

Postsecondary Training

There are several ways to become a nuclear medicine technologist, depending on your prior education and previous medical work experience. Some training programs are based in hospitals, some are offered in technical colleges, and some are a part of four-year colleges. Students can earn either a certificate, an associate's degree, or a bachelor's degree in nuclear medicine technology. All programs that are accredited by the Joint Review Committee on Nuclear Medicine Technology (JRCNMT) prepare students for entry-level positions in hospitals and clinics.

There are 98 JRCNMT-accredited programs nationwide that offer instruction and clinical internship in nuclear medicine technology. These programs can be found mostly on the East Coast, in the Midwest, and on the West Coast. Most programs are open to a small number of students per year (six to 24), although some are larger. They range in length from one to four years, depending on the qualifications of the student entering.

The curriculum includes courses in anatomy, physiology, nuclear physics, mathematics, chemistry, and computer science. Students also study psychology and sociology, medical terminology, and medical ethics. Advanced courses cover how to use the cameras, the nature of radioactive drugs, and federal laws and procedures on handling radioactive materials.

In-depth

Nuclear Imaging

Nuclear imaging is one way of diagnosing problems not easily detected by X rays. In nuclear imaging, the patient swallows, inhales, or is instilled or injected with a radioactive isotope, which acts like a marker or tracer. The isotope goes directly to where the problem is and is then located by a special camera that produces an image.

Two uses of nuclear imaging are the bone scan and the bone density test. These tests are more sensitive than X rays and can often identify a problem months before it shows up on the X ray. They are used when the X rays come back normal, but symptoms persist.

In the bone scan, the patient receives an injection of a bone-seeking nuclide in a vein. Scanning begins two to four hours later. Images are taken of either the entire body or just the concerned part. Injuries, infections, and tumors can all be located with this technique.

The bone density test is used to diagnose osteoporosis, the decrease in bone density that is the major cause of fractures in the elderly. The patient lies on a table while two L-shaped devices (an emitter above the table and a detector below the table) pass over him or her. The emitter emits energy and the detector detects it. Because the energy has to go through the patient's body before it is detected by the detector, the amount that the body absorbs is an indication of the patient's bone density. This procedure is formally called absorptiometry.

Students usually spend time in hospitals while they are completing their academic course work. This clinical training allows them to practice imaging techniques with patients and to gain experience doing laboratory work. According to Tim, it is very important to make sure there is enough clinical training in a program. "I've seen some recent graduates who are really not well prepared to deal with patients."

Training programs in nuclear medicine technology can be rigorous, and because of the small number of openings in each program, competition to gain admittance is stiff. By talking with program directors at several schools about what the academic expectations are, you will be better prepared to choose the right program for your skills and aptitudes.

CERTIFICATION OR LICENSING

In some instances, completion of a training program is enough to be hired for an entry-level position. However, the majority of positions are open only to those who become certified or registered by either the Nuclear Medicine Technology Certification Board (NMTCB) or the American Registry of Radiologic Technologists (ARRT). The certification exams are offered two or three times a year by the NMTCB and the ARRT at locations across the country. The tests measure a candidate's knowledge of radiation safety, instrumentation, clinical procedures, and radiopharmacy. The tests can be taken three times. Any candidate who fails the third time has to complete more course work and can retake the tests. Those who pass certification exams may use the title of either certified nuclear medical technologist (CNMT) or radiologic technologist in nuclear medicine (RTN), depending on the certifying organization.

Many states require state licensure as well as national certification. These states will accept national certification from either the NMTCB or the ARRT. To maintain a license, the technologist must take a certain number of hours of CEUs (continuing education units). For example, Tim has to take 24 credits every two years. These courses are available in day-long workshops as well as in weekend programs. Sometimes, continuing education courses on new diagnostic techniques and tools are offered by pharmaceutical companies right at the hospital.

SCHOLARSHIPS AND GRANTS

You can contact the NMTCB to get a comprehensive list of accredited training programs, many of which offer scholarships. Better yet, visit their Web site where you'll find links to financial aid information at various schools. Individual schools also have their own financial aid programs, so you should talk with a counselor in the financial aid office of wherever you are applying. Stipends (which are living expense allowances given with scholarships) are offered in a small number of institutions.

INTERNSHIPS AND VOLUNTEERSHIPS

Volunteering in a hospital or clinic is a good way to see if you enjoy working with patients. Many facilities offer volunteer opportunities and welcome the extra help that volunteers bring. To explore these opportunities, contact hospital cancer centers, nursing homes,

In-depth

Female Role Model

Manya (Marie) Sklodowska is part of the history of nuclear technology and medicine. Manya learned to read at the age of four and had a remarkable memory. When she was 16 she won a gold medal and many other awards from the Russian school she attended in her native Poland. She became a teacher and also took part in the "floating university," which was forbidden by the Russians who had control of Poland at the time; she secretly read in Polish to women workers.

Manya, a brilliant scientist, eventually went to Paris, and her marriage to Pierre Curie began a partnership that would lead them to major scientific discoveries. Marie Curie coined the term radioactivity, which is the phenomenon that occurs when invisible radiation is emitted from the atoms of certain elements, such as radium. In 1911 she was awarded the Nobel Prize in chemistry for her work in isolating pure radium, which kills diseased cells.

and research facilities near you for more information about their volunteer programs.

Who Will Hire Me?

Hospitals are still the primary employer of nuclear medicine technologists, although clinics, doctors' offices, and research institutions employ 20 percent of them.

Various regional nuclear medicine journals advertise job openings, as do publications geared toward radiologic and nuclear medicine technologists. Some colleges have placement services, and students who have trained in a hospital program may find work at that hospital.

Tim got his job indirectly because of his excellent performance as a student. "One of my fellow students heard that there was an opening here and he applied. The hospital asked the director of my program for a recommendation for this person, which the director felt he was not in position to give. However, he warmly recommended me instead. I came to interview, and here I am."

Where Can I Go from Here?

Staff technologists who do well in their jobs and who have education beyond the associate's degree may advance to *supervisor*, then to *chief technologist*, and on to *department director*. More experienced technologists may also have the opportunity to instruct others in nuclear medicine technology.

Technologists who work in larger hospitals might decide to specialize in a clinical area such as nuclear cardiology or computer analysis. As mentioned earlier, some technologists leave patient care altogether to take jobs in research laboratories. Here, they conduct research aimed at improving laboratory conditions or imaging techniques. Other technologists shift into sales careers for medical equipment or radiopharmaceutical firms. Those who enjoy hands-on training might become *applications specialists* and travel around the country helping hospital staffs learn to use new computer imaging equipment. Still another advancement possibility is to become a *radiation safety officer* for a federal or state regulatory agency.

Advancement Possibilities

Chief nuclear medicine technologists supervise the technologists; write and revise procedures and safety policies and make sure that they are followed; and train staff on how to operate specific equipment.

Nuclear medicine equipment sales representatives sell medical equipment and supplies to doctors, hospitals, and medical schools.

Research technologists assist engineers and physicians in developing improved methods of treating people with nuclear medicine.

Jobs related to nuclear medicine technologists include radiologic technologists. The jobs are similar in that both operate diagnostic imaging equipment. The U.S. Department of Labor classifies nuclear medicine technologists under the headings *Occupations in Medical and Dental Technology* (DOT) and *Nursing, Therapy, and Specialized Teaching Services: Therapy and Rehabilitation* (GOE). Other medical and dental technology occupations include biochemistry technologist, cytogenetic technologist, medical radiation dosimetrist, radiologic technologist, Holter scanning technician, and radiation therapy technologist. Those working in therapy and rehabilitation include dialysis technicians, respiratory therapists, and occupational therapists.

FYI

The U.S. Food and Drug Administration initiated withdrawal of the exemption it granted to radiopharmaceuticals and began regulating them as drugs in 1970, and in 1971 the American Medical Association officially recognized nuclear medicine as a medical specialty.

What Are the Salary Ranges?

The American Society of Radiologic Technologists reports that the average annual salary for nuclear medicine technologists was $65,401 per year in 2004. Technologists with three or more years of experience earned an average of $78,210. Those working in hospitals earned $79,709; in outpatient imaging facilities, $69,995; and in clinics or physicians' offices, $63,400. According to Salary.com, in 2005 the median earnings nationwide for nuclear medicine technologists were $47,472. The lowest paid earned $44,234, and the highest paid earned $51,038. Typical benefits for hospital workers include health insurance, paid vacations and sick leave, and pension plans.

What Is the Job Outlook?

Employment of nuclear medicine technologists is expected to grow faster than the average through 2012, according to the U.S. Department of Labor. In 2002, 17,000 nuclear medicine technologists were employed nationwide. Because the field is relatively small, there is little job turnover each year. The increase in jobs will come from rising numbers of middle-aged and elderly people, the chief users of all diagnostic procedures, including nuclear medicine tests. Thanks to advances in technology, nuclear medicine can be used for an increasing number of diagnostic procedures. For instance, certain radiopharmaceuticals can now detect cancer at an earlier stage than before and without the need for surgery. Nuclear medicine techniques are also used increasingly by cardiologists in order to visualize how effectively the heart is pumping blood.

However, some of the most promising technological advances are prohibitively expensive for hospitals and for patients. Hospitals that wish to use such procedures will have to weigh the cost of equipment against the potential reimbursement and the number of users. These cost considerations will impact how quickly revolutions in research can be put to common use by nuclear medicine technologists.

Other factors could also cause job opportunities in nuclear medicine technology to level off. In an effort to lower labor costs, many hospitals have begun to merge nuclear medicine and radiologic technology departments. Therefore, job opportunities will be best for those trained to perform both nuclear medicine and radiologic procedures. In addition, noninvasive imaging technologies (those that don't involve penetration of the skin, as with injections), such as magnetic resonance imaging (MRI), may supplant nuclear medicine for certain tests because they don't involve radioactivity.

How Do I Learn More?

PROFESSIONAL ORGANIZATIONS

The following organizations provide information on nuclear medicine technologist careers, accredited schools, and employers:

American Registry of Radiologic Technologists
1255 Northland Drive
St. Paul, MN 55120-1155
612-687-0048
http://www.arrt.org

American Society of Radiologic Technologists
15000 Central Avenue SE
Albuquerque, NM 87123-3917
800-444-2778
http://www.asrt.org

Joint Review Committee on Educational Programs in Nuclear Medicine Technology
One Second Avenue East, Suite C
Polson, MT 59860-2320
406-883-0003
jrcnmt@centurytel.net

Nuclear Medicine Technology Certification Board
2970 Clairmont Road, Suite 935
Atlanta, GA 30329
404-315-1739
board@nmtcb.org
http://www.nmtcb.org

Society of Nuclear Medicine
1850 Samuel Morse Drive
Reston, VA 20190
703-708-9000
http://www.interactive.snm.org

BIBLIOGRAPHY

The following is a sampling of materials related to the professional concerns and development of nuclear medicine technologists:

Careers in Focus: Medical Technicians. 4th ed. New York: Facts On File, 2004.

Damp, Dennis V. *Health Care Job Explosion: High Growth Health Care Careers and Job Locator.* 3d ed. Moon Township, Pa.: Bookhaven Press, 2001.

Field, Shelly. *Career Opportunities in Health Care.* 2d ed. New York: Facts On File, 2002.

Foss, Anna M. Gallo. *Review Questions for Nuclear Medicine: The Technology Registry Examination.* New York: Parthenon Publishing Group, 1997.

Karni, Karen R. *Opportunities in Medical Technology Careers.* Lincolnwood, Ill.: VGM Career Horizons, 1996.

Ramesh, Chandra. *Nuclear Medicine Physics: The Basics.* New York: Lippincott Williams and Wilkins, 1998.

NURSE ANESTHETISTS

"Good," Andy Griffin said, looking at the clock. "It's not yet 6:30 and I'm on schedule." Andy, a nurse anesthetist, checks the anesthesia machine and makes sure that the oxygen meter and monitoring devices are working properly. He lays out the tubes and other essentials that will be used in the first operation of the day—the removal of a middle-aged man's diseased gall bladder.

Andy picks up the patient's chart and carefully reviews it. By 7:00 A.M., he will be greeting the patient in the holding room to begin the process of administering general anesthesia.

Definition
Nurse anesthetists are registered nurses (RNs) with advanced education in anesthesiology. They are responsible for administering, supervising, and monitoring anesthesia-related care for patients undergoing surgical procedures.

Alternative Job Title
Certified registered nurse anesthetists (CRNAs)

High School Subjects
Biology
Chemistry

Personal Skills
Helping/teaching
Technical/scientific

Salary Range
$79,929 to $95,049 to $112,869

Educational Requirements
Bachelor's degree, Master's degree

Certification or Licensing
Required by all states

Outlook
Faster than the average

DOT
075

GOE
14.02.01

NOC
N/A

O*NET-SOC
29-1111.00

What Does a Nurse Anesthetist Do?

Nurse anesthetists, also known as *certified registered nurse anesthetists* (CRNAs), are registered nurses (RNs) with advanced training in anesthesiology, the branch of medicine that deals with administering drugs that enable a patient to lose sensitivity with or without loss of consciousness. Reliable methods of putting a patient to sleep were first developed in the 1840s, when the discovery of ether anesthesia revolutionized surgery. Before that time, if a gangrenous leg had to be amputated, for example, all a surgeon could do was offer alcohol or opium to deaden the pain and then saw off the limb as fast as possible before the patient went into shock.

Anesthesiologists are physicians who completed a residency in anesthesiology and passed medical board exams in that specialty. Before World War II, only seven anesthesiology physician residency programs were available; in 1942, there were 17 nurse anesthetists for every anesthesiologist. During the first half of the century, nurse anesthetists often trained medical students and physicians in anesthesiology techniques.

According to the American Association of Nurse Anesthetists, more than 65 percent of anesthetic procedures in the United States are administered by nurse anesthetists. In some states, nurse anesthetists are the only anesthesia providers in rural hospitals. The vast majority of certified registered nurse anesthetists work as partners in care with anesthesiologists, while the rest function as sole anesthesia providers working and collaborating with surgeons and other licensed physicians.

Contemporary anesthesiology is far more complicated than in the early days when an ether- or chloroform-soaked cloth or sponge was held up to the patient's face. Prior to surgery, a nurse anesthetist takes the patient's history, evaluates his or her anesthesia needs, and forms a plan for the best possible management of the case (often in consultation with an anesthesiologist). The nurse anesthetist also explains the planned procedures to the patient and answers questions. On the morning of the operation, the nurse anesthetist administers an intravenous (IV) sedative to relax the patient.

The nurse anesthetist usually administers a combination of several anesthetic agents to establish and maintain the patient in a controlled state of unconsciousness, insensibility to pain, and muscular relaxation. Muscle-relaxant drugs prevent the transmission of nerve impulses to the muscles, which ensures that involuntary movements by the unconscious patient will not interfere with the surgery. Some general anesthetics are administered by inhalation through a mask and tube—the most common are nitrous oxide, halothane, enflurane, and isoflurane. Others are administered intravenously. Because the muscular relaxants prevent patients from breathing on their own, the nurse anesthetist has to provide artificial respiration through a tube inserted into the windpipe.

Throughout the surgery, the nurse anesthetist monitors the patient's vital signs (blood pressure, respiration, heart rate, and temperature) by watching the video and digital displays. The nurse anesthetist is also responsible for maintaining the patient's blood, water, and salt levels at all times by readjusting the flow of anesthetics and other medications to ensure optimal results. After surgery, nurse anesthetists monitor their patients' return to consciousness and watch for complications; they may also be involved in postoperative pain management.

General anesthesia is not necessary for all surgical procedures. Nurse anesthetists also work on cases in which they provide various types of local anesthesia, which results in a numbing or desensitization of one area of a patient's body. Patients are usually awake during a procedure involving local anesthesia.

Lingo to Learn

Analgesics Pain-relieving medications.

Epidural Local anesthesia administered by injection into the space just outside the dural sac that surrounds the spinal cord.

Holding room Room just outside the operating room where the patient is prepared for surgery.

Infiltration Local anesthesia administered by injection directly into the surgical area.

IV Intravenous; refers to anesthetics or any other substance administered through a vein.

Nerve block Local anesthesia administered by injection near the nerves that control sensation in the surgical area.

Spinal Local anesthesia administered by injection into the dural sac that surrounds the spinal cord, resulting in loss of sensation in the entire body below that point in the spinal cord.

Tertiary health care The high-tech specialized diagnosis and treatment available only at large research and teaching hospitals.

Topical Local anesthesia administered by applying a drug to the surface of a mucous membrane that absorbs it; a method often used for surgery on the eye, nose, or throat.

What Is It Like to Be a Nurse Anesthetist?

Andy Griffin sometimes tells people that the existence of the nurse anesthetist is "one of the best-kept secrets in the United States." He discovered nurse anesthetists during a summer job as an operating room assistant (orderly) during his undergraduate days. Andy already knew he was interested in pursuing a career in a medical field, and watching the work of nurse anesthetists in the operating room made him recognize what a challenging job that would be.

After receiving his bachelor's degree in nursing and becoming a licensed RN, Andy worked for two years in a hospital intensive care unit before beginning a master's degree program in anesthesiology. Before he graduated from the Middle Tennessee School of Anesthesia, he had already worked as a nurse anesthetist on nearly 700 cases. After graduation, he went to work for an anesthesia group that has contracts with three Nashville hospitals—St. Thomas, Baptist, and Centennial.

Today is a fairly typical day for Andy. After a procedure such as the 7:30 A.M. gallbladder operation, there would be several other surgical patients.

Occasionally, one complicated operation would take all day; recently Andy worked on an open-heart operation that lasted from 7:30 A.M. to 3:00 P.M.

It might be a typical day, but there are never any merely routine cases. At every moment of the surgery, Andy has to be vigilant—watching the dials on the equipment, adjusting the levels of anesthetic agents being administered (some phases of the operation required deeper anesthesia than others), and monitoring the patient's respiration. During the first month or so of his master's program, Andy had learned the basic facts of anesthesia: the various anesthetic agents available and how to calculate dosage on the basis of the patient's weight. The next two and a half years were spent learning how to anticipate problems; he had to learn what to do in the 5 percent of cases that do not go as planned.

Sometimes, for example, it turns out to be impossible to maintain an airway without performing a tracheotomy (an incision in the throat to insert a breathing tube into the windpipe, or trachea). "The surgeon stays with the surgery," Andy explains. "Life support is the nurse anesthetist's responsibility." At the hospitals where Andy works, an anesthesiologist who is responsible for monitoring four to six operating rooms at the same time is available for consultation in a crisis.

As the surgeon begins closing the incision, Andy simultaneously reduces the anesthesia in order to bring the patient back to consciousness. After the surgery, Andy pulls out the breathing tube as soon as the patient is alert enough to respond to his or her name. When patients are stable, which usually means awake and breathing independently, Andy turns them over to the recovery room nurse.

Carole Rietz is a nurse anesthetist and clinical nurse specialist in Vanderbilt University Hospital's pediatrics division. She works with children and adolescents; her patients range in age from premature infants to 18-year-olds. She occasionally has patients over the age of 18 whose special needs make it appropriate for them to be treated in pediatrics.

Since Carole shares responsibility with anesthesiologists for the care of her patients before, during, and after surgery, she must be skilled in the use of airways, ventilators, IVs, blood- and fluid-replacement techniques, and postoperative pain management.

Some children come to the hospital for one-time operations, such as a tonsillectomy, appendectomy, or hernia repair. Those with long-term medical problems may need to return for surgery and/or other treatment on a regular basis. Many of Carole's patients are children with serious chronic illnesses; some are premature infants with complicated health problems requiring a series of surgeries. Carole works closely with physicians in various pediatric subspecialties (anesthesiology, oncology, orthopedics, urology, and others) and with clinical nurse specialists to ensure the best possible care for each child.

Communicating with children and their parents is an important part of Carole's job. Providing the best possible physical care for patients is obviously essential, yet psychological and social needs are also vital. Vanderbilt tries to provide a nonthreatening hospital environment with approachable staff members. Children and parents can take tours of the facility, where the equipment and medical procedures being planned for the child are explained. Parents need to be trained as primary caregivers in the home, especially in cases of long-term health problems. "If the mother is comfortable, then that feeling of confidence is transferred to the child," explains Carole.

It is essential to answer children's questions at the appropriate age level. A four-year-old with cancer or failing kidneys is still a four-year-old with a child's perspective. Caregivers need to be constantly aware that children do not think like adults.

Carole stresses the importance of giving children choices, whenever possible, to help them feel that they have some say in what is happening to them. They may choose a breathing mask in one of several flavors, or they may bring a favorite toy with them into the operating room. If the child will be returning frequently to the hospital, Carole tries to arrange for care from the same providers each time—to avoid the anxiety of having to meet new staff members on every visit.

Carole especially appreciates the team-oriented, problem-solving approach to health care. After more than 30 years in nursing, Carole strongly believes that health care providers must take an active role in fighting for their patients and prevent the business aspect of medicine from dominating the field.

Life support is the nurse anesthetist's responsibility.

Do I Have What It Takes to Be a Nurse Anesthetist?

Nurse anesthetists must have the ability to concentrate for lengthy periods of time. They are responsible for keeping the anesthetized patient alive, which requires careful attention to every detail. They need to be critical thinkers who can analyze problems accurately and swiftly, make decisions, and take appropriate action. The operating room can be an especially stressful environment. All nurses need the ability to remain calm during emergencies.

Research studies of anesthesia-related problems have demonstrated that most could have been avoided if the anesthesia provider had monitored the patient's condition more vigilantly. The *Journal of the American Medical Association* published new guidelines called the Harvard Minimal Monitoring Standards on Anesthesia Care in 1986. The American Association of Nurse Anesthetists has issued even more detailed monitoring standards.

Nurse anesthetists need to be efficient in their time management. "The surgeons have to be kept happy by having the patients moved along quickly without long delays between cases," was the way one nurse anesthetist put it. If a nurse anesthetist is slow in finishing one case and setting up for the next, the surgeon may be reluctant to work with that nurse again.

How Do I Become a Nurse Anesthetist?

EDUCATION

High School

To become a nurse anesthetist, you must first be a registered nurse. Anyone who is interested in a nursing career needs to take a college preparatory course in high school that gives a good foundation in the laboratory sciences. You need to take biology, chemistry, physics, and mathematics. If your high school offers advanced biology or a human physiology course beyond the introductory biology class, these would be good choices for electives. English classes and other courses that develop communication skills are also important.

High school would be a good time to test your interest in nursing by getting some hands-on experience. There may be opportunities for volunteer work or a part-time job at a hospital, community health center, or nursing home in your community. You might also talk with people in various nursing fields or join a Future Nurses Club.

Postsecondary Training

There are three ways to become a registered nurse: a two-year associate's degree program at a junior or community college, a three-year hospital nursing school program, and a bachelor's degree program (B.S.N.) at a college or university nursing school. Sometimes persons who already have a bachelor's degree in another field enter nursing through a master's level program (M.S.N.) rather than earning another bachelor's degree. All programs combine classroom education and actual nursing experience. Part-time or summer jobs in health care offer additional opportunities for exploring the nursing field.

The bachelor's or master's degree route is strongly recommended since a nurse with less than a B.S.N. has few opportunities for advancement. All applicants to nurse anesthetist programs are required to have at least a bachelor's degree. (The other advanced-practice nursing fields—nurse practitioner, clinical nurse specialist, and nurse midwife—also expect applicants to have a bachelor's degree before beginning specialized training.)

Undergraduate nursing programs include courses in biology, microbiology, human anatomy and physiology, psychology, nutrition, and statistics. Some classes in humanities and social sciences are also required in B.S.N. programs. After completing the nursing degree, it is necessary to pass a national licensing exam; only then are you a registered nurse.

There are 92 accredited nurse anesthesia programs in the United States. They last 24 to 36 months and nearly all offer a master's degree. There are also a few clinical nursing doctorate programs for nurse anesthetists. Applicants to nurse anesthetist programs must have at least one year of experience as an RN in an intensive care unit; many have considerably more. The admissions process is competitive. Andy recently estimated that the average undergraduate grade point average of the students at the Middle Tennessee School of Anesthesia was about a 3.5 on a 4.0 scale.

Students enrolled in nurse anesthetist programs take classes in pharmacology (the science of drugs and their uses), anatomy and physiology, pathophysiology (the physiology of disease), biochemistry, chemistry, and physics. Students also acquire hundreds of hours of anesthesia-related clinical experience in surgery and obstetrics.

CERTIFICATION OR LICENSING

Nurse anesthetists are required to pass national certification exams after completing their educational program. The certification process was initiated by the American Association of Nurse Anesthetists in 1945. All states recognize certified registered nurse anesthetist status. Nurse anesthetists are not required to work under the supervision of an anesthesiologist, although some licensing laws do stipulate that they must work with a physician. All CRNAs must complete at least 40 hours of continuing education every two years in order to maintain their certification.

SCHOLARSHIPS AND GRANTS

There are many sources of financial aid (grants, scholarships, loans, and other forms of assistance) for students in nursing fields. The best way to begin is by consulting the financial aid office of the educational institution you plan to attend.

Other possible aid sources include your state's nurses' association, the National Association of School Nurses, nursing honor societies, state departments of education, the federal government, private agencies, civic and alumni associations, and the U.S. military.

You may be eligible for scholarship aid designated for members of specific ethnic groups. Some nursing scholarship sponsors require recipients to work for their agency for a specified length of time after receiving the degree; generally this means professional employment at full salary.

If you are already an RN employed by a health care agency and want to return to graduate school, your employer may provide full or partial tuition reimbursement.

> **FYI**
>
> **How many anesthetic procedures are carried out each year?**
> Approximately 26 million anesthetic procedures are carried out annually in U.S. medical facilities—and more than 65 percent of these are administered by nurse anesthetists. In 70 percent of rural hospitals, nurse anesthetists are the only anesthesia providers.

Who Will Hire Me?

Many nurse anesthetists are employed by hospitals or outpatient surgery centers (this would include dental and podiatry work as well as same-day surgery). Others are in group or independent practice and provide services to hospitals and other health care centers on a contract basis. Some work for the U.S. Public Health Services. Most rural hospitals rely on nurse anesthetists as their only providers of anesthesia. Nurse anesthetists are eligible to receive direct Medicare reimbursement (under the 1986 Omnibus Budget Reconciliation Act).

The U.S. military also employ nurse anesthetists. In every 20th-century war, nurse anesthetists were the major providers of anesthesia care, especially in forward-positioned medical facilities. In the Vietnam War, there were three nurse anesthetists for every physician anesthetist.

Because the high-quality, cost-effective anesthesia service provided by nurse anesthetists is widely acknowledged, more and more health care institutions are eager to employ them.

Where Can I Go from Here?

Nurse anesthetists who want new professional challenges beyond direct practice might consider teaching or administrative positions or involvement in research for improved or specialized anesthesia equipment and procedures. Some nurse anesthetists choose to acquire other advanced-practice nursing qualifications so they can be involved in a wider range of nursing

In-depth

Nurse Anesthetist History

- The first nurse anesthetist was Sister Mary Bernard, who practiced in Pennsylvania in the 1870s. The first school of nurse anesthetists was founded in 1909 at St. Vincent Hospital in Portland, Oregon. Since then, many schools have been established, including the famous Mayo Clinic Anesthesia Program.
- During World War I, America's nurse anesthetists were the major providers of care to the troops in France. They also trained the French and British nurses and physicians in anesthesia procedures.
- Prior to World War II, anesthesia was considered a nursing specialty. In 1942, there were 17 nurse anesthetists in the United States for every anesthesiologist.
- The nurse anesthesia specialty was formally created on June 17, 1931, when the American Association of Nurse Anesthetist held its first meeting.

activities. Doctoral programs for nurse anesthetists are expected to expand in the near future.

What Are the Salary Ranges?

Nurse anesthetists are probably the highest paid nursing specialists. The National Institutes of Health, for example, pays certified registered nurse anesthetists at a special GS-12 and GS-13 pay scale. At this special GS-12 rate, salaries started at $79,929, and GS-13 salaries started at $95,049 in 2002. The top level of pay for this special GS-13 rate was $112,869, also in 2002. CRNAs working in the private sector frequently have earnings that are higher than these figures.

What Is the Job Outlook?

The American Association of Nurse Anesthetists predicts a very bright future for CRNAs. In addition, the U.S. Department of Labor projects employment for all registered nurses to grow faster than the average through 2012. In fact, registered nurses are predicted to be the fastest growing segment of the U.S. job market in the next decade. In addition, there will be more than 70 million Americans over the age of 65 by 2030. The medical attention required for this age group, in addition to the increasing popularity of areas such as cosmetic surgery, will lead to very healthy job prospects for registered nurses in coming years.

The Health Care Financing Administration recently adopted a rule that removes the federal requirement that nurse anesthetists be supervised by physicians when caring for Medicare patients, and defers to the states on the issue. The immediate effect of the rule, which was published in the January 18, 2001 issue of *Federal Register,* is that hospitals and ambulatory surgery centers will be able to receive reimbursement from Medicare without requiring surgeons or other physicians to supervise nurse anesthetists. For this same reason, many managed care plans see nurse anesthetists as sources of high-quality anesthetic care that result in reduced costs to patients and insurance companies.

How Do I Learn More?

PROFESSIONAL ORGANIZATIONS

The following are organizations that provide information on the career of nurse anesthetist:

American Association of Nurse Anesthetists
222 South Prospect Avenue
Park Ridge, IL 60068-4001
Tel: 847-692-7050
http://www.aana.com

American Society of PeriAnesthesia Nurses
10 Melrose Avenue, Suite 110
Cherry Hill, NJ 08003-3696
Tel: 877-737-9696
Email: aspan@aspan.org
http://www.aspan.org

National League for Nursing
61 Broadway, 33rd Floor
New York, NY 10006

Tel: 800-669-1656
http://www.nln.org

BIBLIOGRAPHY

The following is a sampling of materials relating to the professional concerns and development of nurse anesthetists:

Bankert, Marianne. *Watchful Care: A History of America's Nurse Anesthetists.* New York: Continuum, 1989.

Duke, James. *Anesthesia Secrets.* 2d ed. Philadelphia: Hanley & Belfus, 2000.

Nagelhout, John H., and Karen L. Zaglaniczny. *Handbook of Nurse Anesthesia.* 2d ed. Philadelphia: W. B. Saunders, 2001.

Waugaman, Wynne, R. *Principles & Practice of Nurse Anesthesia.* 3d ed. New York: Prentice-Hall, 1999.

NURSE ASSISTANTS

Hurrying about to answer call lights; helping nursing home residents get showered, dressed, and off to breakfast; taking residents to the bathroom—it had been a hectic morning. Now Dorothy Reeve must make a bed. It may not seem like much, but the resident is bedridden and fragile and can't be moved about much. Dorothy will leave the resident in the bed while making it; she'll work slowly and carefully, a contrast from the fast action that's been required of her all morning.

First Dorothy draws the curtain to protect the resident's privacy. "Are you comfortable, Mrs. Lanning?" she asks, adjusting the pillow and raising the bed. When she's certain that the resident is at ease and unexposed, she lowers the side rail and begins to make up half the bed. She then raises the side rail again and helps the resident to the other side of the bed to finish. Before leaving, she checks again with Mrs. Lanning to make certain she's comfortable and has everything she needs. Mrs. Lanning responds with a smile and she squeezes Dorothy's hand. Dorothy leaves the room with the certainty that her tasks, though small and routine, are important to the residents and the home.

Definition
Nurse assistants care for patients in hospitals and nursing homes under the supervision of nurses.

Alternative Job Titles
Nurse or nursing aides
Nursing assistants
Orderlies
Patient care technicians

High School Subjects
Biology
Health

Personal Skills
Following instructions
Helping/teaching

Salary Range
$12,000 to $16,000 to $23,000

Educational Requirements
High school diploma; completion of training program in either a community college or vocational school

Certification or Licensing
Required for certain positions

Outlook
Faster than the average

DOT
354

GOE
14.07.01

NOC
3413

O*NET-SOC
31-1012.00

What Does a Nurse Assistant Do?

Though the job title suggests someone who assists nurses, *nurse assistants* actually perform many duties independently; in some cases, they become more closely involved with patients or nursing home residents than registered nurses. Nurse assistants work under the supervision of nurses and perform tasks that allow the nursing staff to focus on their primary duties.

Nurse assistants perform basic nursing care in hospitals and nursing homes. Working independently and alongside nurses and doctors, nurse assistants help move patients, assist in patients' exercise and nutrition, and see to the patients' personal hygiene. They bring the patients their meal trays and help them to eat. They push the patients on stretchers and in wheelchairs to operating and X-ray rooms. They also help to admit and discharge patients. Nurse assistants must keep charts of their work for review by nurses.

Most nurse assistants work in nursing homes, tending to the daily care of elderly residents. They help residents with baths and showers, meals, and exercise. They help them in and out of their beds and to and from the bathroom. They also record the health of residents by taking body temperatures and checking blood pressures.

Because the residents are living within such close proximity to each other, and because they need help

Lingo to Learn

Ambulatory care Services for patients who are able to walk.

Acute care Emergency services and general medical and surgical treatment for persons with acute disorders.

Asepsis Methods of sterilization to ensure the absence of germs.

Gerontology A branch of medicine that deals with aging and the problems of the aged.

Neonatal Pertaining to newborns.

Pediatrics A branch of medicine concerned with the development, care, and diseases of babies and children.

with personal hygiene and health care, a nurse assistant also protects the resident's privacy. It is the responsibility of a nurse assistant to make the resident feel as comfortable as possible. Nurse assistants may also work with patients who are not fully functional, teaching them how to care for themselves, and educating them in personal hygiene and health care.

The work can be strenuous, requiring the lifting and moving of patients. Nurse assistants must work with partners, or in groups, when performing the more strenuous tasks so that neither the nurse assistant nor the patient is injured. Some requirements of the job can be as routine as changing sheets and helping a patient with phone calls, while other requirements can be as difficult and unpleasant as assisting a patient with elimination and cleaning up a patient who has vomited.

Nurse assistants may be called upon by nurses and physicians to perform menial and unappealing tasks, but they also have the opportunity to develop meaningful relationships with patients, especially in long-term care facilities. Nurse assistants work closely with patients, often gaining their trust and admiration. When patients are having personal problems or problems with the staff, they may turn to the nurse assistant for help.

Nurse assistants generally work a 40-hour workweek, with some overtime. The hours and weekly schedule may be irregular, however, depending on the need of the care institution. An assistant may have one day off in the middle of the week, followed by three days of work, then another day off. Nurse assistants are needed around the clock, so beginning assistants may be required to work late at night or very early in the morning.

What Is It Like to Be a Nurse Assistant?

Dorothy Reeve works in the Medicare wing of a 90-resident nursing home in Petaluma, California. "I clock in at 7:00 A.M.," she says, "and I hit the floor." She works under the supervision of registered nurses and LVNs (licensed vocational nurses), as well as therapists (physical, occupational, and speech). But mostly she performs her own set of daily responsibilities. Dorothy starts by getting three or four residents out of bed and helps them to start their day. Getting a patient out of bed sometimes requires a mechanical lift. "The lift," Dorothy explains, "supports their weight under a sling and they are lifted like an engine from a car." Also, Dorothy works with another nurse assistant who helps with lifting and feeding. "There are 21 residents on our wing when full," she says. By taking turns with a partner each nurse assistant can take breaks as well as keep watch over residents in the wing.

"I give the person a shower if it's scheduled," she says, "and I get them dressed if they are unable to dress themselves." The residents have set schedules and many must be up at certain times for physical therapy and other appointments. Once her residents are dressed, they are brought out to the dining hall for breakfast. Breakfast is served from 8:00 A.M. until around 9:00 A.M.

"We have to be done with our morning care by 11:00 A.M.," she says. In addition to getting patients ready for the day, Dorothy attends to call lights; call lights are the way residents signal the nurse assistants for help. "You have to make sure that the call lights are answered within three minutes," Dorothy says. "It's the law." Call lights usually have accompanying noises to alert the assistant. "You have to constantly be aware of the sounds that are normal and be alert for the sounds that are not." The call lights are typically going off throughout the morning, and through breakfast and lunch.

Dorothy also takes the residents' vital signs and reports any abnormal readings. She says, "You really have to know your residents individually to know if they're feeling up to par."

When caring for a resident, privacy is important. "We have to make sure that when the residents are receiving personal care," Dorothy says, "that the privacy curtains are pulled and no one can see in. We make sure the door is firmly shut and the drapes are pulled closed for the resident's dignity."

After helping patients with their morning routines and appointments, then helping them with their lunch, Dorothy takes some of the residents to the bathroom and helps them down for a rest. "Then I get all my information together for legal charting," she says. "The charts we keep are legal documents, and when we sign our names we are liable for all the information we chart. If there are any legal questions at some time in the future we had better know why we charted what we did. The state inspectors look at our charting and the RNs get a lot of their information from our viewpoint and from what we chart." Dorothy spends 30 minutes or more preparing the day's chart. To assist in chart preparation, she records her work throughout the day so she doesn't have to try to remember everything she did for each individual resident.

Dorothy's day is usually complete at 3:00 P.M., although she occasionally works overtime. She is paid for 37.5 hours of work a week and works a rotating schedule; this means she works three or four days, then has two days off, followed by another three or four days of work.

The charts we keep are legal documents, and when we sign our names we are liable for all the information we chart.

Do I Have What It Takes to Be a Nurse Assistant?

A nurse assistant must care about the work and the patients and must show a general understanding and compassion for the ill, disabled, and elderly. Because of the rigorous physical demands placed on a nurse assistant, you should be in good health. Also, the hours and responsibilities of the job won't allow you to take many sick days. Nurse assistants must also be of sound mental health. Nurse assistants often work with people who are very sick. Thus, a nurse assistant must be able to deal with the tough realities of terminal illness and death on a daily basis. The job can be emotionally demanding, requiring lots of patience and stability. Nurse assistants should also be able to take orders and to work as part of a team.

Though the work can often be rewarding, a nurse assistant must also be prepared for the worst. "When I first started," Dorothy says, "I had the illusion that the patients would be just like my grandmother was at the time . . . baking, sewing, alert." But she almost quit after the first week. "The residents hit, they screamed, they fell down. You had to feed them their meals and they could not shower themselves." But, after her training, Dorothy came to appreciate the work and to care about the residents. "I like people," she says, "and I love to take care of them. I like to see them smile. In some cases, we caregivers are the only family they have now." Dorothy also appreciates the steadiness of the work and the certainty that experienced nurse assistants will always be in high demand.

How Do I Become a Nurse Assistant?

Dorothy has worked in nursing homes for more than a decade. She completed high school and has had earned some junior college credits. She has also completed a state-required training program and received certification. Dorothy found the training process to be overwhelming at first. "There's so much to remember," she says. "And you need to learn everything quickly so that you can work on your own."

EDUCATION

High School

Communication skills are valuable for a nurse assistant, so take English, speech, and journalism courses. Science courses, such as biology and anatomy, will also prepare you for future training. Because a high school diploma is not required of nurse assistants, many high school students are hired by nursing homes and hospitals for part-time work. Job opportunities may also exist in a hospital or nursing home kitchen, introducing you to diet and nutrition. Also, volunteer work can familiarize you with the work nurses and nurse assistants perform, as well as introduce you to some medical terminology.

Postsecondary Training

Nurse assistants are not required to have a college degree but may have to complete a short training course at a community college or vocational school. These training courses, usually taught by registered nurses, teach basic nursing skills and prepare students for the state certification exam. Nurse assistants typically begin the training courses after getting their first job as an assistant, and the course work is incorporated into their on-the-job training.

Many people work as nurse assistants as they pursue other medical professions; someone interested in becoming a nurse or a paramedic may work as an assistant while taking courses. A high school student or a student in a premedical program may work as a nurse assistant part time before going on to medical school.

CERTIFICATION OR LICENSING

Nurse assistants in hospitals are not required to be certified but those working in nursing homes must pass a state exam. The Omnibus Budget Reconciliation Act (OBRA) passed by Congress in 1987 requires nursing homes to hire only certified nurse assistants. Nursing homes can hire inexperienced workers as nurse assistants, but they must have at least 75 hours of training and pass a competency evaluation program within four months of being hired. Those who fulfill these requirements are then certified.

Dorothy says, "Certification took almost six months of training and class work. California has very strict guidelines." OBRA also requires continuing education for nurse assistants and periodic evaluations.

To Be a Successful Nurse Assistant, You Should . . .

- be a compassionate person
- be in good health
- be able to perform some heavy lifting
- have a great deal of patience
- take orders well
- be a good team player
- be emotionally stable

Who Will Hire Me?

About 40 percent of all nurse assistants work in nursing homes. They also work in hospitals, halfway houses, retirement centers, and private homes. Dorothy started working as a nurse assistant when she was 21 years old. "I had two children to support," she says, "and this field has always interested me because I've always liked older people. And they offered to pay me as I learned." Dorothy heard about the job through a friend and visited the nursing facility directly and filled out an application. She began training in 1984; she worked for the same nursing facility for a year, then worked in a few other homes in the area over the following few years. She then returned to the place where she trained and has stayed there for nine years. It is typical for nurse assistants to try different facilities after receiving training.

Because of the high demand for nurse assistants, you can apply directly to the health care facilities in your area. Most will probably have a human resources department that advertises positions in the newspaper and interviews applicants.

Where Can I Go from Here?

One of the things Dorothy appreciates about her work is that it allows her to perform many of the tasks and duties of a nurse. "Some day I would like to get my nursing degree," she says. But she emphasizes that she is very happy in her current position. "I would like the extra training, but I don't want to just push pills and sit behind a desk and not get to know the residents like I do now." Dorothy would also be interested in trying her work in a different setting, like a hospital.

For the most part, there is not much opportunity for advancement within the job of nurse assistant. To move up in a health care facility requires additional training and education. Some nurse assistants, after gaining experience and learning medical technology, enroll in nursing programs, or may even decide to pursue medical degrees.

A nursing home requires a lot of hard work and dedication so nurse assistants frequently burn out, or quit before completing their training. Others may choose another aspect of the job, such as working as a home health aide. Helping patients in their homes, these aides see to the client's personal health, hygiene, and home care.

What Are the Salary Ranges?

Although the salaries for most health care professionals vary by region and population, the average hourly wage of nurse assistants is about the same across the country. Midwestern states and less populated areas, where a large staff of nurse assistants may be needed to make up for a smaller staff of nurses and therapists, may pay a little more per hour.

According to the U.S. Department of Labor, median hourly earnings of nursing aides, orderlies, and attendants were $9.85 in 2003. The middle 50 percent earned between $8.29 and $11.67 an hour. Wages ranged from less than $7.16 to more than $13.74 an hour. Hospitals paid median wages of $10.53 an hour, nursing and personal care facilities paid $9.83, and community care facilities for the elderly paid $9.31 an hour.

What Is the Job Outlook?

There will continue to be many job opportunities for nurse assistants. Because of the physical and emotional demands of the job, and because of the lack of advancement opportunities, there is a high turnover rate of employees. Also, health care is constantly changing; more opportunities open for nurse assistants as different kinds of health care facilities are developed. Business-based health organizations are limiting the services of health care professionals and looking for cheaper ways to provide care. This may provide opportunities for those looking for work as nurse assistants.

Employment of nursing aides is expected to grow faster than the average for all occupations in response to an emphasis on rehabilitation and the long-term care needs of a rapidly growing elderly population.

How Do I Learn More?

PROFESSIONAL ORGANIZATIONS

The following are organizations that provide information about the career of nurse assistant:

American Health Care Association
1201 L Street, NW
Washington, DC 20005
Tel: 202-842-4444
http://www.ahca.org

National Network of Career Nursing Assistants
3577 Easton Road
Norton, OH 44203-5661
Tel: 330-825-9342
Email: cnajeni@aol.com
http://www.cna-network.org

BIBLIOGRAPHY

The following is a sampling of materials relating to the professional concerns and development of nurse assistants:

Fox-Rose, Joan. *Opportunities in Nursing Assistant Careers.* New York: McGraw-Hill, 1999.

Grubbs, Peggy A. *Essentials for Today's Nursing Assistant.* 2d ed. Upper Saddle River, N.J.: Prentice Hall, 2003.

Hegner, Barbara. *Workbook to Accompany Assisting in Long-Term Care.* 4th ed. Albany, N.Y.: Thomas Delmar Learning, 2002.

Hegner, Barbara, and Barbara Acello. *On the Job: The Essentials of Nursing Assisting.* Albany, N.Y: Thomas Delmar Learning, 2003.

Hegner, Barbara, Barbara Acello, and Esther Caldwell. *Nursing Assistant: A Nursing Process Approach.* 9th ed. Albany, N.Y.: Thomas Delmar Learning, 2003.

Sorrentino, Sheila A., and Bernie Gorek. *Mosby's Essentials for Nursing Assistants.* 2d ed. St. Louis: Mosby-Year Book, 2001.

Wolgin, Francie. *Being a Nursing Assistant.* 8th ed. Upper Saddle River, N.J.: Prentice-Hall, 1999.

NURSE-MIDWIVES

The young woman found out last month that she was pregnant. It would be her second child. When she was pregnant the first time, three years ago, she was seeing an obstetrician for her prenatal care. She also had the obstetrician deliver her baby.

But she wanted to do things differently this time. Last time, she felt that she didn't receive the emotional support she needed from her doctor. And with all the painkilling drugs she was given during delivery, she almost felt as if she weren't in the room when her baby was born.

So this time she has decided she is going to have a nurse-midwife give her prenatal care and deliver her baby. It will be a natural pregnancy and a natural childbirth. And now, after meeting with Deborah Woolley, her nurse-midwife, she knows she has made the right decision.

Definition
A nurse-midwife is a registered nurse who assists in family planning, pregnancy, and childbirth. Nurse-midwives also provide routine health care for women.

High School Subjects
Biology
Chemistry
Psychology

Personal Skills
Helping/teaching
Technical/scientific

Salary Range
$49,550 to $65,000 to $80,000+

Educational Requirements
Two- to four-year registered nursing program; nine-month to two-year certified nurse-midwife program

Certification or Licensing
Required by certain states

Outlook
Faster than the average

DOT
075

GOE
14.02.01

NOC
3232

O*NET-SOC
29-1111.00

What Does a Nurse-Midwife Do?

Midwifery, the act of assisting at childbirth, has been practiced around the world for thousands of years. But in the United States, pregnancy and childbirth are often considered technical medical procedures best left in the hands of physicians known as obstetricians and gynecologists.

Since the 1960s, however, this attitude has been changing as more women insist on natural methods of giving birth. *Nurse-midwives,* particularly those who are certified, have generally become accepted as respected members of health care teams involved with family planning, pregnancy, and childbirth. A number of studies have even indicated that babies delivered by nurse-midwives are less likely to experience low birth weights and other health complications than babies delivered by physicians.

Most nurse-midwives work at hospitals or at family planning clinics or birthing centers affiliated with hospitals. Some nurse-midwives operate independent practices providing home birth services.

Nurse-midwives examine pregnant women and monitor the growth and development of fetuses. Typically, a nurse-midwife is responsible for all phases of a normal pregnancy, including prenatal care, assisting during labor, delivering the baby, and providing follow-up care. A nurse-midwife always works in consultation with a physician, who can be called upon should complications arise during pregnancy or childbirth. Nurse-midwives can provide emergency assistance to their patients while physicians are called. In most states, nurse-midwives are authorized to prescribe and administer medications. Many nurse-midwives provide the full spectrum of women's health care, including gynecological exams.

An important part of a nurse-midwife's work is concerned with the education of patients. Nurse-midwives teach their patients about proper nutrition and fitness for healthy pregnancies and about different techniques for labor and delivery. Nurse-midwives also counsel their patients in the postpartum period (after birth) about breastfeeding, parenting, and other areas concerning the health of mother and child. Nurse-midwives provide counseling on several other issues, including sexually transmitted diseases, spousal and child abuse, and social support networks. In some cases, counseling extends to patients' family members.

Not all midwives are certified nurse-midwives. Most states recognize two additional categories of midwives: *certified* (also *direct-entry* or *licensed*) *midwives* and *lay* (or *empirical*) *midwives*.

Lingo to Learn

Catching babies An informal term used to describe the act of assisting in the delivery of an infant.

Cesarean section A surgical procedure to deliver a baby through an incision in the abdomen. The procedure is named after Julius Caesar, who was supposedly born in this way.

Episiotomy An incision made between the vagina and anus to provide more clearance for birth.

Gynecologist A physician who specializes in the diseases and routine health care of the reproductive systems of women.

Natural childbirth A term used to emphasize pregnancy, labor, and childbirth as natural processes. In natural childbirth, pain-reducing and labor-inducing drugs either are not used or are used conservatively.

Obstetrician A physician who specializes in childbirth and in prenatal and postpartum care.

Pap smear A procedure in which cells are collected from the cervix; the cells are then examined under a microscope for signs of cancer.

Prenatal Before childbirth.

Postpartum After childbirth.

Certified midwives are not required to be nurses in order to practice as midwives. They typically assist in home births or at birthing centers and are trained through a combination of formal education, apprenticeship, and self-education. Certified midwives are legally recognized in 29 states, which offer licensing, certification, or registration programs. Certified midwives perform most of the services of nurse-midwives, and they generally have professional relationships with physicians, hospitals, and laboratories to provide support and emergency services.

Lay midwives usually obtain their training by apprenticing with established midwives, although some may acquire formal education as well. Lay midwives are midwives who are not certified or licensed, either because they lack the necessary experience and education or because they pursue nontraditional childbirth techniques. Many lay midwives practice only as part of religious communities or specific ethnic groups. Lay midwives typically assist only in home birth situations. Some states have made it illegal for lay midwives to charge for their services.

The rest of this article will concern itself only with certified nurse-midwives (CNMs).

What Is It Like to Be a Nurse-Midwife?

Deborah Woolley has been a registered nurse since 1975 and has been practicing as a nurse-midwife since 1983. She currently practices at the University of Illinois Hospital in Chicago, where she also serves as the director of the university's Nurse-Midwifery Educational Program. For Deborah, midwifery offered her the opportunity to have a positive impact on women's health care and childbirth experiences. "I started out as a nurse assigned to the labor and delivery unit. But I became frustrated with the type of care the women were getting," Deborah says. "You'll find that a lot among midwives. Most of the midwives I talk to can point to an event that was the straw that broke the camel's back, as it were—when they realized that they wanted to have more influence over the experience the woman is having. Midwifery's focus is on improving conditions for women and their families. In a way, midwifery is a radical departure from the old way of looking at pregnancy."

Deborah typically arrives at the hospital at 7:00 A.M. and spends the first hour or more seeing patients

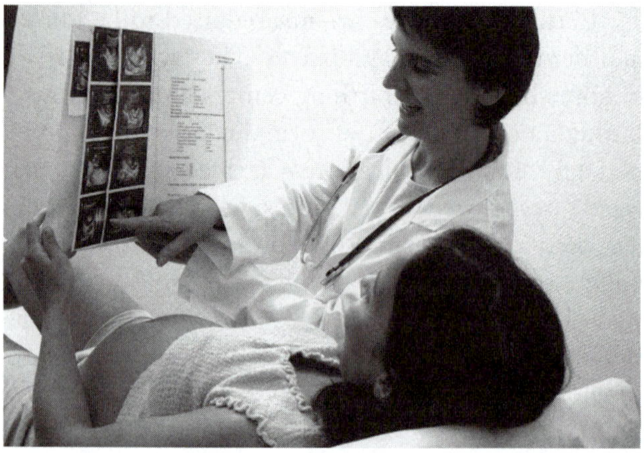

A nurse-midwife reviews sonogram photos with a patient. *(AJPhoto/Photo Researchers Inc.)*

in postpartum—that is, women who have given birth the day or night before. At about 8:30, Deborah goes down to the clinic to begin seeing other patients. "I work a combination of full days and half days during the week. On a half day, I'll see patients for four hours and work on paperwork for one hour. On a full day, I'll see patients for eight hours and work on paperwork for two hours," Deborah says. "But that doesn't mean I always leave exactly at 5:00. At the clinic, we see everyone who shows up."

After Deborah meets a new patient, she'll spend an hour or so taking the patient's medical history, examining her, and getting her scheduled into the prenatal care system. "I also ask about a patient's life. I spend time with the patient and try to get to know her and what's going on in her life. It makes a big difference in the care she's provided. I think one of the things that makes midwives so effective is that they really get to know their patients." Deborah points to one patient to highlight this. "One of my patients was a woman who was having her third child. This woman had always been good about keeping her appointments. Then she stopped coming in. I knew something had to be wrong. So I called people at different agencies, and they helped me track her down. It turned out that she had moved, and she wasn't doing well. We were able to get her back into the system and make sure she had a healthy baby."

Educating her patients is another part of the care Deborah provides. In fact, Deborah believes that education is one of a midwife's most important responsibilities. "I spend a lot of time teaching things like nutrition, the process of fetal development, and basic parenting skills. I refer patients to Lamaze classes. I also screen patients for family problems, such as violence in the home, and teach them how to get out of abusive situations," Deborah says. "In other words, I teach a patient anything she needs to know if she's pregnant. I try to empower women to take charge of their own health care and their own lives."

Apart from seeing patients, Deborah is also responsible for maintaining patients' records. "I have to review lab results and ultrasounds, and fill out birth certificates—things like that. I also have to make sure I have correct addresses on my patients," Deborah says. "There's a lot of writing involved, too. I have to document everything that I do with patients, including what I've done and how and why I've done it."

I have to document everything that I do with patients, including what I've done and how and why I've done it.

Do I Have What It Takes to Be a Nurse-Midwife?

"Speaking as both a midwife and someone who teaches midwives, I think there's one area that seems most difficult for some nurses who get into this profession," Deborah says. "That's making the leap from just being a physician's assistant to having the autonomy of a midwife. As a midwife, you take on more responsibilities for the patient, and that means you have to be prepared to accept the consequences of the decisions you make. There is no more saying, 'I was only following orders,' if something goes wrong. Some nurses find that very stressful. But it's also part of what attracts a lot of us to this field. We really have a lot more direct influence on the quality and nature of our patients' care."

Midwifery is still not accepted by some physicians and other health care providers. "We don't get the slack that docs do," Deborah says. "A lot of people take a doctor's word as law. But a good midwife needs to know her business. She has to have a lot of information at the top of her head—things like statistics, data, and procedures—and she needs to know exactly where that information comes from. This is because people still challenge a midwife's knowledge. And while a lot of obstetricians and gynecologists accept us, there are still many who don't. So you must be confident and poised when working with doctors."

Midwives share both in the joys of childbirth and in the tragedies. "The birth of children is supposed to be fun," Deborah says, "but the reality is that people also die. And in childbirth, when it goes bad, it goes really bad. I've had to hold babies while they die, and I've had to comfort mothers whose babies have died. This is especially difficult for midwives because they become so involved in their patients' lives. So anyone considering midwifery needs to be aware of this part of it, too. But again, most of us become midwives because of the real impact we can have on our patients and their childbirth experiences. It's a great job if you love it. And there really are many more ups than downs."

Giving her patients a sense of empowerment is one of the most important and most satisfying parts of Deborah's career. "Of course I love catching [delivering] babies," Deborah says. "There's nothing as much fun as that. But over the course of my career I've gained more perspective, and I see now that that's not really where a midwife can make the most difference. The biggest part of what I do is to help women learn the stuff they need to make their own lives better. I've learned to ask a woman what she needs, and then to help her get it. The best is when I'm assisting a woman who's giving birth, and she looks up into my eyes and says, 'I did it.'"

Trying to empower patients can be very difficult. "There is a lot of frustration," Deborah acknowledges. "You're dealing with a lot of political and socioeconomic realities, like poverty, violence, and neglect, and this can become overwhelming at times. There's so much that needs to be done, and it's frustrating to recognize that you can't do it all. And these are aspects that cut across all levels of society. It's not just something that you face in a city hospital. It's in the suburbs and in rural areas, too." For Deborah and many midwives, however, this challenge is part of what brought them to this career. "As a midwife," Deborah says, "you have an impact not only on the birth experience, but also on all of a patient's life."

In-depth

Breastfeeding—Benefits and Bothers

Midwifery supports the practice of breastfeeding over bottle-feeding. Human milk contains antibodies that protect infants from infections, and breastfeeding strengthens the psychological bond between mother and child. However, problems sometimes develop with breastfeeding. A breast may become engorged with milk, preventing the infant from sucking properly. In addition, nipples can become sore and cracked, and infections and abscesses can develop in the breasts.

Lactation consultants are health care professionals who help prevent and solve breastfeeding problems. They work in hospitals, public health centers, and private practices. The International Board of Lactation Consultant Examiners certifies lactation consultants. Among the people certified as lactation consultants are many nurse-midwives, dietitians, physicians, and social workers.

Information about becoming a lactation consultant can be obtained from the International Lactation Consultant Association: http://www.ilca.org.

How Do I Become a Nurse-Midwife?

EDUCATION

High School

To begin preparing for a career in midwifery, concentrate on science courses. "I'd advise a high school student to take heavy science," Deborah says. Those science courses may seem inapplicable at the time, but as you move into nursing you'll see how useful they actually are."

A prospective midwife needs to gain a broad range of education and experience. "A midwife is just as people-focused as she is science-focused,"

Deborah says. "So take courses in English, language, philosophy, psychology, and sociology. Language and communication skills are especially necessary because you'll be responsible for maintaining detailed reports on what you do with patients, and you'll be communicating information with patients, doctors, nurses, and insurance companies."

Deborah advises students to gain as much work experience as possible. "You should volunteer at hospitals, especially at facilities where you can work with adolescents. You can also become involved in peer-to-peer counseling." These experiences can make a difference in gaining admission into a midwifery program.

To Be a Successful Nurse-Midwife, You Should . . .

- enjoy working with people
- be independent and able to accept responsibility for your actions and decisions
- have strong observation, listening, and communication skills
- be confident and composed

Postsecondary Training

All nurse-midwives begin their careers as registered nurses. In order to become a registered nurse, you must graduate from either a four-year bachelor's degree program in nursing or a two-year associate's degree program in nursing. After receiving a degree, a registered nurse applies for admission into an accredited certificate program in nurse-midwifery or an accredited master's degree program in nurse-midwifery.

There are 43 nurse-midwifery education programs in the United States that are accredited by the American College of Nurse-Midwives. Four of these are post-baccalaureate certificate programs. Thirty-nine are graduate programs. With an associate's degree in nursing, you are eligible for acceptance into a certificate program in nurse-midwifery. A certificate program requires nine to 12 months of study. In order to be accepted into a master's degree program in nurse-midwifery, you must have a bachelor's degree in nursing. A master's degree program requires 16 to 24 months of study. Some master's degree programs also require one year of clinical experience in order to earn a degree as a nurse-midwife. In these programs, the prospective nurse-midwife is trained to provide primary care services, gynecological care, preconception and prenatal care, labor delivery and management, and postpartum and infant care.

Procedures that nurse-midwives are trained in include performing physical examinations, Pap smears, and episiotomies. They may also repair incisions from cesarean sections, administer anesthesia, and prescribe medications. Nurse-midwives are also trained to provide counseling on such subjects as nutrition, breastfeeding, and infant care. Nurse-midwives learn to provide both physical and emotional support to pregnant women.

According to the American College of Nurse-Midwives, approximately 68 percent of CNMs have a master's degree. Four percent have a doctoral degree.

CERTIFICATION OR LICENSING

After graduating from a nurse-midwifery program, nurse-midwives are required to take a national examination administered by the American College of Nurse-Midwives. Those who have passed this examination are licensed to practice nurse-midwifery in all 50 states. Each state, however, has its own laws and regulations governing the activities and responsibilities of nurse-midwives.

Who Will Hire Me?

Deborah Woolley earned a bachelor's degree in nursing and then began her career as a nurse at a labor and delivery unit in a Texas hospital. While working, she attended graduate school and received a master's degree in maternal child nursing. She then came to Chicago, where she began training as a nurse-midwife. "After earning my nurse-midwifery degree," Deborah says, "I heard there were openings at Cook County Hospital here in Chicago. So I applied for a job there. What I liked about Cook County was that they continued to train me while I was working. They gave me assertiveness training and training in urban health issues."

Hospitals are the primary source of employment for nurse-midwives. Over half of all certified nurse-midwives work primarily in an office/clinic environment, such as family planning clinics (including Planned Parenthood centers) and other health care clinics and agencies. Most list a hospital or physician practice as their place of employment. Some nurse-midwives operate their own clinics and birthing centers, while others work independently and specialize in home birth deliveries.

Where Can I Go from Here?

With experience, a nurse-midwife can advance into a supervisory role or into an administrative capacity at a hospital, family planning clinic, birthing center, or other facility. Many nurse-midwives, like Deborah Woolley, choose to continue their education and complete Ph.D. programs. With a doctorate, a nurse-midwife can do research or teaching. "I spent four and a half years at Cook County while I was working on my Ph.D.," Deborah says. "From there I was recruited to Colorado to head up the midwifery unit at a hospital there. After six years as a director in Colorado, I learned that the director's position here at UIC was open, and I jumped at the chance to come back to Chicago."

What Are the Salary Ranges?

According to the U.S. Department of Labor, the median yearly income for all registered nurses was $49,550 in 2003. This median, however, may actually be closer to the starting salary for a certified nurse-midwife. Career Services of the University of Pennsylvania reports that starting salaries for its School of Nursing master's graduates entering the nurse-midwifery profession ranged from $47,000 to $65,000 in 2000. The average for all starting offers was $59,000. Nursemidwifejobs.com, a division of the company Health Care Job Store that offers job placements to medical professionals, reports the average salary for a nurse-midwife was approximately $62,358 in 2004. Experienced CNMs in the private sector may earn $80,000 a year or more.

Nurse-midwives generally enjoy a good benefits package, although these, too, can vary widely. Most nurse-midwives work a 40-hour week. The hours are sometimes irregular, involving working at night and on weekends. This is partly due to the fact that the timing of natural childbirth cannot be controlled.

FYI

Childbirth Is Natural

The practice of midwifery is many thousands of years old. In most cultures around the world, births are usually attended to by midwives rather than physicians. The United States is one of the few countries where births are usually physician-delivered in hospital settings.

Hospitals began to replace homes as the places of birth early in the 20th century. At the same time, the use of drugs to reduce pain and induce labor became commonplace. In addition, cesarean sections, in which the uterus is cut open for childbirth, increased in frequency.

Though this approach to childbirth undoubtedly decreased infant mortality in the United States, many people began to criticize it during the 1960s. The main criticism was that modern medicine was robbing women of the feelings and sensations associated with childbirth. The natural childbirth movement increased the popularity of midwifery.

Today, midwifery, as practiced by professional nurses who work in consultation with physicians, is generally accepted by the medical establishment.

What Is the Job Outlook?

The number of nurse-midwifery jobs is expected to grow faster than the average for all occupations as nurse-midwives gain a reputation as an integral part of the health care community. Currently, there are more positions than there are nurse-midwives to fill them. This situation is expected to continue for the near future.

There are two factors driving the demand for nurse-midwives. The first factor is the growth of interest in natural childbearing techniques among women. The number of midwife-assisted births has risen dramatically since the 1970s. Some women have been attracted to midwifery because of studies that indicate natural childbirth is more healthful for mother and child than doctor-assisted childbirth. Other women have been attracted to midwifery because it emphasizes the participation of the entire family in prenatal care and labor.

The second factor in the growing demand for nurse-midwives is economic. As society moves toward managed care programs and the health care community emphasizes cost-effectiveness, midwifery should increase in popularity. This is because the care provided by nurse-midwives costs substantially less than the care provided by obstetricians and gynecologists. If the cost advantage of midwifery continues, more insurers and health maintenance organizations will probably direct patients to nurse-midwives for care.

How Do I Learn More?

PROFESSIONAL ORGANIZATIONS

The following organizations provide information on nurse-midwife careers, accredited schools, and employers:

American College of Nurse-Midwives
8403 Colesville Road, Suite 1550
Silver Spring MD 20910
Tel: 240-485-1800
http://www.acnm.org

Midwives Alliance of North America
4805 Lawrenceville Highway, Suite 116-279
Lilburn, GA 30047
Tel: 888-923-6262
Email: info@mana.org
http://www.mana.org

BIBLIOGRAPHY

The following is a sampling of materials relating to the professional concerns and development of nurse-midwives:

Chester, Penfield. *Sisters on a Journey: Portraits of American Midwives.* New Brunswick, N.J.: Rutgers University Press, 1997.

Davis, Elizabeth. *Heart and Hands: A Midwife's Guide to Pregnancy and Birth.* 3d ed. Berkeley, Calif: Celestial Arts, 1997.

Fraser, Diane M., and Margaret A. Cooper, eds. *Myles Textbook for Midwives.* 14th ed. New York: Churchill Livingstone, 2003.

Hobbs, Leslie. *The Independent Midwife: A Guide to Independent Midwifery Practice.* 2d ed. New York: Butterworth-Heinemann, 1997.

Rooks, Judith Pence. *Midwifery and Childbirth in America.* Philadelphia: Temple University Press, 1999.

Sinclair, Constance. *A Midwife's Handbook.* Elsevier Health Sciences, 2003.

Smith, Margaret Charles, and Linda Janet Holmes. *Listen to Me Good: The Life Story of an Alabama Midwife.* Athens, Ohio: Ohio State University Press, 1996.

Van Olphen-Fehr, Juliana, ed. *Diary of a Midwife.* Westport, Conn.: Bergin & Garvey, 1998.

Varney, Helen. *Varney's Midwifery.* 4th ed. Sudbury, Mass.: Jones & Bartlett, 2003.

Wheeler, Linda. *Nurse-Midwifery Handbook: A Practical Guide to Prenatal and Postpartum Care.* 2d ed. Philadelphia: Lippincott Williams & Wilkins, 2002.

NURSE PRACTITIONERS

Definition

Nurse practitioners are registered nurses (RNs) who have advanced education in diagnosis and treatment that enables them to carry out many health care responsibilities formerly handled by physicians.

High School Subjects

Biology
Chemistry
Mathematics

Personal Skills

Helping/teaching
Technical/scientific

Salary Range

$35,290 to $69,203 to $100,000+

Educational Requirements

Master's degree

Certification or Licensing

Recommended (certification)
Required by all states (licensing)

Outlook

Faster than the average

DOT

075

GOE

14.02.01

NOC

N/A

O*NET-SOC

29-1111.00

Harvey Bennett works with college students at Vanderbilt University's Student Health Service. Today the waiting room is full, mostly with patients who are suffering from colds and sore throats. It's easy for a virus to spread quickly through a college community. Harvey, the head nurse practitioner, spends much of his workday seeing students with a variety of health complaints. An average of 150 students visit the Health Service each day. Harvey treats problems ranging from the flu to alcohol-related problems to eating disorders. In working with college students, Harvey says it is essential to establish rapport. "You need to be a good listener and make it clear that confidentiality will be respected," he explains.

He calls his first patient for an initial interview. Careful assessment of each case is important. Hopefully he or one of the center's six nurse practitioners can handle the problem without calling in a staff physician.

What Does a Nurse Practitioner Do?

Nurse practitioners provide health care in a wide range of settings, generally focusing on primary care, health maintenance, and prevention of illness. They carry out many of the medical responsibilities that physicians traditionally handled. They conduct physical exams, take detailed medical histories, order lab tests and X rays, diagnose and treat acute illnesses and injuries, treat and monitor chronic illnesses, such as diabetes and high blood pressure, and prescribe some medications.

The nurse practitioner role developed in the 1960s in response to the shortage of physicians and the need for alternative health care providers, especially in remote rural areas. Harvey Bennett was attracted to the profession during its early years because he valued its goal: to keep people out of the hospital by providing good primary and preventive care.

As a result of their advanced training, nurse practitioners are qualified to work more autonomously than staff nurses. In 1986, a study carried out by the U.S. Congress Office of Technology Assessment found that "within their areas of competence, nurse practitioners provide care whose quality is equivalent to that of care provided by physicians." In preventive care and communication with patients, nurse practitioners were found to excel in comparison to doctors.

A nurse practitioner's exact responsibilities depend on the setting in which she or he works and the field of specialization chosen. A nurse practitioner may work in close collaboration with a physician at a hospital, health center, or private practice office or, as in the case of a rural health care provider, may have only weekly telephone contact with a physician. Nurse practitioners may not function entirely independently of a physician, although the degree of consultation required varies from state to state. As Harvey points out, it is important for nurse practitioners to develop the judgment to recognize when an illness or injury is beyond their level of competence.

Most nurse practitioners have a field of specialization. The most common specialty (and the broadest in its scope) is *family nurse practitioner* (FNP). Family nurse practitioners, who are often based in community health clinics, provide primary care to people of all ages—assessing, diagnosing, and treating common illnesses and injuries. Their interactions with patients have a strong emphasis on teaching and counseling for health maintenance. Nurse practitioners recognize the importance of the social and emotional aspects of health care, in addition to the more obvious physical factors.

Nurse practitioners in other specialties perform similar tasks, though working with different age groups or with people in school, workplace, or institutional settings. *Pediatric nurse practitioners* (PNPs) provide primary health care for children (infants through adolescents). Developmental assessment is an important part of the pediatric nurse practitioner's responsibilities. They must decide whether a child is within the norms of physical and social growth for his or her age group. *Gerontological nurse practitioners* work with older adults. They are often based in nursing homes.

School nurse practitioners work in school settings and provide primary health care for students in elementary, secondary, or higher education settings. *Occupational health nurse practitioners* focus on employment-related health problems and injuries. They work closely with occupational health physicians, toxicologists, safety specialists, and other occupational health professionals to identify potential dangers and to prevent work-related illness or injury. *Psychiatric nurse practitioners* work with people who have mental or emotional problems.

Women's health care nurse practitioners provide primary care for women from adolescence through old age. In addition to handling overall primary care, they do Pap smears and breast exams, provide information on family planning and birth control, monitor normal pregnancies, and offer treatment and counseling for gynecological problems and sexually transmitted diseases. Some nurse practitioners are also certified in midwifery.

In most states, nurse practitioners are allowed to write certain prescriptions, but a physician's signature is often required to validate the prescription.

Lingo to Learn

Acute Describes a disease or symptom that begins suddenly and does not last long.

Advanced practice nurses Nurses with advanced education that enables them to take on many responsibilities formerly carried out by physicians; nurse practitioners, clinical nurse specialists, nurse-midwives, and nurse anesthetists are classed as advanced practice nurses.

Chronic Describes a disease or condition that develops gradually and often remains for the rest of the person's life, such as glaucoma.

Clinical Pertaining to direct, hands-on medical care; from the Greek word for bed.

LPN Licensed practical nurse; an individual trained in basic nursing who usually works under the supervision of a registered nurse.

Pap smear A test that examines cells (taken during a pelvic exam) to detect cancers of the cervix.

Protocol A written plan (prepared in advance) that details the procedures to be followed in providing care for a particular medical condition.

RN Registered nurse; a professional nurse who has completed an approved course of study and passed the National Council of Licensing Examination.

Wellness A dynamic state of health in which a person moves toward higher levels of functioning—a term often used by nurse practitioners.

What Is It Like to Be a Nurse Practitioner?

Harvey Bennett has been a nurse practitioner in Vanderbilt's Student Health Service since 1984. He is certified as a family nurse practitioner. Though he is qualified to provide primary care to persons of all ages, in his present position his practice is confined to the Vanderbilt student population—undergraduates who are generally 18 to 22 and graduate and professional students who may be in their twenties, thirties, and forties.

After completing the nurse practitioner program at Vanderbilt, Harvey spent six years working as a family nurse practitioner based in rural health clinics in Alabama and Georgia. Each clinic was staffed by a nurse practitioner; there was a physician "somewhere in the county." During his Georgia years, the nearest good hospital was 35 miles away. The shortage of doctors and hospitals meant that the nurse practitioners formed long-term relationships with the people they served and had the satisfaction of knowing that they were making a difference in people's lives. It also meant that they were likely to have people knocking on the door in the middle of the night with a medical emergency. In both Alabama and Georgia, Harvey found a high level of acceptance from patients, but in Alabama there was considerable hostility to nurse practitioners from the medical establishment. During the Reagan administration, clinic funding was cut back, so Harvey returned to Nashville.

At Student Health, Harvey spends most of his time seeing students who have come in with health problems. He takes a history from each patient, does a physical, and orders lab tests if indicated. Treatment is based on a protocol developed by the nurse practitioners and doctors; as long as the complaint can be handled within the protocol, the nurse practitioner works without consulting the doctor.

In assessing each case, it is essential to find out whether the reported symptoms may actually reflect a more serious underlying problem. For example, in many cases, students suffering from depression come to the center complaining of headaches, stomach pains, or fatigue.

Teaching and counseling are important parts of the job. College students are at a formative age, and Harvey tries to make a positive impact on their daily health habits. Health topics he discusses with them include alcohol and tobacco use, diet, seat-belt use, and the need to wear bicycle safety helmets. Students often need assistance in making the connection between the symptoms they are experiencing and their behavior (such as smoking or excessive consumption of alcohol). In addition to seeing patients, Harvey, as head nurse practitioner, is also responsible for scheduling and quality control.

Another area of specialization is gerontological nursing care. Kay Grott spent about seven years as a gerontological nurse practitioner in several Tennessee nursing homes. She first encountered this specialty in a junior-year seminar during her undergraduate nursing program at East Tennessee State University. At that time, the lack of appropriate health care for older adults had become a focus of public concern, and Kay decided that she wanted to contribute to solving the problem.

At first, she planned to become a clinical nurse specialist with a concentration in gerontological care, but one of her instructors urged her to become a nurse practitioner instead; he pointed out that nurse practitioners were assuming an increasingly important role in the health care industry. Receiving her MS from the Medical College of Virginia, Kay found the nurse practitioner role to be a good fit.

As a nurse practitioner at a nursing home, Kay was the person responsible for coordinating her patients' total care. She was the liaison between the patient's family, the physician, and the other health care providers. Good communication skills are essential, as well as being comfortable working with older people; that part was easy for Kay, who grew up in an extended multigenerational family. Her work included taking detailed medical histories of each patient, performing physical exams, ordering lab tests and X rays, and monitoring chronic illnesses. It is also important to monitor the patient's progress under the treatment plan drawn up by the health care team. Some typical medical problems are Alzheimer's disease, Parkinson's disease, cardiac conditions, and chronic obstructive pulmonary diseases.

Working with people approaching the end of life, Kay often had to deal with issues of death and dying. Sometimes that meant helping to make people's last months as peaceful and comfortable as possible instead of pursuing an aggressive treatment plan.

A nurse practitioner employed at a nursing home is not always involved in direct patient care. At one point, Kay worked as director of nursing. In that position, she succeeded in raising the nursing home's standards of care to meet new federal standards introduced in the late 1980s.

Do I Have What It Takes to Be a Nurse Practitioner?

A nurse practitioner needs to enjoy working with people and to be strongly committed to making a positive difference in people's lives. Nurse practitioners must develop excellent communication skills. Being a good listener is essential, as is the ability to encourage people to answer questions about personal matters that they may find it difficult to talk about. Anyone going into a health care field needs to have patience and flexibility and the ability to remain calm in an emergency.

Since nurse practitioners work more independently than nurses traditionally do, it is important for them to develop the capacity to take active responsibility in health care situations. At the same time, they must have the judgment to identify those situations that are beyond their competence and to call in a physician or other specialist.

Because the nurse practitioner role is strongly focused on health maintenance and prevention, a person considering becoming a nurse practitioner should find teaching and counseling at least as satisfying as dramatic medical interventions.

A nurse practitioner has to be prepared for the possibility of friction with professional colleagues. The nurse practitioner profession is still new, and some physicians are uncomfortable with it; some display hostility to the idea of nurses functioning in autonomous roles. The nurse practitioner seems to be perceived as a threat by some physicians. Relations with staff nurses can also be a problem for nurse practitioners at times, because some staff nurses resent taking orders from anyone except a doctor. Some patients who have never encountered a nurse practitioner before may be concerned about "just seeing the nurse instead of the doctor." All these situations need to be handled in a mature and professional way.

The problems involved in dealing with insurance companies are also a major source of stress for many nurse practitioners. Although the nurse practitioner is widely recognized as a cost-effective provider of health care, insurance regulations make it difficult for them to receive direct reimbursement.

How Do I Become a Nurse Practitioner?

EDUCATION

High School

Future nurse practitioners should take a well-balanced college preparatory course in high school, with a good foundation in the sciences. Obviously, biology, chemistry, and physics are important courses. If your high school offers anatomy and physiology as a follow up to the basic biology course, that would be a good elective. You also need to take courses in the humanities and social sciences. Classes that improve communication skills are especially helpful for anyone going into a people-oriented field like nursing.

The high school years are also a good time to start getting some hands-on experience in health care. Try doing volunteer work at a local hospital, community health center, or nursing home. There are probably nurse practitioners in your community who would be glad to discuss their work with you and let you follow them around for a few days to observe.

Postsecondary Training

You need to be a registered nurse (RN) before you may become a nurse practitioner. There are three basic kinds of training programs that you may choose from to become a registered nurse: associate's degree, diploma, and bachelor's degree. Which of the three training programs to choose depends on your career goals. A bachelor's degree in nursing is required for most supervisory or administrative positions, for jobs in public health agencies, and for admission to graduate nursing programs. A master's degree is usually necessary to prepare for a nursing specialty or to teach. For some specialties, such as nursing research, a Ph.D. is essential.

A student who begins nursing study in an associate's degree or diploma program may transfer into a bachelor's degree program later. Students with an undergraduate major other than nursing may also enter nursing degree programs, although they may need to fulfill some additional prerequisites. (Harvey Bennett has an undergraduate degree in engineering. After serving in the Navy in the Vietnam War, he decided that he wanted to find a different profession.)

In nursing school, students study the theory and practice of nursing, taking such courses as human anatomy and physiology, psychology, microbiology, nutrition, and statistics. Students in bachelor's degree programs also study English, humanities, and social sciences. After finishing their educational program, students must pass a national examination in order to be licensed to practice nursing in their state and to use the initials RN after their names.

A master's degree is required to become a nurse practitioner. Admission to good nurse practitioner

FYI

The nurse practitioner role developed in the 1960s in response to the shortage of physicians and the need for alternative health care providers.

programs is very competitive. Nurse practitioner programs last one to two years and provide advanced study in diagnostic skills, health assessment, pharmacology, clinical management, and research skills. Usually the student begins with generalist work and later focuses on a specific nurse practitioner specialty.

CERTIFICATION OR LICENSING

Every state requires RNs to pass the National Council Licensing Examination before they are allowed to practice in that state. Some states require continuing education for license renewal.

State requirements for licensing and registration of nurse practitioners vary. All states except Georgia license them to prescribe medications independently, although some states have restrictions regarding the prescription of controlled substances. For specifics, contact your state's nursing board. (See the National Council of State Boards of Nursing Web site at http://www.ncsbn.org for contact information.)

National certification exams for nurse practitioners are available and strongly recommended by professional organizations. At least 36 states require nurse practitioners to be nationally certified by the American Nursing Association or a specialty nursing association.

SCHOLARSHIPS AND GRANTS

There are numerous sources of financial assistance for people studying nursing at both the undergraduate level and advanced levels. The nurses association in your state, the National Student Nurses' Association, nursing honor societies, state departments of education, the federal government, private agencies, civic and alumni associations, and the U.S. military are all possible sources of scholarships.

There may be scholarship aid targeted for members of specific racial/ethnic groups. The National League for Nursing publishes an annual guide, *Scholarships and Loans for Nursing Education.* Students should be aware that some scholarship sponsors require recipients to work for their agency for a certain length of time after graduation, generally at full salary.

If you are already an RN employed by a health care agency and you want to take graduate courses to prepare to become a nurse practitioner, you may be eligible for tuition assistance or reimbursement from your employer.

In addition to the sources mentioned above, you should consult the financial aid office of the educational institution you plan to attend. When applying for any sort of financial aid, always be sure to begin the process in time to get your paperwork in by the deadline.

Who Will Hire Me?

Nurse practitioners are employed in hospitals, clinics, physicians' offices, community health centers, rural health clinics, nursing homes, mental health centers, educational institutions, student health centers, nursing schools, home health agencies, hospices, prisons, industrial organizations, the U.S. military, and other health care settings. In the states that allow nurse practitioners to practice independently, self-employment is an option.

The particular specialty you pursue obviously is a major factor in determining your employment setting. Another important factor is the degree of autonomy you desire. Nurse practitioners in remote rural areas have the most autonomy, but they must be willing to spend a lot of time on the road visiting patients who are unable to get to the clinic, to be on call at all hours, and to make do with less-than-optimal facilities and equipment.

The placement office of your nursing school is a good place to begin the employment search. Contacts you have made in clinical settings during your nurse practitioner program are also useful sources of information on job opportunities. Nursing registries, nurse employment services, and your state employment office have information about available jobs. Nursing journals and newspapers list openings. If you are interested in working for the federal government,

To Be a Successful Nurse Practitioner, You Should . . .

- be strongly committed to making a positive difference in people's lives
- be patient and have the ability to remain calm in an emergency
- find teaching and counseling as satisfying as dramatic medical interventions
- be able to identify those medical situations where it is necessary to call in a physician

contact the Office of Personnel Management for your region. You can also apply directly to hospitals, nursing homes, and other health care agencies.

Where Can I Go from Here?

Nurse practitioners have many avenues for advancement. After gaining experience, they may move into positions that offer more responsibility and higher salaries. Some choose to move into administrative or supervisory positions in health care organizations or nursing schools. They may become faculty members at nursing schools or directors of nursing at hospitals, clinics, or other health agencies.

Some advance by doing additional academic and clinical study that gives them certification in specialized fields. Those with an interest in research, teaching, consulting, or policy making in the nursing field would do well to consider earning a Ph.D. in nursing.

What Are the Salary Ranges?

According to the *2003 National Salary Survey* done by *Advance for Nurse Practitioners,* a news magazine for nurse practitioners, the average salary for nurse practitioners (all specialties) was $69,203 in that year. Details of the survey show that average salaries vary by specialties and settings. For example, nurse practitioners working in their own private practice earned on average $94,313, and those specializing in emergency department medicine earned $80,697 annually. At the other end of the pay scale, however, were nurse practitioners working in family practice, who averaged $66,276, and those in college health service settings, who averaged $56,725 annually. The survey also found that NPs working in New Jersey had the highest average earnings by state, making $78,214. Some practitioners earned even more than this amount, with salaries in the $100,000s.

The U.S. Department of Labor reports that all registered nurses made a median annual salary of $49,550 in 2003. The lowest-paid 10 percent made less than $35,290 per year, and the highest-paid 10 percent made more than $71,210 per year. Nurse practitioners generally make more than RNs.

Geographical location and experience are factors in salary levels. Nurse practitioners must often expect to work long and inconvenient hours, especially if they are in rural practice.

What Is the Job Outlook?

The job outlook for nurse practitioners is excellent. There are approximately 115,000 nurse practitioners working in the United States. A study published in the *Journal of the American Medical Association* in 1998, when there were approximately 60,000 nurse practitioners working in the United States, showed that the nurse practitioner workforce was projected to increase to 106,000 by 2005. Thus, the field has exceeded expectations in terms of growth, and there is no signs of it slowing down. Registered nurses in general, and nurse practitioners specifically, are among the fastest growing occupations in the U.S. workforce, according to the U.S. Department of Labor.

Nurse practitioners are being increasingly recognized as providers of the high-quality yet cost-effective medical care that the nation's health care system needs. More and more, people are recognizing the importance of preventive health care, which, of course, is one of the nurse practitioner's greatest strengths. All nurse practitioner specialties are expected to continue growing. There should be an especially strong demand for gerontological nurse practitioners, as the percentage of the U.S. population in the over-65 age group increases. The Midwest and the South are expected to be the areas of greatest growth in demand for nurse practitioners.

Nurse practitioner organizations are working to promote legislation that will increase the degree of autonomy available to nurse practitioners and make it easier for them to receive insurance company reimbursement. This should make the profession an even more attractive route of advancement for RNs.

At the same time, it is important for those entering the profession to have realistic expectations. Some nurse practitioners report increasing frustration with recent cutbacks in the health care industry that make it difficult to persuade insurance companies to approve for reimbursement the treatment plans considered necessary by health care professionals. Problems with insurance companies and current restrictions on autonomy lead to burn-out and disillusionment for some nurse practitioners, who emerged from their master's degree programs with overly idealistic goals for their profession.

How Do I Learn More?

PROFESSIONAL ORGANIZATIONS

The following are organizations and Web sites that provide information on the career of nurse practitioner:

American Academy of Nurse Practitioners
PO Box 12846
Austin, TX 78711
Tel: 512-442-4262
Email: admin@aanp.org
http://www.aanp.org

National Alliance of Nurse Practitioners
PO Box 40326
Washington, DC 20016
Tel: 202-675-6350

Advance for Nurse Practitioners
http://www.advancefornp.com

Discover Nursing
http://www.discovernursing.com

BIBLIOGRAPHY

The following is a sampling of materials relating to the professional concerns and development of nurse practitioners:

Brown, Kathleen M. P. *Management Guidelines for Nurse Practitioners Working with Women.* 2d ed. Philadelphia: F. A. Davis, 2003.

Burns, Catherine E. et al. *Pediatric Primary Care: A Handbook for Nurse Practitioners.* 3d ed. Philadelphia: W. B. Saunders, 2004.

Fenstermacher, Karen and Barbara Toni Hudson. *Practice Guidelines for Family Nurse Practitioners,* 2d ed. Philadelphia, Pa.: W. B. Saunders, 2000.

Hawkins, Joellen W. et al. *Protocols for Nurse Practitioners in Gynecologic Settings.* 7th ed. New York: Tiresias Press, 2000.

Hoole, Axalla J. et al. *Patient Care Guidelines for Nurse Practitioners.* 5th ed. Philadelphia: Lippincott Williams & Wilkins, 1999.

Katz, Janet R. *Majoring in Nursing: From Prerequisites to Postgraduate Study and Beyond.* New York: Farar, Strauss and Giroux, 1999.

Kidd, Pamela, Denise L. Robinson, and Cheryl Kish. *Family Nurse Practitioner Certification Review.* 2d ed. St. Louis, Mo.: Mosby, Inc., 2002.

Nurse Practitioner's Clinical Companion. Philadelphia: Lippincott Williams & Wilkins, 2000.

Robinson, Denise L. *Clinical Decision Making for Nurse Practitioners: A Case Study Approach.* Philadelphia: Lippincott Williams & Wilkins, 1998.

NURSING SPECIALISTS

"Caring for patients with cancer can be an emotional nursing experience," says oncological nurse Carolyn Panhorst. "Nurses must be aware of the psychological aspects of this type of nursing. They also need to know the effects that this disease can have on the patients, families, and friends.

"A nurse once told me, 'Don't get into this area and think you are going to save anybody.' I thought this was cold," Carolyn says, "but I understand now. You have to want to be there for your patients even though you may not be able to help them. You try to give them what science and technology knows, and then provide them with the best nursing care possible. But, you have to know that you are not God and leave your mind open to the full reality of what the possible outcome may be." She adds, "You must be satisfied that you did the best you could."

Definition
Nursing specialists are registered nurses (RNs) who have advanced training and work experience beyond the RN level in a specialty. Specialties can be related to a specific illness or disease, such as cancer or diabetes; an age group, such as pediatrics or geriatrics; a particular setting, such as community health or schools; or a type of hospital care, such as emergency rooms or intensive care units.

High School Subjects
Biology
English
Mathematics

Personal Skills
Helping/teaching
Technical/scientific

Salary Range
$41,130 to $59,090 to $100,000+

Educational Requirements
Associate's degree through an accredited junior college; diploma from a nursing school; bachelor's degree

Certification or Licensing
Voluntary (certification)
Required by all states (licensing)

Outlook
Faster than the average

DOT
075

GOE
14.02.01

NOC
3152

O*NET-SOC
29-1111.00

What Does a Nursing Specialist Do?

The health care industry in America continues to grow and specialize, and the nursing field is following the same trends. Nurses today have the opportunity to become experts in specific areas of medicine. All nurses care for and treat ill and injured patients and teach them how to prevent illness and injury. Nurses who specialize usually have years of experience working with a particular group of patients and, in addition, have advanced academic training or certification in one field of nursing.

Advanced practice nurses (APNs) are a broad category of registered nurses (RNs) who have completed advanced clinical nurses' educational practice requirements beyond the two to four years of basic nursing education required for all RNs. APNs include four categories of nursing specialties: nurse practitioners (NPs), nurse-midwives, nurse anesthetists, and clinical nurse specialists (CNSs). Each of these specialties is covered in a separate chapter in this book.

Community health nurses organize, promote, and deliver health care services to community groups in urban, rural, and remote settings. They may provide public health services and educational programs to schools, correctional facilities, homeless shelters, elderly care facilities, and well-baby clinics. Some community health nurses provide specialized care in areas where immediate physician services are not available. Community health nurses may also plan, promote, and administer community-wide wellness programs. They may give educational presentations to area organizations, schools, and health care facilities regarding health, safety, exercise, and nutrition.

Critical care nurses provide highly skilled direct patient care to critically ill patients who need intense medical treatment. They not only work in intensive care units (ICUs) and cardiac care units (CCUs) of hospitals but also in emergency rooms, postsurgery recovery units, pediatric intensive care units, burn units, and neonatal intensive care units.

Emergency nurses care for people who need immediate treatment for an illness or injury. When a patient enters the emergency facility, emergency nurses perform a quick preliminary diagnosis and assess the overall condition of the patient. They talk to the patient and family. They record vital signs and observe the patient's symptoms or check for injuries that may not be readily visible. Emergency nurses stabilize patients; prepare them for emergency testing, laboratory procedures, or surgery; and perform resuscitation, if necessary. In many instances emergency nurses perform initial treatments until a doctor can see the patient. This may include setting up or using high-tech medical equipment.

Geriatric nurses care for elderly people in their homes or in hospitals, nursing homes, and clinics. Since older people tend to have different reactions to illness and disease than younger people, treating them has become a specialty. There are specialties within geriatrics, as well. A common geriatrics specialty is medications nursing. *Medications nurses* have additional pharmacology training in drugs and their effects on the elderly. They oversee the administration of medications to patients.

*Home health care nurse*s are often assigned to patients after the patients are discharged from a hospital or after they have had outpatient procedures. They provide follow-up health care on a regular basis and establish a one-on-one patient/nurse relationship. Some home health care nurses also work with patients who have acute, ongoing illnesses such as diabetes or high blood pressure.

Hospice nurses work in hospice facilities or palliative care units in hospitals. Their patients have terminal illnesses and in many cases have decided against further treatment or surgery. Hospice nurses try to make these patients as comfortable as possible during their last days, weeks, or months. They also help family and friends cope with the pending loss of their loved ones.

Legal nurse consultants' job responsibilities vary depending on the case and its medical implications. When working on a case, they may interview clients who feel they have a legal claim against a medical facility, doctor, or nurse or as a result of an accident. They research past medical cases and treatments. They often advise attorneys regarding medical facts, treatments, and other medical issues relevant to a case. Legal nurse consultants obtain and organize medical records and locate and procure evidence. They identify, interview, and retain expert witnesses. They may also assist with depositions and trials, including developing and preparing exhibits for jury or judge trials.

Neonatal nurses care for newborn babies in hospitals. Some neonatal nurses may be in the delivery room and, as soon as a baby is born, are responsible for cleaning the baby, visually assessing it, and drawing blood for screening tests to determine if the baby is normal or needs additional testing or intensive care. Neonatal nurses with more training care for babies who have been born prematurely or who may have an illness, disease, or birth defect.

Occupational health nurses provide health care services to workers. These services may include emergency care in the case of an accident or critical illness, caring for ongoing work-related injuries such as back strain, or monitoring a worker's persistent high blood pressure or diabetes. Occupational health nurses may also be responsible for monitoring and assessing safety aspects of the workplace, including ergonomics, air or noise pollution, chemical exposure, protective clothing, and work procedures. They may also consult with employees regarding medical insurance coverage, and they may serve as a resource for general health and wellness information for employees. Other duties may include conducting company-sponsored health and safety workshops, administering flu shots, overseeing drug testing, and arranging for in-house mammograms and other wellness programs.

Oncological nurses specialize in the treatment and care of cancer patients. Many oncological nurses care directly for cancer patients, but some are involved in patient or community education, cancer prevention, and cancer research. Oncological nurses may work in specific areas of cancer nursing, such as pediatrics, cancer rehabilitation, chemotherapy, biotherapy, hospice, pain management, and others.

Psychiatric nurses focus on mental health. This includes the prevention of mental illness and the maintenance of good mental health, as well as the diagnosis and treatment of mental disorders. They perform a wide range of direct-care nursing duties for the mentally ill, emotionally disturbed, and developmentally handicapped. They may work with individuals, groups, families, and communities. Registered nurses who obtain a master's or doctoral degree can become advanced practice nurses in this specialty. These advanced practice nurses assess, diagnose, and treat psychiatric disorders and potential mental health problems. They provide the full range of primary mental health care services, function as psychotherapists, and in some states they have the authority to prescribe medications.

School nurses focus on students' overall health. They may work in one school or in several. They may also assist the school physician if the school employs one. They work with parents, teachers, and other school and professional personnel to promote health and safety, prevent illnesses, treat accidents and minor injuries, maintain students' health records, and refer students who may need additional medical attention. School nurses may be responsible for health education programs and school health plans. They are also in charge of administering medication to children and for seeing that special needs students' health requirements are met.

Lingo to Learn

Chemotherapy A treatment for diseases, such as cancer, that involves intravenous injections of chemicals that have a toxic effect on specific disease-producing organisms.

Ergonomics The study of humans in their work environment; the science of designing safe ways for workers to operate machines and tools on the job.

Geriatrics The study and treatment of the aging and elderly.

Palliative care A type of care for terminally ill patients that concentrates on alleviating pain and discomfort in patients' last days or weeks.

Triage The technique of prioritizing patient cases in situations of disaster or accident involving a number of people.

Wellness An area of medicine that focuses on the prevention of illness and injury and encourages healthy living.

What Is It Like to Be a Nursing Specialist?

All nursing specialists start out as RNs, so they are trained in direct patient care in a variety of settings. Nurses who specialize have found a unique area of nursing that appeals to them because of the challenges and rewards of dealing with a particular disease, patient profile, or work setting.

Community health nurses work with a wide variety of people, often in a nontraditional health care setting in the communities they serve. They may teach classes for expectant mothers, visit new parents to help them learn how to care for their baby, talk with senior citizens about exercise and nutrition, or give immunizations at a community center or other site. Other community health nurses travel to remote areas where health care is not readily available to the residents. Community health nurses usually work with all ages, from birth to the elderly. They also may work with different groups of people, including immigrants, homeless shelter residents, and persons who are developmentally or physically challenged.

Critical care nurses work in hospitals and medical facilities that have the high-tech equipment needed to care for patients in critical condition. Brandon Frady works in the pediatrics intensive care unit of an Atlanta children's hospital. He works as a bedside nurse and as a relief charge nurse. Brandon is also part of the ground transport team that transports critically ill or injured children to their center. "We care for very sick children here and our skills are challenged on a daily basis," says Brandon. "There is something new to learn every day. We have to learn to operate very high-tech machines, and we are frequently tested on their use and operation. Plus, we need to know the latest research and treatments available for acutely ill children."

Emergency nurses are often confronted with situations that require them to act immediately, independently, and confidently, but they must also be good team players. They must work with other medical, administrative, and law enforcement personnel. Not only are they required to attend to the physical needs of patients, but they may also be involved in crisis intervention in cases such as homelessness, sexual assault, domestic violence, or child abuse.

"Geriatric nursing is a different kind of nursing," says Jean Abdollahian, a retired geriatric nurse and nursing home administrator. "These patients need a special kind of nursing and they almost always need more attention." In Jean's experience, "A geriatrics nurse touches on almost all aspects of nursing—from intensive care, to emergency, to cardiac, to oncology. There are specialties within the specialty."

Home health care and hospice nurses care for patients who are chronically or terminally ill, usually in their homes or other settings away from traditional hospitals and medical centers. Joan Bissing, a hospice nurse in California, says, "While most nurses work directly under a doctor, hospice and home health care nurses must have a specialty in high-tech nursing and a knowledge of different diseases since they are often required to work independently." The hospice nurse is often a source of comfort to the patient and their family and friends. "Some patients may say, 'I've had enough treatments. I just want to live my final days as peacefully and pain-free as possible'," Joan says. "At that point, we focus on giving the patient the best quality of life we can, keeping the patient as comfortable and pain-free as possible."

Legal nurse consultants usually do not have direct patient contact, although they have had considerable past experience caring for patients. As part of legal teams, legal nurse consultants do considerable research and paperwork. "As a legal nurse consultant," says Sherri Reed, president of the American Association of Legal Nurse Consultants, "you must be totally responsible for your part of the job. If information is to be gathered and reports written, you need to get it done. There is no one to take over at shift change. It is entirely your responsibility and you can't pass it on to someone else."

Neonatal nurses are involved in medical situations that usually are happy events. Sharon Stout, who was a neonatal nurse for six years in Georgia, says she loved being in the delivery room and caring for newborns because she enjoyed seeing the interaction with the baby and the new mother and family. "It was usually a very happy time." Neonatal nurses also face the challenges of helping tiny infants who are born prematurely or with critical health problems, such as defective organs, deformities, drug dependencies, and threatening illnesses.

Occupational health nursing is another specialty that is usually practiced outside of a traditional medical setting. Cecelia Vaughn, a certified occupational health nurse specialist, works on a contract basis with a wide variety of clients. "When I go into a facility I have to look at all aspects of the work environment. Is the air clean? Is the worker exposed to harmful pollutants? Are the workplace lighting and the ventilation satisfactory? Are workers tested periodically for chemical exposure, if necessary? Are safety programs presented on a regular basis? And I need to be able to relate personally to the workers. Are they stressed? Is the woman who has bruises a victim of abuse at home? Is a worker on drugs? Is there potential for violence at the workplace? Every day is a new challenge. I never know what the day will bring."

Caring for cancer patients requires a special combination of technical knowledge and emotional support. Carolyn Panhorst worked as an oncological nurse in a small hospital in a small farming community in Indiana. She says, "Although technical expertise is definitely required when caring for cancer patients, the nurse needs to be emotionally and personally attached to the patient. If the nurse cannot give much of herself or himself, this is felt by the patient."

A geriatrics nurse touches on almost all aspects of nursing—from intensive care, to emergency, to cardiac, to oncology.

Psychiatric nurses work in a variety of inpatient and outpatient settings, such as hospitals; community-based or home care programs; and local, state, and federal mental health agencies. The patients that psychiatric nurses care for have illnesses that can sometimes be treated with medications, but also require counseling, emotional support, behavioral conditioning, and lifestyle changes. Psychiatric nurses spend most of their time listening to and talking with patients and guiding them in activities and thought processes that will help patients heal.

"Many people think school nursing is simply putting bandages on skinned knees, but it is much more than that," says Sue Schilb, a school nurse at an elementary school in Iowa for five years. "Of course, we take care of injured and sick children, but what most people don't realize is the amount of paperwork, planning, and record keeping that is involved in the job." Sue adds, "We must assess every child entering kindergarten and make sure the child has had all the required immunizations. In addition, we must main-

In-depth

Nursing Stats

Health Resources and Services Administration's National Sample Survey of Registered Nurses 2000 showed a significant shortage of nurses in the future with reduced enrollments in nursing programs. The survey also found the following:

- Among all RNs, an estimated 22.6 percent have diplomas, 34.3 percent have associate degrees, 32.7 percent have bachelor's degrees, and 10.2 percent have either master's or doctoral degrees.
- Of all RNs, 7.3 percent are advanced practice nurses.
- The average age of all RNs is 45.2 years.
- An estimated 5.4 percent of active licensed RNs are men.

tain records on all the students, including state-mandated immunizations. We take the height and weight of each student every year, check their vision, and work with an audiologist to conduct hearing tests. If special needs children attend our school, we must develop a care plan for them to make sure their needs are met." School nurses may also be required to make presentations, such as disease prevention, health education, and environmental health and safety, to the student body, staff, and parent organizations.

Do I Have What It Takes to Be a Nursing Specialist?

All nurses have a strong desire to help and care for others. Some even describe nursing as a calling rather than a career. Patience, tact, efficiency, and courage are important qualities. You must also be able to work as part of a team of medical professionals. Each nursing specialty has its own set of personal requirements.

Community health nurses, for example, need a great deal of patience and understanding when working with people who do not have access to medical care because of lack of insurance, poverty, or inability to speak English. Since most community health nurses work in public education, they must be able to speak before groups as lecturers or classroom instructors.

Critical care nursing is a very intense nursing specialty. Patients require constant care and monitoring. In many cases, critical care nurses are confronted with situations that require them to act immediately on the patients' behalf. The nurse must be a patient advocate, meaning that the nurse must help the patients receive the best possible care and also respect their wishes. They must also provide support and education to the patients and their families.

Emergency nurses also are often confronted with situations that require them to act immediately and confidently. They must work with other medical, administrative, and law enforcement personnel in situations that require them to be calm and in control, even when the atmosphere becomes very tense.

Jean describes the challenges of geriatric nursing, "In many aspects, geriatric nursing parallels pediatric nursing. Some elderly patients may have illnesses or childlike qualities that demand attention, love, and special medical care. The caregiver must have patience and a good sense of humor to deal with many trying situations."

Home health care and hospice nurses need to be able to work alone, but they must also know how to communicate with doctors, social workers, chaplains, volunteers, counselors, and aides. Sometimes the job requires the nurse to "just listen," says Joan. "We can sometimes sense that our terminally ill patient is unsettled about something, such as past relationships, and then we need to be proactive and get the proper counseling or clergy to help the patient deal with the problem and find peace." One thing Joan wants anyone thinking of going into this profession to remember, "Never forget that it's okay to cry. Shared tears are often part of the patient care."

Legal nurse consultants have less direct patient contact. "Nurses are nurturers by nature," says Sherri. "Because of these predominant traits, many [legal nurse consultants] need to learn to be aggressive and assertive and be their own salespeople if they are going to find work." Legal nurse consultants can expect their jobs to be demanding, but that is what Sherri likes best about her job. "I like my independence and using my knowledge to analyze and research cases. It is challenging and stimulating. There are always new cases and issues."

Neonatal nurses work with patients who haven't yet acquired the language skills to communicate their needs and wants. They must be especially observant and tender with vulnerable newborns. They also need to help and educate new mothers.

Occupational health nurses do not work in a traditional medical setting but in workplaces, such as factories and industrial plants. They treat injuries and illnesses that occur on the job, but they also concentrate on injury and illness prevention, safety procedures, and monitoring of safety regulations.

"Taking care of cancer patients is a different kind of nursing," observes Carolyn, an oncological nurse. "They trust you with their innermost feelings and that's a huge responsibility and also a privilege." There are so many treatment choices available for cancer patients today that the nurse needs to be an educator as well as a caregiver. "You need to be a patient advocate," says Carolyn. "You have to know the difference between giving them information and advising."

Psychiatric nurses have special challenges in working with patients who are mentally, emotionally, or developmentally disabled. Their work does not usually involve bedside care. They spend more time counseling or guiding patients in activities that help them cope with their illnesses. This specialty can be stressful because of nurses' frequent contact with patients who are anxious, unpredictable, unsociable, or depressed.

School nurses provide care for students from elementary grades through high school. They must be able to communicate well with children, parents, and teachers. School nurses who also manage health education must be comfortable in a classroom setting as well as a medical office.

How Do I Become a Nursing Specialist?

All nursing specialists must be registered nurses. After experience, further training, and, in some cases, earning certification, they become qualified as specialists.

EDUCATION

High School

To prepare for a nursing career, you should take science and math classes, including biology, chemistry, and physics. Other classes to take include psychology and sociology. English and speech courses are helpful for learning communication skills.

Postsecondary Training

There are three training programs for registered nurses: associate's degree programs, diploma programs, and bachelor's degree programs. All three programs combine classroom education with actual nursing experience. Associate's degrees in nursing usually involve a two-year program at a junior or community college that is affiliated with a hospital. Many associate's degree nurses (ADN) seek further schooling in bachelor's programs after they have found employment in order to take advantage of tuition reimbursement programs.

The diploma program is conducted through independent nursing schools and teaching hospitals. This program usually lasts three years. A bachelor's degree in nursing (BSN) is recommended for nurses who must compete in an era of cutbacks and small staffs. Bachelor's degree programs are recommended for those who may want to go into administration or supervision. They are also required for jobs in public health agencies and for admission to graduate school.

CERTIFICATION OR LICENSING

Nursing program graduates must pass the licensing exam to become registered nurses. Licensing is required in all 50 states, and license renewal or continuing education credits are also required periodically. In some cases, licensing in one state will automatically grant licensing states with reciprocal agreements.

Additional training is necessary for those wishing to advance into specialized practices, administration, and teaching. Voluntary certification is available for most nursing specialties.

Critical care nursing certification programs are available through the American Association of Critical-Care Nurses. Some institutions may require this certification.

Certification is available for emergency nurses through the Board of Certification for Emergency Nursing and requires recertification every four years.

The Hospice and Palliative Nurses Association offers certification for hospice and palliative nurses who have at least two years of experience in the specialty.

Certification for legal nurse consultants is voluntary and is granted by the American Board of Nursing Specialties. This credential demonstrates that the legal nurse consultant has met practice experience requirements and has passed an examination testing all areas of legal nurse consulting. The certificate is renewed every five years through continuing education or re-examination and continued practice in the specialty.

There are four types of certification available for oncological nurses through the Oncology Nursing Certification Corporation: oncology certified nurse (OCN), certified pediatric oncology nurse (CPON), advanced oncology certified nurse practitioner (AOCNP), and advanced oncology certified clinical nurse specialist (AOCNS). Each subspecialty requires recertification.

Occupational health nurses can take an examination offered by the American Association of Occupational Health Nurses to become certified.

Psychiatric nurses who are advanced practice nurses and have postmaster's degree supervised clinical practice can become certified as specialists in adult or in child and adolescent psychiatric-mental health nursing. Certification is available through the American Psychiatric Nurses Association.

School nurses can earn national certification through the National Board for Certification of School Nurses. Currently North Carolina and Massachusetts require national certification. Some states have state certification programs for school nurses. In addition, some state education agencies set requirements, such as nursing experience and competency in specified areas of health and education. Local or regional boards of education may also have certain qualifications that they require of their school nurses.

SCHOLARSHIPS AND GRANTS

Scholarships and grants are often available from individual institutions, state agencies, and special-interest organizations. Many students finance their medical education through the Armed Forces Health Professions Scholarship Program. Each branch of the military participates in this program, paying students' tuition in exchange for military service. Contact your local recruiting office for more information.

The National League for Nursing publishes information on financial aid. Another source for financial aid, scholarship, and grant information is the Association of American Medical Colleges. Remember to request information early for eligibility, application requirements, and deadlines.

Who Will Hire Me?

A hospital is the most logical place to start looking for a nursing position, but nurses also are needed in retirement communities, government facilities, schools, and private practices. In fact, nursing in hospitals is not expected to grow as fast as other aspects of nursing, due to rising costs and a general trend away from inpatient care. If you are a new nursing graduate, however, a hospital setting offers the best opportunities to work in a variety of specialty areas, which could help you determine whether you have an aptitude for and interest in a particular kind of nursing.

Other employers of nurses include emergency medical centers, long-term care facilities, insurance companies, law firms, home health agencies, and temporary nurses' agencies.

Belonging to an association may make you more marketable to employers because it increases your awareness of what is happening in the nursing community. Associations usually publish magazines and keep members up to date with new practices and advancements in your area of specialization.

Additional training and certification can be a key element in winning nursing specialty jobs. Knowing where you would like to work, earning educational credits in that field, and making sure those in charge of hiring know you are available are the key steps to finding a desirable nursing position.

Where Can I Go from Here?

Experienced nurse specialists can advance in many ways. Those who want challenges beyond direct patient care may become teachers or administrators. Others continue their education to the graduate level and become clinical nurse specialists, nurse practitioners, nurse-midwives, or nurse anesthetists. Nurses are in demand, not only in the United States, but all over the world, so you may find opportunities in other countries on a temporary basis to gain experience or in a permanent position.

What Are the Salary Ranges?

According to the Bureau of Labor Statistics, registered nurses earned an average of $51,230 annually in 2003.

Fifty percent earned between $41,130 and $59,090. The top paid 10 percent made over $71,210 a year. Advanced practice nurses and nurse specialists generally earn salaries that are at the higher end of this pay scale.

Independent legal nurse consultants are usually paid an hourly fee that can range from $50 to $125 per hour. The fee depends on the type of services they are performing, such as testifying, reviewing records, or doing medical research, and also reflects their experience and reputation. In addition, fees vary in different parts of the country. Some legal nurse consultants may work on a retainer basis with one or more clients. Many legal nurse consultants who work for law firms and other businesses and institutions are employed full or part time. The full-time salary range is from under $30,000 to over $100,000.

Neonatal specialty nurses can generally expect to earn more, especially when advancing to administrative positions. According to the National Association of Neonatal Nurses, the median salary is around $50,000 a year.

School nurses' salaries are determined by several factors: the financial status of the school district, the nurse's experience, and the scope of duties. In general, salaries for full-time school nurses tend to slightly less than or equal to teachers' salaries in the same school district.

What Is the Job Outlook?

There are about 2.3 million licensed RNs employed in the United States, making this field the largest of all health care occupations. The U.S. Department of Labor projects registered nurse to be one of the top 25 occupations with fastest growth, high pay, and low unemployment.

Employment opportunities for nurses will be best in home health care and geriatric nursing. The increased number of older people and better medical technology have spurred the demand for nurses to bring complicated treatments to patients' homes.

Employment in nursing homes is expected to grow much faster than the average. Although two-thirds of all nursing jobs are found in hospitals, hospital nursing jobs will experience slower than average growth. This is due to administrative cost cutting, increased work load, and rapid growth of outpatient services.

Nursing specialties will be in great demand. There are, in addition, many part-time employment possibilities; approximately 25 percent of all nurses work on a part-time basis.

The outlook for community health nurses is excellent. The growing numbers of individuals aged 65 or older will increase the need for community-based nursing. In addition, managed care organizations will continue to need community health nurses to provide health promotion and disease prevention programs to their subscribers.

According to the American Association of Critical-Care Nurses, a growing number of hospitals are experiencing a shortage of critical care nurses. Many hospitals needing critical care nurses are offering incentives such as sign-on bonuses. The highest increase in demand is for those critical care nurses who specialize in a specific area of care, such as cardiovascular ICU, pediatric and neonatal ICU, and open-heart recovery units.

The outlook for legal nurse consultants is excellent. According to Sherri, "It is an up-and-coming profession. Our association [AALNC] has grown rapidly and we hope to increase the profession's visibility."

The outlook for neonatal nurses is good, especially for those with master's degrees or higher. According to the National Association of Neonatal Nurses, positions should be available due to downsizing in past years, which has led to a decrease in the number of nurses choosing advanced practice education.

The National Association of School Nurses says that even though school enrollments are projected to increase, school nurse positions are being eliminated in a greater proportion than other positions within the educational system. As educational systems try to find ways to cut costs, professionals such as school nurses may be eliminated. Since cuts may vary by region and state, school nurses should be flexible and willing to relocate or to seek other nursing opportunities, if necessary.

How Do I Learn More?

PROFESSIONAL ORGANIZATIONS

Visit this organization's Web site to access a list of member schools:

American Association of Colleges of Nursing
1 Dupont Circle, Suite 530
Washington, DC 20036-1135
202-463-6930
http://www.aacn.nche.edu

For information on certification in various nursing specialties, contact

American Board of Nursing Specialties
610 Thornhill Lane
Aurora, OH 44202-9756
330-995-9172
http://www.nursingcertification.org

For information about opportunities as an RN, contact

American Nurses' Association
8515 Georgia Avenue, Suite 400
Silver Spring, MD 20910-3403
800-274-4262
http://www.nursingworld.org

For information about state-approved programs and information on nursing, contact

American Association of Critical-Care Nurses
101 Columbia
Aliso Viejo, CA 92656-4109
800-899-2226
info@aacn.org
http://www.aacn.org

American Association of Legal Nurse Consultants
401 North Michigan Avenue
Chicago, IL 60611-4255
877-402-2562
http://www.aalnc.org

American Association of Occupational Health Nurses
2920 Brandywine Road, Suite 100
Atlanta, GA 30341-5539
770-455-7757
http://www.aaohn.org

American Psychiatric Nurses Association
1555 Wilson Boulevard, Suite 602
Arlington, VA 22209-2462
703-243-2443
http://www.apna.org

Emergency Nurses Association
915 Lee Street
Des Plaines, IL 60016-6569
800-900-9659
http://www.ena.org

Hospice and Palliative Nurses Association
Penn Center West One, Suite 229
Pittsburgh, PA 15726
412-787-9301
hpna@hpna.org
http://www.hpna.org

National Association of Neonatal Nurses
4700 West Lake Avenue
Glenview, IL 60025-1485
800-451-3795
info@nann.org
http://www.nann.org

National Gerontological Nursing Association
7794 Grow Drive
Pensacola, FL 32514-7072
850-473-1174
ngna@puetzamc.com
http://www.ngna.org

National League for Nursing
61 Broadway
New York, NY 10006-2701
800-669-1656
http://www.nln.org

Oncology Nursing Society
125 Enterprise Drive
Pittsburgh, PA 15275-1214
877-369-5497
http://www.ons.org

Visiting Nurse Associations of America
99 Summer Street
Boston, MA 02108-1213
617-737-3200
vnaa@vnaa.org
http://www.vnaa.org

BIBLIOGRAPHY

The following is a sampling of materials relating to the professional concerns and development of nursing specialists:

Adelman, Alan M., and Mel P. Daly, eds. *20 Common Problems in Geriatrics.* Columbus, Ohio: McGraw-Hill Higher Education, 2000.

Burgess, Ann Wolbert. *Advanced Practice Psychiatric Nursing.* Upper Saddle River, N.J.: Prentice-Hall, 1998.

Clark, Mary Jo. *Community Health Nursing: Caring for Populations.* 4th ed. Upper Saddle River, N.J.: Prentice Hall, 2002.

Gates, Rose A., and Regina M. Fink. *Oncology Nursing Secrets.* 2d ed. Philadelphia: Hanley & Belfus, 2001.

Iyer, Patricia W. *Legal Nurse Consulting: Principles and Practice.* 2d ed. Boca Raton, Fla.: CRC Press, 2002.

Rodgers Kinney, Marguerite, American Association of Critical-Care Nurses et al., eds. *AACN's Clinical Reference for Critical Care Nursing.* St. Louis: Mosby, 1998.

Sorrell, Jeanne M., and Georgine M. Redmond. *Community-Based Nursing Practice: Learning through Students' Stories.* Philadelphia: F. A. Davis, 2002.

Thureen, Patti J., Jane Deacon, and Patricia Beachy, eds. *Assessment and Care of the Well Newborn.* 2d ed. Philadelphia: W. B. Saunders Company, 2004.

OBSTETRICIANS/ GYNECOLOGISTS

Handel's "Water Music" is playing softly in the background. The lights are dim and a voice says gently, but firmly, "Okay, now, push."

The pregnant woman lying on the bed in the birthing room has broken into a fine sweat, but she nods at her obstetrician's command. Her face screws up with determination and she tries to concentrate on pushing, but the epidural shot the obstetrician gave her an hour ago has kicked in and she has little feeling below her waist.

"Come on, now, Gretchen. You've got to try and push, 'cause this baby of yours wants to say hello." Gretchen's obstetrician, Linda, looks over at Gretchen's sister, Ida. "See if you can help her focus."

Ida takes her sister's hand and begins coaching Gretchen through a focusing exercise. Although this is Gretchen's fourth baby, it's the first time she's had an epidural. Suddenly, Gretchen breaks into laughter as she struggles to push.

Linda looks beneath the drape that covers Gretchen's legs. She smiles broadly and gives the thumbs up sign. Gretchen gives another push and again breaks into laughter.

"Keep laughing," smiles Linda, "every time you laugh, the baby's head comes further out."

Definition
A specialist in obstetrics and gynecology is trained to deliver babies and to provide medical and surgical care for disorders that affect the female reproductive system, the fetus, and the newborn.

High School Subjects
Biology
Chemistry

Personal Skills
Helping/teaching
Technical/scientific

Salary Range
$110,000 to $210,000 to $350,455

Educational Requirements
Bachelor's degree; M.D.; four-year residency program; two years of practice following residency before becoming certified by American Board of Obstetrics and Gynecology

Certification or Licensing
Recommended (certification)
Required by all states (licensing)

Outlook
As fast as the average

DOT
070

GOE
14.02.01

NOC
3112

O*NET-SOC
29-1064.00

What Does an Obstetrician/ Gynecologist Do?

Obstetricians/gynecologists (OBGYNs) provide medical and surgical care for disorders that affect the female reproductive system, the fetus, and the newborn. They care for and treat women before, during, and after childbirth. They commonly serve as consultants to physicians who practice in other areas of medicine.

The specialty of obstetrics and gynecology can be divided into two parts. Obstetrics focuses on the care and treatment of women before their pregnancy, during their pregnancy, and after the child is born. Gynecology is concerned with the treatment of diseases and disorders of the female reproductive system. Because the areas overlap, the specialties are generally practiced together. Preventive measures and testing make up a large part of an obstetrician/gynecologist's practice.

Obstetricians/gynecologists provide many different types of health services to women, from prenatal care to Pap tests to screening tests for sexually transmitted diseases (STDs) to breast exams and birth control. With specialization, the obstetrician/gynecologist's practice may focus on pregnant patients, cancer patients, or even infertile patients.

The subspecialties of obstetrics and gynecology are critical care medicine, gynecologic oncology, maternal-fetal medicine, and reproductive endocrinology. A *critical care medicine obstetrician/gynecologist* has received additional training in vital life-support techniques to treat critically ill patients. This specialist works in the hospital's intensive care unit on a team that includes other specialists. A *gynecologic oncologist* is trained to treat patients with cancers that affect the female reproductive system. A *specialist in maternal-fetal medicine* cares for patients with high-risk pregnancies. This specialty requires advanced knowledge in the medical and surgical complications of pregnancy, and their effects on both the mother and the fetus. A *reproductive endocrinologist,* or an *REI specialist,* is an obstetrician/gynecologist who has been trained in the management of problems relating to reproduction and infertility.

The obstetrician/gynecologist first takes the patient's history and listens as the patient describes the problem or the reason for the visit. He or she performs a physical examination of the patient's vaginal area, cervix, ovaries, and uterus. The obstetrician/gynecologist might use an instrument called a speculum to observe the condition of the vagina and its walls and to see the shape of the cervix. He or she might schedule the patient for tests or X rays. The obstetrician/gynecologist then explains to the patient what the disorder is and the recommended treatment. Disorders that obstetrician/gynecologists commonly treat include yeast infections, pelvic pain, endometriosis, infertility, and uterine and ovarian cancer. Obstetricians/gynecologists prescribe medicines or other therapies, and if necessary, schedule and perform surgery.

When an examination and test indicates that a patient is pregnant, an obstetrician/gynecologist sets up regular appointments with the patient throughout the pregnancy to help her learn about her pregnancy, nutrition, and diet and to make sure the pregnancy is progressing normally. Later in the pregnancy, the frequency of visits increases, and they become important in determining a birthing strategy and any alternative plans. An obstetrician/gynecologist will deliver the baby and care for the mother and child after the delivery.

At these prenatal appointments, the physician listens to the baby's heartbeat and examines its position within the mother's uterus. An obstetrician/gynecologist also checks the mother's health and well-being, since these can directly affect the baby's health.

When labor begins, an obstetrician/gynecologist meets the patient at the hospital, examines her, and periodically checks on her to see that the labor is progressing. Labor can last anywhere from several minutes to several days; the obstetrician/gynecologist supervises the labor and makes decisions based on the health of the mother and unborn child, as well as on previous discussions the obstetrician/gynecologist has had with the patient. For example, some women want to experience as little discomfort as possible. To accommodate those wishes, the patient and the obstetrician/gynecologist discuss the option of having anesthetics administered, such as an epidural. Other women consider the pain and discomfort a natural part of the labor and delivery process, and they ask that no anesthetics be administered. In the event of a serious problem, an obstetrician/gynecologist may have to overrule the wishes of the patient in the interests of the health of both mother and child.

The obstetrician/gynecologist guides the delivery of the baby. If the baby is ready to be delivered but

Lingo to Learn

Cervix The narrow outer end of the uterus. As the time of delivery of a baby approaches, the cervix dilates, or opens, to allow the baby to pass through the uterus, into the birth canal, and out of the woman's body.

Cesarean birth In a cesarean birth a surgical incision of the walls of the abdomen and uterus allows for the safe delivery of the baby. Also called a **cesarean section,** or a **c-section.**

Epidural Anesthesia administered into the spinal cord that numbs the pelvic area of a woman in labor.

Pap smear A method for the early detection of uterine cancer. The method involves the staining of exfoliated uterine cells using a special technique which differentiates diseased tissue. Also called a **Pap test.**

Speculum A medical instrument used to separate the walls of a body cavity for examination.

STD An acronym for **sexually transmitted disease.** Among the most common are such diseases as AIDS, herpes, gonorrhea, syphilis, and chlamydia.

for some reason cannot pass through the birth canal, the obstetrician/gynecologist performs a cesarean section. This involves making an incision in the woman's abdomen, surgically removing the baby from the uterus, removing the placenta, and then closing the incision with sutures.

After delivery, an obstetrician/gynecologist visits the mother and baby in the hospital to make sure they are both well. In the event the obstetrician/gynecologist has performed a cesarean section delivery, he or she checks the closing sutures to make certain they are healing and are not infected. Six weeks after delivery, the mother goes back to the obstetrician/gynecologist for a checkup. Throughout the pregnancy, delivery, and postdelivery period, an obstetrician/gynecologist keeps a detailed medical record on the patient.

What Is It Like to Be an Obstetrician/Gynecologist?

Dr. Carol Cook describes herself as a typical obstetrician/gynecologist. She is in a large single-specialty group practice with seven other obstetrician/gynecologists. "We bridge the office practice typical of internists, with the surgical practice of a general surgeon," she explains. "I see a lot of women for routine checkups," she says. "I would say that around 30 percent of my cases are yearly checkups."

"We see pregnant women on the OB side, and gynecological disorders on the gyn side," says Carol. "There aren't any subspecialists in our group. If I have a patient who's pregnant with triplets, I'll call my person in maternal-fetal medicine, and I'll say, 'let's do it together.' The same goes for a patient with uterine cancer. I'll call the gyn-onc specialist."

Carol is usually in her office by 8:00 A.M. every day. "Today, my 8:00 was an OB patient. She's 38 weeks along, and she came in with her two-year-old and her husband. Her first delivery she had elsewhere, and it was a nine-and-a-half-pound baby by c-section," Carol explains. "This time, she wants to deliver vaginally, if at all possible."

Carol describes her examination of the patient. "I check the size of the cervix. It was two centimeters, getting what we call, ripe. She's almost ready to give birth. Remember, she's already at 38 weeks. Thirty-seven to 42 weeks is term. Then, I see how big the baby is—I do this every visit—by checking the fundal height. *Fundis* is latin for top of the uterus. It felt pretty good-sized, so she's probably going to have another nine pounder. I check the baby's heart tones, and then we discuss what we're going to do. Because she wants to deliver vaginally, we talked it over and decided to wait until 40 weeks, and then we'll probably induce." Carol explains that c-sections are harder to recover from than vaginal births, so many women try and deliver the baby on their own, without surgery.

In the gynecological side of her practice, Carol sees patients with a wide range of problems. Typical gynecological problems that she treats include urinary tract and yeast infections, pelvic pain, infertility, and cancers of the cervix, uterus, and ovaries. She never hesitates to call a specialist in the particular area. "I want my patient to have the best care, and that means getting the person involved who spent extra time studying that particular area, whether that's an REI specialist or a gyn-onc."

Another type of patient Carol treats is the older patient who is in menopause. The onset of menopause can have distressing symptoms, such as interruption of sleep, extreme moodiness, night sweats, and hot flashes, among others. "Some women have such bad symptoms, they can't function," Carol explains. Menopausal women have the choice of taking hormone replacement therapy (HRT), usually a combination of progesterone and estrogen, to counteract and/or mitigate the symptoms of severe menopause. According to Carol, there are actually some advantages to being on HRT. "Women on HRT have less heart disease. When women are in menopause, though, and without HRT, their risk of heart attack is equal to that of men. Women are also at risk of osteoporosis. HRT can help [lower the risk] we believe."

Have I Got What It Takes to Be an Obstetrician/Gynecologist?

Obstetricians/gynecologists, like all physicians, should enjoy helping and working with people. Most of their time is spent with patients, talking to them and listening to their histories and problems. Because of the intimate nature of the profession, they may also end up with a more complete picture of their patients' personal lives than most other physicians ever obtain. "I'm a people person," says Carol. "I really enjoy communicating with my patients. But I also enjoy surgery. Ob/gyn is a nice mix of both." She often finds that her rapport with her patients makes them more likely to use her

In-depth

Cesarean Birth

Cesarean birth is a major surgical procedure requiring some form of anesthesia. There are two basic types of cesarean birth techniques: cervical and classical. The cervical type involves making a horizontal or vertical incision in the lower uterus. Classical cesarean involves making a vertical incision in the main body of the uterus. Today, the horizontal cervical type is by far the most common method of cesarean birth.

There are several reasons for a physician to choose to deliver a baby via cesarean. The most common is dystocia, a catchall term meaning "difficult labor." There are three different conditions that lead many doctors to indicate dystocia: abnormalities of the mother's birth canal, abnormalities in the position of the unborn child in the uterus, and significant abnormalities in uterine contractions. Another cause for cesarean birth is fetal distress—when the unborn child develops a markedly abnormal heart rate, endangering the health of the child.

The procedure of making an incision into the abdominal area to facilitate childbirth can be traced back nearly 5,000 years, to ancient Egypt. There are various theories concerning the source of the name. One states that the name dates back to 715 B.C., when a set of Roman laws, the Lex Caesare, mandated the surgical removal of an unborn child upon the death of the mother. Another theory traces the name to the story that Julius Caesar was born using this procedure.

Cesarean birth was generally used as a last resort until the 1970s. With the refinement of surgical techniques, improved fetal monitoring equipment, the rise of malpractice lawsuits, and the development of new antibiotics, use of cesarean birth technique has increased rapidly—tripling from 5 to 16.5 percent of all births from 1970 to 1980. There has been some controversy surrounding the increased use of this technique, with some who believe that it is used too frequently. Today, about 23 percent of all births in the United States are cesarean sections.

as a sounding board for other medical questions. "I do a lot of primary care," says Carol. "But, according to my insurance, I'm not designated as such, so I can't do it officially. Still, you develop an intimate relationship with your patients—they trust you—and ask you things they might not ask another physician. So I get asked for a lot of medical advice."

Communication skills are essential to all physicians, but especially to an obstetrician/gynecologist. The intimate nature of both the patient's condition and the examination requires that an obstetrician/gynecologist be able to put the patient at ease while asking questions of an intimate nature.

Obstetricians/gynecologists work long, irregular hours. They may be paged at any moment to rush to the hospital to deliver a baby or handle a medical emergency. On a typical day, an obstetrician/gynecologist might have to travel from his or her office to the hospital several times in one day. An obstetrician/gynecologist might start the day by reviewing patient charts at the office and then head to the hospital to perform surgery and make rounds. After returning to the office, an obstetrician/gynecologist might see patients during the afternoon and then finish the day by updating medical records, phoning patients, and reading journals to keep up with new developments in the field.

It is still possible for an obstetrician/gynecologist to have a relatively normal life outside of the world of obstetrics and gynecology. Unlike a trauma surgeon, the obstetrician/gynecologist knows which obstetrics patients are likely to deliver and which gynecological patients are at risk for some emergency.

I really enjoy communicating with my patients. But I also enjoy surgery. Ob/gyn is a nice mix of both.

How Do I Become an Obstetrician/Gynecologist?

EDUCATION

High School

You can prepare for a future in medicine by taking courses in biology, chemistry, physics, algebra, geometry, and trigonometry. Courses in computer science are a must, as well, since the computer is changing the way medicine is communicated and shared by medical professionals. Also important are courses such as English and speech that foster good communication skills.

Postsecondary Training

University or college courses that help prepare you for medical school are math, biology, chemistry, anatomy, and physics, as well as courses in the humanities, such as English composition. Students usually take the Medical College Admission Test (MCAT) in their junior or senior year. This test is required to apply to medical schools.

Admission to medical school is competitive, and applicants must undergo an extensive admissions process that considers grade point average, MCAT score, and recommendations from professors. Most premedical students apply to several schools early in their senior year of college. Competition is stiff; only about one-third of the applicants are accepted.

In order to earn an M.D., you must complete four years of medical school. For the first two years you attend lectures and classes and spend time in laboratories. You learn to take patient histories, perform routine physical examinations, and recognize symptoms.

In your third and fourth years, you are involved in more practical studies. You work in clinics and hospitals supervised by residents and physicians and you learn acute, chronic, preventive, and rehabilitative care. You go through what are known as rotations, or brief periods of study in a particular area, such as internal medicine, obstetrics and gynecology, pediatrics, psychiatry, and surgery.

Upon graduating from medical school, physicians must pass a standard examination given by the National Board of Medical Examiners. Most physicians complete an internship, usually one year in length, that helps graduates decide their area of specialization.

Following the internship, physicians begin a residency. Physicians wishing to pursue the surgical specialty of obstetrics-gynecology must first complete a minimum of four years in residency, three years in obstetrics and gynecology, and a one-year elective.

After completing a residency in obstetrics and gynecology, physicians may pursue additional training to subspecialize in critical care medicine, gynecologic oncology, maternal-fetal medicine, or reproductive endocrinology.

To Be a Successful Obstetrician/Gynecologist, You Should . . .

- be a good clinician
- be an extremely good communicator, capable of putting patients at ease
- have good hand-eye coordination and manual dexterity
- enjoy working with and helping people

CERTIFICATION OR LICENSING

All physicians must be licensed by their state to practice medicine legally. Certification by the American Board of Obstetrics and Gynecology (ABOG) is highly recommended.

In the last months of the obstetrician/gynecologist's residency, he or she takes the written examina-

FYI

During the 1930s Dr. George Papanicolaou found that cervical cancer could be detected by studying cells from a woman's genital tract. This led to the development of the Pap test, now a routine gynecological procedure used to detect cervical cancer. According to the American Cancer Society, the Pap test, along with regular gynecological checkups, has reduced deaths caused by cervical cancer by 70 percent over the past 40 years.

tion given by the ABOG. Candidates for certification take the final oral examination after two or more years of practice. Candidates must have successfully passed the written portion of the certifying exam before they are eligible to take the oral portion.

SCHOLARSHIPS AND GRANTS

Scholarships and grants are often available from individual institutions, state agencies, and special-interest organizations. Many students finance their medical education through the Armed Forces Health Professions Scholarship Program. Each branch of the military participates in this program, paying students' tuitions in exchange for service in the military. Contact your local recruiting office or visit http://www.aamc.org for more information on this program. The National Health Service Corps Scholarship Program also provides money for students in return for public service. Visit http://nhsc.bhpr.hrsa.gov for information. Another source for financial aid, scholarship, and grant information is the Association of American Medical Colleges. Remember to request information early for eligibility, application requirements, and deadlines.

Who Will Hire Me?

Most obstetricians/gynecologists are in private solo or group practices, although some work for public health agencies, women's organizations, and university hospitals and clinics. Obstetricians/gynecologists who work for public health agencies and clinics are active in preventive health care and work in these settings as administrators, consultants, and planners.

A growing number of physicians are partners or salaried employees of group practices. Organized as medical groups, these physicians can more easily afford expensive medical equipment, insurance costs, and other business expenses.

Where Can I Go from Here?

Advancement opportunities for an obstetrician/gynecologist comes by way of acquiring more skill and knowledge and increasing the size of the practice. Going back to school to learn a subspecialty is one way of advancing; however, it also means a serious investment, both of time and finances. Involvement in professional organizations and societies may lead to committee appointments and chairs, which are markers of respect by one's peers.

What Are the Salary Ranges?

Salaries for obstetricians/gynecologists vary according to the kind of practice (whether he or she works individually or as part of a group practice), the amount of overhead required to maintain the practice, and the geographic location. According to Physicians Search.com, OBGYNs receive starting salaries that range from $110,000 to $210,000. Those with three years of experience earn an average salary of $248,294. Salaries range from $184,045 to $350,455. Fringe benefits for OBGYNs typically include health and dental insurance, paid vacations, and retirement plans.

What Is the Job Outlook?

The general population is aging, and health care needs increase dramatically with age. The health care industry, in general, is doing exceptionally well, despite the claims of managed care critics to the contrary. The employment of physicians in almost all fields is expected to grow about as fast as the average for all occupations. Salaries, however, are predicted to drop somewhat, due to managed care.

Specifically, the demand for obstetricians/gynecologists hasn't abated. The specialty is shifting from a male-dominated field to a female-dominated field; of the residents specializing in obstetrics and gynecology in 1998, 64.4 percent were women, according to the American Medical Association.

How Do I Learn More?

PROFESSIONAL ORGANIZATIONS

The following are organizations that provide information on the profession of obstetrician/gynecologist:

American Board of Obstetrics and Gynecology
2915 Vine Street
Dallas, TX 75204
214-871-1619
http://www.abog.org

American College of Obstetricians and Gynecologists
409 12th Street, SW
PO Box 96920
Washington, DC 20090
202-638-5577
http://www.acog.org

American Gynecological and Obstetrical Society
PO Box 387
UVA Health Science Center
Charlottesville, VA 22908
804-923-9937
http://www.agosonline.org

BIBLIOGRAPHY

The following is a sampling of materials relating to the professional concerns and development of obstetricians/gynecologists.

Beckmann, Charles R. et al. *Obstetrics and Gynecology.* 3d ed. Philadelphia: Lippincott Williams & Wilkins, 1998.

Callahan, Tamara L., Aaron B. Caughey, and Linda J. Heffner. *Blueprints: Obstetrics & Gynecology.* 3d ed. Cambridge, Mass.: Blackwell Science, 2003.

Gabbe, Steven G., Jennifer R. Niebel, and Joe Leigh Simpson. *Pocket Companion to Obstetrics: Normal & Problem Pregnancies.* 3d ed. New York: Churchill Livingstone, 1999.

Hacker, Neville, J. George Moore, and Joseph Gambone. *Essentials of Obstetrics and Gynecology.* 4th ed. Philadelphia: W. B. Saunders, 2004.

Mishell, Daniel R. et al. *Comprehensive Gynecology.* 4th ed. St. Louis: Mosby-Year Book, 2002.

Nolan, Thomas E. *Primary Care for the Obstetrician and Gynecologist.* New York: John Wiley & Sons, 1996.

Stenchever, Morton A. et al. *Williams Obstetrics.* 21st ed. New York: McGraw-Hill, 2001.

OCCUPATIONAL HEALTH AND SAFETY WORKERS

Definition
Occupational safety and health workers ensure workplace safety and health, either as governmental regulators or as employees of private companies.

Alternative Job Titles
Industrial hygienists
Industrial safety and health technicians
Safety coordinators
Safety engineers
Safety inspectors

High School Subjects
Biology
Chemistry
Speech

Personal Skills
Helping/teaching
Mechanical/manipulative

Salary Range
$25,900 to $47,580 to $73,630

Educational Requirements
Bachelor's degree

Certification or Licensing
Voluntary

Outlook
As fast as the average

DOT
168

GOE
04.04.02

NOC
2263

O*NET-SOC
29-9011.00, 29-9012.00

Inspections always require Chuck Wilson to be at the office early. This inspection, for a paper recycling plant, was generated by an employee complaint. Chuck checks his paperwork and equipment one last time and heads to his car for the drive to the site. He expects to be gone all day.

When he arrives, he shows his identification and announces the inspection. The management is surprised, but cooperates. Chuck explains that he will take air samples, talk confidentially with employees, and tour the plant looking for possible hazards. Then he begins the inspection. From his interviews Chuck learns that the employees have been telling management for years about health concerns they have. People had complained of nausea, headaches, and dizziness, but nothing was done. Finally, someone filed a complaint with the Occupational Safety and Health Administration (OSHA).

By the time he finishes, it is late afternoon. He talks briefly with managers about what he has found. He cannot be sure until his samples come back from the lab, but experience leads him to believe that the problem is excess carbon monoxide, a deadly and debilitating gas.

What Does an Occupational Safety and Health Worker Do?

Occupational safety and health workers are responsible for preventing accidents and illnesses related to the workplace environment. They work in industries like construction, steel making, automobile manufacturing, and insurance to identify and eliminate potential causes of worker injuries. In the government sector, *safety inspectors* and *industrial hygienists* work to see that companies are following laws governing employee safety and health.

Only since the late 19th century has an attempt been made to protect the lives of people who work in factories, mines, building sites, and offices. Little effort was made before then to protect workers. Even in the first half of the 20th century, common wisdom held that there would be one death for each million dollars spent on construction. The building of the Golden Gate Bridge (1933–37) was a landmark in the progress of safety engineering. Through experimentation with new safety equipment and techniques and rigorous enforcement of work rules, there were no deaths for the first three years of construction. Overall, deaths on this very dangerous project were cut by two-thirds.

Safety and health workers save money, as well. By eliminating lost workdays, workers compensation claims, expensive lawsuits, and by lowering insurance premiums, companies can improve their profitability and competitiveness.

There are a number of different job descriptions that fall under safety and health work. *Safety engineers* try to eliminate conditions and practices that lead to accidents on the job. In construction and demolition they write safety plans for specific projects that reflect the unique nature of each job. They ensure that workers wear safety equipment like hard hats, safety shoes, and eye protection. Safety engineers inspect work sites to see that safety rules concerning digging trenches, excessive dust (which causes breathing problems), and the operation of heavy equipment are followed. In the trucking industry, *safety coordinators* deal with things like driver fatigue, proper loading and lifting, and equipment maintenance. Safety inspectors are employed by public utilities and must have an understanding of electrical safety, proper climbing equipment and techniques, and fire prevention and fighting. All of these people investigate accidents when they occur and write recommendations for preventing future accidents.

Some occupational safety and health workers are employed by insurance companies or as consultants in the field of risk management. Claims resulting from accidents and illness cost the insurance industry many millions of dollars every year. Insurance companies employ experts to recommend ways to prevent costly accidents to their policy holders. These experts may specialize in fire prevention, safety engineering, or industrial hygiene.

Occupational safety and health workers in government service are responsible for enforcing a broad range of laws and regulations governing everything from mine safety to the amount of fresh air someone working in an office must have. Inspectors investigate accidents and complaints. They cite infractions, levy fines, and sometimes testify in judicial proceedings. They work with private industry in an advisory role, too, educating and advising companies about their rights and responsibilities under the law.

In addition to their on-site inspection or laboratory work, occupational safety and health workers must do a great deal of record-keeping and paperwork. They must complete worker compensation, insurance, and hospitalization forms after accidents in addition to any internal documentation that may be required. OSHA requires that a running tabulation of workplace injuries be maintained and displayed.

Lingo to Learn

Abatement date The date set by OSHA, after inspecting a facility and issuing a citation, when required modifications to correct a violation must be completed.

Repetitive motion injuries Injuries caused by doing the same task all day, as data entry or assembly line workers might do. These injuries can be very serious and are a growing source of insurance claims.

Site-specific safety plan A safety plan for construction projects that take special dangers or unusual conditions into account.

Trench safety Each year, workers are killed when improperly supported trenches collapse. Safety engineers help prevent these accidents by making sure excavations are braced.

What Is It Like to Be an Occupational Safety and Health Worker?

Chuck Wilson is an industrial hygienist for OSHA, working out of the Chicago-North office in Des Plaines, Illinois. He is responsible for seeing that workplaces do not have excessive lead, carbon monoxide, silica (tiny particles of sand), asbestos, or any other potentially dangerous substances. The story related above is just one of his inspections. It was a paper recycling company. "They used 20 propane-powered forklifts," he recalls. Tests showed that there was four times the legal exposure to carbon monoxide, which accounted for the headaches and nausea experienced by the employees. "The company had to improve ventilation in the plant and get the trucks serviced more frequently," he says, "but they cooperated. They even requested a reinspection after they made their changes."

The experience at the recycling plant is representative of what Chuck's job is usually like. Inspecting, taking samples, issuing citations where necessary, and occasionally reinspecting. "The inspector is the one who makes the decision on whether a reinspection is needed," Chuck explains. "Requesting a reinspection is pretty unusual." Chuck usually works alone, but there is support available if needed.

Chuck is assigned an inspection by his office supervisor. "Usually they [the assigned inspections] start as employee complaints," he says, "but we can also get referrals from other inspectors who might have been through a particular place." Once he is assigned to a case, he has to prepare. "I try and find out as much as possible about the company and the industry," Chuck says. On the day of the inspection, he calibrates his equipment because accuracy of the devices is critical to an accurate assessment. He arrives at the site unannounced so that he gets a true picture of the situation as it has been maintained. "Most of the time, companies cooperate," he says. "Occasionally, a big company will insist I get a warrant, which takes a couple of days. They use the time to take care of as many violations as they can, to limit their penalty."

Once inside, there are specific steps he follows to ensure the inspection is done properly and the rights of companies are respected. "I explain what is going to happen first," he says. After he briefs management, Chuck conducts a walk through to check for obvious violations, conducts confidential interviews with employees, and takes samples for later testing. "I can usually finish my inspections in one day," he says. Back in the office Chuck writes a narrative of the inspection (explaining exactly what went on during the investigation), prepares samples for shipment to laboratories, writes citations for any violations noted, and once again calibrates his equipment. Between the research prior to inspection and the quantity of paperwork after it, Chuck does not get as many inspections done as he would like. "My goal is two inspections per week," he says, "but I don't always make it."

Tim Lally is a safety supervisor for National Wrecking Company of Chicago. Demolition is very hazardous work. Tim's job is to make it less dangerous. He investigates accidents when they occur, but his biggest responsibility is preventing accidents from happening at all. "You have to play devil's advocate," he explains. "What's the worst thing that could happen here? Then you try and prepare for it." He spends about half of his time doing on-site inspections; the other half is spent on paperwork, in transit, or in meetings.

For many of National's jobs, there are site-specific safety plans that must be written. Whatever task he is performing, Tim must be able to show that what he is doing is having an impact. "You have to justify what you do," he says. "You have to show management how you are improving productivity or profitability. It's a struggle sometimes, but they know that the costs of one bad accident can wipe out the profits from the next three or four [projects]." There is a lot of paperwork—insurance forms, doctors' office reports, accident reports, and government forms. During his on-site inspections, Tim talks to everyone, from laborers to the job foremen. After all, it is they who will suffer if something goes wrong. Speaking about how safety initiatives are received by the workers, Tim has this to say: "The laborers, the equipment operators, they want to do the right thing. Everything comes down to the foremen, though. If they work with you, it makes the job much easier."

Do I Have What It Takes to Be an Occupational Safety and Health Worker?

Safety and health is first and foremost a communication job. Occupational safety and health workers must be able to speak persuasively to every type of person, from top-level management to laborers. They must be confident and articulate. They must be able to think creatively to devise safety plans for changing circumstances. They must also have a good understanding of science and technology. Some types of safety and health work, such as fire prevention engineering, demand even greater technical proficiency. Since safety and health work is frequently performed outside, workers must be willing to endure bad weather and sometimes dangerous conditions.

Chuck has a science background, and he frequently uses his background skills in biology and chemistry. "There are some complex formulas for calculating the final exposures [to airborne contaminants]," he says. "You have to be comfortable with the technical aspects." Using his authority as an inspector took some getting used to. "At first, you're really eager, but you're nervous, too," Chuck recalls.

"Walking into some huge company and telling them that they are about to be inspected was difficult. It's easy now, with experience."

There are many inspections waiting to be conducted at any given time, and unfortunately, not all of them are based on legitimate complaints or problems. "It's frustrating when people make phony complaints just to get back at their employers," Chuck says. "They are a waste of time. We end up not getting to the legitimate complaints as soon as we should, and that means people are in danger."

Tim's safety work requires him to be critical sometimes. "I get tired of finding fault," he says. "People perceive safety people as the bad guys." He addresses this misconception by trying to recognize the good things workers and supervisors do as well as criticize their errors. Managers can be difficult to deal with, especially when they feel that safety restrictions are cutting into the bottom line by requiring additional expenditures to fix problems or prevent possible ones. "Sometimes you have to convince guys that have been doing a job one way for years that they have to change," Tim says. Despite the headaches, Tim finds his work very rewarding. "When things go right, when a dangerous job is finished, and no one got hurt, I get a lot of satisfaction from that," Tim says. "I'm making the company safer. I'm helping people continue to enjoy the things they take for granted."

When things go right, when a dangerous job is finished, and no one got hurt, I get a lot of satisfaction from that.

How Do I Become an Occupational Safety and Health Worker?

EDUCATION

Occupational safety and health work requires at least a bachelor's degree. For most positions, safety engineering, safety management, or industrial hygiene degrees are preferred, but biology, chemistry, chemical engineering, or electrical engineering degrees are also possible routes into the field.

High School

If safety and health work interests you, take courses in biology, chemistry, algebra, and trigonometry. Written and oral communications are very important, so speech and English composition classes are helpful. Practical experience in industrial hygiene might be difficult to find, but if you are interested in safety work in the construction industry, there are often summer construction jobs available. Tim Lally worked in construction and the experience helped him understand what can and cannot be done on a job site. "Having worked in construction increases your credibility," he says.

Postsecondary Training

Neither Chuck nor Tim planned on careers in safety when they went to college. Chuck majored in biology and minored in chemistry before taking a job doing biological research for the Veterans Administration. Tim was studying communications when he decided to change majors to safety management. "I took a safety class to satisfy an elective requirement, and I really liked it," he remembers. There are more than 100 schools offering degrees in safety and health related specialties. Some schools offer safety courses as part of their engineering programs but many have separate departments.

Many companies try to combine safety, industrial hygiene, and environmental management (preventing contamination of air, ground water, etc.) into a single position. People having experience or education in more than one area, for example a bachelor's degree in safety engineering and a minor in environmental engineering, are more attractive to employers than those with a single specialty.

CERTIFICATION OR LICENSING

Certification is voluntary. The Board of Certified Safety Professionals offers a program to become a certified safety professional (CSP). The American Board of Industrial Hygienists offers certification as a certified industrial hygienist (CIH). The American Association of Safety Engineers (ASSE) also offers certification. All certification requires a combination of experience and education plus passing a comprehensive exam.

INTERNSHIPS AND VOLUNTEERSHIPS

Interning is a good way to gain experience and network for a job. Many large firms offer internships. College placement offices and trade publications are good places to look for openings.

SCHOLARSHIPS AND GRANTS

The ASSE Foundation offers scholarships. It accepts applications in the fall every year and announces winners the following spring. For more information, contact the ASSE at http://www.asse.org.

Who Will Hire Me?

Chuck made a drastic career change, going from lab researcher to industrial hygienist, but his employer, the federal government, stayed the same. "It's a good career," he says, speaking of government service. "The benefits are excellent." Government agencies like OSHA are among the largest employers of safety and health workers. Heavy industries (such as steel making, motor vehicle manufacturing, and oil refining), construction, and insurance are also major employers of occupational safety and health workers. Companies advertise openings in industry trade journals or in journals devoted to safety engineering. Large companies often hire safety workers directly. Smaller companies may hire safety consultants who work on a contract basis. Some insurance companies offer industrial hygiene or safety reviews to their clients as a way of lessening the risk of a major claim from a serious accident.

Where Can I Go from Here?

Chuck is a GS-12, a change of three pay grades from when he first came to OSHA. "GS-13 and 14 are where you start to see people getting management positions," Chuck says. As positions in other offices become available, government employees are free to apply for them. This opens up possibilities for advancement for those willing to relocate. Outside government service, there is no single path of promotion that safety workers follow. Successful safety professionals can head company safety programs for several different facilities or move from a branch office to the home office. Tim has advanced through several companies to the position he now holds as head of the National Wrecking Company's safety program.

Advanced degrees in areas such as business or law are helpful for moving into safety management or other executive positions. Those who wish to work for themselves become consultants once they have sufficient experience.

In-depth

Sick Building Syndrome

You find yourself complaining at work about the frequency of headaches, nausea, fatigue, and the inability to concentrate. Many of your coworkers have similar complaints. This might be a sign of a "sick building."

Sick building syndrome can have a variety of causes, all having to do with indoor air quality. Some of these are:

- Poor ventilation of vapors of cleaning compounds, solvents, or other chemicals.
- Poorly designed heating and cooling systems.
- The presence of carbon monoxide because of the proximity of building air intakes to vehicular traffic, a source of carbon monoxide.
- Vapors emitted from new carpet, fresh paint, or photocopy machines.
- Molds or fungi found in humidification systems.

The World Health Organization estimates that nearly one-third of all new or renovated buildings may contain polluted air.

What Are the Salary Ranges?

According to the U.S. Department of Labor, occupational health and safety specialists made median annual salaries of $47,580 in 2003. The lowest-paid 10 percent made less than $25,900, and the highest-paid 10 percent made more than $73,630. Occupational health specialists working for the federal government made the highest average salary: $66,740 a year.

What Is the Job Outlook?

Average growth is expected in the employment of inspectors and compliance officers. This growth reflects a balance of continuing public demand for a safe environment and quality products against the desire for smaller government and fewer regulations.

Economic conditions have little effect on the employment of safety and health workers because the costs of accidents are simply too high. As previously mentioned, those with more than one area of expertise will be the most marketable. As the workforce continues to become less industrial, there will be an increasing need for people specializing in things like repetitive motion injuries and in ensuring safe office environments.

How Do I Learn More?

PROFESSIONAL ORGANIZATIONS

The following organizations provide information on careers in occupational safety and health, certification requirements, training programs, and publications:

American Board of Industrial Hygiene
6015 West St. Joseph, Suite 102
Lansing, MI 48917-3980
517-321-2638
http://www.abih.org

American Industrial Hygiene Association
2700 Prosperity Avenue, Suite 250
Fairfax, VA 22031
703-849-8888
http://www.aiha.org

The American Society of Safety Engineers
1800 East Oakton Street
Des Plaines, IL 60018
http://www.asse.org

Board of Certified Safety Professionals
208 Burwash Avenue
Savoy, IL 61874
217-359-9263
http://www.bcsp.com

National Safety Council
1121 Spring Lake Drive
Itasca, IL 60143-3201
630-285-1121
info@nsc.org
http://www.nsc.org

For information on training and education requirements for the Occupational Safety and Health Administration (OSHA) contact

OSHA Training Institute, Office of Training and Education
1555 Times Drive
Des Plaines, IL 60018
847-297-4810

BIBLIOGRAPHY

The following is a sampling of materials relating to the professional concerns and development of occupational safety and health workers:

Brimson, Terence J. *The Health and Safety Survival Guide: A Comprehensive Handbook for Managers.* New York: McGraw-Hill, 1995.

Cox, Sue, and Tom Cox. *Safety, Systems, and People.* Newton, Mass.: Butterworth-Heinemann, 1996.

Erickson, Paul A. *Practical Guide to Occupational Health and Safety.* San Diego: Academic Press, 1996.

Goetsch, David L. *Occupational Safety and Health: For Technologists, Engineers, and Managers.* 4th ed. Upper Saddle River, N.J.: Prentice-Hall, 2001.

Hasselhorn, Hans-Martin, Alan Toomingaas, and Monica Lagerstrom. *Occupational Health for Health Care Workers: A Practical Guide.* New York: Elsevier Science, 1999.

Leigh, Paul J. et al. *Cost of Occupational Injury and Illness.* Ann Arbor, Mich.: University of Michigan Press, 2000.

Levy, Barry S., and David H. Wegman, eds. *Occupational Health: Recognizing and Preventing Work-Related Disease and Injury.* 4th ed. Philadelphia: Lippincott Williams & Wilkins, 2000.

OCCUPATIONAL THERAPISTS

Definition
Health care professionals who use *occupation,* or purposeful activity, to help people with physical, developmental, or psychological disabilities relearn or maintain the abilities necessary for independent and satisfying lives.

Alternative Job Title
OTR (occupational therapist registered)

High School Subjects
Art
Biology
Physics

Personal Skills
Helping/teaching
Mechanical/manipulative

Salary Range
$35,970 to $52,550 to $75,640+

Educational Requirements
As of 2007, a master's degree in occupational therapy

Certification or Licensing
Required by all states (certification)
Required by certain states (licensing)

Outlook
Faster than the average

DOT
076

GOE
14.06.01

NOC
3143

O*NET-SOC
29-1122.00

Chocolate chips spill from a recently opened package on the counter. Two children, Josh and Ariel, are bustling about the specially designed kitchen facility. With great concentration, Josh measures a cup of flour into a large bowl. Ariel slowly adds a teaspoon of baking soda. Both leave a trail of ingredients in their wake, but Karen Jacobs, who is supervising the exercise, ignores the mess. "That's great work," she says with enthusiasm. "What do we add next?"

The harmony of this scene is suddenly disrupted as Ariel snatches an egg carton from Josh's hands. "I want to put the eggs in," Ariel says belligerently.

Karen intercedes, gently putting a hand on the girl's arm. "Ariel, how would you feel if Josh had taken the egg carton away from you?"

The girl shrugs, but continues to clutch the egg carton tightly. "I wanna do it," she mumbles.

"Well, let's think about this problem," says Karen. "Both you and Josh want to add the eggs to the dough. The recipe says we need two eggs to make the cookies. Can you think of a solution that will make both of you feel good?"

Reluctantly, Ariel answers, "We can both put one egg in the bowl, I guess."

Karen smiles. "That's a good idea," she says. As an occupational therapist, Karen uses activities such as baking cookies, carving pumpkins, or planting flowers to help children with developmental disabilities develop important social skills, such as cooperation and compromise.

"Occupational therapy takes a very holistic approach to working with people," explains Karen. "We work within the individual's—and the family's—physical, emotional, spiritual, and social context to help enhance the client's quality of life. When I work with children, I try to develop real-world exercises that will be fun and rewarding for children, while helping them develop necessary skills. To bake cookies, for instance, the children have to develop a plan for accomplishing the task by breaking it down into steps. They have to measure ingredients, which requires cognitive and small motor skills, and they have to cooperate. These are important skills that can help a person with a developmental disability succeed in an employment situation and live more independently."

Later, Ariel and Josh proudly place the warm cookies they have made on a small plate to share as they discuss the morning's activity with Karen. "I try to develop activities that will enable the children to feel a sense of accomplishment," Karen comments. "Occupational therapists also help clients of every age enhance their self-esteem."

Lingo to Learn

Assistive technology Simple or complex tools that are designed to aid or increase the skills of a person with physical or mental limitations.

Ergonomics The design and placement of tools and equipment so that people can interact with these items at the maximum level of efficiency and safety.

Fine motor skills The fine or precise use of coordinated movements such as for writing, buttoning, and tying shoelaces.

Gross motor skills The use of large muscle groups to coordinate body movements such as for walking, balancing, and throwing.

Psychosocial development The normal and orderly development of trust, autonomy, identity, and intimacy. A person begins this psychological and social development in infancy. Psychosocial dysfunction results from abnormal or arrested development.

Role-playing Exercise in which a simulated situation, such as confronting someone with a disagreement, is acted out in order to give the participants an understanding of their emotions, appropriate behavior, and possibilities for resolution.

What Does an Occupational Therapist Do?

An *occupational therapist* uses everyday activities to help clients learn or relearn the skills necessary to care for themselves and to live more satisfying lives. Professionals in this field strive to help clients become as independent as possible in home, school, and work environments. Unlike physical therapists, who concentrate on helping clients regain physical functions, occupational therapists address the psychological and social dimensions, as well as the physical implications, of their clients' disabilities.

Occupational therapists frequently work closely with other health care providers, such as physicians, nurses, psychiatrists, speech therapists, physical therapists, and social workers. Together these professionals develop an appropriate treatment strategy for each client. Occupational therapists are trained to consider the client's needs, interests, potential, and likes and dislikes when establishing a treatment program. To succeed, treatment programs must be tailored to each client's personal circumstances.

Occupational therapists work with people of all ages who face a wide variety of challenges, including physical, developmental, and psychological disabilities. Some therapists, like Karen, work with children who have physical or developmental challenges, helping them develop gross and fine motor skills, cognitive-perception skills, and psychosocial abilities. Others work with individuals who have become physically disabled through illness or injury. Occupational therapists also work with people who are recovering from work-related injuries, people recovering from substance abuse problems, elderly individuals, and premature infants.

Those who work with people who have disabilities concentrate on helping their clients learn, or relearn, basic daily skills, such as bathing, dressing, and eating. A client who has lost a limb may need to learn how to use a prosthetic device, such as an artificial leg. A client who has suffered a severe spinal cord injury may need to learn how to use a wheelchair or how to eat and dress with limited use of his or her hands. Once clients have mastered these fundamental skills, the occupational therapist helps them develop the skills necessary to care for a home and family, pursue an education, or maintain employment.

Occupational therapists who work in mental health or rehabilitation facilities help individuals who suffer from addiction, depression, eating disorders, and stress-related disorders regain self-confidence and prepare to resume control of their lives. These therapists may engage clients in role-playing exercises or in activities designed to reinforce planning and time-management skills.

Many occupational therapists work in nursing homes, helping older clients adapt to changes in their abilities due to advanced age. A client whose mobility is limited, for example, might need to learn to use a walker and to grip the handrail in the bathroom. An individual with arthritic hands may benefit from activities that emphasize manual dexterity, such as typing or knitting. Occupational therapists also help elderly individuals maintain physical and cognitive abilities through activities designed to exercise clients' muscles and stimulate their minds.

A growing number of occupational therapists today offer home health care services. By visiting clients at home, therapists are able to design real-world activities that can enhance clients' self-sufficiency. These therapists can also help clients adapt their homes to their abilities. Many practitioners apply the concepts of ergonomics to make both the home and work environment user-friendly.

In addition to providing therapy, occupational therapists must maintain records of information about client evaluations, progress reports, staff notes, daily treatment notes, billing statements, and discharge notices. Many also supervise certified occupational therapy assistants and act as consultants or advisers to local or state agencies. For those who obtain advanced degrees, teaching and research positions are also available.

What Is It Like to Be an Occupational Therapist?

Karen Jacobs, who is a clinical associate professor of occupational therapy at Boston University, in Boston, Massachusetts, is in her office by 7:30 A.M., sipping tea as she reviews her lecture notes. At 8:00, Karen hurries to a nearby classroom to deliver a lecture on occupational therapy principles and their application to diverse client groups. Karen draws on her past experiences as a practicing occupational therapist to illustrate the theories and to keep the students focused on the purpose of the profession, which is to help people who are experiencing physical, emotional, or mental challenges.

At 10:30, Karen supervises a clinical laboratory class in which students are designing and constructing assistive technology. One student is building a portable Wheel of Fortune game to help clients who are recovering from strokes improve their vocabulary and memory. Another is cutting out pieces of cardboard that will be used as the foundation for a candy house. By frosting the house and decorating it with candy pieces, children who have cerebral palsy will enhance their fine motor skills. "Be careful not to choose candy pieces that are too small, Laela," says Karen. "It's very important to enable the children to experience success."

Over lunch, Karen grades student papers and works on one of the many papers she is preparing for publication. At 1:00 P.M., she takes two undergraduate students to the William Carter School, a Boston public school for young people with severe learning disabilities. "I believe in giving students exposure to community practice very early in their academic experience," says Karen.

At the William Carter School, Karen's occupational therapy students work with children who have cerebral palsy, seizure disorders, hearing and visual impairments, communication difficulties, and impaired mobility. Karen helps her students lead activities that will encourage the children to develop or enhance important skills. One student helps a child who has difficulty brushing his teeth build a very simple model airplane. While doing something he enjoys, the child is enhancing his fine motor skills. Karen works very closely with her students, and with their clients, to design the best therapeutic strategy for each child.

At 3:00, Karen meets with a graduate student to discuss the progress he has made on his dissertation. At 4:30, she delivers a presentation to several registered nurses at a local hospital. "Occupational therapists work closely with other health care providers," Karen explains. "It's important for the entire health services team to understand the important role occupational therapy can play in accelerating a patient's recovery."

In the evening, Karen spends several hours with her family before preparing lecture notes for the following day.

Because Karen is a professor as well as an occupational therapist, her typical day may be very different from that of an occupational therapist who works in a public school system, a hospital, or a mental health facility. According to Mary Foto, an occupational therapist in California who specializes in industry issues, it is almost impossible to generalize about how occupational therapists spend their days. "This is an extremely diverse field," she explains.

Mary owns a consulting company that helps employers establish return-to-work programs for employees who were injured on the job. Because she works with adults who have employment-related injuries, Mary's job is very different from Karen's. A typical day for Mary might include several appointments with recovering patients and visits to employment sites to implement preventive practices.

"We treat injured employees like injured athletes," says Mary. "Instead of focusing on the injury, we focus on doing exercises that will help the injury heal quickly. We emphasize overall fitness to reduce recovery time and to prevent future injuries. We also do quite a bit of preventive education. At one large grocery chain, for instance, we trained employees to stretch before each shift. By stretching out their muscles before they begin lifting inventory, the employees have dramatically reduced their number of injuries."

Do I Have What it Takes to Be an Occupational Therapist?

Wherever they work, occupational therapists spend most of their time interacting with clients and with other health care providers, so it is very important that they enjoy working with people. Excellent communication skills are also a must. "Academic skills are important," says Karen, "but they're no substitute for the ability to establish a rapport with clients."

Because most occupational therapists work with clients who are recovering from an injury or illness or learning to live with a disability, they must also be extremely compassionate and patient individuals. "Occupational therapy practitioners should be motivated by an intense desire to help people," Karen observes.

Creativity is also an essential characteristic for people entering this profession. Occupational therapists must plan interesting exercises to help clients develop necessary skills. These activities must be designed to meet the unique needs of each client. Creativity also helps occupational therapists design adaptive aids. "As occupational therapists," Karen explains, "we often create adaptive equipment out of inexpensive, readily available materials. For example, I teach my students to make assistive technology out of three layers of cardboard glued together. We use cardboard carpentry to create adaptive puzzles for children to assemble and even portable bowling alleys that help clients develop hand-eye coordination. Any experience a person has with design, construction, or sewing will be useful in this profession."

Like other health care providers, occupational therapists must maintain meticulous records for each client. Organization, attention to detail, and good problem-solving skills are essential to becoming a successful occupational therapist.

> Occupational therapy practitioners should be motivated by an intense desire to help people.

FYI

Occupational therapy services improve rehabilitation for many people, including those with:

- arthritis, cancer, multiple sclerosis, or other illnesses
- head or spinal cord injuries
- work-related injuries such as low back problems or repetitive stress injuries
- sports-related injuries, broken bones, or other injuries from falls or accidents
- amputations
- burns
- limitations following a stroke or heart attack
- mental health or behavioral problems including Alzheimer's, schizophrenia, and post-traumatic stress disorder
- birth injuries, learning problems, or developmental disabilities
- substance abuse problems or eating disorders
- vision problems

How Do I Become an Occupational Therapist?

EDUCATION

High School

High school students who are interested in entering this field should take as many science courses as possible. Biology and physics are extremely important. Chemistry is useful but not essential. Statistics courses, if available, can be extremely helpful. Any courses that will help you understand human behavior, such as basic psychology and sociology, are also useful.

Postsecondary Training

Although you can currently become an occupational therapist with a bachelor's degree, in 2007 a master's degree or greater will become the minimum requirement. In 2003 there were 38 bachelor's degree programs, three post-baccalaureate programs (for people who have bachelor's degrees in fields other than occupation therapy), and 86 master's degree programs. There were also 48 programs that offered a combined bachelor's and master's degree, and five that offered doctoral programs.

Course work at the college level typically includes basic anatomy, physiology and neurophysiology, kinesiology, statistics, psychology, and several occupational therapy practice areas, such as group dynamics, psychosocial dysfunction, and development dysfunction.

Some people begin working in occupational therapy right after college; others have earned a previous degree and worked in other fields before deciding to pursue a career in occupational therapy. Each person brings his or her own unique experience to the field.

CERTIFICATION OR LICENSING

All U.S. states, the District of Columbia, and Puerto Rico regulate the practice of occupational therapy. After completing the course work and internships, occupational therapy students must successfully complete the National Certification Examination of the National Board for Certification in Occupational Therapy. Passing this exam is the final step in becoming an occupational therapist registered (OTR). This certification must be renewed every five years. Many states also require OTRs to obtain a state license to practice.

SCHOLARSHIPS AND GRANTS

The American Occupational Therapy Association (http://www.aotf.org) provides information on scholarships for students of occupational therapy. Contact the association for information on eligibility, application requirements, and deadlines.

INTERNSHIPS AND VOLUNTEERSHIPS

Karen encourages individuals who are considering occupational therapy as a career to take every opportunity to volunteer. "Volunteering is an excellent way to find out if occupational therapy is a good match with your skills and personality," says Karen. "I advise prospective occupational therapy students to work with a broad range of clients—from children with developmental disabilities to adults who are ill or aging—to find out whether they are comfortable working with people with disabilities and whether they have the necessary empathy."

Some occupational therapy programs require prospective students to participate in related volunteer activities prior to admission. College or university admissions counselors should be able to provide this information.

To Be a Successful Occupational Therapist, You Should . . .

- be able to establish a rapport with a wide variety of people
- be creative and enjoy working with your hands
- be patient and supportive of those working with disabilities
- be able to keep accurate and extensive records

Who Will Hire Me?

Karen began her career as a prevocational occupational therapist at school for very young children with disabilities. Prior to earning her Ed.D. and becoming and associate professor at Boston University, Karen also served as a job placement coordinator at a vocational high school and as a consultant for industry, hospitals, schools systems, nursing homes, and rehabilitation centers. Her experience is not unusual. Professionals within this diverse field may choose from a myriad of career opportunities.

The largest number of occupational therapists work in hospitals, including many in rehabilitation and psychiatric hospitals. Other major employers include offices and clinics of occupational therapists and other health practitioners, school systems, home health agencies, nursing homes, community mental health centers, adult day care programs, job training services, and residential care facilities.

The American Occupational Therapy Association publishes a weekly list of job postings and provides networking opportunities. Most occupational therapy academic programs also offer job placement services.

Where Can I Go from Here?

Occupational therapists may advance to management positions that require them to supervise other occupational therapists and occupational therapy assistants. Therapists who earn advanced degrees, like Karen, can also pursue academic careers.

"One of the most exciting things about my job is that I have the opportunity to influence my profession," says Karen. "The students I teach this year will be my colleagues next year."

What Are the Salary Ranges?

The U.S. Department of Labor reports that median annual earnings of occupational therapists were $52,550 in 2003. The middle 50 percent earned between $43,420 and $63,390 a year. The lowest paid 10 percent earned less than $35,970 and the highest paid 10 percent earned more than $75,640 a year. Occupational therapists who worked in hospitals earned average annual salaries of $54,640; in home health services, $61,100 per year; and in elementary and secondary schools, $48,150 per year.

Salaries vary depending on the therapist's area of expertise. Industry occupational therapists may earn higher than average salaries, while the salaries of therapists in public school systems may be below average.

Therapists who are employed by government facilities, public agencies, or schools usually receive full benefit packages that include health insurance, sick pay, and vacation. Self-employed therapists and those who run their own businesses must provide their own benefits.

What Is the Job Outlook?

According to the U.S. Bureau of Labor Statistics, employment in occupational therapy is expected to have faster than average growth. Over the long run, the demand for occupational therapists should continue to rise as a result of growth in the number of individuals with disabilities or limited function requiring therapy services.

In the past, most occupational therapists worked in hospitals. Today, occupational therapists work in industry, school systems, nursing homes, and mental health facilities, as well as in the traditional hospital setting. Many therapists also work in outpatient clinics, sheltered workshops (such as for the mentally disabled or those who have suffered from abuse), and community health agencies. Changes in our health care system are creating new opportunities in home health care and private practice. The aging of our population has also created an increased demand for occupational therapists who work with older clients.

How Do I Learn More?

PROFESSIONAL ORGANIZATIONS

The following organization provides information on occupational therapy careers, accredited schools, and employers:

The American Occupational Therapy Association
PO Box 31220
4720 Montgomery Lane
Bethesda, MD 20824
301-652-2682
http://www.aota.org

BIBLIOGRAPHY

The following is a sampling of books relating to the professional concerns and development of occupational therapists:

Chaffin, Don B., Gunnar B. J. Andersson, and Bernard J. Martin. *Occupational Biomechanics*. 3d ed. New York: John Wiley & Sons, 1999.

Dimond, Bridgit C. *Legal Aspects of Occupational Therapy*. 2d ed. Oxford, U.K.: Blackwell Science, 2004.

Hammell, Karen Whalley, Christine Carpenter, and Isabel Dyck, eds. *Using Qualitative Research: A Practical Introduction for Occupational and Physical Therapists*. New York: Churchill Livingstone, 2000.

Perrin, Tessa, and Hazel May. *Wellbeing in Dementia: An Occupational Approach for Therapists and Carers*. New York, NY: Churchill Livingstone, 2000.

Punwar, Alice J., and Suzanne M. Peloquin. *Occupational Therapy: Principles and Practice*. 3d ed. Philadelphia: Lippincott Williams & Wilkins, 2000.

Reed, Kathlyn L. *Quick Reference to Occupational Therapy.* 2d ed. Gaithersburg, Md.: Pro-Ed, 2000.

Trombly, Catherine A., and Mary Vining Radomsky. *Occupational Therapy for Physical Dysfunction.* 5th ed. New York: Lippincott Williams & Wilkins, 2002.

Weeks, Zona R. *Opportunities in Occupational Therapy Careers.* New York: McGraw-Hill, 2000.

OCCUPATIONAL THERAPY ASSISTANTS

The aroma of grilled cheese sandwiches, toast, and scrambled eggs may linger in the air when Corrine Shields is at work. Dishes may sit in the sink waiting to be rinsed, but Corrine is not a cook or a dishwasher. She is a certified occupational therapy assistant, and she's in the kitchen in order to watch over rehabilitation patients.

Her goal is to teach them skills so that they can regain muscle tone, improve mental abilities, and become more self-sufficient. "By practicing basic living skills," Corrine says, "patients learn to care for themselves once again." Therapeutic activities such as working in the kitchen help rehabilitate patients. "Besides building up their bodies," Corrine says, "it's my job to watch out for their cognitive needs as well. For example, performing the 'simple' task of making toast can be difficult for stroke victims.

"As they move about the kitchen, I evaluate how well they handle safety concerns. I note how well they follow directions and how well they are able to sequence their actions in order to succeed."

When problems arise, Corrine works with her supervisor, a registered occupational therapist, to tailor adaptive strategies for each patient's needs. "It's challenging work," says Corrine. "No two patients are alike. It takes a very creative person to be a good occupational therapy assistant."

Definition
Occupational therapy assistants aid people with mental, physical, developmental, or emotional limitations using a variety of activities to improve basic motor functions and reasoning abilities. Under the supervision of registered occupational therapists, occupational therapy assistants help plan, carry out, and evaluate rehabilitation programs designed to help patients regain self-sufficiency and to restore their physical and mental functions.

High School Subjects
Biology
Health

Personal Skills
Helping/teaching
Leadership/management

Salary Range
$25,830 to $37,400 to $50,290

Minimum Educational Level
Associate's degree

Certification or Licensing
Required by all states

Outlook
Much faster than the average

DOT
076

GOE
14.06.01

NOC
6631

O*NET-SOC
31-2011.00, 31-2012.00

What Does an Occupational Therapy Assistant Do?

Before World War I, there were no occupational therapists or occupational therapy assistants. One consequence of modern warfare is a huge rise in the number of soldiers who survived combat but were disabled, both mentally and physically. These veterans needed special support and training in order to learn to live with the effects of their injuries. Occupational therapy developed in response to the need for services that helped soldiers regain self-sufficiency and mental health. Today, occupational therapy deals with a wide variety of patients.

Occupational therapy assistants work in hospitals, mental health facilities, hospices, substance abuse programs, schools, nursing homes, rehabilitation centers, clinics, and in private physicians' practices. They may work with children, developmentally disabled persons, or victims of accidents or illnesses. Many patients benefit from working with occupational therapy assistants, including people with arthritis, cancer, sports-related injuries, hand trauma, amputation, head or spinal cord injuries, strokes, burns, developmental disabilities, and mental illnesses.

Occupational therapy is not the same as physical therapy. Physical therapy helps people with disabilities or injuries regain movement and is mainly concerned with the well-being of patients' bodies. Occupational therapy also deals with physical rehabilitation, but it goes further and includes concern for the psychological and social effects of disabilities and injuries. The goal of occupational therapy is more than restoring physical mobility. Occupational therapy seeks to help patients develop skills that will allow them to re-enter the workplace and care for themselves at home.

Occupational therapy assistants work under the supervision of registered occupational therapists. In general, occupational therapists are responsible for developing programs while occupational therapy assistants are responsible for carrying out the programs.

Often occupational therapy assistants work more directly with individual patients than do occupational therapists. Occupational therapy assistants teach people with permanent functional disabilities how to use special equipment. For example, a person with a spinal cord injury needs to learn how to get around in a wheelchair. A stroke victim may have lost the use of one hand and has to learn how to put on shoes using a long-handled shoe horn. People with cerebral palsy or muscular dystrophy require special adaptive devices that allow them to feed themselves. Computers and computer-related equipment help speech-impaired patients to talk or amputees to walk. Learning to use such complicated equipment takes time, patience, and the support of occupational therapy assistants.

Occupational therapy assistants also work with people who have mental disorders. These disorders may be developmental or the result of emotional disturbances. They may also result from the effects of alcohol abuse, drug abuse, or eating disorders.

The goal of occupational therapy assistants working with this population is to provide strategies to cope with the tasks of daily life, reduce stress, and increase productivity. For instance, when substance abusers leave their rehabilitation programs, they need new skills in order to avoid unproductive behaviors that might lead to relapses. Recovering alcoholics, for example, benefit from practice with time management and budget preparation. Occupational therapy assistants help them develop these skills and avoid repeated substance abuse.

Working with developmentally disabled children or adults presents a different kind of challenge. Basic personal skills such as hygiene, dressing, or eating may require attention. Occupational therapy assistants observe the level at which developmentally disabled persons function and, after consultation with registered occupational therapists, implement strategies to increase self-sufficiency.

Occupational therapy assistants help developmentally disabled persons learn to ride the school bus or take public transportation to their workplace. They help disabled persons learn to do routine household chores such as cooking and cleaning.

Some occupational therapy assistants work in schools. Along with registered occupational therapists, they assess student needs and provide ways to increase active participation in the school day. For example, a child recovering from cancer therapy may need a desk modified to make sitting more comfortable. Another student needs a special splint in order to hold a pencil better. Other children benefit from game-type activities that improve balance and increase both gross and fine motor coordination.

A special branch of occupational therapy seeks to return injured workers to their jobs. Occupational therapy assistants help these people resume, as closely as possible, their original working roles. When necessary, occupational therapy assistants provide strategies, therapies, or adaptive equipment to modify individual work situations.

What Is It Like to Be an Occupational Therapy Assistant?

Corrine Shields works at St. Joseph's Hospital in Tucson, Arizona. Her primary work area is outpatient services, but she may also work in acute care, rehabilitation, or intensive care. A typical day begins with rehabilitation therapy for transitional care patients. Transitional care is a facility within the hospital for people with cerebral-vascular trauma, or stroke.

Corrine sees these patients once a day, Monday through Friday. She works with them using a variety of exercises. For instance, practice making lists is valuable for people with short-term memory loss. Other people need tasks to improve hand-eye coordination. Some patients need help with balance. To help one patient, Corrine has the patient stand beside an elevated table and play a game of cards with her. Another patient, recovering from a different type of injury but who also needs help restoring balance, stands on a foam mat and plays a more active ball exercise.

A big part of Corrine's morning is spent with patients who require assistance with the activities of daily living. She helps these people learn, or relearn, how to dress and feed themselves, use the telephone, and write messages. She may also teach them how to safely move from a reclining position on a bed to a sitting position in a chair.

In the afternoon Corrine works in the outpatient clinic with people who require a variety of therapeutic strategies. For example, patients who have had hip replacement surgery need exercises to improve their upper body strength. Pulmonary patients sometimes panic when they are unable to "catch their breath." High levels of anxiety can slow the healing process. Corrine helps pulmonary patients recognize approaching anxiety and finds ways to circumvent it when possible.

Some people with perceptual difficulties benefit from visual activities. Corrine sets up a peg board and asks them to complete a design following a pattern on a graph. By observing their progress, she can determine how well the patients are able to follow directions. She notes how they correct errors and evaluates their general problem-solving abilities.

Patients with cognitive disabilities are taken into the kitchen and asked to perform a basic task such as making scrambled eggs. Corrine watches how well they follow directions and how well they sequence the many steps needed to cook. If patients start to make mistakes, Corrine is there to correct them. She also reminds patients how to work safely within the kitchen.

The kitchen is also a great place to teach new skills to arthritis patients, people with hand injuries, or amputees who are learning to use artificial limbs. Occupational therapy assistants teach these people how to reduce their activity levels to basic movements, conserve their range of motion, and save energy.

In between patients, Corrine makes notes on medical charts, describing that day's activities. She consults with her supervisor, a registered occupational therapist, and discusses future patient care. Sometimes she meets with other hospital staff.

Nancy White works in a nursing home, and because she works exclusively with an older population, her job is slightly different than Corrine's. She observes residents and, when needed, devises adaptable equipment. For example, older people sometimes lose their full range of motion and cannot easily bend over to put on their shoes, so Nancy teaches them how to use long-handled shoehorns. "Reachers," a long handle with grippers that open and close, help mobility-impaired seniors pull on their clothing and dress themselves. Other people grow weaker as they grow older and find it difficult to feed themselves. The solution may be something as simple as creating a weighted eating utensil.

"Our goal as occupational therapy assistants," says Nancy, "is to keep nursing home residents as independent as possible, for as long as possible." Some of her work is similar to what goes on in the hospital. For instance, Nancy helps nursing home residents learn how to stay safe while using the bathroom. When necessary, she raises the level of the toilet seat by using special equipment. She checks to see that there is a grab bar in the shower and advises how to use it. She discusses transfer techniques for getting in and out of the bathtub safely.

Lingo to Learn

Adaptive equipment Tools, aids, or devices that persons with reduced or limited mobility use to hold, reach, steady, or pick up objects.

ADL (Activities of daily living) Basic functions (showering, dressing, cooking, eating, going to the bathroom) that the average person performs every day, independently or with the aid of adaptive equipment, such as a sock-aid or a long-handled shoehorn.

Reacher Long-handled implement with a trigger mechanism that "pinches" or "scissors" together to allow the user to grab onto items, such as objects on a high shelf.

Sub-acute care Short-term care facility that patients visit prior to going home in order to learn strengthening and endurance exercises, as well as activities of daily living.

Do I Have What It Takes to Be an Occupational Therapy Assistant?

"I'm a people person," says Corrine. "Being an occupational therapy assistant is a good profession for a people person. I get to work directly with patients and not worry about paperwork as much as an occupational therapist has to." A good occupational therapy assistant is a good observer. "You have to be able to pick up on things," says Corrine, "and watch for subtle emotional signs that telegraph how the patient is really feeling. You have to establish rapport with both the patient and the nursing staff. You need to be able to observe what's going on with patients' minds and bodies, seek out more information when necessary, and then, based on what you've discovered, provide the necessary service.

"You can't be squeamish about being close to people either or worry about dealing with all sorts of bodily functions," she adds. "Also, occupational therapy assistance is a physically demanding field. Sometimes you're supporting the weight of patients or helping transfer them from one place to another."

Barbara Rom, director of the Green River Community College program in Auburn, Washington, emphasizes that occupational therapy assistants should be good with their hands. "You can't be awkward," she says, "because you need to make or adapt all kinds of equipment, such as hand splints. It's a great help if you are nimble, creative, and like to make things with your hands." It's also important that you are able to write clearly, concisely, and legibly. Every activity an occupational therapy assistant does is noted on medical charts. Both written and oral communication skills are important. More and more, computer literacy is also needed.

Occupational therapy assistants always work under the supervision of registered occupational therapists. While you may work as a team in most circumstances, occupational therapy assistants are not the lead members. Above all, occupational therapy assistants must be flexible.

"The methods for delivering health care are changing," Corrine stresses. "Supervisors sometimes change, and patients and their needs change daily . . . if you're not flexible, this is not the profession for you."

Being an occupational therapy assistant is a good profession for a people person.

To Be a Successful Occupational Therapy Assistant, You Should . . .

- enjoy working with people
- be willing to work under supervision
- have good manual dexterity and be physically fit
- be flexible and creative

How Do I Become an Occupational Therapy Assistant?

Corrine Shields has worked as an occupational therapy assistant for nine years. She received her associate's degree from Fox Valley Technical College in Appleton, Wisconsin.

Course work at accredited schools is intense and thorough. Students receive a broad education, including serving a supervised apprenticeship. "The goal," Corrine says, "is to produce graduates who can function immediately as staff members at whatever institution they join."

EDUCATION

High School

Classes in biology, chemistry, physics, social science, health, English, and computer use are helpful to students planning to pursue a career in occupational therapy.

Postsecondary Training

Occupational therapy assistants need more than a high school diploma. There are two ways to enter the profession. Most students attend a two-year program and receive an associate of applied science degree. A few students (those with many years of experience as health care workers or with several years of education past high school) may qualify instead for one-year certificate programs. Both one- and two-year programs include academic study as well as clinical fieldwork.

In-depth

History

Since about the 14th century, physicians have recognized the therapeutic value of providing activities and occupations for their patients. Observations that mental patients tended to recover more quickly from their illnesses led physicians to involve their patients in such activities as agriculture, weaving, working with animals, and sewing. Over time, this practice became quite common, and the conditions of many patients improved.

Occupational therapy as we know it today had its beginning after World War I. The need to help disabled veterans of that war, and years later the veterans of World War II, stimulated the growth of the field. Even though its inception was in the psychiatric field, occupational therapy has developed an equally important role in other medical fields, including rehabilitation of physically disabled patients.

Traditionally, occupational therapists taught creative arts such as weaving, clay modeling, leather work, jewelry making, and other crafts to promote their patients' functional skills. Today, occupational therapists focus more on providing activities that are designed to promote skills needed in daily living, including self-care; employment education and job skills, such as typing, the operation of computers and computer programs, or the use of power tools; and community and social skills.

It is important to note the difference between occupational therapists and physical therapists. Physical therapy is chiefly concerned with helping people with physical disabilities or injuries to regain functions, or adapt to or overcome their physical limitations. Occupational therapists work with physical factors, but also the psychological and social elements of their clients' disabilities, helping them become as independent as possible in the home, school, and workplace. Occupational therapists work not only with the physically challenged, but with people with mental and emotional disabilities as well.

College course work includes medical terminology, basic anatomy and physiology, gerontology and aging, construction of adaptive equipment, note taking and documentation, first aid and CPR, musculoskeletal system disorders, human development, basic health care skills, and therapeutic techniques.

CERTIFICATION OR LICENSING

Every state requires that occupational therapy assistants be certified. Twice a year the National Board for Certification in Occupational Therapy administers a national test to determine certification. The test is rigorous and comprehensive.

SCHOLARSHIPS AND GRANTS

Colleges may reserve scholarships for students pursuing health careers and make specific funds available for students wishing to become occupational therapy assistants. Certain employers, especially long-term care facilities such as nursing homes, may offer stipends to students. In exchange for agreeing to work for the facility after graduation (usually for at least one year), the facility pays a portion of the student's tuition. The American Occupational Therapy Foundation sponsors a number of state association scholarships for students at the associate's degree level and one national scholarship for students pursuing two-year degrees (see "How Do I Learn More?").

Who Will Hire Me?

Occupational therapy assistants work in a variety of institutions including hospitals, mental health facilities, hospices, substance abuse programs, schools, nursing homes, rehabilitation centers, clinics, and private physicians' practices. The majority work for hospitals or nursing homes. Since demand is great for occupational therapy assistants, employers often contact schools to inquire about recent graduates. The American Occupational Therapy Association (AOTA) reports that new occupational therapy assistants find their first jobs, on average, within two months.

FYI

Occupational therapy assistants work with people with a variety of different injuries, disabilities, and illnesses, including:

- Alzheimer's
- arthritis
- depression
- learning disabilities
- multiple sclerosis
- spinal cord injury
- stroke

Where Can I Go from Here?

Because occupational therapy assistants always work under the supervision of occupational therapists, there is not much room for advancement. Unless you are willing to return to school, obtain a four-year degree, and become an occupational therapist, the highest level that occupational therapy assistants can advance to is lead assistant. These people have more responsibility and may assist in making evaluations. They may schedule work for other occupational therapy assistants and help train students.

What Are the Salary Ranges?

According to the U.S. Department of Labor, the median annual salary for occupational therapy assistants was $37,400 in 2003. Those in the lowest 10 percent made less than $25,830, while those in the highest 10 percent made more than $50,290.

Those working in day care programs and within school systems receive slightly lower incomes while those working in skilled nursing facilities, rehabilitation centers, and hospitals receive higher incomes. Generally, full-time occupational therapy assistants receive standard worker benefits, including health insurance.

Occupational therapy assistants may work some nights and weekends, depending on the needs of the facilities where they work. Those assistants involved with schools work more regular hours than those who work in nursing homes, for example.

Advancement Possibilities

Lead occupational therapy assistants are responsible for making work schedules of other assistants and for the training of occupational therapy students.

Occupational therapists select and direct therapeutic activities designed to develop or restore maximum function to individuals with disabilities.

What Is the Job Outlook?

The U.S. Department of Labor predicts that employment of occupational therapy assistants will grow much faster than the average for all other occupations. Contributing to this growth is the aging population and the large numbers of elderly who need therapy. Also, medical advancements are allowing for people with major injuries to live longer and physically improve, requiring the aid of those in occupational therapy. In addition, insurance companies will be encouraging occupational therapists to assign more work to occupational therapy assistants, thereby lowering costs of care. This trend will also encourage job growth for this profession.

How Do I Learn More?

PROFESSIONAL ORGANIZATIONS

For more information about this career, contact

American Occupational Therapy Association
4720 Montgomery Lane
PO Box 31220
Bethesda, MD 20824-1220
301-652-2682
educate@aota.org
http://www.aota.org

American Occupational Therapy Foundation
4720 Montgomery Lane
PO Box 31220
Bethesda, MD 20824-1220
301-652-2682
aotf@aotf.org
http://www.aotf.org

National Board for Certification in Occupational Therapy
800 South Frederick Avenue, Suite 200
Gaithersburg, MD 20877-4150
301-990-7979
http://www.nbcot.org

BIBLIOGRAPHY

The following is a sampling of materials relating to the professional concerns and development of occupational therapy assistants:

Anderson, Laura L. Swanson, and Christine Malaski. *Occupational Therapy as a Career: An Introduction to the Field and a Structured Method for Observation.* Philadelphia: F. A. Davis Company, 1998.

Quinlan, Kathyrn A. *Occupational Therapy Aide.* Mankato, Minn.: Capstone Press, 1998.

Sladyk, Karen. *Ryan's Occupational Therapy Assistant: Principles, Practice, Issues, and Techniques.* 3d ed. Florence, Ky.: Delmar Learning, 2000.

Weeks, Zona R. *Opportunities in Occupational Therapy Careers.* New York: McGraw-Hill, 2000.

ONCOLOGISTS

The tough part about being an oncologist is having to be the bearer of bad tidings. And as tough as it is to tell a patient he or she has a malignant tumor, Dr. Jackson knows it's a million times worse for the patient to hear it. The worst is having to inform a patient that the cancer is Stage IV, inoperable, and extremely difficult to treat.

Fortunately that's not the case for Dr. Jackson's first patient of the day. He looks at Beth's chart. She was diagnosed with breast cancer two years ago. It was caught early and she had surgery to remove the malignant tumor, followed by a course of chemotherapy treatments. Today she has come in for her periodic tests and examination. Dr. Jackson walks into the examination room and smiles.

"Good news!" he says. "Your tests are clean. No sign of any cancer. It's still in remission."

Beth lets out a huge sigh of relief. She knows it will be at least three more years of clean tests before she can say she is cured.

Definition
Oncologists are physicians who diagnose and treat patients who have cancer. They may also be involved in cancer research and clinical trials.

High School Subjects
Biology
Chemistry
Health

Personal Skills
Helping/teaching
Technical/scientific

Salary Range
$120,000 to $215,000 to $473,000+

Educational Requirements
Bachelor's degree; Medical degree plus specialized study in oncology

Certification or Licensing
Recommended (certification)
Required by all states (licensing)

Outlook
About as fast as the average

DOT
070

GOE
14.02.01

NOC
3112

O*NET-SOC
29-1069.99

What Does an Oncologist Do?

An *oncologist* is a physician who specializes in the study, diagnosis, and treatment of cancer. Because cancer affects almost any part of the body and occurs in individuals of any age, there are many different kinds of oncologists. The American Society of Clinical Oncology (ASCO) lists three primary disciplines within the field of clinical oncology.

Physicians who are *medical oncologists* specialize in treating cancer with medicine, hormones, and chemotherapy. *Surgical oncologists* perform the surgical aspects relating to cancer, including biopsy and the removal of cancerous tissue or tumors. *Radiation oncologists* specialize in treating cancer with therapeutic radiation.

In addition to the above three disciplines, ASCO also recognizes pediatric oncology as a fourth discipline. *Pediatric cancer specialists* incorporate all three primary oncology specialties when caring for patients who are infants and children. These oncologists require special skills because young patients with cancer call for specific pediatric care.

Usually when a tumor is discovered, a surgeon performs a biopsy and sends the tissue to a pathologist for evaluation. If the diagnosis is cancer, an oncologist evaluates the patient to determine how advanced the cancer is. This is called staging, which is a precise evaluation of the tumor, lymph nodes, and any metastasis (spreading) that has occurred.

One or more oncologists evaluate the patient's medical history. Information about family medical history is very important since as many as 15 percent of cancers are germline mutations. This means that the parent passes the cancer-causing genes directly to its child.

The oncologist is usually the individual who interacts with the patient, explains the cancer diagnosis, and discusses what this means to the patient. Various treatment options and recommendations are explained.

Once cancer is diagnosed, the oncology team, usually consisting of two or three oncologists, joins with a pathologist, a diagnostic radiologist, and an oncology nurse to form a consulting group. The advantage of creating this group is that it includes a combination of physicians trained in surgery, chemotherapy, and radiation. This group of oncologists and medical specialists attempts to cure the patient of cancer. The cancer cure rate varies, but according to ASCO, cancer is cured in roughly 50 percent of cases.

Oncologists are also involved in clinical trials. Clinical trials are studies that are conducted on consenting patients to identify the most successful strategies for fighting cancer. These studies usually involve two different treatments on two groups of patients with similar symptoms. By analyzing the results of these treatments, clinical oncologists are able to determine which methods are more effective in eliminating or retarding the development of cancer.

Lingo to Learn

Benign Referring to a tumor, it means not malignant (no cancer).

Cancer Any one of a group of diseases in which cells from once normal tissue grow uncontrollably and spread to different sites in the body.

Chemotherapy In the treatment of cancer, the use of drugs to destroy cancer cells. It is often used with surgery or radiation.

Leukemia Cancer of the blood or blood-forming organs.

Malignant tumor A mass of cancer cells that may invade surrounding tissues or spread (metastasize) to distant areas of the body.

Radiation therapy A cancer treatment that uses a high energy rays (such as X rays) to kill or shrink cancer cells.

Remission Complete or partial disappearance of the signs and symptoms of cancer in response to treatment. A remission may not be a cure.

What Is It Like to Be an Oncologist?

Oncologists, like many physicians, divide their time between patient consultations, medical procedures, study, research, publishing, and office or departmental administration. Most oncologists work than 40 hours per week.

Oncologists may see anywhere from 10 to 30 patients each day. In many of these encounters, they may have to deliver devastating health news regarding a malignancy and help patients make extremely difficult choices. They explain the various treatment options, the toxic side effects associated with each option, and give patients realistic assessments of their chances of recovery. As patients undergo treatment, oncologists also help them cope with the pain and discomfort caused both by the disease and the treatment methods.

"It is extremely important to be very direct and honest with a patient at all times," comments Dr. Harmon Eyre, executive vice president of research and medical affairs for the American Cancer Society. "The patient must be able to have absolute trust in his or her physician."

As an oncologist, Harmon has witnessed countless misfortunes. Despite these experiences, he considers his profession extremely rewarding. "It is immensely fulfilling to know that a patient, who might have died if his or her disease had been mismanaged, has been cured and can look forward to resuming a normal life."

According to Harmon, rewarding moments can arise from terribly painful situations. "A few years ago, I treated a 33-year-old man for leukemia. Before he was diagnosed with this disease, he and his wife spent all their time and energy trying to advance in their careers. His cancer caused them to reevaluate their priorities. Before he died, two and a half years after his original diagnosis, he and his wife told me that they had lived more fully during those two and a half years than they had ever lived before."

It is extremely important to be very direct and honest with a patient at all times. The patient must be able to have absolute trust in his or her physician.

Have I Got What It Takes to Be an Oncologist?

"Our understanding of this disease is constantly changing," says Harmon. "We are always discovering new information about genetics, the immune system, and possible treatments. This job is never boring or dull."

If you are considering becoming an oncologist you must be extremely hard working, perceptive, and emotionally balanced. You must also be a voracious reader with an excellent memory, as new information about the cause, prevention, and treatment of cancer is published each day. Staying current with new information also requires that you be proficient and knowledgeable about technology. Your research and writing skills must be well developed, because publishing research results is an important way to advance in this profession.

In addition to the intellectual rigors of the job, you must be prepared to accept emotional and psychological challenges. Every day oncologists interact with people who are very ill and frightened. You must be able to maintain objectivity and composure under intensely emotional circumstances. A balance between compassion and professionalism is essential.

To meet these challenges, you must be an extremely mature and emotionally stable individual. An oncologist must explain very complex information to people who have little or no scientific background, so clear and direct, but passionate communication is necessary. Excellent interpersonal skills are essential to work as part of a medical team. If you work as a surgical oncologist, for example, you may have to work with a medical team that includes a dietitian, a physical therapist, the original referring doctor, nurses, and other staff members.

How Do I Become an Oncologist?

EDUCATION

High School

If you are interested in a career as an oncologist, the first step is to take high school college preparatory courses. Science courses, such as biology, chemistry, physics, and anatomy, will help prepare you for college. Math courses, such as algebra, geometry, and trigonometry, are also important. English and speech classes will help you develop your research, writing, and oral communication skills. Computer science courses are also essential.

If you are certain you wish to pursue a medical career, you may want to consider entering a college or university that is associated with a medical school and offers an accelerated medical education program. In these accelerated programs, you spend either two or three years completing your undergraduate work and then spend four years at the medical school associated with that college or university. More information on such programs is available from high school guidance counselors. If you are considering this option you should look into it in your junior or early senior year.

Postsecondary Training

Your next step in becoming an oncologist is to earn a bachelor's degree at an accredited college or university. Students who plan to go to medical school typically major in a science, such as biology or chemistry. Regardless of the major, course work should emphasize the sciences and include classes such as biology, chemistry, anatomy, and physiology. Other important classes to take include mathematics, such as calculus, English, ethics, and psychology. Volunteering or working at a hospital during your college years is also an excellent way to gain experience working in a medical setting.

After receiving an undergraduate degree, you need to apply to, and be accepted by, a medical school. Admission is competitive, and applicants must undergo a fairly extensive and difficult admissions process that takes into consideration grade point averages, scores on the Medical College Admission Test (MCAT), and professor recommendations. Most students apply to several schools early in their senior year of college. Only about one-third of the applicants are accepted.

For the first two years of medical school, you attend lectures and classes and do laboratory work. Classes include biochemistry, physiology, pharmacology, psychology, and medical ethics. You also learn to take patient histories, perform routine examinations, and recognize symptoms. In the third and fourth years, you spend time working in hospitals and clinics where you are supervised by residents and physicians. It is during this time that you do rotations. Rotations

> **FYI**
>
> Lung cancer is the leading cause of cancer death for both men and women. According to the American Cancer Society, tobacco smoke has at least 43 cancer-causing substances. Smoking is thought to be responsible for eight out of 10 cases of lung cancer.

are brief periods of study in a particular area, such as pediatrics, psychiatry, and surgery. On rotations you learn the distinctive qualities of different medical specialties and work on diagnosing and treating patients. Medical school lasts four years. At the end of this time, you have earned the degree doctor of medicine (M.D.).

After graduating from medical school, you must pass a standard exam given by the National Board of Medical Examiners. You then complete an internship or transition year during which you decide your area of specialization.

Following your internship, you begin a residency. At this point, if you are interested in oncology, you complete a residency in your chosen specialty area. For example, if you are interested in gynecologic oncology, you complete a four-year obstetrics and gynecology residency. Or, if you are interested in medical oncology, you complete a residency in internal medicine. This is paid, on-the-job training, usually in a hospital. Following your residency, you complete a fellowship (specialized study) in oncology. A fellowship in gynecologic oncology, for example, can take from two to four years to complete.

CERTIFICATION OR LICENSING

Licensing is mandatory in the United States. It is required in all states before any doctor can practice medicine. In order to be licensed, doctors must have graduated from medical school, passed the licensing test of the state in which they will practice, and completed their residency. Physicians licensed in one state can usually get licensed to practice in another state without further testing, however, some states may limit reciprocity. Foreign medical school graduates usually must pass an examination and complete a U.S. residency before qualifying for licensure.

Certification is not required for oncologists, but it is highly recommended. Boards in their area of specialty administer certification. For example, the American Board of Internal Medicine administers certification for medical oncologists and the American Board of Obstetrics and Gynecology administers certification for gynecologic oncologists.

SCHOLARSHIPS AND GRANTS

There are usually grants, scholarships, and loans available through most colleges. The easiest way to explore the various financial aid possibilities is to write directly to the financial aid offices of schools and request information and application forms.

There are also various loan programs available through the federal government, including Pell Grants, Stafford Student Loans, National Direct Student Loans, Health Education Assistance Loans, and Health Professions Student Loans. Your high school guidance counselor should have information about these programs.

Many students finance their education through the Armed Forces Health Professions Scholarship Program. Each branch of the military participates in this program, paying students' tuitions in exchange for military service. Contact your local recruiting office for more information on this program.

Who Will Hire Me?

As an oncologist you may work in virtually any health care setting. Because cancer is such a prevalent disease that takes so many different forms, oncologists are in demand in every area of medical practice. A government-funded medical facility, a private hospital, a university health center, an outpatient clinic, a government agency, a pharmaceutical company, or a research laboratory are all possible employers for the oncologist.

Where Can I Go from Here?

As an oncologist, you can advance your career by becoming the head of a research or medical department. Department heads must assume extensive administrative responsibilities in addition to patient care. You can also achieve prominence in the field by publishing articles and medical studies, conducting research, and participating in professional organizations, such as the American Cancer Society and the American Society of Clinical Oncology. Highly respected oncologists, like Harmon, are asked to speak to the public and advise government bodies on health issues.

What Are the Salary Ranges?

According to Physicians Search.com, oncologists receive starting salaries that range from $120,000 to $215,000. Those with three years of experience earn an average salary of $269,298. Salaries range from $155,475 to $473,000. Individual earnings of oncologists will vary, depending on such factors as geographic location, years of experience, professional reputation, and type of oncology practiced. Fringe benefits for oncologists typically include health and dental insurance, paid vacations, and retirement plans.

What Is the Job Outlook?

According to the *Occupational Outlook Handbook,* employment of physicians is expected to grow about as fast as the average for all occupations. Positions in oncology will be abundant. This is due to a growing and aging population, new research, changing diagnostic techniques, and new treatment possibilities.

How Do I Learn More?

PROFESSIONAL ORGANIZATIONS

The following organizations provide information on the profession of oncology:

American Cancer Society
1599 Clifton Road, NE
Atlanta, GA 30329
800-227-2345
http://www.cancer.org

American Society of Clinical Oncology
1900 Duke Street, Suite 200
Alexandria, VA 22314
703-299-0150
asco@asco.org
http://www.asco.org

This organization provides information on careers in oncology radiology.

American College of Radiology
1891 Preston White Drive
Reston, VA 20191
703-648-8900
http://www.acr.org

BIBLIOGRAPHY

The following is a sampling of materials relating to the professional concerns and development of oncologists:

Abeloff, Martin D. et al., eds. *Clinical Oncology.* 3d ed. Philadelphia: Churchill Livingstone, 2004.

Casciato, Dennis A. *Manual of Clinical Oncology.* 5th ed. Philadelphia: Lippincott Williams & Wilkins, 2004.

Devita, Vincent T. Jr., Samuel Hellman, and Steven A. Rosenberg, eds. *Cancer Principles and Practice of Oncology.* 7th ed. Philadelphia: Lippincott Williams & Wilkins, 2004.

Markman, Maurie. *Basic Cancer Medicine.* Philadelphia: W. B. Saunders Company, 1997.

Neal, Anthony J., and Peter J. Hoskin. *Clinical Oncology: Basic Principles and Practice.* 3d ed. London: Arnold Publishing, 2003.

Pazdur, Richard et al., eds. *Cancer Management: A Multidisciplinary Approach: Medical, Surgical & Radiation Oncology.* 8th ed. Philadelphia: F.A. Davis, 2004.

Tannock, Ian F. et al., eds. *The Basic Science of Oncology.* 3d ed. New York: McGraw-Hill, 1998.

OPHTHALMIC TECHNICIANS

Martha is sitting in the examining room with her eyes closed. "I see these shooting silver arrows going back and forth," she explains to Cathy Brown, the eye doctor's assistant. "It's like lightning bolts going on inside my brain or something. And it doesn't really stop when I open my eyes."

Cathy asks Martha more questions about how her eye problem is affecting her. Has it happened before? How long has it been going on this time? Does she experience headaches along with the "lightning bolts"?

"Okay, Martha. I'm going to look at your eyes more closely." Cathy uses a pen-size flashlight to check Martha's eyelids. "There's no infection or inflammation here, so we'll do a few more things." She shines the light into one eye and then the other, noticing that both eyes constrict equally and quickly to the light. Then she checks Martha's eye muscles by covering one eye and then the other as Martha reads the eye chart. Her muscles seem to be fine.

"Martha, I want you to move forward a little; rest your chin here and your forehead here. I'm going to look into your eyes using this machine. I'm looking now at your cornea, your iris, and your lens. Now I'm going to blow a bit of air into your eye, so try to keep it open as wide as you can. . . . Are you still doing a lot of reading in your work? I'm thinking that maybe these shooting arrows are just a sign that you should be resting your eyes more. Okay, here comes the shot of air. Good.

"The last thing I'm going to do is put some drops in your eyes to dilate your pupils. Dr. Berliner will come in to see you then, and he'll look into your eyes with a scope to see what's going on back there."

Definition
Ophthalmic technicians work with ophthalmologists (eye doctors) in examining patients' eye functions. They measure vision, perform routine tests on eyes, and help to diagnose and treat eye diseases and problems.

Alternative Job Titles
Ophthalmic allied health professionals
Ophthalmic assistants
Ophthalmic medical technologists

High School Subjects
Biology
Chemistry
Mathematics

Personal Skills
Helping/teaching
Technical/scientific

Salary Range
$17,840 to $24,170 to $34,200+

Minimum Educational Level
Some postsecondary training

Certification or Licensing
Recommended

Outlook
Much faster than the average

DOT
079

GOE
05.03.03

NOC
6631

O*NET-SOC
31-9092.00

What Does an Ophthalmic Technician Do?

Ophthalmic technicians can be considered eye nurses: They help eye doctors perform their work. If you have had eye checkups in either an optometrist's or an ophthalmologist's office, you have probably been taken care of by an ophthalmic technician. The difference between the two types of eye doctors is that the ophthalmologist works mainly with eye disease and injury and optometrists work mainly with healthy eyes that do not function properly.

Ophthalmic technicians take patient histories, perform lensometries (measure the lens of the eye), and operate various types of ocular equipment. They must be skilled in patient services such as putting on ocular dressings and shields, administering drops and ointments, and otherwise assisting patients. They must know how to work with all kinds of patients:

the elderly, children, the physically disabled, and the visually disabled.

Technicians have knowledge of clinical optics, including retinoscopy, refractometry, spectacle principles, and basic ocular motility. Because contact lenses are popular vision aids, technicians have to understand the basic principles of lenses, fitting procedures, patient instruction, and troubleshooting. In addition, they should have an understanding of general medical knowledge, including anatomy, physiology, and pathology (illness and disease), and they must know CPR (cardiopulmonary resuscitation) and other first aid procedures.

The ophthalmic technician must have the same skills that assistants have, as well as knowledge of more advanced procedures. First, in taking patient histories, they ask about the presenting complaint: why the patient has come to see the doctor. Taking the history is like interviewing the patient. What is the family history? Is there diabetes, glaucoma, or hypertension in the family? What medications is the patient taking: aspirin, steroids, birth control pills? Does the patient have allergies? And finally, if the patient wears glasses or contact lenses, how long have they worn them and how is their vision now?

Working directly with patients is the task with which the ophthalmic technician is involved the most. Many patients are elderly; they visit the ophthalmologist when they have symptoms related to eye problems, such as cataracts and glaucoma. These are the two most common eye conditions leading to loss of sight. (When you have cataracts, it's like trying to see through a steamed-up window; vision is very blurry and opaque.) The technician will help the ophthalmologist to monitor the patient's cataracts, which develop gradually as one gets older, and then will assist the doctor when it is time for the cataracts to be removed.

Certified ophthalmic medical personnel help to bring peace of mind to both patients and the doctors with whom they work. Because ophthalmic technicians work with other professionals, there is a sense of teamwork in the office setting.

Lingo to Learn

Cataract A condition that exists when the eye lens is opaque, causing loss of vision.

Cornea The part of the eyeball that covers the iris and pupil.

Dilate To administer liquid drops to the eye to cause the pupil to enlarge briefly for examination.

Glaucoma An eye disease characterized by such things as loss of vision, hardening of the eye, and a damaged optic disk.

Keratometry Measurement of the cornea.

Ophthalmology The branch of medicine dealing with the structure, functions, and diseases of the eye.

Refraction The ability of the eye to bend light so that an image is focused on the retina; a procedure performed by ophthalmic technicians to determine the eye's refractive characteristics.

Retina The membrane in the eye that allows one to see; it is connected to the brain by the optic nerve.

Retinoscopy Observation of the retina.

Visual acuity The extent to which one can see clearly.

What Is It Like to Be an Ophthalmic Technician?

Cathy Brown works with ophthalmologists at Maine Eye Center, an eye-care clinic in Portland, Maine. She greets patients, settles them into examining rooms, and performs initial tests on patients' eyes. Because of her training and certification, she is qualified to take medical histories, one of the first tasks that need to be done with new patients. She asks new patients about such things as why they need an eye exam, what their family history of disease is, what their vision is like, and what types of medications, if any, they take, all the while keeping up a friendly conversation to set them at ease.

Cathy's other basic skills include measuring and recording visual acuity (that is, how sharp one's vision is). Somewhere in the doctor's office you'll probably find a Snellen chart, which shows 11 lines of progressively smaller letters, starting with the big "E" at the top and ending with PEZOLCFTD at the

Advancement Possibilities

Ophthalmic medical technologists become certified after going through a two-year training program and passing certification exams. Their duties are similar to the technician's but more in-depth and advanced. Basically, technologists might use more specialized equipment, measure intraocular pressure, plot visual fields, and do other jobs that technicians are not certified to do.

Orthoptists are even more specialized than technologists. An orthoptist will assess the patient's eye alignment and measure how the eyes work together.

Ophthalmic surgical assistants work with ophthalmologists in preparing patients for eye surgery. They must be able to identify, select, and maintain ophthalmic surgical instruments; sterilize and set up instruments for surgical procedures; and otherwise assist the ophthalmic surgeon in either an office or a hospital operating room.

bottom. Your visual acuity is determined by how much of the chart you can read without corrective lenses. Cathy also will use color plates to test eyes for color vision.

Many ophthalmologists work in the clinic where Cathy works. Each has a different specialty, such as pediatric ophthalmology (working with children), retinal or corneal ophthalmology, ophthalmic plastic surgery, and cataracts/glaucoma. At this point in her career, Cathy assists mainly with the plastics ophthalmologist, which means that she's involved with conditions like orbital reconstruction and tearing problems. Floating technicians, or technicians who move (or "float") to wherever needed, are required to fill in when any one of the doctors in the office needs help. Cathy says that this is the hardest part of the job, being skilled in just about every specialty so that you can handle any situation that comes up (be it cataracts, corneal problems, or even a simple vision test for a child).

Cathy performs routine exams as well: checking vision, pressure, and muscle reactions and motility; doing retinoscopies and refractometries; and dilating pupils. She does a lot of patient screening, taking histories and basically talking with the patients about their eye conditions. One of the most important things she does is to reassure patients about their particular complaints. Their needs and concerns require patience and understanding.

Although much of the work is routine, every now and then an emergency comes up. Perhaps a patient comes in complaining that her vision is dark or that she sees flashes of light. Cathy says that this should set off an alarm in the technician's mind: Is the retina attached? Is something wrong with the cornea? The patient will be screened by the ophthalmic assistant or technician, examined by the ophthalmologist, and then perhaps will go to the operating room or be sent to the hospital.

Cathy likes her work schedule. Her average workweek is about 36 to 40 hours, and she has Sundays and Mondays off. She is usually finished by about five in the afternoon, but she says that the ophthalmic photographers and those who work with angiograms sometimes have to stay later to wait for photos or X rays to develop.

Do I Have What It Takes to Be an Ophthalmic Technician?

"You definitely must have patience, especially because lots of the people you see are elderly," says Cathy. "You really get to learn a lot about people. It's actually really fun."

Cathy explains that on hectic days, when she might see 40 to 50 patients in one morning, "you need to be as pleasant as you can, but you have to move things along." In other words, you have to be very organized. "The doctors put a lot of trust in your hands. You have to be self-motivated, use your own judgment," Cathy says.

Communication skills are very important, as well as keeping abreast of new technology and knowledge in the field. You should expect to attend meetings, conventions, and a yearly educational program. You need to maintain your continuing education credits within three-year cycles, so you have to be comfortable with taking tests fairly often.

Every now and then there are volunteer opportunities for technicians. For example, Cathy and her colleagues once volunteered at a school for the deaf, where they examined the eyes of about 100 children.

The doctors put a lot of trust in your hands. You have to be self-motivated, use your own judgment.

How Do I Become an Ophthalmic Technician?

There are two general routes to becoming an ophthalmic technician: formal training and on-the-job training. In either case, you need to study for certification exams, take the exams (both written and performance), and continue to periodically update your certification. According to Dr. Melvin Freeman, "certification shows the dedication and professionalism of the employee and their dedication to the best care for patients under the ophthalmologist's guidance."

In Cathy's case, she was in a training program for ophthalmic surgical assisting when a job opened up at Maine Eye Center. She was hired as an on-the-job trainee with the obligation of going through a home-study course and 10 weeks of reviewing with the resident optometrists. She eventually took her exam and was certified as an assistant. Her next step is to take courses leading to certification as a technician.

Cathy says that many doctors hire people to work their way up in the office, as she is doing. At one point, the doctors at Maine Eye Center needed an ophthalmic photographer but realized it was difficult to find a trained worker. They put an ad in the paper and eventually hired someone who was a skilled photographer to be trained on the job.

EDUCATION

High School

Cathy recalls that it was helpful to have taken basic science and math courses in high school. She was able to take certain vocational classes in her junior and senior years, which gave her an awareness of the medical field. These classes included CPR and chemistry lab. Cathy knew that she wanted to work in a medical occupation, so she became involved in a nurses' assistant program. Going on field trips and taking tours of places like hospitals also opened doors for her, and she became further aware of job opportunities in ophthalmology.

As with many careers, it is wise to concentrate on basic subjects like English because in this job you'll find yourself doing various administrative tasks such as writing patient histories. You'll need to be able to communicate well, both on paper and in person. As Cathy mentioned, working for so many doctors involves teamwork and cooperation. Experience with team sports and with groups like the debate team and drama club gives you opportunities to learn how to work with others.

In-depth

20/20

What does 20/20 vision really mean? To test your visual acuity (how well you see), the ophthalmic technician at your doctor's office will have you read the Snellen chart (the one with the big E at the top and the tiny letters at the bottom). This chart hangs at a distance of 20 feet from the examining chair. If you can read all the letters on the chart without glasses or contact lenses, that means you have 20/20 vision. It means that you can see at 20 feet what the "optically normal" eye can see at that distance.

If the technician tells you that you have 20/40 vision, It means that your eyes are less strong; you have to be only 20 feet away from something that the "optically normal" eye can see at 40 feet. The larger the bottom number is, the weaker your visual acuity. So if you can't see the PEZOLCFTD at the bottom of the chart, the ophthalmic technician will probably begin fitting you for glasses!

Postsecondary Training

University degrees are not required for this career. However, you must either successfully complete an accredited ophthalmic technician's program or be certified as an active ophthalmic assistant, have at least one year of full-time work experience as a certified ophthalmic assistant, and finish 18 hours of approved continuing education credits.

The courses involved can be taken while you are working as an ophthalmic assistant, or you can enroll in a one-year full-time training program. You can expect to be quite challenged in most of your courses for this career. At this stage, classes follow a pretty standard outline and curriculum, including basic anatomy and physiology, medical terminology, medical laws and ethics, psychology, ocular anatomy and physiology, optics, microbiology, and diseases of the eye. You also learn about patient services (such as preparing ocular shields, delivering drugs, and otherwise assisting the patient), ophthalmic skills and lensometry, and instrument operation and maintenance (you have to be familiar with such equipment as ophthalmoscopes, retinoscopes, and slit lamps).

Cathy recalls her training experience as somewhat overwhelming. But even though there was so much involved, she continued through her own motivation. She carefully watched others perform their jobs, gained the confidence to try the tasks herself, and eventually learned everything she needed for her own certification. "Everything that was presented in the courses was necessary," she says.

CERTIFICATION OR LICENSING

In brief, to be an ophthalmic technician you have to be certified by the Joint Commission on Allied Health Personnel in Ophthalmology (JCAHPO). The certification requirements are quite straightforward, consisting of five basic elements: (1) evidence of successful completion of education and training; (2) evidence of satisfactory work experience; (3) a current CPR certificate; (4) endorsement by a sponsoring ophthalmologist; and (5) successful completion of a skills evaluation and a written exam.

After becoming certified as a technician, you are required to maintain your credentials by renewing your certification periodically. It is your responsibility to apply for recertification every three years. This means that you must take a certain number of continuing education courses throughout your career. Accepted courses include those offered by JCAHPO at the Continuing Education Program held each year, regional courses, and self-study courses (for example, tapes, readings, and videos).

SCHOLARSHIPS AND GRANTS

JCAHPO selects certain students each year to receive scholarships. These students are usually enrolled in accredited education programs for ophthalmic medical personnel. For more information and application instructions, visit http://www.jcahpo.org/Foundation.htm.

Also, individual schools may have their own financial aid programs, so you should talk with a counselor at the financial aid office wherever you are applying.

Who Will Hire Me?

Ophthalmic technicians work wherever there are ophthalmologists: doctors' offices, eye clinics, and hospitals. They also work in university research and training centers. Some technicians work as teachers, technical writers, and consultants.

Where Can I Go from Here?

Becoming an ophthalmic medical technologist is definitely a step up the career ladder. According to one worker, "Being a COMT [certified ophthalmic medical technologist] is a very rewarding career. There's an abundance of opportunities throughout the country." Lisa Rovick is a COMT in a large multispecialty clinic in the Minneapolis/St. Paul area. She says that other options for advancement include going into the business side of ophthalmology, perhaps becoming a partner with the ophthalmologists at a busy office.

Other ophthalmic workers have become contractors, which means that they offer their services at various medical settings and work on a freelance basis. Education is another area of specialization. Some technicians perform in-service training and teach continuing education courses. Others work as sales representatives or researchers for manufacturers of ophthalmic equipment and pharmaceuticals.

To Be a Successful Ophthalmic Technician, You Should . . .

- be able to communicate well with people
- be able to handle hectic schedules
- be self-motivated
- be organized
- know how to use your own judgment
- not be intimidated by taking tests

Although it is not actually a higher-level position, ophthalmic surgical assisting is a specialty in which you may be examined and awarded a certificate. Cathy has been assisting with surgery and plans to become more involved in that aspect of the work. "I first assist in surgery," Cathy says, "meaning I assist the doctor, and also suture."

What Are the Salary Ranges?

According to JCAHPO, salaries for ophthalmic medical personnel vary from $20,000 to $50,000 a year. The *Occupational Outlook Handbook* reports that median annual earnings for medical assistants were $24,170 in 2003. Those in the lowest 10 percent earned less than $17,840, and those in the highest 10 percent earned more than $34,200. Full-time technicians are usually provided with health and life insurance, and receive vacation pay and sick leave.

What Is the Job Outlook?

The U.S. Department of Labor expects employment of medical assistants to grow much faster than the average for all other occupations. In fact, the medical assistants field is projected to be the fastest growing occupation through 2012. Part of the reason for this growth is the aging population and the number of medical assistants that will be needed to provide eye care to the elderly.

Some programs across the country, such as the Emory University School of Medicine in Atlanta, are beginning to offer higher degrees in ophthalmic technology. Emory awards a master's degree, which allows ophthalmic technologists to advance into management roles. Graduates of these programs also receive better starting salaries; the Emory program has had graduates receive offers of between $36,000 and $55,000 annually.

How Do I Learn More?

PROFESSIONAL ORGANIZATIONS

The following are organizations that provide information on ophthalmic technician careers, accredited schools and scholarships, and employers:

American Academy of Ophthalmology
PO Box 7424
San Francisco, CA 94120-7424
415-561-8500
http://www.aao.org

American Academy of Optometry
6110 Executive Boulevard, Suite 506
Rockville, MD 20852
301-984-1441
aaoptm@aol.com
http://www.aaopt.org

American Optometric Association
243 North Lindbergh Boulevard
St. Louis, MO 63141
314-991-4100
http://www.aoanet.org

Association of Technical Personnel in Ophthalmology
2025 Woodlane Drive
St. Paul, MN 55125-2998
800-482-4858
http://www.atpo.org

Joint Commission on Allied Health Personnel in Ophthalmology
2025 Woodlane Drive
St. Paul, MN 55125-2998
800-284-3937
jcahpo@jcahpo.org
http://www.jcahpo.org

BIBLIOGRAPHY

The following is a sampling of material relating to the professional concerns and development of ophthalmic technicians:

Anshel, Jeffrey. *Smart Medicine for Your Eyes*. New York: Avery Publishing, 1999.

Cassin, Barbara. *Fundamentals for Ophthalmic Technical Personnel.* Philadelphia: W.B. Saunders, 1995.

Ledford, Janice K. *Certified Ophthalmic Technician Exam Review Manual.* 2d ed. Thorofare, N.J.: Slack Inc., 2004.

Stein, Harold A., Bernard J. Slatt, and Raymond M. Stein. *The Ophthalmic Assistant: A Guide for Ophthalmic Medicine Personnel.* 7th ed. St. Louis: Mosby, 2000.

OPHTHALMOLOGISTS

Brenda plops herself down in typical teenage fashion, throwing one leg casually over the arm of the chair and letting it dangle there. Her mother walks into the office a moment later with a resident in ophthalmology who is about to examine her daughter.

"Hi," the resident says. "My name's Thomas Weingeist. It's Brenda, right?" he asks the girl. She doesn't answer, but leans back on one elbow and sweeps a hand through the blonde bangs that fall across her eyes. The resident and the girl stare at one another for a brief moment before the girl blurts out, "Mom thinks glasses are going to help me get better grades. Phfff," she snorts. "Maybe I can't see, but I can hear—and there's no way I'm ever going to get all that sine, cosine crap."

Thomas laughs. Angered by his reaction, Brenda turns her head away. He places his hand on her arm and shakes his head. "No, no, I'm sorry. I'm laughing because I almost flunked trig, and I had 20/20 vision!"

Brenda looks at him skeptically. "Really, I swear," the resident answers. "Come on, let's take a look, and see what's going on." He begins to examine her eyes. "Hey, you've got blue eyes under all that hair."

After the examination, Thomas writes a prescription for corrective lenses. Brenda returns several weeks later for a follow-up checkup and admits, "Dr. Weingeist, you're right, it's better to be able to see, and," she adds timidly, "maybe my math struggles are easing up just a little bit."

Definition
An ophthalmologist is a physician who specializes in diagnosing and treating diseases and injuries of the eye. Ophthalmologists specialize in the treatment and prevention of eye disorders. This treatment may include surgery.

Alternative Job Title
Oculists (mostly used in United Kingdom)

High School Subjects
Biology
Health

Personal Skills
Helping/teaching
Technical/scientific

Salary Range
$120,000 to $256,872 to $417,000

Educational Requirements
Bachelor's degree; medical degree; one-year postgraduate residency in patient care; three- to four-year specialty residency in ophthalmology; optional fellowship in subspecialty

Certification or Licensing
Recommended (certification)
Required by all states (licensing)

Outlook
About as fast as the average

DOT
070

GOE
14.04.01

NOC
3112

O*NET-SOC
29-1069.99

What Does an Ophthalmologist Do?

An *ophthalmologist* is a medical doctor who manages comprehensive care of the eyes. Ophthalmologists are the only practitioners who are medically trained to diagnose and treat all disorders of the eye. Ophthalmologists test the eyes and prescribes glasses or contact lenses to correct nearsightedness, farsightedness, and other visual defects. Newer surgical techniques involving lasers may also be used to correct vision impairments. Ophthalmologists treat eye infections and diseases, such as conjunctivitis and glaucoma, and perform surgery such as corneal transplants.

Most ophthalmologists spend approximately four days per week in the office performing routine eye examinations and screenings and one day per week in the operating room. In a typical week, the general ophthalmologist may see more than 100 patients and perform two major surgical procedures. Cataract removal is the most commonly performed ophthalmic surgery. Other types of surgery include corneal transplants, surgery to correct glaucoma, and surgery to correct cross-eye or other eye muscle deviations. Recent advances now include laser surgery to correct vision problems. Surgery may be performed at a hospital, at a same-day ambulatory care surgical center, or in the doctor's office.

In addition to managing local eye disorders, an ophthalmologist may frequently work with other physicians. For instance, when examining a patient with an ophthalmoscope, the ophthalmologist studies the retina and may discover signs of diseases that involve other parts of the body, such as diabetes, atherosclerosis, and hypertension. This discovery may require that the ophthalmologist consult with another physician regarding the patient's long-term care.

Like many other specialties, ophthalmology has undergone considerable specialization. Some ophthalmologists limit their practice to diseases of the cornea, conjunctiva, and eyelids. The specialty of glaucoma focuses on the treatment of glaucoma and other disorders that may cause optic nerve damage. This practice usually involves the medical and surgical treatment of both pediatric and adult patients. Other specialties include ophthalmic pathology, ophthalmic plastic surgery, and pediatric ophthalmology.

Lingo to Learn

Blepharoplasty Plastic surgery on the eyelid, usually to remove excess or fatty tissue.

Cataract A clouding of the lens of the eye that obstructs transmission of light to the retina.

Conjunctivitis Inflammation of the conjunctiva, the mucous membrane that lines the eyelid and covers the white of the eye.

Iritis Inflammation of the iris of the eye.

Ophthalmoscope Instrument used to view the inside of the eye, especially the retina.

Retina The delicate membrane that lines the eye. It has light-sensitive cells, called rods and cones, that change light rays into electrical impulses that are carried to the brain by the optic nerve.

Vitreous humor The clear, colorless, transparent jelly that fills the eyeball behind the lens.

What Is It Like to Be an Ophthalmologist?

"I love what I do," says Dr. Thomas Weingeist about the work he does as an ophthalmologist specializing in vitreoretinal diseases. Thomas was the resident who helped the teenager see better. "When that girl came in for a routine eye exam, it was like any other assessment. I examined her, refracted her, saw she had poor vision, and wrote a prescription for glasses," he remembers. "I couldn't believe it when she came back and admitted that perhaps I had helped her. What I did for her was so simple, yet it made an impact that may help her have a better future."

Thomas was fortunate enough to have benefited from early exposure to the profession. His father was also an ophthalmologist. "I knew what an ophthalmologist was, and I actually spent a lot of time with him at his office. Originally, I went to graduate school to do research, but then I decided to go to medical school afterwards. Now, my son is studying to be an ophthalmologist." Thomas got his Ph.D. in cell biology at Columbia University and then went on to the University of Iowa for his medical degree, ophthalmology residency, and fellowship in vitreoretinal diseases and surgery.

Today, Thomas is a professor and head of the department of ophthalmology at the University of Iowa. He works with patients who have age-related macular degeneration, detached retinas, and diabetic retinopathy.

A typical patient who comes to Thomas for diagnosis and treatment is one with macular degeneration—the most common cause of severe vision loss in people over 65. Located in the center of our field of vision, the sensitive macula allows us to see fine details. This sharp, straight-ahead vision is necessary for driving, reading, recognizing faces, and doing close work, such as sewing. To help in the diagnosis of macular degeneration, Thomas might use what is called an Amsler Grid—a chart that looks like simple graph paper with a dot at the center intersection. Basically, the chart is a tool for monitoring the patient's central visual field. If, while staring at the center dot, a patient sees wavy lines and blurred or dark areas of the grid, it is a strong indication that the patient has some form of macular degeneration.

Another common patient complaint that Thomas hears appears to have more to do with seeing flying saucers and spaceships at night than modern ophthalmology. "A lot of patients tell me they see flashing lights and floaters," says Thomas. "The floater phenomenon is really nothing more than tiny clumps of gel or cells inside the vitreous—the clear, jelly-like fluid that fills the inside of the eye." He explains that these objects appear to the patient to be in front of the eye, but they are actually floating inside. What the patient sees are the shadows the gel or cells cast on the retina. Floaters can have different shapes: dots, circles, lines, clouds, or cobwebs. "Actually, we ask our patients, 'Do you see shadows?'"

"As people age, the vitreous gel may start to thicken or shrink, and as it does, it can pull away from the back wall of the eye. Sometimes, the retina tears because of this shrinking process."

Thomas uses drops to dilate, or open, the pupils of the patient's eyes so that he can carefully examine the retina and vitreous. "We look into the patient's eye with an ophthalmoscope, checking to see if retinal detachments are causing the shadows."

Flashing lights are similar. When the vitreous shrinks, it tugs on the retina, creating a sensation of flashing lights. The flashes of light can appear on and off for several weeks, even months. The sudden appearance of light flashes could indicate that the patient's retina has been torn.

Although some of the cases Thomas sees may seem routine, he is usually confronted with the unusual and complex medical situations. Because the University of Iowa is one of the premiere ophthalmology research facilities in the country, "this is where patients with the difficult problems go," notes Thomas.

Do I Have What It Takes to Be an Ophthalmologist?

"If you want to be a successful ophthalmologist, you have to love what you do," says Thomas. "You have to become educated, obtain a broad liberal arts background, and you have to be devoted to patient care by being honest, caring, and hardworking."

Prospective ophthalmologists should keep in mind that a typical ophthalmic practice involves the treatment of patients with vision-threatening diseases. These patients may believe that they are losing their sight. Dealing with the prospect of vision reduction or complete loss presents a unique challenge that can be highly stressful and frustrating for both patient and physician. "You must be prepared to offer your patients compassion and understanding, as well as clinical expertise."

If you are considering going into the field of ophthalmology, you should also be aware that certain visual and motor skills are necessary for effective clinical and surgical practice. Ideally, you should have excellent fine motor skills, depth perception, and color vision. Any impairment of these abilities may interfere with the effective use of essential ophthalmic instruments, such as the ophthalmoscope, the operating microscope, and microsurgery instruments.

You must be prepared to offer your patients compassion and understanding, as well as clinical expertise.

You should be patient and have good communication skills. These skills, according to Thomas, come in handy when trying to explain what the profession actually involves. "There's a lot of confusion about what we do. One thing I like to do is clearly define the differences between an ophthalmologist, an optician, and an optometrist. This is something that gets even trickier when you throw in the ocularist and the oculist, not to mention the doctor of osteopathy," laughs Thomas. "A sense of humor helps, too."

How Do I Become an Ophthalmologist?

EDUCATION

High School

"Throughout your education, you have to be a good student," advises Thomas. "And you have to distinguish yourself." High school students should prepare for a future in medicine by taking courses in biology, chemistry, physics, algebra, geometry, and trigonometry. Since college will be your next educational step, it is also important to take English courses to develop your researching and writing skills. Foreign language and social science classes will also help make you an appealing candidate for college admission, as well as prepare you for your future undergraduate and graduate education.

Courses in computer science are a must, as well, since the computer is changing the way medicine is communicated and shared by busy medical professionals.

If you are certain you wish to pursue a medical career, you may want to consider entering a college or university that is associated with a medical school and offers an accelerated medical education program. In these accelerated programs, students spend either two or three years completing their undergraduate work and then spend four years at the medical school associated with that college or university. In accelerated programs, you have the advantage of finishing medical school before your peers who take the normal educational route. More information on such programs is available from high school guidance counselors. Students considering this option should look into it in their junior or early senior year.

To Be a Successful Ophthalmologist, You Should . . .

- be a good clinician
- enjoy helping and working with people
- have good hand-eye coordination and manual dexterity
- be able to listen and communicate well

Postsecondary Training

Following high school, the next step on your educational path to be an ophthalmologist is to earn a bachelor's degree from an accredited four-year college or university. Suggested premedical courses include physics, biology, and organic and inorganic chemistry. Courses in English, mathematics, and the social sciences are also highly recommended.

After receiving an undergraduate degree, you need to be accepted to a medical school. Admission is competitive, and applicants must undergo a fairly extensive and difficult admissions process that takes into consideration grade point averages, scores on the Medical College Admission Test (MCAT), and professor recommendations. Most students apply to several schools early in their senior year of college. Only about one-third of the applicants are accepted.

In order to earn the degree doctor of medicine (M.D.), you must complete four years of medical school study and training. For the first two years of medical school, you attend lectures and classes and spend time in laboratories. Courses include anatomy, biochemistry, physiology, pharmacology, psychology, microbiology, pathology, medical ethics, and laws governing medicine. You learn to take patient histories, perform routine physical examinations, and recognize symptoms.

In your third and fourth years, you are involved in more practical studies. You work in clinics and hospitals supervised by residents and physicians and you learn acute, chronic, preventive, and rehabilitative care. You go through what are known as rotations (brief periods of study) in such areas as internal medicine, obstetrics and gynecology, pediatrics, and surgery. Rotations allow you to gain exposure to many different medical fields.

Upon graduating from an accredited medical school, you must pass a standard examination given by the National Board of Medical Examiners. Most physicians complete an internship, also referred to as a transition year, during which they decide their area of specialization. Following the internship, the physicians begin what is known as a residency.

Physicians wishing to pursue ophthalmology must first complete a one-year postgraduate training program in one of the following specialties: internal medicine, pediatrics, general surgery, emergency medicine, neurology, or family practice. A three-year specialty program in ophthalmology follows this year of training.

"I enjoyed everything," Thomas says. "I loved being a resident. Residents today do a lot of complaining, but we felt lucky to get in, so we didn't complain," he says, referring to the early 1970s when the baby boomers hit the graduate programs, and medical schools and residency programs were inundated with applications. "Every day we saw something intellectually challenging, and then we learned how to take care of those problems."

CERTIFICATION OR LICENSING

Licensing is mandatory in the United States. It is required in all states before any doctor can practice medicine. In order to be licensed, doctors must graduate from medical school, pass the licensing test of the state in which they will practice, and complete a residency. Physicians licensed in one state can usually become licensed to practice in another state without further testing, but some states may limit reciprocity.

To qualify for certification by the American Board of Ophthalmology (ABO) a candidate must successfully complete an ophthalmology course of education and pass written and oral examinations given by the ABO. Certification is valid for 10 years. The ophthalmologist must complete a designated renewal program every 10 years to maintain certification. While certification is voluntary, it is highly recommended. Most hospitals will not grant privileges to an ophthalmologist without board certification. Health maintenance organizations and other insurance groups will not make referrals or payments without certification.

SCHOLARSHIPS AND GRANTS

There are usually grants, scholarships, and loans available through most colleges. The easiest way to explore the various financial aid possibilities is to write directly to the financial aid offices of schools and request information and application forms.

There are also various loan programs available through the federal government, including Pell Grants, Stafford Student Loans, National Direct Student Loans, Health Education Assistance Loans, and Health Professions Student Loans. Your high school guidance counselor should have information about these programs.

Many students finance their education through the Armed Forces Health Professions Scholarship Program. Each branch of the military participates in this program, paying students' tuitions in exchange for military service. Contact your local recruiting office for more information on this program.

Who Will Hire Me?

As an ophthalmologist you will be able to choose from a variety of exciting and challenging work environments. Many ophthalmologists go into private practice, sometimes by themselves, but more commonly in a small group. These small group practices are either multispecialty practices, or single-specialty practices. Other ophthalmologists, like Thomas, choose to work at universities and medical schools, teaching and conducting research. An academic career offers you the clinical exposure of a private practice combined with the opportunity to perform more unusual surgeries.

Usually, academic careers provide the opportunity to teach, as well as handle administrative duties. The additional responsibilities of teaching and running a department are time-consuming, but rewarding. "If they paid me half of what they pay me now, I'd still do it," says Thomas.

Where Can I Go from Here?

You can advance your career by keeping current with new technologies, medications, and techniques. Publishing articles in respected medical journals, such as the *Journal of the American Medical Association,* is another avenue for professional enhancement. Many ophthalmologists combine research and teaching with a private practice. Others work as professors at universities or teaching hospitals and may advance to an administrative position as the head of a university or hospital ophthalmology department.

What Are the Salary Ranges?

Ophthalmologists' salaries vary by the size of the hospital or health care facility where they work and the city or town where they practice. Other factors affecting salary include the ophthalmologist's practice, hours worked per week, and professional reputation. According to Physicians Search, a physician recruitment agency, average starting salaries for ophthalmologists ranged from $120,000 to $190,000 in 2004. Ophthalmologists in practice for three years or more earned salaries that ranged from $161,763 to $417,000, with an average of $256,872.

What Is the Job Outlook?

Employment growth for all physicians is projected to be about as fast as the average through 2012, accord-

In-depth

An Eye Is an Eye Is an Eye—or Is It?

The distinction between ophthalmology and optometry is a frequent source of confusion. Optometrists are often referred to as "eye doctors" even though they don't have medical degrees. And optometrists are confused with opticians, who can't examine eyes at all but just make the lenses. And then there are oculists and ocularists.

Here's the straight story.

Ophthalmologists are the only specialists trained to diagnose and treat all eye and visual problems. Ophthalmologists are physicians—doctors of medicine (M.D.) or doctors of osteopathy (D.O.)—who are trained to medically and surgically care for the eyes. They complete four years of college, four years of medical school, one year of internship, three or more years of specialized medical, surgical, and refractive training and experience. This may be followed by one or more years of subspecialty training. They are licensed to practice medicine and surgery. At a minimum, they train for 12 years after high school.

Optometrists are health service providers who are involved exclusively with vision problems. They are specifically trained for four years by accredited optometry colleges, but they have not attended medical school and are not medical doctors. At a minimum, they train for seven years after high school. Individual states license them to examine the eyes and to determine the presence of vision problems. They determine visual acuity and prescribe glasses, contact lenses, and eye exercises. They perform all the services that an optician performs. Some states even permit optometrists to give limited treatments for some eye conditions.

Opticians are technicians who make and dispense lenses, contact lenses, and other specially fabricated optical devices from prescriptions. Opticians analyze and interpret prescriptions, determine the best lens forms for the customer, and prepare and deliver work orders for the grinding of lenses and the fabrication of eyewear. They help a client select frames and adjust eyeglasses to the client's comfort. At a minimum, they train for two years after high school.

Last, but not least, there are oculists and ocularists. The former are actually ophthalmologists. In the United Kingdom, ophthalmologists are often called oculists. Ocularists, on the other hand, make and fit prosthetic eyes for individuals who have lost one or both of their eyes. Cosmetically, the artificial eye an ocularist makes looks like an eye, but only has an aesthetic purpose and does not function like an eye.

ing to the *Occupational Outlook Handbook*. However, the demand for specialty care may provide more job opportunities for ophthalmologists and other specialists. The increasing number of elderly people will drive demand for vision care. Also, new technology (such as a wider use of lasers to correct vision problems) will allow doctors to treat and detect vision disease and impairments that were previously treatable by invasive surgery or eyewear.

How Do I Learn More?

PROFESSIONAL ORGANIZATIONS

The following are organizations that provide information on the profession of ophthalmology:

American Academy of Ophthalmology
655 Beech Street
San Francisco, CA 94109

415-561-8500
comm.@aao.org
http://www.aao.org

American Board of Ophthalmology
111 Presidential Boulevard, Suite 241
Bala Cynwyd, PA 19004
610-664-1175
info@abop.org
http://www.bop.org

BIBLIOGRAPHY

The following is a sampling of materials relating to the professional concerns and development of ophthalmologists:

Albert, D. M. *Source Book of Ophthalmology.* Boston: Blackwell Science, 1995.

Kaiser, Peter, Neil Friedman, and Roberto Pineda. *The Massachusetts Eye & Ear Infirmary Illustrated Manual of Ophthalmology.* 2d ed. Philadelphia: W. B. Saunders, 2003.

Kanski, Jack J. *Clinical Ophthalmology: A Systematic Approach.* 5th ed. Newton, Mass.: Butterworth-Heinemann, 2003.

Spaeth, George L. *Ophthalmic Surgery: Principles and Concepts.* 3d ed. Philadelphia: W.B. Saunders, 2002.

Stedman, Thomas Lathrop. *Stedman's Ophthalmology Words.* 2d ed. Philadelphia: Lippincott, Williams & Wilkins, 2000.

Vander, James F., and Janice A. Gault. *Ophthalmology Secrets: Questions You Will Be Asked on Rounds, in the Clinic, on Oral Exams.* 2d ed. Philadelphia: Hanley & Belfus, 2001.

OPTICS TECHNICIANS

Definition
Optics technicians produce lenses for prescription eyeglasses. They also assemble the lenses and frame into the finished eyeglass. Some optics technicians also produce lenses for cameras, telescopes, binoculars, and other optical instruments.

Alternative Job Titles
Optical technicians
Precision-lens technicians

High School Subjects
Biology
Mathematics
Technical/Shop

Personal Skills
Following instructions
Mechanical/manipulative

Salary Range
$15,720 to $22,194 to $34,810

Minimum Educational Level
High school diploma

Certification or Licensing
Required by certain states

Outlook
Little change or more slowly than the average

DOT
716

GOE
08.02.02

NOC
N/A

O*NET-SOC
51-9083.02

At 1:00 P.M. the lab at Lenscrafters bustles with activity. The store is packed with business people on their lunch hour, checking their watches, and waiting for their eyeglasses to be finished. Rich Crockett circles the optical lab, checking on the progress of six pairs of glasses that have to be ready within an hour.

One of the optics technicians Rich stops to observe is Ron Miranda. Although on the job for only three months, Ron has already mastered the operation of many high-tech instruments, compounds, and hand tools in the lab. As Rich watches Ron work on a lens, he's pleased with how quickly his newest employee has become proficient at the 20-step process.

As the most experienced member of the lab, Rich offers Ron a few tips on using the precision grinding instruments. Rich glances at the clock. It will be at least another hour before the flurry of business subsides.

What Does an Optics Technician Do?

Lenses are part of countless aspects of daily, scientific, and professional life. Thus, there is a tremendous need for *optics technicians* to make, assemble, and maintain lenses. In addition, optics technicians are needed to help invent new types of lenses and new uses for lenses.

Though most people think of optics technicians as the men and women who grind and polish the lenses for eyeglasses, there are a number of areas in which optics technicians may work. These areas include lens fabrication, product manufacturing, maintenance and operations, and research and development.

Lens fabrication is the area most associated with producing eyeglasses. An optics technician working in lens fabrication might fill any of the following roles: lens molder, lens blocker, lens generator, lens grinder, lens polisher, lens centerer or edger, lens coater, or lens inspector. Depending on the size and organization of the laboratory, an optics technician can perform several or all of these tasks. A technician may also be responsible for supervising the work done by other technicians.

A *lens molder* works with partially melted glass, plastic, or polycarbonate to press and form a lens blank, which is a generic lens used to produce the prescribed finished lens.

A *lens blocker* places the lens blanks into blocks so that they are secured in place during the rest of the grinding and polishing.

A *lens generator* works with an instrument that grinds the lens into its rough curve and thickness.

A *lens grinder* finishes shaping the lens into its prescribed curve and thickness, using cup-shaped tools and fine grinding powders.

A *lens polisher* uses various compounds, pads, and machines to polish the lens so that there are no obstructions when checking the power of the lens and light refraction.

A *lens centerer* or *edger* uses a lensometer to check the degree and placement of the curves that determine the strength of the lens. Using handstones, the edger finishes shaping the lens to fit in the frame.

A *lens coater* performs all the finishing steps in the fabrication of the lens, including the application of tints or coatings and final polishing.

Lingo to Learn

Aberration A condition that causes blurring, loss of clearness, or distortion of shape in the images formed by lenses or curved mirrors.

Diffraction The spreading out of waves as they pass around an obstacle or go through an opening. For example, light waves are diffracted when they pass through a small sheet of glass marked with thousands of parallel lines, producing a spectrum.

Index of refraction The ratio of the speed of light in a vacuum to its speed in the particular substance being measured.

Lens A curved, transparent body that bends (refracts) light rays.

Reflection The bending back of waves, such as light waves, from a surface.

Refraction The bending of waves, such as light waves, when they pass from one substance to another. Refraction occurs because waves travel at different speeds through different substances.

Spherical aberration Rays of light striking near the edges of the lens or mirror are brought to focus closer to the lens or mirror than are the central rays. The result is that the image of a point appears as a small disk.

A *lens inspector* checks the lens for required hardness, inspects for scratches or other defects, and ensures that all government standards have been met.

The area of product manufacturing deals mostly with fabricating lenses for use in products other than eyeglasses. An optics technician working in this field assembles, aligns, calibrates, and tests optical instruments, which include microscopes, telescopes, binoculars, and cameras, as well as less common equipment used for land surveying, night surveillance, or medical research and diagnosis.

Optics technicians in maintenance and operations are responsible for keeping large-scale optical instruments working, such as technical and scientific cameras, large observatory telescopes, and spectrophometers. Most of the work is done at the site where the instrument is being used. These include places such as observatories, hospitals, and missile or satellite tracking stations.

Optics technicians working in research and development help develop new types of lenses and new uses for them. Working closely with engineers or scientists, they conduct tests, take measurements, and fabricate new optical instruments. These technicians may choose to specialize in surveillance equipment, security devices, precision measuring instruments, medical implements, or environmental tools.

What Is It Like to Be an Optics Technician?

The general, day-to-day responsibilities of an optics technician are similar throughout the entire field of optics technology. Whether you are making a pair of glasses for someone, a lens for a NASA telescope, or a crystal for a 16th-century museum piece, the tasks of grinding, polishing, and aligning are usually involved. Work environments, on the other hand, can vary greatly. While the majority of technicians work in laboratories that are clean, ventilated, and well lighted, *maintenance and operations technicians* will find themselves working at night or outdoors at places such as missile and satellite stations. It's not unusual for these technicians to work in cramped positions and on greasy or dirty equipment.

Rich Crockett manages the optics laboratory for a Lenscrafters store in Chicago. He's been an optics technician for more than 25 years. "The size of the lab varies from place to place, and the number of tasks each technician is responsible for may be lesser or greater, but they all look pretty much the same," says Rich.

Ron Miranda is newer to the job. He sees the lab as a very new type of work environment. "I worked as a florist before coming to the lab at Lenscrafters," he says. "Here everything is so bright and clean and organized. At my other job it was completely the opposite."

Lenscrafters provides one-hour service, as do most retail lens fabricators these days. While Rich and Ron try to stick to an eight-hour schedule, the work occasionally extends into the evening. Rich says, "Sometimes I have to be here from before the store opens at 8:00 A.M. until after the store closes at 7:00 P.M. because we have a problem with one of the machines, or maybe someone came in just before we closed and needs their glasses when we open the next day. Usually on those days, though, I'm so busy I don't even realize how long I've been working."

"Yeah, but sometimes you really know you've been working a long day," adds Ron. "Still, when it's over you feel good." He explains that even after a tiring day, he feels proud of having accomplished something tangible. "When you're done, you know you've made a well-crafted product for two or three dozen people." He also notes that the more hours he works, the more money he makes and the closer he is to earning a promotion to lab manager himself.

Optics technicians usually work 40-hour weeks. Some retail eyeglass stores are open seven days a week. Research laboratories at private companies and in the government are generally open Monday through Friday.

An optics technician working in photo-optics maintenance might work at a rocket or missile test range or at a satellite tracking station. A typical day might involve assembling, adjusting, aligning, and operating telescopic cameras that track the missiles or satellites.

Technicians employed by private companies or government laboratories are usually specialized in production or in research and development. *Production technicians* sometimes assemble the entire product, right up to the final inspection, or they may focus on one production task. Other responsibilities include maintaining an inventory of parts and materials, performing precision assembly using microscopes, and working with the engineering staff on special projects. *Research and development technicians* work in laboratories with scientists and engineers. They are often charged with tracking and recording test results and building prototypes.

Regardless of the setting, safety and efficiency are mandatory for optics technicians. Certain chemicals that technicians use can be dangerous if mixed inappropriately, and the fumes they give off can be unhealthy in an unventilated room. Technicians are careful to protect their eyes, especially when they're using grinding instruments, because the particles of glass, plastic, and other materials can be hazardous.

"Everyone wears protective eye gear in the lab, whether they are working on a lens or not," Rich says. "We have emergency equipment all around the lab in case a chemical gets on someone, in their eyes, or explodes. The lab is safer than most people's workplaces. It only seems dangerous when everyone is busy and all the machines are making noise."

Advancement Possibilities

Precision-lens centerers and edgers, also known as *lead technicians,* set up, operate, and train workers on the grinder and collimator. The grinder edges and bevels precision ophthalmic optical lenses, and the collimator centers a beam of light through the lens.

Precision inspectors, also known as **optical elements inspectors** and **lens inspectors,** use precision measuring instruments to inspect optical and ophthalmic lenses at various stages of production and ensure that standards have been met.

Supervisors, also known as **inspecting supervisors** and **lens generating supervisors,** coordinate the activities of workers engaged in fabricating and inspecting optical lenses. The supervisor inspects lenses for defects and adherence to specifications using devices such as a polariscope, magnifying glass, protractor, or power determining instrument.

Do I Have What It Takes to Be an Optics Technician?

An optics technician working in retail has to be good with customers, as well as skilled at the manual aspects of the job. For Rich, the moment when someone puts on that first pair of eyeglasses and looks in the mirror is what makes his job great. "They look around the room and can't believe the detail they can see," says Rich. "Then they look in the mirror and say, 'Hey, I don't look bad at all. I look pretty darn good, in fact.'"

In retail, the production process can be almost nonstop. "It can be a very high-stress job during the times when the store is filled with customers," Rich says. Ron adds, "You have to pay very close attention to detail in every step of lens production." It's important that technicians not be easily flustered. They need to take the time to make sure they're using the right tool and following the specifications of the prescription.

You have to pay very close attention to detail in every step of lens production.

While new, high-tech equipment performs a lot of detail work automatically, most of the precision work still requires a certain feel or manual dexterity on the part of the optics technician. That feel only comes with experience and ability, like any craft work. "You get to believing that every pair of eyeglasses that comes out of this lab is your creation," says Rich. For example, the lens generator encloses the lens in a chamber while it grinds the lens to its prescription rough curve and thickness and then aligns the prism-axes. The technician works entirely by feel and knowledge of the requirements for each lens. Rich likens the work on the generator to peeling a potato blindfolded.

In other areas of optics technology, it's critical that technicians have an aptitude for math and science, as they will be working on complex projects. Good communication skills are also important because optics technicians need to report their findings in a clear manner, whether in a written report or a verbal briefing.

How Do I Become an Optics Technician?

The quickest way to become an optics technician is to apply for a position as a lab technician at a wholesale or retail lens fabricator. Most often these companies are looking for individuals whom they can train according to their own specific needs.

Rich Crockett hires optics technicians for the Lenscrafters labs he manages. "What I am most looking for is someone who gives it all they have in learning the skills. And I want someone who is interested in advancing in a career as an optics tech," he says. "I will train them so they will not only know every detail in making a pair of glasses for Lenscrafters, but also be thoroughly proficient in all phases of setup, grinding, generating, aligning, polishing, and finishing."

After a retail training program, which lasts anywhere from six to 18 months, optics technicians are knowledgeable in the materials that lenses are made out of, the chemicals used as adhesives, polishes, and tints, and also any innovations in optical goods. Some optics technicians are then able to move into other areas of optics. However, most advanced optics positions require some formal postsecondary training as well as on-the-job experience.

EDUCATION

High School

While not all retail lens fabrication laboratories insist on their optics technicians being high school graduates, most prefer hiring individuals with diplomas. If you have your eye on a job in production, maintenance and operations, or research and development, a high school diploma is a must, as you will need to pursue postsecondary training.

High school courses in mathematics, science, and shop are useful. Optics technicians will need some knowledge of algebra, geometry, physics, chemistry, technical reading and writing, mechanical drawing, glass working, and photography. Ideal courses are those that increase your manual dexterity and your ability to follow scientific procedures.

Postsecondary Training

A common way to become an optics technician is to train in an optics laboratory. These are usually on-the-job training programs and therefore provide the added benefit of income while learning. In some of the technical or industrial labs, training is in preparation for a job with the lab and therefore provides no income until training is successfully completed.

Another route is to attend a technical institute or community college that offers a two- or three-year program in engineering, optics, or physics. Useful courses are those that deal with geometrical optics, trigonometry, lens polishing, technical writing, optical instruments, analytical geometry, specification writing, physics, optical shop practices, manual preparation, mechanical drawing, and report preparation.

A handful of colleges and universities offer specific training and degrees for optics technicians. The University of Rochester, for instance, offers a two-year certification program for technicians. For advanced or highly technical positions as an optics technician, you may be required to have a bachelor's degree in optics, engineering, physics, or even astronomy.

CERTIFICATION OR LICENSING

Certification or licensing is usually not required for optics technicians, although some states have a license requirement for retail optics technicians. The licensing examinations in these states may be written, practical, or both. Inquire at an optics laboratory in the state you wish to practice to find out about licensing requirements.

Often, the laboratory will provide a certification upon completion of your training program. You may then be required by the lab to update this certification regularly by completing courses, seminars, conferences, written exams, practical exams, or any combination of them.

To Be a Successful Optics Technician, You Should . . .

- have manual dexterity
- be attentive to detail
- have an aptitude for math and science
- have the desire to learn a craft
- be a good communicator
- work with energy and ambition

SCHOLARSHIPS AND GRANTS

Scholarships are available for students pursuing bachelor's degrees in optics engineering and physics at four-year universities, and to a lesser degree, for students in two-year technical programs. You should contact financial aid offices at the programs you're applying to in order to get information on eligibility, application requirements, and deadlines.

Who Will Hire Me?

Thirty-three percent of all optics technicians in the United States work in labs at retail eyeglass stores. One-hour eyeglass stores such as Pearle Vision and Lenscrafters have sprung up in almost every city, suburb, and town. Department stores often offer eyeglass services as well. With new stores opening up all the time and turnover in existing stores high, opportunities at the retail level are good.

Many other technicians are employed by government laboratories and by private manufacturers who make optical goods for medical, defense, and consumer markets. Several professional organizations offer employment listings and useful contact information. Other optics technicians are employed by optometrists or ophthalmologists in smaller labs.

Where Can I Go from Here?

Rich hopes to be promoted soon from lab manager to district manager of 17 stores. "The next step after I've supervised all the local stores is to move into the regional area." Rich can become a regional lab manager of all the labs in a section of a state, an entire state, or a group of states. This position is also called the RQC (regional quality control) because the individual must make sure that all the labs adhere to company and government standards. At this level, Rich would no longer be responsible for doing hands-on lens fabrication.

Ron sees himself becoming the lead technician in a lab eventually. Lead technicians supervise other optics technicians and handle the lab's administrative tasks.

Experienced technicians who work in production or research and development can aspire to some of the following positions. They can become photographic technicians who operate cameras in research or engineering projects. Advanced production technicians might help produce specialized optical goods such as reticles (the cross hairs in the focus of an optical instrument's eyepiece) or integrate electronic circuits that are used in calculators, computers, and other electronic systems. Instrument assemblers and testers perform the assembly of optical instruments, checking alignment, functioning, and appearance. Technicians can also advance to become optical model makers, who assemble prototypes of new optical devices.

What Are the Salary Ranges?

According to the U.S. Department of Labor, ophthalmic laboratory technicians had median hourly wages of $10.67 in 2003. For full-time workers, this comes to about $22,194 a year. Those in the lowest 10 percent made less than $7.56 an hour ($15,720 annually), while those in the highest 10 percent made more than $16.73 an hour ($34,810).

In a retail setting, technicians may have to complete a probationary employment period before receiving benefits such as health insurance and paid vacation and sick leave. Benefits packages at optics manufacturers and government laboratories are usually generous and include health insurance, paid vacation and sick leave, disability insurance, and some form of retirement plan.

What Is the Job Outlook?

Optics technicians will experience little or no job growth over the next 10 years. Although job growth in the realm of manufacturing lenses for eyeglasses should grow at an average rate, jobs in other areas of optics manufacturing will decrease because of increased use of automation. But even with government cutbacks in space and weapons technology, consumer demand for complex cameras, binoculars, telescopes, and medical tools will sustain employment levels for technicians in production, maintenance and operations, and research and development.

How Do I Learn More?

PROFESSIONAL ORGANIZATIONS

For information on optics technician careers, accredited schools, and employers, contact

American Optometric Association
243 North Lindbergh Boulevard
St. Louis, MO 63141
314-991-4100
http://www.aoanet.org

BIBLIOGRAPHY

The following is a sampling of materials relating to the professional concerns and development of optics technicians:

Belikoff, Kathleen M. *Opportunities in Eye Care Careers.* New York: McGraw-Hill, 2003.

Shannon, Robert F. *The Art and Science of Optical Design.* New York: Cambridge University Press, 1997.

Smith, Gregory Hallock. *Practical Computer-Aided Lens Design.* Richmond, Va.: Willmann Bell, 1998.

OPTOMETRISTS

The little girl's eyes are fixed on the floor, and her head is tucked firmly against her chest. She stands quietly in the pediatric head-trauma unit. Months ago, she'd been hit by a car. Since then, she hasn't raised her head.

A rehabilitation therapist stands beside her. He sees Deborah Zelinsky, an optometrist familiar with the girl's case, and waves her over. "Hi Deb," the therapist says. He shakes his head. "Still no change. We don't know if she can't raise her head or if she won't."

Deborah kneels before the girl. "Hi, Rebecca. You remember me, don't you? I'm the eye doctor lady." Deborah opens a case and takes out a pair of eyeglasses. "Would you like to try these on? They're special for you."

The girl's eyes close as Deborah fits the glasses. "Open your eyes now, Rebecca," Deborah says gently. "It's okay."

Rebecca opens her eyes. Instantly, her head pops up. The therapist exclaims, "We've been trying to get her head up for months! What did you do?"

Deborah smiles. "These glasses make things appear closer. All of a sudden the floor came rushing up at her, so she lifted her head."

Deborah smiles at Rebecca. And Rebecca, her head raised high now, smiles too.

Definition
Optometrists examine people's eyes and prescribe eyeglasses, contact lenses, vision therapy, and drugs to treat vision problems, perceptual problems, and certain eye diseases.

Alternative Job Title
Eye doctors

High School Subjects
Biology
Physiology

Personal Skills
Helping/teaching
Technical/scientific

Salary Range
$45,140 to $95,000 to $114,000+

Educational Requirements
Bachelor's degree; four-year doctor of optometry (D.O.) degree

Certification or Licensing
Required by all states

Outlook
About as fast as the average

DOT
079

GOE
14.04.01

NOC
3121

O*NET-SOC
29-1041.00

What Does an Optometrist Do?

More than half of the people in the United States wear glasses or contact lenses. Even if you do not wear glasses now, there is a good chance that you will require some kind of visual assistance as you get older. The health care professionals on the front lines of vision care are optometrists. *Optometrists* examine the eyes for visual ability, including depth perception, peripheral (side) vision, the ability to focus and coordinate the eyes, and the ability to see color. Optometrists use a variety of tests and instruments to examine the retina, the cornea, and other parts of the eye. During a visit to an optometrist, your eyes will be checked for their overall health.

Many people confuse a vision screening, such as one receives at school or when applying for a driver's license, with an eye examination. But unlike vision screenings, eye examinations are necessary for the health of the eyes. During an examination, an optometrist looks for conditions, including glaucoma, macular degeneration, and cataracts, that directly affect vision. An eye examination can also reveal health conditions, including diabetes and high blood pressure, that can threaten the overall health of a person.

Upon determining that a person's eyesight needs a corrective aid, an optometrist prescribes eyeglasses or contact lenses. Often, the optometrist then provides the patient with glasses or contact lenses and makes certain that they fit properly. An optometrist may also prescribe medications to treat certain conditions of the eyes. When an optometrist's examination

Lingo to Learn

Amblyopia (lazy eye) A partial loss of vision commonly resulting from cross-eye. It may also result from other factors, including exposure to certain toxins.

Astigmatism An irregularity in the shape of the cornea that often causes blurred vision.

Attention deficit disorder A behavioral disorder that is characterized by a short attention span. It is sometimes related to vision problems.

Cataract A clouding of part or all of the lens of the eye that causes blurred or distorted vision.

Conjunctiva A mucous membrane that lines the inner surface of the eyelid and covers the white part of the eye.

Conjunctivitis (pink eye) An inflammation of the conjunctiva.

Cornea The transparent covering at the front of the eye.

Dyslexia A learning disorder in which visual signals are improperly processed by the brain.

Glaucoma A disease caused by the buildup of internal pressure in the fluid of the eye.

Hyperopia (farsightedness) The inability to focus on objects close by.

Iris The colored portion of the eye that opens and closes the pupil to control how much light enters the eye.

Macular degeneration An eye condition related to aging in which the portion of the retina called the macula degenerates.

Myopia (nearsightedness) The inability to see things clearly at a distance.

Presbyopia An eye condition related to aging in which the lens loses flexibility, making near vision difficult.

Strabismus (cross-eye) An eye disorder in which an eye is turned (or both eyes are turned) in, out, up, or down.

reveals the presence of a disease of the eyes or some other serious disorder, the patient is referred to an *ophthalmologist,* a physician who has a medical degree specializing in diseases of the eye and in surgery.

Optometrists have other duties besides caring for patients. Because most optometrists work as independent practitioners, that is, they own their own offices, they are responsible for running the offices and hiring the appropriate personnel. Other optometrists work in group practices or as part of eyewear franchises, where these responsibilities are shared.

Increasingly, optometry is concerned not only with clear vision but also with the effects of vision on people's lives. *Developmental optometrists* provide vision therapy to people who have suffered eye injuries and to people who have such conditions as amblyopia (lazy eye) and strabismus (cross-eye). Developmental optometrists also provide vision therapy to people who have learning disorders and other types of disorders that may be related to perception or vision. Dyslexia and attention deficit disorder, which both adversely affect the ability to learn, may be treated with vision therapy. In some cases, vision therapy eliminates the need for glasses. A developmental optometrist often works with other health care professionals, including neurologists, physical and occupational therapists, psychologists, and learning specialists.

What Is It Like to Be an Optometrist?

Deborah Zelinsky has been an optometrist for 12 years. She has worked as a developmental optometrist for 10 of those years. Deborah operates her own practice, called The Mind-Eye Connection. Her practice is located in an office attached to her home in Northfield, Illinois. Deborah's interest in optometry began when she was young. "I've had a fascination with people's eyes since I was a tiny kid," she says. "I've always found people's eyes fascinating to look at. The concept of eyesight itself was fascinating to me." An experience with vision difficulties helped reinforce Deborah's choice of career. "All of a sudden, when I was 18 or 19, I started seeing double," she says, "and no one could figure out why. Finally, they fitted me with bifocals, and the double vision went away."

As an independent practitioner, Deborah enjoys the freedom to set her own schedule. Generally, she sees patients four days a week, and she reserves one day a week for writing reports and pursuing her own research activities. A typical day for Deborah begins at 7:30 A.M., when she reviews patient records and conducts consultations with other health care professionals over the telephone. "That part of my day usually lasts until 9:00 A.M.," Deborah says. "I don't start seeing patients until 10:30." Deborah is usually finished seeing patients by 5:30 P.M., but one day each week she stays open until 9:00 P.M. to accommodate her patients' schedules.

An optometrist may see 20 or more patients each day. Each examination generally takes about 20 minutes. "But a visit with me can take one to two hours," Deborah says. "I really get involved in the patient's life. And I usually team up with other therapists involved in the patient's life and well-being."

In addition to the typical optometrist's equipment, such as lenses and prisms to measure vision, Deborah uses a variety of other instruments, such as 3-D glasses. "But my most important piece of equipment is my own brain," she says. "I develop tests and activities that go beyond the usual perception tasks, like color or depth perception. I test the patient's eyes in motion, because that's how we really use them. So my tests measure things like focusing, scanning, and searching. I may use lenses that make things seem bigger or smaller, or closer or farther, and even lenses to make the patient walk funny or hear differently. That way I can measure how the patient is using his or her eyes. A patient's eyesight is only part of what I look at."

Once Deborah identifies a problem with a patient's vision, she explains it to the patient and discusses methods of alleviating the problem. "I might prescribe glasses, but not always," says Deborah. "When I do, they're usually part of a program of therapy exercises to help the patient learn how to better use his or her eyes. My goal is to remediate, prevent, or correct the vision problem. Many problems can be corrected completely."

My goal is to remediate, prevent, or correct the vision problem. Many problems can be corrected completely.

FYI

Seeing Is Believing

Vision depends on light. We see objects because they reflect light in different ways. This reflected light enters the eye through the pupil, which is opened and closed by the iris to control the amount of light that reaches the lens. The lens refracts, or bends, the light onto the retina, which is a layer of nerve cells at the back of the eye. The nerve cells in the retina send signals along the optic nerve to the visual center of the brain, which processes this information and interprets what we see.

Many of Deborah's patients are young children. "It's about 50/50, between children and adults. I see infants sometimes. I see kids with reading problems and attention deficit disorder. I work with a lot of adults who are legally blind and with people who have motion sickness. A lot of adults have vision or perception problems, like dyslexia, that were never diagnosed when they were young. Many of my patients are quite complicated. They may have other health problems. They may be on medications. My patients usually require hours of time and effort. It's not like general optometry at all."

Deborah's fascination with eyes has led her into research activities. "I've done some neurological research—examining vision's link with other disciplines. It's interesting to see the connection with my patients. Right now, another doctor and I are studying the various disciplines to examine the relationship between healing and vision."

Do I Have What It Takes to Be an Optometrist?

A career as an optometrist offers a great deal more freedom than many other professions. "I can set my own hours," Deborah says. "And I get a chance to travel when I'm attending seminars and conventions." But in order to be successful, an optometrist must have a great deal of self-discipline and self-motivation. Knowledge of business and accounting practices is also very helpful for the independent practitioner.

Optometrists should have a genuine interest in helping people, and they should be able to work well with others—both with their patients and with other vision and health professionals. Those considering careers in developmental optometry should recognize that they will often be working with people who are under stress and who have a variety of health problems. "But I can't think of any profession more fun," Deborah says. "In a way, I'm at play all day long. I look at this as a lucrative hobby. In fact, most optometrists never retire."

Working as an optometrist has proved very rewarding for Deborah. "You get the chance to help people solve problems that no one else has been able to solve. Like that little girl who wouldn't raise her head. I gave her glasses, but her problem wasn't her vision. It was her perception of what she saw. After her car accident, the signals between her eyes and her brain were mixed up. When I put the glasses on her, the floor seemed to come rushing up at her. As a response, she lifted her head. We're still discovering how intricate the relationship is between our bodies and our perception. It's nonstop new information."

Being an independent practitioner is challenging. "Running your own business gives you the freedom to choose your own future," Deborah says, "but it can be difficult. I really wish I had taken business or accounting classes in school." Opening one's own practice can be expensive, especially in purchasing equipment. Many optometrists, like Deborah, operate their offices in their own homes. "But my office and my personal space are entirely separate. In fact, the office is the largest part of my home. However, one of my long-term goals is to have a family, and having an office in my home means I'll have more time to spend with them."

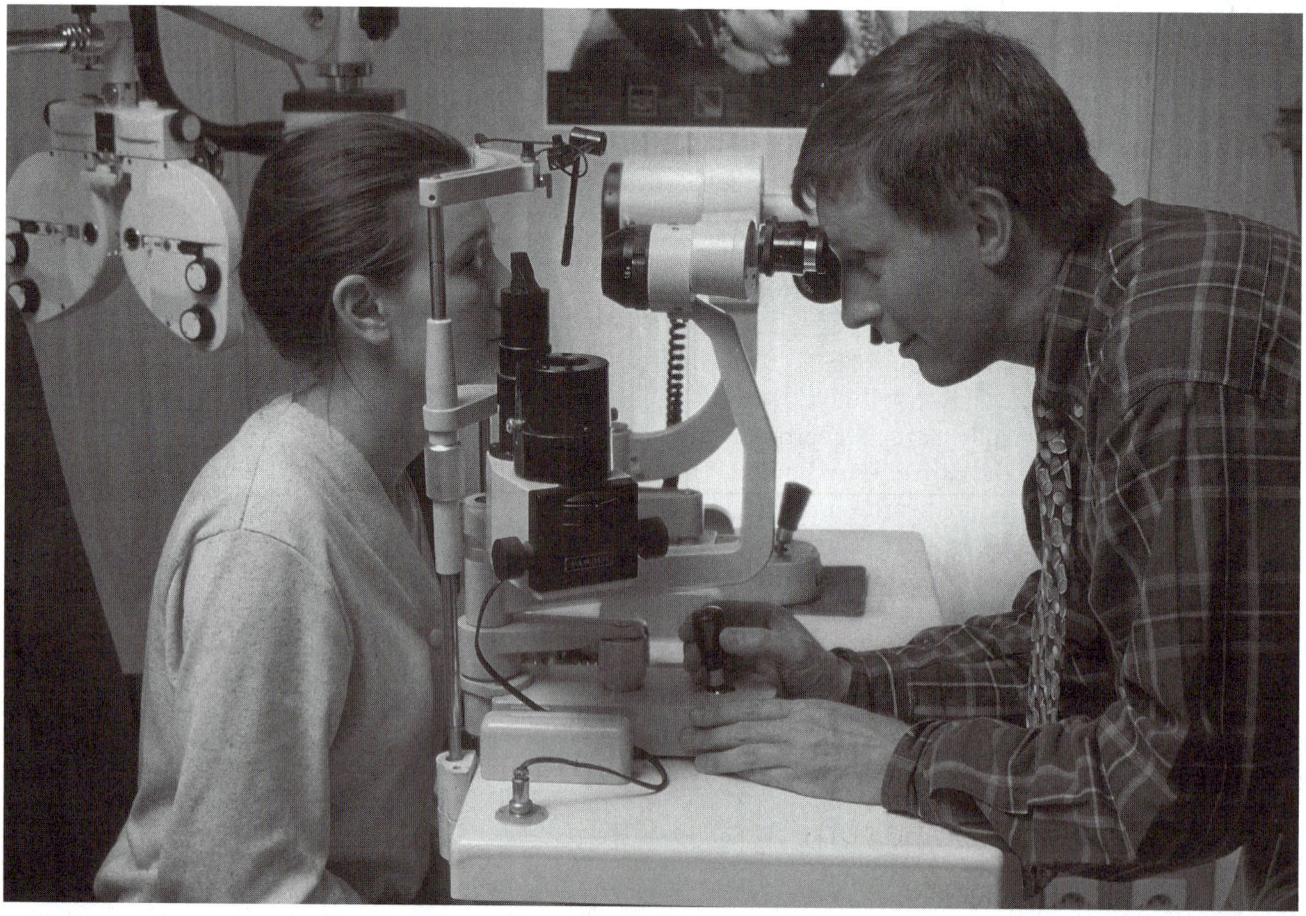

An optometrist conducts an eye examination using a slit-lamp microscope. *(Laurent / Photo Researchers Inc.)*

How Do I Become an Optometrist?

EDUCATION

High School

If you are interested in pursuing an optometry career, follow a college preparatory schedule, with an emphasis on math and science. "I was a math major. I took way more math than what was required," Deborah says. "I wish I had taken more biology classes. Microbiology would have been interesting to take." Because optometrists typically run their own businesses, a background in business and accounting is helpful. "At school, they taught us everything about being an optometrist and nothing about running a business," Deborah says, "but that should be a requirement, too."

While it is difficult to gain practical experience in optometry, you can pursue certain activities that provide insight into how vision and perception work. "I've always juggled," Deborah says, "which helped me develop hand-eye coordination and gave me an awareness of 3-D space." You can gain valuable experience working and communicating with others by finding volunteer work or part-time work at hospitals and other health care facilities. "I lived with my grandmother, which helped me understand the viewpoints of my elderly patients. I'd recommend that students try to volunteer at retirement homes for that," Deborah says.

Postsecondary Training

To become an optometrist, you must first complete at least three years of undergraduate work and then four years in a certified college or school of optometry. In addition to a general liberal arts education, you should follow a course of study that includes mathematics, physics, biology, and chemistry. In order to apply for a graduate degree program in optometry, you must take the Optometry Admission Test.

Postgraduate studies will include laboratory, classroom, and clinical work. You will study pharmacology (the science of drugs), systemic disease (disease that affects the whole body), ocular pathology (the study of eye diseases), and biochemistry (the study of the chemical processes of organisms). Practical courses include theoretical and ophthalmic optics, which discuss lenses and the use of ophthalmic glass and plastics. You learn how to adapt, prescribe, and fit glasses and contact lenses. You also learn about vision therapy. The third and fourth years of an optometric degree program include clinical practice, in which students diagnose and treat the eye disorders of patients. Upon completion of study, graduates receive the doctor of optometry (O.D.) degree. Some optometrists pursue further study leading to a master's degree or doctorate in physiological optics or other fields.

There are 17 accredited schools and colleges of optometry in the United States.

FYI

- The career of optometrist was ranked 39th out of 250 possible careers by Jobs Rated Almanac. The ranking was based on an assessment of factors such as income, stress, physical demands, potential growth, job security, and work environment.
- More than 50 percent of optometrists entering practice today are women.
- Nearly 13 percent of optometrists ages 25 to 40 are minorities.

Source: Association of Schools and Colleges of Optometry

CERTIFICATION OR LICENSING

Every state requires that optometrists be licensed in order to practice. In order to receive a license, you must have a O.D. degree and pass written and practical tests. After being licensed, optometrists are required to continue their education. You must annually fulfill a specified number of course hours. Optometrists must also must pass periodic tests administered by the National Board of Examiners in Optometry and by state and regional review boards.

Optometrists interested in the field of developmental optometry can apply for fellowships in visual development. In order to be certified as a developmental optometrist, you must have at least three years of professional clinical practice, fulfill a specified number of course hours in developmental optometry, and pass an oral and a written examination. Developmental optometrists must also continue their education to keep abreast of advances in the field.

Who Will Hire Me?

Deborah's first job as an optometrist was with a contact lens group in Florida. "I was fresh out of school, and I just went in for an interview," she says. "After a year of working there, I went to work for a pediatric practice. Working with kids led me into developmental optometry." Joining a group practice is a good way for a newly licensed optometrist to start out in this career, because purchasing equipment and setting up an office can be expensive. Optometrists interested in starting up independent practices may have the best luck in rural areas, where there are generally fewer optometrists than in urban areas. Banks and other lenders are a good source for financial backing when starting up a new practice.

Most colleges and schools of optometry offer job placement assistance and will help new optometrists locate potential partnerships. They may also help new optometrists find different locations where optometrists are needed. The American Optometric Association is a professional organization that provides placement services and information on optometrists seeking to hire associates. Working as an associate with an established optometrist is a good way to develop the experience and financial resources needed before setting up an independent practice. An optometrist who starts out as an associate with an established practice may choose to eventually join the practice as a partner. Becoming a partner generally means agreeing to pay a certain amount of money to buy into the practice and then sharing both the costs of running the business and any profits the practice produces.

An optometrist may find employment as part of a health maintenance organization (HMO) or as a member of a hospital's staff. Some optometrists join the military services or work for other government organizations, such as the Department of Veterans Affairs. After receiving a doctorate degree, an optometrist has the option of concentrating on research or teaching.

Where Can I Go from Here?

Advancement in the field of optometry typically means setting up your own practice or becoming a partner with others in a practice. An optometrist then builds up a practice by adding patients. An optometrist may also decide to specialize in a particular area of optometry. Specialization generally requires you to complete an additional one-year clinical residency program in your chosen specialty. Specialties include pediatric optometry, geriatric optometry, developmental optometry, hospital-based optometry, and ocular disease. Some optometrists continue their education to receive doctoral degrees in visual science, physiological optics, or neurophysiology. Some receive doctoral degrees in other areas, such as public health, health administration, health education, or health communication and information.

What Are the Salary Ranges?

According to the U.S. Department of Labor, optometrists made a median annual salary of $95,000 in 2003. The lowest paid 10 percent made less than $45,140 per year, and the highest paid 10 percent made annual salaries of more than $114,000 per year.

An optometrist's income varies according to whether the optometrist owns his or her own practice or works as part of a group or partnership. In-

To Be a Successful Optometrist, You Should . . .

- be interested in helping people
- be able to work well with people
- have good vision and coordination and some mechanical aptitude
- be understanding of a patient's needs, and be tactful when working with patients
- have self-discipline and the ability to motivate yourself
- have business and accounting skills

come also varies depending on how many patients the optometrist treats. An established optometrist with a busy practice can earn much more than the average. Optometry specialists, such as developmental optometrists, also have the potential for higher earnings. In addition, an optometrist's location will affect earnings. Optometrists in rural areas generally earn less than optometrists in urban or suburban areas. Optometrists employed as salaried personnel by the government, by clinics, or by optometry groups often have higher initial earnings than optometrists who set up their own practices. However, as independent practitioners become established, their earnings typically surpass those of salaried personnel. Optometrists who are partners in established optometry groups or practices are generally considered to have the highest earning potential.

What Is the Job Outlook?

Jobs in optometry are expected to grow about as fast as the average for all occupations. The growing elderly population will require many optometric services, such as treatment for presbyopia, glaucoma, cataracts, and macular degeneration. Other areas of optometry, particularly developmental optometry, are expected to grow in importance as researchers and clinicians explore the connection between vision and such disorders as dyslexia and attention deficit disorder.

Optometrists tend to continue working long after the typical retirement age. Therefore, replacement opportunities in this career are fewer than in many other health care careers. Openings for optometrists are created as optometrists retire or as optometrists leave clinic or group practices to set up their own independent practices. Two other factors that contribute to the relative scarcity of replacement opportunities are advancements in optometric equipment technology and the hiring of optometric assistants. Both factors allow current optometrists to see growing numbers of patients, thereby limiting the need for new optometrists.

How Do I Learn More?

PROFESSIONAL ASSOCIATIONS

The following are organizations that provide information on optometry careers, accredited schools, and employers:

American Optometric Association
243 North Lindbergh Boulevard
St. Louis, MO 63141
314-991-4100
http://www.aoanet.org

Association of Schools and Colleges of Optometry
6110 Executive Boulevard, Suite 690
Rockville, MD 20852
301-231-5944
http://www.opted.org

For information on a career as an optometrist in Canada, contact

Canadian Association of Optometrists
234 Argyle Avenue
Ottawa, Ontario K2P 1B9 Canada
888-263-4676
info@opto.ca
http://www.opto.ca

BIBLIOGRAPHY

The following is a sampling of materials related to the professional concerns and development of optometrists:

Belikoff, Kathleen M. *Opportunities in Eye Care Careers.* New York: McGraw-Hill, 2003.

Classe, John G. et al., eds. *Business Aspects of Optometry.* 2d ed. Newton, Mass.: Butterworth-Heinemann Medical, 2003.

Grosvenor, Theodore. *Primary Care Optometry.* 4th ed. Newton, Mass.: Butterworth-Heinemann, 2001.

Kurtz, Daniel, and Nancy B. Carlson. *Clinical Procedures for Ocular Examination.* 3d ed. New York: McGraw-Hill/Appleton & Lange, 2003.

Optometry Admission Test Sample Exams: TopScore Pro for the OAT. Roswell, Ga.: ScholarWare, 2000. CD-ROM.

ORIENTAL MEDICINE PRACTITIONERS

Christina MacLeod's office is an environment of quiet serenity, without the jangling telephones, loud noises, and aggravating voices usually common in so many of today's offices and homes. When her patients come in for an appointment they enter a comfort zone where they can relax to soothing music, soft lighting, and the gentle sounds of nature drifting in through the open windows. Providing a safe place for her patients is just one aspect of Christina's job as an oriental medicine practitioner.

"I am very purposeful about creating an environment that is quiet and peaceful, that feels safe, and offers a space conducive to healing," Christina says. "I prefer natural muted lighting, natural outdoor sounds, and natural temperatures with plenty of warmth to offer a space for calming and relaxation."

Definition
Oriental medicine practitioners are health care professionals who practice a variety of therapies that are part of the ancient healing system of oriental medicine.

Alternative Job Titles
Acupuncturist
OM practitioners
TOM practitioners

High School Subjects
Biology
Business
Psychology

Personal Skills
Helping/teaching
Technical/scientific

Salary Range
$23,058 to $52,000 to $100,000+

Educational Requirements
Some postsecondary training

Certification or Licensing
Required by some states

Outlook
Faster than the average

DOT
N/A

GOE
N/A

NOC
3232

O*NET-SOC
N/A

What Does an Oriental Medicine Practitioner Do?

In the United States, *oriental medicine (OM) practitioners* typically organize their practices around acupuncture, Chinese herbology (oriental medicine), and oriental bodywork (massage).

Acupuncture is the best-known form of traditional oriental medicine (TOM) and it is often considered synonymous with oriental medicine. Acupuncture is a complete medical system that helps improve the body's functioning and promotes natural healing.

An *acupuncturist* treats patients' symptoms and disorders by inserting needles that are not much bigger around than a thick hair into very precise points on the skin. The needles stimulate the area of insertion and work to balance the circulation of energy. During a treatment a patient may feel sensations such as warmth or pressure, but usually not pain. The needles are solid and nothing is injected through them.

Complementing acupuncture is Chinese herbology, also known as the Chinese herbal sciences, which studies the properties of herbs, including their energetics and therapeutic qualities.

Chinese herbalists perform a careful evaluation and diagnosis of each patient to determine which herbs can be used to restore the balance of a patient's qi (life force). Based on the information gathered during the evaluation and diagnosis, the Chinese herbalist then develops a treatment of herbal formulas using the unique combination of the person's characteristics, symptoms, and main complaints.

Oriental bodywork, or massage therapy, is also referred to as oriental physical therapy (tuina). The

Lingo to Learn

Acupressure A treatment similar to acupuncture, but rather than using needles the thumbs and finger tips are used to apply pressure to specific and precise body points to stimulate the area.

Acupuncture A treatment method that involves inserting very thin needles into specific and precise points on the body to stimulate the area and balance the circulation of energy.

Chinese herbology The practice of treating disorders and symptoms using herbs that are divided into three classes: inferior, general, and superior. Inferior herbs are used to remove cold, heat, and other "evil influences" from the body; the general class includes herbs believed to control the preservation of human nature; and the superior class consists of herbs believed to strengthen bodily energies and to help balance a person's emotional and psychic energy.

Meridian Specific channels in the body along which qi flows. Each meridian is related to a particular physiological system and internal organ. It is believed that when the flow of qi along the meridians is blocked or disrupted, disease, pain, and other physical and emotional conditions result.

Qi Pronounced "chee." This was recognized by the ancient Chinese as the vital energy believed to be the animating force behind all life.

Qigong Pronounced "chee goong." This is a Chinese system of exercise, philosophy, and health care. The Chinese character "qi" means life force, and the character "gong" means to cultivate or engage. Translated literally, qigong means to cultivate one's life force or vital energy.

Tuina Pronounced "twee nah." This is a form of oriental bodywork or massage that has been used in China for more than 2,000 years. Practitioners seek to establish a more harmonious flow of qi through the body's meridians.

Yin and Yang The underlying philosophy of oriental medicine that believes everything in the universe can be described in terms of the Yin (shady) and the Yang (sunny) sides of a hill. The Yin and Yang characters are symbols of the fundamental duality in the universe; they are complementary not contradictory concepts.

practice has been used in China for 2,000 years to establish a more harmonious flow of qi through the body's channels.

Tuina practitioners use a variety of methods to accomplish the goal of a harmonious flow of qi, including massage, acupressure (similar to acupuncture but using pressure from their hands and fingers rather than needles), energy generation exercises, and body manipulation. Before beginning, a tuina practitioner will evaluate the patient's specific problems and then create a treatment plan that emphasizes acupressure points and energy channels in addition to pain sites, muscles, and joints.

Oriental medicine practitioners also help their patients through qigong, which is a system of exercise, philosophy, and health care. Medical qigong combines meditation with breathing exercises that can help an ill patient's body functions return to normal or can increase a sense of well-being in a healthy patient.

Dietary therapy is also used by practitioners to help restore harmony to a patient's qi by balancing what the person eats. With this treatment, an oriental medicine practitioner recommends dietary adjustments specific to the individual patient's needs. The therapeutic basis for dietary therapy follows the same principles as those used in Chinese herbology. A practitioner must consider the energetics and therapeutc qualities of each kind of food to be able to choose the right foods to restore balance to the patient's qi.

Oriental medicine practitioners meeting with a patient for the first time carefully document the patient's personal history. That is followed by what is known as the traditional Chinese approach called the "four examinations," which include asking questions, looking, listening/smelling, and touching. While examining a patient the OM practitioner also looks for any signs of disharmony. The practitioner compiles all the information to create an in-depth profile of the patient's whole person: mind, body, and spirit. A patient's first appointment generally takes an hour or longer.

Besides working closely with patients, oriental medicine practitioners who own their own business must keep records of patients' histories and progress under treatment, manage billing and receive payments, and if the services are covered by health insurance, OM practitioners must bill the insurance company.

What Is It Like to Be an Oriental Medicine Practitioner?

Noting the three key elements of her practice, Christina MacLeod describes herself as a facilitator, an educator, and a counselor. "My primary responsibility is to facilitate a healing response so the body can return to a state of balance within. That might look like pain management, mental or emotional rebalancing, or helping to strengthen the physiological functioning of organs of body systems," she says.

As an educator, Christina helps her patients develop an awareness of their bodies, including "what is out of balance, how it got that way, and what can be done to correct it," she explains.

As a counselor, Christina offers patients ideas and suggestions about how to take responsibility for their health. "This might include support for lifestyle changes, healthier nutritional choices, exercise, stress management, and whatever activities might promote their well-being and ultimately prevent other health crises," she says.

A fourth aspect of her practice, Christina says, "is an openness to work cooperatively with other health professionals such as doctors, nurses, physical therapists, dentists, and chiropractors to provide complementary services that meet the needs of the whole person."

Because she owns her own practice, Christina's workday may begin late in the morning and continue long into the evening, or it may begin early and end by mid-afternoon. "I am totally in charge of my work schedule," she says. "I work in a clinical setting and set my hours to offer as much availability to my patients as I can. I sometimes work on Saturday mornings and sometimes on Sundays if there is an emergency."

Christina's office is located in an alternative medicine clinic in a rural Colorado community that also has offices of chiropractors, massage therapists, and other alternative health care practitioners.

While she prefers to see patients in her office, occasionally Christina makes house calls. "If a person can come to the office, that is preferred because I have the environment already set up for relaxation. But if they cannot [come to the office] I may travel to their home."

Since Christina is self-employed, she also must devote time to the day-to-day operation of her business, from scheduling appointments, to ordering supplies, to marketing her services to attract new patients.

Do I Have What It Takes to Be an Oriental Medicine Practitioner?

Oriental medicine is a science of understanding energetics in the body, and it is a healing art. Whether you pursue a career as an oriental bodywork therapist or as an acupuncturist, you should be able to understand and learn this unique approach to health care.

Acupuncturists need sensitive hands and sharp vision. Oriental bodywork practitioners, like massage therapists, must have strong hands and physical stamina. To practice oriental dietary therapy you should have an understanding of nutrition. If you are

FYI

- Traditional Chinese medicine (TCM) has a clinical history of over 3,000 years. The basic principles were first recorded in China about 2,300 years ago in the Classic of Internal Medicine (Huang Di Nei Ching). TCM practitioners have continued to apply, develop, and refine the principles for centuries.
- More than one-third of the world's population uses OM practitioners for the enhancement of health and to prevent or treat disease.
- There are five major traditions of qigong—Taoist, Buddhist, Confucian, martial arts, and medical—and more than 1,000 forms. Kung fu is an example of a martial arts qigong.

planning to open your own practice, you will need strong business skills.

Qualities Christina notes as important for someone planning to pursue a career as an oriental medicine practitioner include an ability to develop trusting relationships with patients, a willingness to accept people at their own level of motivation, strong intuitive skills, an ability to make decisions, strong communication and listening skills, and an ability to know when to intercede for a patient and when to back away from the healing process.

How Do I Become an Oriental Medicine Practitioner?

Christina began her professional life as a dental hygienist, and her studies in that field had courses focused on the sciences, human body, patient education, and clinical care. She left that job and studied massage therapy. "I was a massage therapist for 10 years prior to entering this field [oriental medicine]. I had already established myself as self-employed and as a practitioner working one-on-one with people."

EDUCATION

High School

If you plan to pursue a career as an oriental medicine practitioner you need to learn about and understand the human body, mind, and spirit. Courses in science, especially biology, will help you prepare for the medical courses you will be taking. Psychology, philosophy, sociology, and comparative religion classes can help you learn about the mind and spirit. To prepare for the exercise and massage aspects of oriental medicine you should take physical education classes and sports training. English, drama, debate, and speech classes will help develop your communication skills. You also will need business, math, and computer skills if you plan to open your own practice.

Postsecondary Training

The United States currently has three defined career paths for oriental medicine practitioners: acupuncture, oriental medicine (acupuncture and Chinese herbology), and oriental bodywork (massage). The duration of educational programs vary, but most students choose to attend a master's level program. Generally, schools require at least two years of undergraduate study for admission to a master's level program. Other schools require a bachelor's degree in a related field such as science, nursing, or premed for admission. In addition to covering Chinese herbology, acupuncture techniques, and all aspects of oriental medicine, most programs also provide a thorough education in Western sciences.

Choosing a school for oriental medicine can be complex. You should consider where you want to live and practice since practice requirements vary greatly from state to state. Be sure to attend a school that will prepare you to practice in your desired location. The Accreditation Commission for Acupuncture and Oriental Medicine (ACAOM) lists 46 accredited schools in the United States.

Oriental bodywork is not taught as a separate discipline in schools of oriental medicine, so to become an oriental bodywork practitioner you must meet your state's requirements to become a massage therapist. Accredited massage therapy schools offer studies in anatomy, physiology, kinesiology, ethics, and business practices. After you complete a program in general massage therapy, you can specialize in oriental bodywork, which requires an additional 150 to 500 hours of training. The American Organization for Bodywork Therapies of Asia (AOBTA) can provide additional information about schools that offer training.

SCHOLARSHIPS AND GRANTS

If you plan to apply for federal financial assistance, look for a college accredited by the ACAOM because those programs are recognized by the U.S. Department of Education.

INTERNSHIPS AND VOLUNTEERSHIPS

Most schools of acupuncture and oriental medicine require supervised clinical practice as part of the training. These internships are not optional and may be completed on-site or as a combination of on-site and off-site experiences. Christina notes that some schools also offer a voluntary study program in China as part of the curriculum.

To help you develop an understanding of oriental medicine's approach to healing you may want to study oriental history and philosophy. You also may talk to people who have experienced acupuncture,

To Be a Successful Oriental Medicine Practitioner, You Should . . .

- be compassionate and understanding
- be intuitive
- have strong, sensitive hands and good vision
- have good physical stamina
- have good listening skills
- possess good problem-solving skills

Chinese herbal therapy, or oriental bodywork therapy, or schedule an appointment for yourself so you can experience acupuncture or massage first hand.

A visit to a college of oriental medicine or a massage therapy school may provide additional insight into the profession.

CERTIFICATION OR LICENSING

To qualify to take the National Certification Commission for Acupuncture and Oriental Medicine (NCCAOM) exam students must complete a three-year accredited master's level or candidate program. There are four diplomate designations available: oriental medicine, acupuncture, Chinese herbology, and Asian bodywork therapy.

Licensing requirements vary from state to state, but most use the NCCAOM certification as the standard for licensure. Some states may require certification and additional educational requirements.

Oriental bodywork practitioners are regulated like massage therapists by individual states. Currently 33 states and the District of Columbia require licensure, certification, or registration to practice massage therapy. The American Massage Therapy Association (AMTA) can provide information about specific state requirements.

Who Will Hire Me?

Most practitioners who specialize in acupuncture, Chinese herbology, or other forms of oriental medicine operate private practices or join partnerships with other OM or alternative health care practitioners. Professionals such as chiropractors, osteopaths, and licensed physicians are increasingly including oriental medicine practitioners in their practices.

As oriental medicine and acupuncture become more accepted, there are growing opportunities for practitioners in hospitals and university medical schools. Some practitioners are involved in medical research, conducting studies on the effectiveness of oriental medicine in treating various health conditions. A few practitioners work for government agencies like the National Institutes of Health.

Employment opportunities for oriental bodywork therapists may be found in hotels, spas, fitness centers, cruise ships, nursing homes, and hospitals. Some open their own clinics or establish private practices, and others teach oriental bodywork in massage schools.

Most schools of acupuncture and oriental medicine offer job counseling and placement services. Christina says making professional connections while on an internship rotation or attending a continuing education course may provide job leads. Also, "word of mouth with professional colleagues, networking, or advertising in professional journals may be helpful," she says. "If all else fails, get creative."

Where Can I Go from Here?

Oriental medicine practitioners specializing in acupuncture or Chinese herbology advance their careers by establishing their own practices or starting their own clinics and building a large patient base. Because referrals from physicians and other alternative health care practitioners are important to building a patient base, it is helpful to have strong professional relationships with the medical community in your practice area. Experienced acupuncturist may teach at a school of oriental medicine and may eventually move into a supervisory position or directorship at a school.

Those specializing in oriental bodywork therapies may advance through promotions in the facility where they work. They also may take advanced courses and pursue a higher degree in oriental bodywork, become teachers, or open their own practice.

What Are the Salary Ranges?

According to the Acupuncture School of New York, the standard rate charged per session is $50 to $120 with a median fee of $60 to $70. An acupuncturist starting his or her career typically treats 20 patients per week. Based on those figures, the median earnings for a beginning practitioner is about $62,400 annually. The lowest paid may expect to earn about $52,000 per year, while the highest paid may earn $124,800. The Economic Research Institute reports that acupuncturists starting out should expect earnings of $23,058 to $32,817. Those with 10 years or more of experience may earn $42,886 per year. Salaries will vary, depending on the location of practice, patient base, number of hours worked, and fee charged per hour.

Oriental bodywork therapists may expect incomes similar to those earned by conventional massage therapists. A 2004 survey by the AMTA found that massage therapists practicing in large metropolitan communities may earn between $60 and $100 per hour, and those practicing in other areas may earn $50 to $75 per hour. Due to the physical demands of the work, most therapists are able to see only four or five patients per day for a maximum of 20 billable hours per week. Massage therapist charging $50 per hour may expect to earn about $52,000 annually. Those charging $75 per hour would earn about $78,000, and those charging the highest rate of $100 per hour may earn $104,000 per year.

Places Where Oriental Medicine Practitioners Work

- alternative health care clinics
- health clubs and spas
- hospitals
- nursing homes
- private practice
- wellness centers

What Is the Job Outlook?

Since the 1970s acupuncture and oriental medicine have been among the fastest growing forms of health care in the United States, and during the 1990s a growing interest in alternative medicine moved oriental medicine practitioners to the front of alternative health care.

The NCCAOM reports that since its inception in 1982 it has certified more than 13,000 diplomates in acupuncture, Chinese herbology, and Asian bodywork therapy. In 2000 there were more than 10,000 licensed acupuncturists and some in the field estimate that number will triple by 2015.

The greatest area of growth for acupuncture is in the treatment of addictions. The U.S. government has funded more than $1 million in research investigating acupuncture's effect on cocaine addiction and alcoholism. In addition, many hospitals and prisons now use acupuncture in their substance abuse programs. Besides treating addictions, the use of acupuncture is growing for the treatment of chronic pain, bronchial asthma, and premenstrual syndrome.

Adding to the growth of acupuncture is the 1996 ruling by the Food and Drug Administration that designates acupuncture needles as medical devices, which increases the likelihood that Medicare, Medicaid, and private insurance companies will cover acupuncture treatments for patients.

Oriental bodywork practitioners may expect job growth similar to the practice of massage therapy. Western medicine has become more accepting of alternative therapies like massage, and more than 75 of the 125 medical schools in the United States now offer courses in alternative therapies. The U.S. Department of Labor expects the profession of massage therapist to grow faster than the average through 2012.

How Do I Learn More?

PROFESSIONAL ORGANIZATIONS

The following organizations can provide information about oriental medicine, acupuncture, and massage therapy, including accredited schools, state regulations, certification, and job opportunities:

Accreditation Commission for Acupuncture and Oriental Medicine
7501 Greenway Center Drive, Suite 820
Greenbelt, MD 20770
301-313-0855
info.md@acaom.org
http://www.acaom.org

Acupuncture and Oriental Medicine Alliance
6405 43rd Avenue Court, NW, Suite B
Gig Harbor, WA 98335
253-851-6896
info@aomalliance.org
http://www.aomalliance.org

American Association of Oriental Medicine
PO Box 162340
Sacramento, CA 95816
916-451-6950
info@aaom.org
http://www.aaom.org

American Massage Therapy Association
500 Davis Street
Evanston, IL 60201
877-905-2700
http://www.amtamassage.org

American Organization for Bodywork Therapies of Asia
1010 Haddonfield-Berlin Road, Suite 408
Voorhees, NJ 08043-3514
856-782-1616
office@aobta.org
http://www.aobta.org

National Center for Complementary and Alternative Medicine
PO Box 7923
Gaithersburg, MD 20898
888-644-6226
info@nccam.nih.gov

National Certification Board for Therapeutic Massage and Bodywork
8201 Greensboro Drive, Suite 300
McLean, VA 22102
800-296-0664
info@ncbtmb.com
http://www.ncbtmb.com

National Certification Commission for Acupuncture and Oriental Medicine
11 Canal Center Plaza, Suite 300
Alexandria, VA 22314
703-548-9004
info@nccaom.org
http://www.nccaom.org

BIBLIOGRAPHY

The following is a listing of materials that can provide additional information about oriental medicine:

Alphen, Jan Van. *Oriental Medicine.* Boston: Shambala Publications, 1997.

Aris, Anthony. *Oriental Medicine: An Illustrated Guide to the Asian Arts of Healing.* Chicago: Art Media Resources, 1995.

Cho, Hun Y. *Oriental Medicine: A Modern Interpretation.* Compton, Calif.: Yuin University Press, 1997.

Clinical Manual of Oriental Medicine: An Integrative Approach. City of Industry, Calif.: Lotus Institute of Integrative Medicine, 2002.

Kaptchuk, Ted J. *The Web That Has No Weaver: Understanding Chinese Medicine.* New York: McGraw Hill, 2000.

Lu, Henry C. *Chinese Natural Cures: Traditional Methods for Remedies and Prevention.* New York: Black Dog and Leventhal Publishers, 1999.

Molony, David. *The American Association of Oriental Medicine's Complete Guide to Chinese Herbal Medicine: How to Treat Illness and Maintain Wellness With Chinese Herbs.* New York: Berkley Publishing Group, 1998.

ORTHODONTISTS

"I hate my teeth," 12-year-old Kaela says loudly as she plops onto Dr. Chris Carpenter's dental chair. Her mother sits down next to her daughter and says, "That's why we're seeing an orthodontist, Kaela."

"Mom, I look like Dracula," Kaela says, pointing to her teeth.

"If you've got fangs, I'd better watch my fingers in there," Chris jokes as he walked into the exam room. Kaela and her mother chuckle at the orthodontist's joke, but Chris notices that Kaela quickly covers her smile with her hand. She truly is embarrassed about her teeth.

Pulling up a stool, Chris sits across from Kaela. He looks her in the eye and says, "Kaela, you're not alone. Most people feel their smile could be improved. The wonder of orthodontics is that a patient can come here with an average smile or one that has problems and I can change it. Your smile has great potential. I can make it as beautiful as it can possibly be."

Definition
Orthodontists are dental specialists who diagnose problems with teeth, jaw, and lower facial development and treat malpositioned and misaligned teeth and jaws.

High School Subjects
Mathematics
Science

Personal Skills
Helping/teaching
Technical/scientific

Salary Range
$87,963 to $107,070 to $130,000+

Educational Requirements
Bachelor's degree; four-year doctor of dentistry degree; minimum two-year orthodontic program

Certification or Licensing
Required by all states

Outlook
About as fast as the average

Outlook
Little change

DOT
072

GOE
14.03.01

NOC
3113

O*NET-SOC
29-1023.00

What Does an Orthodontist Do?

Orth means straight and *odont* means tooth. *Orthodontists* straighten teeth that are crooked, crowded, or that have gaps between them. People who benefit from orthodontics include those whose facial profile shows an overbite, underbite, protruding lips, or even a "weak chin."

People who have dental and facial irregularities often have what is termed *malocclusion,* sometimes called a "bad bite." A malocclusion can be corrected for cosmetic reasons, but in some cases crooked teeth can create speech problems or be more susceptible to decay, as they are more difficult to keep clean.

The American Association of Orthodontists recommends that children first be evaluated by an orthodontist by age seven. At that age, even children who have teeth that appear straight may have the beginnings of a jaw malformation that is not detectable by an untrained eye. A malformation can become a serious problem after a child becomes a teen. Parents often bring their children to an orthodontist at the suggestion of their child's general dentist, who may suspect a dental or facial development that should be evaluated and monitored.

When a patient comes to the office, orthodontists take a complete medical and dental history to determine what is influencing health in general and teeth in particular. Next, the mouth is carefully examined to look for oral evidence of disease. The health of teeth is carefully evaluated. The orthodontist notes the size and shape of each tooth and the relationship between the teeth and the gums, the lips, and the face. The patient's facial profile is assessed for uniformity, symmetry, and proportion. At this time, the orthodontist takes a photo of a patient's profile and smile

Lingo to Learn

Arch Describes the group of teeth and connecting bone of either the upper or lower jaw.

Bonding Orthodontic attachments are affixed to teeth using an adhesive.

Crowding The resulting malpositioned teeth from inadequate room for teeth within an arch.

Dental cast A plaster replica of the patient's teeth used for diagnosis and appliance fabrication.

Elastics Rubber bands used with orthodontic appliances as a part of treatment.

Fixed appliance A device that is bonded or banded to a tooth or teeth.

Malocclusion A deviation in the normal relationship of teeth in occlusion (while biting).

Orthodontic appliance A device that influences the growth or position of teeth or position of bones.

Orthodontic band A thin metal ring that is cemented to the tooth through which orthodontic attachments are secured.

Radiograph An image, usually recorded on film. It is sometimes called an X ray.

Retainer An orthodontic appliance that maintains teeth position after corrective treatment.

for the patient's record. After treatment is completed, photos will be taken again to show the results.

To make a diagnosis, orthodontists measure and evaluate relationships. They create casts from plaster by asking the patient to bite into a tray of impression material. The 3-D models made from the casts are mounted on hinges to make a model that shows the biting motion of the patient's teeth. It's difficult for patients to hold their mouths open wide for long periods of time, so these models allow orthodontists to study the dynamics of the bite more easily and to take detailed measurements.

Orthodontists also use radiographic images such as X rays to show the status of tissues that can't be seen by the eye, including problems inside the teeth and with the jaws, facial bones, and tooth roots. X rays can help an orthodontist determine if crowded teeth would benefit from an orthodontic extraction. In other cases, certain jaw discrepancies are detected with radiographs and need correction with orthodontic appliances like braces or orthognathic (jaw) surgery.

Once a problem is diagnosed, orthodontists may give a patient an oral or written treatment plan. This plan includes the diagnosis, the recommended treatment specifics, and a cost estimate of treatment.

There are various types of orthodontic treatment, but almost all involve metal, plastic, or ceramic braces that are banded around, or bonded to, teeth. These braces are made up of brackets and wires that move teeth into, or hold them in, proper position. Moving teeth is a very slow process of adjusting braces slightly every three to six weeks.

In the old days, braces were always metallic. Now braces can be white, clear, or a color. In certain cases, orthodontists sometimes even can place "invisible braces"—those that are attached to the tongue side of the teeth.

Additional orthodontic appliances include headgear, a wire appliance that protrudes from the mouth and is fastened by a strap behind the head. Orthodontists use this approach to orthopedically slow the growth of the upper jaw. Rubber bands are another pulling force that, when changed daily by the patient, help move teeth into position.

Another type of orthodontic appliance is the retainer. When orthodontists finish active treatment, often during two or more years, the patient comes in much less often for appointments or not at all. To make sure the corrected teeth or jaw don't move back into a poor position, an orthodontist may make a removable or permanent retainer for a patient to wear at night and sometimes during the day as well. Retainers are removed when the patients eat and brush their teeth.

While private practitioners make up the majority of orthodontists, other orthodontists teach full or part time at universities, perform research at dental schools or for industry such as dental product manufacturers, work in the military as government employees, or work for the U.S. Public Health Service.

What Is It Like to Be an Orthodontist?

Dr. Chris Carpenter has been an orthodontist for 10 years. He is a private practitioner in a Denver orthodontic practice that employs a staff manager, a receptionist at the front desk, and four dental assistants. The office is open five days a week from 7:00 A.M. to 4:30 P.M. and Chris works four days or 34 hours per week.

Each morning starts off with a "huddle" so that Chris and his staff can review the 40 to 60 patients' treatments for the day and prepare as much as possible beforehand. The office has five treatment chairs. Patients are seated upon arrival. Chris examines each patient, adjusts the wires, and then dictates final instructions to the dental assistant. The dental assistant then completes the final aspects of the treatment and coordinates the next appointment information.

"I see patients about 34 hours a week. I take Wednesdays off, but I usually come into the office anyway to do all the other things involved with running a small business. I pay bills, manage staff members, and do paperwork. I spend a considerable amount of time writing diagnosis and treatment plan letters with copies of radiographs to send to patients' general dentists," Chris says.

Other non-orthodontic responsibilities include working with insurance companies to obtain payment for procedures and overseeing the billing and collection of fees. To ensure the dental office is a safe place for employees and patients alike, Chris conducts a regular evaluation of procedures and conditions in the office to be certain everything is in compliance with the federal Occupational Safety and Health Administration standards.

Staff members are in charge of taking inventory and ordering supplies, but orthodontists oversee the process.

Bookkeeping and accounting duties are another part of Chris's duties—not only for billing purposes but also for keeping track of the staff members' time cards, benefits, social security and tax deductions, and for setting salaries and raises, as well.

On the practical side, Chris says that being an orthodontist means being organized and prepared to work efficiently so that a number of patients can be seen in one day. To accomplish this, Chris may review patient charts in the morning before the workday begins so that he can advise his staff at the morning meeting of the supplies he needs throughout the day. Reviewing the charts helps Chris mentally orient himself to each patient's needs, which helps him stay on schedule.

Being a good time manager is a highly advantageous skill. At any one time during the day, Chris may have five people in dental chairs waiting for treatment and another five in his waiting room. This means efficiently going from one patient to another just to thread, tie, and tighten wires and change bands. Dental assistants help immensely, as well. Chris may be interrupted to check their work or to clip wires and bend them so rough edges don't irritate the patients' cheeks and lips.

Being an orthodontist is physically challenging. Manual dexterity and strength are necessary assets. Fingers, hands, wrists, and arms are in controlled motion within a small space throughout the day. There is little room for error. Keen vision and perception in three dimensions is needed to locate tiny openings and parts of only a few millimeters in size.

To prevent the back injuries that can plague orthodontists as they lean over patients all day, Chris tries to maintain a healthy body. He stretches during the day and exercises about three times a week.

Two years have passed since Kaela's first visit with Chris. Kaela, now 14 years old, is sitting in the dental chair as Chris removes her braces. "Take a look in the mirror at that gorgeous smile," he says with a grin.

Kaela looks in the hand mirror at her teeth without braces and flashes a bright, wide smile.

"Dr. Carpenter, thank you so much! " Kaela says, while practicing versions of her smile in the mirror. "Now I can smile without being embarrassed." In the next couple of months, it is likely that Kaela will be more self-assured and confident when she speaks.

Patients like Kaela are the main reasons Chris enjoys working as an orthodontist. "I think it is the most ideal profession that exists. All day long I have the opportunity to change people's lives by improving their smiles. Patients are excited about the changes. Knowing that I did something that made a difference and made people happy is something that makes me happy to go to work every morning."

FYI

Orthodontics goes back to the ancient Phoenicians and Egyptians. Egyptian mummies have been found with copper bands around their teeth. Researchers speculate that the teeth were pulled together with string made of animal gut. Modern orthodontics dates to 1900, when the father of orthodontics, Dr. Edward Angle, established a system for diagnosing orthodontic problems. His system is still used today.

Do I Have What It Takes to Be an Orthodontist?

Chris was thoroughly trained in dental school, and during his orthodontic postgraduate program he earned a master's degree in orthodontics.

To keep abreast of advancements in orthodontics, Chris takes continuing education courses every year. Although some courses are required for him to maintain his dental license, he also takes other courses because he's interested in providing the latest techniques. He also takes classes to learn to better manage his practice. Business skills help keep the practice running efficiently for maximized profitability while providing the highest quality results.

Chris says, "The business skills and the people skills are almost as important as the orthodontic treatment. Knowing how to run a business while having empathy and a genuine ability to interact well with people is critical. My success is directly related to how well I treat my patients. They need to know I truly care about their concerns."

Being a good communicator while under time pressure is critical. One moment Chris may be discussing the need for good tooth brushing with an eight-year-old patient while another patient's parents are awaiting a consult on a new treatment plan and an insurance company representative is on hold about a claim misunderstanding. "You need to be an effective communicator because you don't have the luxury of a lot of time to make your point," he adds.

Always being able to control your temperament is necessary. "Having all the responsibilities of owning a practice and being your own boss is a lot of pressure. So you don't set yourself up for failure—there's no room for inflexible, perfectionist tendencies. Instead, you need to accept the fact that things will go wrong. You need to have confidence and learn from failure, whether it be with a patient, staff member, or the parent of a patient."

How Do I Become an Orthodontist?

EDUCATION

High School

You should begin preparing for an orthodontics career with a course load that emphasizes, but is not restricted to, math and science subjects. Courses such as algebra, calculus, chemistry, physics, trigonometry, biology, and health are all good courses for college preparation.

Postsecondary Training

Before you can be admitted to dental school you must complete three to four years of undergraduate college education. Maintaining a high grade point average in college is important because dental school admissions are fiercely competitive. While a bachelor's degree is not strictly required, it is a standard that significantly strengthens an applicant's chances of being admitted to a dental school.

Recommended college courses are similar to those suggested in high school. A typical program is a bachelor of science degree in biology. This involves taking math courses, such as algebra, calculus, trigonometry, and geometry. Science courses include biology, anatomy, physiology, anthropology, zoology, botany, and microbiology.

On the practical side, business classes such as marketing, economics, accounting, management, and finance prepare you for owning and operating a business.

Liberal arts courses such as psychology, sociology, English, and drama may also help a future orthodontist become more comfortable in communicating with people.

You must score well on the Dental Admissions Test (DAT) before being admitted into a dental program. Doing well on the DAT helps dental schools determine whether or not you will succeed in dental school. Dental school courses are made up of advanced science classes, clinical work, and laboratory classes. During the last two years of dental school, clinical treatment is emphasized and you begin supervised treatment of patients at a university dental clinic. Graduates receive a doctor of dental surgery (D.D.S.) or doctor of dental medicine (D.M.D.) degree.

This degree qualifies you to work as a general dentist. To be an orthodontist, however, takes more schooling. Postgraduate programs, which are accredited by the American Dental Association Commission on Dental Accreditation, may last from two to three years. Gaining acceptance to a postgraduate program in orthodontics is competitive. Therefore, it is critical that you maintain a high grade point average during dental school.

CERTIFICATION OR LICENSING

New dentists must first pass a licensing examination before they can work in the state of their choice. This test may include working on a patient. In some states, orthodontists must also pass a specialty licensing examination.

Board certification is also available through the American Board of Orthodontists (ABO). To achieve ABO diplomate status, orthodontists must file an application with the ABO, be interviewed and approved as a candidate, pass written and oral examinations, and provide written orthodontic case histories. It may take eight to 10 years to gain ABO diplomate status.

Chris recalls, "After about two years of dental school, I became interested in orthodontics after I took a class on the subject. Following dental school, I attended a 30-month residency in orthodontics. All in all, I went to school for 10 years after high school—a big commitment, but I'd do it again if I had to. That's how much I enjoy the profession."

Orthodontists, as well as all dentists, also must plan on taking courses after they have established a practice. These continuing education courses are taken to maintain a dental license. Other educational activities include attending workshops and seminars, reading professional journals, and participating in study clubs. This helps a practicing orthodontist acquire the most up-to-date skills and knowledge of the best materials to use.

FYI

- The American Association of Orthodontists estimates that up to 75 percent of people could benefit from orthodontic care.
- Almost 5 million people in the United States and Canada are currently undergoing orthodontic treatment; twenty percent of this group are over the age of 18.

Source: American Association of Orthodontists

SCHOLARSHIPS AND GRANTS

Scholarships and grants are often available from individual institutions, state agencies, and special-interest organizations. Many students finance their medical education through the Armed Forces Health Professions Scholarship Program. Each branch of the military participates in this program, paying students' tuitions in exchange for military service. Contact your local recruiting office for more information on this program.

The National Health Service Corps Scholarship Program also provides money for students in return for service. Another source for financial aid, scholarship, and grant information is the Association of American Medical Colleges. Remember to request information early for eligibility, application requirements, and deadlines.

Association of American Medical Colleges
2450 N Street, NW
Washington, DC 20037
202-828-0400
http://www.aamc.org

National Health Service Corps Scholarship Program
U.S. Public Health Service
1010 Wayne Avenue, Suite 240
Silver Spring, MD 20910
800-221-9393
http://nhsc.bhpr.hrsa.gov

Who Will Hire Me?

According to the American Association of Orthodontists (AAO), there are more than 12,000 orthodontists in the United States and more than 90 percent of them are in private practice. Orthodontists may own their own practice or may work as an associate or a partner with other orthodontists. Information about private practice opportunities is available in the *American Journal of Orthodontics and Dentofacial Orthopedics,* the scientific journal of the AAO. The resources required to set up a new private practice are considerable—often a bank-financed endeavor. Some orthodontists work in hospitals and dental clinics.

Other opportunities for orthodontists include teaching at university dental schools, either full time or part time, while also maintaining a practice. Part-time instructors sometimes are not paid, however, because there is prestige associated with university teaching and orthodontists sometimes volunteer to teach a class to build their careers. Some orthodontists also work in a dental school environment where there are research opportunities. Others perform research while testing new materials and procedures and writing about them for industry. Researchers may test new orthodontic materials or techniques by working on anything from model mouths to animals.

Combining one or more aspects of clinical practice, teaching, and research, some orthodontists are employed by the federal government in the U.S. Public Health Service. These orthodontists may be positioned in sites across the country or around the world with the air force, navy, army, veterans hospitals, or other agencies working with public health service, such as the Indian Health Service or the U.S. Coast Guard.

To Be a Successful Orthodontist, You Should . . .

- have dexterity for detail work
- be self-motivated
- have excellent eye-hand coordination
- be able to perceive in three dimensions
- have an artistic eye and be able to judge symmetry
- maintain excellent people skills

Where Can I Go from Here?

Orthodontists in private practice try to build a reputation with the general dentists in the surrounding community who will refer patients. Orthodontists who can effectively communicate with a patient's general dentist and facilitate easy coordination of treatment are more likely to be trusted by the general dentist.

Involvement in orthodontic associations and study clubs may lead orthodontists to active participation in organized dental events. Some orthodontists even become officers and committee chairs of their professional associations.

After many years of working, orthodontists may slow down to part-time status or retire and teach during their retirement years.

What Are the Salary Ranges?

The American Association of Orthodontists says that orthodontists under age 30 often have a starting salary that's double the income of other college graduates.

According to research by Salary.com, a typical orthodontist earned a median base salary of approximately $107,070 in 2004. Half of the people in this job earned between approximately $87,963 and $130,000. The U.S. Department of Labor reports that the median annual earnings for all dentists were $120,330 in 2003.

The location of an orthodontist's private practice may play a role in determining income, as well. Dentists in Pacific, Mountain, Northern, and New England states typically have higher incomes than those in Southern states. Orthodontists in affluent and growing suburbs may have greater income potential than those in all but economically thriving parts of urban or rural areas. Specialists' incomes are also affected by how many other specialists in their area of expertise are working in the community. In an area with few or no other orthodontists, an orthodontic practice may have an edge and find it easier to obtain referrals.

What Is the Job Outlook?

Although employment for dentists is expected to grow more slowly than the average, according to the *Occupational Outlook Handbook,* employment for orthodontists should remain steady. Since our society values physical attractiveness, the motivation to receive orthodontic treatment can be cosmetic in nature, and demand for these services should continue to be strong. However, because orthodontics is largely an optional procedure, problems with national economic health could impact it. Patients or their families without solid income are not likely to pursue or follow through with orthodontic treatment. However, to make the service more accessible, many offices provide financing, accept charge cards, or refer the patient to financing sources where instant over-the-phone approval may be obtainable.

How Do I Learn More?

PROFESSIONAL ASSOCIATIONS

The following organizations provide information on dental careers, accredited schools, and employers:

American Association of Orthodontists
401 North Lindbergh Boulevard
St. Louis, MO 63141-7816
314-993-1700
http://www.aaortho.org

American Dental Association
211 East Chicago Avenue
Chicago, IL 60611
312-440-2500
http://www.ada.org

BIBLIOGRAPHY

The following is a sampling of materials related to the professional concerns and development of orthodontists:

Bishara, Samir E. *Textbook of Orthodontics.* Philadelphia: W. B. Saunders Co., 2001.

Cozzani, Giuseppe. *Garden of Orthodontics.* Chicago: Quintessence Publishing, Inc., 2000.

Fonseca, Raymond J., Robert V. Walker, and Normal J. Betts, eds. *Oral and Maxillofacial Trauma.* 3d ed. Philadelphia: W. B. Saunders Co., 2004.

Graber, Thomas M. and Robert L. Vanersdall, eds. *Orthodontics: Current Principles and Techniques.* 3d ed. St. Louis, Mo.: Mosby-Year Book, 2000.

Mitchell, Laura, Nigel E. Carter, and Bridget Doubleday. *An Introduction to Orthodontics.* 2d ed. New York: Oxford University Press, 2001.

Mitchell, Laura, David A. Mitchell, and Brian Nattress. *Oxford Handbook of Clinical Dentistry.* 3d ed. New York: Oxford University Press, 1999.

Profitt, William R., and Henry W. Fields. *Contemporary Orthodontics.* 3d ed. St. Louis: Mosby-Year Book, 2000.

Sarver, David M. *Esthetic Orthodontics and Orthognathic Surgery.* St. Louis,: Mosby-Year Book, 1998.

ORTHOPEDIC SURGEONS

Definition

Orthopaedic surgeons diagnose and treat patients with musculoskeletal disorders that are present at birth or develop later.

Alternative Job Titles

Orthopedic surgeons
Orthopedists

High School Subjects

Biology
Chemistry

Personal Skills

Helping/teaching
Technical/scientific

Salary Range

$113,000 to $255,438 to $300,000+

Educational Requirements

Bachelor's degree; M.D.; minimum five years postgraduate study; optional fellowships in subspecialties

Certification or Licensing

Recommended (certification)
Required by all states (licensing)

Outlook

About as fast as the average

DOT

070

GOE

14.02.01

NOC

3111

O*NET-SOC

29-1067.00

Grazie," Maria Modarelli says in Italian as she is helped into the doctor's office by the receptionist. She settles into a chair and smiles weakly. Maria looks around at the certificates and diplomas that decorate the walls of the Brooklyn, New York, office. Absentmindedly, she taps the rubber-capped end of her thick, polished cane against the leg of the chair. A few moments go by and she reaches down to pull an ornate gold watch out from the black folds of her coat. She squints at it and sighs and slips the watch back inside. Even as she sits here her left knee aches with pain.

The door to the reception area opens and the orthopedic surgeon enters. He smiles broadly and kneels beside Maria. "Good day, Mrs. Modarelli," he says in Italian. "Where does it hurt?"

She sighs and touches her left leg. The orthopaedist, Dr. Edward Toriello, gets up and moves another chair in the room close to hers. Ed studied medicine in Italy, and today he finds that his knowledge of Italian is an unexpected asset in dealing with a patient. Speaking in Italian in a gentle voice, he begins to tell Mrs. Modarelli how he might be able to help her with the pain in her knee, and how it is possible that she might be able to move it easily again.

What Does an Orthopedic Surgeon Do?

Orthopedic surgeons are concerned with the diagnosis, care, and treatment of patients with musculoskeletal disorders that are present at birth or develop later in life. These musculoskeletal problems include deformities, injuries, and degenerative diseases of the spine, hands, feet, knees, hips, shoulders, and elbows.

In its early days, orthopedics involved treating children with spine or limb deformities, but the specialty quickly expanded. The scope of orthopedics today is immense. Orthopedic surgeons treat a wide variety of diseases and conditions, from such problems as fractures, torn ligaments, bunions, lower back pain, scoliosis, and ruptured discs to degenerative joint diseases, muscular dystrophy, and cerebral palsy.

Orthopedic surgeons treat patients of all ages. Orthopaedists may see children with such problems as bone tumors, hip dislocations, and growth abnormalities such as unequal leg length. Orthopedic surgeons who practice in sports medicine treat injuries to the athlete and are especially involved with knee surgeries and arthroscopic procedures (procedures using fiber-optic instruments). Orthopedic surgeons also treat elderly patients who may have bone disorders, such as osteoporosis, or joint conditions, such as arthritis. Recently, advances in the surgical man-

Lingo to Learn

Arthritis Inflammation of joints.

Arthroscope Fiber-optic instrument used to show the interior of a joint and to perform surgery on a joint.

Arthroscopy The process in which a joint is examined or surgery is performed using an arthroscope.

Bunion Inflammation of the bursa at the joint of the large toe.

Bursa A small, fluid-filled sac found in the area of a joint.

Bursitis Inflammation of a bursa, especially of the shoulder or elbow.

Cerebral palsy A partial or total lack of muscle control, particularly of the limbs, that results from trauma at birth or developmental defects in the brain.

Fluoroscope An instrument used for observing the internal structure of an opaque object (as the living body) by means of X rays.

Muscular dystrophy Any of a group of hereditary diseases characterized by a progressive wasting away of muscles.

Musculoskeletal Involving both the muscles and the skeleton.

Osteoporosis A condition in which bone mass decreases, causing a decrease in bone density and enlargement of spaces within the bone. This loss makes bones vulnerable to breaks and fractures. Older women are especially affected.

Scoliosis Crookedness or curvature of the spine.

agement of degenerative joint diseases have allowed orthopedic surgeons to replace the diseased joint with a prosthetic device in a surgery known as total joint replacement. Similarly, fiber-optic scopes, or arthroscopes, which allow the orthopedic surgeon to look inside a joint, have had an enormous impact on the diagnosis and surgical treatment of internal joint diseases. Other technological advances include microsurgery, which allows orthopedic surgeons to replant limbs, and "space age" metal techniques that create better devices with which to repair damaged bones.

Orthopedic surgeons use medicine and rehabilitative methods as well as surgery to treat their patients. Some disorders require surgery for correction, but others require a cast or brace and work with physical therapists, occupational therapists, and other members of a rehabilitation team. Whatever the prescribed method of treatment, orthopedic surgeons often work closely with other health care professionals, either as the patient's primary care physician or as a consultant to other physicians.

Orthopedic surgeons also have a large role in the organization and delivery of emergency care, working with other specialists in the management of complex trauma injuries, such as from a car accident.

What Is It Like to Be an Orthopedic Surgeon?

"I like putting hands back together," says Dr. Diana Carr, an orthopedic surgeon with a solo private practice in rural Florida. "I like healing sick people. We're a specialty where you can really see what we've done." She remembers as a child growing up in a very small town with no drugstore and the only hospital a long 45-minute drive away. "When the doctor was on vacation, that was it," she says. "There wasn't anywhere to go." For as long as Diana can remember, she wanted to be the person who was the only one for miles who could help people—a doctor. She says she felt that power once when she operated on a man with a World War II injury. "The injury was as old as I was," she says. "After a radial nerve transfer, which was a new procedure at the time, he used his hand for the first time in 50 years. It felt incredible to help him do that."

> I like healing sick people. We're a specialty where you can really see what we've done.

Dr. Edward Toriello, Chief of the Department of Orthopaedic Surgery at Wyckoff Heights Medical Center in Brooklyn, New York, works with patients of all ages, but he tends to see more elderly patients. "They usually come in with their son or daughter. The typical elderly patient I see is healthy, overall, but with an arthritic joint, say. And this changes their whole quality of life. They want desperately to remain independent, but over the course of time—sometimes it's a short period of time, sometimes it's over a period of several months or years—they become trapped physically. They're either housebound, or even chair bound. This can change their entire outlook and personality, making an ordinarily happy person quite bitter." Ed is sensitive to these sorts of changes in people and takes genuine delight in helping them. "I like getting people back on their feet," he says.

As the attending orthopedic surgeon at Catholic Medical Center in Queens, New York, Ed also works with trauma patients. "I see patients in two areas: my office and the ER," he says. Most of his days, though, are spent in the office. He begins an office visit by talking with the patient, and sometimes the patient's relatives, to discover what the problem is. He takes down the patient's history and takes X rays if necessary.

Once Ed has come to a conclusion about the patient's case, he sits down and carefully explains the diagnosis to the patient. "I use a model to show the patient and the patient's family what I'm talking about," he says. "That's what's so great about this specialty, too. You can see it—it's not like I'm trying to describe diabetes or something intangible—it's right there, in black and white." After explaining his diagnosis, Ed talks about the patient's options. "This is an extensive discussion," says Ed, "because each option has risks and advantages." He continues with an example: "A patient diagnosed with an arthritic joint has the option of doing nothing, taking meds, having arthroscopic surgery, or doing a total joint replacement." Depending on the particular characteristics of a patient's case, Ed might recommend arthroscopic surgery. "We won't cure the arthritis," he says, "but it buys time for a lot of people. It's like light housekeeping of the joint. We wash it out, scrape or sand or shave the bone spurs. Clean it up and, hopefully, flush out some of the toxins."

Ed wants patients to take their time deciding which option will make them feel the most comfortable. "I want them to try and figure out what's best," he says. "As much as I love surgery, you don't want to do something that won't help. After we finish talking I give them a booklet that describes what we've just talked about, and I ask them to think about it and talk it over with their families. Some are absolutely positive about wanting the surgery, in which case I might go ahead and schedule them for surgery, but most need to think it over."

In the event that a patient opts for a total joint replacement, Ed sends them to an internist for blood work and a full checkup. "We want to determine that the patient can reasonably survive the procedure," he explains. He then sets a date for the surgery and provides the patient with information about the procedure. The morning of the surgery, Ed meets briefly with the patient, reviews the patient's history, and notes any problems, such as allergies to medications. Most surgeries begin early in the morning, sometime between 7:30 and 8:00 A.M. Ed likes to have music playing during his surgeries. "Preferably, the blues," he adds.

The next several hours consist of cutting, sawing, and measuring. Ed says, "During 'Take Your Daughter to Work Week' my 13-year-old got to see a total knee replacement. She was completely impressed by all the sounds—buzzing, banging, pounding, scraping, the sucking sounds from the suction machine. She loved it." For some surgeries the patient can be awake. A spinal anesthesia allows them to remain conscious without feeling any pain. "During arthroscopic surgeries, I love it when the patient is awake. They can see what I'm doing and what the process really involves."

Following the surgery, Ed is involved with the patient's postoperative care and recovery, including rehabilitation. With the help of a physical therapist and other members of the rehabilitation team, the patient learns how to use the joint again.

Do I Have I What It Takes to Be an Orthopedic Surgeon?

"You've really got to be dedicated—it's not going to be easy. Orthopedics is a macho specialty," says Diana. "You can't be thin-skinned. A sense of humor is helpful." Diana wants women to enter the field, but she wants them to realize it can be a difficult specialty. As the only woman in her orthopedics residency and the only woman in the entire surgery department, she has toughened up and learned to use humor to deal with difficult situations.

Orthopedic surgeons work with a wide variety of instruments, scopes, and technologies. "You should really like working with gadgets," warns Ed. "It's almost like building a room," he adds. "You work with saws, plates, screws, cement, rods." To a certain extent the work of an orthopedic surgeon involves physical activity. "There's a lot of pulling and tugging," Ed says. Women, however, should not worry about not being strong enough. Diana points out, "There is no reason why any woman, regardless of size, cannot successfully practice orthopedics. The correct application of orthopedic principles will allow reductions of fractures and dislocations by any orthopedist." Diana finds that the real problem comes in finding tools and instruments that are properly sized. "The biggest problem I have is the size of the tools don't fit my hand. My hands are small," she says.

Stamina, more than strength, comes into play most often. One reason orthopedic surgeons need stamina is that they wear protective lead aprons during surgeries that involve fluoroscopes. "They seem a lot heavier than their 10 pounds when you're under stress," says Ed. Fluoroscopes provide continuous X rays of the body's interior.

Orthopedic surgeons also need stamina to last through the long surgeries. Some procedures are short and take only 20 to 30 minutes. On the other hand, a total joint replacement can take from two to three hours. And most trauma surgery on bones can take five to seven or more hours to complete. "You just keep telling yourself that no surgery can go on forever," says Ed. "Every surgery has to end sometime."

Knowing the limits of the materials you work with is another necessary quality. As Ed points out, technology has advanced to the point where he and other orthopedic surgeons can use special metals that will last a long time, but in the end, nothing lasts forever. "Titanium, chromium, steel, cobalt—anything will break. It's like a coat hanger, you can keep piling clothes on one, but eventually it's going to give way. It's a race against time." An orthopedic surgeon usually gets to help his or her patients, but there may be moments when the orthopedic surgeon has to tell a star athlete that the days of setting records are over. Compassion, empathy, and understanding will help the orthopedic surgeon to help his or her patient.

To Be a Successful Orthopedic Surgeon, You Should

- have physical stamina
- enjoy working with tools and technology
- enjoy helping people
- have good hand-eye coordination
- be a good listener and effective communicator

How Do I Become an Orthopedic Surgeon?

EDUCATION

High School

If you are interested in pursuing a medical degree, a high school education emphasizing college preparatory classes is a must. Science courses, such as biology, chemistry, and physics, are necessary, as are math courses. These classes will not only provide you with an introduction to basic science and math concepts, but also allow you to determine your own aptitude in these areas. Since college will be your next educational step, it is also important to take English courses to develop your research and writing skills. Foreign language, social science, and computer classes will also prepare you for your future undergraduate and graduate education. As a high school senior you may want to consider applying to colleges or universities that are associated with a medical school. High school guidance counselors should be able to provide you with information about such schools.

Postsecondary Training

Following high school, the next step to becoming an orthopedic surgeon is to receive a bachelor's degree from an accredited four-year college or university. Typical college courses that will help you prepare for medical school include biology, chemistry, anatomy, psychology, and physics. English courses will help you to hone communication skills; other humanities classes, social sciences, and ethics will help prepare you for a people-oriented career.

If you choose to attend a college or university associated with a medical school that offers the accelerated medical program, your undergraduate education will be different from that of other undergrads. An accelerated program typically reduces or consolidates the number of years you spend as an undergraduate, thereby speeding up your entrance into medical school. A med student is actually enrolled for two or three years of undergraduate school, plus the requisite four years of medical school.

After receiving an undergraduate degree, you must then apply to medical school. Most students apply to several schools early in their senior year of college. Admission is competitive: Only about one-third of the applicants are accepted. Applicants must undergo a fairly extensive and difficult admissions process that takes into consideration grade point averages, scores on the Medical College Admission Test (MCAT), and recommendations from professors. Many medical schools also interview applicants.

A student who is not accepted on his or her first attempt to get into medical school should not despair. Many talented and highly regarded physicians were not accepted on their first try. Others have attended and graduated from foreign medical school programs. Ed is one such example.

"I was planning to be a priest," Ed says. "I went to seminary for two years. Having gone to a seminary, I didn't have the grades or the background to get into an American medical school. I didn't want to go to Mexico, so I decided to go abroad to study medicine in Italy." He acknowledges this was a difficult choice to make, since he would have to learn a new language while trying to learn medicine too. "It was a lot of work. All of the courses were in Italian. I went over three months early to go to an intensive language school so that I would learn enough Italian to take the med classes," he explains. "The oral exams were intimidating, I'll tell you that much. It was tough, but I loved every minute of it." The University of Padova's medical school was a six-year program. At the end of five years, Ed transferred to The State University of New York at Buffalo's School of Medicine, where he studied for another two years.

In order to earn the doctor of medicine (M.D.) degree, you must complete four years of medical school study and training. For the first two years of medical school, students attend lectures and classes and spend time in laboratories. Courses include anatomy, biochemistry, physiology, pharmacology, psychology, microbiology, pathology, medical ethics, and laws governing medicine. You learn to take patient histories, perform routine physical examinations, and recognize symptoms. "Anatomy was just pure rote memorization—no finesse, at all," says Ed. "But I loved physiology. Physiology tells you how it all works. That's what put it all together for me."

In the third and fourth years, you are involved in more practical studies. You work in clinics and hospitals and are supervised by residents and physicians. You learn acute, chronic, preventive, and rehabilitative care. You go through what are known as rotations (brief periods of study) in areas such as internal medicine, obstetrics and gynecology, pediatrics, dermatology, psychiatry, and surgery. Rotations allow students to gain exposure to the many different fields within medicine and to learn the skills of diagnosing and treating patients.

Upon graduating from an accredited medical school, physicians must pass a standard examination given by the National Board of Medical Examiners. Most physicians complete an internship, also referred to as a transition year. The internship is usually one year in length and helps graduates to decide on an area of specialization.

Following the internship, the physicians begin what is known as a residency. Orthopedics requires a minimum of five years of postgraduate study. There are more than 160 residency programs in the United States that offer approximately 2,000 residency positions to prospective orthopedic surgeons. Competition for these positions is keen.

"I knew I liked surgery, so I began in general surgery," explains Ed. "I saw how hard everybody worked throughout the residency, but I got discouraged when I saw that general surgery residents who were ahead of me in school were doing more run-of-the-mill surgeries afterwards. It was nothing like what they'd done while in their residencies. The coolest guys were in orthopedics. I liked that it was positive surgery—no amputations," he adds. "And, unlike the general surgeons, the orthopedic surgeons I rotated with were still doing challenging, interesting surgeries once they left their residencies."

Throughout the surgical residency, residents are supervised at all levels of training, with the attending surgeon ultimately responsible for the patient's care. Residents begin their training by assisting on and then performing basic operations. As the residency years continue, residents gain responsibility through teaching and supervisory duties. Eventually the residents are allowed to perform complex operations independently.

The residency years are as filled with stress, pressure, and physical rigor as the previous four years of medical school, perhaps even more so since resi-

FYI

According to the American Academy of Orthopaedic Surgeons, choosing the right shoes for athletic activity is an important step in preventing injury to joints and bones. They offer the following advice for when you are purchasing new athletic shoes:

- Try on athletic shoes after a run or workout at the end of the day, when your feet will be at their largest.
- Wear the same socks that you will wear for the sport.
- Shoes should be immediately comfortable. There should be no "breaking-in" period.
- When the shoe is on your foot, you should be able to wiggle all of your toes freely.
- The shoe should grip your heel firmly, with no slipping as you walk or run.

dents are given greater responsibilities than medical students. Residents often work 24-hour shifts, easily putting in 80 hours or more per week.

CERTIFICATION OR LICENSING

Licensing is mandatory in all states before any doctor can practice medicine. In order to be licensed, doctors must have graduated from medical school, passed the licensing test of the state in which they will practice, and completed their residency.

Certification by the American Academy of Orthopaedic Surgeons, although voluntary, is highly recommended. Hospitals, for example, often refuse to extend privileges to noncertified physicians. Orthopedic surgeons seeking certification must undergo a two-step process. After completing postgraduate training, the candidate must successfully complete the written examination. Then, after two years in practice, the candidate must successfully complete the oral examinations. The orthopedic surgeon who passes both examinations is now eligible for membership in the American Academy of Orthopaedic Surgeons. The candidate must complete an application and interview and be sponsored by two fellows in the academy.

SCHOLARSHIPS AND GRANTS

Scholarships and grants are often available from individual institutions, state agencies, and special-interest organizations. Many students finance their medical education through the Armed Forces Health Professions Scholarship Program. Each branch of the military participates in this program, paying students' tuitions in exchange for military service. Contact your local recruiting office for more information. The National Health Service Corps Scholarship Program also provides money for students in return for service. Another source for financial aid, scholarship, and grant information is the Association of American Medical Colleges. The Ruth Jackson Orthopaedic Society (named for the first woman to become an orthopedic surgeon in the United States) was organized for women orthopaedists. The society offers scholarships and information helpful to women interested in orthopedics. Remember to request information early for eligibility, application requirements, and deadlines.

Association of American Medical Colleges
2450 N Street, NW
Washington, DC 20037
202-828-0400
http://www.aamc.org

National Health Service Corps
U.S. Public Health Service
1010 Wayne Avenue, Suite 240
Silver Spring, MD 20910
800-638-0824
http://nhsc.bhpr.hrsa.gov

Ruth Jackson Orthopaedic Society
6300 North River Road, Suite 727
Rosemont, IL 60018
847-698-1637
http://www.rjos.org

Who Will Hire Me?

Orthopedic surgeons typically practice in one of three settings. One option is to work as a solo practitioner.

FYI

A survey by the American Academy of Orthopaedic Surgeons revealed that 41 percent of surgeons considered themselves generalists. About 36 percent were generalists with a special interest. Only 23 percent considered themselves specialists and confined their practice to a special area, such as the spine, foot, or hand.

Solo practitioners work for themselves, although they may share office space with other orthopedic surgeons or physicians. A second option is to work in an orthopedic group practice. Typically in this setting, two to six orthopaedists work together, sharing costs for the office, seeing each other's patients, and providing continual coverage in hospital rounds. The third typical practice setting is in multispecialty groups. In these groups, a number of orthopaedists work together with other specialists, such as cardiologists or general practitioners.

Many orthopedic surgeons are also involved in education, either as full- or part-time teachers. There are also orthopaedists who work for the military or in administrative positions for health care providers.

Where Can I Go from Here?

Orthopedic surgeons usually advance their careers by increasing the size of their private practice, increasing their specialty knowledge by returning to school, or assuming additional responsibilities of administrative or supervisory positions. Prominence in the profession may also be gained by having papers or research results published in respected medical journals. Many physicians also give lectures at specialty conferences.

What Are the Salary Ranges?

According to the Medical Group Management Association, surgeons had annual earnings of $255,438 in 2002. This figure includes research stipends, bonuses, and other incentives. The U.S. Department of Labor reports that surgeons made anywhere from less than $113,000 to more than $300,000 per year in 2003, depending on their specialty. Keep in mind, however, that medical students and doctors just starting out may make considerably less than this in the early years of their careers.

Factors influencing individual incomes include type and size of practice, hours worked per week, geographic area, and professional reputation.

What Is the Job Outlook?

Orthopedics is an expanding specialty, and the need for surgeons will increase about as fast as the average, according to the *Occupational Outlook Handbook*. Future opportunities in orthopedics will be influenced by major trends in population aging (with its increasing numbers of fractures and reconstructive surgery), by trauma and injuries in sports and the workplace, and by continuing technological advancement.

How Do I Learn More?

PROFESSIONAL ORGANIZATIONS

The following organizations provides information on the profession and certifying process of orthopedic surgeon:

American Academy of Orthopaedic Surgeons
6300 North River Road
Rosemont, IL 60018
847-823-7186
http://www.aaos.org

BIBLIOGRAPHY

The following is a sampling of books relating to the professional concerns and development of orthopedic surgeons:

Brown, David E., and Randall D. Neumann. *Orthopedic Secrets.* 3d ed. Philadelphia: Hanley & Belfus, 2003.

Buckwalter, Joseph A, Thomas A. Einhorn, Sheldon R. Simon, eds. *Orthopaedic Basic Science.* 2d ed. Rosemont, Ill.: American Society of Orthopaedic Surgeons, 2000.

Canale, S. Terry, ed. *Campbell's Operative Orthopaedics.* 10th ed. St. Louis: Mosby-Year Book, 2002.

Duthie, Robert, and George Bentley, eds. *Mercer's Orthopaedic Surgery.* 9th ed. London: Arnold Publishers, 1996.

Miller, Mark D. *Review of Orthopaedics.* 4th ed. Philadelphia: W. B. Saunders Co., 2004.

Skinner, Harry. *Current Diagnosis & Treament in Orthopedics.* 3d ed. New York: McGraw-Hill/Appleton & Lange: 2003.

ORTHOTIC AND PROSTHETIC TECHNICIANS

Definition
Orthotic and prosthetic technicians make, fit, repair, and maintain orthotic and prosthetic devices according to established specifications under the direction of orthotists and prothetists.

Alternative Job Titles
Arch-support technician
Orthotic and prosthetic practitioner

High School Subjects
Art
Biology
Technical/shop

Personal Skills
Helping/teaching
Mechanical/manipulative

Salary Range
$17,600 to $28,500 to $47,300+

Minimum Educational Requirements
Some postsecondary training

Certification or Licensing
Required by all states (licensing)
Voluntary (certification)

Outlook
Faster than the average

DOT
712

GOE
14.05.01

NOC
3219

O*NET-SOC
N/A

The scene is controlled chaos in the Pueblo, Colorado, office of Mike Manship and Russ Miller, orthotic and prosthetic practitioners. From seeing patients who have come in with scheduled appointments and others who have walked in without an appointment, to answering phone calls, and dashing between examining rooms to the office's lab where they adjust patients' orthotic or prosthetic devices, there is never a dull day for the two men.

"If we're not working and talking with people," Russ says, "we are in the lab fabricating devices that will be fit on these people. The people that come into the office that already have the devices, we are oftentimes running from the exam rooms to the lab area to adjust their devices."

What Does an Orthotic and Prosthetic Technician Do?

Orthotic and prosthetic technicians read and follow specific instructions provided by orthotist and prothetists to choose the appropriate materials and tools necessary to make braces. These braces are used to support weak or ineffective joints and muscles, to correct physical defects, or to build artificial limbs for patients.

Mike and Russ are *orthotic and prosthetic practitioners*, a job which involves not only fabricating and fitting orthotic and prosthetic devices like a technician, but also for performing clinical evaluations of patients, for making recommendations regarding the best type of device to meet each patient's needs, and for the patient's post-rehabilitation care. We do "fabrication of these devices, fitting of the devices, and follow up to make sure that the patient is indeed seeing the benefits of orthosis and prosthesis," Russ says.

Similar to the work of orthotic and prosthetic technicians, *arch-support technicians* make steel arch-supports for a patient's foot, following the instructions of a podiatrist, orthotist, or prosthetist.

Like other skilled craftsmen, those working in the field of orthotics and prosthetics must read diagrams and follow written specifications to build medical appliances.

To make a plastic replacement for ears, noses, or hands, prosthetic technicians use wax or plastic to create an impression of the patient's amputated body area. A plaster cast is made from a mold of the impression. To ensure that the final replacement matches the patient's body part, the technician may have to carve, grind, or build up parts of the plaster model. When the basic device is ready, the technician will fit it with an outer cover using a sewing machine, riveting guns, and other hand tools. If necessary, the technician will mix pigments to match the patient's skin coloring and apply them to the outer covering of the prosthesis.

Orthotic devices are built by technicians who use a variety of tools such as hammers, anvils, welding equipment, and saws to cut and shape pieces of metal or plastic into the specified device's structural components. To be sure the finished device fits properly, the technician may shape the metal or plastic parts around a cast model of the patient's torso or limbs. When the technician completes the basic parts of the device, it is assembled with rivets, covered and padded with layers of rubber, felt, plastic, and leather.

Arch-support technicians work with plaster casts of a patient's foot to determine the proper size and shape of the support to be built. They must select stainless steel sheets of the correct thickness and cut the sheets to the correct size. Once the steel is formed to the specified shape the technician checks the support against the plaster model to be sure it fits accurately. The support is then polished with abrasive polishing wheels and leather is glued to it for additional patient comfort.

Lingo to Learn

AFO Ankle-foot orthosis. A brace used to support the ankle and foot.

KAFO Knee-ankle-foot orthosis. A brace used to support the knee, ankle, and foot.

Myoelectrics The technology of taking human nerve impulses or electrical impulses outside of the body and converting them to electric current, which is used to move the artificial parts in a prothesis.

Orthosis Orthotic device. An appliance that supports, aligns, corrects, or prevents deformities. Also used to improve the function of moveable body parts.

Prosthesis Prosthetic device. An artificial substitute for a missing body part such as an arm, leg, hand, or foot that is used for functional or cosmetic reasons or both.

What Is It Like to Be an Orthotic and Prosthetic Technician?

"A typical work day is very chaotic," Russ says, ticking off a list of daily activities that include seeing scheduled and nonscheduled patients, in-house appointments, home visits, hospital calls, and time in the lab fabricating devices.

"In-house appointments, home visits, and hospital calls are often unscheduled so [the job] demands a flexible individual," Russ says.

Russ describes his office as "medical and technical," with examination rooms where he and Mike consult with patients, and a laboratory area where they fabricate orthotic and prosthetic devices for patients.

Not all of Russ's time is spent in the office, he says. "The job involves some travel to see patients that are home bound, or seeing patients in the hospital."

Do I Have What It Takes to Be an Orthotic and Prosthetic Technician?

Technicians generally are not required to work overtime, evenings, or weekends. To be successful you should be comfortable working in workshops with power and hand tools, and with a variety of materials like plastic, metal, and leather. You also must be willing to adhere to strict safety procedures and be able to interpret written directions and follow precise instructions. You must also be committed to learning new technologies and advancements continually being developed in the field.

Russ says that good interpersonal communication skills are key to being successful in this profession. Also, "you need to be able to think on your feet and think outside of the box. In dealing with people there is no recipe, there is no one solution for one problem."

He continues, "This [profession] does require some kind of hand skills and mechanical skills and if you're truly going to advance in the field it would help to have some business experience, such as knowledge of accounting and marketing."

How Do I Become an Orthotic and Prosthetic Technician?

Having worked as a practitioner in orthotics and prosthetics for 20 years, Russ says he has found that working with people is "very rewarding. Being able to impact people's lives is something you will never forget."

EDUCATION

High School

If you plan to pursue a career as an orthotic or prosthetic technician, you should take all the shop classes your school offers. Courses in metal, wood, and machine shop will provide a strong background for working with the tools and materials used in this profession. Algebra and geometry classes will teach you to work with numbers and measurements. To help develop eye-hand coordination, a sense of design and proportions, and to gain skills working with materials like leather, metals, and plastics you should take art classes. Courses in biology, health, and anatomy will provide an understanding of the human body. Because computer technology is used to design devices computer science courses are beneficial, and English will help improve your communication skills.

Postsecondary Training

There are two training options to become an orthotic or prosthetic technician. You may enroll in a two-year program of supervised clinical experience and training under the supervision of a certified orthotist or prosthetist. Upon successful completion of the program technician status is granted.

The second option is to enroll in a one- or two-year educational program that leads to a certificate or an associate's degree in orthotics-prosthetics technology. Educational programs typically include classes in anatomy, physiology, properties of materials, prosthetic and orthotic techniques, building devices, and supervised clinical experience.

To date, the National Commission on Orthotic and Prosthetic Education (NCOPE) accredits only five technician programs: Baker College of Flint, Flint, Michigan; Century College, White Bear Lake, Minnesota; Francis Tuttle, Oklahoma City; Meridian School of Allied Health Careers, Pittsburgh; and Spokane Falls Community College, Spokane, Washington. Each of these programs leads to an associate's degree and certification.

Russ says that to advance and become an orthotic or prosthetic practitioner requires a bachelor's degree in orthotics and prosthetics or in health sciences. "And there is no substitute for on-the-job training," he adds.

FYI

- The ancient Greeks, Egyptians, and Romans were among the first societies that looked for different ways to use artificial methods to replace lost limbs and to support or correct the function of weak body parts.
- Modern orthotics and prosthetics are usually traced back to the 16th century French surgeon Ambroise Paré. Devices dating from that century include metal corsets, splints made of leather and other materials used for deformities of the hips and legs, special shoes, and solid metal hands.
- The Poor Relief Act of 1601, which established some government responsibility for the disabled, helped fuel the rapid development of orthotics in England at that time. Leather-covered wooden hands and single metal hooks to replace lost hands were among the devices developed.
- Improvements in the design and materials used for orthotic and prosthetic devices were prevalent following World Wars I and II, the Korean War, and the Vietnam War. An increase in sports-related injuries and those resulting from automobile accidents have also played a role in improvements to devices.

CERTIFICATION OR LICENSING

Although there are no licensing requirements at this time for orthotic and prosthetic technicians, the American Board for Certification in Orthotics and Prosthetics (ABC) offers a voluntary registration program. The minimum requirements for candidates seeking registration are a high school diploma and either completion of the two-year supervised on-the-job training program or a one- or two-year educational program at an NCOPE accredited school. Depending on the area of specialty, technicians who pass the ABC exam are designated as registered technician-orthotic, registered technician-prosthetic, or registered technician-orthotic/prosthetic. To maintain registration technicians must complete a required number of ABC-approved continuing education credits every five years.

SCHOLARSHIPS AND GRANTS

Qualified students may apply for scholarships through the O & P Educational and Development Fund. In 2004 one $500 scholarship and three $1,000 scholarships were awarded. Century College in Minnesota also offers scholarships, and the Orthotic and Prosthetic Assistance Fund (http://www.opfund.org) provides scholarships.

INTERNSHIPS AND VOLUNTEERSHIPS

Without training it is difficult to find internships or part-time or summer employment in this field, but volunteer opportunities may be available at local hospitals or rehabilitation centers. Since this profession is so specialized, Russ advises, "the best way [to get involved] is to express an interest in a local facility and get some exposure."

To Be a Successful Orthotic and Prosthetic Technician, You Should . . .

- enjoy working with your hands
- have excellent eye-hand coordination
- be patient and detail oriented
- have strong interpersonal communication skills

Who Will Hire Me?

According to a 2004 survey by the American Orthotic and Prosthetic Association (AOPA), 100 percent of O&P program graduates find employment. Orthotic and prosthetic technicians work for hospitals, rehabilitation centers, specialty clinics and home health settings, nursing homes, private brace and limb companies, and the Veterans Health Administration.

Graduates of one- or two-year educational programs generally get job placement assistance through the school they attended. Trade journals and professional organizations also provide job listings.

Where Can I Go from Here?

Many technicians employed by large hospitals or rehabilitation facilities advance to orthotic or prosthetic assistants once they have acquired enough experience, and eventually they may move into supervisory positions. Advancement opportunities are also available to those who specialize in one area of the field.

Significant career advancement is usually only available, however, to technicians who further their educations. By earning a four-year degree in orthotics or prosthetics, or completing a one-year certificate program technicians may become certified orthotists or prothetists.

Russ says, "Advancement in this field is really based on your expertise and longevity in an office. Most offices are independently owned at this time, although 40 to 50 percent are corporately owned." He says advancement in a corporately owned company is usually based on experience and length of employment as well as a proven ability to provide good care and demonstrating good technical knowledge.

If you own your own company, success will be determined by "your ability to be flexible, think on your feet, and to wear as many hats as you can," Russ says.

What Are the Salary Ranges?

Salaries for orthotic and prosthetic technicians vary depending on the location of employment, the size and type of employer, years of experience, and certification. According to the U.S. Department of Labor, in 2003 the median annual earnings for medical ap-

Places Where Orthotic and Prosthetic Technicians Work

- hospitals
- nursing homes
- rehabilitation facilities
- specialty clinics
- private brace and limb companies
- Veterans Health Administration

pliance technicians were $28,500. The lowest paid 10 percent earned $17,600, and the highest paid 10 percent earned $47,300. According to the AOPA 2004 survey, the average annual salary of ABC registered technicians was $40,454, and the average salary for fitters was $34,386. Noncertified licensed orthotists and prothetists with an average of seven years of experience earned $56,040 annually, and ABC-certified orthotists and prosthetists with 15 years of experience reported earning $91,452.

What Is the Job Outlook?

The U.S. Department of Labor projects employment opportunities for orthotic and prosthetic technicians will grow faster than the average through 2012. A study completed for the National Commission on Prosthetic Education reports that the aging baby boom population will increase the demand for orthotics and prosthetics by 2015, and by 2020 the number of people who have amputations and need prosthetic devices is expected to increase by 47 percent. In addition, there are more positions available than there are trained technicians to fill them, so employment opportunities should be good for technicians who graduate from accredited programs.

How Do I Learn More?

PROFESSIONAL ORGANIZATIONS

For information about the profession, accredited educational programs, scholarships, certification, and employment opportunities, contact the following organizations:

American Academy of Orthotists and Prosthetists
526 King Street, Suite 201
Alexandria, VA 22314
703-836-0788
http://www.oandp.org

American Board for Certification in Orthotics and Prosthetics
1521 Technology Drive
Chesapeake, VA 23320
757-548-5653
http://www/americanopcenter.com

American Orthotic and Prosthetic Association
330 John Carlyle Street, Suite 200
Alexandria, VA 22314
571-431-0876
info@aopanet.org
http://www.aopanet.org

National Commission on Orthotic and Prosthetic Education
330 John Carlyle Street, Suite 200
Alexandria, VA 22314
703-836-7114
info@ncope.org
http://www.ncope.org

O & P Educational Development Fund
c/o The Academy
526 King Street
Alexandria, VA 22314
703-836-0788
scholarships@oandp.org
http://www.opcareers.org/education/scholarships.html

BIBLIOGRAPHY

The following is a list of materials relevant to the professions of orthotics and prosthetics:

Edelstein, Joan. *Orthotics: A Comprehensive Clinical Approach*. Thorofare, N.J.: Slack, 2002.

Lusardi, Michelle M., and Caroline C. Nielson. *Orthotics and Prosthetics in Rehabilitation*, Boston: Butterworth-Heinemann, 2000.

Shurr, Donald G., and John W. Michael. *Prosthetics and Orthotics*. 2d ed. Paramus, N.J.: Prentice Hall, 2001.

Wilson, A. Bennet. *A Primer on Limb Prosthetics*. Springfield, Ill.: Charles C. Thomas, 1998.

OSTEOPATHIC PHYSICIANS

Definition
Osteopathic physicians treat diseases using accepted medical and surgical techniques; they also use manipulative treatment to correct impairments in the musculoskeletal system.

High School Subjects
Biology
Chemistry
Physics

Personal Skills
Helping/teaching
Technical/scientific

Salary Range
$51,000 to $133,340 to $250,000

Educational Requirements
Bachelor's degree; D.O. (doctor of osteopathy)

Certification or Licensing
Recommended (certification)
Required by all states (licensing)

Outlook
Faster than the average

DOT
070

GOE
N/A

NOC
3123

O*NET-SOC
29-1069.99

I did it while stepping down off a forklift," says Bill, as he gingerly makes his way to the examining table. Dr. George Pappas helps Bill ease down and carefully inspects the ankle. "You sure did, Bill. Looks like a nasty sprain. Let's begin with some ice for the swelling and then we'll progress with further treatments. Say, how's that shoulder of yours doing?"

Bill, a warehouse worker at a local food processing plant, has sought out the services of his trusted doctor. George, however, is not your typical physician. The initials after the name on his license are D.O., not M.D., yet he has all the professional responsibilities and privileges of a medical doctor. George is an osteopathic physician and part of the growing field of osteopathic medicine.

What Does an Osteopathic Physician Do?

Many people think osteopathic medicine is a medical specialty or a type of alternative medicine. It is neither. *Osteopathic physicians,* like chiropractors, place particular emphasis on the role of the musculoskeletal system in the healthy function of the body. But, unlike chiropractors, osteopathic physicians are trained and licensed to perform all aspects of medical care—including diagnosis, surgery, and the prescription of drugs. Osteopathic physicians care for more than 100 million patients a year in the United States.

For certain conditions, osteopathic physicians use a technique known as osteopathic manipulative treatment (OMT), which involves applying manual force to an interconnected network of nerves, muscles, and bones. Osteopathic doctors use their hands to apply traction, pressure, thrust, and counterforce to body systems. These applications relax muscles, relieve tenderness, and restore mobility and range of motion to joints and muscles.

Osteopathic physicians can be found in virtually all medical specialties, but most are in family practice, internal medicine, and pediatrics. They use the most modern and scientifically accepted methods of diagnosis and treatment. They work in hospitals, clinics, private offices, nursing homes, and other health care settings.

Osteopathic physicians treat a wide range of patients and ailments. They treat children with colds, elderly people with arthritis, athletes with sports-related injuries, new mothers and infants, and workers with occupational injuries.

It is the osteopathic philosophy that distinguishes osteopathic physicians from M.D.'s. Osteopaths are trained to view the human body as a single organism. They consider all body systems as interrelated and dependent upon one another for good health. Osteopathic physicians have a holistic view of medicine, treating specific illnesses in the context of the whole person. In addition to using all forms of medical treatment, osteopaths use OMT to diagnose illness. Reflecting their interest in treating the whole patient, many osteopathic physicians become family practitioners.

Osteopathic medicine was established in 1892 by a physician named Andrew Still. After losing three sons to spinal meningitis, Dr. Still came to believe that some current medical practices were inadequate or even harmful. He developed his own method of treatment, which primarily comprised manipulative techniques applied to the musculoskeletal system. In a departure from the thinking of the day, Dr. Still believed that the body has a capacity for self-healing. He was one of the first proponents of physical fitness as a route to better overall health.

There are more than 45,000 practitioners with D.O. degrees in the United States, according to the American Association of Colleges of Osteopathic Medicine. Both the D.O. and M.D. degrees give their holders the right to practice medicine. However, there is a widespread ignorance of the osteopathic medical profession, not only of how it compares to traditional medical practice but that it exists at all.

Lingo to Learn

Chiropractic A system of health care that emphasizes the relationship between the structure and the function of the body.

Holistic Emphasizing the importance of the whole body and the interdependence of its parts.

Osteopathic manipulative treatment (OMT) Applying manual force to an interconnected network of nerves, muscles, and bones.

Palpation Examining by touching to detect soft tissue changes or structural defects in the body.

Strain-counterstrain therapy An osteopathic treatment technique used to identify trigger points in the body and the use of manipulative techniques to relieve pain caused by these trigger points.

What Is It Like to Be an Osteopathic Physician?

Dr. George Pappas is the medical director and co-owner of Tyler Medical Services, in St. Charles, Illinois. He is an osteopathic physician specializing in occupational medicine, or treating and preventing work-related illnesses and injuries. He views his specialty as being similar to that of a sports physician. "Treating injured workers is not unlike the way a team physician would treat an injured athlete. It's just that you have an industrial athlete. The challenges are the same: getting them back in the game as quickly as possible."

Tyler Medical Services is a comprehensive medical facility. On-site are two other osteopathic physicians, a massage therapist, a physical therapist, and an occupational therapist. In addition, George works with three additional physicians on a contract basis: a neurologist, a neurosurgeon, and an orthopedic specialist. According to him, he does this to "provide a greater ability to treat people in a broader spectrum of care."

George spends about 80 percent of his day with patients and about 20 percent attending to administrative work. He generally works 50 hours a week, with some Saturdays. In the course of a day he sees about 30 patients, half of which have musculoskeletal problems where he can apply osteopathic manipulative treatments, or what he calls "hands-on medicine." He feels that this is the core of his practice—"The actual laying on of the hands, where you are touching a patient and providing them with hands-on medicine is very therapeutic . . . You develop a link with the patient."

Like most osteopathic physicians, George does not forsake traditional medical treatments when needed. He views these treatments as a part of his arsenal, an adjunct to osteopathic treatments. He will prescribe drugs and when faced with a severe condition, such as a herniated disk, will recommend a specialist, who may be an M.D.

Most of the patients who come to his office are there because they feel like he actively involves them in decisions. According to George, "They [patients] are seeking out osteopathic physicians because of their ability to include them in their decisions with health care."

In-depth

U.S. Colleges of Osteopathic Medicine

There are currently 20 osteopathic medical colleges in the United States:

Arizona College of Osteopathic Medicine (Glendale, Ariz.)
Chicago College of Osteopathic Medicine (Chicago, Ill.)
Des Moines University / College of Osteopathic Medicine & Surgery (Des Moines, Iowa)
Kirksville College of Osteopathic Medicine (Kirksville, Miss.)
Lake Erie College of Osteopathic Medicine (Erie, Pa.)
Michigan State University College of Osteopathic Medicine (East Lansing, Mich.)
New York College of Osteopathic Medicine of New York Institute of Technology (Old Westbury, N.Y.)
Nova Southeastern University College of Osteopathic Medicine (Fort Lauderdale, Fla.)
Ohio University College of Osteopathic Medicine (Athens, Ohio)
Oklahoma State University College of Osteopathic Medicine (Tulsa, Okla.)
Philadelphia College of Osteopathic Medicine (Philadelphia, Pa.)
Pikeville College School of Osteopathic Medicine (Pikeville, Ky.)
Touro University College of Osteopathic Medicine (San Francisco, Calif.)
The University of Health Sciences College of Osteopathic Medicine (Kansas City, Mo.)
University of Medicine and Dentistry of New Jersey School of Osteopathic Medicine (Stratford, N.J.)
University of New England College of Osteopathic Medicine (Biddeford, Maine)
University of North Texas Health Science Center/Texas College of Osteopathic Medicine (Fort Worth, Tex.)
Edward Via Virginia College of Osteopathic Medicine (Blacksburg, Va.)
West Virginia School of Osteopathic Medicine (Lewisburg, W. Va.)
Western University of the Health Sciences/College of Osteopathic Medicine of the Pacific (Pomona, Calif.)

George quickly responds when you ask him what he likes most about being an osteopathic physician. He says it's "the reward of the satisfaction of a patient saying 'you made me feel better' . . . it's a high."

Do I Have What It Takes to Be an Osteopathic Physician?

The practice of osteopathy usually involves a lot of personal interaction and touch, which can make some patients feel uncomfortable. Osteopathic physicians need excellent communication skills to let patients know what is going on. Good communication skills are also necessary to treat patients well. "You have to be able to communicate what your thoughts are," says George. "If the patient does not understand what you're telling them, chances are they're not going to do what you tell them to do." George also stresses the need to be a perceptive listener.

Since most osteopathic physicians work in private practices, business and management skills are very useful. You also need to work well with others. Having good manual dexterity is necessary to use osteopathic manipulative techniques effectively.

Most importantly, you need to have a true commitment to caring for people. Lesser goals may not provide sufficient motivation for the completion of difficult medical training.

How Do I Become an Osteopathic Physician?

After college, George worked at a YMCA health care facility. It was here that he was introduced to osteopathic medicine and became intrigued. He took the Medical College Admission Test (MCAT) and later got accepted into programs at an osteopathic as well as a traditional medical school. George says he chose the Chicago College of Osteopathic Medicine because the "philosophies and principals [of osteopathy] fit with who I am."

EDUCATION

High School

Students who plan to become doctors should take a college preparatory program in high school. You should have a good foundation in the sciences, especially biology, chemistry, and physics. You should also take English, foreign languages, and history. If possible, volunteer at a hospital or health care facility. This is an excellent way to observe the workings of a hospital and its staff and to become acquainted with the health care community and its goals.

Postsecondary Training

It generally takes about 11 years to become a physician. Four years of premedical undergraduate courses include physics, biology, mathematics, organic and inorganic chemistry, and English. Premed students who wish to become osteopaths are strongly urged to take psychology, sociology, communications, and history. It is possible to enter an osteopathic school with only three years of undergraduate study, but most applicants have a bachelor's degree. Most schools recommend science majors for premed students.

After completion of the MCAT and acceptance to an accredited osteopathic college, the student studies another four years. Currently, there are 20 colleges of osteopathic medicine in the United States. Most of these schools are in the Midwest and Northeast, although there are some in Florida, Missouri, Texas, and California. Areas of study include biochemistry, anatomy, physiology, pharmacology, psychology, microbiology, pathology, and medical ethics. In addition, students learn the principles of osteopathic manipulation and palpatory diagnosis.

According the American Association of Colleges of Osteopathic Medicine, "The curriculum reflects the osteopathic philosophy, with an underlying emphasis on preventative, family, and community medicine. Clinical instruction emphasizes looking at all patient characteristics (including behavioral, environmental, etc.) and how various body systems interrelate." The philosophical basis of osteopathy is woven into the fabric of the curriculum, giving osteopathic students a holistic approach to health care.

After graduation from medical school, osteopathic students are expected to complete one year of rotating internship in such areas as internal medicine, obstetrics/gynecology, and surgery. Each year George has several students rotate through his practice. Following rotations, students spend two to six years in residency training if a specialty is desired.

One of the difficulties facing the profession of osteopathy is that its schools produce more students than there are available spaces for residents in osteopathic hospitals. Graduates of osteopathic programs must increasingly find residencies in traditional medical facilities. Though increasing the awareness of osteopathy as a profession, some osteopathic physicians feel that residencies in traditional hospitals make it difficult to adhere to the osteopathic philosophy that is central to their training.

CERTIFICATION OR LICENSING

At an early point in the residency period, all physicians must pass a state medical board examination in order to obtain a license and enter practice. Each state sets its own requirements and issues its own licenses, though some states will accept licensing from certain other states.

Many osteopathic physicians belong to the American Osteopathic Association (AOA). To retain membership, physicians must complete 150 hours of continuing education every three years. Continuing education can be acquired in a variety of ways, including attending professional conferences, completing education programs sponsored by the AOA, osteopathic medical teaching, and publishing articles in professional journals. George acquires many of his hours through teaching osteopathic medical students. He finds that teaching is the best way to stay current because "students are going to ask the best questions, they're going to challenge you, [and] they're going to make you stay in touch."

To Be a Successful Osteopathic Physician, You Should . . .

- have excellent communication skills
- be dedicated to helping others
- be a very good listener
- enjoy working with a variety of people
- have good manual dexterity
- be committed to completing an arduous training regimen, including osteopathic medical school, internship, and residency

The AOA offers board certification. Certification has many requirements, including passing a comprehensive exam as well as a practical test where you must demonstrate osteopathic manipulative techniques. The AOA offers specialty certification in more than 100 specialties. Some osteopathic physicians are certified by both the AOA and the American Medical Association.

SCHOLARSHIPS AND GRANTS

Scholarships and grants are often available from individual institutions, state agencies, and special-interest organizations. Many students finance their medical education through the Armed Forces Health Professions Scholarship Program. Each branch of the military participates in this program, paying students' tuitions in exchange for military service.

The National Health Service Corps Scholarship Program also provides money for students in return for their later service. Visit its Web site at http://nhsc.bhpr.hrsa.gov.

Who Will Hire Me?

Osteopathic physicians may begin their career in one of several ways. For example, they may set up a private practice. This route is relatively rare because of the high cost and the need to establish a client base. Many osteopathic physicians begin by taking salaried jobs in group medical practices, clinics, or in health management organizations. These positions offer regular hours, a regular salary, and the opportunity for consultation with peers. After completing his residency, George joined a private group medical practice as an associate.

Osteopathic physicians advance in earnings and stature as they build up a practice. Income usually rises substantially as the practice becomes established. Some osteopathic physicians continue their studies to qualify for a specialty. These fields offer a higher income. Currently, George is working on specialty certification in occupational medicine.

About 65 percent of all practicing osteopathic physicians are currently involved in direct patient care—in a hospital, clinic, or private practice. At present, only a handful of osteopaths are employed as consultants, but this may change as patients become aware of osteopathic options and demand access to osteopathic treatment.

Osteopathic physicians represent 6 percent of the total physician population in the United States and 8 percent of U.S. military physicians. The federal government also employs osteopathic physicians as public health physicians. Government job listings are available in most state and federal institutions.

Sports medicine is a natural outgrowth of osteopathic practice because of its focus on the musculoskeletal system, manipulative treatment, diet, exercise, and fitness. Many professional sports team physicians, Olympic physicians, and personal sports medicine physicians are osteopathic physicians.

Where Can I Go from Here?

Osteopathic physicians may work toward earning a specialty degree—in obstetrics or gynecology, for example—to better serve a general practice clientele. Some choose to go into administration so that they can influence hospital- and public-policy making. There is a also need for research on osteopathic medicine and techniques, and some osteopaths may find this path to be a rewarding alternative to patient care.

About a year after being hired as an associate, George opened Tyler Medical Services. He offers a word of advice concerning hiring associates: "You have to realize that it is much more than just a business. You have to choose associates who have similar philosophies to you, because you are going to be judged on your group as a whole." George has seen his practice grow tremendously and hopes to open another facility in the near future.

What Are the Salary Ranges?

The U.S. Department of Labor reports that the median annual salary for family and general practitioners (the area in which most osteopathic physicians work) was $133,340 in 2003. Physicians may earn as little as $51,000 a year to more than $250,000 a year, depending on the size and type of their practice, hours worked per week, professional reputation of the individual, and the geographic location in which they live.

What Is the Job Outlook?

The outlook for osteopathic physicians is bright. Population growth, longer life spans, and an increase in the number of people covered by medical insurance have contributed to the growing demand for osteopathic physicians. The greatest need is for primary care doctors—family practitioners, internists, pediatricians, and obstetricians. Since most osteopathic practitioners fall into these categories, the outlook for a continued demand for their services is good. Opportunities for new osteopathic physicians are opening up in rural regions, small towns, and the suburban areas. Approximately 52,000 osteopaths are members of the American Osteopathic Association.

How Do I Learn More?

PROFESSIONAL ORGANIZATIONS

The following are organizations that provide information on the career of osteopathic physician:

American Association of Colleges of Osteopathic Medicine
5550 Friendship Boulevard, Suite 310
Chevy Chase, MD 20815-7231
301-968-4100
http://www.aacom.org

American Osteopathic Association
142 East Ontario Street
Chicago, IL 60611
312-202-8000
http://www.osteopathic.org

BIBLIOGRAPHY

The following is a sampling of materials relating to the professional concerns and development of osteopathic physicians:

Digiovanna, Eileen L., Stanley Schiowitz, and Dennis J. Dowling, eds. *An Osteopathic Approach to Diagnosis and Treatment.* 3d ed. Philadelphia: Lippincott Williams & Wilkins, 2004.

Gibbons, Peter, Philip Tehan, and Philip E. Greenman. *Manipulation of the Spine, Thorax and Pelvis: An Osteopathic Perspective.* New York: Churchill Livingstone, 2000.

Greenman, Philip E. *Principles of Manual Medicine.* 3d ed. Philadelphia: Lippincott Williams & Wilkins, 2003.

Lederman, Eyal. *Fundamentals of Manual Therapy: Physiology, Neurology and Psychology.* New York: Churchill Livingstone, 1997.

Marcus, Alon. *Musculoskeletal Disorders: Healing Methods from Chinese Medicine, Orthopaedic Medicine and Osteopathy.* Berkeley, Calif.: North Atlantic Books, 1999.

Ward, Robert C. et al., eds. *Foundations for Osteopathic Medicine.* 2d ed. Philadelphia: Lippincott Williams & Wilkins, 2002.

PATHOLOGISTS

Dr. David Cheng, staff pathologist, walks into an investigative scene. No, there is no yellow crime scene tape stretched across the doorway, nor are there any investigators and detectives roaming about, snapping pictures. David is entering the laboratory where he and his fellow pathologists quietly and earnestly "play detective" every day.

These pathologists make life-altering decisions on a daily basis. One pathologist quickly analyzes a piece of tissue and speeds the results to the operating room. The pathologist's malignant or benign assessment tells the surgeon if further surgery is necessary. Another anatomic pathologist quietly diagnoses viral and bacterial infections. A clinical pathologist reviews an abnormal blood smear, searching for a blood-borne infection or a leukemia diagnosis. In a far corner, a molecular pathologist uses her research and medical skills to determine if genetics play a role in certain types of breast cancer.

As David takes his seat in the laboratory, he realizes the importance of his job and how so many people, families, and generations depend on his skills. When in medical school, he heard that pathologists were called the "doctor's doctor," and every day he understands more fully just what that means.

Definition
Pathologists are physicians who use diagnostic and screening tests to identify and interpret the changes that characterize different diseases in the cells, tissues, and fluids of the body.

High School Subjects
Biology
Chemistry

Personal Skills
Helping/teaching
Technical/scientific

Salary Range
$157,061 to $193,681 to $230,950+

Educational Requirements
Medical degree and a four- to five-year residency

Certification or Licensing
Recommended (certification)
Required by all states (licensing)

Outlook
About as fast as the average

DOT
070

GOE
14.02.01

NOC
3112

O*NET-SOC
29-1069.99

What Does a Pathologist Do?

Pathologists provide information that helps physicians care for patients. When a patient has a tumor, an infection, or symptoms of a disease, a pathologist examines tissues from the patient to determine the nature of the patient's condition. Without this knowledge, a physician would not be able to make an accurate diagnosis and design the appropriate treatment. Because many health conditions first manifest themselves at the cellular level, pathologists are often able to identify conditions before they turn into serious health problems.

Many people associate pathologists only with performing autopsies. In fact, while pathologists do perform autopsies, much more of their work involves working with living patients. Pathologists in hospital laboratories examine the blood, urine, bone marrow, stools, and tumors of patients. Using a variety of techniques, pathologists locate the causes of infections and determine the nature of unusual growths. Pathologists consult with a patient's physician to determine the best course of treatment. They may also talk with patients about their conditions. In a sense, the work of pathologists is much like detective work. It is often through the efforts of pathologists that health conditions are recognized and properly treated.

There are two main divisions of pathology—anatomic pathology (AP) and clinical pathology (CP)—and numerous subspecialty areas. A pathologist may choose to work either in AP or CP, or in both divisions. Anatomic pathology covers three major areas: surgical pathology, cytology, and autopsies. Clinical pathology covers several areas, including toxicology and immunology.

Surgical pathology is concerned with biopsies and the examination of tissues removed from patients. Pathologists examine tumors, for example, to determine if they are malignant (cancerous) or benign (noncancerous). After a surgeon removes a malignant tumor, a pathologist examines it to make sure that the surgeon has not left any of the tumor in the patient's body where it can continue to grow. Pathologists often examine samples of a patient's tissue while the patient is undergoing surgery. The tissue samples, called frozen sections, are prepared for analysis by freezing them with liquid nitrogen. After examining the frozen section, the pathologist immediately recommends to the surgical team the proper course of action for treating the patient, such as the removal of an organ or other body part. For example, after examining tissue from a lump in a patient's breast and discovering a malignancy, a pathologist informs the surgical team that either a lumpectomy (removal of the lump) or a mastectomy (removal of the entire breast) is necessary.

Cytopathology deals with individual cells rather than with larger sections of body tissue. Pathologists working in this area commonly use a technique called fine needle aspiration (FNA) to collect cells from patients. Using this technique, the pathologist aspirates, or collects, a sample of tissue with a thin needle; the cells of the tissue are then analyzed under a microscope. Fine needle aspiration makes it possible to identify the nature of a condition without a surgical procedure.

Pathologists perform autopsies to determine a cause of death. Many people associate autopsies with forensic science, in which pathologists work with law enforcement officials to help solve homicide cases. But the primary purpose of autopsies is to provide greater understanding of diseases. Performing an autopsy enables a pathologist to determine if a physician's diagnosis and treatment were correct. During an autopsy, a pathologist may discover new information that can aid in diagnosing and treating other patients. For example, a patient's family may discover through an autopsy that there is a genetic disorder present than can affect other living family members.

Clinical pathology deals with testing body fluids. *Clinical pathologists* use various laboratory tests to analyze these fluids. There are a number of different specialties within clinical pathology. Toxicology deals with the levels of drugs and toxic chemicals in the body. Clinical chemistry focuses on the levels of such necessary substances as sodium and potassium in the blood and other body fluids. Clinical microbiology concerns bacteria, fungi, and viruses that cause illnesses.

One of the main duties of some clinical pathologists is to make sure that hospitals maintain blood supplies that are free of harmful microorganisms. In most hospitals, the pathologist in charge of the blood bank functions as an *immunohematologist.* This person is in charge of procuring and processing blood and blood products. Clinical immunology deals with the patient's immune system and such diseases as AIDS. Hematopathology focuses on diseases of the blood, such as hemophilia, anemia, and leukemia.

Lingo to Learn

Autopsy, or **post-mortem examination** The inspection and dissection of a dead body to determine the cause of death.

Benign Noncancerous; used in reference to tumors.

Cytology The study of the structure, function, and formation of cells.

Fine needle aspiration A technique in which a thin needle is used to collect cells from a patient; the cells are then examined under a microscope.

Forensic A term denoting a relationship to legal matters and courts of law. Forensic medicine and forensic pathology apply medical knowledge to civil and criminal law.

Frozen section A technique, involving liquid nitrogen, for rapidly preparing tissue specimens for microscopic examination. The term is also used to refer to the specimens themselves.

Lesion Any abnormal change in the structure of a body part.

Malignant Cancerous; used in reference to tumors.

Tumor, or **neoplasm** An abnormal growth or swelling in any part of the body.

What Is It Like to Be a Pathologist?

Dr. David Cheng is a pathologist in a private group practice in Indiana. He and his business partners perform pathological services for health care clinics and hospitals.

"It's a great career," he relates enthusiastically. "I really love my job. I honestly didn't know about pathology before I went to medical school," David admits. "My introduction came in my first year. All medical students have to take pathology courses in their first and second years, and I guess I was amazed by the knowledge that a pathologist has to have."

"Everyone associates pathologists with autopsies," David comments. "However, this profession involves more work with live human beings than dead ones." He goes on to say, "Yeah, I perform autopsies, but the bulk of my work is done in the lab making diagnoses to help the living."

Although there is not much direct patient contact, pathologists do have a lot of contact with physicians and clinical staff. "We may not deal with the patient directly," says David, "but we are definitely involved with the care of almost every patient in a hospital."

David typically begins his work day at 8:00 A.M. "The first few hours I do clinical pathology work. I might review some lab results from the previous day as a quality control measure. I always want to be sure everything is correct." He also segments tissue and makes frozen sections to examine later. "In the afternoon," says David, "I might test fine needle aspirations or do bone marrow biopsies. I'll also process specimens and prepare tissue samples to look at the next day."

"While I'm working, I'm also dictating what I see," he says. "It's very important that our observations are precisely documented. Then of course," he adds, "there is always the paperwork involved with any medical practice." David says he works about 55 to 60 hours a week. "When you have your own group practice, you have to think about the business aspect as well. We contract with physicians or health care facilities, so we have to market our business. We have to keep the clients we have as well as try to get new ones. With the way the medical industry is always in a flux, it is a constant struggle."

"But, I love my job," he relates. "Physicians depend heavily on our diagnoses. It is rewarding to take a challenging case and figure out the disease. Sometimes it is not at all what the doctor expected. Plus," adds David, "the satisfaction is that our analysis is almost always the final word. We are the final authority."

The satisfaction is that our analysis is almost always the final word. We are the final authority.

Do I Have I What It Takes to Be a Pathologist?

David says, "If you are thinking of entering this field, you should love science more than any other specialty." You must be very detail oriented and have strong concentration skills. "The nature of this work requires a lot of attention to detail," notes David. "We get down to the micro-detail." David says an inquisitive mind is also important. "You need to assess what a test means. You need to be able to figure out the puzzles; sometimes the diagnosis is not obvious."

Because the accuracy of your work can affect a patient's life, you must be very precise and you must be a perfectionist. There is no room for error. You must be confident and self-assured and expect only the best of yourself.

You must be able to work independently as well as with others. You need good communication skills,

To Be a Successful Pathologist, You Should . . .

- have an eye for detail
- be able to concentrate intently on your work
- be able to work well with others
- have strong communication skills
- be able to accept a great deal of responsibility and perform well under pressure
- be patient, thorough, and confident in your decisions

since you will often need to interact with other professionals as well as with patients and the public.

You need to be a lifelong learner and be committed to keeping abreast of all the new medical studies and technologies that affect your profession. You should also feel comfortable working with body fluids, tissues, and other potentially unpleasant aspects of health care.

How Do I Become a Pathologist?

Like any medical specialist, a pathologist must complete a medical school program before attending a residency program. You will then need four to five years of accredited residency training to prepare for a career in pathology. Admission to premedical and medical school programs is highly competitive. Prospective pathologists should begin preparing for this career while still in high school.

EDUCATION

High School

If you are interested in pursuing a medical degree, a high school education emphasizing college preparatory classes is a must. Science courses such as biology, chemistry, and physics are necessary, as are math courses. These classes will not only provide you with an introduction to basic science and math concepts, but also allow you to determine your own aptitude in these areas. Especially important are any courses emphasizing laboratory work. Since college will be your next educational step, it is also important to take English courses to develop your researching and writing skills. Foreign language and social science classes will also help make you an appealing candidate for college admission as well as prepare you for your future undergraduate and graduate education. Courses in computer science are a must as well.

If you are certain you wish to pursue a medical career, you may want to consider entering a college or university that is associated with a medical school and offers an accelerated medical education program. In these accelerated programs, you spend either two or three years completing your undergraduate work and then spend four years at the medical school associated with that college or university. In accelerated programs, you have the advantage of finishing medical school before your peers who take the normal educational route. More information on such programs is available from high school guidance counselors. Students considering this option should look into it in their junior or early senior years.

Postsecondary Training

Following high school, the next step on your educational path to be a pathologist is to earn a bachelor's degree from an accredited four-year college or university. Suggested premedical courses include physics, biology, and organic and inorganic chemistry. Courses in English, mathematics, and the social sciences are also highly recommended. Most colleges offer premedical degree programs that prepare students for entry into medical school. Majoring as a premed is not mandatory, however. If you are pursuing other majors you can enter medical school as long as you fulfill certain basic requirements.

After receiving an undergraduate degree, you need to apply to, and be accepted by, a medical school. Admission is competitive, and applicants must undergo a fairly extensive and difficult admissions process that takes into consideration grade point averages, scores on the Medical College Admission Test (MCAT), and professor recommendations. Most students apply to several schools early in their senior year of college. Only about one-third of the applicants are accepted.

In order to earn the degree doctor of medicine (M.D.), you must complete four years of medical school study and training. For the first two years of medical school, you attend lectures and classes and spend time in laboratories. Courses include anatomy, biochemistry, physiology, pharmacology, psychology, microbiology, pathology, medical ethics, and laws governing medicine. You learn to take patient histories, perform routine physical examinations, and recognize symptoms.

In your third and fourth years, you are involved in more practical studies. You work in clinics and hospitals supervised by residents and physicians and you learn acute, chronic, preventive, and rehabilitative care. You go through rotations (brief periods of study) in such areas as internal medicine, obstetrics and gynecology, pediatrics, and surgery. Rotations allow you to gain exposure to many different medical fields.

Upon graduating from an accredited medical school, you must pass a standard examination given by the National Board of Medical Examiners. Most physicians complete an internship, also referred to as a transition year, during which they decide their area of specialization.

Following your internship, you begin a residency, which is graduate medical education in a specialty. If you wish to become a pathologist, you will need four to five years of accredited residency training depending on the certification you desire. During this training, you will become familiar with all of the activities of a pathology department.

CERTIFICATION OR LICENSING

Licensing is mandatory in the United States. It is required in all states before any doctor can practice medicine. In order to be licensed, doctors must have graduated from medical school, passed the licensing test of the state in which they will practice, and completed their residency. Physicians licensed in one state can usually become licensed to practice in another state without further testing, however, some states may limit reciprocity.

The American Board of Pathology is the governing board for pathologist certification. To become certified, the candidate must be a medical school graduate and be licensed to practice medicine in the United States or Canada. Primary certification includes combined anatomic pathology (AP) and clinical pathology (CP), anatomic pathology only, and clinical pathology only. The combined AP/CP certification requires four full years of full-time approved training, plus an additional 12 months of training. The AP or CP certifications alone require three full years of full-time approved training, plus an additional 12 months of training. Subspecialty certifications require additional training in the specialty area.

SCHOLARSHIPS AND GRANTS

There are usually grants, scholarships, and loans available through most colleges. The easiest way to explore the various financial aid possibilities is to write directly to the financial aid offices of schools and request information and application forms.

There are also various loan programs available through the federal government, including Pell Grants, Stafford Student Loans, National Direct Student Loans, Health Education Assistance Loans, and Health Professions Student Loans. Your high school guidance counselor should have information about these programs.

In-depth

Pathology Specializations

Many pathologists, especially those working in university or medical school hospitals, choose to specialize in specific areas of pathology. Specialties include the following:

Cardiovascular pathology: Heart and blood vessels
Cytopathology: Cells
Dermatopathology: Skin
Environmental pathology: Disease caused by environmental factors
Gastrointestinal pathology: Stomach and digestive tract
Gynecologic/obstetrical pathology: Female reproductive system and childbirth
Hematopathology: Blood
Immunopathology: Immune system
Neuropathology: Nervous system
Ophthalmic pathology: Eyes
Pediatric pathology: Children
Pulmonary pathology: Lungs
Renal pathology: Kidneys

Many students finance their education through the Armed Forces Health Professions Scholarship Program. Each branch of the military participates in this program, paying students' tuitions in exchange for military service. Contact your local recruiting office for more information on this program.

The National Health Service Corps Scholarship Program also provides money for students in return for their later service. Visit its Web site at http://nhsc.bhpr.hrsa.gov.

Who Will Hire Me?

About 75 percent of pathologists work in community hospitals directing the activities of pathology laboratories. Most pathologists working in hospitals are responsible for the blood bank supplies. Many also perform laboratory services for physicians and medical clinics affiliated with the hospitals. In most hospitals, pathologists work in a group, sharing various duties. They may, however, specialize in different areas of clinical pathology.

You will probably find that medical schools and university hospitals will offer you the best opportunities for specialization. If you are a pathologist in these settings you may also have opportunities to become actively involved in teaching pathology to medical students.

As health care moves toward more outpatient and ambulatory care services, there will be increasing opportunities to work in clinics, group practices, and your own private practice. Many independent laboratories require pathologists. A relatively small number of pathologists work for local, state, and federal governments as forensic pathologists assisting law enforcement agencies. The military services and government agencies, such as the National Institutes of Health and the Food and Drug Administration, also employ pathologists.

FYI

The following pathologists have been awarded Nobel Prizes for their work.

Karl Landsteine discovered A, B, and O blood groups.

George Whipple recognized that liver contained a substance necessary to prevent pernicious anemia.

Thomas Weller developed methods for the growth of the polio virus in tissue culture.

Peyton Rous discovered that viruses can induce cancerous tumors.

Baruj Benacerraf identified genetically determined structures on the cell surface that regulate immunological reactions.

Source: American Society for Investigative Pathology

Where Can I Go from Here?

After gaining enough experience, you may become director of a hospital pathology laboratory. With even more experience, you may advance to serving in a hospital's administration. A pathologist working in an academic capacity may advance to direct a medical school's pathology program. Some pathologists open independent pathology laboratories or join with other physicians to form private group practices.

Because pathologists have broad medical perspectives, they often serve in leadership positions in medical schools, professional societies, and research organizations.

What Are the Salary Ranges?

Pathologists earned a median annual salary of $193,681 in June 2004, according to Salary.com. Salaries ranged from less than $157,061 to $230,950 or more. Several factors influence earnings, including years of experience, geographic region of practice, and reputation.

What Is the Job Outlook?

According to the U.S. Department of Labor, the employment of physicians is expected to about as fast as the average over the next 10 years. The outlook for careers in pathology is very good. New medical tests are constantly being developed and refined, making it possible to detect an increasing number of diseases in their early stages. The medical community depends on pathologists to analyze results from these tests. Another factor favorably affecting the demand for pathologists is the shifting of health care to cost-conscious managed care services. Testing for, diagnosing, and treating a disease or other health condition in its early stages is much less expensive than treating a health condition in its advanced stages.

How Do I Learn More?

PROFESSIONAL ORGANIZATIONS

The following are organizations provide information on pathology careers, accredited schools, and employers:

American Board of Pathology
PO Box 25915
Tampa, FL 33622
813-286-2444
http://www.abpath.org

College of American Pathologists
325 Waukegan Road
Northfield, IL 60093
800-323-4040
http://www.cap.org

Intersociety Council for Pathology Information
9650 Rockville Pike
Bethesda, MD 20814-3993
301-634-7200
icpi@asip.org
http://www.pathologytraining.org

United States and Canadian Academy of Pathology
3643 Walton Way Extension
Augusta, GA 30909
706-733-7550
iap@uscap.org
http://www.uscap.org

BIBLIOGRAPHY

The following is a sampling of materials relating to the professional concerns and development of pathologists:

Benson, Ellis S., Barbara F. Atkinson, and Martin Flax. *Career Guide in Pathology.* Chicago: American Society of Clinical Pathologists, 1998.

Chandrasoma, Parakrama, and Clive R. Taylor. *Concise Pathology.* 3d ed. New York: McGraw-Hill, 1997.

Kumar, Vinay, Razmi Cotran, Stanley L. Robbins, and James A. Perkins. *Basic Pathology.* 7th ed. Philadelphia: W. B. Saunders Company, 2002.

MacFarlane, Peter S., Robin Reid, and Robin Callandar. *Pathology Illustrated.* 5th ed. New York: Churchill Livingstone, 2000.

Parums, Dinah V., ed. *Essential Clinical Pathology.* Boston: Blackwell Science, 1996.

Sinard, John H. *Outlines in Pathology.* Philadelphia: W. B. Saunders Company, 1996.

Sternberg, Stephen S., and Donald A. Antonioli. *Diagnostic Surgical Pathology.* 3d ed. Philadelphia: Lippincott Williams & Wilkins, 1999.

PEDIATRICIANS

Watery-eyed and flushed, five-year-old Benjamin is sitting on his mother's lap as Dr. David Esary walks into the examining room.

"How are you, Ben?" David asks, sitting down and opening his file. "Are you a sickie today?"

Ben stirs slightly on his mother's lap. "I don't feel good," he says. "My brain hurts."

David smiles and rolls his stool closer. "How long has he been running a fever?" he asks the little boy's mother.

"The fever just started last night," she responds, "but he's had a cough and a runny nose for about three days."

"He may have an infection," David says, making a quick note on the chart. Holding out a hand to Ben, he asks, "Can you stand up for me just a minute, guy? I want to take a peep in your ears and see if any birds have nested in there." Ben giggles and David proceeds with the exam.

Definition
Pediatricians plan and carry out medical care for children, from birth through adolescence.

Alternative Job Title
Children's doctors

High School Subjects
Biology
Chemistry

Personal Skills
Helping/teaching
Technical/scientific

Salary Range
$77,000 to $134,170 to $180,000+

Educational Requirements
High school diploma; bachelor's degree in premedical studies; M.D. degree; three-year residency

Certification or Licensing
Required by all states

Outlook
About as fast as the average

DOT
070

GOE
14.02.01

NOC
3112

O*NET-SOC
29-1065.00

What Does a Pediatrician Do?

Infancy and childhood are the most critical periods of life in a person's development; the body is growing rapidly, and motor, speech, and cognitive skills are evolving. Thorough health care during this time of growth and development is extremely important. An infant or child who doesn't get proper nourishment or medical treatment may face a lifetime of health problems. Likewise, a child who doesn't receive all the necessary immunizations against childhood diseases risks permanent damage, or even death.

Pediatricians are physicians who provide health care to infants, children, and adolescents. Typically, a pediatrician meets a new patient soon after birth and takes care of that patient through his or her teenage years.

A significant part of a pediatrician's job is preventive medicine—what is sometimes called well care. This involves periodically seeing a patient for routine health checkups. During these checkups, the doctor physically examines the child to make sure he or she is growing at a normal rate and to look for symptoms of illness. The physical examination includes testing reflexes, listening to the heart and lungs, checking eyes and ears, and measuring height and weight.

During the checkup, the pediatrician also assesses the child's mental and behavioral development. This is done both by observing the child's behavior and by asking the parents questions about their child's abilities.

Immunizing children against certain childhood diseases is another important part of preventive medicine. Pediatricians administer routine immunizations for such diseases as rubella, polio, and smallpox as children reach certain ages. Yet another part of preventive medicine is family education. Pediatricians counsel and advise parents on the care and treatment of their children. They provide information on such parental concerns as safety, diet, and hygiene.

In addition to practicing preventive medicine, pediatricians treat sick infants and children. When a sick or injured patient is brought into the office, the doctor examines him or her, makes a diagnosis, and orders treatment. Common ailments include ear infections, allergies, feeding difficulties, viral illnesses, respiratory illnesses, and gastrointestinal upsets. For these and other illnesses, pediatricians prescribe and administer treatments and medications.

If a child is seriously ill or hurt, a pediatrician arranges for hospital admission and follows up on the child's progress during the hospitalization. In some cases, a child may have a serious condition, such as cancer, cystic fibrosis, or hemophilia, that requires the attention of a specialist. In these cases, the pediatrician, as the primary care physician, will refer the child to the appropriate specialist.

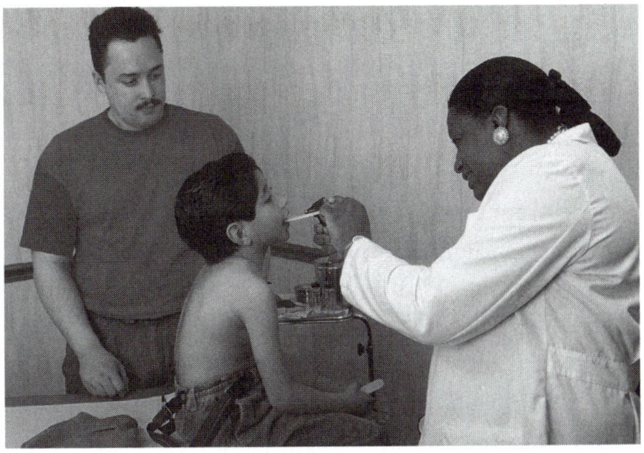

A pediatrician examines a boy's throat while his father looks on. *(Blair Seitz / Photo Researchers Inc.)*

Lingo to Learn

Acute Having a sudden onset, sharp rise, and short course.

Chronic Marked by long duration or frequent recurrence. A chronic illness may become more serious over time.

Health maintenance organization (HMO) A health care organization that is financed by fixed periodic payments. An HMO has member physicians that sometimes refer patients to outside specialists.

Managed care A system of providing health care through a program that is designed to control costs. HMOs and PPOs provide managed care.

Preferred provider organization (PPO) A health care organization that provides economic incentives for people to use certain physicians and hospitals. These physicians and hospitals agree to supervision and reduced fees.

Preventive medicine A branch of medical science emphasizing methods of preventing disease. It is sometimes called well care.

Vaccine A preparation of killed or disabled microorganisms that is administered to produce or increase immunity to a particular disease.

Some pediatric patients may be suffering from emotional or behavioral disorders or from substance abuse. Other patients may be affected by problems within their families, such as unemployment, alcoholism, or physical abuse. In these cases, pediatricians may make referrals to such health professionals as psychiatrists, psychologists, and social workers.

Pediatricians that are in general practice usually work alone or in partnership with other physicians. Their average workweek is 50 to 60 hours, most of which is spent seeing patients in their offices. They also make hospital rounds to visit any of their patients who have been admitted for treatment or to check on newborn patients and their mothers. Pediatricians spend some time on call, taking care of patients who have emergencies. A pediatrician might be called to attend the delivery of a baby, to meet an injured patient in the emergency room, or simply to answer a parent's question about a sick child.

Some pediatricians choose to pursue pediatric subspecialties, such as the treatment of children who have heart disorders, kidney disorders, or cancer. Subspecialization requires a longer residency training than does general practice. A pediatrician practicing a subspecialty typically spends a much greater proportion of his or her time in a hospital or medical center than does a general practice pediatrician. Subspecialization permits pediatricians to be involved in research activities.

What Is It Like to Be a Pediatrician?

A fish tank covers most of one wall. Toys are scattered on the floor and chairs. At a low table in the corner, two toddlers are playing with busy beads, while a five-year-old child painstakingly sounds out words in a Dr. Seuss book. It may sound like a preschool, but it's actually Dr. David Esary's waiting room. The examination rooms, where David takes care of his young patients, are through a set of double doors and down a short hallway.

Although he spends the great majority of his time in the office, David's day always begins with a visit to the hospital. "I usually start out at 7:30 at the hospital, making rounds," he says. "I usually have a few newborns to see and maybe some sick kids in the pediatric ward."

Around 8:30, he returns to his office to see the morning's scheduled patients. On a typical day, he sees anywhere from 15 to 25 patients in the morning, and another 15 to 25 in the afternoon. "I try to have eight to 10 appointments each half day be checkups, and the rest be sick visits," he says. "Sick visits take much less time, because you can just concentrate on what the problem is."

The problem may be anything from recurring difficulties with asthma to an ear infection to a small hole in the heart. David treats anything that falls under the category of general pediatric care. He refers more severe disorders to specialists.

Checkups take up a large part of David's time. These are routine physical examinations that are usually scheduled for certain ages in a child's life. Newborns, for example, are typically scheduled for a visit to David every three months. After a child's first year, checkups are generally less frequent.

A total checkup is a head-to-toe examination. David says, "I check the eyes, ears, nose, and throat, check movement of the extremities, palpate the abdomen, check for hernias, check genitals, and make sure that everything is generally okay neurologically. Plus, I take a little time to play. I also take a developmental history and talk with the parents about habits, appetite, diet, elimination, and any concerns they might have."

Family education is an important element of checkups. "During checkups, I spend a lot of time talking with the parents about things to avoid, proper diet, the importance of immunizations, the risk of poisoning and accidents—that sort of thing," David says.

In addition to treating his existing patient base, David is sometimes called upon to attend the delivery of a new patient, particularly if the baby may be at risk. "If there's a chance that the baby will need immediate care, I'll get called into the delivery," he says. "If, for example, the baby's heart rate drops during labor or if there are other complications." He shares the responsibility of being on call for such emergencies with six other pediatricians, which means that he does a 24-hour on-call shift about four times each month.

While on call, he may be summoned to the emergency room to help attend a sick or injured child. He may take phone calls and answer questions from parents who need to know what to do with a child who is ill or hurt.

Because David practices alone rather than in a physician's group, clinic, or hospital, he serves as his own business manager. This involves overseeing the office finances and supervising his six-person staff. Billing, insurance, and inventory are handled by staff members, as is patient checkin and checkout.

Do I Have I What It Takes to Be a Pediatrician?

What personal quality is most important for pediatricians? "You have to like kids, obviously," David says, laughing. "That's what makes the whole career so great. They're so funny and so much fun."

You have to like kids, obviously. That's what makes the whole career so great. They're so funny and so much fun.

Treating children can be much different than treating adults. Children, especially very young ones, can't verbalize what is wrong with them. They can't control emotions, such as fear and anger, as well as most adults can. Therefore, it takes much patience and understanding to work effectively with them.

"Most kids don't want you to do whatever it is you're trying to do to them, so you can't be too easily frustrated," David says. "You also have to be fairly calm. Someone who's loud and aggressive might do well in another field, but that person would probably scare a child."

It is also important that pediatricians be willing to keep up with newly emerging technologies and medical advances. "I think you have to be a little bit obsessive-compulsive," says David. "You have to keep up on the latest information by attending conferences and reading the literature as much as you can."

Pediatricians need a great deal of commitment in order to cope with the negative aspects of the job. For example, they may be under considerable stress, both during their years of training and in their careers. They work long, irregular hours and often face interruptions to their personal lives. In addition, they must be able to handle very depressing situations. "The downside is the occasional sick child that you lose," says David. "Even though some of the cancers are very curable now, telling a family that a child has leukemia is very hard."

Despite the long hours, the stress, and the occasional loss, pediatrics is a very rewarding career. It is gratifying for a physician to know that he or she has helped a child get well, and it is enjoyable to watch patients grow and develop.

In-depth

An Ounce of Prevention

Some of the most significant breakthroughs in children's health care have been in disease prevention. Perhaps the most well-known method of prevention is the use of vaccines.

The first vaccine was developed in 1796 by Edward Jenner, an English physician. At that time, the viral disease smallpox disfigured and killed thousands of people each year. Jenner noticed that people who had developed a similar but less severe disease, called cowpox, never developed smallpox, even when exposed to it.

Curious about this, Jenner took material from a cowpox sore and scratched it into the arm of a healthy eight-year-old boy. The boy, as expected, developed cowpox. Jenner then scratched material from a smallpox sore into the boy's arm, but the boy did not develop smallpox.

Jenner named the material from the cowpox sore "vaccine," and the process in which he used it "vaccination." Both words are from the Latin *vaccinus*, meaning "of or from cows." The use of the vaccine spread quickly, and within 200 years smallpox had been eliminated from the world.

Vaccines are now available for a wide variety of diseases. Thanks to Jenner's pioneering work, many childhood diseases that once posed serious threats are virtually unheard of.

How Do I Become a Pediatrician?

David knew he wanted to be a doctor when he was in the seventh grade. He didn't, however, plan to be a pediatrician. "I went from the seventh grade all the way through high school and college, and then through my first two years of med school, planning to be an ophthalmologist," he says. He changed his mind in his junior year of medical school when he started doing rotations (specified periods of time in various hospital departments). "Just by coincidence, all the rotations I took were oriented towards kids," David says. "I enjoyed it too much. So, I decided to pursue pediatrics instead of ophthalmology."

EDUCATION

High School

While in high school, take college prep classes, with a heavy emphasis on science and math. Biology, chemistry, physics, and physiology are important science classes. Any advanced math courses are also excellent choices.

Classes in English, foreign languages, and speech will enhance communication skills, which are vital to being a successful physician. Such social sciences as psychology and sociology, which increase your understanding of others, are also beneficial.

In addition to carefully selecting classes, there are other ways you can prepare for medical school and a career in pediatrics. Participation in science clubs, for example, will allow for in-depth explorations of some areas of science. Volunteer work at hospitals or other health care institutions will allow you to see many aspects of medical care. Such volunteer work can also provide a taste of what a physician's career entails, and help you decide if you are suited for it.

Postsecondary Training

After high school, you must attend a four-year college and complete a bachelor's degree in premedical studies. Required undergraduate courses include physics, biology, and organic and inorganic chemistry. Some classes in English, mathematics, social sciences, and the humanities are also required. Medical schools are very selective, so a good grade point average is a must.

In the final year of college, you should apply to medical schools. Applicants must submit transcripts of their premedical studies, letters of recommendation, and scores from the Medical College Admission Test (MCAT). In addition, you typically have an interview with an admissions officer, who evaluates your character, personality, and leadership qualities.

Your first two years of medical school are spent in classrooms and laboratories. Such courses as anatomy, biochemistry, histology (the study of tissues), pathology, physiology, pharmacology, psychology, medical ethics, and medical law make up the standard curriculum. You also learn to take medical histories of patients and to examine patients for symptoms of various diseases.

During the third and fourth years of medical school, you work in hospitals and clinics, under the supervision of experienced physicians. You do rotations in different departments to learn various aspects of medicine. Rotations may include family practice, obstetrics and gynecology, pediatrics, internal medicine, psychiatry, and surgery.

Once you have successfully completed four years of medical school, you take the medical boards. Upon passing the boards, you are granted a medical degree.

In order to become a pediatrician, you must complete a three-year residency program in a hospital. The pediatric residency provides extensive experience in ambulatory pediatrics, the care of infants and children who are not bedridden. Residents also spend time working in various specialized pediatric units, including neonatology, adolescent medicine, child development, psychology, special care, intensive care, and outpatients.

CERTIFICATION OR LICENSING

All physicians must be licensed by their state in order to practice medicine legally. Certification by the American Board of Pediatrics is recommended. A certificate in general pediatrics is awarded after three years of residency training and the successful completion of a two-day comprehensive written examination. A pediatrician who specializes in cardiology, infectious diseases, or other area must complete an additional three-year residency in the subspeciality before taking the certification examination. To remain board-certified, pediatricians must pass an examination every seven years.

SCHOLARSHIPS AND GRANTS

Most medical schools offer scholarships to qualified students. Students should check with the financial aid offices of the schools they are considering to learn what assistance might be available.

There are several organizations offering scholarships and loans to medical students. A good place to look for information on these organizations is a local library, where reference librarians may be able to provide a list of available assistance programs. The Internet is also an invaluable resource for financial aid and scholarship information.

Another option is to contact the National Association of Student Financial Aid Administrators (NASFAA) for a list of possibilities. It can be reached at the following address and Web site.

NASFAA
1129 20th Street, NW, Suite 400
Washington, DC 20036-3453
202-785-0453
http://www.nasfaa.org

Finally, there are some not-for-profit lenders who offer loans targeted at medical students. The following is a list of some of the most popular programs. They may be contacted directly for information.

MEDFUNDS
10515 Carnegie Avenue
Cleveland, OH 44160
800-665-1016
http://www.medfunds.com

Nellie Mae-MedDent
EXCEL Program
50 Braintree Hill Park, Suite 300
Braintree, MA 02184
800-634-9308
http://www.nelliemae.org

The Education Resource Institute, Professional Education Program
PO Box 312
Boston, MA 02117
800-255-8374
http://www.teri.org

Who Will Hire Me?

David Esary found a job during the second year of his residency. "A friend mentioned that she'd seen a letter from a multispecialty clinic saying it needed a pediatrician," he says. "So I contacted them, and we agreed that I would start as soon as I wrapped up my residency." While it's uncommon to win a position so early in one's residency, most pediatricians do not have trouble finding work.

The majority of pediatricians are involved in direct patient care. Of these, about one-third have private practices. The others work in group practices, community clinics, hospitals, university-affiliated medical centers, and health maintenance organizations. Only about 10 percent of pediatricians work in administration, teaching, or research.

For the pediatrician who plans to set up a private practice, it is wise to consult with his or her medical school placement office to find a suitable geographic location in which to do so. Certain locations, such as rural areas and small towns, offer less competition for patients and, therefore, better chances of success.

Many newly licensed pediatricians take salaried jobs until they can pay off some of their medical school debt, which is likely to total more than $50,000. Medical school placement offices should be able to recommend hospitals, clinics, HMOs, and group practices that are hiring pediatricians.

There are some professional organizations of pediatricians that offer job placement and recruitment services for their members. Both the American Academy of Pediatrics and the Ambulatory Pediatric Association offer such services. (See "How Do I Learn More?")

If a pediatrician has a specific location in mind, such as his or her home town, it might be wise to approach potential employers directly.

FYI

Pediatrics became a separate medical specialty during the 19th century. The first pediatric clinic in the United States opened in New York City in 1862. About that same time, several children's hospitals opened in Europe.

Where Can I Go from Here?

The most common method of advancement for pediatricians is subspecialization. There are several subspecialties open to the pediatrician who is willing to spend the additional time training for one. A subspecialty requires three to four more years of residency training.

For a while, David considered entering the subspecialization of neonatology, the care of sick newborns. But he ultimately decided against it. "The problem with neonatology is that once you cure the babies and get them healthy, they go home and you never see them again," he says. "I like general practice because you get to watch the kids grow up."

Some of the other subspecialties a pediatrician might train for include adolescent medicine, pediatric cardiology (care of children with heart disease), pediatric critical care (care of children requiring advanced life support), pediatric endocrinology (care of children with diabetes and other glandular disorders), pediatric neurology (care of children with nervous system disorders), and pediatric hematology/oncology (care of children with blood disorders and cancer).

Some pediatricians pursue careers in research. Possible research activities include developing new vaccines for infections, developing treatments for children with heart disease, and developing treatments for infants born with severe abnormalities.

Another way for pediatricians to advance is to move into the field of education, where they can teach medical students and resident physicians about particular areas of pediatrics.

What Are the Salary Ranges?

Pediatricians, while at the low end of the earning scale for physicians, still have among the highest earnings of any occupation in the United States. The U.S. Department of Labor reports that pediatricians made a median annual salary of $134,170 in 2003. Earnings ranged from less than $77,000 to more than $180,000 for pediatric specialists with many years of experience. The earnings of pediatricians are partly dependent upon the types of practices they choose. Those who are self-employed tend to earn more than those who are salaried. Geographic region, hours worked, number of years in practice, professional reputation, and personality are other factors that can impact a pediatrician's income.

Yet another factor impacting earnings is how much of a pediatrician's revenue comes from patients who are enrolled in managed care plans. Under these plans, insurance companies sometimes reimburse physicians at a relatively low rate.

What Is the Job Outlook?

According to the U.S. Department of Labor, employment of all physicians is expected to grow about as fast as the average for all occupations. The employment prospects for pediatricians—along with other general practitioners, such as family physicians—are especially good. This is because of the increasing use of managed care plans. Pediatricians, under these plans, are considered to be primary-care providers rather than specialists. Since the use of specialists is limited under these plans, however, there may be a decreased need for those pediatricians who choose to pursue subspecialties.

Another factor that may influence a pediatrician's employment prospects is location. Employment possibilities will probably be the best in rural regions and small towns. Some of the larger metropolitan areas, are already well supplied with pediatricians, thus they may offer fewer chances for establishing practices.

To Be a Successful Pediatrician, You Should . . .

- like children and adolescents
- have patience, compassion, and a good sense of humor
- be willing to continually learn
- have a desire to help others
- be able to withstand stress and make sound decisions

How Do I Learn More?

PROFESSIONAL ORGANIZATIONS

The following are organizations that provide information on pediatric careers, accredited schools, and employers:

Ambulatory Pediatric Association
6728 Old McLean Drive
McLean, VA 22101
703-556-9222
info@ambpeds.org
http://www.ambpeds.org

American Academy of Pediatrics
141 Northwest Point Boulevard
Elk Grove Village, IL 60007
847-434-4000
http://www.aap.org

American Medical Association
515 North State Street
Chicago, IL 60610
800-621-8335
http://www.ama-assn.org

American Pediatric Society & Society for Pediatric Research
3400 Research Forest Drive, Suite B-7
The Woodlands, TX 77381
281-419-0052
http://www.aps-spr.org

BIBLIOGRAPHY

The following is a sampling of materials relating to the professional concerns and development of pediatricians:

Behrman, Richard E., ed. *Nelson Textbook of Pediatrics.* 17th ed. Philadelphia: W. B. Saunders, 2004.

Behrman, Richard E., and Robert Kliegman. *Nelson Essentials of Pediatrics.* 4th ed. Philadelphia: W. B. Saunders, 2002.

Hay, William W., Anthony R. Hayward, Myron J. Levin, Judith M. Sondheimer, eds. *Current Pediatric Diagnosis and Treatment.* 16th ed. New York: McGraw-Hill/Appleton & Lange, 2002.

McCarthy, Claire. *Learning How the Heart Beats: The Making of a Pediatrician.* New York: Viking Penguin, 1997.

Milner, Anthony D., and David Hull. *Hospital Pediatrics.* 3d ed. New York: Churchill Livingstone, 1998.

Zitelli, Basil J., and Holly W. Davis, eds. *Atlas of Pediatric Physical Diagnosis.* 4th ed. St. Louis, Mo.: Mosby-Year Book, 2002.

PEDORTHISTS

A deafening roar pours through the stadium. Nearly 7 feet tall, the pro basketball player lopes down the court and moves into position. It's a routine setup. But suddenly he's on the floor, his long body jackknifed in pain, his hands reaching down to grasp one foot. "I think I pulled something," he gasps as a trainer quickly appears at his side. "My arch. . . ." His teammates hover close by and exchange worried glances. Will he be able to get up and play? Will this put him out of commission? For how long?

Watching the game is Ron, a certified pedorthist who works in a nearby sports medical facility. He can't tell how serious the problem is, but he bets this player is on the way to see a doctor. Maybe surgery will be needed. Maybe rehab after that. If footwear can help in any part of the player's recovery, Ron hopes the player comes to see him.

Definition
Pedorthists design, manufacture, fit, and modify footwear aimed at lessening pain or correcting foot problems.

Alternative Job Titles
C.Ped (certified pedorthist)

High School Subjects
Biology
Technical/shop

Personal Skills
Helping/teaching
Mechanical/manipulative

Salary Range
$20,000 to $50,000 to $70,000

Educational Requirements
High school diploma or equivalent plus some postsecondary training

Certification or Licensing
Recommended

Outlook
Faster than the average

DOT
N/A

GOE
N/A

NOC
N/A

O*NET-SOC
N/A

What Does a Pedorthist Do?

A lot of things can go wrong with feet. Some common problems include bunions, claw toes or hammertoes, fallen arches, swelling from arthritis, and ulcers from diabetes. When a doctor examines your feet and decides special shoes or footwear could help, you could be on your way to see a pedorthist.

Pedorthists design, manufacture, fit, and modify shoes or therapeutic devices (such as braces) aimed at lessening pain or correcting foot problems. Trained in anatomy and shoe construction, pedorthists understand what has physically gone wrong with the foot and what shoe, insert, brace, pad, or other device will help. Whether designing a new shoe or just adding a modification, pedorthists play a key role in putting people back on their feet.

A certified pedorthist (C.Ped.) works as part of a team of health care professionals treating a patient. Pedorthists never diagnose problems; that is done by a doctor, surgeon, or podiatrist. These physicians write out a prescription explaining what should be done and send the person to see a pedorthist. Pedorthists also may confer with physical therapists, nurses, orthotists, and other health care professionals.

Patient evaluation is the first step for pedorthists. They gain an understanding of the problem and what the doctor wants to accomplish. During an evaluation, pedorthists may observe the patient's gait (walk) and range of motion. They also may check back with the doctor if there are any questions.

Generally, a corrective or accommodative shoe or device is needed. Corrective footwear fixes a problem, such as bringing pigeon toes into alignment. Accommodative footwear eases but does not fix a problem. It mainly makes the patient more comfortable. For example, feet that are greatly swollen may need shoes that are deeper than normal or that have a wider toebox.

After determining the patient's needs, a pedorthist takes foot impressions. In a floor reaction imprint, the patient walks on a kind of slanted inked mat. The resulting footprints clearly show the foot's shape, pressure points, stride, and other characteristics. The patient also may step barefoot into plaster, wax, or other material. A plaster model of a person's feet can be made from this impression and used in making the patient's shoe or device.

Sometimes, the pedorthist can adapt an off-the-shelf product (like a shoe or insert) for the patient. Perhaps the shoe can be stretched, or the insert cut. Other times, a new shoe or a therapeutic device needs to be made.

To get the proper design, pedorthists may use computer-aided design (CAD) and 3-D computer modeling. They then make the shoe or device or send the specifications to a manufacturing facility. Pedorthists are trained to know the right materials to use, such as plastic or leather. Some pedorthists have equipment in their office for making shoes or devices.

Fitting and follow up are the last steps. Pedorthists put the shoe or device on the patient and check the fit. Any necessary adjustments are made. (Sometimes this requires more than one visit.) Pedorthists make sure the patient understands how to use and maintain the footwear. In some cases the patient will start out using the new footwear for only an hour or so a day, building up gradually to a full day.

In follow-up visits, pedorthists check to see if the desired results are being achieved. They keep careful records and check back with the physician if something else needs to be done.

Pedorthists may work with anyone from babies to elderly people. That's because foot problems can happen at any age. Areas of specialization in pedorthics include adult foot deformities, amputations, arthritis, congenital deformities, diabetes, geriatrics, overuse injuries, pediatrics/rotational disorders, post-polio symptoms or late effects of polio, sports-related injuries, and trauma.

Lingo to Learn

Accommodative shoe or device Eases but does not fix a foot pain or problem. It mainly makes the patient more comfortable. Also may be called functional shoe or device.

Corrective shoe or device Fixes a problem, such as bringing pigeon toes into alignment.

Custom A device or shoe that is made specifically for the patient.

Floor reaction imprint An impression of the bottom of the patient's foot showing foot shape, pressure points, stride, and other characteristics.

Prosthesis A device that replaces a missing body part or improves body function.

What Is It Like to Be a Pedorthist?

Rhona Chick, C.Ped., works for Ballert Orthopedic of Chicago, a health care facility specializing in orthotics and prosthetics (artificial limbs). People come here for everything from braces to prosthetics for amputees. Ballert staff also travel to nearby hospitals, clinics, nursing homes, and other health care facilities to see patients. Rhona has been working in the field for more than 15 years, and she definitely likes her job.

Rhona's cases fall into two major categories: children and adults. "We see a lot of kids from about age one or two to age seven for malalignment of feet," she says. Feet generally should be in a straight line but sometimes a child's foot has not developed properly. For example, a heel may be splayed or tilted to the outside. "These problems often happen in utero [in the womb]," Rhona notes.

Since a child's body is not fully formed yet, the right footwear can encourage the feet to grow in proper alignment. "The body will respond, especially with younger children," says Rhona.

A cast is made of the child's feet and footwear is designed that will hold the foot in the proper anatomical alignment. Ballert has its own on-site facilities for manufacturing the needed shoes or devices. (Although Rhona knows how to fabricate shoes, at Ballert technicians handle this part.)

The child is fitted with the shoes and wears them for about a year until the problem is fixed. During that time, Rhona sees the patient periodically to check on his or her progress.

By contrast, adults are skeletally mature (their bones are fully formed) so it's less likely that footwear will correct alignment problems. Instead, accommodative shoes or devices are prescribed. Rhona's adult patients may also have foot problems caused by diabetes, arthritis, heart disease, or other medical conditions, as well as overuse or years of wearing the wrong shoes.

Each adult case is unique and Rhona has to be careful to think about all aspects of the problem. A patient may need better balance to avoid falls that could cause injury. Ulcers on the feet can become infected and the patient could lose a limb.

For her adult patients, Rhona may adapt an off-the-shelf shoe or device. For example, she may stretch a shoe or trim an insert to accommodate a problem. She may also create a special insert. "All of our footwear is extra-depth to accommodate an insert," says Rhona. Or she may create a shoe or device from scratch.

Rhona learned in school that about 85 percent of the population needs orthotics, but most people don't know it. "Women generally have more problems than men because of high heels and other fashionable shoes," she adds. "Before I was a pedorthist, I always wondered why I'd see women walking to work downtown in bobby socks and gym shoes. But I know now. High heels are the worst thing for feet."

Women generally have more problems than men because of high heels and other fashionable shoes.

Rhona sees fewer sports-related injuries than high-heel injuries. This is partly because athletes protect themselves with good shoes. "Gym shoes today are made with lots of shock absorption," she points out. Still, sports-related injuries do occur, like plantar fasciitis or heel pain, such as what Toni Kukoc of the Chicago Bulls suffered during the 1996–97 season. "Maybe he landed weird on it, maybe it was a weakness that came to climax," Rhona speculates. Heel cups or arch supports might help in his case. Kukoc had a procedure in April 2001 called shock wave therapy to relieve the plantar fasciitis in his right foot. The procedure may also relieve his lower back pain that is possibly caused by the foot problem. Such procedures or any other surgery or treatments are performed by physicians.

Because Rhona is also a prosthetist, part of her job includes working with amputees to ensure proper design, fit, and wear of their artificial feet.

Pedorthists are unusual in that they may also work in retail. For example, Lyle Rosen, C.Ped. spends most of his time working in a shoe store called Corrective Measures Plus in Chicago. Like Rhona, he also sometimes visits patients in various hospitals, clinics, and nursing homes in the area, particularly elderly people, if a doctor calls and asks him to.

"The best way to describe what we do is that we're the pharmacist for a foot doctor," says Lyle. "We fill those doctors' prescriptions." Lyle's workplace looks like a typical shoe store from the outside, with nice-looking shoes on display in the windows.

As a certified pedorthist, Lyle does the same types of things that Rhona does, including evaluations, foot impressions, fittings, and follow-up checks. He does, however, send the fabricating work out to a local manufacturer.

Lyle says he's seeing a lot of foot problems these days from arthritis and diabetes. "Both are going up in numbers," he says. He also sees many stroke and heart disease patients. Many of these people are definitely hurting. For example, heart disease patients can suffer severe edema (swelling). "Their feet become very sensitive," says Lyle.

Do I Have What It Takes to Be a Pedorthist?

A pedorthist needs to be able to talk to patients, ease their fears, teach them about the device or shoe, and make sure the patient complies with the treatment. Some people may resist wearing a corrective or accommodative shoe or device because they think it's not fashionable. Pedorthists should make sure the shoe or device is as appealing as possible. They should also explain how the shoe or device will help the patient and encourage the patient to comply with treatment in order to correct a problem or prevent further damage.

Usually a patient visits a pedorthist several times for evaluation, fitting, and follow up. It's important to be able to develop rapport with patients to make sure you're giving them the best possible care and that they're following your instructions carefully.

"It's definitely a people job," says Rhona. Manual dexterity is also important, she says, for the fabrication parts of the job. Patience, problem-solving skills, and conscientiousness are other desirable traits, she adds. Besides dealing with the public, pedorthists need to be able to work cooperatively with physicians, physical therapists, nurses, and others on the patient's health care team.

To Be a Successful Pedorthist, You Should . . .

- have manual dexterity
- be good at solving problems
- be conscientious
- enjoy working with people
- have good communication skills

How Do I Become a Pedorthist?

"I was premed in college at the University of Illinois-Champaign," recalls Rhona. By junior year, however, she knew she wasn't going to be going on to medical school. She discovered pedorthics through a career guide in the library and decided it was for her.

Lyle had already been in the shoe business for many years when he decided to become certified in pedorthics.

EDUCATION

High School

A high school diploma or equivalent is a requirement to be a certified pedorthist. You do not need to take any special classes in high school but you should take plenty of science courses. Biology is an especially useful class. Because effective communication is always important, classes in English or speech are also useful. Finally, since some pedorthists manufacture footwear or therapeutic devices, classes that teach you how to use various machines are very beneficial.

Postsecondary Training

Many jobs in the field of pedorthics require at least some college-level course work. Appropriate fields of study include courses in medicine, engineering, biomechanics, anatomy, and physical therapy.

CERTIFICATION OR LICENSING

The Pedorthic Footwear Association (PFA), which certifies people in this field, requires at least a high school diploma or equivalent to start training in pedorthics. Beyond the high school requirement, you can take one of three paths to gain admission to the PFA certification program. The first way is to get your associate's degree from an accredited college or university. The degree should be in a health or science-related field.

A second way is to get a bachelor's degree or higher from an accredited college or university.

The third way is to earn 300 points from PFA by doing one or more of the following (PFA assigns the point totals): Complete science courses at an accredited college or university, do an internship in pedorthics working under a C.Ped., or complete PFA-approved courses and seminars.

Once you've fulfilled one of the three options, you qualify to take PFA's certification exam. You must pass this exam to earn your certification. Training doesn't stop after you've earned certification. "There are always continuing education requirements that you must meet," says Rhona. To keep your certification, you need to earn 150 continuing education points every three years as long as you're working in the field. Points are earned by going to approved classes, seminars, and workshops; retaking and passing the certification exam; and taking various other steps spelled out by PFA.

The Board for Certification in Pedorthics (BCP) also offers certification for people in this field. Applicants must complete a minimum of 120 hours of BCP-recognized pre-certification pedorthic courses; take ancillary courses (in anatomy, biomechanics, and patient management, to name a few); gain practical, hand-on experience in pedorthics; and then pass BCP's certification exam. Training doesn't stop after you've earned certification. To keep your certification, you need to earn 32 continuing education points every three years as long as you're working in the field.

Even if a beginning pedorthist does not choose to become certified, he or she should get hands-on experience as an intern in a hospital, clinic, or agency with opportunities in pedorthics. Shoe stores that sell custom-fit and therapeutic shoes are another option for practical experience.

Four states (Oklahoma, Illinois, Florida, and Ohio) require pedorthists to be licensed. Prospective pedorthists who live in one of these states, should contact their state's department of labor to learn more about licensing requirements.

INTERNSHIPS AND VOLUNTEERSHIPS

"An internship is definitely a plus," says Rhona. "It's to one's interest and benefit." Rhona interned at a prosthetics and orthotics facility in Champaign, Illinois, where she mainly did observation. "Hands-on work is the best, though," she says. She recommends that you look in the yellow pages for such facilities and call them to ask about internship opportunities. "For example, there are 56 prosthetic and orthotic facilities or labs listed in the [Chicago-area] yellow pages," says Rhona.

Who Will Hire Me?

Pedorthists are employed in three major areas: manufacturing, retail, and clinical. Rhona is an example of someone from the clinical area. Lyle works in both the retail and clinical areas.

In clinical environments, pedorthists work in hospitals, clinics, nursing homes, or other health care facilities. Some pedorthists own their own companies, specializing in providing pedorthic services to others. Like Rhona, you may work out of one clinical facility but routinely visit other sites because the patients can't come to you.

In manufacturing environments, pedorthists work for shoe and device manufacturers. These companies focus on fabricating pedorthic shoes and devices to supply to other pedorthists. For example, Lyle uses these types of companies because he doesn't have the facilities at his store to make the shoes and devices himself. Having pedorthists on staff can help manufacturers ensure they are properly filling orders for shoes or devices.

In retail environments, pedorthists work in specialty shoe stores. Most of the customers that go to these stores are sent by doctors. But sometimes you will also get people off the street who like the idea of buying extra-care shoes.

Education, government affairs, research, and association work are other possible areas of employment. A source of potential employers is PFA's *Directory of Pedorthics,* which lists all PFA members. You may also wish to contact this association directly for information about employment opportunities in the field.

Where Can I Go from Here?

Bill Boettge, executive director of the Board for Certification in Pedorthics, says ownership and additional duties are two keys to advancement. "The C.Ped. may branch out and open his or her own facility," he says. "Or he or she may take on additional responsibilities besides patient care, such as managing inventory, supervising others in the office, or marketing pedorthic services to doctors or managed care firms," he adds. Each of these things would constitute advancement and command a higher salary.

What Are the Salary Ranges?

Pedorthists just entering the field will usually start out making $20,000 to $28,000 a year. With certification and hands-on experience, pedorthists can make $20,000 to $70,000 a year, according to the Board for Certification in Pedorthics. BCP reports that most certified pedorthists earn between $30,000 and $50,000 a year. These amounts depend on the type of facility and the location. Those working in hospitals and research labs may have a set salary that is very close to the numbers previously cited, while earnings vary at shoe stores and clinics.

Pedorthists working in shoe stores and clinics usually receive paid sick days, holidays, vacation days, and some level of insurance. Retirement savings plans are usually offered as well. Most hospitals provide insurance and other benefits, but usually don't offer as many days off. However, some hospitals offer discounted or free medical services to their employees.

What Is the Job Outlook?

Jobs are abundant for pedorthists for many reasons. Two of the main reasons for the high demand for pedorthists are the popularity of sports and fitness and the fact that as the population ages, people tend to have foot problems.

The sports and fitness boom shows no signs of declining. Many people involved in different sports activities will need special braces, inserts, and devices to maintain a high level of activity. Also, sports-related injuries are increasingly common, so skilled pedorthists able to treat such injuries will be in high demand.

Advancing age brings many chronic conditions such as arthritis and bone disease that require the help of a pedorthist. Many of these people will require special equipment and advice from the pedorthist. The growing elderly population has created a great need for pedorthists. As a result of these factors, the future of pedorthics is stable and ever-growing.

How Do I Learn More?

PROFESSIONAL ORGANIZATIONS

For information on certification requirements and procedures, write to

Board for Certification in Pedorthics
2517 Eastlake Avenue East, Suite 200
Seattle, WA 98102
888-530-2733
info@cpeds.org
http://www.cpeds.org

To find out more about becoming a pedorthist and to receive free brochures, contact

Pedorthic Footwear Association
7150 Columbia Gateway Drive, Suite G
Columbia, MD 21046-1151
410-381-7278 or 800-673-8447
http://www.pedorthics.org

BIBLIOGRAPHY

The following is a sampling of materials relating to the professional concerns and development of pedorthists:

Adelaar, Robert S., and Bob L. Shepherd. *Complex Foot and Ankle Trauma.* Philadelphia: Lippincott, Williams & Wilkins, 1999.

Cailliet, Rene. *Foot and Ankle Pain.* 3d ed. Philadelphia: F. A. Davis Co., 1997.

Marder, Richard A., and George J. Lian. *Sports Injuries of the Ankle and Foot.* London: Springer-Verlag, 1997.

Ranawat, Chitranjan S., and Rock G. Positano, eds. *Disorders of the Heel, Rearfoot, and Ankle.* New York: Churchill Livingstone, 1999.

Tremaine, M. David, and Elias M. Awad. *The Foot and Ankle Source Book: Everything You Need to Know.* 2d ed. New York: McGraw-Hill, 1998.

PERFUSIONISTS

Carol Zografas shuts the door behind her and glances around the sterile cardiac operating room. It is only 7:00 A.M. and she has already read her patient's chart and knows what to expect. It is the first procedure of the day, a neonatal case involving two-month-old Kristen. Carol will be working with Maxine, the anesthesiologist, and Dr. Cardwell, the heart surgeon, as well as with the other operating room staff, to repair complex defects in Kristen's heart.

Carol turns on the heart-lung machine and goes through her preoperative checklist. Is the tubing the right size for the infant? Are all the parts of the machine working properly? She checks off one item after another on her list. Once the operation begins, Kristen's life could depend on Carol's skills and the heart-lung machine.

Finally, she puts the list down, satisfied that she is as prepared as she can be to begin the operation. She looks across the room at Maxine. "I'm all set, Max. Are you ready?" she asks.

Definition
Perfusionists operate and monitor extracorporeal circulation equipment, such as heart-lung machines and artificial hearts, during any medical situation where it is necessary to support or temporarily replace the patient's cardiopulmonary-circulatory function.

Alternative Job Titles
Cardiovascular perfusionists
Extracorporeal technologists
Perfusion technicians

High School Subjects
Biology
Chemistry
Mathematics
Physics

Personal Skills
Helping/teaching
Technical/scientific

Salary Range
$32,000 to $97,424 to $260,000

Minimum Educational Requirements
Bachelor's degree

Certification or Licensing
Recommended

Outlook
About as fast as the average

DOT
078

GOE
14.02.01

NOC
3214

O*NET-SOC
29-2031.00

What Does a Perfusionist Do?

The heart is the main tool of the circulatory system, beating about 70 times a minute to circulate the oxygen and nutrients that provide energy for human action and thought. This tool, basically a pump at the heart of our lives, must move 2,000 gallons of blood through 60,000 miles of arteries and veins every minute of every day.

When one's heart is not functioning correctly, or when one has a heart disease, surgery is often performed to repair the damage or to control the illness. During an operation such as open-heart surgery, coronary bypass, or any other procedure that involves the heart and lungs, the *perfusionist* is indispensable. Before the cardiologist can begin to operate on the heart, it is necessary to interrupt or replace the functioning of the heart by circulating the blood through machines outside of the patient's body. This process of circulating the blood outside the patient's body is called extracorporeal circulation.

Perfusionists are experts in extracorporeal circulation. They perform complex, delicate procedures to transfer the functions of the heart to special machines while the cardiologist operates on the patient. These machines are called heart-lung machines; they take over the job of the heart and lungs. When the surgery is over, perfusionists also may help to start the heart pumping again if it doesn't start up by itself.

During heart surgery, the doctor will pierce the patient's breastbone and the membrane surrounding the heart (called the pericardial sac). Then the perfusionist will activate the heart-lung machine by inserting two tubes into the heart; one tube circulates blood from the heart to the machine, and the other tube circulates blood from the machine back into the heart. Using the heart-lung machine, the perfusionist maintains the functions of the patient's circulatory system and the appropriate levels of the patient's heart, including oxygen, carbon dioxide, and other nutrient levels.

Operating the heart-lung machine is the foundation of the perfusionist's job. During the medical procedure, perfusionists may also administer prescriptive drugs, anaesthetic agents, or blood products through the blood. They may also induce hypothermia, which means that the patient's body temperature is lowered to about 70 degrees (the human body's average temperature is about 98 degrees) so that the metabolism and stress levels are slowed down, allowing for less risk to the patient's bodily functions. Perfusionists use probes in other parts of the body to monitor the blood pressure and kidney activity during the surgical procedures. They also perform blood gas analysis and check for normal brain activity.

Perfusionists perform a technique called blood salvaging, which means that they try to save as much of the patient's blood as possible so they don't have to depend on donated blood. Blood salvaging is especially important these days because of the high rate of AIDS cases; the HIV virus, which causes AIDS, is transmitted through blood (as well as through other body fluids). Some patients donate their own blood supply prior to their surgery. Perfusionists also sometimes work with cell savers, which are machines that separate plasma, damaged platelets, and saline from blood that should not be returned to the patient's body.

During an operation, a patient must have a precise and consistent amount of blood flowing through the body and to the brain. The perfusionist must make sure that the heart-lung machine is delivering the proper amount of blood back into the patient's body to prevent damage to the brain and other major organs. Before the patient is taken off the heart-lung machine, the perfusionist makes sure that the patient's temperature is back to normal; he or she also does a blood test (called a hemocrit) on the patient to ensure that the red blood cell count is normal.

After surgery, the perfusionist slows down the blood flow to the patient and shuts off one of the lines to the heart-lung machine. When the patient's body takes over on its own, the machinery is shut off. If the patient's heart does not start on its own, the perfusionist may have to provide temporary cardiac support (with either the heart-lung machine or an artificial heart) until the patient's heart is ready to beat on its own.

Perfusionists are responsible for assembling, setting up, monitoring, and operating all the equipment that assists the circulation of blood during a medical procedure. They may also be responsible for ensuring that the equipment is maintained in accurate working order.

Specialized perfusionists assist at-risk patients such as premature babies and heart patients who have just had surgery (postoperative, or post-op patients). In these cases, the workers perform extracorporeal membrane oxygenation, using a machine that draws

Lingo to Learn

Blood salvaging Using as much of the patient's blood as possible so as not to depend on donated blood. Some patients donate their own blood supply prior to their surgery.

Cardiac Relating to the heart.

Cardiologist Heart surgeon.

Cardiopulmonary Relating to the heart and lungs.

Cell savers Machines that separate plasma, damaged platelets, and saline from blood that should not be returned to the patient's body.

Extracorporeal circulation Circulation of the patient's blood outside the body.

Heart-lung machine A machine used to take over the function of the patient's heart and lungs during surgery or respiratory failure. The machine draws blood from the patient's body, reoxygenates it, and pumps it back into the patient's body.

Induced hypothermia A condition that the perfusionist may inflict on the patient to reduce body temperature to 70 degrees or below; this slows the patient's metabolism and reduces stress on the heart.

Pulmonary circulation Blood flow to and from the lungs.

blood from the patient's body, reoxygenates it, and pumps it back into the patient through the arteries. For newborns and very young infants, this buys crucial time until the infant's respiratory and circulatory systems can work on their own; for heart patients, it may buy time until the heart is able to pump on its own or until a donor heart is found.

Perfusionists have also recently become important in the treatment of trauma. In such cases, they are called upon to rapidly infuse or replace lost blood or to lower the blood volume. Perfusion is now being used in the treatment of patients undergoing cancer surgery, organ transplants, and orthopedic surgery. As medical technology evolves, new uses for perfusion will most likely be developed.

What Is It Like to Be a Perfusionist?

Carol Zografas is the chief cardiovascular perfusionist at Maine Medical Center in Portland. It is 6:30 in the morning when she arrives at the hospital. She checks the schedule to find out what procedure she will be doing today and finds that she will be assisting the surgical team to repair extensive defects in the heart of a newborn baby.

Carol reads the patient's chart and looks for anything out of the ordinary that she may have to consult with the surgeon about. Does the baby have diabetes? Is the kidney function normal? It will be Carol's job to monitor and adjust the infant's kidney function, blood sugar, brain activity, and other bodily functions while the infant is in surgery.

After she is sure she knows all she needs to know, Carol gathers her equipment together and assembles it in the cardiac operating room. She goes through her page-long preoperative checklist to be sure that all the equipment is running properly. She checks the contents of the prepackaged parts for sterility and integrity. Are the tubes for the artificial heart placed in the right areas to make sure the circuits are complete? Have the proper drugs been administered in the prime fluid? Are all the parts of the heart-lung machine working properly? Are all the alarms operational?

When Carol is satisfied that her checklist is complete, she is ready to begin her work with the rest of the surgical team. She will be in the operating room anywhere from four to six hours for a typical surgical procedure. Her machinery is next to the operating table, and she works closely with the surgeon, the anesthesiologist, and other operating room staff.

Carol and her staff perform approximately 150 procedures each year. As chief of her department, Carol usually performs perfusions two days a week. The remaining hours in her workweek are filled with administrative and managerial tasks and teaching. Maine Medical Center has one of the three largest heart programs in New England and is a clinical teaching site for Northeastern University in Boston.

Carol supervises seven full-time and one half-time staff members. For quality control reasons, she tries not to schedule her staff for more than one procedure a day; she fills in herself when someone gets sick. The rest of her time is spent monitoring quality standards, performing preventive maintenance on equipment, solving staffing problems, chairing department meetings, attending meetings with other departments, counseling staff, and keeping up with the accreditation requirements for the hospital.

In-depth

Heart Surgery through the Ages

Considering the age of humankind and the evolution of the medical sciences, heart surgery is still in its infancy. The first bypass operation was performed in 1944 by Dr. John Blalok, whose patient was a newborn infant with oxygen-poor blood. The baby was born with a bluish tint because blood was not circulating correctly. Dr. Blalock operated on the baby, bypassing a blocked blood vessel.

The most significant breakthrough in open heart surgery occurred 10 years later, when Dr. John Gibbon used a machine to pump blood and supply oxygen to an 18-year-old patient, giving the surgeon needed time for delicate heart surgery. The machine was the heart-lung machine, which is now a standard fixture in cardiac operating rooms.

Although Carol's day begins promptly at 6:30 in the morning, she is never sure when it will end. "All the perfusionists in my department average about five hours of overtime per week. Overtime has its peaks and valleys," she says. "We always have two staff members on call in case of an emergency, and we work every day of the week."

Do I Have What It Takes to Be a Perfusionist?

Perfusionists perform some of the most delicate and vital services for patients during heart and lung surgery, yet most patients have never heard of perfusionists and aren't aware of the services they perform. Although their profession is not well known, perfusionists can take pride in the knowledge that the procedures they perform are crucial to their patients' lives.

Perfusionists make decisions that could affect the well-being of the patient for years to come. "It is so technical," Carol says. "There is always the possibility of us doing some permanent damage. This is why we have so many checklists and check things so often. We build our systems to be as safe as possible."

Carol tries not to schedule her staff for more than one procedure a day, because each procedure takes hours of total focused concentration. "This is not a job you should take because you want to make money," Carol says. "You have to be able to commit yourself to each and every patient, and that takes a lot of compassion. You have to be able to react quickly in emergency situations, keep a cool head. Suppose you've got a patient who comes in to the emergency room, and his heart isn't working. You've got to keep your head and get that patient on bypass as soon as possible." She concludes, "This job is a major commitment on your life, and your family, not unlike that of a surgeon. It can have a major impact on your lifestyle."

You have to be able to commit yourself to each and every patient, and that takes a lot of compassion.

Occasionally, medical situations occur in which all the combined effort and talent of the surgical team are unable to help the patient. Perfusionists must have strength of character to accept the limitations of modern medicine, as well as its successes. "You need to know how to deal with death," Carol says, "and sometimes that only comes with age. It's really hard when you have children you're working with and you lose a patient. You have to learn some way to deal with it."

What Carol likes best about her job is the peace of mind she gets from knowing she's helped another human being. She especially likes working in the neonatal department. It gives her a sense of satisfaction to see a listless newborn with pale, clammy skin transformed through the surgery into a healthy, rosy-skinned infant. Carol's satisfaction comes from knowing that the contributions she makes during any successful surgical procedure help the patient to live a normal life.

Carol likes working in a field where new developments and new technologies are always coming along. She never has time to be bored. She also enjoys teaching. Because Maine Medical Center is a clinical supervision site for Boston's Northeastern University, Carol is able to share her skills with students.

Carol says that it helps to have a great staff. "The surgeons here are wonderful," she says. However, she doesn't really enjoy the administrative work as much as working in the operating room. She also doesn't like what's happening in the health care industry itself. "It's so cost-driven these days," she says. "All you hear is cost, cost, cost; streamline your team. I'm concerned that there isn't much nonprocedural time left for my staff to keep educated about new developments. I'm also concerned that cutting the costs

To Be a Successful Perfusionist, You Should . . .

- have good communication skills
- have a strong sense of responsibility
- work well as part of a team
- think independently
- act quickly and calmly in emergencies
- cope well under extreme stress
- know how to deal with occasional failure

of medical services will adversely affect patient care, although this hospital has assured us over the years that would never happen here." Carol regularly reads various professional journals to keep up with new developments in her field.

How Do I Become a Perfusionist?

Carol was an operating room nurse at Maine Medical Center in 1967 when she entered an on-the-job training program for perfusionists. She characterizes her training as rigorous "baptism by fire." She became board-certified when that became standard, which was in 1972. She says that today you cannot learn perfusionism on the job alone. There is too much technical knowledge required, and too many technological developments have occurred for that to work.

When Carol began her studies, her nursing background was helpful to her, but she had to take a lot of extra classes and study a lot on her own to be successful.

EDUCATION

High School

In preparation for any perfusion technology program, it is very important to take natural science classes such as biology and chemistry. Also essential are courses in higher mathematics and physics. You must have a high school diploma before you can be accepted by an accredited educational program.

Postsecondary Training

On-the-job training and apprenticeships are no longer available for positions in the perfusion field. To prepare for a career in perfusion, you must attend one of the 23 nationally accredited schools in the United States. Some of these schools require you to have a bachelor's of science (B.S.) degree before you enter their program; others include course work toward the B.S. as part of their training. Program length varies from one to four years, depending on the schooling required for acceptance.

Occasionally, an accrediting institution will accept applicants who have trained at nursing schools or other technical schools and who have had experience as nurses or health technicians.

The accredited school carefully examines the student's personal character, academic achievement record, and personal temperament before accepting new students. There is intense competition for admission to these programs. Only 10 to 20 percent of the applicants are accepted.

It takes a unique type of person to work successfully under the kind of stress and challenge required. Intense course work is good preparation for such a challenging job. Courses include physiology, cardiology, respiratory therapy, general surgical procedure, and pharmacology. Also covered are courses in heart-lung bypass for adult, young children, and infant patients undergoing heart surgery; extracorporeal circulation; monitoring of the patient; and special applications.

You'll also receive clinical training for one and a half to two years. Most of the accredited perfusion programs try to begin their students' clinical training as soon as possible. The practice of perfusion requires extensive actual operating room experience. It is in the operating room that you observe and learn about extracorporeal circulation, respiratory therapy, general surgical procedures, and anaesthesia. In clinical

FYI

What is extracorporeal membrane oxygenation?
Used for premature babies suffering respiratory distress and for postoperative heart patients, a machine draws blood from the patient's body, reoxygenates it, and pumps it back into the patient through the arteries. For premature babies, this buys crucial time until the infant's respiratory system can work on its own. For heart patients, it may buy time until the heart is able to pump on its own or until a donor heart is found.

practice, you begin to perform perfusion procedures and perfect their skills.

CERTIFICATION OR LICENSING

Certification currently is not an absolute requirement for perfusionists, but it is rapidly becoming a practical requirement as more than 70 percent of perfusionists nationally are now certified. Certification is administered by the American Board of Cardiovascular Perfusion. Applicants must be graduates of an accredited training program, have performed a minimum of 75 instructor-supervised clinical perfusions during the educational program, and pass a certification examination, which consists of two separate parts: the Clinical Applications in Perfusion Examination and the Perfusion Basic Science Examination. Applicants who successfully complete these requirements may use the designation certified clinical perfusionist.

Perfusionists must renew their certification every year. To be eligible for recertification, perfusionists must have performed at least 40 clinical perfusions per year and complete continuing education programs (45 continuing education units every three years). At present, perfusionists do not need separate state licenses to practice their profession.

SCHOLARSHIPS AND GRANTS

Scholarships for perfusion programs are available from the American Society of Extra-Corporeal Technology (AmSECT). Be sure to write well in advance of your planned study for application requirements and procedures (see "How Do I Learn More?"). In addition, financial aid in the form of scholarships and grants is often available through the financial aid office where the student is applying to go to school.

Who Will Hire Me?

Carol's first job experience was at Maine Medical Center, the hospital where she continues to work today. Typically, the perfusionist works in the cardiac operating room in a hospital as part of the surgery team. The perfusionist might be employed by the hospital itself, by a medical services group, or even by an individual cardiologist.

ADVANCEMENT POSSIBILITIES

Chief cardiovascular perfusionists are in charge of the perfusionists on staff at a hospital. The chief perfusionist supervises others' work, performs administrative tasks, counsels staff, and maintains and monitors quality standards. If the hospital where you work is part of a university or other educational setting, as chief perfusionist you would instruct students and others and perhaps do research on your work.

Many perfusionists are self-employed, meaning that they are independent contractors who offer their services to one or more hospitals. Those who are self-employed must take care of their own business affairs, including purchasing medical insurance, scheduling vacation time, and buying uniforms and other necessary materials.

A clinical perfusionist may find employment in any of the hospitals with open-heart surgery facilities in the United States. Some perfusionists find work as clinical consultants for companies that develop and sell perfusion equipment to hospitals. Perfusionists with graduate school education may conduct research and write about their findings.

AmSECT, the professional society for perfusion technologists, recommends that students who have entered a program investigate the field first with professors and teachers and then join the AmSECT student membership division. This group holds meetings and conferences where you can get information on job openings in the field.

Where Can I Go from Here?

Perfusionism is a highly specialized field. As chief perfusionist in her department at Maine Medical Center, Carol has advanced as far as she can. Her position requires her to be responsible for managing a large staff as well as maintaining quality control. She is also responsible for supervising the purchase of supplies and equipment and for educating her staff about new techniques.

The typical career path involves learning more complex and specific procedures. Carol says that the foreseeable future in perfusionism will be increasingly technical and specialized. Neonatal perfusionism, one of Carol's most rewarding job responsibilities, is a good example of one specialization.

Perfusionists with graduate education and experience may conduct research and write about their work. Others choose to teach in colleges and accredited schools.

What Are the Salary Ranges?

Salaries for perfusionists compare favorably with those of other health technicians. According to a survey by Perfusion.com, the average salary for perfusionists employed by hospitals was $97,424 in 2003, with earnings ranging from $50,000 to $165,000. Those employed by private perfusionist groups earned an average of $88,102, with a range of $32,000 to $275,000. Self-employed perfusionists earned an average of $115,258, with salaries ranging from $50,000 to $260,000. The average national income for all perfusionists was $87,439. Perfusionists usually receive a standard benefits package that includes paid vacation and holidays, insurance, and 401(k) plan options.

Perfusionists employed by hospitals and medical services groups get benefits such as sick leave, vacation, and medical insurance. Self-employed and physician-employed perfusionists usually pay for their own insurance, as well as for such items as uniforms and other minor equipment needed on the job.

What Is the Job Outlook?

This highly specialized field employs only about 3,700 individuals nationwide. However, the job outlook for perfusionists is good. Employment is expected to grow at a rate that is about as fast as the average for all other occupations. The number of Americans age 65 and over continues to rise. This demographic group is at a higher risk for developing cardiovascular disease, therefore requiring the professional expertise of perfusionists.

A number of factors may limit growth in this field. Open-heart surgery is very complex and many hospitals are not capable of performing such procedures; they are usually performed only in medical centers with 300 or more beds. Secondly, many hospitals have tried to cut costs by reducing the number of new perfusionist hires and asking perfusionists to take on more procedures without additional compensation. Finally, the development of new medical techniques, specifically ones that do not require the use of a heart-lung machine during surgery, may limit the need for these workers. It is still too early to tell, though, whether these new techniques will replace existing treatment options.

> **FYI**
>
> **What is a coronary bypass?**
> A surgical procedure performed on patients with diseased or obstructed coronary arteries or veins.
>
> During surgery, a nonessential vein from another part of the patient's body is grafted onto the obstructed coronary artery, thus bypassing it and allowing essential blood flow to and from the heart.

How Do I Learn More?

PROFESSIONAL ORGANIZATIONS

The following are organizations that provide information on perfusionist careers, certification, accredited schools and scholarships, and employers:

American Board of Cardiovascular Perfusion
207 North 25th Avenue
Hattiesburg, MS 39401
601-582-2227
http://www.abcp.org

American Medical Association
515 North State Street
Chicago, IL 60610
800-621-8335
http://www.ama-assn.org

American Society of Extra-Corporeal Technology
503 Carlisle Drive, Suite 125
Herndon, VA 20170
703-435-8556
http://www.amsect.org

The following Web site provides information on all aspects of perfusion:

The Perfusion Home Page
http://www.perfusion.com

BIBLIOGRAPHY

The following is a sampling of materials relating to the professional concerns and development of perfusionists:

Levitzky, Michael G. *Pulmonary Physiology.* 6th ed. New York: McGraw-Hill, 2002.

Wischnitzer, Saul, and Edith Wischnitzer. *Health-Care Careers for the 21st Century.* Indianapolis, Ind.: JIST Works, 2000.

PERIODONTISTS

Tom's gums had shrunk. The 12-year-old boy is nervous as he enters Sara Whitener's periodontal office. What if she can't fix it? What if it gets worse? He already feels self-conscious enough about wearing braces, and now this.

"Well, Tom, it looks like your orthodontist was right. The periodontal, or gum, tissue around your lower front teeth has receded a bit. I've reviewed your medical history, and you don't have any systemic diseases and don't take prescription drugs. So, the cause of this could be hereditary, a reaction to getting braces, or because you may not be effectively cleaning all the plaque off your teeth around your braces. Plaque and tartar irritate gums," Sara says, "and sometimes they react."

"What's going to happen?" Tom asks, looking worried. Sara sits down next to Tom. "Periodontal tissues are important, Tom. They visually frame our teeth, almost like window shades. Some people have too much gum tissue and their teeth look too short. Other people, like you, have too little tissue in some places and those teeth look longer. Gum tissue not only helps our teeth to look attractive, they help support and stabilize our teeth. Teeth with insufficient periodontal tissue can shift and drift, becoming crooked or even loose."

"Can you treat my problem?" Tom asks.

"We can do a tissue graft onto your existing periodontal tissue, which will repair the damage done. It's an uncomplicated in-office procedure that I do every week," Sara says.

"And it works?" Tom asks.

"All the time," she says. "Let me talk with you and your mom about what's involved and then we'll make an appointment."

Definition
Periodontists are dental specialists who specialize in diagnosing, preventing, and treating inflammatory and destructive periodontal (gum) diseases.

High School Subjects
Biology
Health

Personal Skills
Helping/teaching
Technical/scientific

Salary Range
$119,000 to $145,000 to $200,000+

Educational Requirements
Bachelor's degree; four-year Doctor of Dentistry degree; completion of a two-year periodontal program

Certification or Licensing
Required by all states

Outlook
About as fast as the average

DOT
072

GOE
14.03.01

NOC
3113

O*NET-SOC
29-1029.99

What Does a Periodontist Do?

Periodontists treat diseases and conditions of the gum tissue, which is called periodontal tissue in dentistry. Without periodontal care, people with uncontrolled periodontal disease will have irreversible damage to their gums and supporting bone tissue. In advanced cases, teeth will become loose and may even begin to fall out. According to The American Academy of Periodontology, 75 percent of all Americans have some form of periodontal disease. Many don't know it.

People who have periodontal disease can be any age, from children to older adults. The most common group of patients seen in the periodontal office are middle-aged. Smokers have periodontal problems more often than nonsmokers. And, those afflicted often have halitosis (bad breath from decaying gum tissue). The motivation for treating periodontal disease is usually cosmetic—to retain teeth. However, gum diseases can also result in crooked teeth and tooth loss, which can also create functional challenges for speaking and chewing. In addition, crooked teeth are harder to keep clean, and plaque and tartar buildup are the biggest cause of periodontal disease.

Periodontal disease begins with gingivitis, a mild infection and inflammation of the gums from ineffective brushing and flossing, or from not visiting a dentist regularly for a dental prophylaxis (teeth cleaning). The toxins in plaque (bacteria) on teeth irritate gums. If they are allowed to remain irritated, the gums may separate from the teeth, which creates a pocket or space. Food debris and bacteria accumulate in the pockets between teeth and gums, accelerating the destruction to the gums and bone tissue beneath the gums. Simple gingivitis may or may not progress to periodontal disease. But because this disease is often painless, there are symptoms patients can look for: bleeding gums when brushing or flossing; halitosis (chronic bad breath); oozing, infected gums; receding, shrinking, and loosening gums; and new space around or between teeth. Some patients notice these symptoms and get the name of a periodontist from a friend or the phone book. Most likely, however, patients are sent to a periodontist at the suggestion of their general dentist or other dental specialist who may have suspected a periodontal problem. When the patient comes to the office, periodontists take a complete medical and dental history to make sure they know what has affected or is influencing health in general and teeth in particular. Next, the mouth is carefully examined to look for oral evidence of disease. The health of teeth and gums are carefully evaluated.

During the examination, a periodontist judges whether the teeth fit together properly and if gums have receded. As part of the examination, periodontists place small measuring instruments in between patients' teeth and gums to determine depths of the periodontal pockets. By measuring periodontal pockets at each session, periodontists determine if gum health is stabilized, worsening, or improving.

To further make a diagnosis, the periodontist needs to radiographically evaluate health of bone tissue (roots and surrounding jaw bone). X rays are one type of radiograph that reveal status of tissues that can't be seen by the eye, including not only problems with roots and supporting jawbone, but problems inside the teeth and facial bones. To create a baseline of data on periodontal health, X rays are taken at the first appointment. By taking X rays at subsequent appointments, a periodontist can determine if the bone tissues have resorbed, or deteriorated and receded. In some periodontal offices, computer programs are used to take detailed measurements of the changes in a series of X rays taken over time. Other techniques and strategies help periodontists diagnosis gum diseases, but periodontal probing and X rays are relied upon heavily.

Lingo to Learn

Alveolar bone The bone that makes up the tooth socket onto which periodontal fibers attach to the tooth.

Anesthesia Loss of feeling, also known as numbness, caused by an anesthetic agent applied, injected, or inhaled, which permits diagnostic and treatment procedures to be performed comfortably.

Cementum Thin covering of calcified tissue on tooth.

Flap A surgically loosened section of gum or oral tissue that is separated from the tissue while still connected at its base.

Gingiva Gums.

Gingivitis Inflamed gums.

Infection Disease process involving inflammation and sometimes pain caused by microorganisms invading a particular site.

Periodontal pocket A space between a tooth and gum caused when periodontal disease detaches the gum from the root.

Periodontitis Inflammation of the gum and bone tissues around the teeth that can progress and lead to the loss of teeth.

Periodontium Gum and bone tissues around the teeth.

Plaque A mass of microorganisms and protein, food, and other matter that firmly adheres to all hard surfaces in the mouth; can only be removed by brushing and flossing.

Radiograph Sometimes called an X ray, radiographs are images, usually recorded on film, that are produced by ionizing radiation.

Tartar Also called **calculus,** this is a hard, calcified collection of bacteria that adheres to solid surfaces in the mouth; can only be removed with a professional cleaning.

Once a diagnosis is made, periodontists may give the patient an oral or written treatment plan. This plan includes the diagnosis, the recommended treatment specifics, and a cost estimate of treatment.

Early periodontal disease, where the beginnings of gum recession are seen, is treated by nonsurgical deep cleaning around the teeth below the gums. This procedure is called scaling and root planning, and it eliminates plaque and tartar buildup. After this procedure, the teeth above and below the gums are smoother, making it difficult for bacteria to latch onto them. The patients are carefully educated on how to keep their teeth clean and may be given a therapeutic mouth rinse. This may be all the periodontist needs to do to control or reverse the problem at this stage.

For moderate to advanced periodontal disease, periodontists perform other procedures, such as open flap surgery and gum tissue graft. Open flap surgery involves pulling back gum tissue and cleaning the infected side of the root and the bottom of the periodontal pocket. Then the flap is sutured back in place. Gum tissue grafts involve surgically removing a small piece of healthy gum tissue from the mouth, often the roof of the mouth, and placing it where gum tissue has receded.

Guided tissue regeneration is another periodontal procedure. It is a technique for regenerating periodontal ligament and bone that involves placing a meshlike barrier around a tooth root. The barrier keeps the gum tissue away while saving space for the ligament and bone to grow.

Other periodontal procedures include doing osseous grafts. This is where the periodontist takes either the patient's bone tissue or that from a donor or synthetic source and surgically places it around the teeth where bone has been lost due to periodontal disease.

There are many other types of periodontal procedures, including surgical placement of dental implants. Implants function as anchors or tooth root replacements to which an artificial tooth or denture can be attached, an exciting development in modern dentistry for those who have lost teeth.

While private practitioners make up the majority of periodontists, other periodontists teach full or part time at universities, perform research at dental schools or for industries such as dental product manufacturers, work in the military as government employees, or work for the U.S. Public Health Service.

What Is It Like to Be a Periodontist?

Sara Whitener has been a periodontist for 4 years. She is a partner in a group periodontal private practice in Belleville, Illinois. The group also has a satellite office in Mount Vernon, Illinois. The office is open five days a week. Office hours are 8:00 A.M. to 5:00 P.M. and each of the three periodontists works four to five days a week. The senior partner started the practice 21 years ago and the other partner has been with the practice for 12 years. As the youngest periodontist to the practice, Sara worked hard to prove herself. It paid off, and she was made a partner.

Sara's schedule each week is structured. "I see patients Monday through Thursday, and I take Fridays off to teach periodontics at Southern Illinois University School of Dental Medicine. On the days I work in the office, one hour is devoted to paperwork. This involves writing diagnosis and treatment plan letters with copies of radiographs to send to patients' general dentists," Sara says.

To ensure the dental office is a safe place for employees and patients alike, Sara shares the duties of regularly evaluating procedures and conditions in the office to be certain everything is in compliance with the federal Occupational Safety and Health Administration standards. This takes time, as well. And although staff members are in charge of taking inventory and ordering supplies, the periodontist oversees the process.

Sara must also meet with her partners on a regular basis to discuss patient treatment plans and consult on problems. These problems may involve bookkeeping and strategies for keeping track of the supplies, benefits, tax deductions, and setting salaries and raises. They must work together on the overall planning for the practice.

Sara's patient Tom returned to the office for the gingival graft procedure. He was nervous about the shot he had to be given. Sara, however, always places a gel anesthetic on gum tissue to numb it before patients receive anesthetic injections. So Tom didn't feel the pain many people associate with shots. The Novocain so thoroughly numbed him that Tom claims he never felt the surgery.

A week later when he returns, Tom is much more relaxed.

"Well, Dr. Whitener, it looks like you fixed me up. It's healing pretty well, you must know what you're doing" Tom says with a grin.

Taking a look, Sara says, "Why do you think we go to school for so long? It looks like it's healing great. Now I'll show you how to brush properly so it continues to heal and so you'll have less chance of having more gum recession in the future," Sara says.

Tom visibly relaxes. "Thanks a lot, Doc. For awhile there, I thought I was going to be the only toothless 12-year old!" Tom says, getting ready to get out of the dental chair.

"Not so fast, Tom. First let me show you how to floss under your braces," Sara says.

Patients like Tom are the reason Sara enjoys working as a periodontist. The former junior high school math and science teacher likes helping people understand concepts. "I enjoy teaching, not just dental students on Fridays, but patients in the practice. I get a great deal of satisfaction when I see them comprehend their situation and understand what they need to do to improve their oral health and fight their gum disease," Sara says.

Another periodontist, Robert Pick, practices as a partner in a Naperville, Illinois, and in a Chicago university-based group practice. He, too, teaches one day a week, training periodontal residents. In his spare time, he lectures to periodontists and dentists on practice management, periodontal surgical techniques, and how to best use high-tech innovations to improve the practice. For example, his practice files electronic claims using the Internet and has a Web site, an audiovisual room for patient education and consultations, and intraoral cameras for taking photos inside the patient's mouth and projecting their teeth and gums on a TV screen.

"Once they see an 8-inch by 10-inch image of their puffy, receded, and bleeding gums, they are motivated to receive treatment. We also use computer imaging to paint away excess gum tissue or add tissue where the gums have receded. This gives the patient an idea of what they'll look like after the procedure," Robert says.

Robert, who has written a textbook on lasers, uses them instead of scalpels where applicable. "With lasers there's no bleeding, swelling, scarring, suturing, and pain is reduced," Robert says.

Once they see an 8-inch by 10-inch image of their puffy, receded, and bleeding gums, they are motivated to receive treatment.

Do I Have What It Takes to Be a Periodontist?

Sara went through dental school, a periodontal postgraduate program, and obtained a master's degree in periodontics.

For periodontists, manual dexterity and tactile sensitivity are necessary assets, along with good hand-eye coordination. Fingers, hands, wrists, and arms are in controlled motion within small spaces throughout the day. There is little room for error in judgments when performing delicate gum surgery. This is also not a career for the squeamish, as surgical procedures involving blood and bone are common.

Compassion and tolerance are good character traits in those who wish to be periodontists. People with gum disease often have bad breath and poor oral hygiene. It takes a great deal of patience to understand the complexities of human nature. As educators, Sara and Robert are well-suited in this field because they can communicate complex ideas in simple terms that patients can understand.

To keep abreast of advancements in periodontics, periodontists must take continuing education courses every year. Some courses are required to maintain a dental license; other courses help the periodontist better manage the practice. Business skills help keep the practice running efficiently for maximized profitability while providing highest quality results.

Being a levelheaded communicator while under time pressure is critical. Emergencies and other problems may arise at any time. In between seeing patients, periodontists must take phone calls and compose letters and e-mail. If a periodontist gets behind schedule in the morning, all other patients are backed up for the rest of the day. Patients' time is valuable, too, and they can become angry if made to wait an unreasonable amount of time.

Being able to hire and manage an excellent staff is another nonclinical skill that a successful periodontist needs. To make sure that procedures are done quickly and properly every day, periodontists must delegate responsibilities to the staff and oversee their performance in completing them. If a problem or disagreement arises—for example, a patient is angry at a staff member or staff members are in an argument—the periodontist may need to diplomacy skills to arbitrate and smooth things out.

To Be a Successful Periodontist, You Should . . .

- have a knack for detailed work
- be self-motivated
- have excellent eye-hand coordination
- communicate effectively with others: patients, colleagues, and staff

How Do I Become a Periodontist?

EDUCATION

High School

If you are interested in becoming a periodontist, you should begin preparing for this career with a course load emphasizing, but not restricted to, math and science subjects. Courses such as algebra, calculus, chemistry, physics, trigonometry, biology, and health are all solid baseline courses for college preparation.

Postsecondary Training

Being admitted to dental school requires that you first complete three to four years of undergraduate college education. Maintaining a high grade point average is important while in college because gaining acceptance into a graduate program in periodontics is fiercely competitive. While a bachelor's degree is not strictly required, it is a standard that significantly heightens an applicant's chances of being admitted to a dental school.

Recommended college courses are similar to those suggested in high school. Many periodontists earn a bachelor of science degree in biology. This may involve taking math courses such as algebra, calculus, trigonometry, and geometry. Science courses may include biology, anatomy, physiology, anthropology, zoology, botany, and microbiology.

Business classes such as marketing, economics, accounting, management, and finance prepare you for owning and operating a business. Liberal arts courses such as psychology, sociology, English, and drama may help you become more comfortable in communicating with people.

You must score well on the Dental Admissions Test (DAT) before being admitted into a dental program. Doing well on the DAT helps dental schools determine whether or not you will succeed in dental school. Dental school courses include advanced science and clinical and laboratory technique course work. During the last two years of dental school, clinical treatment is emphasized and you begin supervised treatment of patients at university dental clinics. Graduates receive a doctor of dental surgery (D.D.S.) or doctor of dental medicine (D.M.D.) degree.

To become a periodontist, you must complete a postgraduate program accredited by the American Dental Association Commission on Dental Accreditation. Postgraduate programs usually last three years and award a master's degree. Currently, 52 institutions offer advanced training programs in periodontics in the United States.

CERTIFICATION OR LICENSING

For new dentists to be allowed to practice, they must first pass a licensing examination in the state in which they are planning to practice. This test may include working on a patient. Currently in 17 states, specialists must also pass a specialty licensing examination.

Board certification is also available through the American Board of Periodontology (ABP). To achieve ABP diplomate status, periodontists must file an application with the ABP, be interviewed and approved as a candidate, pass written and oral examinations, and provide written periodontic case histories. Periodontists must be recertified every three years. Periodontists seek ABP diplomate status voluntarily to show they've mastered excellence in their abilities.

Periodontists, as well as all dentists, also must plan on taking courses after they are practicing to maintain their dental licenses. Other voluntary educational activities include reading professional journals and participating in study clubs. These activities help a practicing periodontist to acquire the most up-to-date skills and knowledge of the best materials on the market.

SCHOLARSHIPS AND GRANTS

Scholarships and grants are often available from individual institutions, state agencies, and special-interest organizations. Many students finance their medical education through the Armed Forces Health Professions Scholarship Program. Each branch of the military participates in this program, paying students' tuitions in exchange for military service. Contact your local recruiting office for more information on this program.

The National Health Service Corps Scholarship Program (http://nhsc.bhpr.hrsa.gov/) also provides money for students in return for service. Another source for financial aid, scholarship, and grant information is the Association of American Medical Colleges (http://www.aamc.org). Remember to request information early for eligibility, application requirements, and deadlines.

Who Will Hire Me?

More than 90 percent of periodontists are in private practice. There are different types of private practices, such as solo and group. Periodontists may own their own practice or may work as an associate or a partner in another periodontist's practice. Information about private practice opportunities is available in the *AAP News,* the AAP membership newsletter. For those not joining an existing practice, the resources required to set up a private practice are considerable, typically a bank-financed endeavor.

Other opportunities for periodontists include teaching at universities, either full time or part time, while also practicing. Periodontists may volunteer to teach a class since university teaching is a respected endeavor in the field.

Some periodontists also work in a dental school environment but choose to do research. Others perform research while testing new materials and procedures and writing about them for industry. Researchers may test new periodontal materials or techniques by working on anything from model mouths to animals.

Combining one or more aspects of clinical practice, teaching, and research, some periodontists are employed by the Federal Dental Health Services. These periodontists may be positioned all over the country with the air force, navy, army, the veterans affairs department, and Public Health Service. Those who work in the Pubic Health Service typically work with underserved populations, usually in low-income communities.

FYI

Widely considered to be the father of periodontics, John Riggs was the first to have a paper published describing periodontal disease and the recommended therapy, treatment that is still valid now, more than a century later. "Suppurative Inflammation of the Gums and Absorption of the Gums and Alveolar Process" was published in the March 1876 issue of the *Pennsylvania Journal of Dental Science.*

Where Can I Go from Here?

The primary career path for most periodontists in private practice is to build a reputation for the practice with the general dentists in the surrounding community who refer the majority of the periodontist's patients. Periodontists who can effectively communicate with a patient's general dentist and facilitate easy coordination of treatment are more likely to be trusted by the general dentist. These practitioners are more apt to build their practices.

Involvement in periodontal associations and study clubs may lead periodontists to active participation in organized dental events. Some periodontists even become officers and committee chairs of their professional associations. After many years of working, periodontists may slow down to part-time status or retire and teach at a university during their retirement years.

What Are the Salary Ranges?

According to the American Dental Association Survey Center, periodontists under age 40 have an average net salary of about $119,000. This represents the lower end of the salary range. Periodontists who have been in practice for some time generally have higher earnings; the average net salary for periodontists over age 40 is $145,000. Well established periodontists may make over $200,000 a year, but they are the exception.

Salaries also vary by geographic region and are influenced by the number of other periodontists practicing in a community.

Benefits vary by place of employment. Self-employed periodontists often arrange their own benefits through their dental practices.

What Is the Job Outlook?

The demand for periodontists is expected to remain relatively steady, but the procedures that they perform may change over time. As Americans retain more teeth and live longer, they have more teeth at risk for periodontal disease. Furthermore, as the possible links between chronic periodontal infection and medical diseases become more widely known, people may be more motivated to receive regular periodontal care.

Periodontal surgery is expected to be less common as more patients are managed with antibiotics and preventive care. This is good news for patients because periodontal surgery is expensive, but this may mean reduced income for periodontists.

How Do I Learn More?

PROFESSIONAL ASSOCIATIONS

The following are organizations provide information on dental careers, accredited schools, and employees:

The American Academy of Periodontology
737 North Michigan Avenue, Suite 800
Chicago, IL 60611
312-787-5518
http://www.perio.org

American Dental Association
211 East Chicago Avenue
Chicago, IL 60611
312-440-2500
http://www.ada.org

BIBLIOGRAPHY

The following is a sampling of materials related to the professional concerns of periodontists:

Galgut, Peter N., Sherrie A. Dowsett, and Michael J. Kowolik. *Periodontics: Current Concepts and Treatment Strategies.* New York: Thieme Medical Publishing, 2001.

Hall, Walter B., ed. *Decision Making in Periodontology.* 3d ed. St. Louis, Mo.: Mosby-Year Book, 1997.

Hodges, Kathleen. *Concepts in Nonsurgical Periodontal Therapy.* Albany, N.Y.: Delmar Publishing, 1997.

Nevins, Myron, and James T. Mellonig, eds. *Periodontal Therapy: Clinical Approaches and Evidence of Success.* Chicago: Quintessence Publishing, 1998.

Newman, Michael G., Henry H. Takei, and Fermin A. Carranza, eds. *Carranza's Clinical Periodontology.* 9th ed. Philadelphia: W. B. Saunders, 2001.

Schoen, Diane H., and Mary-Catherine Dean. *Contemporary Periodontal Instrumentation.* Philadelphia: W. B. Saunders, 1996.

Watts, Trevor L. P. *Periodontics in Practice.* New York: Thieme Medical Publishing, 2000.

Wilson, Thomas G., Jr., and Kenneth S. Kornman. *Fundamentals of Periodontics.* 2d ed. Chicago: Quintessence Publishing, 2002.

PHARMACISTS

Calling from the front counter, the pharmacy technician asks, "Do you have a second, Mike?" Mike Schaeuble, pharmacist and manager of The Medicine Shoppe, rises from his desk, where he is getting an order ready to phone in to the pharmaceutical wholesaler.

"What do you need, Deb?" he asks as he walks toward her.

"Linda Watson called in with a question on Paxil," Deb replies. "She's going in for elective surgery in a week, and her doctor wanted her to make sure she's been off the Paxil long enough. Apparently, it can cause complications with the anesthesia."

Mike pulls open a drawer and takes out a file. He flips through the contents slowly. "There's nothing in the literature on it," he says. "Get SmithKline Beecham, Paxil's manufacturer, on the phone for me so I can ask them about it. In the meantime, I've got to finish up my order and get it phoned in before 10:00 today."

Definition
Pharmacists dispense drugs prescribed by physicians, dentists, and other health practitioners. They also provide information to pharmacy customers about their medications.

Alternative Job Title
Druggists

High School Subjects
Biology
Chemistry
Mathematics

Personal Skills
Helping/teaching
Technical/scientific

Salary Range
$58,010 to $80,530 to $97,650+

Educational Requirements
Doctor of pharmacy (Pharm.D.) degree

Certification or Licensing
Voluntary for certain positions (certification)
Required by all states (licensing)

Outlook
Faster than the average

DOT
074

GOE
14.02.01

NOC
3131

O*NET-SOC
29-1051.00

What Does a Pharmacist Do?

Pharmacists dispense drugs that have been prescribed by physicians, dentists, and other health care practitioners. They must have a thorough understanding of drug products and how they affect people, and they must counsel their customers about the proper uses of medications. This knowledge is very important because some drugs can be ineffective or even dangerous if they are taken with other drugs or with alcohol. Pharmacists must also warn their customers about such potential side effects as drowsiness, nausea, and increased sensitivity to sunlight.

Pharmacists receive their customers' prescriptions in written form or over the telephone. They then fill the prescriptions with the proper drugs in the strengths indicated.

Pharmacists formerly had to mix many drugs together themselves. Today, most drugs are made and sold in ready-to-take forms by pharmaceutical companies. Because of this, compounding (mixing ingredients to form medications) is a very small part of a pharmacist's job.

Pharmacists keep records of prescriptions filled for each customer. Today, most pharmacies use computers to do this. Each customer has a file that contains pertinent data, such as address, phone number, and insurance information. When filling each prescription, a pharmacist enters new information into the file, including the date, the prescribing doctor's name, and the type, strength, and dosage schedule of the medicine. By referring to customer records, a pharmacist can detect the possibility of negative reactions caused by taking one medicine in combination with others. Referring to customer records also tells a pharmacist if a prescription is being refilled too soon or too often.

Most pharmacists work in community pharmacies, which may be an independent store, a chain, or affiliated with grocery or department stores. These pharmacists, in addition to selling prescription medicines, also sell such nonprescription items as vitamins, aspirin, cough syrup, and cold remedies.

Pharmacists who work in community settings often function as *pharmacy managers* as well. They are responsible for purchasing and tracking inventory, keeping financial records, and billing insurance carriers. They also supervise other pharmacy workers. Among the people that pharmacists supervise are *pharmacy assistants*, whose duties include compounding medications and submitting pharmacy reports, and *pharmacy technicians*, whose duties include filling bottles with tablets and typing labels.

Some pharmacists work in hospitals or other institutional settings. They fill prescriptions, stock pharmaceuticals, keep patient records, and prepare sterile solutions for IVs. In addition to these duties, hospital pharmacists often confer with doctors, nurses, and other staff members about patient treatments. In some cases, pharmacists work directly with physicians to help with drug therapy selection and monitoring.

A growing number of pharmacists today are choosing to work in a variety of positions for pharmaceutical companies. Some of these pharmacists are involved in research and product development, conducting analyses and testing of products. Others work in production and quality assurance, evaluating procedures for manufacturing and packaging drugs. Still others work in marketing or as sales representatives.

Finally, some pharmacists work for managed care organizations. In these settings, they work directly with physicians and other health care providers to ensure that pharmaceutical therapies are prescribed in the most appropriate and cost-effective way. This often involves reviewing medical literature to determine which medications are the safest and most effective. It can also involve gathering data from the organization's patient database and analyzing it.

Lingo to Learn

Compounding The mixing of ingredients to form powders, tablets, capsules, ointments, and solutions.

Contraindication Something that makes prescribing a particular drug inadvisable, such as a patient's medical condition or a patient's use of another drug.

Pharmacokinetic Pertaining to the way a drug interacts with the human body, in terms of the drug's absorption, distribution, and excretion.

Pharmacology The study of the properties of drugs, including their therapeutic values.

Pharmacotherapy The treatment of disease, especially mental illness, with drugs.

Protocol A detailed plan for how a particular drug should be used for medical treatment.

Radiopharmacy The use of radioactive drugs for diagnostic or therapeutic purposes.

Suspension A type of medicine that consists of solid particles mixed with, but undissolved, in a fluid.

What Is It Like to Be a Pharmacist?

Mike Schaeuble is the owner and manager of a franchise pharmacy located a few blocks from a hospital in a mid-sized town. His pharmacy sells only health-related merchandise, instead of the lines of cosmetics, sundries, and hygiene products often found in larger stores.

His days start at 8:30 in the morning, Mondays through Fridays, with a quick check of phone calls that have come in during the night. "A lot of times, we will get calls from doctors or patients needing prescriptions filled," Mike says. "That's the first thing we look at. Then we check our stock for anything we need, and we put together an order for delivery the next day."

Monitoring the pharmacy stock is an important part of Mike's job. Because pharmaceuticals are so expensive, he tries to keep excess product to a minimum. "That's well over $100,000 in inventory right there," he says, pointing to the shelves behind his pharmacy counter. "Part of the business is trying to keep the stock as low as possible without running out." To do this, Mike doesn't warehouse product at all; he reorders only when he needs a particular medicine.

After the morning order has been placed and any other necessary paperwork done, he settles down to the main business of the day. "In this particular pharmacy, 99 percent of our business is filling prescriptions," he says.

Prescriptions are either brought in by patients or called in by the prescribing doctor or nurse. Before any prescription is filled, a certain amount of patient information must be gathered and put into a computerized file. "We need to have name, address, phone, and insurance information," Mike says. "And we try to have a history of the medications that each patient is taking." When the new prescription information is keyed in, a computer software program scans the entire patient record for possible negative drug interactions. Mike also checks the patient record to make sure that no harmful interactions will take place.

Once the necessary information has been entered, Mike fills the prescription. "We make sure that we are reading it accurately. If there's any question at all, we call the physician," he says. "Obviously, the doctors make the biggest part of the medication decisions. We don't have a lot of input into that, unless it's a product that has more than one manufacturer." If there is a generic version of a particular product, the pharmacist must get both the doctor's and the patient's permission before dispensing it.

Because virtually all medicines are now manufactured in ready-to-take form, the actual filling of the prescription is not difficult. It is, in almost every case, a matter of counting out tablets or capsules or measuring liquids. Occasionally, however, Mike must compound a medicine. "The dermatologists are the ones I most often compound a prescription for," he says. "And more frequently now, gynecologists order progesterone suppositories that have to be compounded."

At the same time Mike is filling a prescription, he creates the label for the medicine bottle and sends the necessary information to the patient's insurance carrier for authorization. "We're online with most major carriers," he says. "When I fill a prescription, the information is automatically sent to the carrier, which either authorizes payment for the fill or tells us why they won't." On some occasions, the insurance carrier's records show that the patient is not due for a refill. In these cases, Mike may have to mediate between the carrier, the patient, and the prescribing doctor.

A large part of Mike's job consists of patient education. Many drugs have side effects that can be serious if they are ignored. When a patient gets a prescription that is new, Mike explains the proper way to take the medication and the things to avoid while taking it. "The days of 'just take this' are in the past," he says. "We want to try to educate the patients so they know what they're taking, how they should be taking it, and why. A knowledgeable patient is a better patient."

We want to try to educate the patients so they know what they're taking, how they should be taking it, and why. A knowledgeable patient is a better patient.

Do I Have I What It Takes to Be a Pharmacist?

Pharmacists are an important link in the health care chain. They are responsible for making sure that the patient actually gets what the doctor ordered. There is no room for mistakes. The wrong drug or the wrong dosage could be dangerous or even fatal. For this reason, you must have a high level of personal reliability. "Basically, you have to be a perfectionist," says Mike. "What you do has to be done right every time. There's no real margin for error."

You must also be ethical. Many of the drugs you will deal with are addictive and must be closely regulated. You will be responsible for dispensing drugs in strict accordance with doctors' orders. You cannot take that task lightly.

Your willingness to learn is vital to being a good pharmacist. New pharmaceutical products are being created constantly, and medical research is continually suggesting new approaches to drug therapy. As a pharmacist, you must remain aware of new developments in the field.

"You have to keep up," says Mike. "Our profession is centered around the knowledge of medication. If you don't keep up, that's when mistakes are made."

To Be a Successful Pharmacist, You Should . . .

- have good communication skills
- be accurate and detail-oriented
- have a strong sense of responsibility
- be flexible and willing to keep up on new developments in the field
- have an interest in science and health care

Because you will probably work with the public, as many pharmacists do, you need to have good people skills. "I think you have to like the interaction with the public," Mike says. "In fact, I consider many of my customers as my friends." Even if you don't work directly with the public you need good communication skills to interact with physicians, nurses, researchers, and colleagues.

Finally, you must have a strong interest in health care. Mike especially likes the fact that he is helping others. "You see people come in and they're feeling poorly, and hopefully you can do your little bit to make them feel better and improve their quality of life," he says. "That's what health care is all about."

The downside of pharmacy, for Mike, lies in dealing with insurance companies. "The amount of time spent meddling with the carriers just seems to be increasing," he says. "That gets tedious."

Another problem with the career, he notes, can be irregular hours. "If you're in a department store setting, your hours may not be good. They can include evenings, weekends, and holidays," he says.

How Do I Become a Pharmacist?

EDUCATION

High School

Because so many college courses in the pharmacy curriculum are science-related, you should begin building your math and science skills while still in high school. A good background in chemistry is especially significant. Other science courses, such as biology and physiology, are also good choices, as is mathematics. Taking computer courses is also important. Pharmacies, like most other businesses, are becoming increasingly dependent upon computers. Most pharmacists today use computers to maintain customer information, communicate with insurance carriers, and track inventory.

Business, English, and communication classes, including speech, are important because they will help you develop skills that will be useful throughout your professional career.

Postsecondary Training

The doctor of pharmacy (Pharm.D.) degree is the minimum educational requirement for becoming a pharmacist. (The bachelor's of pharmacy, or B.Pharm. degree, is no longer offered.) Obtaining a Pharm.D. involves at least six years of postsecondary study. In order to be admitted to one of the 85 accredited Pharm.D. programs in the United States, applicants must have completed at least two years of college study. Prerequisites include classes in mathematics, biology, chemistry, physics, and the humanities. Many schools also require applicants to take the Pharmacy College Admissions Test (PCAT).

Classes in Pharm.D. programs are specific to the practice of pharmacy and include organic and medicinal chemistry, biochemistry, pharmaceutics, physiology, pathophysiology, pharmacology, pharmacy law, and laboratory and clinical practice. Students learn how to interact with patients and health care providers and about professional ethics.

Students who are interested in pharmaceutical research and development may go on to pursue a master's or Ph.D. degree in pharmacy. In addition to course work, most of these programs involve performing research at drug companies or universities.

An increasing number of pharmacy graduates are seeking residency training in pharmacy practice. There are over 400 of these pharmacy residencies offered across the country in hospitals, pharmacies, and other facilities.

As a new pharmacist, you may take a residency that focuses on general pharmacy practice, clinical pharmacy, or other specialty areas. Some employers, particularly hospital pharmacies and pharmacy schools, require that you complete one of these residencies as a prerequisite for employment.

CERTIFICATION OR LICENSING

All states and the District of Columbia require that you be licensed to practice pharmacy. In order to become licensed, you must have either a B.S. in pharmacy or a Pharm.D. degree. Most states also require that you spend a specified amount of time in a supervised internship. Internships are usually incorporated into the college curriculum.

All states except California (which has its own licensure exam) require pharmacy graduates to pass the North American Pharmacist Licensure Exam (NAPLEX) and the Multistate Pharmacy Jurisprudence Exam (MPJE) before they can practice. Some states require additional exams that are unique to that state. Although a pharmacy license is valid only in the state in which it is granted, most states grant licenses to pharmacists licensed in other states without extensive reexamination.

After being licensed to practice pharmacy, you must continue your education. Most states require 15 hours of additional education yearly in order to retain your license.

There is currently a certification available in geriatric pharmacy, which is a specialization that deals with the unique health care concerns of the elderly. This credential is administered by the Commission for Certification in Geriatric Pharmacy (http://www.ccgp.org).

SCHOLARSHIPS AND GRANTS

Tuition costs vary depending upon the size of the school, whether or not the school is in the state where you reside, and whether the school is privately or publicly funded.

There are usually grants, scholarships, and loans available through most pharmacy colleges. The easiest way to explore the various financial aid possibilities is to write directly to the financial aid offices of pharmacy schools and request information and application forms.

There are also various loan programs available through the federal government, including Pell Grants, Stafford Student Loans, National Direct Student Loans, Health Education Assistance Loans, and Health Professions Student Loans. Your high school guidance counselor should have information about these programs.

Many students finance their medical education through the Armed Forces Health Professions Scholarship Program. Each branch of the military participates in this program, paying students' tuitions in exchange for military service. Contact your local recruiting office for more information on this program.

Who Will Hire Me?

Mike was recruited for his first pharmacy position while he was still in college. "I went to South Dakota State," he says, "and in January of my senior year, the recruiters for the May graduates came on campus for interviews." He was offered a job with Osco, a chain of drug stores, as a staff pharmacist.

Generally speaking, it is not difficult for new pharmacists to find jobs. You will have many employment possibilities as a pharmacy graduate. Over 62 percent of the pharmacists are employed in a retail or community pharmacy, and 22 percent work in hospitals or institutions. You may also find job opportunities with pharmaceutical companies, health maintenance organizations (HMOs), or government or educational institutions.

Many graduates, like Mike, will be recruited for entry-level positions while still in college. If you do not secure a job with an on-campus recruiter, you may be able to find a job through the pharmacy school's placement office. In fact, this office is usually a good place to initiate your job search.

Another way to find a pharmacist position is to contact employers directly. You should send cover letters and resumes to pharmacies within the region where you would like to work. Some students have success searching for jobs over the Internet. You can search college and university Web sites as well as regional newspapers for job listings. Professional organizations and trade magazines are also good sources for job leads.

Where Can I Go from Here?

Mike started his career as a staff pharmacist. He later moved into a position managing two pharmacies affiliated with a chain grocery store. After several years, he left the chain store and became the manager of an independent franchise pharmacy, where he now plans to remain.

"I like this," he says, looking around his store. "I like the steady hours and the fact that I only deal

In-depth

Outlook Is Promising for Geriatric Pharmacists

There is increased interest in, and a demand for, certified geriatric pharmacists. As America's population ages, and as baby boomers become seniors, there will be a growing need to manage the drug requirements for this older segment of our society. Studies have shown that properly managed drug therapy can help older patients with multiple diseases live better and longer lives. Older people's body systems can react differently to drugs. Even when medication is taken as intended, some adverse reactions can occur that may cause disability and death. There will be an increasing need for pharmacists who specialize in the drug therapy needs of our older population. Pharmacists who have the expertise to know the specifics about the right medication, administered in the right amount and in the right way to an older population, will be in great demand.

with health-related merchandise. It's nice not having to answer questions about where the paper towels or light bulbs are. I'm going to stay with it."

Advancement opportunities in pharmacy depend largely upon where you are employed and your skills. If you work in a drug store chain, you may move into a management position. A common management position is as a district manager in charge of several pharmacies. If you have the necessary experience, capital, and entrepreneurial spirit, you might want to own your own pharmacy.

If you work in a hospital pharmacy, you might advance to the position of chief pharmacist, or director of pharmacy services. In this position, you would be responsible for all the pharmaceutical needs of the hospital, including supervising the pharmacy staff.

Working for a pharmaceutical manufacturer, you may have the opportunity to move into a supervisory position in sales, research, quality control, advertising, production, packaging, or general business management.

If you earn a Ph.D. in pharmacy, you might consider teaching pharmacy or pharmacy-related classes at the college level. Or, you may choose to go into pharmaceutical or pharmacological research.

What Are the Salary Ranges?

According to the U.S. Department of Labor, pharmacists made median annual salaries of $80,530 in 2003. The lowest paid 10 percent made less than $58,010 a year, while the highest paid 10 percent made more than $97,650. Overall, pharmacists working on the West coast earn higher salaries. Pharmacists who work for the federal government generally make less than their private sector counterparts.

In addition to salary, most full-time pharmacists are provided with a full benefits package, which includes paid vacation, medical and dental insurance, and extra pay for overtime. Some employers provide bonuses and profit-sharing plans.

Advancement Possibilities

Directors of pharmacy services supervise and coordinate the activities and functions of hospital pharmacies.

Pharmacy district managers manage several pharmacies in a certain geographic area, usually for a drugstore chain, department store, or grocery store.

Pharmaceutical researchers develop and analyze new drugs.

Professors of pharmacy and professors of pharmacology teach classes to pharmacy students at the college and university levels.

What Is the Job Outlook?

The U.S. Department of Labor predicts that job opportunities for pharmacists will grow faster than the average through 2012. The number of available positions is expected to exceed the number of people entering the field, mainly due to pharmacists who are retiring or otherwise leaving the field. The growing elderly population in the United States is one reason for the good job prospects for pharmacists. Senior citizens are expected to take an increasing number of prescription medications as a result of continuing medical advances and new drug research.

The demand for pharmacists in hospitals will not be as great as other areas of the industry, since hospitals are increasing the amount of outpatient visits and decreasing the length of patient stays; this prompts people to purchase prescriptions from other retail venues, such as drug store and supermarket pharmacies, where job outlooks will be quite good. Other avenues for pharmacists include working for pharmaceutical manufacturing companies, especially those that manufacture drugs designed to treat ailments that affect senior citizens. In such contexts, pharmacists can work in research and development, or even in the marketing and advertising of new drug products.

It appears that pharmacists who are well trained, are willing to keep up with the latest pharmaceutical advances, and are flexible with their career goals should not have difficulty finding jobs. There should also be great advancement opportunities for experienced pharmacists.

How Do I Learn More?

PROFESSIONAL ORGANIZATIONS

The following are organizations that provide information on pharmacy careers, accredited schools, and employers:

Academy of Managed Care Pharmacy
100 North Pitt Street, Suite 400
Alexandria, VA 22314
800-827-2627
http://www.amcp.org

American Association of Colleges of Pharmacy
1426 Prince Street
Alexandria, VA 22314
703-739-2330
pthompson@aacp.org
http://www.aacp.org

American Pharmaceutical Association
2215 Constitution Avenue, NW
Washington, DC 20037
202-628-4410
http://www.aphanet.org

American Society of Consultant Pharmacists
1321 Duke Street
Alexandria, VA 22314
703-739-1300
info@ascp.com
http://www.ascp.com

BIBLIOGRAPHY

The following is a sampling of materials relating to the professional concerns and development of pharmacists:

Gable, Fred B. *Opportunities in Pharmacy Careers*. New York: McGraw-Hill, 2003.

Green, Steven, ed. *Tarascon Pocket Pharmacopoeia: 2005 Classic Shirt-Pocket Edition*. Loma Linda, Calif.: Tarascon Press, 2004.

Lacy, Charles, Lola L. Armstrong, Morton P. Goldman, Leonard L. Lance. *Drug Information Handbook*. Hudson, Ohio: Lexi-Comp, 2004.

McCarthy, Robert L., and Kenneth W. Schafermeyer. *Introduction to Health Care Delivery: A Primer for Pharmacists*. 2d ed. Frederick, Md.: Aspen Publishers, 2001.

Reinders, Thomas P. *The Pharmacy Professional's Guide to Resumes, CVs, and Interviewing*. Washington, D.C.: APhA Publications, 2001.

PHARMACOLOGISTS

The white rat is getting air blown into its face in Dr. Joe DiMicco's laboratory. The rat is in a device called a stress chamber, having its cardiovascular functions monitored with another device, called a telemetric receiver. Joe, clad in a white lab coat, is pointing to the rat while talking to a small group of pharmacology graduate students.

Referring to a three-dimensional model of the rat's brain, Joe points to the part of the brain that his research experiment is focusing on. "This is the dorsomedial hypothalamus. This is where we're going to inject the drug," he explains. "We're going to microinject bicuculline methiodide into this area to block the brain cells known as GABA receptors." He first anesthetizes the rat and then reaches for the cannula, a small tube through which the drug is administered. His students shift slightly to get a better view.

Definition
Pharmacologists are scientists who study the effects of drugs and other chemical agents on human beings and laboratory animals.

High School Subjects
Biology
Chemistry

Personal Skills
Communication/ideas
Technical/scientific

Salary Range
$55,000 to $97,600 to $120,500+

Educational Requirements
Bachelor of science degree; doctoral degree in pharmacology or related field degree

Certification or Licensing
Voluntary

Outlook
Faster than the average

DOT
041

GOE
14.02.01

NOC
2121

O*NET-SOC
19-1042.00

What Does a Pharmacologist Do?

A *pharmacologist* is a scientist who studies the effects of drugs and other chemical agents on animals and humans. One of a pharmacologist's main duties is to develop and test chemical agents that can cure, relieve, or prevent disease. A pharmacologist uses techniques from different sciences, including mathematics, chemistry, biology, physics, and physiology.

Pharmacologists usually conduct their research work in laboratories. The tools and materials they use vary, depending upon the experiment. They may use tissue samples, bodily secretions, body organs, or live animals as test subjects. They use computers and other electronic instruments, various chemical compounds, and radioactive and nonradioactive isotopes (types of atoms).

Different experiments call for different procedures. In some cases, a pharmacologist might inject a chemical into a living tissue sample from a human donor. In other cases, the pharmacologist might inject a drug into a laboratory animal. During these experiments, the pharmacologist monitors the tissue sample or animal closely to see what results the drug has. Test animals are sometimes sacrificed so that necropsies, or autopsies, can be performed to determine the effects of particular drugs on various parts of the body.

Some pharmacologists work for pharmaceutical companies in the development and testing of new drugs. Before any new drug is marketed to the public, it must be extensively tested and refined. Pharmacologists working on a new drug perform tests to determine what side effects it might have, what dosage is most effective, what the best way to administer it is, and how the body absorbs, distributes, and eliminates it.

Pharmacologists also work in academic settings. These scientists, in addition to conducting research projects, teach classes and seminars and direct graduate students in laboratory work.

Pharmacologists may specialize in how chemicals affect certain parts of the body. A *cardiovascular pharmacologist* works with chemicals that affect the cardiovascular and circulatory systems. An *endocrine pharmacologist* studies the effects of drugs on the hormonal balance of the body. A *neuropharmacologist* works with drugs that affect the brain, spinal cord, and nerves. A *psychopharmacologist,* or *behavioral pharmacologist,* works with drugs that affect behavior. A *clinical pharmacologist* specializes in testing various drugs and other chemicals on humans. Studies are made on how certain drugs work, how they interact with other drugs, how their effects can alter the patterns of disease, and how disease can alter the drugs' effects.

There are additional areas of specialization in pharmacology. A *molecular pharmacologist* specializes in studying the precise interactions between drug molecules and cells. A *biochemical pharmacologist* works to determine how drugs influence the chemical activities within organisms. A *veterinary pharmacologist* studies and develops drugs used to treat cats, dogs, and other animals.

Lingo to Learn

Pharmacodynamics The study of the reactions between drugs and living systems.

Pharmacogenetics The science and study of the inheritance of characteristic patterns of interaction between chemicals (drugs) and organisms.

Pharmacognosy The science concerned with the composition, production, use, and history of crude, or unrefined, drugs.

Pharmacokinetics The study of how drugs are absorbed, distributed, metabolized, and excreted.

Therapeutics The study of how drugs and other chemical agents correlate with the physiological, biochemical, microbiological, immunological, and behavioral factors influencing disease. Therapeutics is also concerned with how disease may modify how the body absorbs or disposes of a drug.

Toxicology The study of the adverse effects of drugs and other chemical agents.

What Is It Like to Be a Pharmacologist?

Dr. Joe DiMicco works in the department of pharmacology of a large state university. His office adjoins a high-tech laboratory. Joe splits his time between the office, the lab, and the classroom. "I codirect a course for second-year med students in the fall," he says. "So, when that's in session, I tend to be heavily involved with it on a day-to-day basis." When teaching, Joe arrives at his office at 6:30 A.M. to check his e-mail and respond to questions from students. After that, he assembles the slides and reviews the notes for his lecture. At 8:00, his two-hour lecture begins. He spends afternoons in the laboratory with his students, directing their research experiments. "That's the way my day goes when I'm heavily into teaching," he says.

Besides teaching, the other major part of Joe's work is research. His avenue of research is neuroscience. "I am looking at pathways in the brain that are responsible for generating the physiological changes engendered by stress," he says. "The focus is mostly on cardiovascular indicators, with some endocrine studies, some behavioral, and some gastrointestinal."

Joe has two graduate students in pharmacology working in his lab, and he directs them in planning and conducting research experiments. Earlier in his career he did most of the experiments himself. "One of the ironic things about science is that the more successful you are, the less you get to do the actual science," he says. "You build a little empire of people and then you rarely get into the labs to do the research."

Joe's research work involves testing the stress response in rats. In order to prove his hypothesis that a certain area of the brain—the dorsomedial hypothalamus—is the source of physiological stress symptoms, Joe uses various chemicals to stimulate that part of the rat's brain. "We take a rat under anesthesia and, using a cannula, microinject different drugs to see different results," he says. After the rat has been injected with a drug, it is tested for stress response. "We've developed a model for stress that involves very minimal discomfort for the rat," says Joe. "What we've discovered is that we can take a rat and put him into a little tube and blow air into his face. They hate having air blown in their faces and they have the maximal stress response for that."

While the rat is in the stress chamber, Joe and his students monitor its physical functions. "We can monitor cardiovascular functions using telemetry," he says. "There are little transmitters we implant in the abdomen, with a sensor in the aorta. When we sit the rat on the telemetric receiver, we get a moment-by-moment reading of its cardiovascular functions."

They also monitor the levels of stress hormones in the rat's blood by drawing blood samples. All the data collected for each experiment is carefully documented and compiled. Joe takes the data from the experiments and enters it into a computer, where it is analyzed and used to generate graphs and spreadsheets.

Another part of Joe's work involves reporting the results of his findings to the scientific community. He, like most academic scientists, publishes at least one research paper each year, explaining the nature and findings of his projects. These are typically published in professional journals or as chapters for books.

In addition to teaching and research activities, Joe has a number of administrative duties. Of these, the most significant and time-consuming is writing grant proposals. Securing grant money is the only way to ensure that his research can continue. "It's a struggle to get funding these days because there's a lot of competition," Joe says. "I spend a lot of time writing grant proposals, which can be successful but are more often not successful."

Other responsibilities include periodic trips to Washington, D.C., to work with the National Institutes of Health, the National Institute of Drug Abuse, and the National Aeronautics and Space Administration. He also sits on a number of committees for his university, runs summer internship programs for local colleges, and occasionally does consulting work.

Do I Have What It Takes to Be a Pharmacologist?

Curiosity and problem-solving skills are two vital qualities you need if you want to be a pharmacologist, according to Joe. "It's important to question everything," he says. "You need to be the kind of person who reads a textbook and says 'I wonder why that's so,' instead of just accepting it as fact."

It's important to question everything. You need to be the kind of person who reads a textbook and says 'I wonder why that's so,' instead of just accepting it as fact.

A keen eye for detail and excellent observational skills are also important. Because of the exacting nature of pharmacological experiments and the need for precision when performing them, it is important that you be extremely thorough in your work habits. "If you get tired, you get frustrated, you leave out things, you cut corners—those are the sorts of things that will do you in as a scientist," says Joe.

Good communication skills are also vital to success in this field. Although you may work alone on a specific project, you are nonetheless part of a team. You must communicate clearly. Excellent oral and written communication skills are needed to present the results of research projects. Joe states, "You could be doing the greatest science in the world, and if you can't communicate it, it's worthless."

Finally, you need a great deal of patience and persistence in order to perform your work successfully. Joe says it's easy to get discouraged. "You may put together the most well-supported hypothesis, you can spend weeks in the library putting together all the information, and you can feel sure that it's all going to work," he says, "but then when you get in the lab, it may all fall flat."

Despite the sometimes discouraging and tedious nature of the work, most pharmacologists find their jobs to be very fulfilling. There is a sense of satisfaction in contributing to advances in medical science. There is also the thrill of proving one's hypotheses or discovering something new. "Most of us in this career find ourselves terribly spoiled, I think," says Joe. "To be able to do what fascinates you as your life's work is a tremendous privilege."

How Do I Become a Pharmacologist?

When Joe was an undergraduate, he did not plan to become a pharmacologist. In fact, he wasn't even an enthusiastic science student at first. "I labored under the same misconception that most people have, which is that science is just a lot of facts," he says. It wasn't until he worked as a lab technician for a professor at MIT that he really grew to love science.

"Real science is going in the lab and asking, 'What would happen if I did this?' It's getting a little glimpse into something no one has ever seen or known about before," he says. "I realized that when I worked at MIT. And then the professor I worked for convinced me that I had a talent for doing science and that I could make a contribution."

EDUCATION

High School

A high school diploma is the first essential step to becoming a pharmacologist. High school classes in biology, physics, and chemistry are especially helpful, and they offer opportunities for laboratory research. Mathematics courses, especially calculus, will help you develop the critical thinking skills needed in pharmacology. Math classes also help by emphasizing the importance of precise measurements and calculations. English and speech classes are also important because jobs in this field are likely to include writing about and orally presenting research findings. Computer literacy is another valuable skill that you should acquire in high school. Computers are widely used in pharmacology to calculate, analyze, and document research data.

Postsecondary Training

Because most colleges do not have pharmacology majors, you should probably earn a bachelor of science degree in chemistry or a biological science. Recently, however, some colleges have added pharmacology programs for undergraduate students. Where these programs are available, they are certainly a wise choice.

Whichever undergraduate degree you choose, it will typically have a curriculum heavy in the natural sciences and mathematics. You will be required to take classes in organic and physical chemistry, biology, physics, molecular biology, mathematics, and statistics. Many of these classes include hands-on research experience.

In addition to science-related classes, you should take courses that help you communicate clearly and think critically, such as writing, literature, and humanities.

After completing a bachelor's degree, you must complete four to five years of graduate study in pharmacology. Pharmacy schools, medical schools, schools of biomedical sciences, and schools of veterinary medicine usually have Ph.D. programs in pharmacology.

Pharmacology Ph.D. programs typically have curriculums that include cellular and molecular biology, biochemistry, physiology, neurology, statistics, and research design. Courses in the pharmacological sciences include basic pharmacology, molecular pharmacology, chemotherapy, and toxicology. You should also take courses based on specific organ systems, such as cardiovascular pharmacology, renal pharmacology, and neuropharmacology.

The major component of graduate study in pharmacology is research. Graduate students conduct both supervised and independent research. The primary goal is to complete an original research study that yields new information.

Before taking a permanent position, a new Ph.D. graduate typically spends two to four years of further research training in a postdoctoral position. This provides you with the opportunity to work on a second significant research project with an established scientist.

CERTIFICATION OR LICENSING

The American Board of Clinical Pharmacology administers the examinations for individual certification in clinical and applied pharmacology. There are two certificate categories. Licensed physicians can apply for the certification in clinical pharmacology. Non-physicians and non-licensed physicians can be accredited in applied pharmacology.

"Many times pharmacology is not a physician's only specialty," says Marilyn Hinton, of the American Board of Clinical Pharmacology. "It is usually an additional area of expertise that relates to the physician's specialty. For instance, an internist who deals with patients who have high blood pressure may also be a certified pharmacologist who studies the effects that blood-pressure reducing drugs have on patients with hypertension."

SCHOLARSHIPS AND GRANTS

Tuition costs vary depending upon the size of the school, whether or not the school is in the state where you reside, and whether the school is privately or publicly funded.

There are usually grants, scholarships, and loans available through most colleges. The easiest way to explore the various financial aid possibilities is to write directly to the financial aid offices of schools and request information and application forms.

Universities sometimes offer scholarships for graduate work to qualified candidates. These scholarships often cover all school-related expenses, including room and board. Many require that the recipient serve as an assistant to a professor in the classroom or laboratory.

A good starting point for financial aid research is the SmartStudent Guide to Financial Aid Web site: http://www.finaid.org. This Web site has an extensive list of financial assistance information and links. Research the various loan programs available through the federal government, including Pell Grants, Stafford Student Loans, National Direct Student Loans, Health Education Assistance Loans, and Health Professions Student Loans.

FYI

Although pharmacology and pharmacy are often confused, remember that pharmacology is a separate career in the health sciences. A pharmacist focuses on the preparation, compounding, and dispensing of drugs. Pharmacists use the information provided by pharmacologists. A pharmacologist studies the effects of chemical agents on human and animal biological systems. Pharmacologists use many scientific disciplines, including chemistry, cell biology, and physiology, to solve drug and chemical-related problems that affect human health.

Who Will Hire Me?

You should start looking for a position before you complete your Ph.D. Pharmaceutical companies, universities, and government organizations often recruit pharmacologists who are earning their degrees. University placement offices may also help you find a position.

Your career options depend on your interests and your subspecialty. A medical, dental, or pharmacy school or university may employ you. The government or a nonprofit research organization may also provide a career opportunity. The pharmaceutical industries also hire pharmacologists.

As with many highly skilled professions, networking is key. "The vast majority of people with a new pharmacology degree do some kind of postdoctoral training," Joe says, "and networking is a very important feature of that whole process. A lot of people secure their initial positions just through the contacts they make."

If you know which subspecialty you are interested in, you should contact companies and universities involved with that subspecialty. Sending cover letters and resumes to the personnel directors of these companies and universities may bring results.

If you are interested in government work you may look for employment in various federal agencies. You might consider contacting the U.S. Department of Health and Human Services, the Nuclear Regulatory Commission, the Environmental Protection Agency, the U.S. Department of Agriculture, the U.S. Public Health Service, or the U.S. Department of the Interior for openings and application procedures.

Where Can I Go from Here?

As a new pharmacologist you will probably work with scientists experienced in research. You will learn laboratory procedures, equipment operation and care, and how to perform tests on human and animal subjects for the specific projects you are assigned. You will also learn how to comply with such governmental regulatory agencies as the Food and Drug Administration and the U.S. Department of Agriculture.

During you career, you will gradually take on additional responsibilities. Eventually you will get opportunities to work on your own projects. Advancement from this point usually involves responsibilities such as coordinating major projects or supervising other scientists in laboratories. Supervisory positions and responsibilities are generally awarded to experienced pharmacologists who have proven they are capable scientists.

If you are a pharmacologist in an academic setting you may become a tenured professor and department head. Department heads supervise other professors and, in some cases, oversee all the research projects being conducted within the department. Department heads are frequently asked to present papers and speak at conferences.

What Are the Salary Ranges?

A 2001 survey (the most recent information available) by the American Association of Pharmaceutical Scientists places average base salaries (excluding bonuses) for pharmacologists at $97,600 a year for those working in industry, $95,100 for those in academia, and $81,400 for those in government. The survey also compared salaries by education level and work experience. Pharmacologists with a master's degree and 0 to 5 years of experience earned annual mean salaries of $55,000; with 10 to 20 years, $76,000; and 30 or more years, $106,000. Pharmacologists with a Ph.D. and 0 to 5 years of experience earned annual mean salaries of $72,000; with 10 to 20 years, $108,000; and 30 or more years, $120,500. Bonuses, especially for those in industry, can increase yearly earnings considerably.

Benefits generally include health and dental insurance and paid vacation and sick days.

What Is the Job Outlook?

Employment of pharmacologists is expected to increase faster than the average for all occupations in the next several years. A significant factor in this is the continuing advancement of medical science and technology.

As medical scientists learn more about the human body and how it works, they uncover new possibilities for pharmaceutical treatments. Pharmacologists are needed to explore and experiment with these new treatment possibilities. Specifically, expanded research on such health issues as AIDS, cancer, organ transplants, and other diseases will create jobs in pharmacology. In addition, as more drugs are developed, there is the potential for more drug interactions.

Another reason for the growth in jobs is the deepening concern about environmental toxins. Increasingly, pharmacologists are involved in researching the effects of atmospheric gases, household products, substances used in the workplace, and other environmental materials. This trend is expected to continue and to increase the demand for pharmacologists.

Other expanding pharmacological fields of research are drug abuse and gene therapy. Pharmacologists in the field of drug abuse are working to better understand the effects of abused substances on the fetus and on the body's organ systems. Research in gene therapy focuses on the development of gene products that alter the courses of disease. Both of these fields should provide good career prospects for pharmacologists.

Finally, the need for more pharmacologists involved in research will increase the need for teachers of pharmacology.

Despite the anticipated demand for pharmacologists, it is important to remember that the federal government funds much research and development. Therefore, budget cuts could lead to smaller increases in research and development expenditures, which would limit the dollar amount of each grant and slow the overall growth of research projects.

How Do I Learn More?

PROFESSIONAL ORGANIZATIONS

The following are organizations that provide information on pharmacologist careers, accredited schools, and employers:

American Association of Pharmaceutical Scientists
2107 Wilson Boulevard, Suite 700
Alexandria, VA 22201
703-243-2800
aaps@aaps.org
http://www.aapspharmaceutica.com

American Board of Clinical Pharmacology Inc.
PO Box 40278
San Antonio, TX 78229-1278
210-567-8505
http://www.abcp.net

American Society for Clinical Pharmacology and Therapeutics
528 North Washington Street
Alexandria, VA 22314
703-836-6981
info@ascpt.org
http://www.ascpt.org

American Society for Pharmacology and Experimental Therapeutics
9650 Rockville Pike
Bethesda, MD 20814
301-634-7060
info@aspet.org
http://www.aspet.org

BIBLIOGRAPHY

The following is a sampling of materials relating to the professional concerns and development of pharmacologists:

Asperheim, Mary K. *Pharmacology: An Introductory Text.* 9th ed. Philadelphia: W. B. Saunders, 2002.

Edmunds, Marilyn W. *Introduction to Clinical Pharmacology.* 4th ed. St. Louis, Mo.: Mosby, 2002.

Gauwitz, Donna F. *Administering Medications: Pharmacology for Health Careers.* 5th ed. New York: McGraw-Hill, 2004.

Kalant, Harold and Walter H. E. Roschlau, eds. *Principles of Medical Pharmacology.* 6th ed. New York: Oxford University Press, 1998.

McKim, William A. *Drugs and Behavior: An Introduction to Behavioral Pharmacology.* 5th ed. Upper Saddle River, N.J.: Prentice-Hall, 2002.

Springhouse Staff. *Clinical Pharmacology Made Incredibly Easy.* Springhouse, Pa.: Springhouse Corporation, 2000.

Stringer, Janet L. *Basic Concepts in Pharmacology: A Student's Survival Guide.* 2d ed. New York: McGraw-Hill, 2001.

Walsh, Carol T., and Rochelle D. Schwartz. *Pharmacology: Drug Actions and Reactions.* 7th ed. London: Taylor & Francis, 2004.

Woodrow, Ruth. *Essentials of Pharmacology for Health Occupations.* 4th ed. Albany, N.Y.: Thomson Delmar, 2001.

PHARMACY TECHNICIANS

Definition
Pharmacy technicians work with pharmacists in preparing medication and keeping patient records. They fill and label bottles with prescribed tablets and capsules, prepare IV packs, take inventory, clean equipment, and enter data into a computer.

Alternative Job Titles
Pharmacy assistants
Pharmacy clerks
Pharmacy medication technicians
Pharmacy technologists

High School Subjects
Chemistry
Health
Mathematics

Personal Skills
Helping/teaching
Technical/scientific

Salary Range
$18,740 to $22,755 to $33,780

Minimum Educational Level
Some postsecondary training

Certification or Licensing
Recommended

Outlook
Faster than the average

DOT
074

GOE
14.02.01

NOC
3414

O*NET-SOC
29-2052.00

The medical center pharmacy is brightly lit. The fluorescent light bounces off the clean white shelves and counters, off the glass bottles and beakers. Like scientists in a laboratory, the pharmacy technicians in their white coats hover over vials and weights and measures. One technician prepares an intravenous solution (IV), while another, wearing a special hood, carefully prepares an investigational drug.

A beeper pierces the quiet of the room. It's a Code 5000, the call for the hospital emergency team, and one of the pharmacy technicians moves into action. Critical situations occur every day in the hospital, and he has become very familiar with emergency procedure.

He takes the cart stocked with medications, equipment, and a monitor defibrillator and quickly makes his way through the hospital. At the end of the corridor, nurses, physicians, and an anesthesiologist stream into the patient's room. They all work hurriedly, yet smoothly and precisely. When the pharmacy tech arrives with the cart, it becomes his responsibility to write down everything that happens in order to maintain a legal record of the emergency scene. He listens and watches carefully and also performs his other duties, such as preparing an IV or resuscitation equipment.

What Does a Pharmacy Technician Do?

You've probably stood many times at a pharmacist's counter, waiting for a prescription to be filled. You've watched the pharmacist count out pills or prepare capsules. You've been advised on how to use each medication safely and effectively. And you've probably noticed how much the pharmacist relies on his or her assistants. These assistants are known as *pharmacy technicians,* and they have become a recognized force in the health care industry.

Whether in a drug store, hospital, clinic, or nursing care facility, pharmacy technicians perform a number of duties, many of which require precision and attention to detail. In a retail pharmacy, technicians work under the direction of a pharmacist. Their responsibilities include filling prescriptions and preparing prescription labels, as well as stocking and taking inventory of prescriptions and over-the-counter medications. They also have a number of clerical duties, such as maintaining a database of patient medication records, preparing insurance claim forms, and managing the cash register. The

Lingo to Learn

Defibrillator A device used for arresting chaotic contractions of the heart muscle.

Dosage The amount of medicine to be given.

Floor stock Medication that is kept in the drug cabinet for the nursing unit.

Intravenous (IV) An injection that involves inserting a needle or catheter into a vein to introduce a drug or solution.

Palliative A medicine that relieves without curing.

Parenteral This term pertains to drugs given by injection.

Pharmacopoeia A reference book that describes every drug's purity and the dosage forms in which it is available.

Toxicity A poisonous drug reaction that impairs body functions or damages cells.

pharmacy technician also cleans and sterilizes glassware and equipment.

In a hospital, pharmacy technicians perform many of the same duties as in a retail setting, along with some added responsibilities. For instance, *hospital pharmacy technicians* often assemble 24-hour supplies of medication for patients, prepare commercially unavailable medications, prepare sterile intravenous medications, and deliver medications to patient rooms. They also maintain medications at nursing stations and in operation rooms. Sometimes, a pharmacy technician distributes medications to smaller, outpatient clinics. In large hospitals where computerized or robotic dispensing equipment is used, technicians are usually in charge of operating and maintaining the equipment.

In some hospitals, pharmacy technicians are also important members of the emergency team. They prepare resuscitation equipment and keep a special cart stocked with medications and a monitor defibrillator, which they bring with them when summoned to an emergency in the hospital.

Preparing medication, whether it be for a customer or a hospital patient, often requires more than counting pills and filling bottles. Pharmacy technicians work with a variety of substances and tools, such as a mortar and pestle (typically made of glass or porcelain), which is used to grind crystalline or granular substances. Conical and cylindrical graduates are glasses used for measuring liquids. Technicians use spatulas to prepare ointments or to remove substances from the mortar and pestle. An experienced technician in a hospital or research facility works with investigational drugs: new drugs approved for human use but with unknown side effects; some patients agree to try these new drugs when all other prescribed drugs and treatments have failed. Preparing the investigational drugs requires special gloves and hoods. These experienced technicians also work with chemotherapy agents and live bacteria.

Pharmacy technicians are responsible for the handling and safe delivery of controlled substances, drugs or substances with a high potential for abuse, which, when abused, may lead to severe dependence. Amphetamines, methamphetamines, codeine, and morphine are among these substances. In 1970, Congress passed the Controlled Substances Act to improve the regulation of manufacturing, distributing, and dispensing of these drugs.

What Is It Like to Be a Pharmacy Technician?

Mark McCrory, CPhT, is the senior technician in a hospital pharmacy. His duties include preparing the daily dosing for all the inpatients. "I'm also IV trained," he says, "so I make the IV fluids. I also do a lot of compounding of drugs that are not standard doses. We usually get drugs that are packaged per pill, per unit dose, and sometimes the drugs aren't available as unit doses, or the dosing for the patient requires only half a tab. Our hospital policy is that anytime there's a half a tab, or not a full tab, they're repackaged before they go to the floors." The techs also repackage when drugs have been bought in bulk to save expenses.

To prepare the drugs, the techs work in the manufacturing area of the pharmacy. "Sometimes drugs are not commercially available in suspension [particles of a drug mixed with fluid]. Patients who are in a comatose state are given drugs intravenously, or more often than not, through a gastrointestinal tube. It goes right into their stomachs and is broken down through the body."

The pharmacy also includes a unit dose area, where the unit doses are prepared for the next day.

"That's basically counting pills," Mark says. "We have a sheet of patients generated by units, and each shift has the responsibility for filling certain units. The unit dose techs are also responsible for answering the phones and triaging the questions from nurses. There are certain things that techs can answer. Any kind of dosing or compatibility questions, medication-type questions. We can answer those if we're directed from the pharmacist."

Mark typically works in the IV room, where his first task of the shift is to put labels in order. "The labels are generated by the computer for scheduled doses," he says. "Sometimes they're PRN, as the patient needs them. Those labels come up on a different schedule and printer. Some drugs have short expiration times, and once they're mixed up, they're only good for four or six hours. We do those just before they're due. Other drugs have longer expirations of 24, 48, or 72 hours. We can get those out first thing." Mark also works in a biological safety hood to prepare chemotherapeutic drugs. "We do work with some caustic materials. We work with a lot of acids. Particularly with the chemotherapeutics, there are certain protocols with chemo gloves, chemo gowns. Some of the techs wear full plastic aprons. I wear the paper-type sleeves with heavy-duty rubber gloves."

Mark is also the Pixis coordinator. "The Pixis is the automatic drug dispensing machine," he explains. "Most in-house pharmacies are going with automation. It's robotics. A nurse will ask for a certain drug, a drawer with the drug will pop open, the patient is charged, the drug is dispensed, all through the computer system. I'm sometimes on call, and when there's a problem with the machine, I have to repair it. Usually if there's a problem, it's that the machine has accidentally charged a patient for a drug they don't need." Maintaining the Pixis involves changing drawers, refilling medications, and even replacing a motherboard when necessary.

Cathy Guay works in another area of technician work; she is a pharmacy technician at Palmer's Drugs, an independently owned drug store in Missoula, Montana. As the senior technician at Palmer's, she works the coveted day shift from 9:00 A.M. to 4:00 P.M. The first things she does in the morning is check on the orders that were placed and filled the evening before, to see if there are prescriptions waiting to be filled. If so, she types the prescription and patient data into the computer, prints out a label, gets the medication from the shelf, and counts or measures the appropriate amount. She places the filled order in a designated area where the pharmacist can review it before putting it in a bag for the customer.

In the morning, Cathy also reviews the order that the night technician faxed to their wholesale drug supplier so she'll know what to expect in that day's shipment. She spends most of her day helping walk-in customers and answering phone calls from doctors' offices, customers, and health insurance providers. "I try to answer every call by the second ring," she says. She notes that independent retail pharmacies, as opposed to chain pharmacies, have to compete by offering better customer service. For instance, when customers have a question about their insurance coverage, Cathy finds out the answer. She also delivers prescriptions to customers who are unable to pick them up in person.

Cathy says there's much personal interaction with customers in a retail setting. "You've got that customer on the phone or in front of you," she describes. "You want to take the time to find out how their day is going."

FYI

- Rx, a symbol meaning prescription, was originally a symbol of the gods in early medical writings. The symbol was used as a prayer for healing.
- A 5,000-year-old clay tablet, discovered in the Middle East, records drug remedies used by the Sumerians. Listed on the table are prescriptions for vegetable extracts, ointments, and solutions.
- In ancient Mesopotamia, doctors tested drugs and poisons on slaves and prisoners.

Do I Have What It Takes to Be a Pharmacy Technician?

It's crucial that pharmacy technicians be neat, conscientious, and highly reliable. In this field, mistakes can have serious consequences. If you're the kind of person who pays scrupulous attention to detail and can't stand to leave a room messy, this line of work is probably right for you. "The stress level is very high," Mark says, "because of the demand. You've got somebody's life in your hands. One error could kill a patient. The nurses who call down are under a lot of stress, with doctors breathing down their necks."

During the course of a workday, pharmacy technicians may handle addictive and expensive drugs, so they need to be ethical. "You're working with controlled substances," Mark says. "You're working under the pharmacist's license. They have to be able to trust you." It's also important for pharmacy technicians to not divulge personal information about patients or customers. Good communication skills are also essential because pharmacy technicians are expected to provide customers or patients with instructions on taking the drugs they've been prescribed. Moreover, pharmacy technicians must relate well to a variety of people, including customers, patients, and medical professionals.

You're working under the pharmacist's license. They have to be able to trust you.

Cathy Guay says that retail pharmacy technicians must have especially good interpersonal skills because they're working closely with customers who often have important questions or concerns.

Typing is another essential, if underrated, skill. While pharmacy technicians don't need to be rocket-fast typists, they do need to be accurate. Again, a mistyped prescription label could have a dire effect on a patient's health. Because pharmacy technicians must handle needles and syringes while they're preparing drugs, good hand-eye coordination and finger dexterity are essential. In addition, technicians need good eyesight in order to identify the various pills and medications. Correct color vision is a must since some drugs are color-coded.

To Be a Successful Pharmacy Technician, You Should . . .

- be able to work both independently and as part of a team
- be responsible and reliable
- be able to type accurately (rather than quickly)
- have good finger dexterity
- have good eyesight and normal color vision

How Do I Become a Pharmacy Technician?

Mark went through a pharmacy technology program at a local community college. "It involves a lot of memorization of drugs, body parts, physiology," he says. Mark also believes that certification is important. "You're given more respect. It's not required to work here, but it helps. Also, we pay 50 cents more an hour to certified techs." For retail pharmacy technicians, informal, on-the-job training is still the most common way to enter the profession. However, many employers can no longer afford to train technicians and prefer to hire formally educated technicians.

Cathy Guay entered the field by working as an errand runner for a nursing home pharmacy in Seattle. When her employer offered to pay for a nine-month technician training program, Cathy jumped at the chance. Training is offered at community colleges, vocational/technical schools, and hospital community pharmacies throughout the United States. The programs usually last from six months to two years, leading to a certificate or an associate's degree.

EDUCATION

High School

To become a pharmacy technician, you need a high school diploma or its equivalent. You should take courses that develop your basic math skills, since a pharmacy technician's job demands accuracy in numerical calculations and record keeping. To test your aptitude for the scientific nature of a pharmacy tech's job, take some courses in biology and chemistry. By working on projects in your high school's chemistry lab, you learn how important it is to follow instructions to the letter. Health courses can familiarize you with medical and pharmaceutical terminology. Finally, taking English and speech courses will polish your communication skills for the job.

Postsecondary Training

Formalized pharmacy technician training was first offered by the armed forces and is now offered by many hospitals, vocational and technical schools, and community colleges. Some courses offered in these training programs include introduction to pharmacy and health care systems, pharmacy laws and ethics, medical terminology, anatomy, therapeutic agents, biology, and higher math. In addition, courses in microcomputers, writing, IV preparation, and interview and intercommunication skills are also part of some programs. In addition to the class work, you may be required to perform an internship or clerkship in a pharmacy. Since 1983, the American Society of Health-System Pharmacists (ASHP) has accredited pharmacy technician programs in order to ensure certain standards of training. To find out what programs are offered near you, contact the Pharmacy Technician Educators Council (http://www.rxptec.org).

CERTIFICATION OR LICENSING

While certification is not required, it is highly recommended. In the past, certification was handled on a state-by-state basis. However, in 1995 the Pharmacy Technician Certification Board (PTCB) was established to create a single, national voluntary certification program for pharmacy technicians. Since that time, more than 195,000 pharmacy technicians in the United States have taken the National Pharmacy Technician Certification Examination and received the designation certified pharmacy technicians (CPhT). Certification shows an employer that you have received the training and gained the knowledge needed to perform the duties of a pharmacy technician. On-the-job experience or a hospital training program is usually adequate preparation for taking the exam. Some national drugstore chains have developed incentives for their pharmacy technicians to become certified. Walgreens, for instance, has created its own training program and materials, and the company offers a pay raise to technicians who become certified.

After passing the exam, pharmacy technicians must take 20 hours of continuing education every two years in order to maintain their certification. Certification must be renewed every two years.

FYI

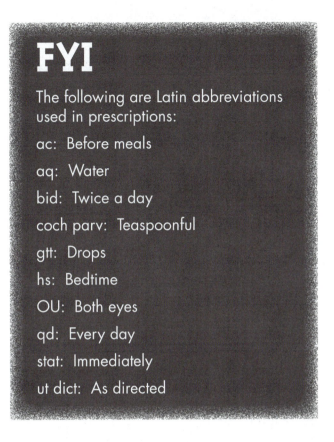

The following are Latin abbreviations used in prescriptions:

ac: Before meals

aq: Water

bid: Twice a day

coch parv: Teaspoonful

gtt: Drops

hs: Bedtime

OU: Both eyes

qd: Every day

stat: Immediately

ut dict: As directed

Who Will Hire Me?

Mark got his job as a tech immediately following his community college program. "My program required an internship," he says, "where I had to work in an inpatient and outpatient setting. I was offered my job before I was even finished with my internship, which is often the case. We hire a lot of our techs from internship programs."

Most pharmacy technicians begin their job search on the local level. Newspaper ads, employment agencies, and hospital job listings are all good starting points. Graduates of training programs sometimes move into technician positions with the hospital or retail pharmacy where they served as interns.

The majority of pharmacy technicians will find work in hospital pharmacies, retail drugstores, and home health care pharmacies. There are also positions available in nursing home pharmacies, clinic pharmacies, and mail-order prescription pharmacies. In addition, experienced technicians are sometimes hired by nontraditional employers, such as medical insurance companies, medical computer software companies, drug manufacturers, food processing companies, and as instructors in pharmacy technician training programs.

More job opportunities are available in those areas with an older population, because more medical services are generally required by the elderly. These areas typically include New York, Florida, California, Arizona, and New Mexico.

Where Can I Go from Here?

The advancement prospects for pharmacy technicians are somewhat determined by the size of the pharmacies where they work. Mark describes the line of advancement at his workplace: "You start off as a tech trainee. You do tests and skill evaluations to move up the ladder. We have Tech 1, Tech 2, then Senior Tech. Many of our techs tend to go into pharmacy school. A number of the pharmacists we work with started at the hospital as pharmacy techs." This is the path Mark wants to take, with plans of getting his Pharm.D.

Experienced pharmacy technicians may also choose to specialize in a particular area of pharmacy work, such as in narcotics control or chemotherapy preparation. Others may choose to work primarily in the emergency room or operating room of a hospital or clinic. In a smaller retail pharmacy, advancement is not always possible.

What Are the Salary Ranges?

According to the *Occupational Outlook Handbook*, the median hourly wage for pharmacy technicians was $10.94 in 2003, or $22,755 annually for full-time employees. The middle 50 percent earned between $9.01 and $13.50 an hour, while those in the highest 10 percent earned more than $16.24 an hour.

Graduates of accredited training programs, along with technicians who are certified, are usually paid in the higher ranges. In addition, salaries are higher on the East and West coasts and in large cities. Benefits for pharmacy technicians often include medical and dental insurance, retirement savings plans, and paid sick, personal, and vacation days.

Advancement Possibilities

Directors of pharmacy services direct and coordinate, through subordinate supervisory personnel, activities and functions of hospital pharmacies.

Pharmacists compound and dispense prescribed medications, drugs, and other pharmaceuticals for patient care, according to professional standards and state and federal legal requirements.

Radiopharmacists prepare and dispense radioactive pharmaceuticals used for patient diagnosis and therapy, applying the principles and practices of pharmacy and radiochemistry.

What Is the Job Outlook?

According to the *Occupational Outlook Handbook*, employment for pharmacy technicians will grow faster than the average for all other occupations. This demand can be attributed to the changing role of pharmacists, the increasing pharmacy workload due to the growing elderly population, and the need to control health care costs. In particular, as pharmacists spend more time in consultation with customers, skilled pharmacy technicians will be needed to handle the assembly and dispensing of medications. While the use of computerized and robotic dispensing equipment eliminates some traditional duties, there will always be a need for a skilled technician to maintain these devices, as well as to handle the other technical and clerical responsibilities.

Pharmacists are getting jobs with many different kinds of health care providers, which means more opportunities for pharmacy technicians as well. As technicians continue to gain recognition for their skilled and specialized work, more career, training, and scholarship opportunities will arise. Those interested in pursing a career as a pharmacy technician should keep an eye on health care trends and government health care reform. Also watch for the changing role of hospitals, as hybrids between hospitals and nursing homes develop.

How Do I Learn More?

PROFESSIONAL ORGANIZATIONS

To learn about continuing education, contact

American Association of Pharmacy Technicians
PO Box 1447
Greensboro, NC 27402
aapt@pharmacytechnician.com
http://www.pharmacytechnician.com

To learn about an online certification course, contact

National Pharmacy Technician Association
PO Box 683148
Houston, TX 77268
888-247-8700
http://www.pharmacytechnician.org

To learn about certification, contact

Pharmacy Technician Certification Board
2215 Constitution Avenue, NW
Washington, DC 20037-2985
800-363-8012
http://www.ptcb.org

BIBLIOGRAPHY

The following is a sampling of materials relating to the professional concerns and development of pharmacy technicians.

Generali, Joyce A. *The Pharmacy Technician's Pocket Drug Reference.* 2d ed. Washington, D.C.: APhA Publications, 2003.

Reddy, Indra K., and Mansoor A. Kahn. *Essential Math and Calculations for Pharmacy Technicians.* Boca Raton, Fla.: CRC Press, 2003.

Reifman, Noah. *Certification Review for Pharmacy Technicians.* Washington, D.C.: PTCB Books, 2004.

WetFeet. *Careers in Biotech and Pharmaceuticals: The WetFeet Insider Guide.* Reissue ed. San Francisco: WetFeet, 2004.

PHLEBOTOMY TECHNICIANS

It's my job to draw blood from donors," says Sherry Southerland, who works as a phlebotomy technician at a branch office of the Bonfils Blood Center, a blood bank that supplies most of the hospitals in Colorado. "I go over the donors' medical histories, ask them additional questions, scrub the skin, find the vein, collect, and label the blood. Like any job, after a while, things can get pretty routine." She sighs and adds, "But when my dad got sick and I saw him being transfused, I realized that phlebotomy technicians are not just some cog in a machine. I could see the other end of the process and it made a real difference."

Sherry stresses the vital role phlebotomy technicians serve in the collection of the nation's blood supply. "We've got to have this resource," she says, "and it must be screened well. When my dad was sick, I hoped that the phlebotomy technicians who had drawn the blood that he was receiving had done a good job screening donors. Did they ask enough questions, I wondered. Did they take time to explain why those questions were necessary? The importance of what I was doing as a phlebotomy technician suddenly came through."

Definition

Phlebotomy technicians draw blood from patients or donors in hospitals, blood banks, clinics, physicians' offices, or other facilities. They assemble equipment, verify patient identification numbers, and withdraw blood either through a finger puncture or with a needle syringe.

Alternative Job Titles

Blood technicians
Phlebotomists

High School Subjects

Biology
English
Health

Personal Skills

Helping/teaching
Technical/scientific

Salary Range

$18,720 to $21,944 to $33,488

Minimum Educational Level

Some postsecondary training

Certification or Licensing

Required by certain states

Outlook

About as fast as the average

DOT

079

GOE

14.05.01

NOC

3212

O*NET-SOC

N/A

What Does a Phlebotomy Technician Do?

Ancient people did not understand the role of blood, but they knew it was vital. Some believed that it might even be the home of the soul. Early Egyptians bathed in blood, hoping this act would cure illness or reverse the aging process. Some Romans drank the blood of dying gladiators in order to acquire the athletes' strength and bravery.

Over time, scientists began to understand how blood functioned and they searched for ways to collect it or transfer it from one person to another. Quills or silver needles were attached to silver tubing and the tubings were attached to animal bladders in order to construct blood-collection devices. Arteries were punctured and blood gushed out. Sometimes the donor died, as well as the patient. Little care was taken with the cleanliness of instruments. No one understood why blood sometimes failed to coagulate or coagulated too quickly. No one could explain why blood could not always be transferred successfully from one person to another.

Modern techniques of blood collection, typing, and transfusion developed in the 20th century. Blood is now drawn by professionals called *phlebotomy technicians* or *phlebotomists*. They work in clean, well-lighted laboratories, hospitals, and clinics.

Blood is used for a variety of medical tests or is stored in blood banks for future use. There are three main methods by which blood can be drawn: venipuncture, arterial puncture, and capillary collection. Collecting through veins is the most common method, followed by artery collection, then capillary collection, which involves punctures of the fingers or heels.

The first steps in drawing blood are to take the patient's medical history and match the physician's testing order with the amount of blood to be drawn. Then the patient's temperature and pulse are taken. Next, the site of the withdrawal is located. Typically, the large vein that is visible on the underside of the arm near the elbow is used.

Finding a suitable vein, however, is not always easy because there is a great deal of anatomical difference among people. Once a suitable site is located, a tourniquet is wrapped high on the patient's upper arm, as far from the elbow as is convenient. The phlebotomy technician checks the site for lesions, other needle marks, and any skin disorders that might interfere with the collection process. Then the site is cleansed by swabbing with a sterile solution. The phlebotomy technician grasps the patient's forearm and retracts the arm downward in order to immobilize the soft tissue and steady the vein. Sometimes the patient is asked to open and close his or her hand a few times to make the vein more prominent. Making a proper puncture takes practice. After the sterile needle is uncovered, it must be grasped tightly but passed through the skin gently. The needle is inserted almost horizontal with the vein and as parallel to the skin as possible. Then the hub of the needle is raised and the angle toward the skin increased so that the needle can pierce the wall of the vein. After the needle is advanced slightly into the vein itself, blood may be withdrawn. Generally this is done by releasing a clamp attached to the blood collection device or to the tubing. When the required amount of blood is collected, the needle is removed and sealed, the site covered, and the tourniquet removed.

After collection, the phlebotomy technician labels the blood, coordinates its number with the worksheet order, and transports the blood to a storage facility or to another laboratory worker. The phlebotomy technician also checks to make sure that the patient is all right, notes any adverse reactions, and administers first aid or other medical assistance when necessary.

Specialists in blood-bank technology are professionals who perform a variety of tasks associated with blood banking. They test blood for compatibility, type and match it, and store it until needed. Phlebotomy technicians who are employed by blood banks may be supervised by specialists in blood-bank technology. Phlebotomy technicians who work in hospitals or clinics are supervised by other laboratory personnel.

Lingo to Learn

Autologous donation A blood donation that is stored and reserved for return to the original donor during surgery.

Blood bank A facility responsible for collecting blood from donors, separating blood into its components, typing, and matching blood in order to ensure safe transfusions.

Blood components The red cells, white cells, platelets, and plasma that constitute blood.

Hematology The science of blood and blood diseases.

Plasma The liquid portion of blood, including protein, but excluding cellular components.

Platelets The cells in blood that are involved with clotting.

Transfusion A medical procedure to transfer blood from one body into another.

Typing A procedure to determine the blood group (A, B, AB, or O) within a particular sample.

Venipuncture The puncture of a vein with a hypodermic needle, commonly known as a needle stick.

What Is It Like to Be a Phlebotomy Technician?

"When I come to work," says Sherry Southerland, "I never know whether the lobby of the blood bank will be full or whether no one will show up for an hour or two. The day after a disaster occurs anywhere in the

U.S., however, we're always mobbed by donors. Regardless, 80 percent of the people we see are repeats, folks who come here every 56 days because they know how great the need is for blood. They know that blood banks like ours are on the front lines and that together, we're the ones fighting this war to keep people healthy."

Sherry's job as a phlebotomy technician begins by greeting donors when they arrive at the Bonfils Blood Center branch office in Lakewood, Colorado. If they are first-time donors, she enters their names and medical information into the computer and if they are repeats, she pulls up their medical history cards. To give blood, donors must weigh more than 110 pounds, not have infections such as colds or the flu, not be taking certain medications, and not be engaging in a variety of at-risk behaviors. At-risk behaviors include illegal intravenous drug use and certain types of sexual activity.

Sherry asks each donor several questions, some of which are repeats of medical history information. "People skills are very important in this job," she says. "I'm not trying to be nosy when I ask these questions. We're trying to retain donors and yet we need to weed out the high-risk volunteers too. You have to be dedicated to the donors and to putting out a safe product."

Updating medical histories and asking questions help screen out people with illnesses or behaviors that might jeopardize the safety of the blood supply. In particular, phlebotomy technicians try to screen donors who might have active cases of or have been exposed to tuberculosis, malaria, hepatitis, syphilis, and HIV virus.

If the donors' medical histories are satisfactory, Sherry checks their temperatures and then, using a small centrifuge, does a quick blood test to verify iron levels. A low iron level indicates that the donor's body is in a weakened condition and there isn't enough hemoglobin present. (Hemoglobin is the iron-containing protein within red blood cells that carries oxygen.) If a patient should receive such hemoglobin-poor blood, there wouldn't be enough red blood cells to perform vital functions within the body. If, however, iron levels are sufficient, Sherry directs the donors to a reclining bed where she takes their pulse and blood pressure and swabs the skin with antiseptic.

Next comes the needle stick. "I can't look when it's my turn to give blood," she says. "And the first time I had to make a needle stick on someone else, I was so nervous. It's still a bit scary. You don't want to hurt people. Practice, that's the only way to learn."

It takes about five minutes to collect a pint of blood. When the required amount is collected, Sherry uses a hematron, a device that heat-seals the tubing that extends from the needle in the donor's arm to the collection bag. Then the needle is removed and disposed of, and the blood is transported to the laboratory where it is typed by other workers. Next, she makes sure that the donor drinks some juice, eats cookies or crackers, and rests for 10 to 15 minutes before leaving the blood center. "Everybody reacts a bit differently to giving blood," she says. "Here, it's not like in a doctor's office where phlebotomy technicians draw only a small vial of blood." Taking a pint of blood makes some people turn white, others break out in cold sweats, and some people pass out completely. Still, only 1 percent of donors have any adverse reactions, at all.

Phlebotomy technicians are trained to watch for a range of responses from mild light-headedness to loss of consciousness. Each year Sherry renews her first aid and CPR training. She also has emergency medical training and a certificate that enables her to set up IVs, intravenous drips used to replace body fluids. Other portions of her day are spent performing quality checks on equipment, taking inventory of supplies, and attending meetings.

Specialists in blood-bank technology (persons who have advanced degrees) process the blood collected, type it, make cross matches with patients, check the blood for communicable diseases and infections, and store it for future use.

Do I Have What It Takes to Be a Phlebotomy Technician?

"Being a phlebotomy technician is challenging work," says Sherry. "You're constantly working with people. Good communication skills are essential because you have to stick the patient or donor with a needle in order to draw blood. Yes, you're following orders and doing routine work, but a sense of humor helps too."

Mary Anderson, program director at the Wichita Area Vocational Technical School in Wichita, Kansas, adds, "The patients have to feel like they are the most important thing in your world at that moment. Even when you have to work at a quick pace, you should not make the patients feel like they're on an assembly line. That's not always easy," she says, "particularly for phlebotomy technicians who work in hospitals. They have to deal with a variety of people under difficult circumstances. Often you're called to the bedside of a patient to draw blood, and not only are you dealing with a sick person who doesn't want to have another needle stuck in them, the doctors, the nurses, and sometimes the families are after you to hurry up and finish your work."

According to the American Society of Phlebotomy Technicians, phlebotomy technicians are "often the only part of the lab staff that a patient sees. . . . Yet, phlebotomists work difficult hours, the pay is low, the turnover rate high, and they often find themselves faced with cantankerous patients. . . . Although phlebotomists serve as valuable liaisons between the patient and the clinical laboratory, many times they suffer low professional esteem."

"No matter what the working situation," says Mary, "phlebotomy technicians have to be patient and not get upset. This is essential because the blood test won't be any better than the samples they collect."

No matter what the working situation, phlebotomy technicians have to be patient and not get upset. This is essential because the blood test won't be any better than the samples they collect.

Phlebotomy technicians need to have excellent interpersonal communication skills. They should be good listeners and able to speak precisely and clearly. They should be able to reassure patients as well as be able to explain medical procedures. Some shift work may be required. Those working in hospitals, in particular, can expect to work some weekends and holidays as well. People in this profession work with precise, often small, medical supplies. Good manual dexterity is essential.

Persons who are squeamish at the sight of blood or have difficulty working with needles would find it hard to succeed as a phlebotomy technician. There is a small risk of exposure to contaminated blood and other illness in this profession, but phlebotomy technicians always wear gloves and, when necessary, additional protective clothing. This, along with common sense and attention to procedure, minimizes risk.

To Be a Successful Phlebotomy Technician, You Should . . .

- enjoy working with people
- be patient
- be able to work under pressure
- be attentive to detail
- be an effective communicator and a good listener
- have good manual dexterity

How Do I Become a Phlebotomy Technician?

Sherry had been a home health care aide and a hospice volunteer before she started working for Bonfils Blood Center. "I was trained on the job. That was a common practice then," she says. Now, in order to achieve certification and to move ahead professionally, formal training programs are highly recommended.

EDUCATION

High School

Biology, health, and other science courses are helpful for students wishing to become phlebotomy technicians after graduation. Computer science, English, and speech classes are also important. In addition, if you plan on entering a formal phlebotomy training program, you should be sure to fulfill the entrance requirements for the program you plan to attend.

Postsecondary Training

Until recently, on-the-job training was the norm for phlebotomy technicians. Now formal programs are offered through independent training schools,

In-depth

Blood: Its Function and Purpose

Blood is a distinctive and recognizable type of tissue, but this does not mean it is a stable, uniform substance with a fixed proportion of ingredients. Quite the opposite is true; its composition is always changing in response to the demands of other body systems. Other organs are constantly pouring sources into the blood, or removing things from it. Blood in one part of the body at any given moment may be vastly different in chemical makeup from blood in another part of the body.

Blood does have certain basic components. A sample of blood left to stand for an hour or so separates into a clear, watery fluid with a yellowish tinge and a darker, more solid clump. The clear, yellow liquid is plasma and it accounts for approximately 55 percent of the volume of normal blood. The darker clump is composed mainly of the red cells that give blood its characteristic color.

Plasma enables our blood to carry out most of the transportation tasks our bodies assign it. Being more than 90 percent water, plasma, like water, can carry substances within it in two ways: in solution and in suspension. A substance in a water solution, such as salt in salt water, must be removed from the water by chemical or physical action, such as boiling. On the other hand, a substance in suspension, such as red blood cells in whole blood, separates more easily, particularly when its watery carrier has been contained and its flow stilled.

Red blood cells number in the trillions and are carried in suspension by the plasma. In turn, the red blood cells carry the single most important substance needed by the body's cells: oxygen. A complex iron-protein substance called hemoglobin is responsible for the oxygen-carrying capacity of red blood cells. Although water and plasma can also carry oxygen, hemoglobin is special because it increases by more than 50 times the oxygen-carrying capacity of our blood.

White blood cells are larger than red blood cells, but there are far fewer of them in our blood. We need every last one of them, however, as the white blood cells are the ones that attack foreign bodies that invade our tissues. Autoimmune diseases, such as multiple sclerosis, result when the white blood cells mistakenly attack healthy areas of our bodies.

Platelets, while not equipped with nuclei and therefore not fitting the definition of a cell, are nonetheless crucial. More like bits of cell substance, platelets initiate some of the first steps in the complex biochemical process that leads to the clotting of blood. Without them, we could easily bleed to death from the smallest of injuries.

community colleges, or hospitals. Most programs last from 10 weeks to one year and should be approved by the National Accrediting Agency for Clinical Laboratory Sciences or the American Society of Phlebotomy Technicians. They include both in-class study and supervised, clinical practice. Course work includes anatomy, physiology, introduction to laboratory practices, communication, medical terminology, phlebotomy techniques, emergency situations, and CPR training. Most of these programs are structured to prepare students for certification exams.

CERTIFICATION OR LICENSING

Certification and licensing for phlebotomy technicians varies according to state and employer. Several agencies grant certification. To be eligible to take the qualifying examination from the American Society of Phlebotomy Technicians or from the Board of Registry of the American Society of Clinical Pathologists (ASCP), applicants must have worked as a full-time phlebotomist for six months or as a part-time phlebotomist for one year, or have completed an accredited phlebotomy training program.

SCHOLARSHIPS AND GRANTS

Many community colleges offer general scholarships and financial aid, as do some hospitals and training programs. In addition, institutions with specific phlebotomy programs are sources of information on work-study and student internships.

Advancement Possibilities

Blood bank technologists are responsible for all the activities within blood banks, including the collection, testing, storage, and transportation of blood.

Phlebotomy supervisors oversee the work of other phlebotomy technicians, coordinating schedules and making certain the strict safety guidelines of the field are followed.

Training instructors work in technical schools, community colleges, and hospital educational programs to train phlebotomists in their duties. They might also supervise the clinical practice portion of the training in a hospital.

Who Will Hire Me?

Phlebotomy technicians work in a variety of health care settings. The majority of them work in hospitals or in outpatient settings such as clinics, physicians' offices, reference laboratories, or blood banks. A few are hired by private industry or by insurance companies. The greatest need for phlebotomy technicians is in small hospitals (that is, those with fewer than 100 beds). Many of the publications serving health care professionals list job advertisements, as do daily newspapers. In addition, some employers actively recruit graduating students through visits to accredited programs.

Where Can I Go from Here?

Sherry worked in the Bonfils Blood Center's mobile units for several years. Her next move was to become a supervisor at the Lakewood branch office. After a few years as supervisor, however, she stepped out of administration and moved back to working directly with donors. "Ten minutes after the 1995 explosion at the Federal Center in Oklahoma City, we were flooded with donors," she says. "People know the need for donated blood is always there. Working with generous, concerned people is what I like best about my job and I wanted to continue doing just that."

One of the most common career paths for phlebotomy technicians is to work for a few years in a hospital or laboratory and then return to school to study medical laboratory technology or some other branch of clinical laboratory medicine.

If you are interested in advancing within blood-bank centers, one option is to return to school, obtain a bachelor's degree, attend a specialized fifth-year program, and become a certified specialist in blood-bank technology. Specialists in blood-bank technology are responsible for all the activities and staff within blood banks. They coordinate educational programs, oversee blood collection, direct testing, and arrange for storage and transportation of blood and blood products.

What Are the Salary Ranges?

Experience, level of education, employer, and work performed determine the salary ranges for phlebotomy technicians. According to a survey by the American Society of Clinical Pathologists' Board of Registry, the median annual salary for phlebotomy technicians was $21,944 in 2002. Salaries ranged from $18,720 to $25,168. Phlebotomist supervisors had median annual salaries of $33,488 in 2002.

A specialist in blood bank technology with a bachelor's degree and advanced training can usually expect a starting salary of approximately $40,000 a year.

Benefits such as vacation time, sick leave, insurance, and other fringe benefits vary by employer, but are usually consistent with other full-time health care workers.

What Is the Job Outlook?

According to the *Occupational Outlook Handbook,* employment of clinical laboratory workers is expected to grow about as fast as the average for all other occupations over the next 10 years. Across the United States, demand for phlebotomy technicians is highest in small hospitals. Demand for all kinds of health care professionals, including phlebotomy technicians, will grow as the percentage of Americans aged 65 and older continues to rise. There is a particular demand for workers who are qualified to draw blood at patients' bedsides. The number of patients with certain diseases, such as HIV and AIDS, also increases the need for phlebotomy technicians.

How Do I Learn More?

PROFESSIONAL ORGANIZATIONS

For information on careers and answers to questions about the field, contact

American Association of Blood Banks
8101 Glenbrook Road
Bethesda, MD 20814-2749
301-907-6977
aabb@aabb.org
http://www.aabb.org

For a career brochure, contact

American Society for Clinical Pathology
2100 West Harrison Street
Chicago, IL 60612
312-738-1336
http://www.ascp.org

To learn about phlebotomy programs, contact the following organizations:

American Society of Phlebotomy Technicians
PO Box 1831
Hickory, NC 28603
828-294-0078
http://www.aspt.org

National Accrediting Agency for Clinical Laboratory Sciences
8410 West Bryn Mawr Avenue, Suite 670
Chicago, IL 60631
773-714-8880
info@naacls.org
http://www.naacls.org

BIBLIOGRAPHY

The following is a sampling of materials relating to the professional concerns and development of phlebotomy technicians:

Garza, Diana, and Kathleen Becan-McBride. *Phlebotomy Handbook: Blood Collection Essentials.* 6th ed. Upper Saddle River, N.J.: Prentice Hall, 2002.

McCall, Ruth E., and Cathee M. Tankersley. *Phlebotomy Essentials.* 3d ed. Philadelphia: Lippincott Williams & Wilkins, 2002.

Pendergraph, Garland E., and Cynthia Barfield Pendergraph. *Handbook of Phlebotomy and Patient Service Techniques.* 4th ed. Philadelphia: Lippincott Williams & Wilkins, 1998.

PHYSICAL THERAPISTS

"There's no hope," the patient says in despair. For two weeks, his leg has been in constant pain, the result of a displaced disc in his spine. "I've taken painkillers, but they haven't helped. My doctor says I'll have to be operated on next. But I'm a waiter. How can I do my job if I can't walk?"

Gabor Sagi, the physical therapist assigned to the young man's case, helps him onto a mat on the floor. "Don't give up just yet. I'm going to lead you through a series of positions. I want you to tell me how each one feels."

Gabor pushes on the patient's shoulders and shifts the patient's pelvis forward. The young man cries out, "Wait!"

Then he starts to laugh. "Gabor, this is incredible! What did you do? It's gone! The pain, I mean. Like you just shut it off. "

Gabor smiles. "So there's hope for you after all? Okay, now I'm going to show you some exercises to do at home. I'll bet you'll be back at the restaurant in a week."

"You'll come in then," the young waiter says, "and I'll serve you the biggest meal you've ever had!"

Definition
Physical therapists help alleviate pain, prevent disability, and restore mobility and function in patients with injuries, diseases, or birth defects. They also help improve the physical conditions of healthy people.

Alternative Job Title
Physiotherapists

High School Subjects
Biology
Health
Physical education

Personal Skills
Helping/teaching
Technical/scientific

Salary Range
$40,380 to $57,710 to $86,310

Educational Requirements
Master's degree from an accredited physical therapy program

Certification or Licensing
Recommended (certification)
Required by all states (licensing)

Outlook
Faster than the average

DOT
076

GOE
14.06.01

NOC
3142

O*NET-SOC
29-1123.00

What Does a Physical Therapist Do?

Many illnesses, injuries, birth defects, and other health conditions can have a drastic effect on a person's mobility and overall quality of life. *Physical therapists* (PTs) work with patients to help to relieve their pain and restore them to full function, if possible, or to help them adjust to life after disabling illnesses or injuries so that they can live independent lives. Physical therapists work as part of a team of health care professionals, which may include general practitioners, specialists, radiologists, occupational therapists, and social workers.

A physical therapist first consults a patient's medical history. The physical therapist may then speak with the patient's physician to discuss the patient's health and treatment options. The physical therapist also speaks to the patient to learn about the kind and amount of pain the patient feels. The therapist seeks to identify aspects of the patient's behavior, activity, and lifestyle that cause an onset of pain.

The next step is to conduct clinical tests to measure the patient's strength, range of motion, and ability to function. The physical therapist may observe the patient as he or she performs certain tasks, such as walking up and down stairs, walking on a treadmill, bending and stretching, and lifting objects. Once the patient's problems have been identified, the physical therapist will discuss them with the patient and with a team of health care professionals in order to set treatment goals and design a plan that will help the patient accomplish these goals.

Treatment is specifically designed according to the patient's needs and abilities. A physical therapist treating a patient who is paralyzed or otherwise immobilized may begin with passive exercises, such as stretching and manipulating joints and muscles. The therapist may use electrical stimulation, hot or cold compresses, or ultrasound in order to stimulate muscles and relieve pain. Traction and deep-tissue massages can also help relieve a patient's pain and restore function. As treatment progresses, the therapist may design a program of movements and exercises that help the patient regain strength and mobility.

For certain patients, such as a person who has suffered a stroke or lost a limb, a return to full function is not possible. Physical therapists work with such patients to help them adjust to their new conditions. They may help a patient adapt to wearing a prosthetic device, such as an artificial limb, or to using crutches or a wheelchair. Other patients must relearn certain activities, such as walking, dressing, and climbing in and out of bathtubs, in order to return to independent lives. Physical therapists work with cardiac patients to increase their endurance and minimize the risk of further heart problems. Burn patients require treatment that will reduce scarring and maintain flexibility.

Physical therapists also work with athletes and other people who seek to improve their physical conditions. A physical therapist may devise an exercise program designed to enhance a person's athletic performance. The therapist will observe the person's movements and suggest ways of improving posture and technique to achieve the person's goals. Other professionals besides physical therapists who do this type of work include athletic trainers, personal trainers, and physical instructors.

The American Physical Therapy Association recognizes seven specialty areas within physical therapy: cardiopulmonary, clinical electrophysiology, geriatrics, neurology, orthopedics, pediatrics, and sports physical therapy.

Lingo to Learn

Modalities are the various technical procedures used in physical therapy during treatment. They include the following:

Cryotherapy The therapeutic use of cold.

Diathermy The production of heat in parts of the body, using electric currents, microwaves, or ultrasound.

Hydrotherapy The therapeutic use of water on the outside of the body, including the use of exercise pools, whirlpools, and showers.

Laser therapy The use of lasers to reduce pain, inflammation, and swelling.

Traction A therapeutic procedure in which part of the body is placed under tension, as by the attachment of a weight.

Ultrasound The use of sound waves to treat soft tissues.

What Is It Like to Be a Physical Therapist?

Gabor Sagi has been a physical therapist for 10 years. He works as a full-time therapist at Mercy Hospital and Medical Center in Chicago, Illinois. "I was attracted to physical therapy as a career because of my interest in sports. In high school, I started lifting weights, and that made me more aware of my muscles and how the body works," Gabor says. "I became interested in the mechanics of the body and how it works." An injury to his back increased his interest. "I had to undergo therapy myself. What I liked was that physical therapy would give me a chance to work with both my mind and my hands."

Gabor generally works four full days (nine hours each) and one half day each week. "I set my appointments with my patients, so that gives me a lot of flexibility for setting my own schedule," he says. "But I usually put in at least a 40-hour week."

A typical day for Gabor begins at 8:30 A.M. "I spend the first half-hour or so sending reports on my patients to their physicians and updating and reviewing notes on my patients. Then I'm ready to receive my first patient of the day," Gabor says. During the day, Gabor may see as many as 20 different patients. "I'll see a patient two or three times a week, for about 30 minutes each session. A patient's therapy program may last anywhere from two weeks to three months or more."

When Gabor receives a new patient, he performs an initial assessment of the patient's condition and what the patient expects to achieve from physical therapy. The initial assessment generally lasts from 45 minutes to an hour. "The first thing I explore is the history of the patient's complaint. I want to know what his or her life is like. Usually, patients come to me because they're having trouble functioning. So I want to see what their functions are, their jobs or hobbies, and I set goals with them to return them to full function." Gabor speaks with patients at length about their conditions. "I learn the details of how their conditions affect them. I want to know what makes them feel better and what makes them feel worse. I try to find the pattern in a patient's behavior."

After this assessment, Gabor performs a physical examination of the patient. "I need to make sure that whatever treatment I use won't be dangerous or detrimental to a patient. The first thing I do is observe the patient's condition. I look for any deformities, swelling, muscle wasting, or scars. I'll palpate the patient, which means I'm touching the patient to look for tender areas and checking the quality of tissue texture. Then I'll examine the patient's movement. I look at the range of movement the patient is able to achieve and the quality of the movement. I'll test muscles, overall strength, and speed and endurance. I'll also do a neurological exam to look for any motor or sensory deficits."

Once this examination is completed, Gabor and his new patient move on to more specific physical tests to better evaluate the patient's particular condition. Gabor says, "I also observe the patient performing certain tasks, like dressing and undressing, climbing stairs, using the treadmill, or reaching up or down and picking up objects."

After Gabor has completed examining his patient, he devises a treatment program. "It's important to set goals with a patient to bring back full physical function, if that's possible. I try to make each patient responsible for his or her own progress." Gabor prescribes an exercise or movement program, and other treatments the patient may need. He also schedules follow-up appointments with the patient. "I'm constantly assessing the patient. If something's not working, I need to know that so I can adjust the treatment plan."

It's important to set goals with a patient to bring back full physical function, if that's possible. I try to make each patient responsible for his or her own progress.

Do I Have What It Takes to Be a Physical Therapist?

Physical therapists have become respected members of the team of health care professionals involved in a patient's treatment and rehabilitation. "When I first started working as a PT," Gabor says, "a lot of physicians still took the old approach to physical therapy. That is, the physician would prescribe the treatment and the physical therapist would be expected to carry it out. They'd tell you what to do even if they didn't really know anything about physical therapy. But nowadays the relationship has changed a lot. It's become much more of a two-way communication." Because physical therapists work not only with patients but also with other health care professionals, good communication skills are essential to this career. "I have to be able to explain things to my patients in ways they can understand," Gabor says. "It's important to be clear about what I expect of them and what they must expect of themselves."

For Gabor, his relationship with his patients is very rewarding. "You really get to work one-on-one with people. You get involved in their lives and you become close to them on a fairly intimate level. But there's always a limit to that closeness. It's pretty much confined to the therapy center. And I like that, too." Physical therapists usually work with people who are in pain or who are undergoing a particularly stressful period in their lives. "There's a nice sense of responsibility, of taking charge, and of taking care of people and having them trust you," Gabor says. "But there's a downside to that, too. It can be quite overwhelming. A lot of the patients I see have given up. They'll be dependent on me. But it's important to help them take responsibility for themselves. I have to give the responsibility for their treatment back to them. And that can be difficult."

Physical therapy requires a great deal of creativity on the part of the therapist. No two patients are alike, and no two will respond the same way to the same treatment. The physical therapist must be aware of a patient's needs and condition and be flexible enough to adapt therapy specifically to the patient. "But that's the part of physical therapy I like the most. Not only do I get to work with my hands, but I'm constantly working with my mind," Gabor says. "In a way, examining a new patient, especially someone with spinal problems, is like detective work. Often, a patient will be referred to me with a general diagnosis, like sciatica, which just means the patient has pain in his or her leg. So it's up to me to know what kinds of questions to ask, like questions about the patient's symptoms and behavior, to track down the source of the pain and map out a treatment plan."

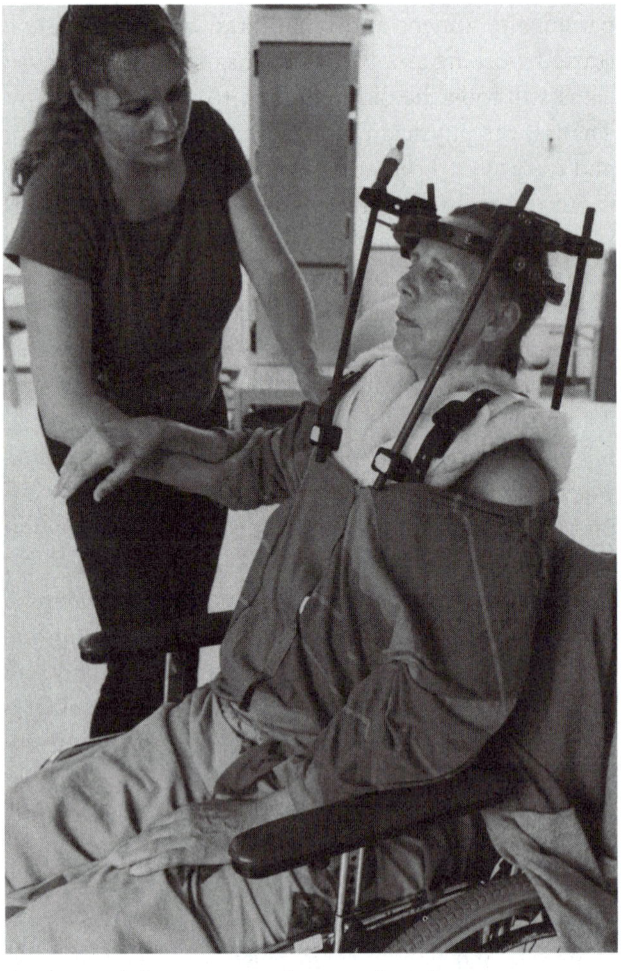

A physical therapist performs rehabilitation exercises with a woman suffering from compression of the spinal cord. *(Henny Allis / Photo Researchers Inc.)*

To Be a Successful Physical Therapist, You Should . . .

- like working with people
- have strong communication skills
- be able to work independently and as part of a team
- be creative
- be in good physical condition

Gabor enjoys coming into contact with people. "I meet lots of different people in my job. I've treated chairmen of companies, politicians, police officers, people who haul garbage, you name it. Each patient is entirely new." Being a physical therapist has also given Gabor a chance to travel. "I've worked in maybe 20 different settings in the last 10 years. I trained as a physical therapist in France, where I was born. But I worked for years in London, England, before coming to work here. Everywhere that there are people, there's a need for physical therapists."

How Do I Become a Physical Therapist?

Physical therapists undergo rigorous educational and clinical training to prepare for their careers. Pam Johnson, who works as a physical therapist at Swedish Covenant Hospital in Chicago, completed her master's degree in June 1996. "I have a bachelor's degree in biology. After college, I volunteered in the physical therapy department of a hospital. That led to my being trained as a physical therapy aide," Pam says. "I think that experience helped me get into the master's degree program. It definitely gave me a good picture of what physical therapy is all about."

According to the American Physical Therapy Association (APTA), there were 203 accredited physical therapist programs in 2003. Of the accredited programs, 113 offered master's degrees, and 90 offered doctoral degrees. Previously, the

Commission on Accreditation in Physical Therapy Education (CAPTE) had accredited bachelor's degree programs; however, CAPTE now only accredits programs that offer master's degrees and higher. This change was made to give students an appropriate amount of time to study liberal arts as well as a physical therapy curriculum.

EDUCATION

High School

Competition for entering both master's degree and bachelor's degree physical therapy programs is intense, so you should begin planning your career while still in high school. Courses in mathematics, biology, chemistry, and other sciences should be part of your curriculum. "Taking physics is really important," Gabor Sagi says, "because physical therapy is really all about mechanics, the way things move." Students should also work on developing strong communication skills. "You have to be able to write reports and speak to other members of the medical and health care staff," Gabor says. "And you also need to be able to communicate with your patients."

An interest in sports and physical education will give you more insight into the functions of the body. Social sciences and psychology courses will give you a deeper understanding of people. A physical therapist works with many different people from a variety of cultures, and therapists should be sensitive to each individual's concerns. Volunteer work at local hospitals, health clinics, retirement homes, and other places that involve contact with both health care professionals and their patients will also help prepare you for this career. "It isn't like you see on television at all," Pam says. "Patients aren't always easy to work with. Sometimes they're not cognitively aware. And in real life you're dealing with people on respirators, catheter bags, IV lines, and other equipment. I admit I was uncomfortable with that as a student. But volunteering and working as an aide meant that I knew what I was getting myself into."

Postsecondary Training

A bachelor's degree program in physical therapy generally begins with courses in biology, chemistry, and physics. Then you will take specialized courses in biomechanics, neuroanatomy, manifestations of disease and trauma, human growth and development, evaluation and assessment techniques, and therapeutic treatment techniques. You also receive laboratory and clinical experience. You visit hospitals to observe physical therapy treatments and begin supervised treatment of patients. While in college, you can volunteer in physical therapy departments of hospitals or clinics. You can also participate in meetings and lectures organized by the American Physical Therapy Association.

A master's degree program provides intensive education in physical therapy. "I'd say one of the hardest parts was being in class or in the lab all day, from eight in the morning to five in the evening," Pam says. "I think the bachelor's degree program is less intense that way. But the toughest of all was what are called practicals. That's when you are given a case from an actual patient history. The professor plays the patient, and you have to go through an evaluation and assessment, give your diagnosis, develop goals for treatment, and suggest a treatment plan. The professor will then tell you how you did. It really forces you to think on your feet and confront things that aren't clear-cut. Practicals were a great learning experience."

CERTIFICATION OR LICENSING

All states require physical therapists to pass a licensure exam after graduating from an accredited physical therapist educational program before they can practice. Gabor says, "Because I was trained overseas, I had to first take an exam to have my training recognized, even though I'd already worked as a professional physical therapist for many years. I was given a provisional license to practice while I prepared to take the actual licensing exam." Licensed physical therapists should also expect to continue their education. "I've taken a lot of practical courses to learn specific techniques," Gabor says. "These are usually short courses lasting a few days."

A physical therapist is encouraged to become certified as a clinical specialist in one of the seven specialty areas recognized by the American Board of Physical Therapy Specialists. The seven areas of specialization are cardiovascular and pulmonary (or cardiopulmonary), clinical electrophysiology, geriatrics, neurology, orthopedics, pediatrics, and sports. Certification is available to any physical therapist with several years of clinical experience and postgraduate education in a specialty area.

In-depth

Seven Specialties of Physical Therapy

Cardiopulmonary physical therapy is concerned with the heart and lungs.

Clinical electrophysiology physical therapy is concerned with the effects of electrical stimulation on the body.

Geriatrics physical therapy is concerned with elderly people.

Neurology physical therapy is concerned with the nervous system.

Orthopedics physical therapy is concerned with the skeleton.

Pediatrics physical therapy is concerned with children.

Sports physical therapy is concerned with athletics and exercising.

Who Will Hire Me?

Physical therapy offers a broad range of employment opportunities. Many physical therapists work in hospitals, but APTA reports that almost 80 percent of the 137,000 PTs in the United States work in rehabilitation centers, health care clinics, physical therapy centers, community health centers, nursing homes, schools, pediatric centers, sports facilities, and research institutions. Many companies in manufacturing and other areas employ physical therapists in corporate and industrial physical therapy departments.

Pam Johnson performed her internship at the Rehabilitation Institute of Chicago (RIC). "That was a pretty intense place to work," Pam says. "I was offered a permanent job there, but I didn't want to specialize yet. So I went to a physical therapy job fair, and that's where I found out about Swedish Covenant. I also spoke to the people I was working with at RIC, and they recommended Swedish Covenant, too. So I applied for a position and was given an interview. They also let me come in and observe the physical therapy department, which was very helpful. I got to see what kind of atmosphere they had." Pam was lucky enough to have several job offers within a couple of weeks. "There still are jobs out there, but it's not as easy as it was, say, 10 years ago. A friend of mine in San Francisco, for example, has had a horrible time of finding work."

Pam's choice of Swedish Covenant came because of the flexibility the hospital environment offered. "They have us on a rotating schedule. Every three months we're assigned to a different area of the hospital. Right now, for example, I'm assigned to the acute care unit, treating patients who are just out of surgery. It gives me exposure to the whole range of physical therapy, so I'll be able to choose a specialty later on. Working in a hospital also gives you a chance to move up to senior positions, something that isn't always available in other places. And here at Swedish Covenant, we have a very international staff. This gives me exposure to physical therapy techniques all over the world."

Gabor Sagi's career path has been different from Pam's. "My first jobs were as a contract PT in France. I'd fill in full time for vacationing physical therapists who had their own private practices. After a year of that, I moved to England, where I was self-employed. I worked on a part-time contract with a medical center, and another part-time contract with a hospital in the National Health System there." Gabor came to the United States after being offered his current position. "For a long time, there was a shortage of physical therapists in the States," Gabor says, "but that's changing."

Where Can I Go from Here?

"Physical therapy is really a broad profession," Gabor says. "There are so many areas to specialize in. Right now, I tend to specialize in backs. But one day I could decide to move into a different area."

Gabor's interests include several areas. "I plan to go back to France eventually and start up my own private practice or a group practice with a couple of others. I also want to continue my interest in the spine and become more expert in that field. Then I'd like to teach others interested in that specialty." Gabor also plans to conduct clinical research; he is actively involved in studying a physical therapy technique called the McKenzie Method. "I'm training to be an instructor now. Then I'll be bringing McKenzie to France," Gabor says.

For Pam Johnson, the future is still wide open. "I'm just starting out, so it's great that I get exposed to so many different areas of physical therapy," she says. "In the future, I might decide to get into aquatic therapy. Another area I'm interested in is working with spinal cord injuries. These patients tend to be pretty young. So the work I'd do would really have an impact on the rest of their lives."

Physical therapists go on to earn doctorate degrees in physical therapy and conduct research.

What Are the Salary Ranges?

Physical therapists earned median annual salaries of $57,710 in 2003, according to the U.S. Department of Labor. Salaries ranged from less than $40,380 to more than $86,310. Salaries vary according to location, setting, and position. Supervisory and administrative personnel earn more than the average, as do many physical therapists who operate their own private practices. Physical therapists in home health care setting make the highest average annual salaries at $67,000 a year.

In-depth

The McKenzie Method

The McKenzie Method is a unique approach to assess and treat problems relating to the spine through a series of individualized exercises. The method is based on a belief in the body's ability to heal itself without needles, injections, heat, cold, or force dependent on a therapist. After a thorough assessment by a certified McKenzie physical therapist, patients trains with the therapist until they can self-administer, or do the exercises on their own. The end goal is to reduce a patient's therapy visits, to promote natural healing, and to educate the patient about reducing the risks of future injuries. For more information, visit the official Web site of the McKenzie Institute at http://www.mckenziemdt.org.

What Is the Job Outlook?

Employment of physical therapists is expected to grow faster than the average, according to *Occupational Outlook Handbook*. This positive may be tempered by federal legislation that imposes limits on reimbursement for therapy services.

Over the long run, the demand for physical therapists should continue to rise as a result of growth in the number of individuals with disabilities or limited function requiring therapy services, such as the elderly population. As the baby boom generation enters the prime age for heart attacks and strokes, there will be increasing demand for cardiac and physical rehabilitation. Future medical developments may also increase the survival rates of trauma victims who will need rehabilitative services. In addition, a growing number of employers are using physical therapists to evaluate worksites, develop exercise programs, and teach safe work habits to employees in the hope of reducing injuries.

How Do I Learn More?

PROFESSIONAL ORGANIZATIONS

The following organization provides information on physical therapy careers, accredited schools, and employers:

American Physical Therapy Association
1111 North Fairfax Street
Alexandria, VA 22314
800-999-2782
http://www.apta.org

BIBLIOGRAPHY

The following is a sampling of materials related to the professional concerns and development of physical therapists:

Cameron, Michelle, ed. *Physical Agents in Rehabilitation: From Research to Practice*. 2d ed. Philadelphia: W. B. Saunders, 2003.

Cavallaro Goodman, Catherine, Kenda S. Fuller, and William G. Boissonnault. *Pathology: Implications for the Physical Therapist.* 2d ed. Philadelphia: W. B. Saunders, 2002.

Lesh, Steven G. *Clinical Orthopedics for the Physical Therapist Assistant.* Philadelphia, PA: F. A. Davis, 2000.

Lippert, Lynn S. *Clinical Kinesiology for Physical Therapist Assistants.* 3d ed. Philadelphia: F. A. Davis, 2000.

Meadows, James T. S., ed. *Differential Diagnosis for the Orthopedic Physical Therapist.* New York: McGraw-Hill, 1999.

Shepard, Katherine F., and Gail M. Jensen. *Handbook of Teaching for Physical Therapists.* 2d ed. Newton, Mass.: Butterworth-Heinemann, 2002.

PHYSICAL THERAPY ASSISTANTS

Tracey Anderson believes that the most demanding aspects of her work as a physical therapy assistant (PTA) are also the most rewarding. "We're working with people who are hurting, angry, and some of their families don't understand," she says of the patients who visit the private clinic for which she works. "We have one patient who is very young and has had multiple surgeries. Her body is covered with scars. One time she told me, 'No one's going to love me like this.' These people are stressed out and they tell you so many things."

This level of closeness isn't surprising to Tracey. "You do develop relationships with these people. You're very close to them physically, working with their bodies, helping them with exercises. They're in pain, they're crying." Though Tracey finds it difficult to separate herself from her patients' suffering, she's happy to have the opportunity to make her patients feel better. "I've had people who come in and who are cantankerous and mean, and I've seen them lose that anger. You make a lot of friends. It's amazing."

Definition
Physical therapy assistants work under the supervision of physical therapists to help patients improve mobility, relieve pain, and prevent or lessen long-term physical disability.

Alternative Job Titles
Physical therapist assistants
Physical therapy technicians

High School Subjects
Health
Physical education
Psychology

Personal Skills
Following instructions
Helping/teaching

Salary Range
$24,230 to $36,610 to $49,650

Minimum Educational Level
Associate's degree

Certification or Licensing
Required by certain states

Outlook
Much faster than the average

DOT
076

GOE
14.06.01

NOC
6631

O*NET-SOC
31-2021.00

What Does a Physical Therapy Assistant Do?

Disease and injury can profoundly impair the performance and mobility of the human body. For centuries, forms of exercise, massage, and the use of heat and other techniques have been used to treat disabling conditions. Modern physical therapy has evolved, becoming more sophisticated and broader in scope. In addition to restoring mobility and alleviating pain and suffering, physical therapy now aims at preventing and mitigating permanent disability. Under the supervision and direction of a physical therapist, the *physical therapy assistant* works with patients to instruct and assist them in achieving the maximum functional performance of their bodies.

Injuries to the back, a common source of pain and immobility, often respond well to physical therapy. For some conditions, such as stroke, therapy may involve relearning such basic tasks as standing, eating, bathing, and walking. Other patients may be required to adapt to the permanent use of a wheelchair or an artificial limb. Patients with such severe impairments are often emotionally overwhelmed by these limitations of their bodies. A physical therapy assistant must also work with them to improve their state of mind. Ultimately, the goal of a physical therapy assistant is to help patients regain a maximum degree of independence.

As part of a team including the patient's physician, nurses, physical therapist, and, often, a psychologist and social worker, the physical therapy assistant participates in the evaluation of a patient's condition. An evaluation can include measuring the patient's strength, range of motion, and functional ability; that is, how well the patient performs certain physical tasks. Once the physical therapist has developed a treatment plan, it is the responsibility of the physical therapy assistant to carry out the therapy, to take notes on the patient's progress, and to report observations, particularly if he or she perceives that a patient is having severe difficulties or experiencing problems with the prescribed therapy. During complicated therapeutic procedures, the physical therapy assistant works side-by-side with the physical therapist; more routine procedures are usually carried out by the physical therapy assistant alone.

An important role of the physical therapy assistant is teaching patients the use of canes, walkers, crutches, or wheelchairs, and how to apply, remove, care for, and live with devices such as braces, or artificial limbs and joints. Many patients, especially geriatric (elderly) patients, need to learn how to climb stairs, or to transport themselves from bed or from a wheelchair to the shower or toilet.

The emotional and psychological condition of a patient is often a key factor in their response to therapy. A physical therapy assistant plays a part in helping their patients overcome the feelings of hopelessness, loss, and fear that often accompany illness and disability.

Physical therapy assistants work with a variety of patients, ranging from the elderly to the very young. In an acute care hospital, patients may include those with back problems, severe burns, cancer, and those recovering from motorcycle or car accidents. In a rehabilitation facility, physical therapy assistants work closely with newly disabled patients to help restore them as fully as possible to an independent lifestyle. These intensive therapy sessions—lasting three hours or more—often involve helping the patient relearn the basic tasks of life. They sometimes incorporate occupational and speech therapy as well (see the article Occupational Therapy Assistants).

Home health therapy allows still more individual contact with the patient. The physical therapy assistant visits a patient in his or her home, which allows the assistant to assess the patient's abilities for performing everyday tasks like sweeping, washing dishes, or making a bed. The assistant teaches the patient how to accomplish these tasks safely. Many home health patients are elderly and confined to their homes, and the physical therapy assistant provides a welcome link to the outside world.

Other physical therapy assistants work with disabled children at schools and children's hospitals. By doing "play" therapy, a physical therapy assistant can work on a child's motor control, vestibular stimulation, balance, and coordination. The physical therapy assistant helps children learn to crawl, sit, stand, or walk, and over the years, helps them achieve the most possible independence.

In all of these job settings, a physical therapy assistant may also perform clerical duties, such as filling out reports, devising schedules, maintaining patient records, and coordinating inventory and supplies. A physical therapy assistant may also be responsible for coordinating the patient's treatment with the patient's insurance plans.

Lingo to Learn

Disassociation Passive exercises performed on the patient by the physical therapist or PTA that involve stretching parts of the body in order to loosen rigid or locked joints.

Iontophoresis Using electrical impulses to introduce anti-inflammatory medication through the skin into an inflamed area.

Quality of life In medicine, quality of life refers to the overall nature of a patient's physical and psychological well-being.

Traction A therapy that uses mechanical equipment to stretch, pull, or hold a part of the patient's body into position. It is used for fractures, muscle spasms, or other injuries to aid proper healing and to relieve pain caused by physical pressure.

Ultrasound Ultrasound is commonly used in physical therapy to relieve pain and swelling of joints and improve muscle condition.

Vestibular stimulation The vestibular nerve in the ear affects a person's balance; some patients require therapy to restore their sense of balance.

What Is It Like to Be a Physical Therapy Assistant?

"A patient usually requires a procedure prior to the therapist seeing them," says Tracey Anderson, a physical therapy assistant in a private clinic, "such as hot pack, electrical stimulation, or ultrasound. That takes about 20 minutes, then you prepare them for the therapist to see them."

When Tracey first gets to work, she prepares the procedure room. "I make sure everything's ready, turning on equipment, making sure we have hot packs and cold packs. There are some procedures that require an injection that freezes the area to be worked on. So I get everything set up, then go through the schedule to see which patients are coming in, then I pull their records." Tracey is also required to keep her work area clean, which includes making the bed and doing some laundry. Though Tracey doesn't have to deal with progress reports or the maintaining of files, she mentions that PTAs in some offices must transcribe notes, keep records, schedule, and perform other administrative duties.

"Our office has a casual atmosphere," she says. "We've found that really does make people much more comfortable. We don't wear lab coats. Our waiting room has a dining room table, and we give the patients coffee or tea. If a patient has to wait a little while, we sit with them and talk. Once they're comfortable, it's easier to work with them."

Many physical therapy facilities focus on sports medicine, but Tracey's clinic primarily provides wound care. She often works with people who have scar tissue from multiple surgeries. When a patient arrives, Tracey leads them to the back where the patient can change clothes and get into the bed. "I then apply electrical stimulation to whichever part of the body we're working—the lower back or shoulder, for example. Usually we cover patients with hot packs and they stay that way for about 20 minutes. If an ultrasound is required in that area, then I'll do that. Then the therapist takes over." Patients at the clinic are scheduled for every half hour, so Tracey sees about 16 patients a day.

Tracey learned how to use the electrical stimulation machine while on the job. "We attach electrodes to the area of the body being worked on. The electricity sort of grabs the muscles and works them. The idea is that it will tire the muscles so that they will relax. That makes it much easier for the therapist to work on the patient. You have to be very careful, though; it's easy to apply too much electricity."

The clinic also features a gym area. "A patient may require 15 or 20 minutes of therapeutic exercises. The therapist gives me the exercises, and then I teach the patient how to do them."

A patient may require 15 or 20 minutes of therapeutic exercises. The therapist gives me the exercises, and then I teach the patient how to do them.

Tracey also provides emotional support, as well. "I can't tell you how many stories I've heard," she says. "Many patients need to talk about their circumstances, and how their families are reacting to their injuries. You really have to be able to talk to them and listen."

Do I Have What It Takes to Be a Physical Therapy Assistant?

Some of the most important qualities for a physical therapy assistant to have are physical stamina, patience, and good communication skills. If you are thinking of entering this field, you must also genuinely enjoy working with people, including those under the stress of illness, aging, or injury. When a condition will not permit patients to regain full use of their bodies, the physical therapy assistant helps them to adjust to this, and to discover ways to become as self-sufficient as possible. "You're dealing with people who are in pain," Tracey says. "Usually by the time they get to the physical therapist, they've been through doctors, insurance companies, and paperwork, and they're not always the nicest people. You just have to love what you're doing and really get along well with people."

Physical therapy assistants are often responsible for many patients in a day, so they need to be organized, efficient, and realistic about what can be accomplished. Mastery of the many therapy techniques

To Be a Successful Physical Therapy Assistant, You Should . . .

- like to work with people
- have an outgoing personality and strong communication skills
- be patient, encouraging, and creative
- have stamina, good physical dexterity, and coordination
- enjoy physical activity
- have good decision-making abilities and be able to follow directions
- be organized and self-motivated

is obviously essential. A physical therapy assistant must also have good observational skills in order to recognize what is and is not working for a patient. These observations must then be communicated to the patient's physical therapist and physician.

A physical therapy assistant is constantly challenged in his or her work. Not only does this career require a great deal of stamina and physical strength, but, because of the often slow healing process and the repetitive nature of many therapy techniques, the therapy assistant must have patience as well. The ability to communicate enthusiasm and encouragement is a great asset. "You have to have a great personality," Tracey says. "I find a sense of humor to be very important. You have to make people very comfortable. People need to trust you."

How Do I Become a Physical Therapy Assistant?

EDUCATION

High School

While you are in high school, you should take courses in biology, health, math, psychology, speech, and English to prepare for a career as a physical therapy assistant. Classes that enable you to become comfortable on computers are also useful.

Some high schools offer work-study programs in health, which combine classes in health and medical subjects with practical work experience. Volunteering at a local hospital is also an excellent way to explore the hospital environment and to become familiar with aspects of this career. Working with children, the physically disabled, or the elderly is another way to gain practical experience.

Postsecondary Training

Students must attend an accredited physical therapy assistant program, offered at many community and junior colleges, vocational schools, and universities. The American Physical Therapy Association (APTA) sets the standards for accreditation and educational requirements for these programs. There are about 245 accredited physical therapy assistant programs in the United States, according to APTA.

Physical therapy assistant programs are designed to last two years and result in an associate's degree. The programs are divided into academic course work and hands-on clinical field experience. The course work includes anatomy, physiology, biology, the history and philosophy of rehabilitation, human growth and development, chemistry, and psychology. In addition, students take some courses in mathematics and applied physical sciences in order to gain an understanding of the apparatus and the principles behind the therapeutic procedures they will use. Students also receive training in the variety of physical therapy techniques, including massage, therapeutic exercise, and heat and cold therapy. Before students can begin their clinical work, many programs require that they gain certifications in CPR and first aid. During the clinical rotation period, students apply the education, techniques, and skills they have learned in various health facility settings, under the supervision of senior physical therapy assistants and physical therapists.

CERTIFICATION OR LICENSING

Upon graduation from an accredited program, most states require that a candidate pass a written examination administered by the state in order to become a licensed physical therapy assistant. The process for renewing the physical therapy assistant license also varies by state. In addition, physical therapy assistants must be certified in CPR and first aid.

SCHOLARSHIPS AND GRANTS

The APTA offers a minority scholarship to students enrolled in physical therapy assistant programs accredited by the APTA. This award is given to outstanding minority students on a competitive basis. Visit the APTA Web site, http://www.apta.org, for more information

INTERNSHIPS AND VOLUNTEERSHIPS

If you are interested in becoming a physical therapy assistant, look for a summer or part-time position working or volunteering in the physical therapy department of a hospital or clinic. Many public and private schools also enlist volunteers to work with their disabled students. Jobs at summer camps for disabled children are also excellent experience for prospective physical therapy assistants. Nursing homes and other elderly facilities are another source of work experience and volunteerships. Any of these volunteer positions will help you determine whether you have the personal qualities needed for this career.

Another way to gain more knowledge about this field is to speak with physical therapists and physical therapy assistants.

Who Will Hire Me?

Tracey first started working for the clinic in a clerical position. "I started talking to some of the therapists," she says, "and they decided to start training me for working with patients."

There are about 50,000 physical therapy assistants in the United States, about three-quarters of whom work in hospitals or the offices of health care practitioners. Physical therapy assistants also find employment in rehabilitation centers, home health therapy, extended-care facilities, schools for disabled children, nursing homes, physicians' offices, and private physical therapy offices. The clinical rotation you do during your training program will give you a good feel for which environment is right for you.

Your training program's placement office offers an excellent route to finding your first job. (In fact, one way to evaluate a prospective school is to ask how many of its graduates find work as physical therapy assistants.) Once you've graduated, your placement office should provide listings of available jobs in the area, along with advice on putting together your resume.

Other ways to find a job include looking at classified ads, visiting employment agencies, and browsing hospital and job sites on the Internet. Many newspapers have a section in their classified ads specifically for health care positions. Employment agencies sometimes handle all hiring for local hospitals; call around to see if that's the case in your area. You should also check the Web sites for your local hospitals, as they may post job openings online. There are also a num-

In-depth

Physical Therapy (PT) vs. Occupational Therapy (OT)

Assessment

In physical therapy, the therapist assesses the patient's body structure and physiology.

In occupational therapy, the therapist conducts activity analysis, in which a person's ability to do an activity is compared to the demands of that activity.

Treatment Goals and Methods

Physical therapy treatment seeks to moderate pain and enhance healing through applications of heat and cold, ultrasound, and electrical stimulation; improve normal function and movement through joint mobilization, stretching, and exercise; and improve overall conditioning to allow for an improved level of physical activity.

Occupational therapy treatment seeks to enable a person to perform activities that are necessary or desirable by improving the patient's technique, adapting the environment, or modifying the task itself.

ber of free Internet sites dedicated to helping people in certain health professions locate work nationwide.

Where Can I Go from Here?

A physical therapy assistant's responsibilities may increase as his or her level of experience increases. At a larger facility, a physical therapy assistant may receive promotions to a supervisory position; in a smaller facility, an assistant may gradually receive more and more responsibility for the coordination of the physical therapy office. As physical therapy assistants develop greater experience and responsibilities, they can expect to earn higher salaries.

Physical therapy assistants may also choose to advance by changing facilities, such as moving from a hospital setting to a home health setting, or from the acute care facility to the outpatient unit of a physical therapy department. Each area of physical therapy brings its own challenges and rewards.

Some physical therapy assistants return to school in order to become fully qualified physical therapists. Many universities and colleges offer bachelor's-to-master's degree programs in physical therapy. (The master's degree is now the minimum requirement for employment as a physical therapist.) Competition for placement in a physical therapy program is expected to remain keen; a physical therapy assistant with a degree from an accredited program, good grades, and strong work experience may find acceptance into a physical therapy program easier than those with no prior experience in this field. There are APTA-accredited programs in California, Ohio, and Pennsylvania that allow physical therapy assistants to keep working during the week while they pursue a master's degree in physical therapy on the weekends.

Some physical therapists and physical therapy assistants may find opportunities for conducting research into the effectiveness of physical therapy techniques or participating in the development of new therapies. Still others may develop a desire to move into other health and medical careers.

Advancement Possibilities

Physical therapists plan and administer medically prescribed physical therapy treatment for patients suffering from injuries, or muscle, nerve, joint, and bone diseases, to restore function, relieve pain, and prevent disability.

Physiatrists are medical doctors who specialize in clinical and diagnostic use of physical agents and exercises to provide physiotherapy for physical, mental, and occupational rehabilitation of patients.

What Are the Salary Ranges?

Physical therapy assistant salaries vary according to facility type, geographical location, employer, and the physical therapy assistant's experience level. The U.S. Department of Labor reports that median annual salaries for physical therapy assistants were $36,610 in 2003. Salaries ranged from less than $24,230 a year to more than $49,650. Benefits for physical therapy assistants vary but usually include paid holidays and vacations, health insurance, and pension plans.

What Is the Job Outlook?

"For a long time," says Tracey, "physical therapy wasn't seen as a medical profession. Many people didn't take it seriously, and insurance companies didn't want to pay [for it]. But I've seen that change a lot over the last 10 years. People are recognizing physical therapy as a very viable procedure, not just a glorified massage."

According to the *Occupational Outlook Handbook,* employment of physical therapy assistants is expected to grow much faster than the average for all other occupations over the next 10 years. As medical technology advances, more patients will be saved and will be in need of physical therapy. New abilities to treat disabling conditions will also prompt more demand for physical therapy assistants to work with these patients. Also, as the population grows older and as more and more people survive into advanced age, the number of elderly people with chronic and debilitating conditions will also increase as will their need for physical therapy. Also, the technologies that permit more infants and young children to survive severe birth defects are also a factor in the forecast for strong growth in jobs in the field.

An additional factor in the growth of the number of jobs for physical therapy assistants is the need for containing the rise of medical costs: Many hospitals will look for physical therapy assistants to fill out their physical therapy staff, rather than increasing the number of higher-paid physical therapists.

How Do I Learn More?

PROFESSIONAL ORGANIZATIONS

The following are organizations that provide information on physical therapy assistant careers, accredited schools, and employers:

American Physical Therapy Association
1111 North Fairfax Street
Alexandria, VA 22314-1488
http://www.apta.org

American Congress of Rehabilitation Medicine
5987 East 71st Street, Suite 111
Indianapolis, IN 46220-4049
acrm@acrm.org
http://www.acrm.org

BIBLIOGRAPHY

The following is a sampling of materials relating to the professional concerns and development of physical therapy assistants:

Curtis, Kathleen A. *Physical Therapy Professional Foundations: Keys to Success in School and Career.* Delmar Learning, 2002.

Krumhansl, Bernice, and Kathy Siebel. *Opportunities in Physical Therapy Careers.* New York: McGraw-Hill, 1999.

Moffat, Marilyn, and Steve Vickery. *The American Physical Therapy Association Book of Body Maintenance and Repair.* New York: Henry Holt, 1999.

Quinlan, Kathryn A. *Physical Therapist Assistant.* Careers Without College. Mankato, Minn.: Capstone Press, 1998.

PHYSICIAN ASSISTANTS

Definition
Physician assistants are formally trained to practice medicine under the supervision of a licensed physician. They may provide medical care as determined by their supervising physicians and their state's laws.

Alternative Job Titles
Child health associates
Physician associates

High School Subjects
Biology
Chemistry
English

Personal Skills
Communication/ideas
Helping/teaching

Salary Range
$35,980 to $78,257 to $91,380+

Educational Requirements
Graduation from accredited P.A. program; Bachelor's degree recommended.

Certification or Licensing
Required by all states

Outlook
Much faster than the average

DOT
079

GOE
14.02.01

NOC
3123

O*NET-SOC
29-1071.00

As soon as she arrives at the clinic, Mary Murray, physician assistant, checks the list of patients she will see that day. Her first patient is Fred Applebee, an older man with a rash that has spread on his forearms and is beginning to ooze and scale over.

She checks the chart and notes the comments made by the nurse who initially saw Fred. When Mary enters the room, she offers Fred a friendly handshake and says, "Hi, Mr. Applebee, I'm Mary, the physician's assistant. Have you ever been seen by a physician's assistant before?"

As expected, Fred's answer is no. Mary finds that many patients have never been treated by a physician's assistant. So Mary sits on the examining stool and explains what she does and what her scope of medical practice is. She tells Fred about her formal medical training and that she is licensed to work under the supervision of a physician. She further explains that she is able to perform many of the duties of a physician, including writing prescriptions. She tells him that if she has any questions about his medical problems, she discusses them with her supervising physician. She then asks Fred if he is comfortable with being treated by her.

After winning Fred's confidence, Mary proceeds to examine Fred and diagnose his skin problem. She writes a prescription for a topical ointment and an antibiotic and tells Fred to keep a close eye on the infection and to call if it gets worse.

Mary then goes on to the next patient, a young boy with a fever and a cough. As Mary enters the room, she shakes hands with the mother and the young patient, and proceeds once again to explain the duties of a physician assistant.

Because physician assistants are relatively new to some medical practices and their patients, Mary's first goal when seeing patients is to make sure they understand her role and feel comfortable being seen by her. "I always introduce myself and explain the duties of a physician's assistant. It's important to me that they trust me and recognize that I am a medical professional who will provide them the best medical care possible. I think establishing that confidence initially is the key to establishing a relationship." Mary adds, "I find that some patients are more open with me than they are with their doctors. I think they feel less intimidated."

In most cases, patients are more than satisfied with the services of a physician assistant. "Mary took more time to listen and she didn't seem so rushed," says Fred. "I'll ask for her next time I have a medical problem. I felt like she really cared."

Lingo to Learn

Ambulatory care centers Doctors' offices, clinics, hospitals, or other "walk-in" health care facilities that provide medical care.

Chart A collection of written materials relating to the health care of a patient.

Clinical rotation Supervised clinical training in family medicine, emergency medicine, pediatrics, surgery, and other areas.

Family practice An area of medicine that provides general health care to patients of all ages.

Primary care A specialty that includes family practice, internal medicine, pediatric care, and obstetrics/gynecology.

What Does a Physician Assistant Do?

Physician assistants, or *PAs,* are formally trained, licensed health professionals who practice medicine under the supervision of a physician. They provide some of the skilled patient care usually done by physicians, allowing the physicians to spend their time on more serious medical care. Much of the patient care that physician assistants provide used to be limited to physicians. The profession was started in the 1960s to relieve a physician shortage in some areas of the country and to improve access to high-quality care. Physician assistants hold about 63,000 jobs in the United States.

Physician assistants practice as part of a team, always under the supervision of a licensed doctor of medicine or osteopathy. Physician assistants perform many essential tasks. They are educated to recognize when patients need the attention of a supervising physician or another specialist. They provide a wide variety of routine diagnostic, therapeutic, and preventive health care services. They take medical histories, examine patients, order and interpret laboratory diagnostic tests and X rays, diagnose common illnesses and disorders, develop treatment plans, provide counseling, manage infections, and treat minor problems, such as burns and abrasions. They suture wounds and set simple fractures. In most states they are permitted to prescribe medications. Some physician assistants perform surgical procedures. They may also perform managerial duties and supervise technicians and assistants.

Physician assistants are also trained to provide medical emergency care. They deal with such emergencies as severe drug reactions, heart attacks, psychiatric crises, and uncomplicated deliveries until a physician becomes available.

The medical cases they handle depend on their education, experience, state laws, and the type of practice they are in. In some states, the state regulatory agency determines what duties they may perform; in others, the supervising physician does. Physician assistants have to know the laws and regulations in the state in which they practice. Not being independent practitioners, physician assistants do not work in solo practices.

"The practice lends itself to what the physician feels comfortable letting the physician assistant do," explains Mary. "For example, I haven't had much experience in splinting and casting, so a supervising physician is not likely to give me this type of work. Instead, the physician will give this duty to a physician assistant who has this type of experience, perhaps someone who has worked in orthopedics."

Physician assistants help reduce waiting time for patients. They usually spend more time examining patients and answering their questions than physicians do. They also help relieve the physician shortage in rural areas where access to health care is a problem. Physician assistants working in rural or inner-city clinics may provide most of the patient care there and consult with the supervising physician by telephone as needed and as required by law. In these situations, a physician may be available in a clinic only one or two days a week. Or physician assistants may work in a satellite clinic that has no physician on site. In that case, they use telecommunications to maintain contact with the supervising physicians. Physician assistants may also visit patients in their homes or in hospitals and nursing homes, again consulting with their supervising physicians.

According to the American Academy of Physician Assistants (AAPA), about 42 percent of all PAs practice what is known as primary care medicine, which is family medicine, internal medicine, pediatrics, and obstetrics and gynecology. About 24 percent are in surgery or the surgical subspecialties. Some also work in specialized areas such as emergency medicine, occupational medicine, psychiatry, orthopedics, and geriatrics.

What Is It Like to Be a Physician Assistant?

Mary Murray has been a physician assistant for 10 years, working mainly in a family practice clinic and in family practice/urgent care in hospitals. After she graduated from high school, she went to college and received a bachelor's degree in nursing. "After working as a nurse I decided I wanted to do more in patient care, but I didn't want to make the time commitment required to attend medical school and practice as a physician," says Mary. "Becoming a physician assistant seemed to be the answer. It allowed me to learn more and become more involved with patient care. I'm happy with it."

Mary likes working with people. "I enjoy the challenge each day brings with new patients to diagnose and treat." Mary sees patients with any number of medical problems, from lacerations to abrasions, to burns to high blood pressure. She also spends some of her time counseling patients and discussing preventive health care with them.

"Like any profession," says Mary, "there are positive and negative aspects of the job." She goes on to explain, "You can usually choose the type of setting you want to work in. This generally determines the hours you work. You work longer hours in a hospital or in obstetrics/gynecology than in a clinic setting."

Physician assistants who work in surgery may have to stand for long periods. Physician assistants who work in hospital emergency departments may work long shifts, such as 24-hour shifts twice a week or 12-hour shifts three times a week. Physician assistants who work in physicians' offices, group practices, or hospitals may have to work weekends, nights, and holidays. Some PAs may be required to be on call. As in any medical profession, exposure to infectious diseases is a reality.

A few years ago, Mary added teaching to her professional duties. She now teaches in the physician assistant program at Midwestern University in Downers Grove, Illinois. She teaches medical Spanish to those who plan to practice with a Spanish-speaking population. In addition, she still works part time as a physician assistant in family practice/urgent care at MacNeal Hospital in Berwyn, Illinois, and in urgent care one day a week in the emergency department of another hospital. The patients she treats are not as seriously ill as those seen by physicians.

> **FYI**
>
> Physician assistants perform many types of patient care, such as
> - examining patients
> - taking medical histories
> - ordering and interpreting laboratory tests
> - ordering X rays
> - diagnosing common illnesses
> - treating minor injuries
> - promoting disease prevention

"As faculty, we are trying to keep our clinical skills as up to date as possible so we can keep abreast of medical advances in order to teach them," Mary says of her dual roles as a teacher and practitioner. "It adds credibility when you are practicing and keeping up on changes in the medical field, such as AIDS."

The amount of supervision that physician assistants have is up to the supervising physician. Some physician assistants work in clinics where a physician is not present, so supervision has to be via telecommunications. Supervision is greatest for practitioners who are recent graduates.

Mary explains, "As soon as you graduate and are certified, you can practice. The supervising physician is available to answer questions or deal with issues that you do not feel prepared for.

"With experience, physician assistants practice more independently, but we are not independent practitioners," she emphasizes. "We could never hang up our shingle and practice by ourselves. Supervising physicians are there to lend us assistance and share the experience and knowledge they get through medical school and residency."

Do I Have What It Takes to Be a Physician Assistant?

Because you deal directly with patients, you must enjoy working with people and be able to relate to people effectively. You need good communication skills so you can converse with patients at a level they will understand. You also need to be conscientious and patient, always treating people tactfully and respecting their confidentiality.

"People skills and interpersonal skills are necessary. Communication skills are vital. You also have to like working with people," Mary says.

You should be able to demonstrate self-confidence and good judgment. You will be required to respond to emergencies calmly and be responsible for making decisions quickly. Of course, you must also be interested in health care and science.

Mary adds that "shadowing" is encouraged for those interested in a physician assistant career. That is, if you think you would like to work as a physician assistant, you should try to spend some time with someone in that profession so you can see what the job involves and determine if you have an interest in this type of work.

Physician assistants should also have a love for learning and be self-motivated to stay abreast of new medical treatments and new developments in technology.

How Do I Become a Physician Assistant?

EDUCATION

High School

If you are thinking of a career as a physician assistant, you should take well-balanced college preparatory courses in high school. Science and health courses are essential preparation for the work you will be doing later. English and communication courses are also important for developing verbal abilities. Taking computer courses is also imperative in today's work world. Taking a foreign language, especially Spanish, can also be advantageous.

If possible, you should explore the career field by finding part-time or volunteer work in a hospital, nursing home, or clinic.

Postsecondary Training

To become a physician assistant, most states require that you complete course work in an accredited educational program. According to AAPA, there are 133 accredited programs throughout the United States. Most physician assistant programs require that applicants have previous health care experience and two years of college education. According to AAPA, the typical applicant has a bachelor's degree and over four years of health care experience. Competition for admission to physician assistant programs is usually intense.

"The field has become so competitive that having a background and experience in health care will help those applying to physician assistant programs," Mary says. "Science-oriented classes will help, as will anything you can do to expose yourself to health care careers, such as volunteering at a hospital."

Physician assistants are educated in intensive medical programs accredited by the Accreditation Review Commission on Education for the Physician Assistant (ARC-PA). The average PA program lasts two years. Most programs are affiliated with two- and four-year college and university schools of medicine and allied health. Some are offered in hospitals; others in the armed forces.

Midwestern University, where Mary teaches, offers a two-year physician assistant program. "Most of the PA programs are 18 to 24 months in length," she said. "It is a rigorous, very intense program. Students do not get a summer break; the program runs straight through. Working full time while going to school is out of the question. Working part time is difficult."

The educational program at Midwestern University includes classroom instruction and clinical training. The classroom instruction, which usually lasts from six to 24 months, includes biochemistry, human anatomy, physiology, pharmacology, microbiology, physiology, medical ethics, pathology, clinical laboratory, and health promotion. Mary compares the program to a "mini-medical school." "It is almost like taking medical school in one year. Students take 60 some credit hours the first year," she said. "There are courses in neuroscience, introduction to clinical medicine, agricultural medicine, and corrective medicine."

The supervised clinical work, which lasts nine to 15 months, includes training (called clinical rotations) in areas such as family medicine, internal medicine, emergency medicine, pediatrics, geriatric medicine, obstetrics/gynecology, surgery, orthopedics, psychiatry, radiology, and general surgery. Students take these clinical rotations in private medical practices or hospitals, and many students receive a job offer from the supervising physician they worked under during a rotation.

Four-year programs generally include liberal arts courses that include the biological and behavioral sciences. Postgraduate residency training programs, which are not accredited, are available in gynecology, geriatrics, surgery, pediatrics, neonatology, and occupational medicine. Candidates must have graduated from an accredited program and be certified by the National Commission on Certification of Physician Assistants (NCCPA) before entering these programs.

If you plan to enroll in a PA program you should try to make financial arrangements in advance, such as applying for grants, scholarships, or loans.

CERTIFICATION OR LICENSING

All states require physician assistants to be certified by the NCCPA. To become certified, you must successfully complete the Physician Assistants National Certifying Examination. NCCPA also offers an optional examination in surgery for PAs who conduct a variety of health care functions related to surgery.

Only physician assistants with current certification may use the designation physician assistant-certified (P.A.-C.). Most states also require physician assistants to register with the state medical board.

To maintain a valid NCCPA certificate, PAs must complete 100 hours of continuing education every two years and pass a recertification exam every six years. In lieu of the recertification exam, PAs can also complete an alternative program that combines learning experience with a take-home examination.

Mary says that attending conferences and seminars and reading professional journals can meet the continuing education requirements. She belongs to the American Academy of Physician Assistants and the Illinois chapter of the AAPA. Through these organizations, she receives professional journals to help her meet the continuing education requirement. These organizations also sponsor continuing education seminars.

SCHOLARSHIPS AND GRANTS

There are many sources of financial aid for students. Contact the financial aid office of the academic institution you plan to attend to learn about scholarships, fellowships, grants, work/study opportunities, loans, and other sources of financial aid. Be sure to allow plenty of time for the paperwork.

FYI

The following are some of highlights of a 2004 survey taken by the American Academy of Physician Assistants:

- Females accounted for 60 percent of the respondents.
- The average age of respondents was 42 years.
- The average age when respondents graduated from PA school was 31 years.
- Half of respondents held a bachelor's level PA degree; 22 percent held a master's level PA degree.
- Almost 90 percent of respondents were in clinical practice.
- The average workweek of respondents was 42 hours a week.

The American Academy of Physician Assistants has a listing of scholarship and grant programs on its Web site: http://www.aapa.org/paf/pafprog.html.

Many students finance their education through the Armed Forces Health Professions Scholarship Program. Each branch of the military participates in this program, paying students' tuitions in exchange for military service. Contact your local recruiting office for more information on this program.

Many public and private organizations and businesses offer scholarships as well. Libraries, the Internet, and your guidance office should be able to provide you with more information. A good starting point for financial aid research is the SmartStudent Guide to Financial Aid Web site. This site has an extensive list of financial assistance information and links: http://www.finaid.org.

There are also various loan programs available through the federal government, including Pell Grants, Stafford Student Loans, National Direct Student Loans, Health Education Assistance Loans, and Health Professions Student Loans. Your high school guidance counselor should have information about these programs.

Who Will Hire Me?

Most schools have placement offices that will have information about job openings. In addition, many schools sponsor job fairs. "Recruitment is phenomenal as the profession grows," Mary comments.

As a physician assistant you may find work in any number of settings. Historically, PAs worked in areas where there was a shortage of physicians and where residents lacked access to high-quality health care. Today, they work in major cities as well as rural areas in most health care settings. However, about one-third of all PAs continue to provide health care to communities having fewer than 50,000 residents and experiencing a physician shortage.

According to AAPA, 65 percent of PAs were employed in the offices of physicians, dentists, and other health practitioners in 2004. About 22 percent were employed in hospitals. The remainder was employed in public health clinics, prisons, home health care agencies, nursing homes, and the Department of Veterans Affairs.

Physician assistants who were employed in health care fields prior to entering their PA training program should contact their former employers about job possibilities.

Membership in professional organizations can also provide job-networking possibilities. "Networking is very important in such a fast-growing profession," Mary notes. Professional organizations enable members to learn what their colleagues are doing, what advances are occurring in various types of work settings, and where jobs are available. Some trade and professional organization publications contain job listings.

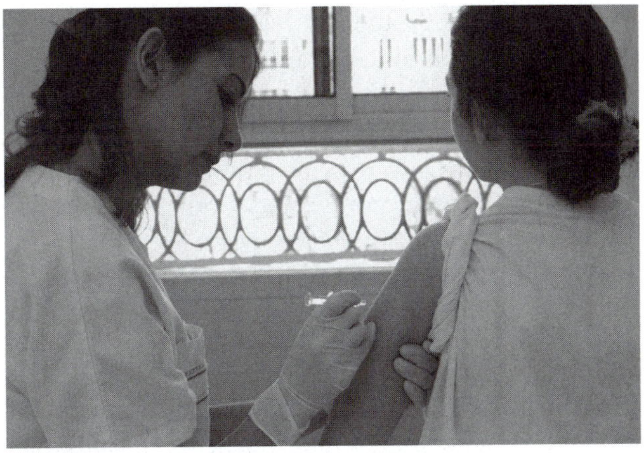

A physician assistant administers an injection. *(Hop American / Photo Researchers Inc.)*

Where Can I Go from Here?

"I'm very clinically minded, so I do not plan to move into management," Mary says. "I enjoy providing patient care. However, opportunities exist for physician assistants who are interested in moving into management positions. Their health care skills are an asset. Clinical areas need managers with a health care background to perform managerial duties. Also, employers who are increasing their physician assistant staffs will need coordinators and supervisors for those staffs. Physician assistants can move into these positions."

The physician assistant profession is still relatively young, and there are no formal lines of advancement yet. You can find career advancement opportunities by taking on greater responsibility with higher salary, completing graduate study and practicing in a specialty, or moving to a larger hospital or clinic. Some physician assistants join a private partnership practice. Others teach in a program for physician assistants or become administrators in hospitals or clinics.

Opportunities exist for physician assistants who are interested in moving into management positions. Their health care skills are an asset.

What Are the Salary Ranges?

Salaries vary by employer, amount, and type of training, experience, geographical location, and specialty. According to a survey conducted in 2004 by the American Academy of Physician Assistants, the average total income for PAs working full time (32 or more hours per week) was $78,257. Physician assistants working in hospitals and medical offices may earn more than those in clinics. Physician assistants working for the federal government are generally paid slightly less. The U.S. Department of Labor reports that the lowest paid 10 percent of PAs earned less than $35,980, and the highest paid 10 percent earned more than $91,380 a year.

Benefits such as insurance, sick leave, and vacation are usually standard for full-time workers. Some government jobs also provide retirement plans.

What Is the Job Outlook?

Employment of PAs is expected to grow much faster than the average during the next decade. Demand for PAs far outpaces supply. Employment opportunities are expected to be excellent, especially in locations where physician shortages exist. As physician assistants take on greater responsibilities and move into diverse work settings, they are being increasingly recognized as providers of high-quality patient care. Health care organizations are being restructured for cost economies, and the restructuring of health services is expected to bring standardized regulations for physician assistants. The continued growth of the profession depends on their growing acceptance by physicians.

Physicians and institutions are expected to employ more PAs to provide primary care because they are cost-effective and productive members of a health team. PAs should find good employment opportunities in hospitals, academic medical centers, public clinics, and prisons.

Insurance companies are increasingly paying for the use of physician assistants, and the public's acceptance of them is growing. Medicare now lets physicians bill the government for services provided by physician assistants in hospitals and nursing homes. The best job opportunities for physician assistants will be in states where they have a wider scope of practice.

How Do I Learn More?

PROFESSIONAL ORGANIZATIONS

The following are organizations provide information on physician assistant careers and accredited schools:

American Academy of Physician Assistants
950 North Washington Street
Alexandria, VA 22314
703-836-2272
aapa@aapa.org
http://www.aapa.org

Association of Physician Assistant Programs
950 North Washington Street
Alexandria, VA 22314
703-548-5538
http://www.apap.org

National Commission on Certification of Physician Assistants
12000 Findley Road, Suite 200
Duluth, GA 30097
678-417-8100
http://www.nccpa.net

BIBLIOGRAPHY

The following is a sampling of materials relating to the professional concerns and development of physician assistants:

Blessing, J. Dennis. *Physician Assistant's Guide to Research and Medical Literature.* F. A. David, 2001.

Hooker, Roderick S., and James F. Cawley. *Physician Assistants in American Medicine.* 2d ed. New York: Churchill Livingstone, 2002.

Labus, James B. *The Physician Assistant Surgical Handbook.* Philadelphia: W.B. Saunders Company, 1998.

Rodican, Andrew J. *Getting into the Physician Assistant School of Your Choice.* Rev. ed. New York: McGraw-Hill, 2003.

Sacks, Terence J. *Opportunities in Physician Assistant Careers.* 2d ed. New York: McGraw-Hill, 2002.

Springhouse Staff. *Physician Assistant's Clinical Companion.* Springhouse, PA: Springhouse Corporation, 2000.

PHYSIOLOGISTS

Doctors tell him to use a cane but John refuses. He is a proud man, and he wants to remain independent, but he has become frail and is having trouble keeping his balance when he walks.

"I'm going to get stronger," says John to his exercise physiologist, Fred Kronk. So Fred begins working with him two or three times a week, designing and monitoring his exercise regimen. After several months he sees John progress from not being able to walk more than a tenth of a mile to walking a full mile. Regaining his independence makes John proud. "I can make it around myself. I can make it to the bus. I can make it to work."

Watching John recover also makes Fred proud. "When I see this, I realize that I am the tool that came into play to help him accomplish this. And when I see something like this happen, I know that everything is going right in my life."

Definition
Physiologists are scientists who study life. Over the years, physiology has diversified into many areas such as respiratory, cardiovascular, and cell physiology. Physiologists conduct research that ranges from studying the workings inside single living cells to the interactions between humans and the environment. These studies try to determine the effects that stress and environmental changes can have on organisms.

High School Subjects
Biology
Chemistry

Personal Skills
Helping/teaching
Technical/scientific

Salary Range
$18,000 to $77,000 to $200,000

Educational Requirements
Bachelor's degree, master's degree recommended for exercise physiologists, doctorate for medical physiologists

Certification or Licensing
Voluntary

Outlook
Faster than the average

DOT
N/A

GOE
N/A

NOC
N/A

O*NET-SOC
N/A

What Does a Physiologist Do?

Physiologists study the systems of living organisms. They answer key questions about the human population and the environment. They focus on the effects that stress and environmental changes have on people and animals. Physiologists' work is essential in understanding how to treat disease.

There are two general types of physiologists closely associated with health care: *medical physiologists* and *exercise physiologists.* Medical physiologists are subdivided into many specialties, most of which deal with a specific bodily system (respiratory, endocrine, neurological, and circulatory) or a specific anatomic level (cellular or molecular).

Medical physiologists conduct research to increase scientific knowledge about the functions of the human body. A medical physiologist may study the systems of other animals and plants and apply this knowledge to humans. For instance, the cardiovascular system of a baboon may be studied to answer questions pertaining to heart disease in humans.

In an experiment at Northwestern University's Medical School in Chicago, Dr. Don McCrimmon tries to determine how the brain controls an animal's breathing. "I work on neuro-control breathing," he says. "We look at the mechanisms for generating basic respiratory movement and how the brain controls it. We look at methods that the body has for controlling and adjusting our breathing as we change our activity levels. How does all of this happen? It turns out that one of the interesting aspects of how we breathe when we exercise appears to be actually a learned response."

Research consumes a large portion of a medical physiologist's career. It is difficult to determine the expected length of an experiment because the findings of one experiment may lead to many additional projects and studies. In fact, an experiment may last from a few months to several years before it is completed. The number of projects being conducted in a particular laboratory can vary greatly as well.

Currently, Don has a staff of four assisting him with his experiments. In addition to his research, Don is a professor. He teaches physiology to students in the medical and dental schools and to students studying physical therapy.

The responsibilities of exercise physiologists vary greatly depending on their place of employment. When working in a clinical setting, exercise physiologists conduct research on both humans and animals to measure their physical responses before, during, and after exercise.

When employed in a nonclinical setting, such as at a health club or a local YMCA or YWCA, exercise physiologists work with their clients to develop exercise programs that help them develop and maintain physical fitness.

During his initial interview with new health club members, Fred, an exercise physiologist and director of Health and Fitness at Gold Coast Multiplex in Chicago, tries to develop a clear understanding of their fitness goals. He also learns their medical history and vital health statistics. "If somebody comes in and says, 'Oh, I just want to tone up,' well, that means a lot of different things to a lot of different people. So I need to ask questions and find out her current physical activity level. I ask her, Do you like exercise? Do you like fitness? Does it work for you? What are your goals?"

When people join Fred's club they must complete a physical activity readiness questionnaire. From the answers, the exercise physiologists learn if members have any health problems that may pose a potential risk when they exercise. In some cases, Fred asks members to get permission from their doctors before they begin their programs. He may also contact the physician's office to notify the doctor that their patient has joined the club. If the physician indicates that there are exercise restrictions for the client, the exercise physiologist and the doctor may work together to devise the best program for the individual.

Fred is also responsible for ensuring that all the equipment on the floor is well maintained and that members are receiving adequate instructions on their use. His responsibilities also include supervising any athletic leagues, such as volleyball or softball, that may be organized by the club, managing group exercise classes, and acting as a personal trainer for clients requesting one-on-one biomechanical analysis of their exercise routines.

Because the health club is a nonclinical setting, fitness testing is not extensive. "We do things like measure their resting heart rate and blood pressure. We look at their upper body strength, their endurance levels. How many sit-ups can they do? We estimate their oxygen consumption. It's a good indicator of general health," comments Fred.

The responsibilities for exercise physiologists working in a clinical setting are somewhat different

Lingo to Learn

Aerobic exercise A form of exercise that promotes cardiovascular fitness. An aerobic exercise sustains activity long enough to require the cardiovascular system to fuel muscles with oxygen. Aerobic exercises include running, bicycling, and cross-country skiing.

Anaerobic exercise A form of exercise in which the muscles are able to provide energy through a chemical process that does not involve oxygen. These exercises are usually used to build strength. Weightlifting is a form of anaerobic exercise.

Electron microscope A microscope that uses beams of electrons to scan cell surfaces. The final image is viewed on a monitor or photographic plate.

Magnetic resonance imaging (MRI) A medical imaging device that uses magnetic fields to produce images of internal organs.

Oscilloscope An electronic instrument that graphically displays an electrical signal as a glowing line on a fluorescent screen. The pattern on the screen is actually a rapidly moving point of light.

Target heart rate (THR) The ideal pulse rate to strive for during aerobic exercise. The rate varies according to age and is generally between 70 and 85 percent of your maximum heart rate. One method of calculating your maximum heart rate is by subtracting your age from 220.

than in a health club. Those working in a clinic or lab are generally under a physician's supervision and may be involved in health testing such as stress tests—a test that measures a patient's heart activity while running on a treadmill. Or they may study the amount of fat in the body, analyze the patients' blood for cholesterol, and update the patients' charts.

What Is It Like to Be a Physiologist?

Medical physiology generally involves working in a laboratory in a hospital, university, government agency, or private industry. Some medical physiologists may venture outside the confines of the laboratory to pursue research in the field. In other words, they work in the natural habitat of the subjects they are studying.

Although some research may deal with different plants and animals, research is ultimately conducted to benefit humans. There is a certain level of interaction between medical physiologists and their experiments. Don McCrimmon explains the relationship this way: "Our work becomes more of a calling rather than just a career. It is a way of life, a way of thinking. It's not something you do eight hours a day, it's something you do as a career. You think about it on weekends and evenings—pretty much on and off all the time."

For a medical physiologist working at a university, there are rarely two days in a row that are the same. Don's juggles his responsibilities daily. In the morning he may initiate an experiment that will run from eight to 10 hours. With the assistance of his research associate, who performs a great deal of the basic preparations, Don is also able to focus on his teaching responsibilities, as well as any administrative work he needs to complete.

Don finds the research and teaching very rewarding. He says the research gives him an opportunity to satisfy his natural curiosity and advance scientific understanding. He sees teaching as an added benefit. "Students with a scientific curiosity, in particular, are fun to work with. It's particularly rewarding when you can help them understand some concepts and see them work through problems."

While working in an academic environment offers medical physiologists the opportunity to conduct research and help their students, they must also set aside time in their schedules to attend to any administrative duties they may have. They may also spend time in organizational and departmental meetings.

Fred Kronk believes a career as an exercise physiologist offers many different challenges every day and that the job is always interesting and new. As he explains, "It can be really varied, and that's why I like the job. I can do so many things."

Throughout the day, exercise physiologists work with many different people on both an individual and group basis. During a typical day, Fred meets with clients to discuss their exercise goals and then creates and schedules their specific exercise programs.

Exercise physiologists who work in health clubs are limited in the types of fitness testing they can conduct without a doctor present. However, they can test the client's resting heart rate, blood pressure, upper body strength, and endurance level. They can also analyze the client's oxygen consumption to determine the efficiency of the client's heart muscles and lungs. Exercise physiologists who work in clinic or hospital settings conduct, record, and analyze more sophisticated fitness tests that may help a physician diagnose a patient's health problems.

Do I Have What It Takes to Be a Physiologist?

If you would like to be a medical physiologist, you need a great deal of curiosity. You need to be a detective of the natural world. You should have a strong interest in how organisms work and how different organisms are related. You should be results oriented, always seeking an outcome or solution to a problem or experiment.

You should be comfortable working with new technology. Physiologists use a wide variety of tools in their research, such as oscilloscopes, polygraphs, electron microscopes, and nuclear magnetic resonance imagers. Computers are also used for data acquisition and analysis and to help interpret experimental results. As technology advances, you will be required to learn how to use new equipment.

You should be a good teacher. Medical physiologists are usually involved in teaching students or research assistants. You must be able to relate information and create an interest in research. Some research projects can be lengthy and involved. You must be able to dedicate yourself to a project, moti-

To Be a Successful Medical Physiologist, You Should . . .

- have a great deal of curiosity
- be a meticulous researcher
- enjoy laboratory work
- have good observation skills
- be a good teacher
- be adept at using scientific instruments

To Be a Successful Exercise Physiologist, You Should . . .

- have an intense interest in fitness
- be a good teacher
- have excellent people skills
- be a committed caregiver
- be a team player
- be a good motivator
- have the ability to understand and use a wide variety of exercise equipment

vate others, and be able to see a project through to its conclusion. You need good managerial and leadership skills. In either career you will probably have to manage people, projects, budgets, and grants.

If you choose to be an exercise physiologist, you must also be a good teacher. You will be required to teach your clients how to use the exercise machines effectively. If you are the head of a department or a club, you will also have to instruct your coworkers about policies and safety procedures. Clients will come into health clubs with questions regarding the latest trends in diet and exercise. Exercise physiologists need to be able to separate fact from fiction for their clients and explain the correct ways to achieve fitness goals.

Both medical and exercise physiologists should have a love for learning. Many developments and studies will raise new questions that must be answered. You will continually be challenged to make new discoveries. You should love change and be adaptable. As a physiologist, you will see many changes in your field during your career.

Like medical physiologists, exercise physiologists must be dedicated to their career to succeed. Competent exercise physiologists are good caregivers. You should be able to assure, help, and motivate someone who is struggling with an exercise program. Exercise physiologists who cannot give this support usually end up changing careers.

Being a good communicator is a necessity for both exercise and medical physiologists. You must be able to communicate with coworkers and clients and be able to document your work. Each profession requires that you generate reports, make presentations, and keep accurate records.

How Do I Become a Physiologist?

Don was introduced to the subjects of physics and chemistry in high school. He was immediately intrigued by physics. He received his undergraduate degree in Canada and earned his Ph.D. at the University of Wisconsin at Madison. It was while he was at graduate school that he first attended a physiology class, and the subject immediately captured his interest. He completed his postdoctoral work at Northwestern University's Medical School in Chicago, where he now teaches and conducts research.

Fred received an undergraduate degree in the fine arts. However, to earn money while he was working toward his degree, he worked at health clubs in his area. He found he liked working at clubs and that the members seemed to like him. He decided to attend Northeastern Illinois University's graduate program, where he earned a master's degree in physiology.

EDUCATION

High School

If you are interested in a career as a physiologist, the first step is to take college preparatory courses in high school. Science courses, such as biology, chemistry, physics, and anatomy, will help prepare you for college as well as give you the opportunity to test your ability and enjoyment in these areas. Math courses, such as algebra, geometry, and trigonometry, are also important. English and speech classes will help you develop your research, writing, and oral communication skills. Computer science courses are also essential. Finally, courses such as social studies, government, and foreign languages will not only broaden

FYI

Medical physiologists might do research to answer questions like these:

- Why does one cell develop cancer, and another one doesn't?
- Why do some viruses invade the immune system?
- Why does blood clot after an injury but flow freely through blood vessels?
- Why do some athletes perform better than others?
- Why does the smell of a favorite food stimulate the appetite?

your educational background but will also help make you an appealing candidate for college admission. In addition, if you think you would like to work in the area of exercise physiology, you should take classes in physical education and health.

While attending high school, you should think about what specialty you might wish to pursue. Most colleges that offer undergraduate degrees with majors in physiology also have special areas of study within the subject. In addition to exercise, these may include cellular, environmental, or nutritional physiology. Once you think you know what area you are most interested in, you should enroll in the college that offers a degree in that specialty. Contact the American Physiological Society for a booklet that lists schools that award academic degrees with a major in physiology. This booklet also lists the special areas of study these colleges offer.

Postsecondary Training

If you are interested in working in exercise physiology, you need to earn a master's degree in order to be competitive in the job market. Even though some health clubs may employ you with only a bachelor's degree, the potential to move into any independent or administrative position usually requires an advanced degree.

Few fields require a doctoral degree for entry-level positions, but medical physiology is one of them. If you are interested in teaching in medical physiology programs at the college level or in pursuing independent research, you must earn a Ph.D. Researchers with a bachelor's or master's degree in physiology generally work under the supervision of a physiologist with a doctorate.

The course work will differ depending on your prospective employment. All physiologists must take a concentration of science courses, including biology, anatomy, chemistry, and physics. Also important are classes in composition, statistics, and mathematics. If you wish to be an exercise physiologist, you should also take courses in physical education, nutrition, kinesiology, and physical therapy.

Medical physiologists begin to focus more closely on their chosen field at the master's and doctoral levels. The course work and research will reflect your focus. Because an advanced degree requires several more years of study, you must have a strong commitment to your area of study.

CERTIFICATION AND LICENSING

There is no certification or licensing for medical physiologists. For exercise physiologists, however, the American College of Sports Medicine (ACSM) offers several certification programs, which vary according to the candidate's educational and clinical experience. The designations are ACSM certified personal trainer, ACSM health/fitness instructor, ACSM exercise specialist, and ACSM registered clinical exercise physiologist. Visit the ACSM Web site for more information on each of these certification programs: http://www.acsm.org.

To be certified by the American College of Sports Medicine is considered a hallmark within the exercise physiology industry. As Fred states, "ACSM tends to be considered by some as the gold standard." To retain certification, members must take a required number of continuing education hours. This helps ensure that exercise physiologists are up-to-date with the latest research.

SCHOLARSHIPS AND GRANTS

Many public and private organizations and businesses offer scholarships as well. Libraries, the Internet, and your guidance office should be able to provide you with more information. A good starting point for financial aid research is the SmartStudent Guide to Financial Aid Web site. This Web site has an extensive list of financial assistance information and links: http://www.finaid.org.

There are usually grants, scholarships, and loans available through most colleges. The easiest way to explore the various financial aid possibilities is to write directly to the financial aid offices of schools and request information and application forms.

INTERNSHIPS AND VOLUNTEERSHIPS

In the fields of medical and exercise physiology there are several opportunities to gain practical experience as either an intern or as a volunteer. These experiences provide you with a great chance to learn about the many different types of employment opportunities available and to help you decide your specialty. In addition, you can speak with professionals within the field and gain by their experience. It is an opportunity to find out what the people who are working in physiology like and dislike about their careers.

Many teaching hospitals across the country have excellent volunteer programs. You should contact the hospitals in your area and inquire about volunteer opportunities. In some instances, it may be possible for volunteers to work in the laboratories as a technician for a term. This opportunity would give you the chance to learn from basic researchers. You should also contact the American Physiological Society, which has outreach programs to help students interested in physiology.

If you are interested in exercise physiology, you should contact health clubs in your area and speak to the exercise physiologists on staff.

The internship process should be formalized and managed through your college. Some health clubs, like Fred's, have internship programs with the colleges in their area. These are formal internships set up with the student's internship department. When working with an intern, Fred receives a syllabus from the college and there is a formal review at the end of the internship. An internship can last a few days or a few weeks, but it offers valuable information because as Fred states, "The most valuable experience is to see what actually goes on at a club."

Who Will Hire Me?

Exercise physiologists can find work in a variety of places, including health clubs, hospitals, universities, athletic organizations, and large corporations that have exercise programs available for employees. You may also be employed as a research scientist at a private laboratory. Self-employment as a personal trainer is also a possibility for an ambitious exercise physiologist. Because of their advanced training and clinical understanding of the human body, exercise physiologists have an advantage over many other fitness experts when it comes to becoming a personal trainer.

The majority of medical physiologists work for colleges and universities or for the federal government. If you are interested in teaching and research, there are hundreds of educational institutions across the country that offer degrees in physiology that need qualified physiology professors. At most of these colleges you would be responsible for both teaching and research. You may also be responsible for acting as an adviser to students who are earning their doctorates.

Medical physiologists may also find employment opportunities with pharmaceutical companies in research and testing labs. You may also find employment at hospitals and doctors' offices.

Where Can I Go from Here?

Obtaining an entry-level position as a medical physiologist at a university requires that applicants have a doctorate in physiology. After earning their doctorates, medical physiologists then complete postdoctoral fellowships at a different institution. By changing lab settings, beginning physiologists can increase their basic skills as well as increase their knowledge of techniques and gain more insight into different scientific problems and issues. After their fellowships are complete, physiologists move into careers either in the medical area or at academic institutions.

To move into management positions, exercise physiologists must have proven technical skills, exhibit a firm commitment to customer service, and work well as team players. Advancement opportunities are often more abundant to employees who are creative and approach problems from a new perspective. Exercise physiologists who establish an excellent reputation and become well known may decide to open a business as a personal trainer or may find a position with a professional sports organization.

Exercise physiologists who earn master's degrees and certification may find employment with college and professional sports teams. Basic and applied research and teaching are also options for those who earn advanced degrees.

What Are the Salary Ranges?

According to a survey conducted in 2000 by the Association of Chairs of Departments of Physiology, medical physiologists breaking into the field with a bachelor's degree can expect to earn approximately $38,000. Instructors may begin with an annual salary of about $42,000. A physiologist who holds a master's or doctoral degree and who teaches as a full professor may earn more than $100,000. However, department chairpersons in some higher education institutions may earn between $200,000 and $300,000. In addition to full benefits, such as insurance, retirement, and vacation, many institutions offer their professors sabbaticals to pursue additional education or to conduct research.

Exercise physiologists generally make less than medical physiologists. Exercise physiologists who have an undergraduate degree and no experience can expect a starting salary of $18,000 to $30,000 per year, according to the American College of Sports Medicine. However, some exercise physiologists who are involved in medical studies regarding exercise and body functions earn more. Working as a researcher or with a sports team can also increase your earnings.

What Is the Job Outlook?

There has been an explosion in the research and knowledge of genetics and molecular biology recently. These changes may have a positive effect on the overall field of medical physiology. Being able to manipulate and analyze an organism at a genetic level helps researchers understand what is going on with the organism systematically. As Don explains, "We can manipulate DNA and alter an animal and find out how these alterations affect the ability of that animal to adapt to various situations." These and other new discoveries will lead to the future demand for medical physiologists.

The future for exercise physiologists is quite healthy. Research is presently being conducted to investigate different ways the aging process can be slowed down with a good exercise program. In addition, more insurance companies are considering a good fitness program to be a form of preventive care and are considering reimbursing their members for their health club costs.

How Do I Learn More?

PROFESSIONAL ORGANIZATIONS

The following are organizations that provide information on medical and exercise physiologist careers, accredited schools, and possible employers:

American College of Sports Medicine
P.O. Box 1440
Indianapolis, IN 46206-1440
317-637-9200
http://www.acsm.org

American Physiological Society
9650 Rockville Pike
Bethesda, MD 20814-3991
301-634-7164
http://www.the-aps.org

BIBLIOGRAPHY

The following is a sampling of materials relating to the professional concerns and development of physiologists:

Axen, Kenneth, and Kathleen Axen. *Illustrated Principles of Exercise Physiology.* San Francisco: Benjamin Cummings, 2000.

Ganong, William F. *Review of Medical Physiology.* 21st ed. New York: McGraw-Hill, 2003.

Guyton, Arthur C., and John E. Hall. *Textbook of Medical Physiology.* 10th ed. Philadelphia: W. B. Saunders, 2000.

Heitzmann, William Ray. *Opportunities in Sports and Fitness Careers.* New York: McGraw-Hill, 2003.

Johnson, Leonard R., ed. *Essential Medical Physiology.* 3d ed. New York: Academic Press, 2003.

MacKenna, B. R., and R. R. Callander. *Illustrated Physiology.* 6th ed. New York: Churchill Livingstone, 1997.

Tortora, Gerard J., and Sandra R. Grabowski. *Principles of Anatomy and Physiology.* Hoboken, N.J.: Wiley, 2002.

PLASTIC AND RECONSTRUCTIVE SURGEONS

A team of plastic surgeons, anesthesiologists, and nurses arrives in Guatemala City, Guatemala, to find that three boxes of their surgical equipment have been lost by the airline. Working with the nonprofit group Casa de Guatemala, the team has come to perform surgery on underprivileged children. Now one of their precious operating days is lost in the effort to replace the missing equipment. The medical team is donating their time and talent. They realize that the experience will not be like doing surgery at a hospital back home. The loss of one operating day, however, is a disappointment. Dr. Mimis Cohen of Chicago, Illinois, has taken these trips for years. "With work like this," he says, "you have to be prepared for the worst. If you go with the attitude that it's going to be like operating in Chicago, it won't succeed."

Mimis explains the set up, "On the first day, we have a clinic and we sort the kids out. We treat primarily birth defects. Often the parents will travel for 24 hours from remote villages, and it's heartbreaking when you have to turn kids down." Parents and children fill the clinic, waiting to be helped. Dr. Cohen begins his day by operating on a small boy with a cleft lip and palate. "We each operate on between 15 and 16 children a day," he says, "many with double- and triple-procedure surgeries." Despite the long hours and limited resources, these professionals believe their work is well worth the effort. They know that the corrective surgeries they perform have the potential to greatly improve the quality of the children's lives.

Definition
This surgeon deals with the repair, replacement, and reconstruction of defects of the form and function of the skin and its underlying musculoskeletal system.

Alternative Job Title
Plastic surgeons

High School Subjects
Biology
Chemistry

Personal Skills
Mechanical/manipulative
Technical/scientific

Salary Range
$40,788 to $255,438 to $400,000

Educational Requirements
Bachelor's degree, medical degree, three-year residency in general surgery, two-year residency in plastic and reconstructive surgery, optional fellowships

Certification or Licensing
Recommended (certification)
Required by all states (licensing)

Outlook
About as fast as the average

DOT
070

GOE
14.02.01

NOC
3111

O*NET-SOC
29-1067.00

What Does a Plastic and Reconstructive Surgeon Do?

A *plastic and reconstructive surgeon* deals with the repair, replacement, and reconstruction of defects in the form and function of the skin and its underlying musculoskeletal system. The plastic and reconstructive surgeon is especially skilled in working on such areas of the body as the head, neck, face; upper and lower limbs, breasts, and external genitalia. Besides performing surgery to correct medical problems, the plastic and reconstructive surgeon also can perform surgery for purely cosmetic results.

Special knowledge and skill in the design and transfer of skin flaps, in the transplantation of tissues, and in the replantation of structures are vital to the performance of plastic surgery. The plastic surgeon must also possess excellent skills in the performance of excisional surgery, in the management of large wounds, and in the use of synthetic materials. In addition, a vast knowledge of surgical instruments and how to use them is necessary for this specialty.

Some the most commonly performed procedures include surgery to correct cleft lip and cleft palate, surgery to the outer ear (otoplasty), scar revision, dermabrasion, breast reconstruction, hand surgery, abdominoplasty ("tummy tuck"), rhinoplasty ("nose job"), liposuction, chemical peel, and hair replacement surgery. Surgeons working on trauma victims may perform several of these surgeries at once, or in stages to allow for proper healing.

The profession breaks down into two areas of expertise: plastic (also called cosmetic) surgery and reconstructive surgery. Physicians complete training in both disciplines, although some surgeons may specialize in one area by taking additional years of fellowships in one or more areas.

The main goal of reconstructive surgery is to restore, or allow for, normal function of an abnormal body structure. Abnormalities are caused by such things as birth defects, injuries, infections, tumors, and diseases. A secondary result of reconstructive surgery may be an approximation of normal appearance. The goal of cosmetic surgery, on the other hand, is to reshape normal structures of the body to improve the patient's appearance and self-esteem.

Plastic and reconstructive surgeons must have extensive knowledge of wound treatment and closure. A wound may be the reason for a procedure or the by-product of the procedure. In either case, treatment is necessary and can be accomplished in several ways, depending on such factors as amount of skin missing and extent of nerve damage. Skin grafts, tissue expansion, and skin flaps are among the commonly used methods of closing, growing, and transplanting skin. Plastic and reconstructive surgeons take great pains to render the surgical areas as scar-free and aesthetically pleasing as possible, although scarring is sometimes unavoidable. Many patients having reconstructive surgery often return to have scarring reduced or to have cosmetic surgery performed to improve their post-reconstruction appearance.

Plastic and reconstructive surgeons routinely use a variety of lasers to perform reconstructive surgery. The carbon dioxide laser is used to cut tissue and seal blood vessels simultaneously. The YAG laser is effective in treating skin growths with heavy concentrations of blood vessels. The YAG delivers its highly focused beam right to the skin's surface, allowing the surgeon to use it like a scalpel. Argon and copper vapor lasers are used, respectively, to treat abnormalities with a proliferation of blood vessels, such as bulky vascular tumors, and brown or red pigmented areas.

Cosmetic surgery is usually done to correct minor defects and should not leave large, visible scars. Surgeons frequently perform endoscopic surgery for cosmetic procedures. In a typical endoscopic surgery, only a few small incisions, each less than one inch long, are needed to insert the endoscope and other instruments. The endoscope is a flexible, fiber optic instrument that allows the surgeon to see the interior of a hollow organ. Because incisions for endoscopic surgery are small, bleeding, bruising, and swelling may be reduced, as is the patient's recovery time. Endoscopic surgery is commonly used in abdominoplasties, breast augmentations, face-lifts, and forehead lifts.

Lingo to Learn

Alloplasty In plastic surgery, implanting synthetic materials to replace or build up a tissue or organ.

Blepharoplasty Surgery of the eyelid.

Excisional surgery Surgery that cuts out something, such as a tumor.

Flap A section of living tissue that carries its own blood supply and is moved from one area of the body to another.

Maxillofacial Having to do with the jaw and face.

Skin graft A patch of healthy skin that is taken from one area of the body, called the donor site, and used to cover another area where skin is missing or damaged. The three basic types of skin grafts are the split-thickness graft, the full-thickness graft, and the composite graft.

Tissue expansion A procedure that enables the body to grow extra skin by stretching adjacent tissue. A balloon-like device called an expander is inserted under the skin near the area to be repaired and then gradually filled with saltwater over time, causing the skin to stretch and grow.

The future of plastic surgery may also include the use of lasers to resurface the skin. Lasers remove old layers of skin in a manner that is less harsh and aggressive than deep chemical peels or abrasions. This is a new technique and long-term data on results are not yet available.

What Is It Like to Be a Plastic and Reconstructive Surgeon?

Dr. Mimis Cohen, professor and chief, division of plastic, reconstructive, and cosmetic surgery, University of Illinois at Chicago, has taken a team of surgeons, anesthesiologists, and nurses with him to Guatemala to perform reconstructive plastic surgery on disadvantaged children. "There are such a huge number of problems, I could have a full-time job down there," he says.

Months and months of planning go into one of Mimis's trips. He arranges for a hospital in Guatemala City to screen surgery candidates. "They have scattered clinics, so if a candidate for surgery comes along, they make sure he or she gets to us," he explains. "Then we fly down with our equipment: computers, lasers, syringes, gowns, IVs." Mimis takes two or three other surgeons, three pediatric anesthesiologists, and six or seven operating room and recovery nurses. All of the surgeons are highly experienced. Mimis says, "I don't use the trip as a training ground. These kids only have one shot." The doctors donate their time and expertise and pay for the hotel, food, and transportation of the nurses.

The first day the children are sorted into three groups headed by one of the three surgeons. Each surgeon will operate on 30 to 40 patients. They only have one week to get there, set up, screen the children, and then perform the surgeries and provide as much postoperative care as they can before leaving for the United States. "The surgeon examines the child with the parents, and then the anesthesiologist examines the child to make certain there aren't any complications, like a heart condition," Mimis explains. "If the child is okay, we accept him or her for surgery. After we've finished screening all the kids, we have a priority conference to determine the order of the surgeries." Generally, those who will need the longest postoperative care will go first. "So, newborn babies go first, complex patients go next. We don't want to have some complication develop after I've left," says Mimis. "The local doctors are involved in the postoperative and follow-up care, but we want to make certain we leave them in the best shape."

When Mimis is not planning one of these trips to Guatemala, or on one, his time is taken up with his responsibilities as chief of plastic surgery at the University of Illinois. "At the university, I do a fair amount of reconstruction on children with deformities. Mainly facial, but also hands and birthmarks. I do a fair amount of cancer reconstruction on the breast and face," he says. "I do a lot of trauma, maxillofacial work," he says. "And I also do a fair amount of cosmetic surgery." Teaching responsibilities, conferences, and presentations also take up a great deal of Mimis's time and attention. "Some people have the notion that you just teach in classrooms, but that's not true. You teach surgery in surgery," he says. "You teach through patient care."

Dr. Roxanne Guy, a plastic and reconstructive surgeon who practices in Melbourne, Florida, estimates that half of her practice is reconstructive and the other half is cosmetic. "Breast reconstruction after mastectomy, breast reductions, skin cancer resections, and trauma cases, facial fractures, and burns," she lists the reconstructive surgeries she frequently performs. "Accidents where the patient has lost part of an ear, or a cancer that takes part of the patient's face—no surgery is ever the same. The defects are all different and individual. It's sort of like a puzzle, somewhat exciting and different. As a surgeon, you have to use imagination and skills and the principles of wound healing and grafting to fill in the puzzle."

For new patients, Roxanne says, "We send information, a brochure on the problem, to the prospective patient to help educate him." On the day of the appointment, the patient fills out a brief questionnaire about his or her medial history, which Roxanne will add to when she meets with the patient. "A nurse would take the patient's history—allergies, et cetera—and show the person an informational video on the problem and the various options for treatment, including the surgical procedure. Then, I meet with the patient and review the patient's history, as well as the procedure, including any complications, risks, and the prescribed postoperative care. Afterwards, I would examine the patient and decide what would be the best solution for that patient."

Roxanne then provides the patient who wants cosmetic surgery with a cost sheet outlining the costs of the various procedures. For patients who are seeking reconstructive surgery, insurance preapproval forms are provided to be completed and sent to their health insurance company. If the patient decides to go ahead with the surgery, he or she comes back for a detailed health history and physical. Roxanne sends the patient's blood work to the lab to rule out any further complications, schedules the surgery, and explains any pre-operative care instructions to the patient. A procedure may be performed in her office, in an ambulatory surgery center, or in a hospital; it all depends on the complexity of the surgery and whether or not a one- to two-night stay in the hospital is necessary. "Microsurgery cases I do at the hospital, for example," she says. The day of the surgery, Roxanne sees the patient in preop and then performs the surgery.

Do I Have What It Takes to Be a Plastic and Reconstructive Surgeon?

"It's drama, it's theater, it's fun, it's positive," Roxanne says of her work. "And I like providing something that is a happy experience. If it's a reconstructive case, I'm fixing something damaged, and if it's an aesthetic case, I'm helping to create or fix something." Roxanne explains, "*Plasticos* is Greek for 'to shape or remold.' People who have cosmetic surgery experience a positive rise in self-esteem following the procedure."

Plastic and reconstructive surgeons must possess excellent manual dexterity and the ability to make and execute decisions promptly. Any operation involves risks, and during surgery a plastic and reconstructive surgeon may have to deal with the unexpected, such as a patient's sudden drop in blood pressure or a bad reaction to anesthesia. The surgeon must be able to cope with such situations while maintaining his or her composure.

Another essential quality in surgeons is a genuine concern for people. Those who aspire to be plastic and reconstructive surgeons must be able to deal compassionately with patients and their families. Surgeons should be effective communicators, able to address any fears, questions, and needs their patients have. Plastic and reconstructive surgeons must also have good judgment and know when to refuse to perform a surgery that would not benefit the patient.

How Do I Become a Plastic and Reconstructive Surgeon?

EDUCATION

High School

If you are interested in pursuing a medical degree, a high school education emphasizing college preparatory classes is a must. You must take science courses, such as biology, chemistry, and physics, and math courses. These classes will not only provide you with an introduction to basic science and math concepts, but also will allow you to determine your own aptitude in these areas. Since college will be your next educational step, it is also important to take English courses to develop your research and writing skills. Foreign language, social science, and computer classes will also help make you an appealing candidate for college admission as well as prepare you for your future undergraduate and graduate education. High school juniors or seniors should also be aware that some colleges or universities are associated with a medical school and can offer a medical degree through an accelerated program. You may want to consider applying to one of these schools. High school guidance counselors should be able to provide you with information about such schools.

Postsecondary Training

Following high school, your next step to becoming a plastic and reconstructive surgeon is to receive your bachelor's degree from an accredited four-year college or university. Often those planning to attend medical school major in a science. No matter what your major, however, the typical college courses that help you prepare for medical school include biology, chemistry, anatomy, psychology, and physics. English courses will help you to hone research and communication skills. Social sciences and ethics courses will help prepare you for a people-oriented career.

If you choose to attend a college or university associated with a medical school that offers the accelerated medical program, your undergraduate education will be slightly different from that of other undergraduates. An accelerated program typically reduces or consolidates the number of years you spend as an undergraduate, thereby speeding up your entrance into medical school. A six- or seven-year medical student is actually enrolled for two or three years, respectively, of undergraduate school, plus the requisite four years of medical school.

After receiving an undergraduate degree, you must apply to and be accepted by a medical school. Most students apply to several schools early in their senior year of college. Admission is competitive; only about one-third of the applicants are accepted. The admissions process takes into consideration grade point averages, scores on the Medical College Admission Test (MCAT), recommendations from professors, and extracurricular activities, such as volunteering at hospitals. Often schools also conduct interviews with prospective students.

In order to earn the doctor of medicine (M.D.) degree, you must complete four years of medical school study and training. For the first two years of medical school, you attend lectures and classes and spend time in laboratories. Courses include anatomy, biochemistry, physiology, pharmacology, psychology, medical ethics, and laws governing medicine. You learn to take patient histories, perform routine physical examinations, and recognize symptoms of diseases.

In their third and fourth years, students are involved in more practical studies. They work in clinics and hospitals supervised by residents and physicians and they learn acute, chronic, preventive, and rehabilitative care. They go through rotations (brief periods of study) in such areas as internal medicine, obstetrics and gynecology, pediatrics, psychiatry, and surgery. Rotations allow students to gain exposure to the many different fields within medicine and to learn firsthand the skills of diagnosing and treating patients.

After graduating from an accredited medical school, physicians must pass a standard examination given by the National Board of Medical Examiners. Most physicians complete an internship, also referred to as a transition year. The internship is usually one year in length and helps graduates to decide on an area of specialization.

Following the internship, physicians begin what is known as a residency. Physicians wishing to pursue the surgical specialty of plastic and reconstructive surgery must first complete a minimum of three years in a general surgery residency. This general surgery training is followed by two years of training in plastic surgery. Most physicians add another six to 12 months of training to focus on a particular field of interest. At this point, for example, a surgeon may choose to focus on one of the subspecialties of plastic surgery, such as hand surgery.

CERTIFICATION OR LICENSING

Licensing is a mandatory procedure in the United States. It is required in all states before any doctor can practice medicine. In order to be licensed, doctors must have graduated from medical school, passed the licensing test of the state in which they will practice, and completed their residency.

In order to receive certification from the American Board of Plastic Surgery (ABPS), a candidate must have successfully completed the approved residency program in plastic surgery. The plastic and reconstructive surgeon then applies to the ABPS and, once the application is approved, takes the qualifying written examination. After passing the written examination, the applicant must then pass the oral examination.

In order to become certified, the plastic and reconstructive surgeon must also practice the specialty of plastic surgery for two years. The candidate can take the written examination any time during the two years of practice, but the oral examination cannot be

FYI

According to the American Society of Plastic and Reconstructive Surgeons, in 2003:

- More than 8.7 million cosmetic plastic surgery procedures were performed
- Botox injection was the top cosmetic plastic surgery procedure performed
- Women made up 85 percent of cosmetic plastic surgery procedure patients
- Forty-five percent of cosmetic plastic surgery procedures were performed on patients in the 35 to 50-year age group

taken before the candidate has finished the two-year practice requirement.

SCHOLARSHIPS AND GRANTS

Scholarships and grants are often available from individual institutions, state agencies, and special-interest organizations. Many students finance their medical education through the Armed Forces Health Professions Scholarship Program. Each branch of the military participates in this program, paying students' tuitions in exchange for military service. Contact your local recruiting office for more information. The National Health Service Corps Scholarship Program (http://nhsc.bhpr.hrsa.gov) also provides money for students in return for service. Another source for financial aid, scholarship, and grant information is the Association of American Medical Colleges (http://www.aamc.org). Remember to request information early for eligibility, application requirements, and deadlines.

Who Will Hire Me?

Many plastic and reconstructive surgeons go into private practice. Others work full time in academic and research institutions. Still others combine a private practice with academic and research work.

A private practice in plastic surgery can be devoted to one area of expertise, such as hand surgery, or the practice can be considered general. In a general practice, the plastic and reconstructive surgeon performs a wide range of cosmetic and reconstructive procedures. Most plastic and reconstructive surgeons in private practice divide their time between cosmetic and reconstructive work, simply because their work is more interesting if it is varied. It is possible, however, to have a private practice devoted entirely to cosmetic surgery, since these procedures can easily support an entire practice.

Where Can I Go from Here?

Plastic and reconstructive surgeons can advance by attending conferences featuring discussions of new procedures or by reading about and learning new techniques. Surgeons must also continue to master new technologies that will improve the operations they perform. They may also advance their careers by conducting research, teaching, and developing a larger client base.

Plastic and reconstructive surgeons may go back to school to train in a subspecialty through a fellowship. Many plastic and reconstructive surgeons, however, achieve a level of expertise simply by doing something better than anyone else. This, of course, is accomplished through practice and much refinement of technique. Publishing articles in respected medical journals, such as *Journal of the American Medical Association,* is another way to increase one's professional stature.

What Are the Salary Ranges?

Average salaries of medical residents ranged from about $40,788 in 2004–05 for those in their first year of residency to about $50,258 for those in their sixth year, according to the Association of American Medical Colleges. Salaries vary depending on the kind of residency, the hospital, and the geographic area.

Surgeons are among the highest paid of all occupations. The Medical Group Management Association reports that general surgeons made average annual salaries of $255,438 in 2002. This figures includes base salary, bonuses, and research grants. A plastic surgeon in the first five years of private practice can earn between $75,000 and $150,000. Someone who has been practicing five to 10 years can earn between $150,000 and $250,000. A few plastic surgeons earn $400,000 a year or more.

Incomes vary, depending on such factors as a surgeon's reputation, the geographic location, and the types of procedures the surgeon performs. Currently, plastic and reconstructive surgeons in private practice tend to earn more than those in academic and managed care settings.

What Is the Job Outlook?

The job growth for surgeons is expected to increase about as fast as the average over the next 10 years, according to *Occupational Outlook Handbook.* Both men and women will continue to want cosmetic surgery. Reconstructive surgery will continue to be performed on anyone—young or old, male or female—who needs it. If health insurers do not pay for certain procedures, individuals will cover the cost themselves. In addition, as technology advances, plastic and reconstructive surgeons develop new, increasingly safe and easy ways to eradicate deformities and improve appearances. With such advances, many people will seek out the plastic surgeon's services.

How Do I Learn More?

PROFESSIONAL ORGANIZATIONS

The following are organizations that provide information on the profession of plastic and reconstructive surgery:

American Board of Plastic Surgery
Seven Penn Center, Suite 400
1635 Market Street
Philadelphia, PA 19103
215-587-9322
info@abplsurg.org
http://www.abplsurg.org

American Society for Aesthetic Plastic Surgery
11081 Winners Circle
Los Alamitos, California 90720
800-364-2147
asaps@surgery.org
http://www.surgery.org

American Society of Plastic Surgeons
444 East Algonquin Road
Arlington Heights, IL 60005
888-475-2784
http://www.plasticsurgery.org

BIBLIOGRAPHY

The following is a sampling of books relating to the professional concerns and development of plastic and reconstructive surgeons:

Aston, Sherrell J., Beasley, Robert W., Thorne, Charles H., eds. *Grabb and Smith's Plastic Surgery.* 5th ed. Philadelphia: Lippincott Williams & Wilkins, 1997.

Berger, Karen J., and John Bostwick. *A Woman's Decision: Breast Care, Treatment & Reconstruction.* 3d ed. New York: St. Martin's/Griffin, 1998.

Daver, B. M., Antia, N. H., and Furnas, D. W. *Handbook of Plastic Surgery for the General Surgeon.* 2d ed. New York: Oxford University Press, 2000.

Evans, Gregory R. *Operative Plastic Surgery.* New York: McGraw-Hill, 2000.

Moore, Charles Edwards. *The Good, the Bad, & the Homely: Essays from an Old-Fashioned, Country, Plastic Surgeon.* New York: Ardor Scribendi, 2000.

PODIATRISTS

The bright lights of the operating room shine on Gerry Hash as he pulls latex gloves over his hands, preparing for the morning's first surgical procedure. "Is she ready to go?" he asks the anesthesiologist as he nears the operating table. The patient on the table, who has received general anesthetic, is a 60-year-old woman and a longtime patient of Gerry's.

The anesthesiologist looks up from the monitor on which he is closely observing the patient's vital signs. "She's stable," he says. "You're ready to go."

Gerry assesses different sites on the patient's left foot to determine the best place to make the incision. "Scalpel," he says to the scrub nurse standing beside him.

Taking the scalpel from the nurse, Gerry leans forward slightly and makes a small incision on the inside of the patient's foot. As the scrub nurse blots the incision site with a sterile sponge, Gerry hands the scalpel back to her.

The surgical procedure is a relatively uncomplicated one that Gerry has performed many times before. He proceeds in a relaxed and confident manner, and he chats with the nurse as he operates.

Definition
Podiatrists diagnose, prevent, and treat foot disorders by prescribing medication, performing surgery, and fitting corrective orthotic devices.

Alternative Job Titles
Doctors of podiatric medicine
Foot doctors

High School Subjects
Biology
Physics

Personal Skills
Mechanical/manipulative
Technical/scientific

Salary Range
$40,920 to $95,550 to $145,090

Educational Requirements
High school diploma; bachelor's degree from an accredited college or university; four-year degree from an accredited college of podiatric medicine; one-year residency

Certification or Licensing
Required by all states

Outlook
About as fast as the average

DOT
079

GOE
14.04.01

NOC
N/A

O*NET-SOC
29-1081.00

What Does a Podiatrist Do?

Podiatrists, or *doctors of podiatric medicine,* are specialists dedicated to treating disorders of the foot and ankle. Podiatrists see patients who are having problems with their feet. To determine the nature of foot problems, podiatrists talk with patients and visually examine their feet. Sometimes, in order to make diagnoses, podiatrists take X rays, perform blood tests, or prescribe other diagnostic tests.

Podiatrists treat many common disorders, including corns, calluses, warts, ingrown toenails, and athlete's foot. Bunions, deformed toes, arch problems, and cysts are other examples of common foot disorders treated by podiatrists. Among the relatively uncommon foot disorders treated by podiatrists are infections and ulcers related to diabetes. Podiatrists also treat injuries to the foot and ankle, such as breaks and sprains.

The method of treatment varies considerably depending on the patient's problem. For some patients, podiatrists prescribe physical therapy sessions or give instructions on how to perform certain exercises. For other patients, podiatrists prescribe medications, either to be injected, taken orally, or applied in ointment form.

Some foot disorders, such as ingrown toenails and warts, may require minor surgical procedures. Podiatrists typically perform these kinds of procedures in their offices. Other disorders require more extensive surgery, for which patients may be anesthetized. For this kind of surgery, a podiatrist must use a sterile operating room, usually either in a hospital or an outpatient surgery center.

Lingo to Learn

Achilles tendon The tendon connecting the heel bone to the calf of the leg; the strongest tendon in the body.

Athlete's foot A skin disease, usually occurring between the toes, caused by ringworm fungi.

Bunion An inflamed swelling of the joint at the base of the big toe. A bunion often results from wearing narrow, high-heeled shoes.

Closed reduction Realignment of a fractured bone by manipulation (without incision).

Corn A cone-shaped mass of thickened skin on a toe; it is caused by long-term friction and pressure.

Flatfoot Lack of an arch in the foot. Though almost everyone is born with flat feet, arches usually develop by age six.

Metatarsals The bones between the toes and the ankle.

Open reduction Realignment of a fractured bone after incision into the fractured site.

Phalanges The bones that make up the toes and the fingers.

Plantigrade Walking with the heel touching the ground, as humans, bears, and raccoons do.

Tarsals The bones that make up the ankle.

Another responsibility of podiatrists is to fit patients with corrective orthotic devices, or orthoses, such as braces, custom-made shoes, lifts, and splints. For a patient who needs an orthotic device, a podiatrist makes a plaster cast of the patient's foot, determines the measurements and other characteristics needed to make the device, and sends the information to a manufacturing plant called a brace shop. When the device is complete, the podiatrist fits it to the patient and makes follow-up evaluations to ensure that it fits and functions properly. The podiatrist may also make any modifications or repairs that are needed.

Podiatrists frequently treat patients who have injured their feet or ankles. A podiatrist may wrap, splint, or cast a foot to keep it immobile and allow it to heal. In more complicated cases, podiatrists may perform corrective surgery.

A key responsibility of podiatrists is recognizing serious health disorders that sometimes show up first in the feet. For example, diabetics are prone to foot ulcers and infections because of their poor blood circulation. Symptoms of kidney disease, heart disease, and arthritis also frequently appear in the feet first. A podiatrist must be alert to symptoms of these diseases in his or her patients and refer them to the appropriate doctors and specialists.

There are three subspecialties of podiatric medicine recognized by the American Association of Colleges of Podiatric Medicine: orthopedics, surgery, and primary medicine. Although any licensed podiatrist is considered qualified to address all areas of podiatric medicine, certification as a specialist in one of these three areas requires completion of specialized training.

Podiatrists who specialize in orthopedics use mechanical devices, physical treatments, medications, and exercises to treat structural disorders of the foot. Podiatrists who specialize in podiatric surgery are trained in the use of prosthetic joint implants, plastic surgery, and other surgical techniques to correct foot deformities. Podiatrists with a specialization in primary podiatric medicine, or general podiatric medicine, focus on prevention, diagnosis, and general care of the foot and ankle.

The average workweek for a podiatrist is 35 to 40 hours. Most podiatrists work in private offices and see their patients in examining rooms. Some podiatrists work in outpatient clinics, nursing homes, or hospitals.

Some podiatrists are helped by *podiatric assistants.* A podiatric assistant prepares patients for treatment and assists the podiatrist in administering treatments. A podiatric assistant also develops X rays, sterilizes instruments, and performs general office duties.

What Is It Like to Be a Podiatrist?

"My day starts like almost anyone else's workday," says Gerry Hash, a podiatrist in a mid-sized midwestern city. "I come in and look at my schedule, return phone calls, and catch up on paperwork." Gerry works as a private practitioner. As such, he is basically the owner and manager of his own business, in addition to being a doctor.

"I don't have a business manager, so I do all the business stuff," he says. "I pay the phone bills, the nursing staff, the lease on the office, the yellow page ads." The only part of the business that he does not deal with directly is billing. For that, he has a contract with a company that bills both patients and insurance carriers.

After the phone calls and paperwork have been taken care of, Gerry begins seeing his patients. On Mondays, Tuesdays, and Wednesdays he sees patients in the office, with appointments scheduled 15 to 30 minutes apart. Thursdays are set aside for surgeries. On Fridays, he visits local nursing and retirement homes to see patients who can't come into the office.

Gerry's days are extremely varied. "The thing about podiatry is that even though it is a limited area, there is such a wide variety of things you see and do on a daily basis," he says. "There may be days when the hardest thing I do is an ingrown toenail. Other days, I may see a diabetic who's in danger of losing his foot."

There may be days when the hardest thing I do is an ingrown toenail. Other days, I may see a diabetic who's in danger of losing his foot.

"There are so many different things and so many different methods of treatment," he says. "I write prescriptions, drain abscesses, remove nails, prescribe home exercises, give injections, order X rays or bone scans . . . on and on." The only surgeries that Gerry performs in his office are wart removals and procedures involving toenails. All other surgical procedures require sterile operating rooms and are done in either hospitals or outpatient surgery centers.

Surgeries that must be done in operating rooms are scheduled on Thursdays for Gerry. Surgery may last anywhere from 30 minutes for minor procedures to four hours for more complicated cases. Injuries and problems with the back part of the foot typically require the most time to correct.

"Today, for example, was my surgery day," Gerry says. "I reduced a dislocated toe. That means that I made an incision, put the toe back in place, and fixed it in place with a pin. Then, I did an bunionectomy, in which I reduced the bone on the inside of the foot. After that, I corrected a hammertoe, a toe that curls under." While the surgical lineup varies from week to week, the procedures he describes are fairly common ones.

Gerry prescribes orthotic devices for some of his cases. "Orthoses don't necessarily correct the problem, but they accommodate for it by increasing the efficiency and mechanics of your foot." When a patient needs an orthotic device, Gerry measures the joint motion in the foot and ankle, as well as the leg length. He also analyzes the patient's gait, or manner of walking. Finally, he makes a plaster cast of the foot. Using the cast, measurements, and results of the gait analysis, he fills out a prescription form that tells the brace shop how to make the device. After the device is made, Gerry fits it to the patient and makes periodic adjustments and evaluations of its effectiveness.

Gerry's job frequently requires him to work closely with other medical specialists. "Diabetes and vascular or neurological problems often manifest themselves first in the feet, so I may be the first doctor that patient comes to," he says. "For example, a patient might come in with her feet getting numb. This could mean she's got compression of some nerve group. It could mean she's got diabetes. I've got to recognize the problem and know who to send her to."

Do I Have What It Takes to Be a Podiatrist?

Gerry believes there are three facets to being a good podiatrist. "There's skill, there's personality, and there's commitment," he says. "And while skills can be taught, commitment and personality cannot."

A high level of commitment is required for success both in school and in a career, according to Gerry. "You've got to have the want and the desire to do it. If you don't have that, you won't make it," he says. "Residency is tough. When it's 3:00 in the morning and you're just getting off your shift, and you have an early paper to present, you've got to be determined."

To Be a Successful Podiatrist, You Should . . .

- enjoy working with people
- have good manual dexterity
- be caring and understanding of others
- be self-motivated and confident in making decisions
- have an aptitude for both science and business

Being able to work well with people is also high on Gerry's list of necessary qualities. "You need to be good with people. You need to be caring and empathetic," he says. "If a patient has a problem with his body, he wants someone who can help him understand what's going on and not make him feel dumb." Gerry enjoys the patient interaction. He says that the time he spends with his patients is the best part of his job.

What he does not enjoy about the job, however, are the paperwork and administrative duties. Because he is a private practitioner, he also functions as a manager—of staff, of supplies, and of finances. "The most difficult part is the red tape, the paperwork, the business aspects of medicine," he says. "When I went through med school, I imagined being the best doctor I could be. I did not envision or anticipate how much of a business person I would have to be." Since the vast majority of podiatrists work as private practitioners, Gerry cautions that anyone considering this field should be aware of the managerial aspects of the job.

How Do I Become a Podiatrist?

From the time he entered high school, Gerry knew that he wanted to pursue some kind of medical career. Although he didn't settle on podiatry until he started his undergraduate study, he tailored both his high school and college curriculum to fit the requirements for medical school.

His advice for prospective podiatrists is as follows: "Science classes are going to be very important. Your undergrad studies are going to be the same as if you were going to medical school, and to get through that, you need a strong background in math and science."

EDUCATION

High School

If you are considering a career in podiatry, take as many natural science courses as you can. Any courses that teach the workings of the human body, such as biology, physiology, and anatomy, will be especially helpful, both in college courses and in practice. Chemistry and physics are also helpful courses to take.

Courses that teach basic business skills help provide the background needed to run a podiatry practice. Among these courses are business math, accounting, computer science, and keyboarding.

Math courses are important, both in postsecondary schooling and on the job. English classes will improve your written and oral communication skills.

Postsecondary Training

After high school, you will need to enroll in a four-year college program leading to a bachelor's degree. The majority of students choose to major in biology, although some major in other physical sciences. In order to be eligible for acceptance into a college of podiatric medicine, your undergraduate curriculum must include eight credit hours each of biology, general or inorganic chemistry, organic chemistry, and physics. Six credit hours of English are also required.

In rare cases, a college of podiatric medicine accepts a student who does not have a bachelor's degree, but who has completed at least 90 semester hours of college credit. Over 90 percent of students who enter a college of podiatric medicine do, however, have at least a bachelor's degree.

There are eight colleges of podiatric medicine in the United States; they are located in Florida, California, New York, Ohio, Pennsylvania, Illinois, Iowa, and Arizona. They each offer a four-year course of study leading to a doctor of podiatric medicine (DPM) degree. Links to all of these schools can be found on the Web site of the American Podiatric Medical Association (http://www.apma.org).

During the first two years in a podiatric medicine program, students spend most of their time in the classroom and laboratory. Courses include basic medical sciences, such as anatomy, physiology, microbiology, biochemistry, pharmacology, and pathology. During the third and fourth years, students do clinical rotations in private practices, hospitals, and clinics. They study different areas of podiatric medicine such as general diagnosis, therapeutics, surgery, anesthesiology, and operative podiatric medicine. They also gain experience in the clinical sciences by spending time in college or community clinics and accredited hospitals.

CERTIFICATION OR LICENSING

All practicing podiatrists must be licensed in the United States. As part of the licensing requirements for all states, podiatrists must pass a two-part National Board exam. These National Boards are taken during the second and fourth years of podiatric medical school. In addition, most states require written and oral examinations and a postgraduate residency of at least one year prior to licensing.

There are four categories of residencies: rotating podiatric residency, primary podiatric medical residency, podiatric orthopedic residency, and podiatric surgical residency. There are also extended podiatric surgical residencies, lasting from 24 to 36 months, for podiatrists who want to learn advanced surgical skills.

Residencies take place in accredited teaching hospitals, where residents from other disciplines may also be training. Rotations during the podiatric residency may include anesthesiology, internal medicine, radiology, general surgery, plastic surgery, orthopedics, emergency room, vascular surgery, biomechanics, and pediatrics.

In order to become certified in one of the three specialty areas of podiatry, a podiatrist must pass additional written and oral examinations and demonstrate experience in his or her specialty area.

SCHOLARSHIPS AND GRANTS

There are several federal and private loan programs available to students considering a podiatric medical education. Interested students should contact the American Association of Colleges of Podiatric Medicine (http://www.aacpm.org) for information on loan programs.

In addition to loans, there may be scholarship or grant money available through private sources, such as community groups, corporations, or churches. Students should check with local libraries for information on scholarship and grant possibilities.

FYI

In the average lifetime, a person walks about 115,000 miles—more than four times the distance around the earth.

Who Will Hire Me?

There are more than 13,000 practicing podiatrists in the United States. Most of them work independently in their own practices. Gerry is no exception: He has been in private practice since he finished his surgical residency.

"It is very expensive to set up a practice," he says. "It's going to take anyone who's new three to five years to get established. Anyone who wants a get-rich-quick scheme isn't going to find it here."

Although most podiatrists work as solo practitioners, there are some who join partnerships or multispecialty group practices. Others are employed by hospitals, nursing homes, clinics, health maintenance organizations (HMOs), and public health departments.

Because most of these organizations are unlikely to advertise openings, podiatrists looking for positions should contact them directly. Talking with someone in an organization's personnel office might be a way to begin. In addition, a podiatrist may have made valuable contacts during his or her education and residency. Some of these contacts may be able to offer guidance in the job search or even help locate potential employers.

Podiatrists also work in the armed forces, the U.S. Public Health Service, and the Department of Veterans Affairs. The Veterans Omnibus Health Care Act of 1976, which launched an expanded VA podiatric medical program, greatly increased the number of podiatrists in federal service. Podiatrists interested in working for the Department of Veterans Affairs should contact a local VA office for more details.

Where Can I Go from Here?

The most common way that podiatrists advance their careers is by pursuing specialization. Gerry is following that path by specializing in surgery. Currently, his goal is to increase the amount of time he spends performing surgeries.

"Right now, I do one whole day of surgery each week," he says. "If that's your interest, then hopefully you'll start doing a day-and-a-half or two days of surgery. Some who start out doing general podiatric medicine eventually do all surgery." Gerry doesn't want to do surgery exclusively, however. "I'd like to spend maybe 30 percent of my time doing surgery and 70 percent with my patients," he says.

There are other areas of specialization for podiatrists. Some focus on caring for diabetic patients. Others might focus on foot diseases common in children or elderly patients. Still others specialize in sports medicine, treating athletes who have sustained foot or ankle injuries.

A podiatrist can also advance his or her career by becoming a professor at a college of podiatric medicine or the head of a hospital's podiatric department.

What Are the Salary Ranges?

The earnings of podiatrists who work in private practice depend on the location and size of the practice and on the length of time the podiatrist has been in the field. The *Occupational Outlook Handbook* says that median annual earnings of salaried podiatrists were $95,550 in 2003. Salaries ranged from less than $40,920 to more than $145,090. In general, salaried podiatrists tend to earn less than self-employed podiatrists. A survey by *Podiatric Magazine* reports that the average net income for all podiatrists was about $114,200 in 2003.

Podiatrists who work independently in their own offices must arrange for their own health insurance and retirement planning. Podiatrists who are employed by hospitals, nursing homes, and public health departments are typically provided with benefit packages that include insurance, paid vacations, and pension plans.

What Is the Job Outlook?

Employment of podiatrists is expected to grow about as fast as the average in the next decade. This expected growth is due in part to the increasing number of elderly people in our society. Elderly people, after years of standing, walking, and bearing weight on their feet, are especially prone to foot and ankle disorders.

Another reason for the expected growth in podiatry is the increasing number of people who are sustaining injuries related to sports and exercise. As more and more people become exercise conscious, the number of foot and ankle injuries increases.

Finally, the demand for podiatric services is expected to grow as health insurance coverage for such care becomes more common. Currently, Medicare and private insurance plans often cover acute medical and surgical foot care, X rays, and leg braces. Coverage for routine foot care, such as the removal of corns and calluses, is ordinarily not covered by most insurance plans, unless the patient has a systemic condition that has resulted in severe circulatory problems or areas of desensitization in the legs or feet.

The number of job opportunities available for a new podiatrist will depend largely upon where he or she hopes to practice. For example, states containing colleges of podiatric medicine have few available openings. In the south and southwest, where there is a shortage of such practitioners, the opportunities should be considerably better.

How Do I Learn More?

PROFESSIONAL ORGANIZATIONS

The following are organizations that provide information on podiatric careers, accredited schools, and employers:

American Association of Colleges of Podiatric Medicine
15850 Crabbs Branch Way, Suite 320
Rockville, MD 20855
800-922-9266
http://www.aacpm.org

American Podiatric Medical Association
9312 Old Georgetown Road
Bethesda, MD 20814
800-366-2273
http://www.apma.org

BIBLIOGRAPHY

The following is a sampling of materials related to the professional concerns and development of podiatrists:

Copeland, Glenn. *The Foot Book: Relief for Overused, Abused & Ailing Feet.* With Stan Solomon. New York: John Wiley & Sons, 1997.

Edmonds, Michael E., Althea V. M. Foster, and Lee J. Sanders. *A Practical Manual of Diabetic Footcare.* Oxford, U.K.: Blackwell, 2004.

Gerbert, Joshua, ed. *Textbook of Bunion Surgery.* 3d ed. Philadelphia: W. B. Saunders, 2000.

McMinn, Robert M. H., Ralph T. Hutchings, and Barri M. Logan. *Color Atlas of Foot & Ankle Anatomy.* 2d ed. St. Louis, Mo.: Mosby, 1996.

Merriman, Linda M., and Warren Turner, eds. *Assessment of the Lower Limb.* 2d ed. New York: Churchill Livingstone, 2002.

Tollafield, David R., and Linda M. Merriman. *Clinical Skills in Treating the Foot.* New York: Churchill Livingstone, 1997.

Weatherfield, M. Lisa, ed. *Podiatry Sourcebook.* Detroit, Mich.: Omnigraphics, 2001.

PSYCHIATRIC TECHNICIANS

A young boy charges through the adolescent psych ward, raging, his words choked in screams and tears. Full of fury, he pounds the walls with his fists. The boy has just been told he is being discharged from the hospital that day. Sue Jones, a psychiatric technician, stands nearby with a junior technician.

"Should I take him down?" the junior technician asks Sue.

"No," Sue answers, "Let him work it out."

It is a calculated risk.

Sue has worked with the boy. She knows that he comes from the streets, out of control, neglected by a mother who sold her body for drugs right in front of him. After four months in the ward, he's made little progress. But this is only his first time in treatment. Given time . . .

The boy stands there, screaming. The staff moves between him and the other patients, ready to restrain him if he turns violent.

But it is better to do it this way, Sue thinks. Let him feel his anger. For the first time in his life he's found a structured environment, and now they are sending him away. And in this anger, there is hope, a chance to heal.

Definition
Psychiatric technicians provide skilled nursing care and assist in treatment programs for patients with mental illnesses and emotional disturbances and patients with developmental disabilities.

Alternative Job Titles
Human services technicians
Mental health technicians
Psychiatric nursing specialists
Psychiatric technologists

High School Subjects
Health
Psychology

Personal Skills
Communication/ideas
Helping/teaching

Salary Range
$17,390 to $25,667 to $43,805

Minimum Educational Requirements
Associate's degree or some postsecondary training

Certification or Licensing
Voluntary (certification)
Required in some states (licensing)

Outlook
More slowly than the average

DOT
079

GOE
14.07.01

NOC
3413

O*NET-SOC
29-2053.00, 31-1013.00

What Does a Psychiatric Technician Do?

People with mental illnesses and emotional disturbances, and those with developmental disabilities, require special care to prevent them from becoming a danger to themselves or others and treatment toward the possibility of functioning to the fullest extent possible in mainstream life. Whether in a psychiatric hospital or clinic, a residential halfway house, or a school for the developmentally disabled, the health professional with whom these patients most often interact is the *psychiatric technician.*

Psychiatric technicians work intensively with patients and perform a variety of tasks, including participating in prescribed treatment programs, such as group therapy; administering oral and hypodermic medications; and taking basic health measurements, such as blood pressure and temperature readings. Psychiatric technicians are also responsible for maintaining patient hygiene and assisting in other routine activities, including feeding and bathing patients and keeping their clothing and living areas clean; when possible, the psychiatric technician encourages and trains patients to perform these activities for themselves.

One of the most important roles of the psychiatric technician is to observe patients and to provide written and oral reports on their observations to the patients' medical and psychiatric physicians. A psychiatric technician spends a great deal of time with patients, speaking with them, playing cards, chess, and other games, and escorting patients to medical appointments, church services, movies, museums, sports events, and other places. The psychiatric technician also facilitates patient-to-patient interaction, encouraging patients to participate in social and recreational activities as a means of promoting the rehabilitative process. By developing a relationship with patients, psychiatric technicians provide regularity and trust in a structured environment, which may be beneficial and necessary to the patient's progress.

Under the supervision of psychiatrists, psychologists, and other mental health professionals, the psychiatric technician participates in the planning of treatment strategies and is chiefly responsible for their implementation. Activities may include physical and mental rehabilitation exercises in recreational and occupational settings designed to build social and mental skills, modify behavior, and encourage a sense of personal responsibility and confidence often lacking in psychiatric patients.

Because of their direct association with patients, psychiatric technicians are an important component of the psychiatric team. Their observations provide insight into the effectiveness of treatment strategies so that each patient will receive the most appropriate care possible. Close contact with a patient also allows the psychiatric technician an important awareness into the patient's behavior and state of mind, which enables the psychiatric staff to recognize times of stress and possible harmful behavior. Timely intervention may prevent the patient from becoming a danger to him- or herself or others.

Psychiatric technicians may also be responsible for maintaining contact with the patient's family, arranging family meetings, and conducting initial admission interviews and psychological testing. In a hospital setting, the psychiatric technician becomes involved in every part of their patients' lives. In other settings, such as clinics, halfway houses, and day centers, the psychiatric technician sees many patients who have left the hospital and are making the transition to everyday life. These patients require special attention from the psychiatric technician who, while working with families, government services, and other mental health agencies, will help to coordinate the patient's housing, finances, and employment. The psychiatric technician will also establish continuing psychiatric and medical treatment.

Lingo to Learn

Neurosis A mental and emotional disorder that affects only part of the personality. A neurosis does not disturb the use of language and is accompanied by various physical, physiological, and mental disturbances, the most usual being anxieties or phobias.

Obsessive-compulsive A neurosis that results in the patient's compulsion to carry out certain acts, no matter how odd or illogical or repetitive they are. This sort of neurosis is evident once the obsession or compulsive act interferes with normal life. For example, a person obsessed with cleanliness might take a dozen or more showers a day.

Paranoid schizophrenic The most common and destructive of the psychotic disorders, characterized by departure from reality, inability to think clearly, difficulty feeling and expressing emotions, and a retreat into a fantasy life.

Phobias An irrational or overblown fear that prevent a person from living a normal life.

Psychosis A more complete disintegration of personality and a loss of contact with the outside world than with neuroses.

Community mental health is another area that employs psychiatric technicians. In this particular setting, patients generally do not require hospitalization, but nonetheless need help in dealing with such problems as drug and alcohol abuse. Sometimes called *human services technicians,* the patients of these psychiatric technicians may also include the elderly, victims of spousal and sexual abuse, and clients of social welfare programs, child care centers, vocational rehabilitation workshops, and schools for people with developmental disabilities.

What Is It Like to Be a Psychiatric Technician?

Sue Jones has been a psychiatric technician for almost 10 years. She is a senior member of a nursing staff, working with adolescent inpatients at a private psychiatric hospital in New Hampshire. "The unit I work on is very violent at times. But not all are like that. It's quieter to work with adults, because many of them have been in the system a long time, and they're often depressed," Sue says. "I prefer to work with adolescents because you seem to have more of a chance to help them. There's still a chance to get them out of the system and back into normal life."

Typically, there are 30 patients in Sue's unit, ranging in age from 12 to 17, with varying degrees of emotional and mental disabilities, and with varying levels of functional ability. Assigned to this unit are 10 or more staff, including nurses, psychiatric aides, and psychiatric technicians. The high ratio of staff to patients allows intensive supervision, observation, and interaction, which are key elements to psychiatric treatment.

"We keep patients on a highly structured schedule, from the moment they wake up to the time they go to sleep," Sue explains. "Their day begins at 8:00 A.M., when they're expected to have prepared their rooms, made their beds, cleaned, showered, and dressed. We call this 'milieu' therapy, which is an important part of their treatment. By holding them responsible for their own behavior, we encourage them to function at the highest level possible for them."

Patients are divided into two groups according to their functional level. Throughout the day, Sue and the other psychiatric staff lead patients through a variety of group and individual activities, each designed to coordinate therapeutic and rehabilitative skills that may allow the patient to leave the hospital setting and return to the community. The typical day for these patients includes group therapy and individual counseling sessions, schooling, group and individual activities, and therapies such as art therapy. Sue also leads "life school" classes in which patients are exposed to and taught skills they will need in the community, such as how to handle money and shop for groceries. Relieving the stressfulness of these activities may be an important factor in a patient's successful return to the community.

As a senior member of the staff, and because she is continuing her studies, Sue is considered a psychology intern. As such, she leads group counseling sessions under the supervision of a staff psychologist. "By talking about their problems, patients can help each other feel better. In group, they can talk through their problems and maybe learn to avoid the behavior that brought them here in the first place."

Sue is also responsible, along with the other members of the staff, for maintaining a safe environment in her unit. "Things can get physical two or three times a shift," Sue says. "Often, I eat lunch on the fly. If there's a crisis, for example, if one of the patients begins to attack someone on the staff, or themselves, or one of the other patients, I have to be ready to help intervene. But a big part of my job is observing my patients, recognizing when things are going badly for them, figuring out where they are in an emotional cycle and at what point to intervene. I try to get to them before they turn violent, to talk it through, and help them resolve an emotional crisis themselves.

"It's part of what we call MAP, or Managing Aggressive Patients. By first recognizing anxiety and working with patients to create an alliance, we assist them in verbalizing their conflict instead of acting it out," Sue explains.

Despite the stressfulness of her work, Sue finds being a psychiatric technician very rewarding. "For me, it's exciting watching these kids grow, seeing the things that happen in the course of the day that make them feel better or worse about themselves. Although I've had many traumatic experiences here, I do have the reward of seeing a few people heal."

Do I Have What It Takes to Be a Psychiatric Technician?

Psychiatric technicians work with people who, because of their illnesses, may exhibit extreme forms of behavior. Often they may be unpleasant or disagreeable to work with, or even abusive to themselves and others. The job of psychiatric technicians requires them to work closely with these patients; compassion, sensitivity, and a strong motivation to help others are necessities. Sue Jones agrees. "I really care for my patients, and I love the work I do. It's very hard work, and I had to grow a lot to do it."

It's very hard work, and I had to grow a lot to do it.

Patience is often required on the job, especially with patients whose disabilities allow for only slow, often insubstantial, improvement. What may outwardly appear to be a minor event may, for these patients, be a major moment of progress. Through encouragement, empathy, and an awareness of the patient's condition, the psychiatric technician is instrumental in motivating patients to reach these accomplishments and encouraging them to continue. A keen sense of observation allows the psychiatric technician to recognize not only times of stress in the patient but also the activities, events, and situations that help the patient's condition. Being able to relate to their patients and to present their observations to the patients' psychiatric and medical doctors allows the psychiatric technician to function as an important bridge in the therapeutic process.

This field also requires physical prowess, if not strength. Restraining individuals who become violent can be a traumatic experience. "I've had to rescue one boy who tried to hang himself. Another girl tied her neck off with a strip of cloth she tore off her shirt. I've also had to interfere with a kid who reduced a room full of furniture to nails and boards," Sue says. "We diffuse situations like that as a team. We also process and debrief traumatic events as a team, and we'll discuss them informally with each other, too. Some of us have also had individual sessions to overcome traumatic events." But, at 5'6" and 125 pounds, Sue says that she is stronger than she looks. "I'm very active physically, anyway, and I've developed physically as a result of the job. And I know what I'm doing—I know when to ask for help. I would say that my strength is as much in my honesty and consistency as in my physical preparedness. I don't hesitate. And I don't bargain."

Sue finds the work very challenging. But there are frustrations too, Sue says. "Before we dispose—that is, transfer a patient to another facility—sometimes, the best we're able to achieve is to function as a sort of bandage. We have to work within the patient's insurance requirements," she explains, "which often means we can only provide the lowest level of care. Their insurance won't pay for anything more."

Sue's work as a psychiatric technician is never boring. "There's never a dull moment. I go in each morning knowing that I have to deal with what happens or has happened in the shift before, and that I will deal with it no matter what. I've amazed myself by doing this. I do what has to be done. It's the ultimate internship, and I have very little fear about the work I do."

To Be a Successful Psychiatric Technician, You Should . . .

- be patient, compassionate, and mature, with a strong sense of responsibility
- enjoy working with and relate well to people
- be motivated to help others achieve their highest potential
- be observant and articulate
- be in good physical condition

How Do I Become a Psychiatric Technician?

The educational requirements for becoming a psychiatric technician can vary widely from state to state and from facility to facility. In some cases, no specialized schooling is required and training is given on the job. Elsewhere, a psychiatric technician may be required to have a two-year associate's degree or even a four-year bachelor's degree from a psychiatric technician program. These schools also feature clinical fieldwork in which a student participates in on-the-job training at a variety of facilities requiring psychiatric technicians. Sue Jones, for example, has continued her studies while working and expects to receive her bachelor's degree shortly. "It's because I'm still studying that I've received more and more responsibilities, and now I'm considered one of the senior staff in my unit," Sue says.

EDUCATION

High School

Students considering this field should plan to continue their education in either a two-year or four-year academic program. This will allow them greater growth in the field, increasing their responsibilities as they gain experience with corresponding increases in pay. While in high school, students should take on courses in psychology, biology and other natural sciences, and mathematics. Developing good communication skills is important, too, so taking English and other courses that will build strong written and verbal skills is highly recommended. Because a psychiatric technician becomes intimately involved in the lives of his or her patients, subjects that prepare you for human interaction, such as social sciences courses, peer counseling, and tutoring programs, will also be an asset as you begin your career.

"Looking back," Sue reflects, sighing, "I wish I had concentrated more on biology, because that is the basis of much of psychiatric work. But one course I had in high school really helped—government. We're part of a system here, and it's helped me to understand why certain things like the insurance system are the way they are. And I deal with a lot of governmental agencies on behalf of my patients. I think it's important to understand the structure of our society."

Postsecondary Training

For those students pursuing postsecondary education as a psychiatric technician, two-year programs leading to an associate's degree and four-year programs leading to a bachelor's degree will usually include courses in human development, personality structure, and the nature of mental illness; anatomy, physiology, and basic medical science; and training in nursing techniques. Social science courses give the prospective psychiatric technician understanding of family and community relationships, and programs will also offer an overview of the mental health and medical system.

An important element of all programs is the practical and clinical phase of study in which students receive training and experience in the actual work of psychiatric technicians. A student's field experience may comprise as much as one-third of his or her study program.

Other postsecondary courses a psychiatric technician can expect to take include English, psychology, sociology, and mental health-related courses, including early childhood development, general and abnormal psychology, classes in family and social welfare institutions, psychopathology, general nursing, community mental health, and techniques of therapy.

Apart from field experience, many programs offer training in interviewing and observation skills. Students may be trained in recognizing meanings behind certain tones of voice, in what people say and do, and ways of speaking and behaving. Because psychiatric technicians often administer psychological tests, students may also be trained in the proper administration of such tests, which are often in the form of questionnaires and have been designed to give health professionals insight into a patient's state of mind. Psychiatric technician students also receive training in crisis intervention, group counseling, behavior modification, child guidance, and family therapy, as well as training in consulting and working with the variety of agencies, both public and private, concerned with mental health and the public welfare.

Finally, prospective psychiatric technicians may also enter the field through military service. Military personnel may request, as part of their military service, secondary schooling as a hospital corpsman and choose to specialize as a psychiatric technician. The Navy, for example, offers a 15-week general course at a hospital corpsman school, followed by two six-week training periods in psychiatric technology. The first of these periods features course work; the second period is the clinical phase.

CERTIFICATION OR LICENSING

The American Association of Psychiatric Technicians (AAPT) offers four levels of national certification. According to the AAPT, first level certification is achieved by passing a comprehensive test, but requires no postsecondary training or practical experience. Level II requires 30 hours of college course work and one year of practical experience; Level III requires 60 college course credits, or an associate's degree, and two years of field experience. Level IV certification is available to psychiatric technicians with at least three years of experience and a bachelor's degree in psychiatric technology or a related psychology major. AAPT certification is voluntary, but it will probably be helpful when you seek your first job in the field. In addition, certification may make you eligible for increases in salary and responsibilities as you progress in your career (see "How Do I Learn More?").

Currently only four states—Arkansas, California, Colorado, and Kansas—require psychiatric technicians to be licensed. These four states also have various agreements regarding reciprocity. Licensing requirements may include completing specific amounts of classroom instruction and hands-on experience and passing a written test. Continuing education courses are usually required for license renewals.

INTERNSHIPS AND VOLUNTEERSHIPS

It is possible to find work in the field during high school, either part time or during the summer. Students may apply for positions as psychiatric aides, trainees, or orderlies or find work in housekeeping, maintenance, or administrative positions. These positions generally do not require formal education or training and are excellent opportunities for gaining experience and insight into the field.

Prospective psychiatric technicians may also gain practical experience by applying for jobs as a nurse's aide at a local hospital or clinic or participating in volunteer programs related to this field. Many schools also offer peer counseling experience, and schools with developmentally delayed students may have need of student volunteers or tutors. This kind of work will help you decide if the field is right for you.

In addition, volunteering in local mental health and community service organizations or working at playgrounds, swimming pools, and summer camps will help you gain both experience and insight into the field and the nature of the work involved.

Students interested in these opportunities should talk to their school guidance counselor or contact local hospitals and mental health clinics.

ADVANCEMENT POSSIBILITIES

Senior psychiatric technicians supervise and instruct junior psychiatric technicians, help coordinate schedules, and serve as the liaison between management and the technicians.

Psychiatric technician instructors work in hospitals and at technical schools to train psychiatric technicians. They may also teach certification courses.

Psychiatrists are physicians who treat patients with mental, emotional, and behavioral symptoms. They have completed all of the training required to become licensed medical doctors (M.D.'s) and then have taken additional training to specialize in psychiatry.

Psychologists teach, counsel, and work in research and administration to help understand people, their capacities, traits, and behavior and to explain their needs. They normally hold doctorates in psychology, but they are not medical doctors and cannot prescribe medication.

Who Will Hire Me?

Apart from state mental institutions and private psychiatric hospitals and clinics, there are a great many facilities that need skilled psychiatric technicians. For example, nursing homes, family service centers, public housing programs, public schools, prisons, and courts of law are all places that employ psychiatric technicians.

A growing number of psychiatric technicians are finding employment in the community, rather than in the hospital setting. The trend is toward treating psychiatric patients in the home or school, allowing them to continue to be a part of the community. A psychiatric technician may work in a school or participate in half-day programs where patients can receive therapy and specialized attention without disrupting their daily life. Psychiatric technicians specializing in patients with developmental disabilities may find employment in training centers devoted to teaching these patients job and life skills.

In addition, a growing number of psychiatric technicians are working as part of privately funded family stabilization teams. Much like social workers, these psychiatric technicians are assigned to specific patients and the family and are available to intervene in periods of difficulty or crisis, working with the entire family to resolve personal relationship issues, coordinate their access to community support services, such as welfare, medical treatment, and housing, and resolve financial and legal issues. This work involves visiting patients in their own homes and communities, where living and social conditions may vary widely. Many members of family stabilization teams are required to carry beepers and to be on call 24 hours a day. Their intervention can often make a great difference in resolving a situation before it reaches a crisis point.

Where Can I Go from Here?

For Sue Jones, her work is part of a career path that will eventually result in her receiving a Ph.D. in clinical psychology. "Although, looking back on it," she says, "if I had started early enough, I would have gone to medical school to become a psychiatrist."

Apart from gaining practical experience that will help in future studies, many aspiring psychologists and senior nursing staff find that their work as a psychiatric technician combines well with continued educational efforts, allowing them an opportunity to study, as well as to see in practice, many of the theoretical concepts included in their class work.

For psychiatric technicians, the increase in experience will lead to increased responsibilities and increased pay. With the proper experience, a psychiatric technician can also achieve positions with supervisory duties.

In general, continuing educational growth will greatly expand a psychiatric technician's advancement opportunities. A psychiatric technician may choose to enter other specialties in the psychiatric field, which may require more specialized training. With experience and education or additional training, psychiatric technicians may also choose to become instructors for other psychiatric technicians.

What Are the Salary Ranges?

Salary depends on a variety of factors, including geographical location, the type of facility, and the level of education and experience. The U.S. Department of Labor reports that psychiatric technicians earned a median hourly wage of $12.34 in 2003, which translates into about $25,667 a year, based on a 40-hour workweek. The lowest paid 10 percent earned less than $8.36 an hour ($17,390 a year), and the highest paid 10 percent earned more than $21.06 an hour ($43,805 a year). Technicians employed in physicians' offices generally receive higher pay than those in institutional settings.

Most psychiatric technicians work a 40-hour week, which may include at least one weekend shift. Many psychiatric facilities require trained staff 24 hours a day, and psychiatric technicians may have their choice of day, evening, night, or weekend shifts. Fringe benefits often include health insurance, paid sick days, and paid vacations. Some state institutions and agencies may also grant financial assistance for continuing study.

What Is the Job Outlook?

The U.S. Department of Labor projects employment for psychiatric technicians to grow more slowly than the average through 2012. Demand for technicians, though, is expected to continue in large part because of a well-established trend of returning hospitalized patients to their communities after shorter and shorter periods of hospitalization. This trend has encouraged development of comprehensive community mental health centers and has led to a strong demand for psychiatric technicians to staff these facilities.

Concerns over rising health care costs should increase employment levels for technicians, because they and other paraprofessionals can take over some functions of higher paid professionals. This kind of substitution has been demonstrated to be an effective way of reducing costs without reducing quality of care.

How Do I Learn More?

PROFESSIONAL ORGANIZATIONS

The following are organizations that provide information on psychiatric technician careers, accredited schools and scholarships, and employers:

American Association of Psychiatric Technicians
2000 O Street, Suite 250
Sacramento, CA 95814
800-391-7589
aapt@psych-health.com
http://www.psychtechs.org

American Psychiatric Association
1000 Wilson Boulevard, Suite 1825
Arlington, VA 22209
703-907-7300
apa@psych.org
http://www.psych.org

Child Welfare League of America
Child Mental Health Program
440 First Street, NW, Third Floor
Washington, D.C. 20001-2085
202-638-2952
http://www.cwla.org/programs/bhd/mhdefault.htm

BIBLIOGRAPHY

The following is a sampling of materials relating to the professional concerns and development of psychiatric technicians:

Careers in Focus: Medical Technicians. 3d ed. New York: Facts On File, 2004.

McClelland, Lucille Hudlin. *Textbook for Psychiatric Technicians.* 2d ed. St Louis, Mo.: Mosby, 1971.

Sternberg, Robert J. *Career Paths in Psychology: Where Your Degree Can Take You.* Washington, D.C.: American Psychological Association, 1997.

PSYCHIATRISTS

Fidgeting uneasily in her chair in the patient lounge, Cheryl Vanden waits for Dr. Jenny Kane, her psychiatrist, to say something. Sunlight streams through the broad wall of windows. Sitting on the couch next to Cheryl, Jenny looks over the notes she took during yesterday's session.

Cheryl is suffering from a depression severe enough to provoke a series of suicide attempts. She was admitted to the hospital four days ago, after overdosing on prescription painkillers. Although not antagonistic, she is very reluctant to talk about herself, and Dr. Kane has made little headway.

"Cheryl, this morning in group [therapy], you seemed very uneasy when John talked about parents," Dr. Kane notes. After receiving no response, she continues. "Did you feel distressed by that?"

Cheryl picks at a fingernail, looks away. "I don't know," she finally says.

Definition
Psychiatrists are medical doctors who specialize in treating patients who have mental, emotional, and behavioral disorders.

High School Subjects
Biology
Chemistry
Psychology

Personal Skills
Helping/teaching
Technical/scientific

Salary Range
$110,000 to $163,144 to $189,499

Educational Requirements
Medical degree

Certification or Licensing
Required by all states

Outlook
About as fast as the average

DOT
070

GOE
14.02.01

NOC
3111

O*NET-SOC
29-1066.00

What Does a Psychiatrist Do?

Just as cardiologists specialize in treating heart diseases and neurologists specialize in treating disorders of the brain and nervous system, *psychiatrists* specialize in treating mental and emotional disorders. These problems might stem from fairly common ailments—anxiety, stress, eating disorders, or addiction to drugs and alcohol—or less common disorders, such as schizophrenia or manic depression.

Doctors of psychiatry may work in private practice or for a private hospital. They also work in state mental hospitals, medical schools, community mental health centers, and in government agencies. Many psychiatrists combine a private practice with work in a clinic, hospital, or medical school.

Psychiatrists first evaluate their patients by examining them physically, talking with them about their problem or problems, and asking them questions designed to provide diagnostic information. They may order laboratory tests and X rays. If a patient's problem appears to be caused by a physical condition, the psychiatrist may refer the patient to another specialist, such as a neurologist, for treatment.

Once the doctor has obtained patient information, he or she sets up an appropriate treatment plan. The method of treatment depends upon the type of illness and the patient's needs. Psychiatrists may prescribe medications, such as tranquilizers or antidepressants, which affect the patient's feelings and/or behavior.

They may also use psychotherapy. Psychotherapy is sometimes called "talking therapy." The psychiatrist spends several sessions talking with the patient to help him or her overcome emotional pain. By listening, asking questions, and pointing out important points, the doctor guides the patient through an exploration and interpretation of the feelings at the core of his or her problem. This type of therapy may be given to an individual in a one-on-one setting. It can also be used in groups of patients. It is often used with families.

Some psychiatrists use other forms of therapy. *Behavior therapists* use specific techniques to help patients learn how to change troublesome behaviors. These techniques might include the use of rewards

A child psychiatrist meets with a young girl. *(Voisin / Photo Researchers Inc.)*

or deterrents to bring about or eliminate behaviors. Some behavior therapists use meditation, biofeedback, and relaxation training to help their patients.

Psychiatrists try to help their patients uncover, understand, and deal with subconscious memories and emotions. They do this by encouraging the patient to express random thoughts, or free associate. They may also analyze their patients' dreams for clues to the subconscious mind.

Some psychiatrists focus on a particular type of patient. *Child psychiatrists* work specifically with children and their parents. *Geriatric psychiatrists* work with elderly patients. *Industrial psychiatrists* are employed by companies to deal with employee problems that may affect their job performance, such as alcoholism or absenteeism.

Forensic psychiatrists combine a knowledge of law with a knowledge of psychiatry. They evaluate defendants and testify in court on their mental states. They may help determine whether defendants understand the charges brought against them, and whether they are able to help in their own defense.

Psychiatrists may also serve as mental health consultants to schools, day-care centers, and senior citizen's groups. In addition, they may work with courts, probation officers, police departments, and other community agencies.

What Is It Like to Be a Psychiatrist?

Dr. Jenny Kane oversees the stress-care ward in the psychiatric unit of a hospital. Her ward is one of five in the unit; others include the crisis-care ward for patients who are extremely agitated, the med/psych ward for psychiatric patients who also require extensive medical treatment, the chemical dependency ward, and the adolescent ward.

Jenny's ward usually houses 23 or 24 patients with disorders that vary in type and degree of severity. She is fully responsible for their psychiatric care during their stay on the ward.

"Maybe the easiest way to describe my job is to compare it to parenting," she says. "Whatever and whenever a patient needs me, it's my job to be there, or at least to make arrangements to have them taken care of."

For her, this means being on call practically all the time. "I can have another physician cover my ward for me, yes," Jenny says. "But it's not uncommon for a patient to want to talk to me specifically. The patients on this ward are usually in very precarious mental health, and they sometimes really need stability and continuity." Because of this, even when another doctor is covering her ward, Jenny remains available to answer questions or talk with patients.

It's not uncommon for a patient to want to talk to me specifically. The patients on this ward are usually in very precarious mental health, and they sometimes really need stability and continuity.

The nature of her position also means that she does not have a set work schedule. She often spends time on the ward on Saturdays and Sundays. It's also not unusual for her to stop by in the evenings to check on patients. And, of course, she might be called in at any time if a patient is having a crisis severe enough to require her presence.

On an average weekday, Jenny arrives on the ward between 7:00 A.M. and 8:00 P.M. The first thing she does is make rounds. This involves talking with each patient and reviewing his or her chart to see what, if anything, occurred during the night.

Each patient is different, says Jenny, so the nature of treatment is different. Most often, however, a patient's treatment involves some combination of psychotherapy and medication. "These days, medication is a very strong component of psychiatric care," she says. Jenny is responsible for prescribing medication and for monitoring its level and effect on the patient.

Treatment also involves psychotherapy, or talking with the patients to help them work through their problems. This is done both one-on-one with individual patients and in group sessions. Jenny conducts four group sessions each week. The patients in the group are assigned to sessions that are appropriate for their problems. For example, one group session might focus on addictive tendencies, another on dealing with stress and anxiety.

While all patients on her ward are psychiatric patients, many of them have minor physical disorders as well. "For example, yesterday we admitted a patient who was diabetic. As her mental condition had worsened, she'd stopped taking her insulin and her blood sugar was way too high," Jenny said. "Other times, patients come in off the streets. They may have frostbite, if it's in the winter. They may have infections because they haven't been capable of taking care of themselves."

Jenny treats her patients' physical ailments as well. "I treat anything that a family practitioner would treat," she says. "If it's necessary, I call in a specialist."

In addition to dealing directly with patients, Jenny also spends a considerable amount of time in

Lingo to Learn

Biofeedback The technique of making unconscious or involuntary bodily processes (such as heartbeats or brain waves) perceptible to the senses (through the use of an electronic monitoring device) in order to manipulate them by conscious mental control.

Neurosis An emotional disorder that arises due to unresolved conflicts, with anxiety often being the main characteristic.

Phobia An obsessive, persistent, unrealistic fear of an object or situation.

Psychoanalysis A method of treating mental disorders by bringing unconscious fears and conflicts into the conscious mind.

Psychosis A major mental disorder in which the personality is seriously disorganized and contact with reality is impaired.

Psychosomatic A physical illness caused or aggravated by a mental condition.

Psychotherapy The treatment of mental disorders by psychological, rather than physical, means.

various types of meetings. The ward staff meets every morning to review patient cases.

"At least three to four times a week, we have treatment planning meetings," she says. "These meetings are multidisciplinary, so anyone who is involved with treating the patient is in attendance." This could include medical specialists, therapists, nurses, and representatives from outside agencies.

Jenny also meets periodically with patients' families and with community mental health agencies to ensure that patients being released from the hospital will continue to receive the necessary care.

Another part of Jenny's job is dealing with the justice system. She, along with the other hospital psychiatrists, treat inmates of the county jail. They may also be called upon to testify in competency or commitment hearings in court regarding the mental state of patients.

Do I Have What It Takes to Be a Psychiatrist?

Not all psychiatrists' schedules are as irregular as Jenny's. She is quick to point out that those doctors who work in a private practice usually set their own office hours. Although they may occasionally get phone calls at odd hours or see some patients on weekends or evenings, for the most part their schedules are more routine than hers.

Whatever type of practice they are in, however, psychiatrists must realize that they have a certain responsibility to their patients. "Some patients come to rely very heavily on their psychiatrists," says Jenny. "And when you're dealing with emotionally and mentally fragile people, you must take that reliance very seriously."

Part of a psychiatrist's ability to form relationships with patients is his or her compassion for them. "You must be able to empathize with them, you must have a desire to help them," says Jenny. "If that is lacking, I would imagine that you'd be constantly frustrated in your patient dealings."

To balance that empathy, however, a certain amount of detachment is needed. While the psychiatrist should have compassion for patients, he or she must not become emotionally involved with them. "It's sometimes very difficult not to become emotionally tangled up with the patients you care for," says Jenny. "You grow to know them, you grow to care for them. But getting too involved can ultimately be hard on you emotionally. And it can get in the way of effective treatment as well."

> **To Be a Successful Psychiatrist, You Should . . .**
>
> - be able to analyze human behavior
> - be compassionate, yet be able to be objective
> - be a good listener and a good communicator
> - be able to form positive relationships

Psychiatrists need to be good listeners and good interpreters. They need to be aware of what patients mean as well as what they say. An inquiring mind and good analytical skills are also important.

Finally, psychiatrists should be emotionally stable themselves in order to deal with their patients, some of whom may be extremely depressed, hostile, or defensive. "Working with emotional disturbances on a daily basis can be draining and exhausting, even discouraging," says Jenny. "Of course, the flip side is when you see people improve, when you know without a doubt that you've helped them. That's a real high."

How Do I Become a Psychiatrist?

EDUCATION

High School

If you want to become a psychiatrist, you can begin preparing in high school. While psychology classes are an obvious and natural choice, you must remember that you are, first and foremost, aiming for admission into medical school.

A well-rounded college preparatory curriculum should include courses in English, natural and physical sciences, math, social studies, and a foreign language.

It will be particularly helpful to take as many science classes as possible. Biology, chemistry, physiology, physics, and, of course, psychology are all excellent choices.

The ability to comprehend quickly and communicate well is extremely important to being a successful psychiatrist. Advanced English classes and speech classes both offer good ways to develop and refine comprehension and communication skills.

In addition to making wise curriculum choices, there are other ways to explore your aptitude for a career in psychiatry. A summer job or volunteer work at a hospital might provide a taste of what a medical profession is like. It may even be possible to work or volunteer at a psychiatric hospital or community mental health clinic.

Postsecondary Training

After high school, it takes between 12 and 14 years of schooling and training to become a psychiatrist. These include four years of undergraduate school, four years of medical school, and three to four years of postgraduate residency training.

The first phase is undergraduate work. Most students who hope to attend medical school focus on science and math classes, often majoring in biology or chemistry. A concentration on psychology classes is also appropriate. In addition to these subjects, undergraduate students will take classes in English, arts and humanities, a foreign language, and social studies.

During your second or third year in college, you should take the Medical College Admission Test (MCAT), which most medical schools require. Medical schools have very high admission standards, so a good score on the MCAT is important, as is a good grade point average. Most medical schools also require letters of reference and a personal interview with applicants.

Medical school consists of four years of advanced training. During the first two years, students take such courses as anatomy, physiology, pharmacology, microbiology, psychology, pathology, medical ethics, and medical law. They learn how to examine patients and take medical histories.

The remaining two years of medical school involve hands-on learning. Students spend time in hospitals and clinics, working with patients under the supervision of practicing physicians. They get experience in various medical specialties, such as family practice, obstetrics and gynecology, pediatrics, internal medicine, surgery, and psychiatry. Upon completion of these four years, students receive the M.D. degree.

After graduation from medical school, students must complete a residency. First-year residents work in several specialties, such as internal medicine, pediatrics, or family practice. The next three years are spent in either a psychiatric hospital or the psychiatric ward of a general hospital, learning how to diagnose and treat various emotional and mental disorders.

Some psychiatrists continue their professional training even beyond the four-year residency period. To become a child psychiatrist, for example, psychiatrists must complete at least three years in general residency and two years in child psychiatry.

CERTIFICATION OR LICENSING

At an early point in the residency period, all candidates are required to pass a medical licensing examination administered by their state's board of medical examiners. At the end of an accredited residency training program, physicians must pass certification examinations in their field. The evaluation and examination program is directed by the appropriate specialty board (in this case, psychiatry) of the American Board of Medical Specialties.

SCHOLARSHIPS AND GRANTS

Scholarships and grants are often available from individual institutions, state agencies, and special-interest organizations. Many students finance their medical education through the Armed Forces Health Professions Scholarship Program. Each branch of the military participates in this program, paying students' tuitions in exchange for military service. Contact your local recruiting office for more information on this program.

The National Health Service Corps Scholarship Program (http://nhsc.bhpr.hrsa.gov) also provides money for students in return for service. Another source for financial aid, scholarship, and grant information is the Association of American Medical Colleges (http://www.aamc.org). Remember to request information early for eligibility, application requirements, and deadlines.

Who Will Hire Me?

Dr. Jenny Kane 's first position, which she was recruited for during her residency, was in a private

In-depth

Bipolar Disorder

Bipolar disorder, also known as manic depression, is a mental illness that psychiatrists treat successfully. People who suffer from this disorder experience mood swings from mania to depression. During periods of mania, they feel indestructible, hyperactive, and overly self-confident. They may be extremely irritable, have increased energy, and sleep less, among other symptoms. During periods of depression, those with bipolar disorder feel intensely sad and hopeless. They may lose interest in normal activities, have sleep problems, have trouble concentrating or making decisions, or think about suicide. The periods of mania and depression vary in length and are unpredictable. Some people with bipolar disorder experience "rapid cycling," which means they alternate between periods of mania and depression at least four times a year.

Bipolar disorder can be treated with both medication and psychotherapy. Without treatment, people with bipolar disorder, along with their families, experience constant disruption and distress throughout their lives. In psychotherapy, the psychiatrist has a series of sessions with the patient to discuss the feelings, thoughts and behavior that cause difficulty. The goal of psychotherapy is to help patients and their families identify early warning signs of bipolar episodes. A psychiatrist also can help people with the disorder manage emotional stress, which helps people stay well and may prevent bipolar episodes.

The most common medication used to treat bipolar disorder is lithium, a mood stabilizer. It helps control mania and may prevent future manic and depressive episodes. Some anticonvulsant medications, such as valproate and carbamazepine also are effective in treating bipolar disorder. Antidepressants, combined with lithium or anticonvulsants, are sometimes used to treat the depressive phase of the illness.

practice. After seven years in private practice, she interviewed with the hospital where she now works.

Employment options for new psychiatrists include private practice, general hospitals, state and private mental hospitals, medical schools, community mental health centers, and government agencies. Approximately one-half of practicing psychiatrists work in private practice; many others combine a private practice with work in a health care institution or community mental health center.

While still in your residency, you should start considering where you would like to practice. You may find positions through networking with other mental health professionals that you meet during your training. In other cases, the hospitals or agencies where you train may offer permanent positions.

There are several professional journals for psychiatrists, and they may list job openings in their classified advertising sections. Also, members of the American Psychiatric Association have access to an online job bank that lists hundreds of available positions all over the nation.

Where Can I Go from Here?

Advancement for most psychiatrists takes the form of increased income. By building a reputation and expanding his or her patient base over time, the psychiatrist earns more money.

Psychiatrists who work in psychiatric hospitals, clinics, and mental health centers may work their way up to administrative positions. Those who go into teaching or research may eventually become department heads.

What Are the Salary Ranges?

Psychiatrists' earnings are determined by the kind of practice they have and its location, their experience, and the number of patients they treat. Like other physicians, their average income is among the highest of any occupation.

According to Physicians Search, a physician recruitment agency, average starting salaries for psychiatrists ranged from $110,000 to $180,000 in 2004. Psychiatrists who have practiced for three years or more earned salaries that ranged from $121,000 to $189,499. The median for psychiatrists was $163,144 in 2003, according to the Medical Group Management Association.

What Is the Job Outlook?

Employment opportunities for psychiatrists are expected to grow about as fast the average, according to *Occupational Outlook Handbook*. As a society, we are becoming more aware of the importance of good mental health. While in the past emotional and mental disorders were often viewed as shameful and were not dealt with, people today recognize mental disorders as genuine illnesses that can be treated. This changing viewpoint has encouraged many people to seek psychiatric treatment who might not have a decade ago.

Psychiatry itself has made advances that make treatment more effective. Perhaps most significant is the increased use of drugs to treat various forms of mental, emotional, and behavioral disorders. In many instances, pharmaceutical treatments are replacing the more traditional forms of therapy.

Since medicine can only be prescribed by a medical doctor, some patients who might otherwise be treated by a counselor or a psychologist are choosing to see a psychiatrist instead.

The need for more psychiatrists in the field should promote the need for more teachers of psychiatry at the university level. Also, these doctors are needed as researchers to investigate the causes of mental illness and continue to develop and refine treatments.

How Can I Learn More?

PROFESSIONAL ORGANIZATIONS

The following organizations provide information on the psychiatric careers:

American Medical Association
515 North State Street
Chicago, IL 60610
800-621-8335
http://www.ama-assn.org

American Psychiatric Association
1000 Wilson Boulevard, Suite 1825
Arlington, VA 22209
703-907-7300
apa@psych.org
http://www.psych.org

BIBLIOGRAPHY

The following is a sampling of materials relating to the professional concerns of psychiatrists:

Coles, Robert. *The Mind's Fate: A Psychiatrist Looks at His Profession.* 2d ed. Boston, Mass.: Little, Brown, 1996.

Fadem, Barbara, and Steven S. Simring. *High-Yield Psychiatry.* 2d ed. Philadelphia: Lippincott Williams & Wilkins, 2003.

Gelder, Michael G., Juan J. Lopez-Ibor Jr., Nancy Andreasen, eds. *New Oxford Textbook of Psychiatry.* New ed. New York: Oxford University Press, 2003.

Jenkins, Susan C., Joyce A. Tinsley, Jon A Van Loon. *A Pocket Reference for Psychiatrists.* 3 ed. Washington, D.C., American Psychiatric Association, 2001.

Klitzman, Robert. *In a House of Dreams and Glass: Becoming a Psychiatrist.* New York: Simon & Schuster, 1996.

Lazarus, Arthur, ed. *Career Pathways in Psychiatry: Transition in Changing Times.* Hillside, N.J.: Analytic Press, 1996.

PSYCHOLOGISTS

Dr. Murphy Thomas steps into the attractive 19th-century house in Murfreesboro, Tennessee, that has been converted into an office. He has come in early this morning to work on a report about a murder case.

Murphy, a clinical psychologist, begins going through his interview notes. For a number of years, he has been doing consulting work in forensic psychology for both civil and criminal cases. The case at hand involves a young man accused of murder and Murphy has been asked to interview him.

The accused's lawyer wants an expert opinion as to whether the prisoner is competent to stand trial. Or should the lawyer present an insanity defense? It looks like a difficult case.

Definition
Psychologists study human (and animal) behavior and the mental, social, and biological processes that are involved in their behavior. They evaluate and counsel clients, teach, administer programs, and conduct research.

High School Subjects
Mathematics
Psychology
Science

Personal Skills
Helping/teaching
Leadership/management

Salary Range
$31,250 to $53,230 to $85,000+

Educational Requirements
Bachelor's degree; master's degree required; doctoral necessary for employment in most fields of psychology

Certification or Licensing
Required for certain positions

Outlook
Faster than the average

DOT
045

GOE
12.02.01

NOC
4151

O*NET-SOC
19-3031.00, 19-3031.01, 19-3031.02, 19-3031.03, 19-3032.00

What Does a Psychologist Do?

Psychology as a scientific discipline has not been in existence for much longer than a century, though, of course, people have been interested in human behavior and mental processes for thousands of years. In the late 19th century, the field of psychology developed dramatically under the leadership of such pioneers as Wilhelm Wundt, William James, and Sigmund Freud.

Psychologists are specialists in human behavior. It is a very diverse field with hundreds of career paths. Some psychologists focus on research into the mental, social, and biological aspects of behavior, while others are mental health service providers who apply this knowledge in their work with clients. It is interesting to note that psychologists may also be involved in the design of advanced computer systems or the redesign of an office layout to generate productivity. Many psychologists are involved in both research and the treatment of clients.

People often confuse psychologists with psychiatrists. A psychiatrist is a medical doctor (M.D.) who specializes in psychology. Psychologists are not medical doctors, although they usually have a doctorate in psychology (Psy.D.) or philosophy (Ph.D.).

The field of psychology is divided into many specialties (with some overlap in subject matter and methodology), all of which address mind and behavior in some way. Students typically choose their area of specialization early in their graduate school years.

Clinical psychology is the largest single specialty. The *clinical psychologist,* or *psychotherapist,* works with clients who have mental, emotional, or behavioral disorders. They interview clients and administer diagnostic tests. They also provide psychotherapy sessions, behavior modification programs, and other forms of treatment.

Some clinical psychologists serve as directors of community mental health programs. Some specialize in work with children or the elderly. Other specialists within the clinical psychology field include *neuropsychologists,* who work with people undergoing rehabilitation after strokes or head injuries, and *health and rehabilitation psychologists,* who work with medical and surgical patients in overcoming such problems as chronic pain or illness. Most clinical psychologists are in individual or group practice. Others work at hospitals, clinics, or universities.

Counseling psychologists work with clients who are not mentally ill but have problems dealing with the stresses in their lives, such as family crises, interpersonal conflicts, or vocational decisions. They help people make decisions and develop better problem-solving skills. Like clinical psychologists, counseling psychologists provide individual, family, and group therapy.

Social psychologists make use of the insights of psychology, psychiatry, sociology, and cultural anthropology to study the different ways individuals and groups influence each other in their interactions. They analyze group structures, attitudes, and leadership patterns.

Developmental psychologists study behavioral and psychological developments from infancy through old age. They seek to identify and explain typical age-related patterns of behavioral and emotional change in the personality as a whole, and in specific areas, such as language comprehension and moral reasoning. Many developmental psychologists concentrate on research or teaching, but some work in programs for children or the elderly.

School psychologists work with children, teachers, parents, and educational administrators to identify and treat children's learning and behavioral problems. They test children who are thought to have special educational needs or who have been referred for evaluation because of their behavioral problems. In cooperation with teachers and other educational experts, school psychologists design remedial and preventive programs to help all children develop to their fullest potential. Sometimes school psychologists also work with parents and children to address problems in family relations.

Educational psychologists do research on the processes of teaching and learning. They evaluate learning outcomes and seek ways to make both teaching and learning more effective.

Experimental psychologists do research on human and animal behavior. (Rats, pigeons, and monkeys are common experimental animals.) They study such areas of behavior as motivation, thinking, learning and retention, sensory and perceptual processes, genetic factors, and the effects of substance abuse.

Industrial/organizational (I/O) psychologists apply psychological knowledge to the workplace. They work with the personnel department and management in screening job applicants. They also help train employees to improve both productivity and the quality of life in the workplace.

Consumer psychologists study consumer attitudes to products and services. They give advice on consumer preferences and effective advertising and marketing techniques.

Quantitative and measurement psychologists design, administer, and evaluate intelligence, personality, and aptitude tests. These psychologists also design the research tools used to gather and analyze psychological data.

Lingo to Learn

Developmental tasks The achievements and skills considered necessary for a person to acquire at each stage of life in order to function well.

Experimental variable A condition or factor that is systematically manipulated by the experimenter in order to observe and assess its influence on behavior.

MMPI (Minnesota Multiphasic Personality Inventory) One of the most widely used psychological tests.

Psychoanalysis The method of psychotherapy developed by Sigmund Freud.

Self-image A person's view of himself or herself, which may be quite different from an observer's perception of that person.

Stimulus Any object, action, or situation that causes a person or animal to respond in some way.

Survey research The gathering and assessing of data from large numbers of people by the use of questionnaires and sampling methods.

Transference The client's transferral to the therapist of past emotional attachments to parents or other significant figures.

Other psychologists include *correctional psychologists* (working with inmates of correctional institutions) and *sports psychologists* (working with athletes to help them overcome anxiety and become more motivated and competitive).

What Is It Like to Be a Psychologist?

After reviewing his notes on the murder case, Murphy glances through his calendar of appointments for the upcoming week. It will be a typical week of 10- to 12-hour workdays. His first patient will be here any minute for his 9:00 A.M. appointment. After this session, the entire 10-member professional staff will gather for their weekly two-hour meeting to discuss their cases with a senior consulting psychologist who is not a member of the practice. Murphy believes strongly in the importance of collegiality. It is all too easy for a psychotherapist to become isolated and overwhelmed.

After the group meeting, he goes out for lunch. Although the next client is not scheduled until 2:00 P.M., Murphy intends to return to the office early to do paperwork and return phone calls from insurance companies. He calculated recently that he was averaging an hour a day on the phone with insurance companies because of managed care. It is the hardest part of his job these days. (The goal of managed care is to contain health care costs by tightly regulating authorizations for treatment and reducing or eliminating reimbursement for treatment plans considered unnecessary or not cost-effective.)

Murphy will see clients in individual appointments this afternoon. He averages 25 to 30 direct-contact hours weekly with patients in his office. Since he has a very active consulting practice, he also spends many work hours out of the office—another 20 to 27 a week. Much of this time is devoted to work with various community training programs. Later this week, for instance, he will be advising the police department on its performance evaluation system. (Could the system be improved to offer greater motivation, and if so, how?) Next week, he will start a new project that will take him out of the office for two mornings a week for a month. He will be working with the city's management training program.

Murphy also does consulting at area hospitals, clinics, and hospices. Tomorrow he is scheduled for a consultation at a sleep-disorders clinic. Other clients include organizations that want his advice on health benefits and disability claims. There is also the criminal- and civil-court work. Courts and attorneys often request input from psychologists on matters ranging from custody disputes to insanity pleas. As a member of the American Psychological Association's ethics panel, Murphy is sometimes called on to testify as an expert witness in professional malpractice suits. A recent case he dealt with concerned a psychologist accused of having sexual relations with a client.

When Murphy started his undergraduate work at Emory University in Atlanta he was planning to become a doctor. He has always been drawn to the helping and healing professions. To his disappointment, however, he found premed course work unrewarding. Then he registered for a course in psychology and was fascinated. He became a psychology major.

Dr. Kathleen Hoover-Dempsey, developmental psychologist at Vanderbilt's Peabody College, had a less promising introduction to psychology. "It was the heyday of behavioral psychology," she recalls more than 30 years later. "I had a miserable psych course about rats, pigeons, and snakes." (An equivalency between animal and human behavior had been assumed.) Kathleen concluded that she was not interested in studying psychology.

After graduating as a political science major, she became an elementary schoolteacher and soon found herself wanting to learn more about how children learn, how they change over the course of their education, and how their family situations affect their development. She enrolled in graduate school to study developmental psychology.

After completing her Ph.D. at Michigan State, Kathleen remained in the academic world, teaching undergraduate and graduate students, and conducting research. Her current activities include directing Peabody's undergraduate major in child development and working with a team of faculty colleagues and graduate students on a long-term research project on parent/school/child relationships. She interviews parents about what they do (or don't do) to help their children succeed in school.

This project addresses such questions as how parents' views of their roles develop over their children's school years and how children's understandings of parental roles change. The evidence strongly suggests, Kathleen reports, that parents continue to be important to their children's school achievement and psychosocial development all through adolescence, contrary to some previous assumptions.

Do I Have What It Takes to Be a Psychologist?

The most important personal qualities for a successful career as a psychologist depend, in part, on which field of psychology you choose. Clinical and counseling psychologists (and others involved in direct patient care) must have emotional stability, patience, and excellent communication skills. You need to be people-oriented and enjoy helping others. If you are thinking of becoming a school psychologist you must enjoy working with children of all ages.

If you are planning to focus on research, you must have a logical mind and the ability to analyze data. You must also have patience for detail and precision. Computer skills are becoming increasingly important in psychological research. It is important for researchers and teachers to have good speaking and writing skills for communicating with both students and professional colleagues.

Since a master's degree is the minimal educational requirement and a doctorate is strongly recommended for psychologists in most fields, you need to be an above-average student who enjoys academic work and scientific inquiry.

"A psychologist should be good at asking the how-and-why questions," says Kathleen. "How does environment influence people's development? Why are some people more effective than others?" A strong curiosity about what makes people tick is basic for all psychologists, whether they are in applied or research fields, sums up Kathleen.

"A psychologist must have a desire to make sense out of chaos," is the way clinical psychologist Murphy puts it. "You need to have respect for scientific theory and empirical research." He comments that psychology is not the right career for people who want to help others but lack an interest in scientific research and analysis.

A psychologist must have a desire to make sense out of chaos. You need to have respect for scientific theory and empirical research.

How Do I Become a Psychologist?

EDUCATION

High School

If you are thinking of a career in psychology you should take well-balanced college preparatory courses in high school. Science and mathematics courses are an essential preparation for the scientific and quantitative work you will be doing later. English and communications courses are also important for developing verbal abilities. If your high school offers an introductory psychology course, that would be a good choice. Since Ph.D. programs generally require that students demonstrate a reading knowledge of two modern foreign languages, high school would be a good time to get started on French, German, or Spanish.

If you want some hands-on experience with the work that psychologists do, you might find volunteer opportunities or part-time jobs at hospitals, nursing homes, day care centers, or social service organizations.

Postsecondary Training

Your next step in becoming a psychologist is to earn a bachelor's degree at an accredited college or university. Nearly all colleges and universities offer a psychology major.

Although a bachelor's degree in psychology does not qualify a person to be a professional psychologist, the psychology major's communication and analytical skills and knowledge of the principles of human behavior are good preparation for employment in many fields, including business, sales, service industries, and administrative support. In fact, according to the American Psychological Association (APA), psychology is the second most popular undergraduate major behind business administration.

A bachelor's degree in psychology is the most obvious way to prepare for graduate work. It is not necessary, however, to major in psychology at the undergraduate level to become a psychologist. Some graduate programs require that applicants be psychology majors, but others welcome applicants with any major provided that they have had some undergraduate psychology courses, along with work in the social, biological, and physical sciences, mathematics, and statistics. Getting into a good graduate program is competitive.

A master's degree program typically lasts two years and, according to the APA, the most commonly required courses in the master's program are statistics, research design, and those courses with industrial/organizational content.

Doctoral degrees require two to five years of graduate work beyond the master's degree (or a total of four to seven years of graduate work if one enters a Ph.D. program without a master's degree). Early in the program you will probably take classes in the core areas of psychology. You will work with a professor and learn how to do research and study how this research is applied to certain situations. When you have completed the course work, you must pass a comprehensive exam and write a dissertation based on original research.

If you are going to be a clinical, counseling, or school psychologist, a year of supervised internship is also required.

The Psy.D., offered at some professional schools of psychology and some universities, is also an option if you want to work as a clinical, counseling, or school psychologist. The Psy.D. program is less research-oriented than the Ph.D. and puts more stress on clinical work. It usually does not require a dissertation. Instead, the degree is awarded on the basis of the successful completion of course work, supervised clinical/practical work, and examinations.

If you are going into clinical, counseling, or school psychology, it is important to earn a doctoral degree from an accredited institution. Membership in the APA requires that the doctoral degree (or equivalent) be from an accredited school. Most state licensing boards also have the same requirement, although some may require graduation from an accredited doctoral program in psychology. This is referred to as specialized accreditation and is granted by the APA Committee on Accreditation. This applies only to doctoral programs, internships, and postdoctoral residency programs in health service areas of professional psychology.

CERTIFICATION OR LICENSING

All states and the District of Columbia and Canada have licensing or certification requirements for clinical, counseling, and school psychologists who are involved in direct client care. Other psychologists in private practice, such as social psychologists, must also meet licensing or certification requirements. The precise requirements vary from state to state.

There are certifications available in certain specialties within psychology. You can earn the Certificate of Proficiency in the Treatment of Alcohol and Other Psychoactive Substance Use Disorders through the APA. The National Association of School Psychologists (NASP) also has a certification program for school psychologists.

SCHOLARSHIPS AND GRANTS

There are usually grants, scholarships, and loans available through most colleges. The easiest way to explore the various financial aid possibilities is to write directly to the financial aid offices of schools and request information and application forms. The APA and NASP Web sites list funding and scholarship opportunities for students. Graduate students also need to contact their psychology department for information about research and teaching assistantships.

Various loan programs are available through the federal government, including Pell Grants, Stafford Student Loans, National Direct Student Loans, Health Education Assistance Loans, and Health Professions Student Loans. Your high school guidance counselor should have information about these programs.

A good starting point for financial aid research is the SmartStudent Guide to Financial Aid Web site. This site has an extensive list of financial assistance information and links: http://www.finaid.org.

Who Will Hire Me?

When it comes time to look for your first professional position as a psychologist, your university placement office and the psychology professors you have worked with in your department (especially your dissertation adviser) may be able to help you.

You can also seek assistance from your internship supervisors and other contacts in clinical and academic settings. You can make useful connections by getting involved in professional organizations such as the APA. Professional publications and Web sites list job openings in psychology.

There are approximately 139,000 psychologists in the United States. According to the APA's 2001 survey of psychologists with Ph.D.'s, about 40 percent of graduates with Ph.D.'s were either self-employed

In-depth

All in a Day's Work

School psychologists are involved in the education and social atmospheres of schools. Here are a few things they do:

Assess: Use a wide variety of techniques to assess students' academic and social skills.

Intervene: Work with children and families to help solve conflicts through counseling and behavior management.

Prevent: Help foster tolerance for diversity and develop initiatives to make schools safer.

Educate: Develop programs on topics such as substance abuse and crisis management.

Research and Plan: Contribute to planning and evaluating schoolwide reform and restructuring.

Source: The National Association of School Psychologists

or worked for for-profit organizations. Thirty-five percent worked for academic institutions. The rest worked for non-profit organizations and state and local governments. The same survey reports that 69 percent of recent Ph.D. graduates were employed full time after graduation.

After gaining some work experience, many psychologists who have doctoral degrees go into individual or group private practice or set up research and consulting firms. Many psychologists employed by educational, clinical, or other institutions also see clients or do consulting on a part-time basis.

Where Can I Go from Here?

Advancement depends largely on the setting in which you work and your skills and initiative. In academic institutions, you are usually promoted from instructor to assistant professor to associate professor to full professor. Promotion is based on one's record of achievement in research and teaching.

Promotion to administrative positions is often the goal of psychologists working in business, industry, education, or government agencies. School psychologists may be promoted to direct pupil personnel services, special education programs, or a school system's psychological services.

Many psychologists advance by going into private practice as therapists or setting up consulting or research firms (on either a full-time or part-time basis). Clinical and consulting psychologists are likely to go into private practice, either as individuals or as groups.

According to the APA, the greatest range of jobs and the highest pay in psychology are available to doctoral graduates. For psychologists without doctorates, the route to advancement may be to return to graduate school to earn a Ph.D. or Psy.D.

What Are the Salary Ranges?

Psychologists with doctorates consistently earn more than psychologists with master's or bachelor's degrees. A 2001 survey by the APA revealed that the median salary for a psychologist with a doctorate working as assistant professors was about $43,000. Those working in research positions made median starting salaries of about $53,000 a year. Those working in human services in schools made median starting salaries of about $57,000. The APA also reports that psychologists working as full professors with more

To Be a Successful Psychologist, You Should . . .

- have emotional stability and patience
- be good at asking "how and why" questions
- have excellent speaking and writing skills
- be able to analyze complicated data
- be curious about what makes people tick

than 12 years of experience make more than $90,000 a year.

The U.S. Department of Labor (USDL) reports that clinical, counseling, and school psychologists made median annual salaries of $53,230 in 2003. The lowest paid 10 percent made less than $31,250, and the highest paid 10 percent made more than $88,930. The USDL reports that industrial-organizational psychologists made median salaries of $67,740 a year in 2003, with the middle 50 percent making between $52,730 and $85,120 a year.

What Is the Job Outlook?

According to the U.S. Department of Labor, employment of psychologists is expected to grow faster than the average for all occupations as the demand for psychological services grows in schools, hospitals, and other settings. Employment opportunities are expected to be particularly good in school settings, as there is an increased awareness of how developmental problems affect students' ability to learn. Research and data collection jobs should also be a good employment field for all psychology majors.

Those with advanced degrees in school psychology should have the best prospects, according to the *Occupational Outlook Handbook,* as schools are expected to increase student counseling and mental health services. In addition, a master's degree in industrial/organizational psychology will open employment opportunities.

How Do I Learn More?

PROFESSIONAL ORGANIZATIONS

The following are organizations that have information on careers in psychology:

American Psychological Association
750 First Street, NE
Washington, DC 20002
800-374-2721
http://www.apa.org

American Psychological Society
1010 Vermont Avenue, NW, Suite 1100
Washington, DC 20005
202-783-2077
http://www.psychologicalscience.org

The National Association of School Psychologists
4340 East West Highway, Suite 402
Bethesda, MD 20814
301-657-0270
http://www.nasponline.org

BIBLIOGRAPHY

The following is a sampling of materials relating to the professional concerns and development of psychologists:

Buskist, William, and Thomas R. Sherburne. *Preparing for Graduate Study in Psychology: 101 Questions and Answers.* Needham Heights, Mass.: Allyn & Bacon, 1995.

Coon, Dennis. *Introduction to Psychology: Gateways to Mind and Behavior.* 10th ed. Belmont, Calif.: Wadsworth Publishing, 2003.

DeGalan, Julie and Stephen Lambert. *Great Jobs for Psychology Majors.* 2d ed. New York: McGraw-Hill, 2000.

Grodzki, Lynn. *Building Your Ideal Private Practice: A Guide for Therapists and Other Healing Professionals.* New York: W. W. Norton, 2000.

Hess, Allen K., and Irving B. Weiner, eds. *The Handbook of Forensic Psychology.* 2d ed. New York: John Wiley & Sons, 1999.

Perlman, Stuart D. *The Therapist's Emotional Survival: Dealing with the Pain of Exploring Trauma.* Northvale, N.J.: Jason Aronson, 1999.

Sayette, Michael A., Tracy J. Mayne, and John C. Norcross. *Insider's Guide to Graduate Programs in Clinical and Counseling Psychology.* Rev. ed. New York: Guilford Press, 2004.

Sternberg, Robert J. *Career Paths in Psychology: Where Your Degree Can Take You.* Washington, D.C.: American Psychological Association, 1997.

Yalom, Irwin D. *Love's Executioner and Other Tales of Psychotherapy.* New York: HarperCollins, 2000.

PUBLIC HEALTH WORKERS

Mark Macchiano conducts routine inspections of restaurants and investigates reports of food-related illnesses for the McHenry County Health Department in northern Illinois. "I remember one restaurant where there was a party and over 70 people became ill," he says. We didn't know at first what was going on. Was it in the water, or maybe in the ice? Was the contaminated food still being served? It's hard to locate one source of bacteria, though. We tried to contact all the people that had been there and find out their symptoms."

Mark checked food storage and preparation methods, water quality, and sanitation practices, such as hand washing and garbage disposal. He says, "We basically tried to paint a picture of what most likely happened. It appeared to be the way the food was cooled down, combined with poor personal hygiene, and cross-contamination of bad chicken and lettuce."

Definition
Public health workers are health care professionals employed in the public sector. They are involved in the prevention and control of illness or disease, and in the promotion of health in the general population. Public health workers incorporate virtually all health care professions.

High School Subjects
Biology
Chemistry

Personal Skills
Helping/teaching
Technical/scientific

Salary Range
$24,770 to $53,660 to $137,670+

Educational Requirements
The same requirements needed to practice any health care profession in the private sector are required for public health workers.

Certification or Licensing
The same certifications or licenses in the private sector are required for public health workers.

Outlook
Faster than the average

DOT
N/A

GOE
NA

NOC
N/A

O*NET-SOC
NA

What Does a Public Health Worker Do?

Public health workers are many different health professionals who have a variety of expertise and education. Almost any health professional that works in the private sector—nurses, doctors, technicians, researchers, therapists, counselors, aides—may be employed in the public health area as well. Public health workers generally work for government-funded institutions, agencies, or departments. Their services are usually community-based. They interact with huge and diverse populations within a community. Public health services may also be part of the care provided by some private organizations.

One of the focuses behind public health is preventive medicine. According to the National Association of County and City Health Officials, public health workers' efforts help assure the quality and accessibility of health services to everyone in the community. They focus on preventing epidemics and the spread of disease. They help protect against environmental hazards, and they promote and encourage healthy behaviors and mental health. They also respond to disasters and assist communities with their recovery efforts.

Several specific jobs fall under the heading of public health. *Health officers* act as chief administrative officers of local health departments. They create policies for health care in the community and are responsible for recognizing the needs of the community. They advise residents and elected officials of ways to improve the community's health. Other responsibilities include creating appropriate community programs and monitoring the budget and program results. In about half of the states, health officers are required to be licensed medical practitioners for that state, and in the other half, non-physicians with administrative backgrounds may hold this position. A few states have no formal requirements.

Community health center administrators perform functions similar to a health officer, but on a slightly larger scale. They coordinate public health efforts and direct other health care workers in their states. They also enforce state health regulations.

Public health nurses, physicians, dentists, and medical assistants generally work in the same capacity as private-sector members of their professions. However, they add community-based prevention to their focus. They are involved in the primary care of their patients as well as educating them about health issues. *Public health physicians* may be assigned to a specific population that is underserved by the medical community. Or, they may concentrate on a specific problem that faces the community, such as sexually transmitted diseases.

Public health dentists treat residents of state institutions or patients at local clinics. *Public health nurses* may be responsible for the immunization of school children and the neonatal training of expectant parents. *Public health medical assistants* carry out various tasks, from scheduling patients in community clinics to giving routine physicals.

Public health nurse practitioners provide evaluations and treatment plans for clients. They also conduct regular checkups and provide counseling. *Public health nurse-midwives* assist with childbirth and the care of newborns. *Public health nutritionists* inform people about proper diet and nutrition. They oversee some institutional food preparation areas, and educate food service workers. Nutritionists act as advisers to other health care workers. They may also educate community members about specific nutritional needs.

Public health workers also provide counseling and referrals. They analyze each client's situation, determine a cause or factor for the client's illness, make sure that the client has access to the proper care, and then address the problem within the larger framework of the community.

In addition to medical programs, some public health professionals work with environmental health issues. There are many types of careers involved in maintaining safe water, air, and food. *Environmental specialists* conduct surveys, inspections, and investigations to ensure compliance with environmental safety guidelines and laws. Environment, in this instance, can mean the water in a fishing pond or community pool, the air quality in a school building, or the soil in a local park.

Epidemiologists, or *public health investigators,* work with those exposed to outbreaks of certain diseases. They work to control the spread of an illness and give assistance to those who are affected. Epidemiologists develop policies and procedures for investigations, analyze incidents of outbreak, and advise other health care professionals about public health concerns.

Registered sanitarians regularly inspect restaurants, grocery stores, and any other place food is sold or served to the public.

Most public health providers are involved in public education as well. Many create programs to emphasize good health in their communities, such as sponsoring a wellness day or a mobile blood-pressure testing unit. Public health workers may also speak to schools and civic groups to educate people about the dangers of unhealthy behaviors, or about the benefits of regular health screenings. *Community health educators* coordinate these programs and use the media to promote public health issues in their communities. They provide health education materials, determine attitudes about health in their communities, identify and advertise available health resources, and train other people in health education.

Public health also includes social workers. *Caseworkers* often help people determine their eligibility for support from government-assisted programs and other agencies. *Case coordinators* help people apply for Medicaid, and may provide child care and transportation for clients who need public health assistance resources. They also target populations for outreach and intervention programs. *Social workers* work with state agencies as advocates for the mental and physical health of their clients. They may investigate cases of reported abuse, provide protective services for the abused or neglected, or counsel families on proper child care.

What Is It Like to Be a Public Health Worker?

Public health is a huge job and it takes many skilled and dedicated professionals to make it work. Where does it begin? One of the major concerns for public health workers is prevention of disease. Primary care

Lingo to Learn

Accessible care The ease with which a patient can initiate interaction with a health care worker for any health problem. It takes into account efforts to eliminate barriers such as those posed by geography, administrative tasks, financing, culture, and language.

Botulism Acute food poisoning caused by a toxic by-product of bacteria. Characterized by muscle weakness and paralysis, disturbances of vision, slurred speech, or difficulty swallowing.

Communicable disease A disease capable of being transmitted from one person to another; diseases may be airborne, bloodborne, distributed through direct contact or contamination, or sexually transmitted.

Epidemiology The study of diseases affecting many people at one time, how they spread, and their origins.

Reportable diseases A list of approximately 30 communicable diseases whose outbreaks in the community must by law be reported to local health officials. This list includes rabies, typhoid, hepatitis, and tuberculosis.

doctors are in the business of prevention, as are public health nurses and educators. Janie Weller is a public health nurse at the Delta Public Health Center in Delta Junction, Alaska. "It's not really a center, it's a 9-by-13 [foot] room!" she laughs. Janie serves a community of about 1,200 in the heart of Alaska, and she deals mainly with children and parents. "One of the things I do is immunizations. There is a big focus on children from birth to age five, because that's when they are developing so much and undergoing so much change." She also conducts well-child checkups and health screening. "We look for illnesses, especially tuberculosis, or exposure to Hepatitis A. I also work with pregnant teens and new moms. I teach childbirth classes and I do testing and counseling. I make sure people are plugged into the appropriate programs."

It seems like a lot of work, particularly since Janie works alone with only occasional volunteer support. "It forces you to be pretty creative in the programs you set up and work on," she says, adding that she still hopes to hire a full-time person to help her with the clerical duties that consume so much of her time. Janie likes the flexibility that being a public health nurse gives her. "I've recently gotten into parenting. I've enjoyed that and have created a parenting group that is more for moms' mental health than anything else."

In addition to providing flexibility and autonomy, working within a smaller community also allows Janie to keep track of her clients more closely. She can see if what she has suggested is working, and she is able to maintain contact with those she has treated. "In a large town you might see a person, suggest something, and never see them again. You don't know how they're doing. In Delta, I experience a lot of closeness with the people. I have the chance to establish a good working relationship with them." If Janie encounters something beyond her scope of practice, she refers clients to the local doctor. "He gets the emergencies," she says. "In fact, some people like to come and see me for the easy stuff, because my schedule is not so hectic. I have time to talk to them."

Janie works mostly out of her small office, but she also makes visits to local schools and travels to workshops that may be held out of town. She visits a village called Dot Lake, approximately 90 miles away, about once a month to provide health services for its residents. In Alaska, many communities are severely underserved, and traveling nurses may serve many small towns that do not have enough money to support a full-time public health nurse.

Another job at the preventive end of the public health spectrum is that of registered sanitarian. Mark Macchiano, sanitarian for the McHenry County Health Department in northern Illinois, conducts routine inspections of eating establishments and advises them on their food preparation and storage methods. Mark is also responsible for inspecting septic systems and water wells that are being installed for homes not connected to the public sewage systems.

The typical day for Mark, if there is such a thing, usually begins with planning the day. "You never really know where you will end up," he says. "We investigate complaints and do regular checkups on the restaurants we are responsible for." In a normal inspection of a food service establishment, Mark checks the temperature at which food is stored; ensures the availability of hand-washing materials and the regularity with which the staff washes their hands; watches for unsafe practices, such as using hand-washing sinks for food disposal; checks for a correct Ph balance and cleanliness of washing water; and performs other routine investigations. "We do have a lab that does water testing," he says, "but we don't use much hard science out there. Most of it is common sense. Are people washing their hands? Are the employees sick?"

Mark finds that most places are cooperative but he mentions that many owners and workers see him as the enemy. "We're trying to change that," he says. "Personally, I try to educate people as much as I can as to why they need our inspections, why specific regulations are important, and so on. I take the inspection as an opportunity to let people know that we're working with them, not trying to close them down."

Despite the watchful eyes of Mark and his coworkers, episodes of contamination still occur. When that happens, Mark's job becomes more intervention-oriented. "If they score a 60 or below on a regular inspection, they must be shut down by the director of the department," Mark notes. "Most owners will close down when we ask them to. Then we try to identify the cause. If 10 people got sick here, what made them sick? We might take food samples to the lab for testing; we might have them throw out all of their open food; we might have them clean everything. We will also interview the cooks and ask them questions about meal preparation and storage."

While Mark is working it is important that he set a good example for the workers of the establishment. "If I'm going to be taking temperatures of their meat, I make sure I wash my hands well before I handle their food. We have to watch ourselves and see what message we're sending as regulators."

Mark's office also fields many questions. "We answer what we can and refer some to other agencies like the Occupational Safety and Health Organization or the Environmental Protection Agency." He states, "The office also provides some instructions on how to keep food safe in the home as well as ways to care for septic systems and wells." Mark sometimes attends wellness fairs, where he promotes general knowledge of public health issues and information about the job he does for his community.

If a sanitarian discovers a disease outbreak in Karen Moore's region of suburban Cook County, Illinois, chances are that she will be on the scene, too. Karen is an epidemiologist and public health investigator in communicable diseases for the Cook County Department of Health. Her job often takes her to restaurants and other sites of suspected outbreaks of disease. Her job is to identify the source of the illness and how it was spread, eliminate the cause, and investigate those people who may have been exposed to the source. She then provides treatment information to exposed persons or health care professionals. She might investigate outbreaks of lice in schools or a case of typhoid reported by hospital workers. There are about 30 diseases that by law must be reported to the county health department, including meningitis, hepatitis, and typhoid. Karen also investigates cases of botulism from food service establishments in her region.

"For food-borne diseases, outbreaks are defined as two or more people sick from the same establishment who have not shared any other meals for the past 72 hours," explains Karen. "If there is evidence of an outbreak, I'm the first one called out to investigate. I usually go with an environmental inspector and a health inspector." She adds, "We interview ill persons. We ask them what they ate, whom they were with, how soon they got sick, what kind of symptoms they had, and request any other information about anyone else that was there. I ask the manager if any of his employees were sick, look for hand-washing procedures that may or may not be in use, or anything that might fill in the picture."

In cases that are not readily identified as restaurant contamination, the questions must be just as thorough, and sometimes more personal. Karen says, "We ask, where do you work? Where do you buy your groceries? Because of confidentiality, we can't say 'Did so-and-so down the block baby-sit for you this week,' but we can ask if they have small children and questions like that." Even though epidemiology involves a lot of phone work from the office, as well as substantial written documentation of events, it still requires investigative work and creative thinking. Karen states, "For the most part you're somewhat of a detective, and you have to have a certain amount of intuition about asking the questions that will give you the whole picture."

How does Karen find out about an outbreak? Sometimes citizens call in complaints about an establishment; sometimes hospitals report cases of diseases; sometimes potentially contaminated establishments call if they have been hearing health complaints related to their business. After she knows about an outbreak, Karen does what she can to intervene in the situation and prevent the further spread of the disease.

Janie, Mark, and Karen all find that the best part of their jobs is the satisfaction that they are truly helping to make a difference in the quality of life in their communities. Additionally, Karen likes to be able to relieve people's fears. "A parent might call and say they just found out their child has lice. It seems like a little thing but if you don't know anything about it, it can be very scary. I like being able to make people feel better. If they are informed, they feel safer."

All seem to appreciate the variety their jobs have. "It's never the same day twice," Mark says, and Karen agrees, saying, "My work is almost seasonal—summer for me is a busy, food-born illness season, but fall will bring something else. It's always changing."

FYI

The problem of overweight and obese children and adolescents has nearly doubled since 1980. This weight problem is also increasing in adults. Being overweight or obese increases the risk of many illnesses including diabetes, high blood pressure, high cholesterol, heart disease, and stroke.

Do I Have What It Takes to Be a Public Health Worker?

A public health worker must have many of the attributes that a medical worker in the private sector needs. You must have compassion for people and be able to relate to all social levels. You must be detail-oriented and able to keep accurate records. Flexibility is also important. Many days your job will take an unexpected turn and the best-laid plans become only a dream. You should like to learn and be a voracious reader. It is important that you remain knowledgeable about current laws, government social issues, and newly developed treatments and drugs. You must also be an educator and be willing and able to share your knowledge with others. You must be tactful and able to communicate with others without being judgmental.

Mark believes that patience is very important for anyone who will be working with the public. You also need to be able to work well with colleagues. "Public health is really a team effort. In our office everyone is pretty compatible, and that helps."

Public health workers need problem-solving skills and the ability to think creatively. "As a public health investigator, you have to be quick with information, be able to speak off the top of your head," says Karen. "You deal with professionals all day who are asking your advice. 'How do I approach this situation?' or 'What are the guidelines for this disease?'" Karen also notes that you should have excellent communication and listening skills, as well as empathy.

In addition, Janie says, "You need to have organizational skills to deal with the paperwork required to document public health records. Above all," she emphasizes, "you must have the sincere desire to help people live better lives. This is a key characteristic for a public health worker."

How Do I Become a Public Health Worker?

EDUCATION

Some careers, such as that of public health physician, require much more education than others. For educational requirements for specific careers, see the chapters pertaining to those careers in the private sector. Administrative positions generally require a master's degree or extensive experience in either administration or in the specialty under consideration. Technical aides or assistants may require less education initially, but in most cases it is difficult to advance without a four-year degree.

High School

Public health careers are varied and have a wide range of educational requirements. However, if you take college preparatory courses you will have a good foundation to enter any higher education program. Certainly communication, written and oral, is a part of every public health job. Classes in biology, chemistry, health, social sciences, and psychology will help you understand the nature of diseases and other problems that face communities and the nation at large. Computer science courses are also essential.

Volunteering for public service agencies or in medical facilities while in high school is an excellent way to discover the different aspects of public health.

Postsecondary Training

Higher education requirements are determined by the public health field you wish to enter. Karen, Mark, and Janie all have their bachelor's degrees and agree that most positions in public health require at least that level of education.

Some health careers require a specialized training program; others require undergraduate, graduate, and doctoral degrees. Refer to the requirements listed in this book for the specific profession you are interested in.

CERTIFICATION OR LICENSING

In general, you need to fulfill the same licensing requirements for your profession in public health as you would if you practiced in the private sector. For instance, physicians must be licensed by the state in which they practice. Likewise, if your profession, as practiced in the private sector, requires certification by a professional association, then you need that certification.

Mark is a registered sanitarian and he must take continuing education courses in order to keep his license. The same is true for Janie and Karen, and for most workers in this industry.

SCHOLARSHIPS AND GRANTS

Tuition costs vary depending upon the size of the school, whether or not the school is in the state where you reside, and whether the school is privately or publicly funded. The profession you choose will also determine your costs.

There are usually grants, scholarships, and loans available through most colleges. The easiest way to explore the various financial aid possibilities is to write directly to the financial aid offices of schools and request information and application forms.

There are also various loan programs available through the federal government, including Pell Grants, Stafford Student Loans, National Direct Student Loans, Health Education Assistance Loans, and Health Professions Student Loans. Your high school guidance counselor should have information about these programs.

FYI

More than 6 million illnesses and 9,000 deaths in the United States are believed to be food related. The National Association of County and City Health Officials works to address food safety issues by distributing food safety materials and promoting food safety practices.

Many public and private organizations and businesses offer scholarships as well. Libraries, the Internet, and your guidance office should be able to provide you with more information. A good starting point for financial aid research is the SmartStudent Guide to Financial Aid Web site. This site has an extensive list of financial assistance information and links: http://www.finaid.org.

INTERNSHIPS AND VOLUNTEERSHIPS

Internships are usually required for public health careers. Karen wrote protection orders for a domestic violence clinic; Janie worked a nurse internship in a hospital, rotating among several units including intensive care, pediatrics, and emergency medicine. Though neither is directly involved in the area of their internship anymore, both believe it was invaluable for teaching them what they wanted out of a career in public health.

"Seeing all the sick people, I decided to be on the well-people end of things," Janie recalls. "The people who want to see me generally want my help. They're interested in learning. I find this pace much better for me than hospital nursing was. Also, when you're in a hospital, you have a lot of other nurses and doctors telling you what to do all the time. I'm pretty unsupervised here in Delta."

Karen found out about her first job by way of her position as an intern. She ended up working for the sexually transmitted disease (STD) department of her facility, and her experiences with survivors of domestic violence as well as work in STD control gave her insight into how to deal with the public. In effect, experience is the best education after one has received a bachelor's degree.

> The people who want to see me generally want my help. They're interested in learning.

Who Will Hire Me?

State and federal departments of health are the primary employers of public health workers. Numerous other facilities also exist to promote health among various populations and most of these facilities rely on grant money and other government funding to operate.

Calling local health departments will give you an idea of the jobs available in your area and can help you determine the qualifications that each field or department requires. The U.S. Department of Health and Human Services can provide a national overview of available jobs. The department also has information on several operating divisions, including the Food and Drug Administration and the Centers for Disease Control and Prevention.

You should contact state employment agencies as well as call the agencies where you would like to work. Janie moved to Delta shortly after they had already hired a public health nurse. She then got to know the nurse and her supervisor. When the nurse left, Janie already knew the person who was in charge of hiring a new public health nurse. Similarly, Karen stepped into the epidemiology department as a volunteer while the regular epidemiologist took a maternity leave.

Where Can I Go from Here?

Though some public health workers find jobs as consultants in the private sector, many choose to stay in public health for the same reason they started there: to benefit the whole population.

As with any other profession, you may choose to further your education in order to create additional advancement opportunities. Karen points out that although her employer does not offer tuition reimbursement, it does allow flexible hours for those who commit to extra schooling.

One route of advancement may be in administration. Administrative positions generally require more education and experience. As an administrator, you may create health policies, such as deciding to focus on a particular disease that is showing signs of emerging as an epidemic. You may be given responsibility for a region or department. You may write proposals for grant money, allocate funds for the development of projects, or identify a far-reaching goal of public health workers and implement a program to address a specific problem.

State and federal government agencies often offer many advancement opportunities to their workers who demonstrate excellent skills and professional commitment.

What Are the Salary Ranges?

Salary ranges are as broad as the careers of public health workers. As in most industries, those workers who have higher education levels, more experience, and greater responsibility generally command higher salaries.

Salaries are based on the relevant field, amount of education and experience, area of the country, and length of time in the same position. Salaries for jobs in public health are generally less than those for equivalent jobs in the private sector. The benefits, however, are usually competitive or better than those found in private-sector health care jobs.

According to the Bureau of Labor Statistics (BLS), public health social workers and health educators average $39,160 annually. Salaries range from less than $24,770 to more than $58,030 a year. The BLS reports the average salary for epidemiologists as $53,660. Physicians who are general practitioners earned a median annual salary of $137,670 in 2003.

Benefits such as insurance, sick leave, and vacation are usually standard for full-time workers. Some government jobs also provide retirement plans.

What Is the Job Outlook?

Public health and social services are a huge concern in the United States. According to the Bureau of Labor Statistics, occupations in the social services are expected to be some of the fastest growing in the nation, with growth of about 49 percent in the industry, compared to 16 percent growth for all industries combined. In addition, the bureau predicts that employment in the health services industry will also experience rapid growth in the next decade.

Growth is also predicted because of expanded services for the elderly, the mentally and physically disabled, and families in crisis. The increasing elderly population will generate a need for more social and community health services. In addition, the continuing influx of immigrants will continue to place demands on public health services and health education programs.

Many Americans believe that everybody has the right to good health, and it is also increasingly recognized that the availability of health care and health education are important factors in some of the social problems faced today. In response to this realization, public health is enjoying some attention that it had not traditionally received. "People might not know what an epidemiologist is, but if I say I am from the Public Health Department, they recognize that. Most people are really cooperative and glad to see us," notes Karen.

Despite the growth predictions, it should be noted that health care in general is experiencing some budget constraints, and public health is not excluded from the critical eyes of those who finance it. Many public health jobs depend on grants and government funding.

How Do I Learn More?

PROFESSIONAL ORGANIZATIONS

The following organization provides information on careers in public health:

National Association of County & City Health Officials
1100 17th Street, 2nd Floor
Washington, DC 20036
202-783-5550
http://www.naccho.org

The U.S. Department of Health and Human Services has several agencies and institutions devoted to public health. Most provide information concerning their specific area. For general information contact

U.S. Department of Health and Human Services
200 Independence Avenue, SW
Washington, DC 0201
202-619-0257
http://www.os.dhhs.gov

Some of the agencies and institutions of the U.S. Department of Health and Human Services are:

Agency for Healthcare Research and Quality
540 Gaither Road
Rockville, MD 20850
301-427-1364
info@ahrq.gov
http://www.ahcpr.gov

Agency for Toxic Substances and Disease Registry
1600 Clifton Road, NE
Atlanta, GA 30333
888-422-8737
ATSDRIC@cdc.gov
http://www.atsdr.cdc.gov

Centers for Disease Control and Prevention
1600 Clifton Road, NE
Atlanta, GA 30333
404-639-3534
http://www.cdc.gov

Food and Drug Administration
5600 Fishers Lane
Rockville, MD 20857
888-463-6332
http://www.fda.gov

Health Resources and Services Administration
5600 Fishers Lane
Parklawn Building
Rockville, MD 20857
301-443-3376
http://www.hrsa.gov

National Institutes of Health
9000 Rockville Pike
Bethesda, MD 20892
301-496-4000
nihinfo@od.nih.gov
http://www.nih.gov

The following federal agency also deals with public health concerns:

U.S. Environmental Protection Agency
1200 Pennsylvania Avenue, NW
Washington, DC 20460
202-272-0167
http://www.epa.gov

BIBLIOGRAPHY

The following is a sampling of materials relating to the professional concerns and development of public health workers:

Garrett, Laurie. *Betrayal of Trust: The Collapse of Global Public Health*. New York: Hyperion, 2001.

International Medical Publishing Staff. *Healthy People 2010.* Washington, D.C.: International Medical Publishing, 2001.

Snook, I. Donald, and Leo D'Orazio. *Opportunities in Health and Medical Careers.* New York: McGraw-Hill, 2004.

Tarlov, Alvin R., and Robert F. St. Peter, eds. *The Society and Population Health Reader, Volume 2: A State Perspective.* New York: New Press, 2000.

Teutsch, Steven M., and R. Elliott Churchill, eds. *Principles and Practice of Public Health Surveillance.* 2d ed. New York: Oxford University Press, 2000.

Tulchinsky, Ted, and Elena A. Varavikova. *The New Public Health: An Introduction for the 21st Century.* Burlington, Mass.: Academic Press, 2000.

Turnock, Bernard J. *Public Health: What It Is and How It Works.* 3d ed. Sudbury, Mass.: Joes and Bartlett, 2000.

RADIOLOGIC TECHNOLOGISTS

A boy, frightened and still wearing his baseball cap and uniform, is wheeled into radiology. The radiologic technologist, who has significant experience in dealing with worried young children, instinctively knows that the best way to calm the boy and accomplish her job is to divert his attention from his throbbing leg.

With a smile and a few quick questions, she learns the boy's name—Billy; the position he plays—pitcher and sometimes second base; and his team's record—not that great.

The boy grows more relaxed as she explains the X-ray procedure. As she talks, she positions the boy beneath the X-ray camera for the optimum filming angle. She sets the controls of the X-ray machine so as to be able to produce a picture of the correct density, contrast, and detail. She then adjusts a columnator, which is a knob that reduces the size of the X-ray area, therefore ensuring that the boy's leg will be exposed to the least amount of radiation for the shortest duration of time.

The radiologic technologist is acutely aware of the potential harmful effects of the radiation on both herself and the boy, and as a result, she wears protective clothing and a radiation badge as a matter of rule. Most importantly, she properly and professionally covers the boy with lead shielding before beginning the procedure. She makes the exposure, removes the film so that it can be developed, and then tells the boy the procedure is complete.

Billy is wheeled away and she reloads the "bucky" with X-ray film and prepares for her next assignment. Before the day is over, she will have completed 20 to 25 X-ray procedures; among those are scans that reveal broken bones, chest examinations, lung cancer, and pneumonia, as well as scans to determine problems in the spinal column, kidneys, and upper and lower gastrointestinal tract.

As a result of his fracture, the boy will be lost to his team for the rest of the season, but his leg will heal perfectly as the result of the technologist's competent imaging, which provided the physician with the precise view he needed to accurately set the broken bone and begin the healing process.

Definition
Radiologic technologists operate equipment that creates an image of the human body for the purpose of medical diagnosis. They are responsible for accurately positioning the patient and ensuring that the minimum amount of radiation is used to produce a quality diagnostic image.

Alternative Job Titles
Radiographers
X-ray technologists

High School Subjects
Health
Mathematics
Physics

Personal Skills
Helping/teaching
Technical/scientific

Salary Range
$29,340 to $41,850 to $58,300

Minimum Educational Level
Associate's degree

Certification or Licensing
Required by all states

Outlook
Faster than the average

DOT
078

GOE
14.05.01

NOC
3215

O*NET-SOC
29-2034.01

What Does a Radiologic Technologist Do?

Radiologic technologists, sometimes called *radiographers* or *X-ray technologists,* operate equipment that creates images of the human body for the purpose of medical diagnosis. Since all work is done at the request and under the supervision of a supervisor, radiologist, or attending physician, radiologic technologists do not complete any procedures on their own.

To do their job, radiologic technologists, or RTs, must help prepare the patient by explaining the procedure and answering any questions the patient might have. In some instances, an RT may administer, under the supervision of a radiologist, a substance called a contrast medium, which is usually barium sulfate given orally or rectally, so as to make specific body parts, such as the kidney or abdomen, better able to be viewed. They must also make sure that the patient is free of jewelry or any other metal that would obstruct the X-ray process. RTs position the person sitting, standing, or lying so that the correct view of the body can be radiographed. Technologists are also responsible for protecting the test subject from radiation, covering adjacent areas with lead shielding. Special attention and protection is given to the very young and women in their childbearing years, since they are the most susceptible to the effects of radiation. Radiologic technologists are keenly aware of the welfare of the patient in relation to radiation, ascribing to the term "ALARA," which means, "as low as reasonably allowable."

The technologist is responsible for the positioning of the X-ray equipment at the proper angle and distance from the part to be radiographed, and determining exposure time based on the location of the bone or organ and the thickness of the body in that area. Universal formulas that relate to body weight, degree of illness, and density of tissue and bone exist to help the RT determine the appropriate settings. The RT must set the controls of the X-ray machine to produce pictures of the correct contrast, detail, and density. The RT then places the photographic film on the far side of the patient's body to make the necessary exposures. The film is then developed for the radiologist or other physician to interpret.

Secondary duties for RTs may include the performance of routine administrative tasks such as maintaining patient files and keeping detailed records of equipment maintenance and usage. RTs may also be responsible for managing a radiation quality assurance program and, with considerable experience, manage other technologists in regard to work schedules and assignment of duties.

Lingo to Learn

Bucky The tray in which X-ray film is loaded.

Columnator A dial on the X-ray machinery that controls and adjusts the area of radiation exposure.

Contrast medium A solution of barium sulfate that is administered orally or rectally to highlight organs such as the abdomen, which normally can't be distinguished. This medium is used for upper and lower gastrointestinal examinations(GIs).

Diagnostic imaging Preliminary testing of the body tissues and skeletal structures through the use of X rays, sound waves, tomographic scans, and magnetic scans.

Fluoroscopy A procedure that examines the upper or lower gastrointestinal areas.

Pigastat A device used for children that immobilizes them during an examination, lifting arms and holding them in place.

Radiographs X-ray films.

What Is It Like to Be a Radiologic Technologist?

Diane Libertini has been a radiologic technologist for 25 years and has worked in hospitals and in private practice. Currently, she works at an imaging center, where she works as a billing manager and quality control manager and also performs mammograms. "Before you see the first patient," Diane says, "you must perform quality control tests on the CT [computerized tomography] machine, mammo machine, and processors. We have one CT room, one tomographic/radiographic room, one flouroscopy/radiographic room, one sonogram room, one mammogram room, one DEXA [dual energy X-ray absorptiometry, which measures bone mass], and a nuclear medicine department." The technologists must rotate through the different rooms each day. "We begin seeing patients at 8:30. We start with the patients who must be without food and water and do the exams that require prep first. The CT room begins by feeding the patients who need an oral contrast and then waiting one hour to scan the patient."

While waiting, scans not requiring prep can be performed. A CT scan takes from 15 minutes to over an hour. "Each CT is set up on a computer," Diane explains. "A machine scans the patient, making 360 degrees around the patient. We usually perform five to seven CTs per day."

Technologists also perform IVPs (intravenous pyelograms), diagnostic X rays of the kidneys, ureters, and bladder. "The tomographic/radiographic room is used for IVPs," Diane says. "You inject a contrast material and then take timed pictures of the urinary tract. These tests are done first thing in the morning and usually take one hour. In this room, the X-ray tube moves in a linear fashion."

The fluoroscopy/radiographic room is reserved for prepped tests such as upper GIs, (gastrointestinal), which are X-ray examinations of the esophagus and stomach. "The fluoroscopy unit allows the radiologist to watch as the test is being done. The tests require a contrast material called barium to be administered. The oral cholecystogram requires pills to be taken ahead of time to show up the gallbladder. Each of these takes about 30 minutes, and we schedule four or so a day."

The imaging center schedules many mammograms (X rays of the breast) throughout the day, one every 15 minutes. "The screening mammogram consists of four images. Each patient leaves with a preliminary report. The radiologist must check and speak to every patient."

Common tests performed in the sonogram room are pelvic, obstetrical, and breast sonograms. This exam uses sound waves instead of X ray. "We also do vascular sonograms that measure flow and velocity of the blood. Each patient receives their results before they leave and they talk to the radiologist." In the DEXA room, 20-minute tests are performed that involve a small amount of X ray to take a picture of the hip and lumbar spine.

The nuclear medicine department requires a specially licensed technologist. "Each patient is injected with a small amount of radioactive isotope and the images are obtained with a gamma camera."

Diane says each technologist is also expected to take on front desk duties. Her schedule is 6:30 A.M. to 3:30 P.M. Monday through Friday, with every other Friday off.

Do I Have What It Takes to Be a Radiologic Technologist?

Radiologic technologists should be skilled at technical work and have a mastery of medical technology. They must enjoy helping and working with the sick, who are sometimes worried or frightened. Clearly, a personal touch is mandatory for success in the field. "It's a 'people' business," Diane says, "where the people are often being sick, scared, and not wanting to be at the doctor's office. You must be very patient, very detail oriented, and willing to work late if an emergency comes up."

> It's a "people" business, where the people are often being sick, scared, and not wanting to be at the doctor's office.

Communication skills, as previously mentioned, play a significant role in an RT's daily duties. The RT must be able to relay information to radiologists and other technologists, and help patients into the proper position so a procedure can be completed.

Prospective RTs should be aware of the repetitiveness of the job and that RTs spend long hours on their feet and are subject to frequent overtime. The physical stress of lifting and moving patients and the emotional stress, especially in a hospital setting, of knowing a patient, sometimes a child, has a life-threatening illness can be difficult.

FYI

A beam of tiny particles from the nuclei of atoms might help cure some cancers. In boron neutron capture therapy, the patient is injected with a boron compound. The compound accumulates in cancerous tumors only. A nuclear reactor or particle accelerator is used to generate a beam of neutrons, which is focused on the cancerous area. The beam stimulates the boron compound, which kills the cancer cells but does no harm to healthy tissue.

"You are exposed to radiation," Diane points out, "so there is an element of hazardous duty. Also, some techs have developed chemical allergies to the darkroom chemicals." RTs wear lead aprons when performing fluoroscopies and other procedures. They also wear radiation badges that are checked once a month for exposure levels. In terms of disease exposure, RTs prescribe to universal standards when dealing with diseases such as AIDS, hepatitis, and tuberculosis, wearing rubber gloves, gowns, and masks to maintain health and safety standards. Although radiation and disease pose a risk, RTs can be diligent and aware so as to avoid exposure in the fulfillment of their duties.

How Do I Become a Radiologic Technologist?

After graduating from high school, Diane stepped right into an approved two-year school of radiologic technology in a hospital-based program. "At the end of the program," she says, "you take the exam from the American Registry of Radiologic Technologists to receive your license, which enables you to perform X rays. You then may sit for the advanced certification exams in mammography, computed technology, magnetic resonance imaging, quality management, radiation therapy, nuclear medicine, and sonography. New exams are coming down the road."

EDUCATION

High School

Students who intend to pursue a career as a radiologic technologist should take courses in the sciences—namely, biology, anatomy, physics, and chemistry. You should also take courses in mathematics and take advantage of writing and speech classes, which will allow you to hone your communication skills. Unlike a few other technical careers, a high school degree is required for entry into radiologic technology training programs.

> **To Be a Successful Radiologic Technologist, You Should . . .**
>
> - have compassion and a personal touch
> - have patience and a flexible personality
> - be extroverted and able to communicate in a clear and concise manner
> - have an understanding of medical terminology and procedures

Postsecondary Training

Instruction in the radiologic sciences is offered at universities and colleges in the form of four-year baccalaureate programs and two-year associate degree programs, in hospitals in the form of a two-year hospital certificate program, and also in the armed forces.

A two-year associate's program consists of a mixture of theory and practical hours. Due to the intense nature of the education, many students take an additional year to complete the educational requirements.

The curriculum that aspiring RTs will experience includes instruction in anatomy and physiology, radiation physics and biology, pathology, medical technology instruction and procedures, principles and techniques of diagnostic imaging, patient care and medical ethics, and radiation safety and protection. Programs should be accredited by the Joint Review Committee on Education in Radiologic Technology (JRCERT). See http://www.jrcert.org for more details.

CERTIFICATION OR LICENSING

Most medical employers require certification by the American Registry of Radiologic Technologists (ARRT). Radiologic students, upon completion of their education, are expected to take and pass the National Registry Boards to allow employment. All students must be registry-eligible, which means registered with the ARRT to take the test the next time it is offered. The Registry Boards are offered four times a year.

In addition to standard certification, a significant amount of continuing education exists in the radiologic field. In order to maintain proper certification, RTs must take 24 hours of continuing education in the course of two years. These courses are offered by technical-type programs and also the Institute for Professional Growth (IFPG), which offers X-ray seminars at area hotels.

Currently, 38 states require that radiologic technologists be registered.

FYI

According to a 2004 survey conducted by the American Society of Radiologic Technologists, the "typical" radiologic technologist is

- female
- holds an associate degree
- has been practicing in the profession for more than 16 years
- works an average 40-hour workweek in a hospital, clinic, or physician's office
- is certified in radiography, mammography, or computed tomography

INTERNSHIPS AND VOLUNTEERSHIPS

Radiologic technologists gain valuable internship experience in the course of the practical hours that are required to gain a degree. Those in a hospital certificate program will gain experience on-site throughout their education. "I was lucky," Diane says. "I was in a work-study program in high school. I worked in the radiology department of a hospital for school credit, so I knew what I was getting into, and I had a head start when I actually got into X-ray school."

A guidance counselor may be able to set up a meeting with a professional radiologic technologist at his or her place of work. This way, you could observe the duties, facilities, and equipment used, as well as ask questions of the technologist. Another way to gain more information and make a good contact in the field is to speak with a teacher of radiology at an educational program.

Who Will Hire Me?

While most RTs work in hospitals, others may work in physicians' offices, HMOs (health maintenance organizations), mobile imaging clinics, nursing homes, or extended health care facilities. "My first job was at the hospital where I trained," Diane says. "I worked part time during training and was offered a job at graduation."

Hospitals provide radiologic technologists with the best opportunity for employment. Half of RTs work in hospitals. Application through employment services or through the personnel officers of potential health care employers is a good way to locate job openings.

While rural areas and small towns offer more opportunity for employment than cities, pay and benefits are usually better with an urban employer.

Where Can I Go from Here?

Those interested in moving beyond a career in radiologic technology should be aware that advanced jobs can only be acquired through further education. This education may be provided in-house, at a teaching hospital, or in a technical school or college setting. Those obtaining a bachelor's degree will have the best chance for advancement. Further education will al-

Advancement Possibilities

Computed tomography (CT) technologists, working closely with physicians, are responsible for taking detailed cross-sectional pictures of the internal structures of the human body.

Magnetic resonance imaging (MRI) technologists use computers, radio waves, and powerful magnets to create images of specific parts of the body.

Diagnostic medical sonographers use high-frequency sound waves, not radiation, to create images of internal body structures.

Chief technologists and technical administrators are radiologic technologists who have, through experience and further education, risen to supervisory positions in hospitals and other health care settings.

Radiologic instructors teach in university settings, teaching hospitals, and in two-year technical programs.

low RTs to become certified in CT, ultrasound, MRI (magnetic resonance imaging), nuclear medicine, and other fields, thereby gaining experience and flexibility to prosper in the workplace.

"I first worked on the third shift," Diane says, "pulling 40 hours from Monday to Friday. I then went to nuclear medicine and CT working days, weekends, and on call. We worked all the time."

With considerable experience, radiologic technologists can move into teaching positions or train new technologists in-house or at other locations. Other RTs may use their experience to work in sales and marketing, demonstrating new equipment for medically oriented businesses.

Radiologic technologists employed in hospitals have the opportunity to advance to administrative and supervisory positions. Those who gain their bachelor's degree and then a master's degree in health administration may choose to seek a position as a hospital administrator or manage a business for radiologists.

What Are the Salary Ranges?

According to the *Occupational Outlook Handbook*, radiologic technologists had median annual earnings of $41,850 in 2003. Those in the lowest 10 percent earned less than $29,340, while those in the highest earned more than $58,300 annually. On average, RTs working for medical and diagnostic laboratories earned the highest salaries in this field.

Compensation and pay scales will vary based on the location of the employer—with urban areas more lucrative than rural areas and small towns—and on the level of education attained, the experience, and the responsibilities of the technologist.

What Is the Job Outlook?

The field of radiologic technology is expected to grow faster than the average for all other occupations. This is due to the vast clinical potential of diagnostic imaging. New uses for radiologic technology will continue to be discovered, therefore increasing demand. Opportunities in small towns and rural areas exist for those flexible about location and compensation.

Another factor that will influence growth is the aging of the American population. As the median age rises, more attention will be focused on diseases that are prominent in older people. Many of these diseases require the use of imaging equipment and technologists. The Southeast and Southwest regions of the United States offer significant employment opportunity due to their large populations of retirement-age Americans. The aging workforce will also create more positions in the radiology field, since may radiologic technologists will reach retirement age. The ARRT and ASRT have found that the majority of RTs are 40 years or older, part of the reason the organizations are predicting a severe shortage of RTs by 2010.

Another reason for this shortage is that fewer people are entering the field than ever before. The career may be unattractive to some because of the long hours and wages that don't properly compensate. In an effort to bring some standardization to the field, ARRT is considering requiring technologists to have a bachelor's degree in order to become certified. Currently, RT students are putting in nearly four years of training anyway, because of the practical requirements of associate's degrees.

While a shortage in the workforce may exist, prospective RTs should be aware that there is stiff competition for good jobs. One must be prepared to be flexible in order to prosper in the field. Education will provide the best tool for competition and advancement. Those technologists with advanced training in mammography, CT imaging, MRI, ultrasound, and other technologies stand to prosper in the years ahead.

How Do I Learn More?

PROFESSIONAL ORGANIZATIONS

To learn about certification, contact

American Registry of Radiologic Technologists
1255 Northland Drive
St. Paul, MN 55120-1155
651-687-0048
http://www.arrt.org

For extensive information about careers in radiologic technology, visit the ASRT Web site.

American Society of Radiologic Technologists (ASRT)
15000 Central Avenue, SE
Albuquerque, NM 87123-3917
505-298-4500
http://www.asrt.org

To learn about accredited educational programs, contact

Joint Review Committee on Education in Radiologic Technology
20 North Wacker Drive, Suite 2850
Chicago, IL 60606-3182
312-704-5300
mail@jrcert.org
http://www.jrcert.org

BIBLIOGRAPHY

Following is a sampling of materials relating to the professional concerns and development of radiologic technologists.

Anderson, Anthony, ed. *The Radiology Technologist's Handbook to Surgical Procedures.* Boca Raton, Fla.: CRC Press, 1999.

Bushing, Stewart C. *Radiologic Science for Technologists: Physics, Biology, and Protection.* 8th ed. St. Louis, Mo.: Mosby, 2004.

Statkiewicz Sherer, Mary Alice, Paul J. Visconti, and Russell E. Ritenour. *Radiation Protection in Medical Radiography.* 4th ed. St. Louis, Mo.: Mosby, 2002.

Stedman's Radiolology Words. 4th ed. Philadelphia: Lippincott Williams & Wilkins, 2003.

RADIOLOGISTS

Dr. Arildsen steps into his office at Vanderbilt Medical Center's Radiology Department and checks the messages on his desk: A biopsy has to be rescheduled, a colleague wants to arrange a consultation, and there is a request for a consultation with a sports medicine specialist concerning a football player's injured knee.

Ronald Arildsen is a diagnostic radiologist specializing in work with body CT scans and MRIs. Diagnosing sports injuries is one of his favorite parts of his job.

Ron frowns intently at the MRIs of the athlete's knee. It shows a torn ACL (anterior cruciate ligament), a ligament directly behind the patella (knee cap). The knee is the most commonly injured joint in football, a sport that requires running, cutting, pivoting, jumping, and stopping, in combination with tackling and other contact. This athlete's injury is likely to require reconstruction surgery followed by six to eight months of rehabilitation. He will be out for the rest of the season. Fortunately Ron doesn't have to break the news to the patient. His job is to make the diagnosis and discuss it with the athlete's team of physicians and therapists.

Definition
Radiologists are physicians who specialize in radiology—the area of medicine that uses X rays, high-frequency sound waves, high-strength magnetic fields, and radioactive compounds to diagnose and treat illness and injury.

High School Subjects
Biology
Chemistry
Math

Personal Skills
Helping/teaching
Technical/scientific

Salary Range
$150,000 to $200,000 to $317,000+

Educational Requirements
Bachelor's degree, medical degree

Certification or Licensing
Required by all states

Outlook
About as fast as the average

DOT
070

GOE
14.02.01

NOC
3111

O*NET-SOC
29-1063.00

What Does a Radiologist Do?

Radiologists are physicians who specialize in the diagnosis and treatment of injury and disease by means of X rays, high-frequency sound waves, high-strength magnetic fields, and radioactive compounds. Radiologists read and interpret the images produced by radiological technologists and sonographers. The field of radiology is divided into several subfields, including diagnostic radiology (diagnosis through the use of various imaging techniques), radiation oncology (the treatment of tumors by various forms of radiation), and nuclear medicine (diagnosis and/or treatment by the introduction of radiopharmaceuticals [radioactive materials] into the body).

Radiology came into existence in 1895 when the discovery of X rays by Wilhelm Roentgen revolutionized medicine by making it possible for doctors to see inside the body without cutting it open. In taking an X ray, streams of high-energy photons penetrate the body and produce images of internal structures that can be preserved on photographic film. Before the discovery of X rays, the only ways to study the body's bones and organs were by touching the outside of the body (which gave very limited knowledge of the inside of the body), through surgery, and through autopsy of the body after the patient's death.

Diagnostic radiologists still use X rays today, but they also have many other more sophisticated imaging techniques that have been invented in recent decades. The CT (computed tomography) scan, developed in the early 1970s, makes use of computer technology to turn ordinary X-ray images into three-dimensional composite cross-sections. CT scans provide far more detailed information than ordinary X rays about the location, extent, and characteristics of the injury or disease. They are especially useful in planning reconstructive surgery and cancer therapy.

MRI (magnetic resonance imaging) is an advanced diagnostic technique in which the patient is exposed to powerful electromagnetic fields. Computer technology turns the data obtained into two-dimensional images that enable radiologists to examine abnormalities of the spinal cord, abdomen, pelvis, brain, and other organs, bones, and tissues.

Ultrasound techniques use high-frequency sound waves (instead of radiation) to produce images. Because pregnant women should not be exposed to radiation, ultrasound images are obtained in order to discover the number, age, position, and condition of the fetus. Other ultrasound procedures are the echocardiogram (used to examine the heart) and Doppler ultrasound (used to study the blood flow in the veins and arteries).

Radiation oncologists are specialists in the use of various forms of radiation in the treatment of tumors. It is necessary to determine the location and extent of the tumor as precisely as possible, since the goal is to target the radiation (such as gamma rays, electron beams, or other forms) to destroy the cancer cells without doing serious harm to the healthy cells that surround the tumor. Usually the radiation is administered by external beam, but sometimes radioactive sources (such as iodine or cesium) are inserted directly into the body at the site of the tumor. Cancer treatment often combines radiation therapy, surgery, and chemotherapy. Even when the cancer cannot be cured, radiation treatment often reduces pain and other symptoms.

Nuclear medicine radiologists produce images and treat disease by placing radiopharmaceuticals (radioactive materials) in the body. When radioisotopes are inserted into the circulatory system and tracked by special cameras, they yield information not obtainable by X rays. The PET (positron emission technology) technique, for example, is used to study blood flow and brain function and is an important tool in the diagnosis of Alzheimer's disease and cancer. SPECT (single photon emission computed tomography) is used to monitor heart function. Radioisotopes are also sent through the bloodstream to treat certain cancers.

Interventional radiological techniques are used to do biopsies, drain abscesses, and open blocked or narrowed arteries (balloon angioplasty). Through these high-tech, minimally invasive procedures, radiologists often make it possible for patients to avoid having to undergo surgery.

Lingo to Learn

Angioplasty An interventional radiological procedure that uses a balloon-tipped catheter to open blocked or narrowed arteries.

CT (computed tomography) scan or **CAT (computed axial tomography) scan** A diagnostic procedure that uses computer technology to produce three-dimensional composite cross-sectional images of internal structures from X rays.

Echocardiogram An ultrasonic technique for examining a patient's heart.

Mammography X-ray examination of the breasts to detect cancer in its earliest stages.

MRI (magnetic resonance imaging) A diagnostic procedure that produces two-dimensional visual images of internal structures by placing the patient in a powerful electromagnetic field.

Oncology The branch of medicine that deals with tumors and cancer.

Pathology The branch of medicine that identifies and studies disease processes by examination of body organs, tissues, and fluids obtained during surgery or autopsy.

Plain film Ordinary X rays (as distinguished from more sophisticated radiological images).

Ultrasound The use of high-frequency sound waves to produce images of structures within the body.

What Is It Like to Be a Radiologist?

Like most radiologists, Ronald Arildsen spends the greater part of each day sitting in a darkened room reading and interpreting various kinds of images, preparing reports of his findings, and holding consultations with surgeons, internists, and other doctors. "Radiologists are often called doctors' doctors," he says, meaning that radiologists work more closely with other doctors than with patients.

"When doctors don't know what to do," explains Dr. Lisa Sheppard Boal, a diagnostic radiologist in basic community practice at Passaic Beth Israel Hospital in Passaic, New Jersey, "the first people they consult are the radiologists and pathologists." (Pathologists are physicians who specialize in examining tissues, organs, and body fluids for clues to the diagnosis and prognosis of disease.) Because Lisa is in community practice, she works in all fields of diagnostic radiology, although her special area of interest is neuroradiology (radiology of the head and spine). Ron is a specialist in body CT scans and MRIs. In addition to working with CT scans and MRIs, he also reads "plain film" X rays of the body.

When doctors don't know what to do the first people they consult are the radiologists and pathologists.

As the morning wears on, Ron studies one set of images after another, reads the notes from the clinicians who originally examined the patients, and forms his conclusions. One patient's problem is gallstones, painful but not life-threatening. And another one has a compound fracture of the tibia and a torn ligament. But here is some encouraging news, Ron thinks as he examines new film of a tumor that was currently under treatment. He can see definite evidence that the tumor has shrunk, which means that the treatment strategy is working.

Ron checks his watch. This year, he is teaching the basic radiology course for second-year medical students, and he needs to take time to go over his lecture notes before class. He is also codirector of the fourth-year radiology elective, which gives him the pleasure of working with future radiologists. Since coming to Vanderbilt in 1991, he has found that he particularly enjoys teaching at the medical school and working with radiology residents.

After class, he will take care of that rescheduled liver biopsy. Guided by radiological imaging, needles can be inserted into almost any part of the body with a high degree of precision, which makes it possible to do biopsies and drain internal abscesses without performing surgery.

Lisa is having a busy day, too, at Passaic Beth Israel. She has been sitting in the viewing room reading X rays, ultrasounds, upper GIs (images of the upper gastrointestinal tract), CT scans, and MRIs for several hours, when the emergency room calls. A stroke patient has just been brought in and Lisa, as a specialist in neuroradiology, is needed to evaluate the damage.

In the afternoon Lisa will be working at the outpatient center, interviewing women coming in for mammograms (X-ray examination of the breasts) and then interpreting the results for them. She will also be working with some pregnant women who are having ultrasounds. As a mother of two small children, reading ultrasounds is one of the parts of her job that she finds especially enjoyable.

Being in community practice is always stimulating for Lisa because it offers the opportunity to be involved with diagnostic work in so many different areas of medicine. With the recent introduction of managed health care, radiologists are also becoming increasingly involved in helping to make decisions about how the hospital can provide the best possible care for the lowest price.

Lisa likes the intellectual challenge involved in diagnosis and feels a deep satisfaction when she is able to hit on the right answer in a perplexing case. She has never forgotten the advice of one of her professors at Jefferson Medical School: "If you hear thundering hoofbeats in the distance (and you're not in Africa), they're probably horses, not zebras." In other words, first consider the most likely explanations for the patients' symptoms before you start exploring rare diseases.

Do I Have What It Takes to Be a Radiologist?

The first question to ask yourself is, "Have I got what it takes to be a doctor?" Becoming a doctor is a long and gruelling process, requiring strong academic ability (especially in the sciences), commitment, and perseverance.

The next question is whether radiology is the right medical specialty for you. Diagnostic radiology would not be the right field for a doctor who wants to have a lot of direct contact with patients, since diagnostic radiologists spend most of their time examining film and consulting with medical colleagues. Radiation oncologists and radiologists who specialize in interventional radiological procedures spend more time with patients than diagnostic radiologists.

Radiologists describe their work as intellectually stimulating and full of variety. "You must be very alert to detail," stresses Lisa Sheppard Boal. Another radiologist describes the field as attractive for "cerebral types who like to think things through," while also having opportunities for performing procedures and working as part of a medical team. One radiologist mentions a colleague who found radiology a very satisfying field after developing a hearing loss that made it difficult to have a lot of direct patient contact.

Radiology is one of the best-paid medical specialties. It is not physically draining like some fields, especially surgery. After radiologists complete their residencies, they can generally count on "normal" working hours. Lisa, for example, works eight-hour days at Passaic Beth Israel. When she is on call, she is able to receive film images on a home computer screen, an innovation that she welcomes.

Because they do so much of their work behind the scenes, radiologists have more job-security concerns than doctors in some other fields. Patients will often insist on having a particular internist or obstetrician, but no one demands that a particular radiologist interpret their X rays. One result of this anonymity is that cost-conscious hospitals and HMOs are tempted to save money by replacing experienced radiologists with less experienced, and therefore lower-salaried, colleagues.

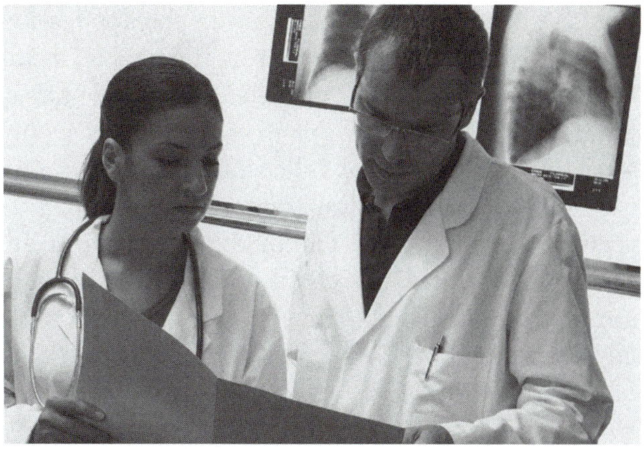

Two radiologists discuss a patient's X rays. *(AJ Photo/ Photo Researchers Inc.)*

How Do I Become a Radiologist?

EDUCATION

High School

To become a radiologist, you should take a good college preparatory program in high school. The sciences—biology, chemistry, and physics—are especially important, as is a solid foundation in mathematics. You also need to take English, foreign languages, history, and other humanities courses. Future physicians should work on developing effective study habits and communication skills.

> **To Be a Successful Radiologist, You Should . . .**
>
> - have a good foundation in the sciences
> - enjoy intellectual challenges
> - have strong powers of concentration and an eye for detail
> - have the ability to work well with physicians in other fields of medicine

Postsecondary Training

In college, you should enroll in a liberal arts program with a strong emphasis on the sciences. Biology and chemistry are the most obvious choices for a major. Many colleges offer a premed course of study for students who plan to apply to medical school; this is the most appropriate track to follow if it is available at your college. Whatever your major, you need to take as many courses as possible in biology, chemistry (both organic and inorganic), and physics. Humanities and social sciences (psychology, sociology, economics, anthropology) are also important in providing a well-rounded education. High grades are essential.

You should begin planning for medical school well in advance. Examine the admissions requirements for the medical schools you'd like to attend and plan your undergraduate program accordingly. You should make arrangements to take the Medical College Admission Test (MCAT) before your senior year. This is a standardized test required by all U.S. medical schools, and your score is an important factor in admissions decisions. The test covers verbal ability (language skills), quantitative ability (mathematics), and the humanities and social sciences, in addition to biology, chemistry, and physics.

When it is time to apply to medical school, the American Medical College Application Service

(AMCAS) is available to assist with the application process. You should apply to at least three medical schools to improve your chances of acceptance. Sometimes students are able to enter medical school after only three years of college, but the usual practice is to complete the four-year undergraduate program first. About half of all qualified applicants are accepted into medical school each year. If you are not accepted the first year you apply, consult your adviser about how to become a stronger candidate for the following year (by doing a year of graduate work in biology, for example).

Medical school is four years of rigorous study. Medical students usually feel overwhelmed, but it's important to remember that nearly everyone who starts medical school really does complete the program and graduate. The first two years of medical school are generally devoted to basic science work: human anatomy and physiology, biochemistry, microbiology, pathology, pharmacology, and human behavior. During this period, you attend lectures and seminars and do laboratory work. The first two years may also include actual experience with patients and early instruction in giving physical examinations, interviewing, diagnosing, and counseling.

The last two years of medical school concentrate on the clinical sciences (the various medical specialties): internal medicine, surgery, pediatrics, obstetrics, gynecology, psychiatry, and family medicine. While remaining closely supervised, you are actively involved in patient treatment as part of a hospital medical team. You also continue to do course work. In addition to the clinical sciences, there may be work in such areas as medical ethics and decision analysis cost containment. During these years, you begin to focus on a future specialty such as radiology

CERTIFICATION OR LICENSING

After finishing medical school and receiving the M.D., you go on to do a hospital residency. At an early point in the residency period, you are required to pass a medical licensing examination administered by the board of medical examiners in each state. The length of the residency depends on the specialty chosen. Radiologists spend five to seven years in advanced training as resident physicians. As all doctors warn, the residency years are tough—long hours of demanding work and intensive study that are physically draining and often put a severe strain on family and personal life. At the end of an accredited residency training program, physicians must pass certification examinations in their fields. The evaluation program is directed by the appropriate specialty board of the American Board of Medical Specialties.

FYI

Radiology was developed in 1895 when the discovery of X rays revolutionized medicine by making it possible to see inside the body without cutting it open.

SCHOLARSHIPS AND GRANTS

Becoming a physician is expensive, but strongly committed students should not be deterred by the financial obstacles involved. Consult the financial aid office of the academic institution that you plan to attend to find out about scholarships, grants, loans, work-study programs, and other possible sources of assistance. Ronald Arildsen attended Columbia Medical School on a U.S. Navy scholarship. In return, he spent five years working as a general practitioner in the Navy after graduation. Then he returned to Columbia for his radiology residency.

More than 80 percent of medical students need to take out loans, and many graduate deeply in debt. Keep in mind, however, that physicians can expect high earnings after they complete their medical school and residency training.

Who Will Hire Me?

About 90 percent of radiologists are in group practice. Some groups are composed exclusively of diagnostic radiologists or radiological oncologists, while others have members from both areas. The American College of Radiology (the professional association for radiologists and radiological physicists) defines a radiology group as any practice with at least two radiologists; this includes private groups, the radiology units of multispecialty groups, academic groups, and groups on the staffs of government facilities.

A job-listing service for radiology groups and a job-placement service for radiologists seeking employment are provided by the American College of Radiology, but relatively little use is made of these services. Professional contacts and recommendations play a much more important role in recruitment and placement.

Where Can I Go from Here?

Advancement for a radiologist, as for other medical specialists, means gaining the respect of colleagues and progressing in professional skill, knowledge, reputation, and income. Radiologists who are interested in research and teaching advance through involvement with university medical schools and teaching hospitals. A radiologist with an interest in administration might have the goal of becoming a hospital's director of radiology or chair of a medical school's radiology department.

Radiologists typically report a high level of satisfaction with their work. "I wouldn't be happy doing anything else," declares Dr. Lisa Sheppard Boal.

What Are the Salary Ranges?

Radiologists are among some of the highest paid physicians. A strong demand for radiologists has contributed to rising salaries. For example, according to a survey conducted by Merritt, Hawkins & Associates of Irving, Texas, in 2003 the average salaries of radiologists in the United States were $317,000, which represented 13 percent growth from the 2002 average of $286,000. Additionally, an article in the Chicago *Tribune* of June 2001 notes that salaries for those who have just completed their residencies may range from $150,000 to $200,000. Factors that influence annual income include size and type of practice, hours worked per week, professional reputation of the individual, and geographic location.

What Is the Job Outlook?

The U.S. Department of Labor reports the employment outlook for physicians will grow about as fast as the average for all occupations. Radiologists will enjoy an especially good job outlook for two reasons. Since 2001, all residency programs are five-year programs, as mandated by the American Board of Radiology. This means there will be fewer graduates entering the workforce than in past years, as they complete this extra residency year. In addition, many radiology groups limited hiring of new radiologists in the 1990s because of concerns over managed care cost-cutting practices. The demand for radiologists has remained steady, however, and as a result, many of these groups are now understaffed and looking for new workers and offering competitive salaries.

How Do I Learn More?

PROFESSIONAL ORGANIZATIONS

The following are organizations that provide information about a career as a radiologist:

American College of Radiology
1891 Preston White Drive
Reston, VA 20191
703-648-8900
http://www.acr.org

American Medical Association
515 North State Street
Chicago, IL 60610
800-321-6335
http://www.ama-assn.org

BIBLIOGRAPHY

The following is a sampling of materials relating to the professional concerns and development of radiologists.

Brant, William E., and Clyde A. Helms, eds. *Fundamentals of Diagnostic Radiology.* 2d ed. Philadelphia: Lippincott Williams & Wilkins, 1999.

Callaway, William J. *Mosby's Comprehensive Review of Radiology: The Complete Study Guide and Career Planner.* 3d ed. St. Louis: Mosby-Year Book, 2002.

Chen, Michael Y., Thomas L. Pope, and David J. Ott, eds. *Basic Radiology.* New York: McGraw-Hill, 2004.

Hall, Eric J. *Radiobiology for the Radiologist.* 5th ed. Philadelphia: Lippincott Williams & Wilkins, 2000.

Mettler, Fred A., Jr. *Essentials of Radiology.* Philadelphia: W. B. Saunders, 1996.

Novelline, Robert A. *Squire's Fundamentals of Radiology.* 5th ed. Cambridge, Mass.: Harvard University Press, 1997.

Ouelette, Hugue, and Patrice Tetreault. *Clinical Radiology Made Ridiculously Simple*. Miami, Fla.: MedMaster, 1999.

Weir, Jamie. *Imaging Atlas of Human Anatomy.* 3d ed. St. Louis: Mosby-Year Book, 2003.

Weissleder, Ralph, Jack Wittenberg, and Mukesh G. Harisinghani. *Primer of Diagnostic Imaging*. 3d ed. St. Louis: Mosby-Year Book, 2002.

RECREATIONAL THERAPISTS

Definition
A recreational therapist uses medically approved recreation programs to help patients with mental, physical, or emotional disabilities.

Alternative Job Title
Quality of life professionals
Therapeutic recreation specialists

High School Subjects
Physical education
Psychology

Personal Skills
Communication/ideas
Helping/teaching

Salary Range
$19,930 to $32,540 to $65,000

Educational Requirements
High school diploma, bachelor's degree

Certification or Licensing
Required by certain states

Outlook
More slowly than the average

DOT
076

GOE
14.06.01

NOC
3144

O*NET-SOC
29-1125.00

Four people show up at a restaurant five minutes before their dinner reservations. They are talking, sometimes laughing as they wait. Two of them appear to be a little nervous, perhaps, but they are smiling and enjoying themselves just the same. They order, snack on appetizers, and then eat, taking time to savor the food and the evening out. When the meal is over, they pay and leave.

Sound ordinary? For thousands of people with cognitive or physical disabilities, a night like this one might rarely happen. This is not because they are unable to go out to dinner and enjoy themselves. It is because nobody has shown them the skills they need to take part in everyday life and to enhance their well-being. A recreational therapist is trained to assess the recreational needs of a disabled person and to help find leisure activities that will be fulfilling, interesting, and accessible.

During dinner at the restaurant, one of the party leaves the table to find the rest room. Coming back she is beaming. In her wheelchair she has successfully navigated the tables and chairs in her way, and she receives the congratulations of her therapist and other dinner companions.

What Does a Recreational Therapist Do?

Recreational therapists, often referred to as *therapeutic recreation specialists,* work with people who have mental, physical, or emotional disabilities. They plan, organize, direct, and monitor recreation programs for patients in hospitals, clinics, and various community settings. These therapists use sports, games, music, arts and crafts, and other activities to assist clients in developing, improving, or maintaining functional skills.

Some clients need help in recovering from a recent injury or in learning how to stay active despite a disability. Therapists might design seniors' programs that use leisure activities to improve general health and well-being. Therapists who work with developmentally disabled people may use recreation to introduce clients to social interaction in a nonthreatening, supportive, and fun environment. Among substance abusers or people in prison, recreational therapists use recreational activities as a way of stimulating acceptable social behavior and interests, and to raise self-awareness and self-esteem. Other clients use recreational therapy as a way to relax and to manage stress to maintain mental and physical health.

Some recreational therapists work in a clinical setting, where the emphasis is on recovery or rehabilitation from a specific illness, disease, or disability. They work as part of a team with other health professionals and develop recreational activities as a form of treatment. Clinical recreational therapists may work in hospitals, outpatient clinics, rehabilitation centers, and long-term care facilities. Other therapists work in a community setting, where the emphasis is on outreach and continuing education. Community recreational therapists work with people in public and private schools, adult day care centers, community agencies, and neighborhood and county parks.

Recreational therapy often groups people with similar interests or similar abilities. Even pursuits such as reading or sewing encourage interaction when they are set up as group activities, such as a reading club or sewing circle. Recreational therapists help their clients find meaningful ways to participate in society. In doing so, they promote health, adjustment, growth, and independence.

It is commonly known that stress can lead to mental instability and breakdown. Stress has also been implicated in the weakening of the immune system, which protects the body from infections and other physical ailments. Imagine how much added stress a person is under when faced with chronic illness or long-term interruption of the abilities they rely on—walking, seeing, memory retention. For people in this predicament, realizing that they can still be independent and enjoy themselves is as beneficial to their physical rehabilitation as are the skills they learn from their therapeutic program. Therapists in this situation are instrumental in getting their clients to taking the first step in that rehabilitation process, by encouraging them to press past the barriers they encounter as a result of their disability or illness.

For people with paralysis or other disabilities, sports has become a hugely popular and successful recreational therapy. People with limited mobility and skill can play basketball and rugby, go skiing, and race in marathons. Professional wheelchair athletes may obtain corporate sponsorships and train year-round for national and international competitions. Being physically active is a way these athletes express their competitive spirit and earn appreciation for their athletic abilities. The success of wheelchair athletes in high-profile events such as the Boston Marathon has gone a long way toward establishing acceptance and opportunities for all people with disabilities.

Recreational therapists who specialize in sports educate people with disabilities and limitations about activities that are available to them. The therapist may also be a part of developing adaptive equipment for a particular individual based on his or her knowledge of that person's abilities and goals.

Lingo to Learn

Geriatrics and **gerontology** The medical study of the physical processes and problems of old age. Either of these terms may be used in hospital departments with elderly patients.

Leisure education The use of sports, hobbies, and other activities to acquire skills and abilities to lead an independent lifestyle.

Orient To acquaint with an existing situation or environment. For example, to indicate obstacles for a blind person in a place he or she frequents so that they may make a mental "map" of the area and be able to guide themselves.

Recreation The opportunity to participate in leisure activities that improve health and well-being.

Special Olympics A program of physical fitness, sports training, and athletic competition for children and adults with mental retardation.

What Is It Like to Be a Recreational Therapist?

Therapists in hospitals and clinics generally have regular 40-hour weeks, though they may need to be involved with special events that occur after hours or on weekends. The kinds of programs that therapists initiate depend on the people with whom they work. The clinical recreational therapist first consults with other medical professionals to determine the therapeutic needs of the client. They may work with several other therapists, such as speech pathologists, occupational therapists, and physical therapists, to achieve a common goal for a particular client. Then they will interview the client to discover his or her activities and interests.

After determining the therapeutic needs of a client, the recreational therapist plans a program that uses levels of accomplishment as steps in measuring progress. For instance, a person who has nerve damage may go through a physical therapy program to develop dexterity in the hands. This client may also take part in a recreational therapy group that engages in gardening. Progress may be measured by the recreational therapist in terms of the increasing levels of confidence with which the client repots plants or the length of time the client can hold pruning scissors. Therapists evaluate the client's interests to create a program that will not only fulfill therapeutic requirements but also will be enjoyable. The recreational therapist also periodically evaluates these programs for their effectiveness and may restructure the therapy if a client does not respond as expected.

Cynthia Kowalski works with elderly hospitalized patients at the Ravenswood Hospital Medical Center in Chicago. "The trend in hospitals these days is to have a rehab department with speech therapy, recreational therapy, occupational therapy, all under one roof. I work on the geriatric floor and I basically deal with getting patients into the community to practice physical, cognitive, and social skills in a realistic setting." What works for one person may not work for another, so programs are as individually oriented as they can be, given the limitations of working within a hospital.

"First I do a planning session with the patient. Then once a week we put the program into effect, usually with other skilled coworkers like a physical therapist or occupational therapist. For instance, we might plan to go out to eat with someone who has a new disability, to focus on increased awareness. Now that they have a disability, they need to think about accessibility—does the restaurant have ramps? How much time will we need to give ourselves to get there? We also start them thinking about things like safety and judgment." All of these issues may seem simple, but they are things that a person with a disability might never have thought through before. The goal of recreational therapists is to eliminate the uncertainty that might prevent their clients from continuing to live as well as they did before the disability or illness occurred.

Cynthia also works with cognitive disabilities, like those which may be incurred from a head trauma or stroke. In a program called Advanced Reality Orientation, she gathers a group of such patients for a one-hour newspaper reading group. This serves several purposes for its participants. "We work on different cognitive functions," Cynthia relates. "Do they remember what they've read? Can they follow the thread of the conversation, and do they contribute? For this group, I really focus on the people who liked reading in the past. Sometimes, speech therapy will want [a client] there so they can practice taking part in a conversation group, but I usually suggest this program for people who are interested in current events and reading." Such a group also makes clients aware that there is a world outside the hospital, and that they can still actively participate in it.

If a reading group is not something that a client is interested in, Cynthia may suggest other therapeutic recreational programs. "I usually have a one-on-one evaluation for people who were active before; I may give them community resources on older adult programs. This kind of community re-entry depends on the functional level of the client, though." In this way, the clinical and community aspects of recreational therapy can overlap and be mutually supportive. Cynthia knows of programs in her area that will help her clients once they are out of her care, and can suggest them as a means of continuing therapy.

Other recreational therapists might have days that are completely different from Cynthia's. They might work at summer camps for disabled children and live at the camp with their clients seven days a week. Their work might be seasonal or oriented around events like the Special Olympics or sporting seasons. Therapists who work within community settings often spend time creating outreach programs and other social events in which disabled members of the community can voluntarily participate. Because there is less contact with participants than in hospitals, the focus of the community recreational therapist is on creating general events or activities such as games or day trips that any member of a specific group can enjoy. Because of this, recreational therapists are sometimes called quality of life professionals by the National Recreation and Park Association.

Do I Have What It Takes to Be a Recreational Therapist?

To be a recreational therapist, you must have a strong desire to help people live independently and meet their personal goals. Interest in recreational and leisure activities is also a requirement. Therapists come into contact with segments of the population, such as disabled or elderly people, who are often neglected or forgotten

In-depth

Special Olympics Do a World of Good

In 1968 Eunice Kennedy Shriver organized the Special Olympics for mentally challenged children and adults. The First International Special Olympics Games were held at Soldier Field, Chicago, Illinois. The idea started in the early 1960s when Shriver started a day camp for people with mental retardation. She saw that they were far more capable in sports and physical activities than many experts believed. Since 1968, millions of children and adults with mental retardation have participated in Special Olympics. Special Olympics now has chapters in all 50 states, the District of Columbia, Guam, the Virgin Islands, and American Samoa. And there are now accredited Special Olympics programs in nearly 150 countries.

by traditional recreational programs. It is important to be able to recognize the value of these people as individuals, and to believe in their right to live active, healthy, and full lives. Working with other therapists and clients can be very stressful, and patience is very important when considering any job in therapy.

One of the most rewarding things about working with people in recovery and adjustment is seeing how the programs designed to help them do help. Because this kind of therapy is designed around what a client already likes to do, it can be fun to participate in the activities along with the clients. Leadership skills help the recreational therapist run programs efficiently and well. Open communication is critical to the success of the therapist-client relationship. A good therapist is willing to listen to clients' concerns and incorporate individuals into the therapeutic goals.

A therapist with an aptitude for analysis and evaluation makes therapeutic treatment plans that are best designed for each client, and therefore most effective. An ability to focus on both short- and long-term goals allows the therapist to continue with programs that will be optimal for each client. Finally, the ability to see when a program is not working is key to helping speed recovery and adjustment.

How Do I Become a Recreational Therapist?

EDUCATION

High School

To prepare for a career as a recreational therapist, you should take biology, sociology, and psychology, as well as develop interests in sports and other leisure-time activities. Anatomy and kinesiology are also valuable; you can more readily understand common dysfunctions of the body if you understand common functions. Communication skills are very important to the success of the therapist, so speech and writing classes are also suggested.

While still in high school, it is possible to get some clinical experience by volunteering in hospitals or retirement communities. Duties may include bringing newspapers or magazines to patients, visiting with them, and generally being supportive of their rehabilitation efforts.

Cynthia has noticed that employment opportunities are based on the kind of volunteer work you have done. "For some reason it's hard to get a job in the park districts [community settings] if all your experience is clinical, and vice versa. So I would recommend getting as much experience in both settings as you can." Some examples of community settings include park district programs, day care facilities, summer camps, and independent programs organized by parents of children with developmental disabilities. Clinical experience might come from volunteering in a hospital, a residential facility for seniors or mentally disabled, or a correctional facility in which therapy might be part of an inmate's social rehabilitation.

Postsecondary Training

Approximately 140 academic programs in recreational therapy are offered at colleges and universities in the United States. Course work includes natural sciences (anatomy, biology, and behavioral science) as well as social sciences (psychology, criminology, and sociology). Cynthia's major course work included classes in recreation programming. These taught her how to evaluate clients to determine their course of therapy, develop goals, and understand the activity needs of various populations. Academic programs also require a minimum of 360 hours of internship under the supervision of a certified therapeutic recreation specialist.

Since the primary purpose of recreational therapy is to take into consideration and use the clients' needs and interests to help them take an active part of their therapy, it might be valuable to target a group with whom you are interested in working and take classes that provide information that group might find interesting.

CERTIFICATION OR LICENSING

Certification is not required in most states. It does, however, indicate that the holder has met requirements set by the National Council for Therapeutic Recreation Certification. There are two standards of recognition: therapeutic recreational specialist (professional level certificate) and therapeutic recreation assistant (paraprofessional level certificate). There is only an exam for the professional level certificate, which earns the therapist who passes it use of the designation certified therapeutic recreation specialist (CTRS).

Who Will Hire Me?

The most pressing need for recreational therapists is expected to be in nursing homes and senior retirement communities, because of the increasing number of older Americans. Check with facilities in your area to see if they have recreational therapists on staff and what they expect from their therapists. How many hours of internship do they prefer? Do they look for a certain specialty more than others? How many therapists do they employ? Do they accept interns or volunteers?

Rehabilitation centers hire recreational therapists to work with the physically disabled and to develop adaptive sports programs, such as wheelchair basketball and marathon racing. Similarly, park districts, mental health facilities, and group homes use recreational therapists to teach and encourage participation in sporting events, such as the Special Olympics, for mentally and physically disabled people.

Correctional institutions hire recreational therapists to coordinate activities for inmates in order to reduce stress and depression, and to develop skills that will allow them employment opportunities when they are reassimilated into society.

General hospitals, veterans' hospitals, children's hospitals, and psychiatric hospitals provide a large number of recreational therapy jobs. Other potential employers include camps or day care centers that serve the needs of disabled or elderly people.

FYI

Park districts in many communities provide special activity programs for developmentally disabled people as well as for senior citizens. The National Therapeutic Recreation Society is part of the National Recreation and Park Association. The NRPA campaigns to recognize the link between recreation and good health for everybody.

To Be a Successful Recreational Therapist, You Should . . .

- be comfortable working with elderly and disabled people
- be creative, patient, and flexible
- have good organization and communication skills
- enjoy group activities

Where Do I Go from Here?

Therapists with three or four years of experience and a master's degree may advance to supervisory or administrative positions. Continuing education is another path to advancement. Approved classes are offered by numerous recreational therapy associations, including the American Therapeutic Recreation Association (ATRA) and the National Therapeutic Recreation Society (NTRS). Earning continuing education credits may increase a therapist's responsibility and salary levels. Some therapists teach or conduct research.

What Are the Salary Ranges?

Recreational therapists earned median salaries of $32,540 in 2003, according to the U.S. Department of Labor. The lowest paid 10 percent earned less than $19,930 a year, while the highest paid 10 percent earned more than $50,760 annually. Supervisors earned top salaries of $50,000 per year; administrators reported maximum earnings of $65,000 per year; and some consultants and educators reported even higher earnings. Recreational therapists employed by hospitals generally earn higher wages than those employed in nursing care facilities.

What Is the Job Outlook?

The U.S. Department of Labor predicts that employment for recreational therapists will grow more slowly than the average over the next 10 years, mainly due to hospitals shifting more procedures to outpatient settings in an effort to contain costs. Thus, recreational therapists will a lessened role in the hospital setting.

However, increased life expectancies of the elderly and people with developmental disabilities will create opportunities for recreational therapists. Significant growth is also projected for therapists who work with the physically and mentally handicapped. The increase of alcohol and drug dependency is also creating a demand for qualified therapists to work in short-term alcohol and drug abuse clinics.

Most openings for recreational therapists will be in nursing homes because of the increasing numbers and greater longevity of the elderly. There is also greater public pressure to regulate and improve the quality of life in retirement centers, which may mean more jobs and increased scrutiny of recreational therapists.

How Do I Learn More?

PROFESSIONAL ORGANIZATIONS

For career information and resources, contact

American Therapeutic Recreation Association
1414 Prince Street, Suite 204
Alexandria, VA 22314
703-683-9420
http://www.atra-tr.org

For information on certification, contact

National Council for Therapeutic Recreation Certification
7 Elmwood Drive
New City, NY 10956
845-639-1439
nctrc@nctrc.org
http://www.nctrc.org

The following organization has career information, a journal, and other resources:

National Therapeutic Recreation Society
National Recreation and Park Association
22377 Belmont Ridge Road
Ashburn, VA 20148-4501
703-858-0784
http://www.nrpa.org/branches/ntrs.htm

BIBLIOGRAPHY

The following is a sampling of materials relating to the professional concerns and development of recreational therapists:

Austin, David, and Michael E. Crawford. *Therapeutic Recreation: An Introduction.* 3d ed. San Francisco: Benjamin Cummings, 2000.

Boik, Barbara Labovitz, and E. Anna Goodwin. *Sandplay Therapy: A Step-By-Step Manual for Psychotherapists of Diverse Orientations.* New York: W. W. Norton & Co., 2000.

Dattilo, John. *Facilitation Techniques in Therapeutic Recreation.* State College, Pa.: Venture Publishing, 2000.

Hobday, Angela M., and Kate Ollier. *Creative Therapy with Children & Adolescents.* Atascadero, CA: Impact Publishers, 1999.

Hogan, Susan. *Healing Arts: The History of Art Therapy.* New York: Taylor & Francis, 2001.

Kaduson, Heidi Gerard, and Charles E. Schaefer. *Short-Term Play Therapy for Children.* New York: Guilford Press, 2000.

Lowenstein, Linda. *Creative Interventions for Troubled Children & Youth.* Beverly Hills, Calif.: Champion Press, 1999.

Stumbo, Norma J., and Carol Ann Peterson. *Therapeutic Recreation Program Design: Principles and Procedures.* 4th ed. San Francisco: Benjamin/Cummings, 2003.

REFLEXOLOGISTS

In Wendi Humphryes's therapy room she gives her patient careful instructions about how to lie on the treatment table. The patient, with bare feet, is then made as comfortable as possible with pillows, including an extra pillow under her knees, a blanket covering, and soft music playing in the background.

"Once a client is comfortable I check for injuries, ingrown toenails, and areas [on the feet] to avoid," Wendi says. With the preliminaries out of the way, Wendi, a certified reflexologist, gets down to business, making her patient feel better by carefully massaging specific points on her patient's feet, hands, or ears.

Definition
Reflexology is a complementary health therapy in which practitioners use their hands to apply pressure to specific points on a patient's hands and feet that correspond to specific parts of the body in order to promote health, relaxation, and speed the healing process.

High School Subjects
Biology
Health
Psychology

Personal Skills
Communication/ideas
Helping/teaching

Salary Range
$7,000 to $35,000 to $78,000+

Educational Requirements
Some postsecondary training

Certification or Licensing
Recommended

Outlook
Faster than the average

DOT
N/A

GOE
N/A

NOC
3232

O*NET-SOC
N/A

What Does a Reflexologist Do?

The practice of reflexology is based on the theory that the human body is divided vertically into 10 zones, with five zones on each side. Matching zones also appear on the hands and feet. *Reflexologists* believe that massaging a spot in a zone on the foot can stimulate or affect the corresponding zone on the body. For example, massaging the reflex in the middle of the big toe is an attempt to affect the pituitary gland, which is the body part that corresponds to the center of the big toe.

Reflexologists believe, as well, that their treatments may help their clients in two other ways. Treatments may reduce the amount of lactic acid in the feet. Lactic acid is believed to be unhealthful when found in large quantities in the feet. And treatments may break up calcium crystals that build up in the nerve endings of the feet. It is believed the calcium crystals inhibit the flow of energy, which increases with the removal of the crystals. Reflexologists stress that their methods can improve circulation and promote relxation.

A reflexologist treating a first-time patient will ask the person a variety of questions related to his or her overall health, medical conditions, and why the patient sought the help of a reflexologist. Following the question and answer session, the reflexologist will make the patient as comfortable as possible before conducting a physical examination. The reflexologist uses information gathered during the consultation and examination to determine a course of treatment appropriate for the patient's physical condition.

In some cases, such as a patient who is extremely ill, the reflexologist will refer the patient back to his or her primary physician to be sure the proposed reflexology treatments will not be in conflict with the physician's course of treatment. For example, most practitioners will not treat someone who is running a fever. Also, because reflexology increases circulation, if the patient is on medication the dose may have to be adjusted, on the primary physician's advice, to compensate for the changes in the body's utilization of the drug.

Because of the differences in people—size, weight, foot shape, health condition—one of the primary skills a reflexologist must possess is knowing how much pressure to apply to each patient's feet.

A large, healthy adult requires a different amount of pressure than a young child. The practitioner also must know how long to work on the foot, since treatments that last too long may offset the benefits of the procedure.

Because the human foot is so sensitive, most reflexologists work primarily on the feet, but if a foot has been injured or amputated it is acceptable to work on the hands. Some practitioners also work on the patient's ears, back, and other body points as needed.

The modern practice of reflexology originated in the early 20th century when physician William Fitzgerald, an ear, nose, and throat specialist, discovered that applying pressure to a patient's hands or feet prior to surgery decreased the pain experienced by the patient.

Fitzgerald believed that "bioelectrical energy" flows from the feet or hands to specific points in other parts of the body. Based on his theories, Fitzgerald mapped the energy flow from the hands and feet to the corresponding areas throughout the body.

Eunice Ingham, a physiotherapist and follower of Fitzgerald, advanced his work with additional mapping of the correspondence between the reflexes and parts of the body. She eventually became known as the mother of modern reflexology and founded the organization that is now the International Institute of Reflexology (IIR).

Lingo to Learn

CAM (Complementary and alternative medicine); Complementary medicine is used with conventional medicine; alternative medicine is used in place of conventional medicine.

Lactic acid A natural waste product of the body's metabolic process that is unhealthful in large quantities.

Reflexes Specific points on the hands and feet that correspond to specific points elsewhere in the body.

Zones The 10 sections of the body, five on each side of an imaginary vertical line that divides the body in half. The section closest to the middle is zone one and the section farthest from the middle is zone five. It is believed that zones are found in the hands and feet that correspond to the body's zones.

What Is It Like to Be a Reflexologist?

By Wendi Humphryes's definition, her primary responsibility as a reflexologist "is to work mainly with pressure on the feet, hands, and ears of individuals to activate reflex zones or areas of the feet, thus stimulating the body's own natural healing process into action. An increased state of well-being [in the patient] often follows."

Most patients visit with Wendi first when they call her office to schedule an appointment. During the initial phone conversation, Wendi asks the patient if the requested appointment will be the person's first appointment with a reflexologist and why the person feels he or she needs treatment.

"On the day of the session a new client is given an information/release form to complete," Wendi says, "and then a verbal history of the situation is taken. Sometimes a client is in for relaxation and has very little [health] history. Other times a client has a long condition history, and I take notes based on the client's complaints."

Once the patient is comfortably settled in Wendi's therapy room, he or she receives an explanation of the treatment Wendi will perform. The patient also will share with Wendi what type of work is expected and how much time should be spent in that day's session. "The [patient's] reflex points are then worked thoroughly on the areas desired for the amount of time requested," Wendi says. "Notes and sore point documentation are recorded before and after the session."

At the end of the session the patient stops by Wendi's front desk to check out and at that time often schedules a follow-up appointment. Wendi explains that the average person usually experiences "re-congestion" within three to four days of therapy, so repeat visits are usually beneficial. In addition, Wendi trains patients in self-applied reflexology. "I instruct a client on how to work some of their own points at home so the results obtained from my treatments may be extended."

Wendi has a private practice so she has created an environment in her Englewood, Colorado, office that she believes meets her patients' needs. "The environ-

FYI

- According to the National Center for Complementary and Alternative Medicine (NCCAM), 62 percent of adults in the United States use some form of CAM to treat a variety of health conditions, including back, neck, head, and joint pain; depression, and sleeping problems.
- The Chinese first used foot massage as a supplement to acupuncture in 2,000 B.C. or earlier.
- A 4,000-year-old fresco depicting foot massage was found in the tomb of the physician to a pharaoh in the Egyptian city of Saqqara.
- Zone theory, the theoretical basis for reflexology, dates back to the 1500s in Europe.
- In the United States, Native Americans, specifically the Cherokees, have emphasized the importance of foot health because feet are what connect human beings with the earth.

ment I have created for my clients feels warm, sunny, family-like, clean, and non-cluttered," she explains, also pointing out that her office is accessible for patients with disabilities.

She notes that the environment in a reflexologist's office typically varies based on the practitioner's personal tastes and clientele. "Sometimes a practitioner's offices will have a spa-type environment and cater more to relaxation therapy," Wendi says. "Oftentimes, reflexology offices are more closely related to medical offices."

Besides taking care of her clients' physical needs and treatments, because she is self-employed Wendi must also handle the business aspects her practice, such as documenting client information, billing, ordering supplies, and more.

Do I Have What It Takes to Be a Reflexologist?

Since reflexologists work closely with their clients it is essential that you be friendly, open, and sensitive to the feelings of others. You also must be able to gain your patients' trust and make them feel comfortable and relaxed. Communications skills are important to enable you to gather the information needed in order to effectively treat your patients. If you plan to go into private practice like Wendi you must be comfortable making decisions and have the skills to handle the basics of your business such as advertising, finances, and legal requirements.

Wendi says having the heart to help others is the most important characteristic of a reflexologist. "Whether you choose to work in a spa setting to relax clients or an office geared toward addressing medical complaints, this field is all about helping people find wellness."

How Do I Become a Reflexologist?

Wendi worked for 18 years in medical reimbursement. She mentions that by keeping an eye towards trends in health care and medicine, she noticed there was a large increase in public interest in complementary and alternative medicine. Armed with that knowledge, Wendi studied to become a reflexologist and opened her practice in 2003.

EDUCATION

High School

The practice of reflexology involves using the correspondence between reflexes and other parts of the body, so having knowledge of medicine and anatomy will be beneficial. You should take courses in biology, chemistry, health, and other subjects related to the medical sciences. Courses in psychology will also help you learn about dealing with different types of people. You may want to investigate areas of bodywork and alternative medicine in your community that are not taught in high school. Knowledge of massage therapy will be particularly helpful since some states require reflexologists be licensed massage therapists.

POSTSECONDARY TRAINING

Completion of a rigorous course of study and practice is the most important part of a reflexologist's training. A variety of courses are available, from one-day workshops designed to teach you how to work on yourself to comprehensive courses that require a commitment of nine months or longer. Some correspondence courses are available, but any reputable correspondence course will require completion of supervised, hands-on training. Many reflexologists train in other therapies such as massage, aromatherapy, or other types of bodywork to increase the services they may offer clients. The IIR provides an extensive course of study in reflexology. Information about accredited schools is available from the American Commission for Accreditation of Reflexology Education and Training. On the Internet, a listing of schools offering training in reflexology and is available at http://www.naturalhealers.com.

CERTIFICATION OR LICENSING

In some states reflexologists who have completed a course of study through a reputable school of reflexology can be licensed specifically as a reflexologist. However, in most states reflexologists are regulated by the same laws that govern massage therapists. In these states, you must complete a state-certified course in massage before being licensed to practice reflexology. Because the laws are so varied, anyone wishing to work as a reflexologist should be aware of state and local regulations before opening a practice. National certification is available through the American Reflexology Certification Board (ARCB). For certification you must have a high school diploma or equivalent, have completed a hands-on reflexology course with a minimum of 110 hours of study, and have documented completion of 90 hours of post-graduate client sessions.

SCHOLARSHIPS AND GRANTS

Some schools of reflexology offer scholarships and grants to qualified students. Check with the school you plan to attend to see what type of financial aid is available.

INTERNSHIPS AND VOLUNTEERSHIPS

The best way to learn about the career of reflexology is to talk with a reflexologist. Contact reflexologists in your area and arrange to interview him or her. Also, since certification requires hands-on training, you may have an opportunity to complete an internship through the school you are attending.

Wendi says that before she enrolled in the Modern Institute of Reflexology in Lakewood, Colorado, she attended a hands-on weekend course offered by a practicing reflexologist in her area to learn more about reflexology. Wendi says the Modern Institute of Reflexology also provided her an opportunity to intern at a local clinic.

To Be a Successful Reflexologist, You Should . . .

- be in good physical condition
- be friendly and sympathetic
- be able to make people feel relaxed and comfortable
- have strong, sensitive hands
- have good decision-making skills

Who Will Hire Me?

Most reflexologists open their own practices, but others may work for chiropractors, spas, and other alternative therapy providers that offer reflexology as one of their services.

Where Can I Go from Here?

Because most reflexologists are self-employed, advancement is directly related to the quality of treatment they provide and their business skills. Wendi notes that as the field grows and is more accepted by the public there may be opportunities in teaching reflexology. "I expect the need for teaching will expand and be another service I add to my business."

What Are the Salary Ranges?

Generally, reflexologists working in large metropolitan areas earn between \$30 and \$60 per hour. Those practicing in rural areas often earn less, or between $20 and $40 per hour. Like massage therapists, a reflexologists work can be physically exhausting, so most practitioners consider working four or five billable patient hours per day to be full time employment. Based on those numbers, a practitioner in a rural area charging $20 per hour with four client-contact hours per day would earn about $400 per week or $20,800 annually. A reflexologist in a city charging $60 an hour with a large client base may earn as much as $1,500 per week or $78,000 annually or more. Practitioners just starting out or those working part time may earn as little as $7,000 per year, while those with experience, an established practice, or who combine reflexology with other therapies in their practice such as massage or oriental medicine, may earn as much as $100,000 annually. The median annual salary for most practitioners is estimated to be about $35,000.

What Is the Job Outlook?

While the scientific community is still skeptical about the effectiveness of reflexology, it has grown in popularity as a complementary or alternative therapy in recent years, particularly because it is a holistic practice that focuses on treating the whole person rather than just the symptoms of disease. In addition, reflexology treatments pose little risk to most clients, so it provides a safe, convenient way to improve health.

The U.S. Department of Labor projects that employment of massage therapists will grow faster than the average through 2012, and it is likely that employment of reflexologists will have similar growth.

How Do I Learn More?

PROFESSIONAL ORGANIZATIONS

For additional information about the career of reflexology, accredited training programs, certification, workshops, and seminars, contact the following organizations.

American Reflexology Certification Board
PO Box 740879
Arvada, CO 80006-0879
303-933-6921
info@arcb.net
http://www.arcb.net

International Institute of Reflexology
5650 First Avenue North
PO Box 12642
St. Petersburg, FL 33733-2642
iir@tampabay.it.com
http://www.reflexology-usa.net

Reflexology Association of America
79 Hudson Road
Boston, MA 07140
978-779-0255
http://reflexology-usa.org

BIBLIOGRAPHY

The following is a selection of materials that will provide additional information about reflexology:

Byers, Dwight C. *Better Health with Foot Reflexology*. 10th ed. St. Petersburg, Fla.: Ingham Publishing, 2001.

Carter, Mildred, and Tammy Weber. *Body Reflexology: Healing at Your Fingertips*. Upper Saddle River, N.J.: Prentice Hall, 2002.

Cosway-Hayes, Joan. *Reflexology for Every Body*. North Hills, Calif.: Footloose Press, 2003.

Dreyfus, Katy. *The Reflexology Deck: 50 Healing Techniques*. San Francisco: Chronicle Books, 2004.

Kluck, Michelle R. *Hands on Feet: The New System That Makes Reflexology a Snap*. Philadelphia: Running Press Book Publishers, 2001.

Kunz, Kevin, and Barbara Kunz. *Reflexology: Health at Your Fingertips*. New York: DK Publishing, 2003.

Voner, Valerie. *The Everything Reflexology Book*. Avon, Mass.: Adams Media Corporation, 2003.

REGISTERED NURSES

It is three in the morning in the intensive care unit. Nurses on the night shift are making their rounds, listening to the instruments that monitor their patients, changing IV bags, and giving medicine. In the emergency room it has been a slow night; only a few cases have come all at once. The flurry of activity there involves quick thinking and decision-making that could make the difference between life or death. This is quite a bit to ask of the trauma nurses who are seven hours into their shift.

Meanwhile, at a retirement community, a live-in nurse assists her client to the bathroom, walking slowly to help her navigate the long hallway from her bedroom safely. It is 11:00 at night. People need help at all hours, not only from nine to five. Nurses are there to provide the support, the medicine, the regimen prescribed by the doctor, to analyze a patient's progress. They also offer suggestions and emotional support to the friends and families of their clients.

Definition
Registered nurses (RNs) administer medical care to sick or injured individuals and help people achieve health and prevent disease.

High School Subjects
Biology
Health
Math

Personal Skills
Helping/teaching
Technical/scientific

Salary Range
$36,420 to $51,020 to $100,000+

Educational Requirements
Associate's degree through an accredited junior college, diploma from a nursing school, or bachelor's degree

Certification or Licensing
Required by all states

Outlook
Faster than the average

DOT
075

GOE
14.02.01

NOC
3152

O*NET-SOC
29-1111.00

What Does a Registered Nurse Do?

Just as the title *doctor* encompasses numerous specialties and branches of study, the title *registered nurse* is an umbrella term, covering many different aspects of nursing. Although nurses work in various health care facilities, they have three basic goals: to assist the ill, disabled, or elderly in the recovery or maintenance of life functions; to prevent illness and relapse of illness; and to promote health in the community. Most nurses come into contact with patients more frequently than other members of the health care community. Doctors are busy with diagnosis and the creation of treatment plans, and often do not have time to carry out the plans themselves. Because of this, nurses often provide a human element in a patient's treatment. They observe a patient's symptoms and evaluate progress or lack of progress. Nurses are also responsible for educating their patients and families on how to cope with a long-term illness or disability.

The field of nursing is broken down by the setting in which a nurse works. A registered nurse typically works under the guidance of a physician, who will develop a care plan for a patient that the nurse helps to administer. But the specific work of each nurse can take many forms. About two-thirds of all nurses work in hospitals, where they are assigned to different areas. *General duty nurses* offer bedside nursing care and observe the progress of the patients. They may also supervise licensed practical nurses and aides. *Surgical nurses* are part of a logistical team in the operating room that supports the surgeon. They sterilize instruments, prepare patients for surgery, and coordinate the transfer of patients to and from the operating room. A *maternity nurse* looks after newborn infants, assists in the delivery room, and educates new mothers and fathers on basic child care. A *head nurse* directs and coordinates the activities of the nursing staff. Other hospital staff nurses are trained to work in intensive care units, the emergency room, and in the pediatrics ward.

Registered nurses work in varied settings. *Home health nurses* provide nursing care, prescribed by a physician, to patients at home. They assist a wide range of patients, such as those recovering from illnesses and accidents, and must be able to work independently. *Private duty nurses* may work in hospitals or in a patient's home. They are employed by the patient they are caring for or by the patient's family. Their duties are carried out in cooperation with the patient's physician.

Office nurses work in clinics or at the private practice of a physician. Their duties may combine nursing skills—taking blood pressure, assisting with outpatient procedures, and patient education—with administrative or office duties such as scheduling appointments, keeping files, and answering phones. Nurses in this field may work for a health maintenance organization (HMO) or an insurance company.

Nursing home nurses direct the care of residents in long-term care facilities. The work is similar to that done in hospitals; however, a nursing home nurse cares for patients with conditions ranging from a hip fracture to Parkinson's disease. *Public health nurses,* or *community health nurses,* work with government and private agencies to educate the public about health care issues. *Occupational health nurses,* or *industrial nurses,* provide nursing care in a clinic at a work site. For a more detailed discussion of these and other nursing specialties, see the chapter Nursing Specialists.

What Is It Like to Be a Registered Nurse?

"A lot of people see nursing as bedpans and sponge baths, but that isn't the case anymore," says Jen Macri, who works in an intensive care unit (ICU) at Christ Center and Medical Hospital in Oak Lawn. Her workday runs from about 3:00 P.M. to 11:00 P.M., four days a week. Although she acknowledges that new nurses often get night and evening shifts, she points out that that isn't necessarily a bad thing. "I like second shift because it doesn't interrupt my sleep patterns. Some people like the rush of first shift—there's always a lot going on then. Some people really like nights, and wouldn't give them up for anything. Night staff are a special breed." Because most of the hospital administrative staff goes home at the end of the first shift, hospitals usually quiet down during second shift; fewer nurses are assigned to night and evening duty.

Jen's regular duties in the ICU include administering medicines that patients are supposed to receive. "Any kind of patient care—bathing, changing linens, monitoring support systems—that is also our responsibility. We do all the things nurses in other parts of the hospital do for their patients." What makes the ICU different is its uncertainty. Jen's patients are stable but monitored. "If a patient becomes unstable, we address the problem ourselves. We can't just call for a doctor and wait for him to show up. We have to begin dealing with the situation ourselves."

Nurses often provide a human element to hospital stays. Because of the life-threatening conditions of her patients, comfort and support for concerned family members is a significant part of Jen's day. "Sometimes you'll end up doing part of the doctor's job. The doctor might sit the family down and explain a condition to them and they nod their heads and have no idea what he was talking about. You kind of have to interpret what the doctor meant for people; you are more accessible to the patient and to the family than the doctors usually are."

Jen also finds that ICU nurses are allowed a certain freedom that is not usual on the other floors. "The doctors rely on us pretty heavily to keep track of patient status," she notes, and with the added responsibility comes an added amount of independence. Additionally, some ICU nurses may find that the restrictions placed on other hospital nurses by insurance companies or administrative staff are lessened for them because of the immediate and critical nature of the care they provide.

Jen works with about 10 other nurses per shift, and in her ICU there are 22 beds, so the nurse-to-patient ratio is about 1 to 2. In other parts of the hospital, this ratio can be 1 to 5 or as high as 1 to 25, depending on the type of care that is required and on the shift that is being scheduled. The general trend in hospitals is towards a higher nurse-to-patient ratio, which makes nurses responsible for more patients at a time. Jen works overtime if she is in the midst of a situation that has occurred on her shift. "You don't just go home when the shift is over. If somebody goes unstable in the last half hour of your shift, it is still your responsibility to handle it."

Lingo to Learn

Case manager A nurse or administrator who coordinates the medical care of a patient.

Crash cart The cart that carries medicines, equipment, and machines that may be needed in an emergency situation.

Intubate To insert breathing apparatus into the throat of a patient who is unable to breathe satisfactorily.

Nursing home A long-term care facility that provides the elderly and chronically ill with health care and assistance with daily activities, such as bathing, eating, and dressing.

Skilled nursing facility A facility that provides round-the-clock medical care by registered nurses and other licensed health care professionals.

Vital signs The pulse rate, breathing rate, and body temperature of a person.

Nursing demands alertness, education, and a certain amount of mental and physical stamina. "Intensive care can be stressful physically, because you are moving people who aren't able to move themselves. And it can be mentally tiring, too, because you see a lot of sickness and death. Not everybody dying is 80, either; I have seen 20- and 30-year-old patients in ICU." Occasionally, nurses in Jen's unit will have a debriefing to help them cope with a traumatic event or a death in their unit. "The people that you work with are so supportive. It's kind of the nature of the job. You really have to be there for each other."

Like other aspects of health care, nursing has become increasingly cost-conscious and somewhat political in recent years. Some nurses have a difficult time adjusting to the requirements of insurance companies and administrators and resent the fact that they are allowed less contact with their patients than before. Because Jen is new to nursing, she was trained with the current health care issues in mind and finds that she is not as critical about some requirements as some of her older coworkers.

Do I Have What It Takes to Be a Registered Nurse?

To be a successful nurse, says Jen Macri, you have to be adept at problem solving. "You have to be pretty organized, especially now that [hospital administration] is laying more and more in your lap and you have less time to do everything." More than anything else, nurses must have genuine concern for the people with whom they are working. "Ultimately, you're there to do good for the people," Jen summarizes. "People who aren't into that don't last very long."

Bunny Sendelbach, a nurse of almost 20 years, agrees. Bunny currently works in a retirement community where she provides care to elderly residents. "A nurse should be someone who has an aptitude in science, psychology, and who knows how to get along with a huge team. Most of all, you have to be able to inspire confidence and make your patients feel secure and good about themselves. That's the key to good health." Bunny feels that nursing is really still a calling, though this has gotten lost in the increasingly technical and financial aspects of the work. "To be a good healer, you have to be able to put aside your own ego, and give the patient the best environment you can so they can heal themselves. Nurses have to have heart, but they have to have brains as well."

To be a good healer, you have to be able to put aside your own ego, and give the patient the best environment you can so they can heal themselves.

The benefits of nursing are not limited to patients. Asked what made nursing worth the emotional stress and responsibility, both Jen and Bunny answered immediately. Jen appreciates the gratitude of patients and family; she also appreciates being able to contribute. "It's the people that get well and come back to say thank you, even if you only did a little smidge of something. You feel like you contributed by helping somebody. That's well worth everything else. When you know you've done something caring to help somebody else, you know you've done well."

To Become a Registered Nurse, You Should . . .

- have keen observational skills
- be able to work under pressure
- be well-organized
- be caring and sympathetic
- handle emergencies calmly

Patience, tact, and efficiency are qualities that make a good nurse. A strong sense of purpose and courage are qualities that will keep a good nurse in the career for years to come.

How Do I Become a Registered Nurse?

EDUCATION

High School

While still in high school, you should take core science and math classes, including biology, chemistry, and physics. Other classes to take include psychology and sociology. Communication skills are vital to successful nurses, so English and speech courses will be useful.

It is possible to volunteer in many of the places nurses work, in order to decide if nursing is the career you want. Hospitals will take high school volunteers as candy stripers or assistants to deliver mail and flowers, visit with patients, and do routine office work. While volunteerships at this level are not really concerned with patient treatment, they enable you to understand the way the hospital works and who is responsible for what duty.

While volunteering, you may be given more opportunity as a technician or as an aide to contribute to patient care. In many cases, according to Jen, if hospitals know you are seriously considering a career in nursing, they will give you better opportunities for hands-on involvement and experiences. "They'll say, come in here and help intubate Mr. So-and-so. One of the great things about being a volunteer is that it can be a direct line into a job at that hospital." Hospitals have a vested interest in training people to be nurses, especially if it means they will be able to hire somebody who is already familiar with the workings of their administration and setup.

Postsecondary Training

There are three training programs for registered nurses: associate's degree programs, diploma programs, and bachelor's degree programs. All three programs combine classroom education with actual nursing experience. Associate's degrees in nursing usually involve a two-year program at a junior or community college or nursing school that is affiliated with a hospital. Many associate's degree nurses (A.D.N.) pursue further schooling in bachelor's programs after they have found employment in order to take advantage of tuition reimbursement programs.

The diploma program is conducted through independent nursing schools and teaching hospitals. This program usually lasts three years and is the type that Jen went through and heartily recommends. "There are big differences in the programs. I think the best ones are done from big teaching hospitals, where you have the opportunities to see things that you wouldn't see in community hospitals or in associate's degree programs. I saw things at Rush [Presbyterian in Chicago] that I would never have seen in a suburban hospital, and will probably never see again."

A bachelor's of science degree in nursing (B.S.N.) is recommended for nurses who must compete in an era of cutbacks and small staffs. Additionally, bachelor's degree programs are recommended for those who may want to go into administration or supervision. It

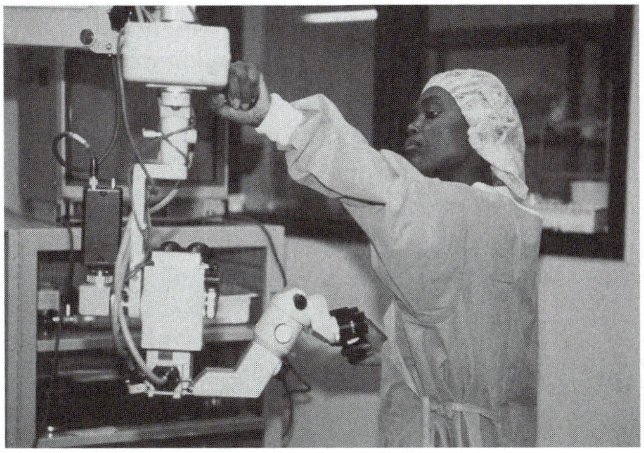

An operating room nurse prepares equipment before surgery. *(Photo Disc)*

is also required for jobs in public health agencies and for admission to graduate school.

There are also accelerated B.S.N. and master's degree programs for students who hold a bachelor's degree in another field. Many of these programs take three years to complete and require the student to complete courses in anatomy and physiology, statistics, chemistry, nutrition, and other subjects before starting the program. To review a listing of these programs, visit http://www.aacn.nche.edu/Media/FactSheets/AcceleratedProg.htm.

CERTIFICATION OR LICENSING

Those who pass an accredited nursing program are known as nurse graduates, but must still pass the licensing exam to become a registered nurse. Licensing is required in all 50 states, and license renewal or continuing education credits are also required periodically. In some cases, licensing in one state will automatically grant licensing in reciprocal states.

Additional training is inevitable for those wishing to advance into specialized practices, administration, and teaching. This may include further clinical training within a hospital in an area such as pediatrics or gerontology, or through a master's or Ph.D. level program.

SCHOLARSHIPS AND GRANTS

Scholarships and grants are often available from individual institutions, state agencies, and special-interest organizations. Many students finance their medical education through the Armed Forces Health Professions Scholarship Program. Each branch of the military participates in this program, paying students' tuitions in exchange for military service. Contact your local recruiting office for more information on this program.

The National League for Nursing publishes information on financial aid. Another source for financial aid, scholarship, and grant information is the Association of American Medical Colleges. Remember to request information early for eligibility, application requirements, and deadlines. (See "For More Info" for contact information for these organizations.)

Who Will Hire Me?

Jen believes that belonging to an association makes you more marketable to employers because it increases your awareness of what is happening in the nursing community. "I joined an association to put it on my resume, but the magazines they sent me ended up being really helpful and interesting. They keep you up-to-date with new practices and also advancements in the medical community and what that means to nursing. They have articles about medicine written for the layperson; they aren't written like medical trade journals. And managers love to see that stuff on applications. They know it keeps you aware and informed."

As with most jobs, persistence pays off, and special education can be a key element in winning specific jobs. "Right out of school I started knocking on doors. I wanted to work in the Surgical Heart Unit (SHU). I had extra cardiac training in watching monitors that other grads didn't. I interviewed with them but I didn't have the experience. From there I just bugged them every three months or so. Finally, the recruiter had an ICU position come up and she called me because I had kept in touch, because she knew me." Jen suggests keeping in touch with the recruiters at desired locations, introducing yourself with a letter or by getting their names and calling them, and then making sure they remember that you are waiting for them. "Part of it is just luck; if they need you when you are looking, you might luck into something that you'd be waiting forever for otherwise."

The most obvious place to look for a nursing job is in a hospital. Nurses also are needed in retirement communities, in government facilities, in schools, and in private practices. In fact, nursing in hospitals is not expected to grow as fast as other aspects of nursing, due to rising costs and a general trend away from inpatient care. The slack caused by fewer available hospital jobs will be taken up by increased opportunities in newer fields. Insurance companies now hire registered nurses to assist in case management and to ensure that insured patients are getting the correct kind of care from their health care pro-

FYI

The first U.S. school of nursing was established in 1872 at the New England Hospital for Women and Children in Boston.

viders. One of the fastest growing fields in nursing is home health care. Nurses who care for people on a part-time basis in their homes are in great demand for a variety of reasons. Technology has enabled many people to live free of health care institutions, but these people may still require assistance with some of their treatments.

Many surgical centers and emergency medical centers are taking the place of hospital emergency rooms. This will provide work for nurses who require a flexible schedule but who do not wish to work in a hospital. The number of older people with functional disabilities is growing, and jobs will be available in long-term care facilities for specialized conditions such as Alzheimer's disease.

Registered nurses should look in local papers and on the Internet for positions, in addition to contacting a preferred employer to ask what it may have available. Knowing where you would like to work, achieving educational credits in that field, and making sure those in charge of hiring know you are available are the key steps to finding a desirable nursing position.

Where Can I Go from Here?

Experienced registered nurses can advance in many ways. Those who want challenges beyond direct patient care may become teachers or administrators. Others continue their education and become clinical nurse specialists, nurse practitioners, nurse-midwives, or nurse anesthetists. Master's degrees and doctorates are required for many of these positions. (See the individual chapters on each of these types of nurses.)

What Are the Salary Ranges?

According to the U.S. Department of Labor, registered nurses earned median annual salaries of $51,020 in 2003. The lowest paid 10 percent made less than $36,420 a year, and the highest paid 10 percent made more than $73,020 a year. Nurses working in home health services made average salaries of $50,530 a year, while those working in nursing care facilities made $47,770 a year. Some nursing specialists, such as nurse anesthetists, can make well over $100,000 a year.

Salary is determined by several factors: setting, education, and work experience. Most full-time nurses are given flexible work schedules as well as health and life insurance; some are offered education reimbursement and year-end bonuses. A staff nurse's salary is limited only by the amount of work one is willing to take on. Many nurses take advantage of overtime work and shift differentials. About 10 percent of all nurses hold more than one job.

Most health care employers provide a good benefits plan for their workers, as well as flexible work schedules, child care, and bonuses. Educational incentives take the form of in-house training and tuition reimbursement, which enable nurses to increase their skills and potential for advancement at a reduced or no cost to themselves.

What Is the Job Outlook?

Registered nurses are the largest segment of the health care field, with about 2.3 million nurses currently working in the United States. Job opportunities for registered nurses are excellent. The U.S. Department of Labor projects that more new jobs will be available for registered nurses than any other occupation through 2012.

Increasing numbers of nurses who have entered to the profession in recent years have, however, lessened the demand for nurses in some areas. Even so, there are still many employment opportunities for nurses, especially in the inner cities and in rural areas. Employment opportunities for nurses will be best in home health care. The increased number of older people and better medical technologies have spurred the demand for nurses to bring complicated treatments to patients' homes.

Employment in nursing homes is expected to grow much faster than the average. Though more people are living well into their 80s and 90s, many need the kind of long-term care available at a nursing home. Also, because of financial reasons, patients are being released from hospitals sooner and admitted into nursing homes. Many nursing homes are acquiring facilities and staff capable of caring for long-term rehabilitation patients, as well as those afflicted with Alzheimer's. Many nurses will also be needed to help staff the growing number of outpatient facilities, such as HMOs, group medical practices, and ambulatory surgery centers.

Two-thirds of all nursing jobs are found in hospitals. However, because of administrative cost cutting, increased nurse's workload, and the rapid growth of outpatient services, hospital nursing jobs will experience slower than average growth.

Nursing specialties will be in great demand. There are, in addition, many part-time employment possibilities—approximately one in five of all nurses work part time.

How Do I Learn More?

PROFESSIONAL ORGANIZATIONS

The following organizations provide more information on nursing careers and to access a list of member schools:

American Association of Colleges of Nursing
1 Dupont Circle, NW, Suite 530
Washington, DC 20036
202-463-6930
http://www.aacn.nche.edu

American Nurses Association
8515 Georgia Avenue, Suite 400
Silver Spring, MD 20910
800-274-4262
http://www.nursingworld.org

Discover Nursing, sponsored by Johnson & Johnson Health Care Systems, provides information on nursing careers, nursing schools, and scholarships.

Discover Nursing
http://www.discovernursing.com

For information about state-approved programs and information on nursing, contact

National League for Nursing
61 Broadway, 33rd Floor
New York, NY 10006
800-669-1656
nlnweb@nln.org
http://www.nln.org

BIBLIOGRAPHY

The following is a sampling of materials relating to the professional concerns and development of registered nurses:

Bozell, Jeanna. *Anatomy of a Job Search—A Nurse's Guide to Finding and Landing the Job You Want.* Springhouse, Pa.: Springhouse Publishing, 1999.

Katz, Janet R., and Carol Carter. *Majoring in Nursing: From Prerequisites to Postgraduate Study and Beyond.* New York: Farrar, Strauss & Giroux, 1999.

Nettina, Sandra M. *The Lippincott Manual of Nursing Practice.* 7th ed. Philadelphia: Lippincott Williams & Wilkins, 2000.

Smith-Temple, Anthelyn Jean, Joyce Young Johnson. *Nurses' Guide to Clinical Procedures.* 5th ed. Philadelphia: Lippincott Williams & Wilkins, 2005.

Springhouse staff. *Nursing Procedures.* 3d ed. Philadelphia: Lippincott Williams & Wilkins, 2000.

Tucker, Susan Martin, Mary M. Cannobio, Eleanor Vargo Parquette, and Marjorie Fyfe Wells. *Patient Care Standards: Collaborative Planning & Nursing Interventions.* 7th ed. St. Louis, MO: Mosby, 2000.

Vallano, Annette. *Kaplan Careers in Nursing: Manage Your Future in the Changing World of Healthcare.* New York: Kaplan, 1999.

REHABILITATION COUNSELORS

Definition
Rehabilitation counselors help people with disabilities find employment and lead lives that are full and productive.

Alternative Job Titles
Case managers
Job placement specialists
Vocational rehabilitation specialists

High School Subjects
Physical education
Psychology
Sociology

Personal Skills
Communication/ideas
Helping/teaching

Salary Range
$18,000 to $27,410 to $60,000

Educational Requirements
High school diploma; a bachelor's degree in rehabilitation services or related field for employment in limited areas; a minimum of a master's degree in rehabilitation counseling is required for some employment

Certification or Licensing
Required by certain states

Outlook
Faster than the average

DOT
045

GOE
12.02.02

NOC
4153

O*NET-SOC
21-1015.00

Mario has always been a hardworking man. In the mornings he works as a short-order cook and in the evenings as a landscaper. But in one instant everything changed. Mario fell from a roof, struck his head, and sustained a disabling brain injury. Fortunately for Mario, there are no other physical complications. He is eager to return to his job at the restaurant. However, now disabled, he discovers there are new challenges he will have to face before he can begin working again. Mario has someone there to help him meet those challenges: his rehabilitation counselor.

Greg Cusick works for the Vocational Rehabilitation Services Department, an academic affiliate of the Rehabilitation Institute of Chicago. First, Greg puts Mario through initial assessment testing to determine his functioning levels. Then he develops a work-trial program for him in the hospital's cafeteria. It only takes a few days to see that Mario is ready to return to the restaurant. The restaurant owner agrees to let Mario return after Greg arranges for him to observe Mario working in the cafeteria. It is, as Greg describes it, "one of the better success stories."

What Does a Rehabilitation Counselor Do?

Rehabilitation counselors help people with disabilities find employment and lead full and independent lives. How people feel about themselves is significantly influenced by their careers and their ability to contribute to society. Because of that, the services of rehabilitation counselors play a crucial role during a patient's transition back into the work environment. Rehabilitation counselors develop programs that include client assessments, training programs, and job placement.

The majority of the clients Greg Cusick sees have physical disabilities and are outpatients of the Rehabilitation Institute of Chicago (RIC). Before clients can begin vocational rehabilitation therapy, an in-house psychologist must determine that they have adjusted psychologically to their physical disability. Though clients may still be involved in physical, occupational, or psychological therapy, most are ready to begin considering their vocational goals for the future.

Rehabilitation counselors first meet with other members of their client's treatment team to learn the client's medical history and current physical and emotional status. At RIC, the first time that clients and rehabilitation counselors meet face-to-face is during the initial consultation. During the consultation, rehabilitation counselors gather information regarding the client's employment and educational history, as well as any vocational goals the client may have for the future. Rehabilitation counselors may do a job analysis of a client's previous career to determine if it is possible to return to that career.

If it is impossible for clients to return to their former careers, rehabilitation counselors discuss the possibility of clients entering new fields and beginning new careers. However, rehabilitation counselors do not force anything on clients. As Greg explains, "We don't have a bunch of jobs and try to fit people into those jobs. I'm not going to tell clients what to do. The clients are going to tell me what they are interested in doing and then I'm going to see if that's appropriate, and, if so, then try and help them reach that goal."

Clients must go through extensive testing. After the tests are completed, rehabilitation counselors have an understanding of the clients' vocational goals and their current level of skills and abilities. Furthermore, the results of the testing determines if any additional training may be needed before clients can return to work.

One of the first tests clients must complete is an interest test. This gives rehabilitation counselors direction as they look for areas of employment that clients may find interesting. Abilities testing assesses the clients' verbal and numerical skills, as well as their general learning potential. There are also additional tests for finger dexterity, motor coordination, and balance. Additionally, if appropriate to their interests, clients undergo clerical tests, which assess office, computer, and keyboarding skills.

During a work-trial assessment, rehabilitation counselors try to place their clients in real work environments that simulate the field they are planning to enter. They are evaluated by their counselor on a daily basis. The program gives rehabilitation counselors an opportunity to assess their clients' skill levels, work behaviors, interaction with other people, and memory, in real-life environments. The work-trial program usually lasts from two to four weeks and the positions are unpaid.

The next step is developing a tentative plan for employment. "Sometimes that means receiving some type of training," says Greg, "and we work with a lot of different training programs as well as community colleges."

In addition to working as *vocational rehabilitation specialists,* rehabilitation counselors can also work as job placement specialists. *Job placement specialists* help clients who have completed their training programs find jobs. The job placement specialists receive referrals describing the vocational goals of the clients, their level of skills, and their experience. Many job placement specialists work to cultivate strong relationships with the human resources managers of corporations in their area to learn of openings and potential employment opportunities for their clients.

However, even after clients become employed, the vocational rehabilitation counselors' responsibilities concerning the client still continue. They check in regularly with both the employer and the client to see if everything is running smoothly. The counselor

Lingo to Learn

Caseload management The ratio of clients to counselors, takes into account characteristics of each case.

Disability management The process of returning a person with a disability to work.

Peer counseling Guidance and support given to a person by a person who has had similar experiences.

Prevocational services The evaluation, training, and assessment that a rehabilitation counselor uses prior to training a person with a disability for a vocation.

Rehabilitation engineering Encompasses many disciplines including engineering and medicine with the aim of improving the quality of life for persons with disabilities.

Supported employment Competitive employment for persons with severe disabilities who require ongoing support.

Work adjustment Training designed to help persons with disabilities form work habits that will increase their productivity. Seeks to promote self-confidence, tolerance, and interpersonal communications.

may need to make an on-site visit to observe clients at work. Rehabilitation counselors arrange for any additional training if necessary.

The length of time a counselor may work with a client varies greatly. Each case is determined on a client-by-client basis. If a job placement fails, the rehabilitation counselor works with the client to try again. It is not enough for a counselor to find the client a job, but to find the client a career, because, as Greg explains it, the primary responsibility of the vocational rehabilitation counselor is "to get people to work. That's what our goal is, that's our bottom line."

What Is It Like to Be a Rehabilitation Counselor?

Although many people have earned a degree in rehabilitation counseling, their job titles can vary greatly. Some rehabilitation counselors, like Greg Cusick, work as vocational rehabilitation specialists, while others work as job placement specialists or case managers. Furthermore, even working as a vocational counselor, Greg's responsibilities change as his clients progress through therapy. First he works as a vocational evaluator. Then, once the clients begin working with job placement specialists, Greg's role becomes more of a case manager, overseeing their progress.

The number of clients rehabilitation counselors see during a week depends on their specialization, as well as their place of employment. At the Vocational Rehabilitation Services Department for the Rehabilitation Institute of Chicago, Greg sees 10 to 12 clients in a week. However, he may speak with as many as 12 more on the phone, checking on their status. Most rehabilitation counselors work a 40-hour week. To accommodate clients who may not be able to come in during the day, some rehabilitation counselors work in the evenings or on weekends.

Some clients seek out the help of rehabilitation counselors on their own, after they have become disabled through an accident or illness. Others are referred to rehabilitation counselors by members of their treatment team, which may include a physician, psychologist, or social worker.

Rehabilitation counselors work with clients who face incredible challenges every day and are very vulnerable. Even though the clients Greg sees are there because of physical disabilities, they may also be struggling with psychological or emotional problems, like depression or anxiety. Often clients do not begin their vocational therapy immediately after they are released from the hospital. Some clients may have been discharged for up to six months before they begin their vocational therapy.

When asked to describe one of the major rewards of being a rehabilitation counselor, Greg replies, "Right here, this." He picks up a green form. "This is a placement notice for one of our clients. He just got a job today. To see clients find the jobs they want, to be happy, to stop receiving Social Security, to start receiving a wage, to start to become independent again. That's the fun part of the job."

On the other hand, the job of rehabilitation counselors can be very stressful. The job market is very competitive. And besides helping clients prepare for the job hunt, they also have to help potential employers see past a client's disability. However, vocational rehabilitation counselors have a great deal of confidence in their clients once their vocational therapy has concluded. Rehabilitation counselors do not expect special considerations for their clients. "We feel that we have clients that are just as competitive as anyone else," Greg explains.

Working as a rehabilitation counselor can have its share of disappointments and frustrations. A counselor may work several months to find the perfect placement for a client and still not succeed. For various reasons, either the employer or the client may become unhappy in the situation and the rehabilitation counselor has to start all over again with the client. Greg recently placed a client in what he thought was the ideal environment, but it did not work out. Rehabilitation counselors cannot let their clients become discouraged. Instead they work just as hard to find their clients better placements the next time.

Do I Have What It Takes to Be a Rehabilitation Counselor?

Successful rehabilitation counselors have strong problem-solving skills. When clients realize that they cannot return to their old jobs, it is the responsibility of rehabilitation counselors to give them direction toward new careers. They have to answer any questions the clients have about working with a disability. They also have to explain to clients that they can begin new

To Be a Successful Rehabilitation Counselor, You Should . . .

- have strong problem solving skills
- be adept at interpersonal communication
- be sensitive to others
- be able to persevere
- understand organization of businesses
- enjoy working with a variety of people
- be a good listener

careers that will accommodate their disabilities and be just as exciting and fulfilling as their former careers.

It is important that rehabilitation counselors have strong interpersonal communication skills. They need to let their clients express their fears and disappointments. They need to know when they can encourage their clients to go a little further and when to leave them alone. Also, rehabilitation counselors need effective communication skills when they are interacting with the other members of the treatment team. Each member of the team needs to know how the client is progressing in his or her respective therapies to effectively treat the whole client.

Rehabilitation counselors must be sensitive people who care about the well-being of others. They must have an almost unending source of patience. Because placements sometimes fail, rehabilitation counselors have to be able to help clients until they find the right placement that offers long-term employment. Most rehabilitation counselors are dedicated to their profession and believe that by helping people find employment and lead productive lives they are helping society, one person at a time.

Finally, successful rehabilitation counselors are often better salespeople than their contacts in the business community with whom they may place their clients. In some cases they must help potential employers overcome a reluctance to hire someone with a disability. Furthermore, because clients may become discouraged while trying to find employment, rehabilitation counselors have to help their clients keep their self-esteem high. A positive attitude is important. As Greg explains, "They need a positive outlook and attitude if they're to go out and get a job. Because if they're not positive, no one is going to hire them."

How Do I Become a Rehabilitation Counselor?

EDUCATION

High School

To prepare for a career in rehabilitation counseling, take courses in psychology, sociology, economics, and statistics. These classes will provide useful insight into human nature. Also, you will begin to realize how different economic factors can affect the job market.

Speech and communication classes can help you develop the skills necessary to express yourself clearly and effectively, both to your clients and to potential employers. Additionally, because listening skills are so important, communication classes can teach you an understanding of both verbal and nonverbal communication.

Business classes are beneficial because rehabilitation counselors need to understand how businesses are organized and structured. When inquiring about potential job opportunities for clients, you need to know whom to contact in a business.

Anatomy and biology classes will give you a basic understanding of your clients' disabilities and see how they affect vocational training and goals.

Postsecondary Training

In the field of rehabilitation counseling, your academic degree determines your level of responsibility and place of employment. Counselors with only a bachelor's degree in rehabilitation counseling are usually employed as counseling or rehabilitative aides.

Currently, there are more than 50 rehabilitation education programs across the country offering bachelor's degrees. Undergraduate course work includes classes in sociology, psychology, history, and statistics.

A counselor with a master's degree in rehabilitation counseling will have many more employment opportunities in a wider range of areas. In fact, vocational and rehabilitative agencies hire only applicants with master's degrees. Also, an advanced degree is required to apply for certification by the Commission on Rehabilitation Counselor Certification.

Most master's degree programs last for two years. At present there are more than 80 accredited master's programs across the country. Accreditation of rehabilitation counseling educational programs is granted by the Council on Rehabilitation Education. Some of the graduate course work includes classes in the medical and psychosocial aspects of disability and techniques of counseling, as well as training in vocational evaluations and job placement. In addition to course work, graduate students complete about 600 hours of supervised clinical training.

CERTIFICATION OR LICENSING

The Commission on Rehabilitation Counselor Certification offers certification for counselors. Applicants must hold a master's degree from an accredited graduate rehabilitation counseling program to become a certified rehabilitation counselor (CRC). Also, the applicant must have completed an internship program and must pass a written examination. To retain their status, CRCs are required to complete 100 hours of continuing education within five years of receiving their certification. Two designations available to CRCs are the master addictions counselor (MAC) and clinical supervisor (CS) designations.

Most states require some form of licensing for rehabilitation counselors. This usually involves passing a written exam and an evaluation by a state board of examiners. Also, most states require license applicants to be CRCs.

SCHOLARSHIPS AND GRANTS

The U.S. Department of Education Rehabilitation Services Administration (RSA) offers scholarships and grants to students pursuing advanced studies in rehabilitation counseling. For more information on these scholarships and affiliated schools, visit RSA's Web site at http://www.ed.gov/fund/grant/apply/rsa/scholarships.html.

INTERNSHIPS AND VOLUNTEERSHIPS

High school students interested in gaining practical experience in the field of rehabilitation counseling should contact the volunteer office of the hospital in their area. Many hospitals have large volunteer programs. Volunteers are often placed in the department they are interested in; furthermore, the volunteer office may be able to arrange for the student to spend a day with rehabilitation counselors. Most rehabilitation counselors enjoy talking about their careers and are happy to answer any questions the student may have.

The Rehabilitation Institute of Chicago has several different programs that bring together professionals of different backgrounds to discuss one particular issue at area high schools.

Who Will Hire Me?

Because rehabilitation counselors work with people of all ages and backgrounds, places of employment can vary greatly. Rehabilitation counselors who work with clients with physical disabilities may work for rehabilitation or vocational agencies. Some rehabilitation counselors work at halfway houses and correctional institutions with clients who are struggling with drug and alcohol addictions. Many licensed counselors have begun to work for HMOs and other insurance agencies.

Greg Cusick's first position as a rehabilitation counselor was for the students' center for disabilities at a community college in San Diego. Greg was supervised by a certified counselor. He explains, "So for a year and a half she would meet with me once a week and show me the ropes. We would go over cases and she supervised [me] very closely."

You can contact different professional associations. The National Rehabilitation Counseling Asso-

FYI

In 1990, Congress passed the Americans with Disabilities Act. This measure recognized the rights and needs of people with disabilities and developed federal guidelines and regulations aimed at eliminating discrimination and other barriers preventing people with disabilities from participating fully in school, workplace, and public life. Many government programs have since been created to aid people with disabilities.

ciation and the American Rehabilitation Counseling Association collect information regarding employment opportunities. Also take advantage of the placement office at the school from which you earn your degree.

State and federal governments hire a large number of rehabilitation counselors to work for agencies that are funded with state or federal money. To assist disabled veterans, the Department of Veterans Affairs hires hundreds of rehabilitation counselors.

Where Can I Go from Here?

Students who earn their bachelor's degree in rehabilitation services may consider working in a supervised position to gain practical experience before committing the time and money required to earn a graduate degree.

However, to widen the scope of career possibilities, it is mandatory that you earn a master's degree. Counselors with graduate degrees have a greater choice of counseling areas that they can work in. After becoming certified, rehabilitation counselors can move into supervisory or administrative positions. However, supervisors or managers may be required to work additional hours due to their increased responsibilities. Also, in some instances this may require additional training before they can move into managerial positions.

Often rehabilitation counselors decide to specialize and work in only one area of counseling. They may also choose to move into private practice.

Finally, many rehabilitation counselors find fulfillment as teachers, helping students become competent rehabilitation counselors. When rehabilitation counselors return to the academic environment to teach, they bring with them their real-world experience, which helps their students gain a better understanding of the demands of the job.

What Are the Salary Ranges?

The U.S. Department of Labor reports that rehabilitation counselors made median annual salaries of $27,410 in 2003. The middle 50 percent made between $21,720 and $35,650 a year. The lowest paid 10 percent made less than $18,000 a year, and the highest paid 10 percent made more than $47,100. Rehabilitation counselors with advanced degrees working in supervisory positions can make more than $60,000 a year.

Self-employed counselors who have well-established practices, as well as counselors employed in group practices, usually have the highest earnings, as do some counselors working for private firms, such as insurance companies and private rehabilitation companies.

What Is the Job Outlook?

Demand for rehabilitation and mental health counselors is expected to be strong through the next decade, with job growth that is faster than the average for all occupations. Managed care systems and insurance companies are increasingly providing reimbursement for counselors, enabling many counselors to move from schools and government agencies to private practice.

New medical technologies are saving lives in greater numbers and continue to improve functionality for people with disabilities. This increasing population should increase the need for rehabilitation counselors.

Legislation regarding the rights of people with disabilities has further increased opportunities in rehabilitation counseling. Not only do counselors help people back into the workforce, they also help companies comply with Americans with Disabilities Act regulations. More employers are also offering employee assistance programs that provide mental health and alcohol and drug abuse services.

How Do I Learn More?

PROFESSIONAL ORGANIZATIONS

The following organizations provide information on rehabilitation counseling and possible sources of employment information.

American Counseling Association
5999 Stevenson Avenue
Alexandria, VA 22304
703-823-9800
http://www.counseling.org

Commission on Rehabilitation Counselor Certification
1835 Rohlwing Road, Suite E
Rolling Meadows, IL 60008
847-394-2104
http://www.crccertification.com

Council on Rehabilitation Education
1835 Rohlwing Road, Suite E
Rolling Meadows IL 60008
847-394-1785
http://www.core-rehab.org

National Rehabilitation Counseling Association
P.O. Box 4480
Manassas, VA 20108
703-361-2077
http://nrca-net.org

BIBLIOGRAPHY

The following is a sampling of materials relating to the professional concerns and development of rehabilitation counselors:

Garner, Geraldine O. *Careers in Social and Rehabilitation Services*. New York: McGraw-Hill, 2001.

Parker, Randall M., and Edna Szymanski, eds. *Rehabilitation Counseling: Basics and Beyond*. 3d ed. Austin, Tex.: Pro-Ed, 1998.

Riggar, T. F., and Dennis R. Maki, eds. *Handbook of Rehabilitation Counseling*. Springer Series on Rehabilitation. New York: Springer: 2003.

Robb, Daniel. *Crossing the Water: Eighteen Months on an Island Working With Troubled Boys—A Teacher's Memoir*. New York: Simon & Schuster, 2002.

Roessler, Richard T., and Stanford E. Rubin. *Case Management and Rehabilitation Counseling: Procedures and Techniques*. 3d Edition. Austin, Tex.: Pro-Ed, 1998.

RESPIRATORY CARE WORKERS

Definition
Respiratory care workers administer general respiratory care to persons with heart and lung problems.

Alternative Job Titles
Inhalation therapists
Respiratory care practitioners

High School Subjects
Biology
Chemistry
Health

Personal Skills
Helping/teaching
Technical/scientific

Salary Range
$31,420 to $42,050 to $56,480

Minimum Educational Level
Associate's degree

Certification or Licensing
Required by certain states

Outlook
Faster than the average

DOT
079

GOE
14.06.01

NOC
3214

O*NET-SOC
29-1126.00, 29-2054.00

Tom Garcia reports to work at 7:00 P.M. at Northwestern Memorial Hospital, one of Chicago's major teaching hospitals. He greets coworkers as he gets a cup of coffee and collects the reports of the day shift. When he sits down to read them over, he looks for important messages, patients who have undergone surgery that morning, and new admissions requiring evaluation. He makes notes of changes in therapy or medication. When Tom finishes scanning the last report, he realizes that one chart is missing. He dials the nurse's station on the pediatric floor.

"Hi, Joanie, it's Tom Garcia. Where's Jessica Brandon's chart?" Tom has been giving Jessica chest physiotherapy since she was admitted a month ago with complications of cystic fibrosis. There is a pause on the other end, then a sigh.

"Tom," Joanie says finally, "Jessica died this afternoon."

Tom covers his eyes with his hand and sits quietly for a moment. This is the part of the job Tom hates. He sees Jessica's smile as he left her room just last night. "You be sweet now," he told her, "and I'll see you tomorrow." Sometimes all the knowledge and skilled care in the world are not enough. The feelings of failure—however irrational—and having to witness the grief of survivors can be excruciating.

But right now Tom can't indulge his feelings. It's going to be a tough night. Two other respiratory care workers are out with the flu bug that's going around. He'll have to work twice as hard, yet give each patient the same focused attention as he would on a slow day.

What Does a Respiratory Care Worker Do?

In extraordinary circumstances, it is possible to go without food for a few weeks or without water for a few days. But without air, brain damage occurs within minutes; death follows after about nine minutes.

Respiratory care workers include *therapists, technicians,* and *assistants* (or *aides*). Assistants clean, sterilize, store, and maintain inventory and care for equipment. They are usually beginners on their way to certification and registration and have little patient contact. The duties of *registered respiratory therapists* (RRTs) and *certified respiratory therapists* (CRTs) are similar. They both treat patients with cardiorespiratory problems.

RRTs have more clinical experience, however. They apply scientific knowledge and theory to the practical problems of respiratory care under the supervision of doctors. They may be required to exercise independent clinical judgement. Sometimes they even advise doctors on appropriate therapy. Licensed RRTs can also order medication with a physician's approval. In addition, their responsibilities often entail training, teaching, and supervising other workers, such as CRTs.

Respiratory care workers review clinical data, patient histories, and respiratory therapy orders. They interview and examine patients and perform or recommend X rays and laboratory tests. They evaluate patient information in order to determine the appropriateness of specific therapies. They perform and modify prescribed therapeutic procedures, such as the administration of aerosol inhalants that confine medication to the lungs. They are also responsible for assembling, maintaining, and monitoring equipment and for ensuring cleanliness and sterility. Equipment includes ventilators (respirators), positive-pressure breathing machines, or environmental control systems. The patients of respiratory care workers may be recovering from surgery and need respiratory care to restore full breathing capacity and to prevent respiratory illnesses. Other patients suffer from chronic conditions like asthma or emphysema. Victims of heart failure, stroke, drowning, or other trauma need life support. Respiratory care workers observe patients' physiological responses to therapy and consult with physicians if there are adverse reactions. They are often called to emergency rooms and intensive care units where their skill and devotion can mean the difference between life and death. Now that home care is becoming more widespread, respiratory care workers sometimes instruct patients and their families in the use of respiratory equipment at home.

An important aspect of the job is record keeping. Respiratory care workers record critical information on patients' charts, make reports, and keep track of the cost of materials and charges to the patients. There is always a lot of paperwork.

Lingo to Learn

Bronchodilator Drug that aids expansion of the bronchial airway.

Cardiorespiratory Relating to the heart and lungs.

Clinical Involving direct observation of the patient.

Intubation Introduction of a breathing tube into the throat.

Pulmonary Relating to the lungs.

Ventilator A machine that maintains breathing for a patient who cannot breathe independently.

What Is It Like to Be a Respiratory Care Worker?

In the intensive care unit, Tom Garcia, a registered respiratory therapist, inspects ventilators for recent surgery patients. Since these people are intubated and cannot speak, Tom asks yes or no questions that can be answered with hand squeezes. He takes a few moments to reassure these critical patients and let them know he's there for them. As he finishes up, the pager summons him to operating room seven. A young woman, the victim of a drunk driver, has just come out of emergency surgery. Tom connects her to a ventilator and confirms that the equipment is operating properly.

The surgeon asks Tom questions about an oddity in the patient's blood gas analysis. It's something Tom has seen before. He explains it to the surgeon and makes a recommendation. Tom smiles to himself as he leaves the intensive care unit, reflecting that only a few years ago, doctors didn't ask the advice of lower-level professionals. But that's changing with specialization, the increasing sophistication of equipment, and new options in therapeutic technique.

It's nearly midnight when Tom sits down to eat a quick lunch. After leaving the ICU, Tom administered bronchodilator aerosols to two pulmonary disease patients. He coached them on how to cough in order to clear their lungs. He also performed chest physiotherapy on a man recovering from pneumonia. This technique involves placing the patient in a posture to promote drainage and thumping and vibrating the rib cage. Tom expands the sketchy notes he made on his rounds. Finally, he writes out a to-do list for the remainder of his shift. He has to check on the car accident victim again and call the equipment manufacturer about a recurring problem with one of the ventilators. Since one of the aides has the flu, he'll check to see that there are enough supplies for the next shift.

"This is not a job for someone who wants a nice, predictable nine-to-five existence," Tom says. "And you'll never get rich. On the other hand, you'll never be bored either. The rewards of a career in respiratory therapy are the constant challenge and knowing that you help people. You see results. What you do makes a difference."

The rewards of a career in respiratory therapy are the constant challenge and knowing that you help people. You see results.

Advancement Possibilities

Pediatric neonatal specialists work with premature newborns and newborns with respiratory problems. The needs of these infants are unique; since many more premature infants now survive, this is a rapidly growing field.

Pulmonary function technologists use advanced techniques to diagnose pulmonary diseases.

Do I Have What It Takes to Be a Respiratory Care Worker?

Because people can die so quickly if they stop breathing, respiratory care workers play a critical role in medical institutions. In cases of cardiac arrest, drowning, electric shock, and other kinds of trauma, they may literally hold people's lives in their hands. For this reason, respiratory care workers need to develop maturity, the capacity to accept grave responsibilities, and a genuine desire to care for others.

"You can't be squeamish," says Tom. "Especially in a big city hospital, you see lots of bad injuries. You've got to keep your cool because the patient and the trauma team depend on you. And since you work with ventilators and other sophisticated machinery, it helps if you're good with your hands or have mechanical aptitude."

Pat Adney is director of respiratory care and rehabilitation services at Chicago's Weiss Memorial Hospital. In addition to the qualities already described, Pat says having a natural curiosity and interest in the field is a plus. "A really good respiratory care worker possesses intellectual curiosity. Most of your education comes from the job; you constantly have to figure things out and learn on your own initiative because there's always something new." Pat also stresses emotional equilibrium. "You must strike a balance so you neither burn out nor become heartless and unfeeling."

Since respiratory care workers have to process a lot of paperwork, writing skills are a must. "You work with doctors and other highly educated people," says Tom. "In order to have credibility, you must be articulate and well read in your field. There's always so much to read because there are new things happening all the time."

Another factor to keep in mind is the necessity for shift work. Medical facilities operate 24 hours a day, so there are three shifts. Most respiratory care workers are expected to be flexible about shift changes, overtime, and holidays. Remember, too, that they are on their feet for most of the 40-hour week. They must also be able to take orders from superiors—even when they come from people who are not always pleasant. "You have to deal with professional egos," Tom comments, "and sometimes you're pulled in different directions because of great needs and a too small staff."

Finally, one important factor to consider is safety. The pressurized gases used in respiratory therapy are potentially hazardous; and every respiratory care worker runs the risk of contracting an infectious disease from a patient. Following safety precautions, regular maintenance, and equipment testing reduce the possibility of injury from pressurized gases, while strict adherence to proper procedure minimizes the risk of exposure to infectious disease.

How Do I Become a Respiratory Care Worker?

Tom's career grew out of two major boyhood interests. "I always liked fooling around with mechanical things, and I was interested in science. Applying mechanics to the human body is fascinating." Tom recalls his training period as being a tough two years. "There was a lot of memorization. Everything was very concentrated. In the second year you get thrown into patient care—you have to be an adult right away."

EDUCATION

High School

Respiratory care requires a lot of fundamental mathematical problem solving. For instance, in their daily work, respiratory care workers must compute medication dosages and calculate gas concentrations. Tom advises that high school students take courses in algebra, physics, chemistry, biology, English composition, and reading comprehension. Classes in health, computer skills, general mathematics, and bookkeeping are also helpful.

A summer job in a hospital is a good way to see what the field is like. Although the job assignment may not relate to respiratory therapy, there will be chances to observe and perhaps get acquainted with respiratory care workers. If no part-time or temporary work is available, you might consider volunteer service.

Postsecondary Training

To work as an aide, you may only need a high school degree and on-the-job training. Formal training in respiratory care is provided in one-year certificate programs, which certify an individual for entry-level respiratory therapy work, or two-year associate degree or four-year bachelor degree programs that prepare you for the registry examination and advanced work. There are 59 entry-level and 319 advanced respiratory therapy programs in the United States and Puerto Rico. A high school diploma or equivalent is required for all. Training is available through hospitals, medical schools, colleges and universities, trade schools, vocation-technical institutes, and the armed forces. It is imperative that the training institution be accredited by the Committee on Allied Health Education and Accreditation (CAHEA) of the American Medical Association (AMA) or the Committee on Accreditation for Respiratory Care (CoARC). A list of accredited programs is available from the American Association for Respiratory Care (AARC) (see "How Do I Learn More?").

Two-year schools should include enough credit hours of clinical training (treating patients under supervision) to qualify the student to take both the certification and registry examinations. (Certification is required in order to sit for the registry examination.)

Course work consists of anatomy, physiology, medical terminology, chemistry, mathematics, microbiology, physics, therapeutic procedures, clinical medicine, and clinical expressions. Students learn to do procedures such as venous punctures, arterial blood draws, intubation, stress testing, and electrocardiograms. Social science classes in communication skills, psychology, and medical ethics support the basic science studies.

In respiratory care, as well as all other areas of medicine, education is ongoing. Constant improvements in equipment, medication, and therapeutic technique make continuing education a must. In addition to registry, a respiratory care worker may pursue specialties in pulmonary function technology, pulmonary function therapy, pediatric neonatology, and many other areas. Supervising RRTs or equipment manufacturers often present in-service training seminars. Good hospitals support additional training.

CERTIFICATION OR LICENSING

Typically, a hospital hires uncertified new graduates providing that they pass the certification exam in six months to a year. Tom took the registry exam two years after certification. As an RRT, Tom is now a supervisor. "I enjoy teaching," he says. "I like to pass on knowledge, to help shape the careers of new people."

Certification and registry examinations are offered by the National Board for Respiratory Care (see "How Do I Learn More?"), usually through a state licensure agency. Forty-two states license respiratory care personnel. The certified respiratory therapists (CRT) designation is the standard for licensure in most states. As of 2006, candidates for the CRT must hold an associate's degree from an accredited respiratory therapy education program. To sit for the registered respiratory therapist (RRT) exam, applicants must hold the CRT designation and an associate's degree from an accredited program.

SCHOLARSHIPS AND GRANTS

The American Respiratory Care Foundation (the philanthropic organization of the AARC) offers scholar-

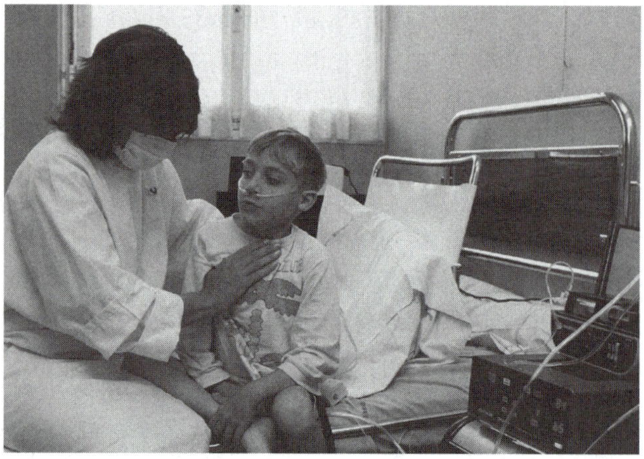

A respiratory therapist works with a young child with cystic fibrosis. *(Alix / Photo Researchers Inc.)*

ships specifically for respiratory care education (see "How Do I Learn More?"). Some hospitals may sponsor students on an as-needed basis. Individual states sponsor general scholarships.

Who Will Hire Me?

AARC reports that there are more than 110,000 respiratory therapists in the United States. According to the *Occupational Outlook Handbook,* 90 percent of respiratory care workers had jobs in hospitals in departments of respiratory care, anesthesiology, and pulmonary medicine. The remaining jobs were in home health care services, medical equipment rental companies, and nursing homes. Nevertheless, more and more respiratory care workers are now finding employment in skilled nursing and rehabilitation facilities, doctors' offices, companies that provide emergency oxygen services, and municipal services such as fire departments.

Many CAHEA-accredited schools have placement services to help graduates find jobs. The American Association for Respiratory Care publishes a monthly magazine, *The AARC Times,* which features classified job ads (see "How Do I Learn More?"). Networking with people already employed in the profession is also a source of job referrals.

Many new graduates apply directly to potential employers. They do research by talking to respiratory care workers already working there. They ask about the quality of training and the general quality of health care available through the employing institution. It's a good idea to find out whether there will be support for additional training. Will the employer reimburse tuition expenses? Will it allow a flexible schedule to accommodate class time? Teaching hospitals are especially good places to begin a career. Equipment, technology, and training are likely to be first rate, with opportunities for varied duties and working with a range of patient needs.

Employers look for applicants who have made good grades and who have excellent attendance records. They evaluate personal qualities too, like courtesy, communication skills, enthusiasm, maturity, and a responsible, cooperative attitude.

Where Can I Go from Here?

Tom Garcia started out as respiratory therapy technician and later took the registry exam. "It's common to go into nursing or medical school or several ancillary fields once you acquire some technical skills," Tom says. "Many decide to stay in respiratory care, but usually a CRT will want to become an RRT so that he or she can get into supervisory or administrative levels."

Pat Adney, who started her medical career as a physical therapist, says, "Many respiratory care workers go into home care after a few years. At first, you're on call on a rotating basis. You may have to go out on weekends or holidays, but eventually you get some options that allow more flexibility."

To Be a Successful Respiratory Care Worker, You Should . . .

- have compassion, courtesy, and flexibility
- be able to articulate your thoughts, ideas, and opinions
- have a cool head under stress
- be willing to follow instructions and be a team player
- pay attention to details
- have mechanical aptitude and good manual dexterity

What Are the Salary Ranges?

An AARC study found nearly half of the respiratory therapists in the United States made more than $48,000 a year in 2002, which was an increase of $10,000 from the previous year. According to the *Occupational Outlook Handbook,* respiratory therapists earned a median salary of $42,050 in 2002. Those in the lowest 10 percent earned less than $31,420 annually, while those in the highest 10 percent earned more than $56,480.

Hospital workers usually enjoy excellent fringe benefits including health insurance, paid vacation and sick leave, and pension plans. Additional benefits may include free parking, cafeteria discounts, uniform allowances, tuition reimbursement for job-related studies, and on-site day care.

What Is the Job Outlook?

Employment in respiratory care is expanding rapidly. The U.S. Department of Labor expects employment to increase faster than the average for all occupations over the next decade.

Even though efforts to control rising health care costs have slowed down job opportunities in hospitals in recent years, this slow-growth trend is not expected to last. On the contrary, respiratory care professionals with credentials in neonatal care and pulmonary disease will be particularly in demand.

Several factors are involved, including the rapid increase in the middle-aged and elderly populations. The elderly are the most likely to suffer heart and lung ailments such as pneumonia, chronic bronchitis, emphysema, and heart disease. As the Baby Boomers move from middle age into old age, the need for respiratory care workers will increase.

Advances in the treatment of heart attack, traumatic injury, and premature birth also bode well for the respiratory care field, since all these groups require respiratory care for some part of their treatment. The AIDS epidemic also continues to spread, and these patients often have secondary lung ailments. This and other disease populations will boost the demand for respiratory therapy professionals.

The home health care field is also expanding. This expansion has been fostered to some extent by the insurance industry's demand for less expensive alternatives to hospital care. Equipment manufacturers and rental firms, as well as companies that provide respiratory care on a contract basis, will also employ more respiratory care professionals.

How Do I Learn More?

PROFESSIONAL ORGANIZATIONS

For career and accredited programs information, contact

American Association for Respiratory Care
9425 North MacArthur Boulevard, Suite 100
Irving, TX 75063
(972) 243-2272
info@aarc.org
http://www.aarc.org

For accreditation information, contact

Committee on Accreditation for Respiratory Care
1248 Harwood Road
Bedford, TX 76021-4244
817-283-2835
http://www.coarc.com

For a list of accredited respiratory care programs, contact

National Board for Respiratory Care
8310 Nieman Road
Lenexa, KS 66214-1579
http://www.nbrc.org

BIBLIOGRAPHY

The following is a sampling of materials relating to the professional concerns and development of respiratory care workers:

Egan, Donald F., Craig L. Scanlan, Robert L. Wilkins, and James K. Stoller, eds. *Egan's Fundamentals of Respiratory Care.* 7th ed. St. Louis, MO: Mosby Year-Book, 1999.

Persing, Gary. *Respiratory Care Exam Review: Review for the Entry Level and Advanced Exams.* Kent, U.K.: W. B. Saunders, 2004.

Wilkins, Robert L., Thomas J. Butler, and James R. Dexter. *A Pocket Guide to Respiratory Disease.* Philadelphia: F. A. Davis, 2001.

SCIENCE AND MEDICAL WRITERS

It is the early 1980s, and M. J. Friedrich, works in a lab doing gene sequencing. She is explaining her job to a friend and stops to ask him if he has any questions. He asks, "How do you put those sequins on your jeans—by hand or by machine?"

M. J. is now a part-time in-house writer for CancerSource and a contract writer for *JAMA* (*Journal of the American Medical Association*). She recalls that incident and reflects, "What that illustrated to me was just how much there's a gap between people who work in science and people who don't. And it's really important to understand who your audience is and try to gauge your writing to them so that they're not misunderstanding what you're saying."

M. J. continues, "I contend that molecular biology's not that hard, it's not that complicated. But it's off-putting because people don't study it and don't really know what genes are and don't know what DNA is. And I think that that's the job of a science writer—to make these seemingly complicated and mysterious concepts less scary."

Because of the significance science has in our daily lives, which will only increase as advancements are made in the field, M. J. is convinced that people really need to understand science. And that's where science and medical writers come in. They play a key role by making technical information more accessible to the general public.

Definition
Science and medical writers research and interpret technical, scientific, and medical, information and then write about it in such a way as to make it accessible to the appropriate audience—the general public or professionals in the field.

High School Subjects
English
Journalism

Personal Skills
Communication/ideas
Technical/scientific

Salary Range
$20,000 to $43,260 to $100,000+

Educational Requirements
High school diploma, bachelor's degree

Certification or Licensing
Voluntary

Outlook
About as fast as the average

DOT
131

GOE
01.02.01

NOC
5121

O*NET-SOC
27-3042.00, 27-3043.00

What Does a Science or Medical Writer Do?

Science and medical writers write about issues related to these fields. Because the medical and scientific subject areas may sometimes overlap, writers often find that they do science writing as well as medical writing. For instance, a medical writer may write about a scientific study that has an impact on the medical field.

Some science and medical writers specialize in their subject matter. A medical writer may write only about heart disease and earn a reputation as one of the best writers in that particular area. Science writers may limit their writing or research to environmental science subjects, or they may be even more specific and focus only on air pollution issues.

According to Jeanie Davis, former president of the Southeast Chapter of the American Medical Writers Association, "Medical writing can take several different avenues. You may be a consumer medical writer, write technical medical research, or write about health care issues. Some choose to be medical editors and edit reports written by researchers. Sometimes this medical research must be translated into reports and news releases that the public can understand. Today many writers write for the Web." She adds, "It is a very dynamic profession, always changing."

Science and medical writers have many options open to them, says Barbara Gastel, M.D., coordinator of the master of science program in science and technology journalism at Texas A&M. She points out, "Opportunities exist in the popular media. Newspapers, radio, TV, and the Web have writers who specialize in covering medical and scientific subjects." Science and medical writing appears in books, technical studies and reports, magazine and trade journal articles, newspapers, company newsletters, on Web sites, and in radio and television broadcasts. It can be specific to one product and one type of writing, such as writing medical information and consumer publications for a specific drug line produced by a pharmaceutical company. Research facilities, government agencies, and high-tech companies hire writers to write reports or press releases about their scientific or medical studies. These materials may be used to inform the public about the organization's latest scientific or medical research or to assist other researchers who are gathering information on those findings. Educational publishers use writers to write textbooks and manuals for the medical profession. Science and medical writers also write online articles and interactive courses.

Depending on their employment status, science and medical writers may be given a specific writing assignment by their employer or client. An experienced writer with contacts may pitch, or suggest, a story idea to a science or medical magazine or a newspaper having a section devoted to science or medicine. In order to pitch a story idea, writers first have to develop a relevant, interesting topic based on their ongoing research into advancements in science and medicine. One way to stay on top of what's happening in science or medicine is to read industry magazines. M. J. says that this is extremely important and she regularly reads *Science, Nature, JAMA, New England Journal of Medicine, Discover,* and *New Scientist.*

Writers always need good background information regarding a subject before they can write about it. To gain a thorough understanding of the subject matter, science and medical writers may spend hours doing research on the Internet or in corporate, university, or public libraries. Science and medical conferences also offer a wealth of information, so writers frequently attend them in search of topic ideas or data. They often supplement this research by conducting interviews with professionals such as doctors, pharmacists, scientists, engineers, managers, and other experts.

It's also important to present the information so it can be understood. This requires knowing the audience, whether it is the general public or professionals in science or medicine. Once science and medical writers have collected background material, they organize everything into a logical order. Science and medical writers who write for the general public translate high-tech information into articles and reports that are accurate and easily understood. M. J. says, "The challenge for a science writer who writes for any audience whether it's a general audience or professional . . . is still to make it compelling."

Some science and medical writers must be skilled in public relations. These writers report on advances made by their employers (for example, research facilities, government agencies, or high-tech companies) in such a way as to promote their work. Other writers try to remain unbiased in their reporting, illustrating to their readers both the pros and the cons of the scientific or medical achievements they're writing about so that readers can evaluate the merits of each particular achievement for themselves.

An article may be enhanced by the use of graphs, photos, or historical facts. Writers sometimes enlist the help of technical or medical illustrators or engineers in order to add a visual dimension to their work. If reporting on a new heart surgery procedure that will soon be available to the public, writers may need to discuss how that surgery is performed and what areas of the heart are affected. They may give a basic overview of how the healthy heart works, show a diseased heart in comparison, and report on how this surgery can help the patient. The public will also want to know how many people are affected by this disease, what the symptoms are, how many procedures have been done successfully, where they were performed, what the recovery time is, and if there are any complications. In addition, interviews with doctors and patients add a personal touch to the story.

Writers for the broadcast media need to write short, precise articles that can be transmitted in a specific time allotment. They need to work quickly because news-related stories are often deadline-oriented. Writing for the Web encompasses most journalistic guidelines, including time constraints and, sometimes, space constraints.

Some writers choose to be freelance writers either on a full- or part-time basis or to supplement

Lingo to Learn

Byline Line appearing in an article or story giving the name of the writer.

Clip Published work sample usually clipped from a publication.

Pitch To suggest a story idea to a publication hoping that it will be accepted and then printed.

Portfolio Collection of clips (news stories, magazine articles, or other pieces written) that serve as work samples for a person seeking employment.

Trade journal Periodical having content geared toward members of a particular industry.

other jobs. Freelance science and medical writers are self-employed writers who work with small and large companies, health care organizations, research institutions, and publishing firms on a contract or hourly basis. They may specialize in writing about a specific scientific or medical subject for one or two clients, or they may write about a broad range of subjects for a number of different clients.

What Is It Like to Be a Science or Medical Writer?

Generally, writers work in an office or research environment. They usually travel in order to gather research information and conduct interviews. Certain employers may confine research to local libraries or the Internet. In addition, some employers require writers to conduct research interviews over the phone rather than in person.

Although the workweek usually runs 35 to 40 hours in a normal office setting, many writers may have to work overtime to cover a story, interview people, meet deadlines, or disseminate information in a timely manner. The newspaper and broadcasting industries deliver the news 24 hours a day, seven days a week. Writers often work nights and weekends to meet press deadlines or to cover a late-developing story.

Each day may bring new and interesting situations. "One of the things I like about my job is there aren't really typical days," comments M. J. Instead, her workweeks may be basically pretty similar, consisting of time spent at the library conducting research, looking through journals to find background material, coming up with topic ideas, attending conferences, finding contacts and setting up interviews, compiling interview questions, and writing stories. M. J. says she often "might be preparing for one article in the middle of another one."

Going to conferences is something else that M. J. enjoys. She says, "I'll try to talk to people who are attending to see what they think the hot topics are. Sometimes I'm going to conferences that are primarily given by basic scientists, so their take on what's being presented is a little different than what a physician might be interested in." Conferences afford "an opportunity not only to meet people and find story ideas but just to learn. If I go for three days to a conference, I try to go to every talk that I can, even if I'm not going to write about it, because I'm usually trying to come up to speed on a topic." This has been particularly important for M. J., given that she writes articles on a wide range of topics for *JAMA*. "One assignment might be on osteoarthritis and the next assignment might be on mild cognitive impairment, which is sort of a precursor to Alzheimer's disease. I may or may not have any background in that area, so it really behooves me to learn as much as I can when that opportunity is provided." This thirst for knowledge serves her well since M. J. rarely writes on the same topic twice.

Because the fields of science and medicine are evolving at such a rapid pace, it's essential that science and medical writers stay aware of developments. What M. J. likes most about being a science and medical writer is that she is always learning. She emphasizes that while being equipped with a solid foundation in the sciences will definitely prove beneficial to science and medical writers, it's that love of learning and curiosity along with a passion for writing that are of utmost importance.

Potential drawbacks to a career as a science or medical writer are that certain assignments may be boring or they may take place in less-than-desirable settings. Some of the most difficult elements for writers may be meeting deadlines, gathering information, tracking down appropriate interview subjects, or getting people to talk about their research.

Full-time, part-time, and freelance science and medical writers alike should be prepared to deal with the ebb and flow of their own productivity as well as the number of assignments received. Sometimes writers have "good" days or periods of time when it takes very little effort to write, and other times they struggle to come up with an idea of a topic to cover or the right words to explain a little-known disease or complex scientific achievement. M. J. stresses that it's important to realize that not every day will be a great day for writing. Sometimes "ideas don't leap off the page, things seem dull." Freelancers face a work life of feast or famine—that is, dry spells when few assignments come in and periods filled multiple assignments and rush jobs.

Do I Have What It Takes to Be a Science or Medical Writer?

According to Barbara Gastel, "This career can have various appeals. People can combine their interest in science or medicine with their love of writing. It is a good field for a generalist who likes science and doesn't want to be tied to research in one area. Plus," she adds, "it is always fun to get things published."

It is a good field for a generalist who likes science and doesn't want to be tied to research in one area.

If you are considering a career as a science or medical writer, you should enjoy writing, be able to write well, and be able to clearly express your ideas and those of others. "There's dreary science writing," M. J. maintains. "That's because people are just writing about science. They're not tying it to other things. They're not making associations." She believes that good science writing has the potential of capturing the interest of readers who normally wouldn't be interested in science, perhaps because "they haven't had it presented to them in a good way."

It's not essential that you take every science course available in school, but you should at least have a solid grasp of and interest in basic science. Without an interest in science or medicine, a writer may become bored or feel incapable of producing content that appeals to the target audience. You should be curious and take pleasure in learning new things since science and medicine are ever-changing. Good writers who cover their subjects thoroughly have inquisitive minds and enjoy looking for additional information that might enhance their articles. Persistence comes in handy if data or people are hard to track down.

To Be a Successful Science or Medical Writer, You Should . . .

- enjoy learning, reading, and writing
- be curious
- like talking to people
- be able to deal with deadline pressure
- be persistent

Excellent knowledge of the English language and superb grammar and spelling skills are required. You should be skilled in research techniques and be computer literate and familiar with software programs related to writing and publishing. You need to be detail-oriented since many of your writing assignments will require that you obtain and relay accurate and detailed information. Interpersonal skills are important, too, since many jobs require that you interact with and interview professional people such as scientists, engineers, researchers, and medical personnel. You must be able to meet deadlines and work under pressure.

Freelancers should be resourceful in scouting out a range of publishers to whom they can submit article ideas. They also should be self-motivated. It is up to the freelance writer to keep track of deadlines and to garner enough assignments to make ends meet financially. An enjoyment of working alone is also vital. But science and medical writers considering a freelance career should be aware that it's a lot of hard work and can get very isolating no matter how much a person likes to be alone.

How Do I Become a Science or Medical Writer?

There are many paths that lead to a career as a science or medical writer. Some people develop an early interest in writing and later discover an interest in science or medicine, while for others the reverse might be true. And still others may simultaneously become interested in writing and in science or medicine. Often those who become science or medical writers start out working in another field entirely. M. J. worked for nine years in a University of Virginia microbiology lab and "sort of parlayed that into an editing job with the American Society of Clinical Pathology" because she wanted to write.

EDUCATION

High School

If you are contemplating a career as a writer, you should take English, journalism, and communications courses in high school. Computer classes are also helpful. If you know in high school that you want to do scientific or medical writing, it is to your advantage to take biology, physiology, chemistry, physics, math, health, and other science-related courses.

To get some hands-on writing experience, you should strongly consider working on your school newspaper or yearbook. In hindsight, M. J. wishes that she had written for her school newspaper. She suggests that students might want to write a science column for their school paper reporting on what they're learning in science class: something that has relevance to them, something that is beautiful or challenging, something that "knocks their socks off."

If you can find no opportunities for science or medical writing, then writing of any kind will be beneficial. "Whatever you're pulled to, whatever turns you on," M. J. says, "incorporate that into your writing."

Part-time employment at health care facilities, newspapers, publishing companies, or scientific research facilities can also provide training, background information, and insight that can be beneficial in this career. Volunteer opportunities are usually available in hospitals and nursing homes as well.

Postsecondary Training

Although not all writers are college-educated, today's jobs almost always require a bachelor's degree. Many writers earn an undergraduate degree in English, journalism, or liberal arts and then obtain a master's degree in a communications field such as medical or science writing. A good liberal arts education is important since you are often required to write about many subject areas.

Two of M. J.'s favorite classes in college were Masterpieces of World Literature (going back to Homer's *Odyssey*) and Contemporary Fiction. Studying great works of literature helped her to appreciate language (which she believes to be key to a writer's success), both as it's written and as it's read aloud. M. J. offers this advice to those thinking about a career as a science or medical writer: Read "good works, bad works, everything."

Graduate work in religious studies and philosophy prepared M. J. to become a more critical thinker. Studying with the best teachers regardless of subject area is another of her recommendations, as is being sure to take plenty of science and medical-related courses, at least enough to be very familiar and comfortable with basic science.

In addition to your classroom studies, you should write whenever you can and keep copies of anything you're proud of, particularly if it has to do with science or medicine but even if it doesn't. These clips, whether published or not and whether on paper, in electronic format, or both, should be added to your portfolio to serve as samples of the kind of work you can do. They should demonstrate your writing skills and style as well as how you deal with difficult issues. Remember, too, whenever you write something for publication, request a byline (your name printed on your article).

CERTIFICATION OR LICENSING

Certification is not mandatory; however, certification programs are available from various organizations and institutions. The American Medical Writers As-

FYI

According to the Society for Technical Communications, the following are just some of the industries in which technical communicators work:

- computing
- biotech
- aviation
- manufacturing
- medicine

sociation Education Program offers an extensive continuing education and certification program.

INTERNSHIPS AND VOLUNTEERSHIPS

Internships provide an invaluable opportunity to make contacts in the field and excellent ways to build your portfolio. You should investigate internship programs that give you experience in the communications department of a corporation, medical institution, or research facility. Some newspapers, magazines, and public relations firms also have internships that give you the opportunity to write.

Employers in the communications field are usually interested in seeing samples of your published writing assembled in an organized portfolio or scrapbook. Working on your college's magazine or newspaper staff can help you build a portfolio. Sometimes small, regional magazines also buy articles or assign short pieces to writers.

Who Will Hire Me?

A fair amount of experience is required to gain a high-level position in this field. Most writers start out in entry-level positions. These jobs may be listed with college placement offices, or you may apply directly to the employment departments of corporations, institutions, universities, research facilities, nonprofit organizations, and government facilities that hire science and medical writers. Many firms now hire writers directly upon application or recommendation of college professors and placement offices. Want ads in newspapers and trade journals are another source for jobs. Serving an internship in college can give you the advantage of knowing people who can give you personal recommendations.

You may need to begin your career as a junior writer or editor and work your way up. This usually involves library research, preparation of rough drafts for part or all of a report, cataloging, and other related writing tasks. These are generally carried on under the supervision of a senior writer.

Many science and medical writers enter the field after working in public relations departments, the medical profession, or science-related industries. They may use their skills to transfer to specialized writing positions or they may take additional courses or graduate work that focuses on writing or documentation skills.

Pharmaceutical and drug companies, medical research institutions, government organizations, insurance companies, health care facilities, nonprofit organizations, manufacturers, chemical companies,

In-depth

Then and Now

The modern publishing age began in the 18th century when printing became mechanized, and the novel, magazine, and newspaper developed. Developments in the printing trades, photoengraving, and retailing and the availability of capital produced a boom in newspapers and magazines in the 19th century. Further mechanization in the printing field, such as the use of the Linotype machine, high-speed rotary presses, and special color reproduction processes, set the stage for still further growth in the book, newspaper, and magazine industries.

In addition to the print media, the broadcasting industry has contributed to the development of the professional writer. Film, radio, and television are sources of entertainment, information, and education that provide employment for thousands of writers. Today, the computer industry, and the Internet and its proliferation of Web sites, have also created the need for more writers.

As our world has become more complex and people are seeking even more information, the professional writer has become increasingly important. And, as medicine and science are taking giant steps forward and discoveries are being made every day that impact our lives, skilled science and medical writers are needed to document these changes and disseminate the information.

medical publishers, medical associations, and other medical-related companies employ medical writers.

Many science and medical writers are employed, often on a freelance basis, by newspapers, magazines, and the broadcast industries. Internet publishing is a growing field that hires science and medical writers. Corporations that deal with the medical or science industries also hire specialty writers as their public information officers or to head up communications departments within their facilities.

Where Can I Go from Here?

Writers with an undergraduate degree may choose to get a graduate degree in science or medical writing, corporate communications, document design, or a related program. An advanced degree may open doors to a prestigious career.

Some writers enjoy writing so much that they simply continue to write and become recognized experts in their field. Their writings may come to be in demand by trade journals, newspapers, magazines, and the broadcast industry. Many experienced science and medical writers are promoted to head writing, documentation, or public relations departments within corporations or institutions. Others may move into managerial positions, perhaps becoming managing editor of a trade journal or magazine or director of publications at a university.

As freelance writers prove themselves and work successfully with clients, they may be able to demand increased contract fees or higher hourly rates.

What Are the Salary Ranges?

The Council for the Advancement of Science Writing (CASW) provides salary information specifically for science writers. The CASW reports that newspaper writers in entry-level positions covering general topics may begin at about $20,000 to $30,000 per year, while those with experience may earn $60,000 or more. Science writers with magazines may start at about $30,000 with salaries going as high as $100,000 for experienced writers and writers with the most reputable magazines.

The Society of Technical Communicators' 2003 salary survey of its members reported that the average salary for entry-level technical writers was $43,260. The U.S. Department of Labor reports that the mean annual wage for writers and editors in 2003 was $43,340. Writers working in pharmaceuticals and medicine manufacturing made average salaries of $62,900.

Freelance writers' earnings vary depending on their expertise, reputation, and the kinds of articles they are contracted to write. Rates may be paid by the piece, hourly, or per word.

Most full-time writing positions offer benefits such as insurance, sick leave, and paid vacation. Some jobs also provide tuition reimbursement and retirement benefits. Freelance writers must pay for their own insurance. However, certain professional associations offer group insurance rates for members.

What Is the Job Outlook?

According to the Bureau of Labor Statistics, there is a lot of competition for writing and editing jobs, and the overall demand for writers and editors is expected to as fast as the average for all occupations. However, opportunities for technical writers with specializations in science, medicine, and law are expected to be among the best in the field. The continued growth of medical and scientific knowledge will create an increased need to disseminate information about these fields. Skilled writers are essential in this regard.

The Society for Technical Communication also states that there is a growing demand for technical communicators. They report that it is one of the fastest growing professions and that this growth has created a variety of career options.

How Do I Learn More?

PROFESSIONAL ORGANIZATIONS

The following are organizations that provide information about a career as a science or medical writer:

American Medical Writers Association
40 West Gude Drive, Suite 101
Rockville, MD 20850-1192
301-294-5303
amwa@amwa.org
http://www.amwa.org

Council for the Advancement of Science Writing
PO Box 910
Hedgesville, WV 25427
304-754-5077
diane@nasw.org
http://nasw.org/users/casw

The following organization provides information on the field of science writing and offer the booklet A Guide to Careers in Science Writing:

National Association of Science Writers Inc.
PO Box 910
Hedgesville, WV 25427
304-754-5077
info@nasw.org
http://www.nasw.org

The Society for Technical Communication offers student memberships for persons enrolled in a program in preparation for a career in technical communication. This organization also has a scholarship program.

Society for Technical Communication
901 North Stuart Street, Suite 904
Arlington, VA 22203
703-522-4114
stc@stc.org
http://www.stc.org

BIBLIOGRAPHY

The following is a sampling of materials relating to the professional concerns and development of science and medical writers:

Alley, Michael. *The Craft of Scientific Writing*. 3d ed. New York: Springer, 1997.

Blum, Deborah, and Mary Knudson, eds. *A Field Guide for Science Writers*. Reprint ed. New York: Oxford University Press, 1998.

Bremer, Michael. *Untechnical Writing: How to Write About Technical Subjects and Products So Anyone Can Understand*. Concord, Calif.: Untechnical Press, 1999.

Iles, Robert L. *Guidebook to Better Medical Writing*. Rev. ed. Washington, D.C.: Isles Publications, 2003.

Iverson, Cheryl, ed. *American Medical Association Manual of Style*. 9th ed. Philadelphia: Lippincott, Williams & Wilkins, 1998.

Rubens, Philip, ed. *Science and Technical Writing: A Manual of Style*. New York, NY: Routledge, 2000.

Worsley, Dale, and Bernadette Mayer. *The Art of Science Writing*. New York: Teachers & Writers, 2000.

SOCIAL WORKERS

Definition
Social workers help individuals, families, and communities find solutions to personal and social problems. They address such issues as mental illness, family conflict, racism, poverty, and unemployment. Social workers do counseling and advocacy, link clients with public agencies that offer resources, and help develop social programs and policies.

High School Subjects
Health
Psychology

Personal Skills
Communication/ideas
Helping/teaching

Salary Range
$24,770 to $39,160 to $60,000

Educational Requirements
Bachelor's degree; master's degree recommended

Certification or Licensing
Required by all states

Outlook
Faster than the average

DOT
195

GOE
12.02.02

NOC
4152

O*NET-SOC
21-1021.00, 21-1022.00

"I've got to catch up with my paperwork before my first client comes in," remarks Carolyn Campbell. She and another social worker have just left the weekly staff meeting at the Lorene Replogle Counseling Center in Chicago. After briefly working on her records, Carolyn checks her watch and steps out into the waiting room.

"Hello, Julie." She greets the tired-looking young woman with a smile. "Please come in."

Ever since her marriage broke up, Julie has been having trouble sleeping. Through counseling, Carolyn hopes that she might help Julie lose some of her anxieties. It seems to Carolyn that, despite her fatigue and discouragement, Julie's self-confidence is gradually returning.

Since this is staff meeting day, Carolyn has fewer counseling sessions scheduled than on her other workdays. After meeting with Julie, she has a few minutes to write her notes. Carolyn's recordkeeping, like that of most health care professionals, has become more complicated over the last few years as a result of the stricter requirements of cost-conscious insurance companies. Of course, Carolyn has always written detailed case notes on each of the clients she is counseling. Reviewing her notes helps her to see the client's personal situation and issues more clearly and to recognize the progress he or she is making. She also keep notes on her conferences with the master's level social work student she is supervising at the center.

What Does a Social Worker Do?

The social work profession grew out of the 19th-century realization that the problems of the poor could not be solved by the charitable efforts of well-meaning individual volunteers. The establishment of charitable organizations in the late 19th century and the settlement house movement (pioneered by Jane Addams at Chicago's Hull House) led to the creation of formal social work education programs.

Social workers serve human needs and work for social justice in a wide range of institutional and community settings. The National Association of Social Workers (NASW) has defined the profession's core values as commitment to service, social justice, the dignity and worth of the person, the importance of human relationships, integrity, and competence.

Most social workers are involved in what the profession calls direct practice, meaning that they work directly with clients in agency offices, schools, hospitals, outpatient clinics, prisons, and other settings. Some social workers have chosen to specialize in indirect practice. Instead of working directly with clients, they work with institutional and social structures—developing, administering, analyzing, and evaluating programs and policies. Nearly 40 percent of all social workers are employed by government agencies. The others work in many parts of the private sector.

One of the most familiar areas of social work is child welfare and family services. The purpose of child welfare agencies is to protect the well-being of children. *Child welfare workers* counsel children and adolescents who have social adjustment problems. They also work with parents and teachers to help identify and address problems and locate appropriate resources. Social workers make home visits to investigate reports of child abuse, neglect, and abandonment. Sometimes they need to remove the children from the home and place them in shelters or find foster homes for them.

Social workers in child welfare and family services provide counseling on family relationships and teach parenting skills. They also counsel and evaluate potential adoptive parents and help families find the resources they need for disabled, ill, or elderly members. Parents may also need help obtaining child support payments or finding day care.

In recent years, social workers in child and family services have had to develop social services for children born with HIV-related conditions or congenital disabilities resulting from the mother's use of drugs like crack cocaine.

Clinical social workers specialize in providing mental health services to children, adolescents, and adults. They may offer individual and group therapy, crisis intervention, social rehabilitation, outreach services, marital counseling, stress management, and preventive mental health programs.

Health care social workers (also called *medical social workers*) help hospital patients and their families cope with serious medical problems, such as AIDS, cancer, and Alzheimer's. They help educate the family about the illness and its treatment, as well as the changes it will bring to their lives. Health care social workers arrange for at-home services (visiting nurses, home oxygen equipment, or participation in a meals on wheels program, for example) that will be needed after the patient's discharge from the hospital. Sometimes they organize support groups for caregivers and other family members.

Gerontological social workers specialize in work with older people. They counsel the aged and their families and help make arrangements for housing, transportation, adult day care, and long-term care. Sometimes they organize support groups for caregivers or arrange respite services to give the principal caregiver some time off. They are also responsible for investigating reports that elderly persons are being abused or neglected.

School social workers are employed in school settings to provide counseling, education, and advocacy. They address such problems as teen pregnancy, the spread of AIDS and other sexually transmitted diseases, alcohol and drug abuse, racial discrimination, and conflicts related to multiculturalism. Since passage of the Education for All Handicapped Children Act, school social workers have also been helping to integrate children with disabilities into the mainstream of public education.

Lingo to Learn

Advocacy Defending the rights of individuals or communities.

Defense mechanisms Various mental processes, such as denial or displacement, through which individuals protect their personalities from guilt, anxiety, or unacceptable thoughts.

Empowerment The process of assisting individuals and groups to acquire greater effectiveness with the goal of enabling them to make positive changes in their lives.

Family therapy Therapy that focuses on the family group as a unit, rather than on the separate individuals of the family.

Grass-roots organizing Educating and mobilizing the people of a local community for action toward a common goal.

Intervention The social work equivalent of treatment; it includes all the professional activities through which social workers try to prevent or solve clients' problems.

Mediation Intervention in disputes between opposing groups with the goal of reconciling differences and/or achieving a mutually satisfactory compromise.

Norms The rules and expectations for appropriate behavior held collectively by any community, culture, or society.

Public assistance Government-provided financial aid for persons who are unable to support themselves.

Other areas of social work include working with the inmates of correctional institutions and their families, personnel department work for corporations, work with the homeless, and community organizing at the grass-roots level.

What Is It Like to Be a Social Worker?

Carolyn Campbell has been a licensed clinical social worker on the staff of the Lorene Replogle Counseling Center for 19 years, yet every day continues to offer new challenges. Every client's situation is different. When she first came, she had no idea she would still be at the center nearly 20 years later. At that time, she was planning to concentrate on building up her private practice. As it turned out, she liked working at the center so much that she decided to make it the focus of her professional life, though she continues to maintain a small private practice out of her home office. One of the most positive features of the center's policies, Carolyn thinks, is its sliding-fee scale that makes it possible for clients with low incomes to receive the benefit of individual counseling services.

Maria is her next client. Like Julie, she has been in therapy with Carolyn for about six months. Maria is dealing with interpersonal issues that go back to her childhood in a somewhat dysfunctional family.

After her session with Maria, Carolyn prepares to go out on an errand but her telephone rings. It is the center's receptionist asking Carolyn to do an intake interview with a potential client who wants to talk to a counselor. Usually the center director takes care of the intake interviews, but he is leading a seminar on depression at another location. Carolyn carries on a short conversation with the young man on the other end of the line and soon realizes that the services offered by the center will not meet his needs. What he really wants is to find a good drug-rehabilitation program, so Carolyn offers an appropriate referral.

Later that day, Carolyn meets with Alan, one of the students who is doing supervised work at the center as part of Loyola University's master of social work program. They discuss some of the frustrations that are making Alan wonder if counseling is really the right field of social work for him. Carolyn reminds him that one of the hardest truths for all counselors to learn is that they will not be able to "cure" all their clients or solve all their problems. "There are some circumstances in people's lives that cannot be changed, no matter how much we wish we could bring about those changes," she reflects.

Since most social workers enter the profession because they want to help people, having to acknowledge the limitations of intervention can be hard to accept. Fortunately, the occasional frustrations are usually balanced by the sense of satisfaction one gets from seeing individuals and families begin making positive changes in their lives.

"What drew me to social work was the opportunity it offered to combine my interests in psychology and sociology. I was interested in individuals and in larger groups," explains one licensed clinical social worker. Harrison Taylor, the clinical coordinator of the Adolescent Intensive Outpatient Program at the Tennessee Christian Medical Center in Madison, decided to specialize in family therapy after some early work experience with Children and Family Services in Nashville.

In his current position, Harrison is responsible for running a group therapy program for troubled adolescents between the ages of 13 and 17. The teenagers participate in adventure-based activities and the creative arts with the goal of learning problem-solving skills. Once a week, their parents come in to work on parenting skills. The purpose is to "rebuild the bridges between parents and teenagers," says Harrison. "Family members learn from each other when they are given tools and guidelines to help them get unstuck."

Family members learn from each other when they are given tools and guidelines to help them get unstuck.

Do I Have What It Takes to Be a Social Worker?

Social workers must be strongly committed to helping other people, but it is not enough simply to like people and enjoy working with them. The satisfaction experienced by social workers when they are able to help people improve their lives is great, but the work is not easy. Social workers need to develop excellent communication skills, especially listening skills. They must have patience, emotional maturity, self-control (even when confronted with tragic situations), and the ability to assess a client's circumstances with clarity and objectivity. It is essential for social workers to be able to demonstrate acceptance of their clients as people, even when they are not able to endorse the clients' actions.

Social workers are often responsible for making recommendations that will have a lasting impact on people's lives. Is there sufficient evidence to believe that this child is being abused and should be removed from his parents' home? Is this person still able to live alone despite her illness? Would this couple be suitable adoptive parents?

Despite the educational efforts of the National Association of Social Workers, many people still know little about the profession. One social worker cites the common misconception that social workers are just "people who bring food to the poor." Another misconception is that social workers are interfering busybodies or troublemakers who exaggerate social problems.

One licensed clinical social worker (LCSW) suggests that this situation may be changing with the advent of managed care (which stresses health care cost containment). Since services provided by LCSWs are less expensive than those offered by other mental health professionals, insurance companies and other organizations are turning more and more toward LCSWs as providers. At the same time, LCSWs are expressing frustration with the decrease of professional autonomy that results from these cost-containment measurements.

How Do I Become a Social Worker?

EDUCATION

High School

To prepare for a career in social work, take a well-balanced college preparatory program. Classes that improve your communication skills (speech and writing courses) are especially helpful. Classes that provide an introduction to psychology, sociology, and the other social sciences are also good choices. Knowledge of history is important for developing an understanding of contemporary social problems.

You can also look for ways to gain experience in working with people. You might find part-time work or volunteer opportunities at a local social-service agency, the YMCA, summer camp programs, or tutoring programs. There may also be volunteer opportunities available through social-justice groups or religious organizations.

Postsecondary Training

Most social work jobs require a bachelor's degree, though the degree does not necessarily have to be a bachelor of social work (B.S.W.) degree. Sociology, psychology, or other social sciences are also appropriate majors. For many positions, especially those in health and mental health settings, a Master of Social Work (M.S.W.) degree is necessary.

As an undergraduate, Carolyn had a double major in psychology and sociology, with a minor in history. One summer, she did an internship at a public-aid office; she spent another summer as a houseparent in a children's home. After graduation, she worked at a small public assistance office in southern Illinois for three years.

This hands-on experience convinced Carolyn that social work was the right career for her, so she enrolled in the MSW program at Loyola University in Chicago. Harrison majored in sociology as an undergraduate and then earned an MSW at the University of Chicago. As an undergraduate, he worked part time as a mental health assistant at an inpatient adolescent unit.

There are 158 graduate and 453 undergraduate programs that are accredited by the Council on Social Work Education. There are also Ph.D. programs in social work and D.S.W. (doctor of social work) programs. An accredited B.S.W. program must include work in the following five areas: human behavior and the social environment, social welfare policies and services, social work practice, research, and a practicum (supervised field experience) of at least 400 clock hours.

MSW programs are generally two years in length and require at least 900 hours of supervised field experience. In their fieldwork, most students focus on a specialized area of social work, such as child welfare, health or mental health, work with the elderly, or community organizing.

"I think social workers receive a greater amount of close supervision during their training period than members of any other profession," says Carolyn. "We had some really tough supervisors, but they gave us what we needed."

CERTIFICATION OR LICENSING

All 50 states and the District of Columbia have requirements for the certification, licensing, or registration of social workers. The precise regulations vary by state. Becoming a licensed social worker (LSW) generally requires meeting certain educational and work-experience requirements, as well as passing a written examination.

Because Carolyn decided to specialize in mental health (clinical) work, she had to gain additional experience and take the LCSW examination after becoming an LSW. Continuing education is also required for remaining licensed in Illinois.

In addition to the state licensing requirements, there are also various voluntary certifications offered by the National Association of Social Workers (NASW), such as School Social Work Specialist. Social workers who are accepted for membership in the NASW have an M.S.W. and two years of experience and pass an examination may use the title ACSW (Academy of Certified Social Workers).

Professional credentials are especially important for social workers thinking of going into private practice, because many insurance companies require certain credentials for recognition as a provider of reimbursable services. In some cities and counties, it is also necessary for social workers in private practice to obtain local permits or registration certificates.

Social workers who want to be employed by federal, state, or local government agencies usually need to pass a civil service exam.

SCHOLARSHIPS AND GRANTS

For information about scholarships, fellowships, grants, student loans, and other financial aid, consult the financial-aid office of the academic institution that you plan to attend. Allow plenty of time for the paperwork.

There are also a few scholarships and fellowships specifically targeted for women, African Americans, Hispanics, and Native Americans who want to study social work.

Contact the National Association of Social Workers for additional information on applying for financial aid.

To Be a Successful Social Worker, You Should . . .

- be strongly committed to helping other people
- have excellent communication skills
- have patience, maturity, and self-control
- have the ability to assess a client's circumstances with both compassion and objectivity

Who Will Hire Me?

Social workers are employed by federal, state, and local government agencies in the following departments: social services, human resources, child welfare, health and mental health, housing, education, and corrections.

Four out of 10 social workers are employed in state, county, or municipal government agencies, primarily in departments of health and human services, mental health, social services, child welfare, housing, education, and corrections. If you would like to work for a government agency, you usually need to arrange to take a civil service exam. For most government jobs, the applicant's scores on the civil service exam are considered the most important factor.

Most private sector jobs are in social service agencies, hospitals, nursing homes, home health agencies, and other health centers or clinics. Some social workers teach and do research at colleges and universities; these faculty positions usually require a doctoral degree.

Some social workers choose to go into private practice after a few years at an agency. This seems to be a growing trend. Most social workers in private practice are clinical social workers who offer counseling and psychotherapy to individuals, families, and groups. Before venturing into private practice, a social worker must have an M.S.W. and supervised experience. To succeed as a private practitioner, it is necessary to have a reliable network of professional contacts for client referrals.

Students looking for an entry-level social work position will receive assistance from their college or university placement service. It is also a good idea to ask for suggestions about job openings from your social work professors, fieldwork supervisors, and other contacts made through your fieldwork.

Information about job openings is also available through the local chapter of the National Association of Social Workers or your state's society for clinical social work. Professional journals and newsletters publish job openings. These publications should be available at your college or university library.

Where Can I Go from Here?

Harrison Taylor, who received his M.S.W. eight years ago, is currently preparing to go into private practice as an organizational development consultant. He wants to do what he calls *change management* by moving beyond individual and family therapy to apply his knowledge to corporate and nonprofit organizations. As Harrison points out, family issues often get projected into the workplace. His potential clients would be organizations that have problems with conflict management, lack of teamwork, diversity issues, low morale, and high turnover. Harrison's change of focus was prompted in part by his desire to work for the benefit of the wider society and in part by his hope of regaining some of the professional autonomy he has recently lost through the coming of managed health care.

Carolyn Campbell is not planning any changes in her professional life at this time. She has long known that she does not want to move into administration, the traditional route of advancement in social work. Because she enjoys supervising clinical social work students, she sometimes thinks of teaching in a university social work program.

Social workers with a master's degree have better opportunities for advancement to administrative or supervisory positions in social welfare or health care. Some choose private practice as their route of advancement. Social workers who earn doctoral degrees have opportunities for teaching, research, policy analysis, and program development.

What Are the Salary Ranges?

According to the U.S. Department of Labor, medical and public health social workers made median annual salaries of $39,160 in 2003. Salaries ranged from a low of $24,770 to a high of $58,030. Child, family, and school social workers made median annual salaries of $37,190, with the middle 50 percent making between $27,370 and $44,460 a year.

Social workers in teaching, research, administration, and private practice generally have higher salaries than most social workers, but very few earn more than $60,000.

In general, salaries on the east and west coasts are higher than in the Midwest, while jobs in rural areas tend to pay less than those in the city.

What Is the Job Outlook?

Social workers hold about 477,000 jobs. Social work positions are expected to increase faster than the average for all occupations because of the population's growing need for social services, as well as the number of social workers leaving the field for other occupations. More gerontological social workers will be needed as the percentage of elderly persons in the population increases. The strong trend toward early discharge of hospital patients will increase the need for hospital social workers, who make arrangements for at-home medical services and social supports. The need for school social workers is also expected to grow, as schools will have to provide expanded social services for children with serious adjustment problems, as well as those with disabilities.

Employment opportunities in government agencies will depend on how much funding is available for social programs.

Although private practice is a growing field in social work, its viability will depend in large part on the willingness of vendors and insurance companies to pay for the services offered by clinical workers. Private practitioners who contract with businesses and corporations will probably do well.

The impact of lower budgets, combined with the need for more staff members, has resulted in some social-service agencies hiring less qualified human-services workers instead of professional social workers. This trend is a cause of concern to some social workers, who fear a decline in professional standards and the quality of service offered to clients.

How Do I Learn More?

PROFESSIONAL ORGANIZATIONS

The following are organizations that provide information on social work careers:

Council on Social Work Education
1600 Duke Street
Alexandria, VA 22314
703-683-8080
http://www.cswe.org

National Association of Social Workers
Information Center
750 First Street, NE
Washington, DC 20002
202-408-8600
http://www.socialworkers.org

BIBLIOGRAPHY

The following is a sampling of materials relating to the professional concerns and development of social workers:

Grant, Gary B., and Linda May Grobman. *The Social Worker's Internet Handbook*. Harrisburg, Pa.: White Hat Communications, 1998.

Grobman, Linda May, ed. *Days in the Lives of Social Workers: 50 Professionals Tell "Real-Life" Stories from Social Work Practice*. 2d ed. Harrisburg, PA: White Hat Communications, 1999.

Hepworth, Dean H, Ronald H. Rooney, and Jo Ann Larsen. *Direct Social Work Practice: Theory and Skills*. 6th ed. Belmont, Calif: Wadsworth Publishing Co., 2001.

Hopps, June G., and Robert Morris, eds. *Social Work at the Millennium: Critical Reflections on the Future of the Profession*. New York: Free Press, 2000.

Morales, Armando T., and Bradford W. Sheafor. *Social Work: A Profession of Many Faces*. 10th ed. New York: Allyn & Bacon, 2003.

Parent, Marc. *Turning Stones: My Days and Nights with Children at Risk*. New York: Ballantine, 1998.

Simpson, Carolyn, and Dwain Simpson. *Exploring Careers in Social Work*. Rev. ed. New York: Rosen Publishing Group, 1999.

SPECIAL PROCEDURES TECHNOLOGISTS

Something was wrong. Maybe David Brown felt it before he thought it. Maybe his years of training and experience as a cardiac catheterization technologist made him sense that Mrs. Smith was in trouble. She lay calmly, still under the anesthesia but disconnected from the EKG monitor now, as he transferred her from the table.

The other members of the cardiology team were in the second swing room, prepping for the next patient. The procedure had gone well—they'd found and removed significant blockage from Mrs. Smith's artery; she was stable . . . but something was wrong.

David lifted her eyelids. Only the whites showed. He called out: "She's crashed!" He lifted her back onto the table and hooked her up again to the monitor, as the rest of the team rushed to his side. To the cardiologist he said, "Seizures. She's fibrillating."

The team's response was immediate. With the third shock from the defibrillator, her heart beat again. The cardiologist snaked the catheter through the artery to her heart. Studying the image on the fluoroscope, he said, "Vessel wall collapsed. Good catch, David. You just saved her life. Now, let's get a stent in there."

Definition
Special procedures technologists operate medical diagnostic imaging equipment, such as computer tomography (CT) scanners and magnetic resonance imaging (MRI) scanners. They also may assist in procedures involving imaging, such as angiography and cardiac catheterization (CC).

Alternative Job Titles
Angiographers
Cardiac catheterization technologists
Computer tomography technologists
Special vascular imaging technologists

High School Subjects
Biology
Health

Personal Skills
Technical/scientific
Helping/teaching

Salary Range
$29,340 to $44,460 to $58,300+

Minimum Educational Level
Associate's degree

Certification or Licensing
Recommended (certification)
Required by certain states (licensing)

Outlook
Faster than the average

DOT
078

GOE
14.05.01

NOC
3215

O*NET-SOC
29-2031.00, 29-2034.00

What Does a Special Procedures Technologist Do?

Although X rays are a valuable diagnostic tool, advances in technology have allowed medical staff to capture even more precise images of the human body. Tools such as computer tomography (CT) scanners and magnetic resonance imagers (MRI), and techniques such as angiography and cardiac catheterization, allow physicians and specially trained technologists to pinpoint areas of medical concern. In some cases, intervention procedures may be performed right away, saving valuable time and allowing patients to avoid riskier surgical procedures.

Cardiac catheterization, computer tomography, angiography, and magnetic resonance imaging are four special procedures that are often grouped together, because each technique involves the making or using of visual images to assist physicians in treating their patients. Many of those who do this work began as radiologic technologists and then went on to receive advanced training in their specialized area. These professionals with advanced training are known as *special procedures technologists*. They are generally responsible for positioning the patient for examination, immobilizing them, preparing the equipment to be used, and monitoring the equipment and the patient's progress during the procedure.

Special diagnostic procedures may be grouped into two areas: invasive and noninvasive. CT scans and MRI scans are considered noninvasive because the equipment does not enter the body. Angiography and cardiac catheterization are considered invasive techniques because the imaging work is done from within the body. Sometimes patients will undergo more than one of these procedures so that their physicians will have a better understanding of their health conditions.

ANGIOGRAPHY

Blood vessels do not normally show up on X-ray photographs. Yet physicians need to be able to see the vessels of the circulatory system in order to detect and locate such life-threatening conditions as aneurysms, narrowing or blockage of the vessel, or the presence of clots in the vessel. Angiography accomplishes this by coating the vessels of the affected areas with a contrast medium, a substance that allows blood vessels to be seen because the contrast makes the vessels opaque to the X rays. In patients with tumors or injuries to their organs, an angiogram can show any changes that have occurred to the pattern of the vessels. Studying the flow of the contrast medium through the vessels also gives the physician important information about the way the patient's blood flows. With this information, the physician can assess the extent of damage or the progression of disease and determine the necessary treatment.

In order to perform an angiography, a small tube, called a catheter, is first inserted into the patient and moved through an artery to the area the physician wishes to examine. The special procedures technologist, called an *angiographer* in this case, assists the placement of the catheter by operating and monitoring an X-ray fluoroscope. The angiographer next prepares the contrast medium to be injected and is responsible for controlling the amount and rate of flow of the contrast medium into the patient's body. Using a video display, the angiographer will adjust the density and contrast of the image in order to make certain that the highest possible quality X rays will be taken. The angiographer then initiates the filming sequence, taking a rapid series of X rays that will function as a

Lingo to Learn

Aneurysm A saclike bulging of a blood vessel, usually an artery; an extremely dangerous health condition.

Artery A vessel that carries blood away from the heart to the rest of the body.

Catheter A small, flexible, strong tube made of plastic, rubber, or metal, inserted into the body to inject medicines, drain fluids, and perform diagnostic procedures.

Catheterization The introduction of a catheter into the body.

Coronary stent A device inserted into a blood vessel in order to support a weakened or collapsed area of the vessel.

Diagnosis The determination, after examination, of the nature of the patient's health condition and extent of disease.

Electrocardiogram (EKG or **ECG)** A record of the electric current produced by the contractions of the heart. The EKG machine and monitor provide a graphic, real-time representation of this electric current.

Fluoroscope X-ray apparatus that uses a fluorescent screen of calcium tungstate to produce images of the varying densities of the body.

Imaging The creation of images of the parts of the body.

Intravenous Refers to the injection of medicines, contrast mediums, and other drugs directly into a vein.

Stroke A condition, often accompanied by seizures, brought on by the collapse or rupture of a blood vessel in the brain.

Vascular Pertaining to or containing vessels.

Vein A vessel that carries blood from other parts of the body back to the heart.

X ray A type of radiation beam used to record on film shadow images of the portions of the body.

movie of the vessel. This will allow the physician to study the blood flow within the vessel.

An angiography procedure can last a few minutes or up to three hours. Once the X rays have been taken, the angiographer takes them to the hospital's darkroom to be developed. The angiographer then reviews the finished X rays for their quality and to be certain that they properly record the area under examination.

Recent advances in technology allow angiographers to inject far less contrast medium into patients. Computers, in what is called digital subtraction angiography, enable the technologist to delete parts of the X rays that reduce the quality and visibility of the vessels. In some cases, this means that the contrast medium can be injected intravenously, eliminating the riskier catheterization procedure. Advances in intervention procedures, such as expanding a blocked artery or injecting medications directly into a tumor, mean that these can be performed while the catheter is still in place. In this way, surgery can often be avoided.

CARDIAC CATHETERIZATION

Like angiography, the cardiac catheterization (CC) procedure is invasive, in that it involves the introduction of a catheter into the patient's body in order to examine and treat heart conditions. As part of a team assisting the cardiologist, the *cardiac catheterization technologist* performs one or more of several functions, including positioning the patients and explaining to them the procedure they will undergo; monitoring such vital signs as the patient's blood pressure and respiration rates; documenting the procedure by inserting patient data into a computer system used to control the amount, quality, and sequence for filming the X rays of the patient's heart; and assisting the cardiology team in preprocedure sterilization by retrieving supplies and equipment necessary to the procedure.

During a cardiac catheterization procedure, a catheter is introduced through a small incision into a vein or artery and guided into the patient's heart. When the catheter is in position, it can be used for various diagnostic and intervention procedures, such as directly reading the heart's blood pressure, withdrawing blood to determine the amount of oxygen reaching the heart, injecting contrast medium for filming X rays, or introducing tools and medications to repair damaged vessels. When these procedures are called for, the cardiac catheterization technologist will assist in preparing whatever tools and medications are needed.

When X rays are required, the CC technologist will enter data on the amount, quality, and filming sequence of the radiation beam, initiate the introduction of the contrast medium into the heart, and activate the fluoroscope that will film the heart. CC technologists are also responsible for positioning the X-ray device and the table, raising and lowering them according to the cardiologist's request.

Finally, an important function of the cardiac catheterization technologist is to remain alert to changes in the patient's response throughout the procedure. Because patients undergoing this procedure generally suffer from life-threatening conditions, and because there remains a measure of risk to the procedure, the cardiologist and the other members of the cardiac catheterization team must be kept continually informed of the patient's progress.

CT (COMPUTER TOMOGRAPHY) SCAN

CT scanning (also known as CAT scanning, which stands for computer axial tomography) represents an important breakthrough in diagnostic imaging. While invasive techniques such as angiography entail not only a degree of risk to the patient, but are also limited in their usefulness in highly complex organs like the brain, CT scanning combines X rays with computer technology to create clear cross-section images. These cross sections, or slices, provide more detailed information than standard X rays, while the technique minimizes the patient's exposure to the X-ray radiation. First developed in the early 1970s for studying the brain, CT scanning has proven a useful technique for examination of much of the body.

A CT scanner is a large device consisting of a rotating scanner and a table that may be placed in a variety of positions as it enters the scanner. The *CT technologist* is responsible for positioning the patient on the table, making certain that the head and body are immobilized. The placement of the patient must be precise and according to the radiologist's instructions in order to achieve the necessary images of the area under examination. Contrast media are also used in CT scanning. The medium is sometimes taken orally, at other times given intravenously. The CT technologist enters data into the scanner's computer control, including the type of scan to be performed, the time required, and the thickness of the slice to be made.

As the CT scan begins, large numbers of low dosage X rays are passed through the patient from a great many angles. These angles enable the computer to construct three-dimensional images of the parts of the patient's body. Different tissues in the body absorb X rays in different amounts; sensors allow the computer to gather this information and build the images. During the procedure, the CT technologist observes the patient through a window in the control room and speaks to the patient over an intercom system. Because the CT scan can be an uncomfortable procedure, the CT technologist is able to provide reassurance to the patient.

MAGNETIC RESONANCE IMAGING (MRI)

MRI is the latest advance in imaging technology. Unlike the other procedures, it does not involve X rays and, therefore, presents no risk to the patient. MRI scans also produce the most detailed and flexible images among the various imaging techniques. Because it is relatively new, however, it remains an extremely costly procedure.

As its name implies, MRI uses a strong magnetic field to affect the positioning of hydrogen protons (the nuclei of hydrogen) in the body. Normally, hydrogen protons are randomly positioned; when subjected to the magnetic field of the MRI, however, these protons will line up parallel to each other. A pulse of radio waves is then used to knock the protons out of this alignment. As the protons return to their magnetic alignment, they produce radio signals, and the MRI scanner reads these radio signals in order to construct its images. Because the different tissues of the body contain different levels of hydrogen, each tissue will produce a radio signal of a different strength. The MRI computer interprets the strength of the signals as it builds the images of the section of the body under examination.

The *MRI technologist* first speaks to the patient, explaining the MRI procedure, and makes certain that the patient is not carrying any metal objects. These can be hazardous to the patient and can damage the equipment once the magnetic field is activated. The MRI technologist is responsible for positioning the patient on the table that will be introduced into the MRI scanner. Special coils, or receivers, are positioned on the patient over the area the radiologist wishes to examine. A microphone inside the scanner allows the patient and technologist to communicate throughout the procedure, which generally requires half an hour, and the MRI technologist will explain the microphone's operation to the patient.

In the computer control room attached to the MRI scanning room, the MRI technologist enters the necessary data, such as the patient's history, the position for entry into the scanner, the part of the body to be scanned, and the orientation of the scan, into the computer. The MRI technologist initiates the scan and observes the patient through a window in the control room and on a closed-circuit video display, while maintaining voice contact. In this way, the MRI technologist can offer comfort and reassurance to the patient while remaining alert to the patient's safety.

MRI scans are particularly useful for examining the brain, spinal cord, and the eyes and ears and for determining the precise extent of tumors that may be present in the patient's body. MRI scans can provide detailed images of the heart, the circulatory system, as well as joints and soft tissues and organs such as the intestines. Continual refinements to MRI techniques are making possible the imaging of areas of the body that have previously resisted detailed examination.

What Is It Like to Be a Special Procedures Technologist?

Before the introduction of these special imaging procedures, physicians were dependent on X rays to give them an understanding of the conditions affecting their patients. X rays, however, are not usually precise enough to supply detailed images of many vital areas of the body. For some health conditions, exploratory surgery was the only way a physician could locate the source of a health problem. Yet even minor surgery can expose a patient to risk. Special imaging procedures have greatly enhanced the physician's diagnostic abilities; in some cases, these procedures allow the patient to avoid surgery altogether.

Special procedures have created a need for personnel trained to operate the equipment and assist the medical and nursing staff. The quality and precision of the images determine their usefulness in treating the patient. Technologists are the people responsible for this quality and precision.

David Brown is a cardiac catheterization technologist at the Texas Heart Center in St. Luke's Episcopal Hospital in Houston. "We're one of the premier cardiac centers in the world," David says.

"We're a large facility, with 11 cath labs, which may be more than most places. But we're involved in research too. A lot of the procedures we perform are still experimental."

Typically David works in a team of four, including two nurses and two technologists, who assist the cardiologist. Teams are assigned to one of several different rooms, with each room set up according to the needs of its diagnostic specialty. Assignments to these rooms are rotated according to a daily schedule. In addition to these rooms, "swing labs," which are really two rooms joined together, allow the cardiac team to perform more than one procedure. "That way, when we finish one procedure, one of us will manipulate the patient from the table while the others are already preparing for the next procedure.

"The nature of the room's specialty determines its schedule. A room set up for peripheral vascular work, for example, may only see one or two patients in the day," David explains. "In a swing lab, we'll work on eight to 11 patients a day. Compare that to an X-ray lab, where it's more like an assembly line—they'll do 200 to 300 patients in one day. Because what we do may be very intensive, our schedule operates according to a specific structure."

When David arrives at the hospital at 7:00 A.M., he first meets with the other members of the cardiac staff to coordinate the day's schedule and receive his assignment. "There's a specific amount of time allotted for each procedure, based on how long they usually take. So I know at the beginning of the day what my schedule will be like." As part of the team, David is assigned to one of the four areas of the cardiac catheterization procedure described above.

"Each one is important, and I've been trained for all of the different fields of the procedure. Sometimes I drive the table, that is, position the patient, manipulate the X-ray camera. Other times, I do the procedural documentation, or I do what we call human dynamic monitoring, which means watching the EKG monitoring, reading the patient's blood pressure and other vital signs. Or I'll be the 'go-fer,' running supplies, sterilizing the equipment, and scrubbing up the other members of the team."

David's days are busy, and sometimes procedures can take longer than expected. "The nature of cardiac catheterization means that the procedure must always come first. So sometimes we're lucky when we can break for lunch, if there's another team available to fill in for us," David says. "And I'd say we run late almost every day."

The daily schedules of other special procedures technologists vary according to the size of the hospital, their patient load, and the type of imaging technique they perform. An angiographer's day may be similar to David Brown's, as they too assist in an invasive procedure. MRI technologists and CT technologists may find their schedules to be much different. "Also," David says, "the other special procedures are generally assigned to the radiology department, while we're a part of the cardiology department."

Do I Have What It Takes to Be a Special Procedures Technologist?

Special procedures technologists, as with all personnel involved in health care, work with people undergoing extremely stressful periods of their lives. "That can be a down side," says Kelly Yu, an MRI technologist at a New Haven, Connecticut, hospital. "Our job can be very stressful and full of hard situations. But the fact that I feel I am helping mankind helps balance the equation."

David Brown agrees. "We work with sick and dying people, and they are often pretty scared. I like it that I can interact with the patients, and I do my best to make them more comfortable. You really get to know your patients, and there's an extra satisfaction when the intervention is successful. But when things don't go well, it can be pretty rough."

You really get to know your patients, and there's an extra satisfaction when the intervention is successful.

Good communication skills are important not only for interacting with the patients, but also for working with other members of the medical staff. As a member of a cardiology team, David's contact with physicians, nurses, and other technologists is more intensive than Kelly's work in MRI. "But I like it that I'm allowed to interact with professionals on an equal level," says David, who is currently completing his premedical studies and expects to become a general surgeon. "I think being a cardiac tech allows me to prove myself to the others. There's more respect here than in other areas of radiology. They see me working; I'm part of the team, and really, the only thing that counts here is how well you perform your job. I think there's an attitude toward other radiology technologists that you're just a tech. I don't find that in cardiology."

For Kelly, the recent initiation of board certification for MRI technologists brings an added respect to her work. "Certification is a big step toward acknowledgment," she says. But Kelly finds a lot of satisfaction in the work itself. "I chose radiology and MRI because it's an up-and-coming career that's always taking steps toward being at the forefront of medicine in the years to come. Each year we get better upgrades, and we're able to do things that were never even imagined before, like magnetic resonance angiography, breast imaging, and imaging of heart, abdomen, and prostate. I like the fact that this career is always moving on, challenging me to become a better and more competent tech."

No matter where they work, though, technologists must have the desire to keep learning and stay current with new developments in the field. One of the exciting parts of David's work is the sometimes experimental nature of the procedures with which he assists. "A lot of the work we do is as part of major research studies into techniques and types of medication. For example, we pioneered the use of coronary stents. I like being involved in new technologies. And I get to see procedures that never make it to being approved too."

David, who began his radiology career as a radiologic technologist in the army, finds his work in cardiology to be an important step in his future career. "I've dreamed of becoming a surgeon since I was young. And the work I do here is a lot like surgery. It's giving me a real exposure to what I hope to do in the future. I get to put into practice a lot of the things I'm studying in school too. For that reason, I recommend this work to anyone considering a medical career."

Technologists must be able to concentrate on several tasks at once. Cardiology patients are often confronted with life-threatening conditions, and David must always be alert to signs that they are in trouble during the procedure. "I'm working with critical patients. I have to be able to see what can go wrong and be prepared for it. If a patient crashes suddenly, or if they can't tolerate the procedure, I have to know to call the anesthesiologist or to call for respiratory support. That can be stressful, knowing that a person's life depends on what you do."

Patients undergoing these procedures may require extra sensitivity from the technologists and other personnel involved in their care. "You have to be able to inspire confidence in them," Kelly says. "That's a big factor in a patient's health and whether they'll get better." Technologists, therefore, should enjoy working with people and be able to give reassurance.

Hospitals are, of course, sterile, well-lit work environments. However, working conditions may vary. A busy hospital, a critical care ward, or an emergency room may present a much more stressful environment than a health care clinic, a health maintenance organization (HMO), or a diagnostic imaging center. Hours may also vary widely. David Brown, for example, generally works eight hours a day, five days a week. "Although," David says, "they're considering adding a second shift, because of the increasing volume of patients we see." Other special procedures technologists may be assigned to work night or weekend shifts, or they may be on call, meaning they must be available to work 24 hours a day.

Advancement Possibilities

Radiologic equipment specialists test, repair, calibrate, and assist in the installation of radiological and related equipment used in medical diagnosis or therapy, applying technical knowledge of electronic, radiological, and mechanical systems, as well as user knowledge of computers, manuals, test equipment, measuring instruments, hand tools, and power tools.

Chief radiologic technologists direct and coordinate activities of radiology or diagnostic imaging departments in hospitals or other medical facilities.

Radiologists diagnose and treat diseases of the human body using X rays and radioactive substances.

Radiology administrators plan, direct, and coordinate administrative activities of radiology departments in hospital medical centers.

How Do I Become a Special Procedures Technologist?

Most special procedures technologists begin their careers in radiology as radiologic technologists. Generally, they are required to hold an associate's degree in radiology, and then they receive additional training and education in their special procedure. In addition, many states and Puerto Rico require that radiologic technologists be licensed.

EDUCATION

High School

"In tenth grade," David says, "I sort of fell into an advanced course—human anatomy and physiology—where we had to dissect a cat. Ever since I've dreamed of becoming a surgeon." Biology, chemistry, and algebra were also important classes for David. "Having good math skills makes everything go easier," he adds. "And I'd say that my English and social science classes were really helpful, especially when I'm relating to patients and the other members of the cardiology team."

Advanced courses were also a feature of Kelly Yu's high school curriculum. "I found taking advanced courses in anatomy, physiology, math, and physics to be very useful," she says. Classes in communication, such as speech, and classes that reinforce written and verbal skills will help you throughout your career. Because most imaging specialties depend heavily on computer technology, you should gain a good understanding of the use of computers. Depending on where you will work, you will probably find yourself confronted with people from a great variety of cultural backgrounds and experiences. Therefore, you will do well to take a variety of social studies classes and gain an awareness of, and respect and understanding for, issues confronting other cultures.

Postsecondary Training

A high school diploma or equivalent is a requirement for anyone interested in entering this field. After high school, most students will find it necessary to attend a two-year program and earn an associate's degree in radiology before finding employment. These programs can be found at community colleges, vocational and technical training schools, or in the military.

David, for example, began his career in the army. "Actually, I applied for the physical therapy program, but that was filled. So I went into radiography. It was a pretty extensive course, with 20 weeks in the classroom and 23 weeks doing clinical practice. I was sent to a lot of different hospitals around the country for that part."

After he left the army, David applied for his job in the cardiology department. "I was taught everything I needed to know about cardiac catheterization, as well as EKG monitoring, here at the hospital. The training program here usually lasts from three to six months, depending on how quickly you pick it up and how much experience you've already had."

Kelly Yu received her associate's degree in radiology. "Then I was lucky enough to get into the Yale School of Medicine for a year to specialize in MRI."

Most radiologic technologists receive training through a program accredited by the Joint Review Committee on Education in Radiologic Technology (JRCERT). These programs include classroom work, laboratory training, and clinical experience. You can expect to study such subjects as human physiology; medical terminology; radiation physics and protection; diagnostic imaging techniques, principles, procedures, evaluation, and pathology; computer science; quality assurance; medical ethics and law; and patient care.

In all cases, special procedures technologists must complete additional training in their specialty area, which is usually offered through a hospital, medical center, college, or vocational or technical training school.

CERTIFICATION OR LICENSING

Graduates of accredited programs are eligible to take the certification examination offered by the American Registry of Radiologic Technologists (ARRT). Most states and Puerto Rico also require licensing for radiologic technologists. This requirement is usually satisfied by successfully receiving ARRT certification, but you will need to check with your state's licensing board for specific information. Certification requirements and opportunities vary by state for the individual special procedures. However, where certification is available, technologists are strongly advised to complete those requirements. This will enhance your chances of finding employment (see "How Do I Learn More?").

INTERNSHIPS AND VOLUNTEERSHIPS

If you are interested in entering the health care field, you can begin your involvement while still in high school. Most hospitals have volunteer programs that will allow you to explore the hospital environment and gain valuable insight into medicine and patient care. Many nursing homes, mental health centers, and other treatment facilities need dedicated volunteers to assist with patients. You may also be able to find part-time work in one of the lower-skilled medical fields; for example, as a nurse's aide or as an orderly. A job in administration, such as clerking at a hospital, health clinic, or health care center, will also give you valuable experience and exposure to the field. Because careers in health care can be as stressful as they are rewarding, you should consider if your personality is right for the field, and if the field is right for you. You can locate volunteer and employment opportunities by consulting with your high school guidance counselor, contacting local hospitals and health care facilities, or by searching job ads and contacting other employment services.

Who Will Hire Me?

As noted, special procedures technologists are employed in a variety of health care settings. Hospitals are the most likely source for employment, especially for techniques such as CT and MRI scanning, which require extremely costly equipment. Health maintenance organizations and other health care clinics and centers also need personnel trained to carry out the variety of testing procedures needed for medical care. There are also a great number of diagnostic imaging centers, often associated with hospitals, that are specifically dedicated to performing the battery of special imaging procedures. Also, the U.S. government employs radiologic and other imaging personnel, usually through the Department of Veterans Affairs or as members of the armed forces.

Where Can I Go from Here?

Advancement in special procedures fields is generally limited, as these specialties already represent advanced areas of radiology. With experience, however, a special procedures technologist may advance to greater responsibilities and to supervisory positions. Chief radiologic technologists, for example, oversee a radiology or imaging department at a hospital or other medial facility. Radiology administrators direct and coordinate the administration of hospital radiology departments. After working as a technologist you may also choose to continue your education in order to reach advanced positions. Radiologists, for example, have medical degrees and use X rays to diagnose and treat illnesses. David sees his special imaging procedures work as a valuable bridge to becoming a doctor. David, in fact, credits his decision to pursue a medical career to his work as a cardiac catheterization technologist.

Special procedures technologists will find demand for their skills throughout the country. Travel to other countries is also a possibility, as some countries, including Great Britain, South Africa, and Canada, recognize U.S. certification.

What Are the Salary Ranges?

According to the *Occupational Outlook Handbook,* radiologic technologists had median annual earnings of $41,850 in 2003. Those in the lowest 10 percent earned less than $29,340, while those in the highest 10 percent earned more than $58,300 annually. Medical and clinical laboratory technologists had median annual earnings of $44,460 in 2003. The lowest paid 10 percent earned less than $31,410, and the highest paid 10 percent made more than $60,790.

Compensation and pay scales will vary based on the location of the employer—with urban areas more lucrative than rural areas and small towns—and on the level of education attained, the experience, and the responsibilities of the technologist. Benefits vary widely from state to state and from employer to employer. Most packages, however, include paid vacation and holidays, as well as sick leave, medical and dental insurance, and some form of retirement plan. Some employers may offer additional benefits such as on-site day care and tuition reimbursement.

What Is the Job Outlook?

The job outlook for special procedures technologists is quite favorable. The U.S. Department of Labor expects employment of radiologic technologists to increase at a faster than average rate over the next 10 years. For certified special procedures technologists the outlook should be even better. Heart disease and cancer continue to be among the primary health concerns in the U.S. population, and there will be a high demand for skilled technologists to assist in the diagnosis and treatment of these and other conditions.

Because these procedures can reduce or even eliminate the need for riskier and costlier surgical interventions, their use can be expected to become more and more common in the health care industry. The ability to diagnose ailments precisely and accurately, and even before they become life-threatening, is an important factor in the increasingly cost-conscious health care arena. In addition, health insurance companies, especially malpractice insurance underwriters, will also require more and more testing in order to limit physician and hospital liability. While these procedures themselves may be expensive, they can reduce both hospital and physician liability costs and litigation and also reduce the need for the much more expensive treatment of advanced diseases and conditions.

Another factor that will influence growth is the aging of the American population. As the median age rises, more attention will be focused on diseases that are prominent in older people. Many of these diseases require the use of imaging equipment and technologists. The Southeast and Southwest regions of the United States offer significant employment opportunity due to their large populations of retirement-age Americans. The aging of the work force will also mean more retirement within the field and more positions to fill. ARRT has found that the majority of radiologic technologists are 40 years or older, part of the reason the organizations are predicting a severe shortage of technologists by 2010.

Another reason for this shortage is that fewer people are entering the field than ever before. The career may be unattractive to some because of the long hours and wages that don't properly compensate. In an effort to bring some standardization to the field, ARRT is considering requiring technologists to have bachelor's degrees in order to become certified. Currently, radiologic technology students are putting in nearly four years of training anyway, because of the practical requirements of associate's degrees.

How Do I Learn More?

PROFESSIONAL ORGANIZATIONS

The following are organizations that provide information on special procedures technologist careers, accredited schools and scholarships, and possible employers:

American Registry of Radiologic Technologists
1255 Northland Drive
St. Paul, MN 55120-1155
651-687-0048
http://www.arrt.org

American Society of Nuclear Cardiology
9111 Old Georgetown Road
Bethesda, MD 20814-1699
301-493-2360
admin@asnc.org
http://www.asnc.org

American Society of Radiologic Technologists
15000 Central Avenue, SE
Albuquerque, NM 87123-3917
800-444-2778
http://www.asrt.org

Joint Review Committee on Education in Radiologic Technology
20 North Wacker Drive, Suite 900
Chicago, IL 60606-2901
312-704-5300
mail@jrcert.org
http://www.jrcert.org

To learn more about credentialing in cardiovascular technology:

Cardiovascular Credentialing International
4456 Corporation Lane, Suite 120
Virginia Beach, VA 23462
804-497-3380
http://www.cci-online.org

BIBLIOGRAPHY

The following is a sampling of materials relating to the professional concerns and development of special procedures technologists:

Brant, William E., and Clyde A. Helms, eds. *Fundamentals of Diagnostic Radiology.* 2d ed. Baltimore: Lippincott Williams & Wilkins, 1999.

Careers in Focus: Medical Technicians. 4th ed. New York: Facts On File, 2004.

Juhl, John H., and Andrew B. Crummy, eds. *Paul and Juhl's Essentials of Radiologic Imaging*. 7th ed. Philadelphia, PA: J. B. Lippincott, 1998.

Mettler, Fred A., Jr., and Milton J. Guiberteau. *Essentials of Nuclear Medicine Imaging*. 4th ed. Philadelphia: W. B. Saunders, 1998.

SPORTS PHYSICIANS

Definition
Sports physicians typically treat patients who have incurred injuries to their musculoskeletal systems during physical activity, usually a sporting event.

High School Subjects
Biology
Chemistry
Health

Personal Skills
Helping/teaching
Technical/scientific

Salary Range
$47,710 to $115,020 to $145,600+

Educational Requirements
Medical degree

Certification or Licensing
Required by all states

Outlook
Faster than the average

DOT
070

GOE
14.02.01

NOC
3111

O*NET-SOC
29-1062.00, 29-1069.99

"Your shoulder needs more rest and treatment before you can play again," says Dr. Jim Johnson. It's not what Mike, the star quarterback, wants to hear. If he doesn't play in tomorrow night's game, the chances of the team winning aren't very good. A loss could mean the team won't make it to the playoffs and his own chances for a scholarship will be in jeopardy. Jim is getting pressure from the coach, the athlete, and the athlete's family to let Mike play in this one crucial game.

Mike has had a cortisone injection to relieve the pain from his rotator cuff injury. He is taking nonsteroidal anti-inflammatory drugs, icing his shoulder regularly, and taking care not to raise his arm above his shoulder.

"Can't you give me another one of those injections?" asks Mike. Jim shakes his head. "It's not safe to give you another injection so soon, Mike. It might make you feel better, but if you go back out on that field, you are in real danger of tearing that tendon even more, and that could mean, at the very least, surgery and two to three months of recovery and rehabilitation."

It's difficult to watch Mike's disappointment, but Jim has to stand firm against all the pressures to sway him from what he knows is best for Mike. Mike is worried about tomorrow night's game. Jim is thinking not only about Mike's ability to play next season and the season after that, but about helping him have a healthy, pain-free future.

What Does a Sports Physician Do?

Sports physicians are doctors who treat patients suffering from injuries to their musculoskeletal systems due to some form of physical activity, usually a sporting event. These injuries include broken bones, pulled or strained muscles, torn ligaments, and sprains. The majority of sport physicians are either general practitioners or orthopedic surgeons. The spectrum of clients they treat ranges from professional athletes making millions of dollars a year to the weekend warrior who overdoes it during a Saturday afternoon tennis game. Also, many general practitioners and orthopedic surgeons work as team physicians in addition to their duties in private practice.

For example, Dr. Rick Wilkerson, D.O., an orthopedic surgeon in Spencer, Iowa, treats patients with sports injuries, as well as patients in need of joint reconstructions or general orthopedic care. In addition to his work as an orthopedic surgeon, Rick is the team physician and surgeon for Buena Vista University in Storm Lake, Iowa. He is also responsible for the sports medicine care of 19 area high school sports teams.

Team physicians are typically responsible for the health and well-being of athletes from preseason training to postseason play. They develop and implement preventive programs that help athletes avoid injuries. They also develop specific rehabilitation programs that help injured athletes recover as quickly and as safely as possible. One of the most serious responsibilities of sports physicians is ensuring that athletes have completely recovered from their injuries before they return to the field.

Sports physicians often conduct pre-sports physicals of athletes. During the physicals, doctors learn the athletes' medical history as well as determine their fitness to participate in athletics.

Often, certified athletic trainers conduct performance testing that evaluates the speed, strength, and flexibility of athletes. The test results are used by both the athletes and the coaches to recognize the athletes' strengths and weaknesses. Conditioning programs are developed based on the results of the testing. The goal of conditioning programs is to increase the athletes' strength and endurance while minimizing their risk of injury. A general conditioning plan is also created for the entire team.

When an athlete does become injured, sports physicians conduct clinical examinations of the injury to determine the degree of damage. Orthopedic surgeons can use several different diagnostic tools to evaluate their patients' status. During a procedure called arthrography, physicians inject a dye into the injured joint. Then an X ray is taken of the joint that reveals the exact site and extent of the injury. During a procedure called arthroscopy, orthopedic surgeons insert a fiber optic device, which acts as a video camera, into the injured area. The inside of the injured joint then appears on a monitor for the surgeon to evaluate. In some cases arthroscopy can also be used as a surgical procedure.

After athletes have become injured, sports physicians are responsible for developing and overseeing their rehabilitation program. The goal of the rehabilitation program is to return athletes to their normal performance level as quickly and as safely as possible.

The rehabilitation program may include a combination of surgery, physical therapy, and rest. Surgical procedures include arthroplasty. This is an operation often used to treat ligament injuries around the joint. In some cases during arthroplasty, artificial joints made of metal or plastic are fitted to replace damaged joints. As a surgical treatment, arthroscopy is used to remove torn cartilage or bone fragments from an injured joint.

The field of sports medicine is relatively new and research is constantly being conducted to discover better and more effective ways of preventing and treating injuries. The new discoveries help advance rehabilitation programs. As Rick explains, "Over the years we have developed rehabilitation programs between myself and the physical therapists. These programs are continually being modified as new information becomes available in clinical and research studies in the area of sports medicine."

Lingo to Learn

Arthrography A diagnostic tool in which the physician injects a dye into an injured joint which then reveals in an X ray the exact site and extent of the injury.

Arthroplasty An operation used to treat ligament injuries around joints. It can also be used to create new joints from plastic or metal materials.

Arthroscopy A diagnostic or surgical tool. As a diagnostic tool, a tiny camera is inserted into the injured area to reveal the extent of the damage. As a surgical tool, it is used to remove torn cartilage or bone fragments from an injured joint.

Computerized tomography (CT) A computerized diagnostic tool that combines X-ray images of the injured joint to create a detailed view of the injured area.

Magnetic resonance imaging (MRI) A computerized diagnostic tool that measures the effects of a magnetic field on an injured area to determine the status of the injury.

What Is It Like to Be a Sports Physician?

Unlike most other medical specialties, sports physicians generally treat fit, active people. They work with otherwise healthy people who have incurred an injury and may be in a great deal of pain, but usually are not suffering from a chronic or long lasting illness. There are tragic cases of athletes becoming permanently disabled due to a sports injury. However, there is a great deal of optimism in the field of

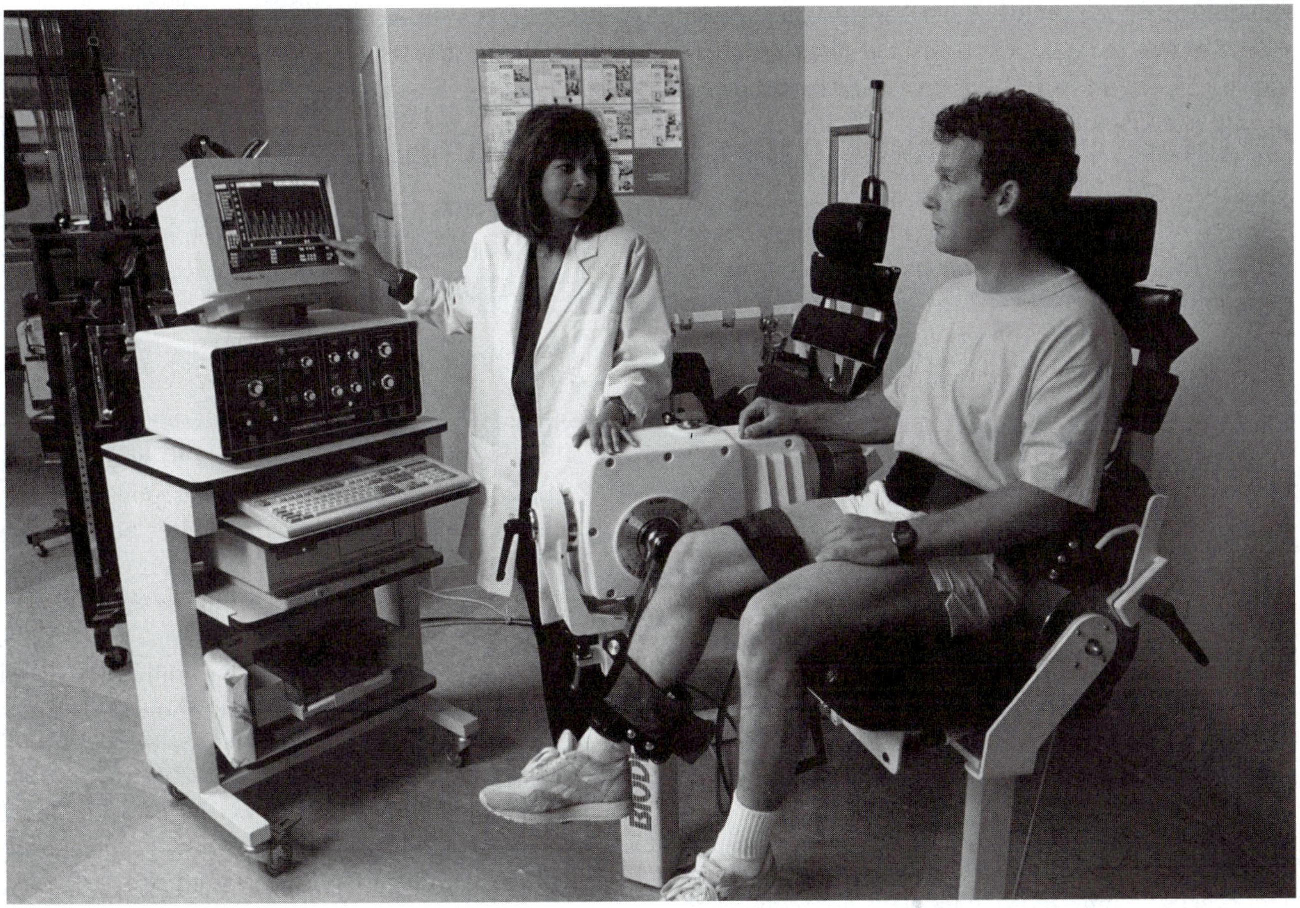

A sports physician treats an athlete with a leg injury. *(Photodisc)*

sports medicine, mainly because the vast majority of patients are expected to recover completely.

For many sports physicians, treating sports-related injuries is just part of their job. Only half of Rick's time is devoted to patients who have been injured during a sporting event. The other half of his time is concentrated on joint reconstructions or general orthopedics. Furthermore, the cases Rick treats at the Sports Medicine Northwest Clinic, in Spencer, Iowa, are equally divided between sports-related injuries and general orthopedics.

Working in small towns, sports physicians may be responsible for the well-being of athletes from many different high schools. Team physicians may be hired by large college athletic departments or professional athletic organizations and may be responsible for the medical care of the members of only one team.

The actual responsibilities of team physicians vary. Some team physicians may be required to be on call or attend every game both at home and on the road. They can be hired to work on staff as team physicians or be hired as consultants. Many team physicians have staffs that include physical therapists and certified athletic trainers. Team physicians have to be aware of staff activities to ensure that athletes are being well-served.

One of the foremost responsibilities of sports physicians is the determination of athletes' eligibility to return to athletic events after they have recovered from an injury. If athletes return before they have fully recovered they are extremely vulnerable to injuring themselves again. As Rick explains, "The most difficult portion of this career is basically the occasional conflict between trying to care for the patient's well-being, while at the same time being pressured by the athlete, coach, and possibly family to get them back to playing sports at the earliest time possible."

The careers of sports physicians can be incredibly exciting. They often get the opportunity to travel across the country. They may also treat professional athletes who are known throughout the world. Unfortunately, some athletes may not recover fully from an injury and that may mean they never play again. And often, it is sports physicians who have to tell the athletes that they have sustained a career-ending injury.

Do I Have What It Takes to Be a Sports Physician?

Successful sports physicians have strong communication skills, even temperament, good people skills, and a high level of dedication to their field. They need to understand the role of sports in society.

Strong communication skills are a necessity because you must be able to clearly express yourself to staff, patients, and coaches. For example, to effectively treat an athlete, trainers must know what parameters the physician has determined to be most important. Furthermore, it is very important that you be able to speak to athletes so they understand why they should not play. As Rick explains, "[Sports physicians must have] the ability to communicate with the athlete and convey the physician's interest in returning them to the sport at the earliest and safest time."

The field of sports medicine demands a high level of dedication. In addition to the time dedicated to private practice, some sports physicians are required to put in additional time on the field and in the training room. Some sports physicians travel with the team from preseason to the play-offs. Furthermore, because research is constantly being conducted in the field, you must always be aware of new developments so you can best treat your patients.

Finally, you should have a clear understanding of the role of sports in today's popular culture. You need to realize the objectives of the coaching staff, as well as the pressures on the injured athlete, so you can provide the best treatment.

To Be a Successful Sports Physician, You Should . . .

- have the ability to communicate effectively with a variety of people
- be a good listener
- have an even temperament
- be an effective motivator
- enjoy working with athletes
- be able to focus on patient's medical needs

How Do I Become a Sports Physician?

EDUCATION

High School

Acceptance into medical school is extremely competitive, so it is never too early for you to begin preparing. Take as many science classes as possible, such as biology, chemistry, and anatomy. It is beneficial to take these classes at an advanced level, if possible.

If there are any communication classes available, consider taking them. Good communication skills will help throughout your academic and professional life. Furthermore, good communication skills are a necessity to help you successfully interact with your staff, patients, and coaches.

While in high school, contact your athletic department to discuss the possibility of assisting the department's athletic trainers. If the high school has a team physician, the department may be able to arrange for an interview.

Postsecondary Training

Sports physicians must have a medical degree. Acceptance into medical schools is based on many things. Though an undergraduate degree is a requirement, not all medical schools require applicants to have earned an undergraduate degree in premedical studies.

In fact, Dr. Rick Wilkerson earned a degree in international relations before beginning his medical career. Some people believe that a well-rounded, liberal, undergraduate education is beneficial to a doctor. They believe that physicians with a fuller educational experience interact more effectively with their patients. Also, it is not unusual for medical students to have worked for a few years before deciding to enter medical school.

Many students follow a premed program for undergraduate studies. Typically, these programs require many courses in the sciences, including anatomy, biology, chemistry, and physiology. All medical schools in the country require applicants to take the Medical College Admissions Test (MCAT). Students usually take this exam during their third year of college. MCAT results are an important tool for medical schools in determining acceptance into a program. Admission to medical school is highly competitive and a superior grade point average is a must.

Medical students spend the first two years immersed in science classes. Course work may include classes in anatomy, biochemistry, physiology, pharmacology, and microbiology. For the next two years you work in clinical environments, treating patients and developing diagnostic skills.

After medical school, students spend at least one year in an internship program. This will be followed by several years in a residency program, training in a specialty. In the case of a sports physician, this will usually mean a specialty in orthopedics or general practice.

CERTIFICATION OR LICENSING

To become a licensed physician, you must pass the state board examination of the state in which you plan to work. A doctor cannot practice medicine without a license.

After completion of a residency programs, you apply for certification in your particular specialty. There are over 20 specialty boards that certify candidates based on their qualifications. The American Board of Family Practice will only consider certifying candidates who have three years of experience in postgraduate training. To become board certified by the American Board of Orthopedic Surgery, applicants must have completed five years of postgraduate training, three years of which must be in the area of orthopedic surgery.

Continuing education is an important part of a sports physician's career. As Rick explains, "The area of sports medicine is a fairly new area of medicine and new information regarding rehabilitation, training techniques, and injury prevention are continually being published."

The American College of Sports Medicine offers several opportunities for continuing education. Their annual meeting provides one such opportunity. It is a four-day event during which more than 1,000 case studies and workshops are presented.

SCHOLARSHIPS AND GRANTS

Scholarships and grants are often available from individual institutions, state agencies, and special-interest organizations. Many students finance their medical education through the Armed Forces Health Professions Scholarship Program. Each branch of the military participates in this program, paying students' tuitions in exchange for military service. Contact your local recruiting office for more information on this program. The National Health Service Corps Scholarship Program (http://nhsc.bhpr.hrsa.gov) also provides money for students in return for service. Another source for financial aid, scholarship, and grant information is the Association of American Medical Colleges (http://www.aamc.org).

In-depth

Sports Medicine to the Rescue

In July 1995, New York Yankee pitcher Jimmy Key underwent surgery to repair a completely torn rotator cuff in his left shoulder. Though rotator cuff injuries are not uncommon for major league pitchers, Key's prognosis was grim. A complete return from a total tear had never been done before.

Advances in sports medicine allowed Key's surgeon, Dr. James Andrews, to use state of-the-art materials to create a strong repair that could withstand an aggressive therapy program. Key returned to pitching in the spring of 1996, a testament to his drive and the capabilities of his surgeon and physical therapist.

His problems, however, were far from over. He had a slow start in the 1996 season and was sent down to the minors to work out the kinks.

Many thought his career was over. Undaunted, Key and his rehabilitation crew made a spectacular comeback. He returned to the Yankees and finished the season with an 11-6 record. The Yankees went to the World Series and in game six, what would be the deciding contest, Key pitched five and a third innings as the Yankees defeated the Braves, with Key getting the win.

INTERNSHIPS AND VOLUNTEERSHIPS

To gain practical experience in the area of sports medicine, speak to the physical education teachers at your school. They will be able to direct you to either the athletic trainer or team physician. It may be possible for you to volunteer to work as an assistant. Furthermore, the team physician or athletic trainer may be able to answer questions you may have regarding the field.

Another option is to contact a local hospital's volunteer department. Most hospitals have excellent volunteer programs and in some instances you can work in the departments you are most interested in, including orthopedics or rehabilitation.

Who Will Hire Me?

After receiving certification and licensing, either as general practitioners or as orthopedic surgeons, most sports physicians begin to work in private practice. Although some recently licensed physicians open their own private practices, many doctors join partnerships with other physicians. This provides an opportunity to share the expenses of opening a new medical practice. Once physicians have developed a good reputation and have successfully treated many patients, they may decide to open an office of their own.

To begin working as team physicians, doctors may contact their local school board or the athletic department of local high schools and colleges to describe their qualifications and to determine if there are any employment opportunities. There are several thousand high schools, colleges, and universities across the United States. Most have athletic departments. Often team physicians can work for several high schools on a part-time basis. At any level, sports physicians may be employed as staff members, or as consultants.

Sports physicians may also seek employment at sports medicine clinics. Work at these clinics may be part time or full time. Established sports physicians may open a clinic themselves or in partnership with other sports medicine professionals.

Competition for positions with professional sports organizations is intense. Professional sports teams usually hire well-respected experts in the field with several years of experience. The salaries of professional athletes often run into the millions and organizations must ensure that these athletes have the best medical care and training that money can buy.

In-depth

Sportsmed Profile

In 1960, as the team physician for the New York Titans (later the Jets), Dr. James A. Nicholas developed a keen interest in treating and preventing sports-related injuries. In 1973 he founded the Institute of Sports Medicine and Athletic Trauma at Lenox Hill Hospital, New York City. It was the world's first hospital-based sports medicine institute. Since then, Dr. Nicholas has gone on to work as a team physician for seven other professional teams and has also worked with professional dancers. He was a founding member of several sports medicine societies, including the Orthopedic Society for Sports Medicine.

In 1986, Lenox Hill Hospital changed the name of the Institute to the Nicholas Institute of Sports Medicine and Athletic Trauma. This institute has become a renowned center for the study of the treatment and prevention of sports-related injuries.

Because research is so important, many sports physicians are hired by universities to conduct research and testing to develop new and better ways of preventing and treating athletic injuries. In addition, sports physicians at universities may also teach.

Where Can I Go from Here?

For sports physicians, like most doctors, advancement in the field consists of successfully treating patients and building a highly respected reputation. Usually, sports physicians working as team doctors begin their careers working for high schools and then move up to the college level. Professional athletic organizations and big-time college programs usually only employ physicians who are highly regarded in their field and have many years of experience.

What Are the Salary Ranges?

Physicians, as a group, have among the highest annual earnings of all occupations. The private sports physician of a professional individual athlete, such as a figure skater or long distance runner, will most likely earn far less than the team physician for a professional football or basketball team, primarily because the earnings of the team are so much greater so the organization can afford to pay more for the physician's services. On the other hand, the team physician for the professional basketball team probably wouldn't have time for a private practice, although the sports physician for the figure skater or runner would, in all likelihood, also have a private practice or work for a sports health facility.

According to the U.S. Department of Labor, general practitioners and family practice physicians earn an annual net income of approximately $115,020 in 2002. Ten percent of these physicians earned less than $47,710 annually in that same year, and some earned more than $145,600 per year. This general figure does not include the fees and other income sports physicians receive from the various athletic organizations for whom they work. Again, these fees will vary according to the size of the team, the location, and the level of the athletic organization (high school, college, or professional, being the most common). The income generated from these fees is far less than what they earn in their private practices. On the other hand, those team physicians who are employed full time by a professional organization will likely make more than their nonprofessional sports counterparts, even as much as $1 million or more.

What Is the Job Outlook?

The job outlook for sports physicians is excellent. First of all, there will always be a demand for competent physicians who can treat injuries associated with athletic activity. It is the nature of competition that athletes are constantly trying to do better than their competitors. They try to push themselves to the limit to jump a little higher or run a little faster than their competition. The associated strain means there will always be a risk of injury.

Furthermore, the demand for sports physicians is increasing as professional organizations and collegiate athletic departments realize that sports physicians and research in the area of sports medicine is helping athletes avoid injuries. It is common sense that a healthy athlete is more productive than an injured one and so more and more athletic organizations are hiring sports physicians to help prevent injuries before they happen.

How Do I Learn More?

PROFESSIONAL ORGANIZATIONS

The following are organizations that provide information on sports physicians and sports medicine:

American College of Sports Medicine
401 West Michigan Street
Indianapolis, IN 46202
317-637-9200
http://www.acsm.org

American Orthopaedic Society for Sports Medicine
6300 North River Road, Suite 200
Rosemont, IL 60018
847-292-4900
http://www.sportsmed.org

BIBLIOGRAPHY

The following is a sampling of materials relating to the professional concerns and development of sports physicians:

Andrews, James R., William G. Clancy Jr., and James A. Whiteside, eds. *On-Field Evaluation and Treatment of Common Athletic Injuries.* St. Louis, Mo.: Mosby-Year Book, 1997.

Brukner, Peter, and Karim Khan. *Clinical Sports Medicine.* 2d ed. New York: McGraw-Hill, 2002.

Harries, Mark, Clyde Williams, William Stanish, and Lyle Mitchell. *Oxford Textbook of Sports Medicine.* 2d ed. New York: Oxford University Press, 1998.

Heitzmann, William Ray. *Opportunities in Sports Medicine Careers.* Lincolnwood, Ill.: VGM Career Horizons, 1999.

Kent, Michael, ed. *The Oxford Dictionary of Sports Science and Medicine.* 2d ed. New York: Oxford University Press, 1998.

Puffer, James. *20 Common Problems in Sports Medicine.* New York: McGraw-Hill, 2001.

Wilmore, Jack H., and David L. Costill. *Physiology of Sport and Exercise.* 3d ed. Champaign, Ill.: Human Kinetics, 2004.

SURGICAL TECHNOLOGISTS

The operating lounge is empty, except for two people sitting at one of the round tables, quietly joking around and drinking their coffee while they draw up the following week's schedule. A high-pitched series of beeps jars their banter and the surgical technologist reaches down for his pager. Through a background of static, he hears: "Stab wound. OR. Stat." John Houck is on his feet and headed toward the operating room before the message clears from his pager.

In emergencies like this, there is no time to set up for surgery. John has nearly finished scrubbing when the patient, a woman in her mid-30s, is wheeled into the operating room. Within minutes, a nurse, anesthesiologist, and surgeon arrive. John has to be doubly efficient in emergencies, not having had the time to organize the instruments, sutures, or sponges. He helps the other members of the surgical team to scrub, and the operation begins.

John hands instruments to the surgeon as needed and counts the sponges. He will help with suturing at the close of the surgery. Once the initial frenzy is over, surgery becomes a familiar rhythm, everyone working together to ensure the survival of the patient.

"I think we've got her," the doctor says finally, as he finishes stitching up the woman. "She's going to hurt a little, but she'll make it."

An orderly wheels the woman to the recovery room. The members of the surgical team pull off their gloves and masks. John collects the instruments that need sterilizing, throws the garbage away, and begins cleaning the operating room in preparation for the next operation.

Definition
Surgical technologists are integral members of the surgical team. They work closely with surgeons, nurses, anesthesiologists, and other personnel to ensure the success of operations and assume appropriate responsibilities before, during, and after surgery.

Alternative Job Title
Operating room technicians

High School Subjects
Biology
Chemistry

Personal Skills
Following instructions
Helping/teaching

Salary Range
$23,290 to $33,150 to $45,000+

Minimum Educational Level
Some postsecondary training

Certification or Licensing
Recommended

Outlook
Faster than the average

DOT
079

GOE
14.02.01

NOC
3219

O*NET-SOC
29-2055.00

What Does a Surgical Technologist Do?

Surgical technologists are an integral part of the surgery team, providing assistance and assurance that, from start to finish, operations run as smoothly as possible.

During World War II, there was a shortage of doctors and nurses to perform operations. From this need came the idea of specially training someone to assist in the surgical process. Today, there are thousands of certified surgical technologists, without whom successful operations would be difficult.

The role of a surgical technologist begins before the patient arrives in surgery and continues after surgery is completed. The operating room must be set up for whatever kind of surgery will be performed, from organizing drapes and equipment to preparing the sterile field, which means placing the necessary sterilized instruments on a special sterilized tray and making sure nothing unsterilized touches them. The technologist scrubs and puts on a gown, cap, mask, shoe covers, and gloves, and then helps the surgeons and nurses get gloved and gowned after scrubbing. The surgical technologist's most important role is maintaining the sterile field. "It could be so easy for a patient to get infected if someone's not monitoring the room," John Houck says.

Once the surgery is underway, the technologist pays attention to the needs of the surgeon, handing instruments, sutures, and sponges, perhaps holding back flaps of skin with forceps if need be. "You are the surgeon's right-hand person," John says. "You have to be almost a mind-reader. You definitely have to know your procedures."

You are the surgeon's right-hand person.

Technologists count the sponges, sutures, and needles frequently to make sure nothing is left inside a patient. If there are specimens to be taken to the lab to be analyzed, it is the technologist who helps prepare, care for, and dispose of these specimens. They help apply dressings to the patient and may be asked to operate sterilizers, lights, or suction machines.

After the operation, the technologist makes sure the patient is transported to the recovery room by an orderly. If an orderly is not available, then the technologist transports the patient. They are responsible for cleaning up after the surgery, including disposing of soiled drapes and disposable instruments and equipment, sterilizing instruments, and restocking the operating room for the next operation.

What Is It Like to Be a Surgical Technologist?

John Houck has worked as a surgical technologist since 1982. He works the 3:00 P.M. to 11:00 P.M. shift at Illinois Masonic Hospital. He likes to arrive early for his shift so that he can relax for a few minutes, hear about the morning from his coworkers, and organize his schedule for the evening. Surgical technologists who work the morning shifts handle scheduled surgeries. At hospitals, surgeries are scheduled in the mornings or early afternoons, so it's rare that there are a lot of scheduled surgeries for John's shift. A morning technologist may have back-to-back surgeries through his or her entire shift. John's shift involves simply finishing with the scheduled surgeries and then waiting for emergencies to come in. "The

Lingo to Learn

Drape Sterile cloth used to surround and isolate the actual site or location of the operation on the patient's body.

-ectomy Surgery that involves the partial or complete removal of an organ, as in appendectomy (removal of the appendix).

Forceps Instrument that is very similar in appearance to cooking tongs. Used by surgeons to hold back skin or other soft tissue.

On call Surgical assistants remain available via pager to come to work on a moment's notice in case of an emergency.

-otomy Surgery that involves the perforation or incision of organs or tissue, as in radial kerototomy (laser surgery performed on the eye).

-plasty Surgery to restore, reconstruct, or refigure body parts, as in rhinoplasty (surgery to reshape the nose).

Scalpel A thin-bladed knife that is used as a surgical tool.

Scrub The process of thoroughly washing the hands and forearms before surgery to ensure sterility.

Scrubbing Literally, the physical cleaning of the hands, wrists, and forearms of the surgeon and each member of the surgical staff. Scrubbing is performed prior to all surgeries in order to kill germs and harmful bacteria.

Sterile field The part of the operating room where the instruments, equipment, and surfaces are entirely free of germs.

Sterilize A procedure in which living microorganisms are removed from an area or instrument.

Sutures The stitches used to close a wound or surgical incision.

day-shift people don't get much emergency action," John says. "This shift, we see a lot of trauma cases—stabbings, shootings, accidents. We get at least three unscheduled cases a night, even during the slowest times."

In emergency situations, John says, a technologist has to move fast. "You'll get a call, 'gunshot coming up in five,' and you've got five minutes to get everything ready—to prepare the sterile field, to prepare the room. Sometimes you don't even get five minutes." He laughs. "One thing you get good at around here is fast set-up."

In any situation, John makes sure that the operating room is ready for the surgery that is about to take place. He helps the surgeons with their gowns and gloves and stands by during surgery ready to pass whatever instruments are needed and keeping careful count of everything: sponges, needles, sutures.

At the end of an operation, an orderly comes to wheel the patient to the recovery room and John cleans up. He throws away used surgical drapes and throws away, washes, or sterilizes equipment and instruments.

"You don't have a lot of awake contact with the patient," he says, "so it's not like you get to know them, but it's rewarding work. It's a good feeling when you hear that someone who was near death made it and is doing well."

Do I Have What It Takes to Be a Surgical Technologist?

"I used to get adrenaline rushes," John says. "And I'll admit, it gets crazy. But now I'm used to the pace. Now it's just part of my job." There is no doubt that surgical technologists work under great pressure and tension. Not only do they need to be able to react quickly and efficiently to high-stress emergency situations, but they also need to realize that flaring tempers are a part of the work. They have to learn not to take anger personally. "This is a place where you need to stand up for yourself," says John. "You need to be confident and good at your job. No one has time for someone who doesn't know what they're doing. If you're meek and timid in this business, you get yelled at and walked all over."

Technologists must be good at organizing, pay attention to details, and be very attentive to the surgeon during surgery. "There is a lot of responsibility here," John says. "But I like that there's a lot of variety to the work."

To Be a Successful Surgical Technologist, You Should . . .

- be a fast learner
- be a good decision maker
- be able to think on your feet
- react calmly and efficiently to crises
- be self-confident
- have the ability to remain focused and handle multiple tasks simultaneously
- be flexible and able to respond to unexpected conditions at a site

Technologists often stand for long periods of time. They should have manual dexterity as they are often required to quickly handle instruments. They should be interested in helping people and sensitive to the needs of the patient, even though most often the patient is not conscious. They should be able to withstand strong odors and unpleasant sights.

The operating room environment, whether in a hospital or private setting, is a clean, brightly lit, fairly quiet, and cool environment. Technologists must be able to focus on the task at hand, even when it may be long and tedious. They must be able to adapt to emergency situations. While most technologists work 40-hour weeks, schedules are not always fixed, and technologists may be expected to work different shifts as a part of that work week. Most technologists are expected to be available to work on call from time to time.

How Do I Become a Surgical Technologist?

As a member of the military, John decided that work as a surgical technologist would be interesting to him, and he was sent to the training program on the Texas base where he was stationed. He became certified and worked in the hospital on his army base for some time. John was a fairly good student in high school, where his favorite subject was science.

EDUCATION

High School

Surgical technologists are required to have their high school diplomas to enter a training program. Students who haven't finished high school are encouraged to complete their GED, which enables them admission to surgical technology programs at hospitals and community colleges. High school courses in basic sciences are important, as well as anatomy and physiology if possible.

Postsecondary Training

Surgical technologists receive their training in programs offered by community colleges, technical schools, hospitals, and the military. There are 150 accredited programs for surgical technology throughout the country.

Training programs last anywhere from nine to 24 months and lead to a certificate, diploma, or associate's degree. In 2002 there were 361 surgical technology training programs accredited by the Commission on Accreditation of Allied Health Education Programs (CAAHEP). Required courses include anatomy, physiology, pharmacology, microbiology, and medical terminology. Students learn about the safety and care of patients during surgery, surgical procedures, and aseptic techniques. They learn to sterilize instruments, to prevent infection, and to handle drugs and equipment. Graduates of surgical technology programs know how to apply their knowledge appropriately, are prepared to assume the full range of responsibilities encompassed by their profession, and have received extensive clinical experience in circulating and scrubbing. They are comfortable handling equipment and maintaining a sterile field, monitoring fluids, and organizing the operating room.

CERTIFICATION OR LICENSING

Certification is recommended but not required; however, to advance in the profession, becoming certified is a good idea. "Being certified is not the only way to work as a technologist," John says, "but it's smart. Employers look on it as a sign of commitment. You put time in to get certified. They think: This person is serious about this type of work. Employers like that."

Advancement Possibilities

Assistant operating room administrators are responsible for ordering all of the medical supplies necessary for any surgery that might take place and making certain that they are available to the operating team during surgery. They are also responsible for creating shift schedules, as well as for supervising and monitoring the other surgical technologists.

Assistant operating room supervisors direct and monitor the work of the surgical technologists working as part of the surgical team. Should any problem arise during a surgery, it is up to the operating room supervisor to make certain the problem—whether it is a missing instrument or a personality conflict—does not affect the surgery being performed.

Medical supplies salespeople work for sterile equipment companies or operating room equipment companies and sell medical supplies and/or equipment to hospitals, clinics, and private practices.

National certification is provided by the Liaison Counsel on Certification for the Surgical Technologist. Applicants must either be currently certified or must be graduates of surgical technology programs accredited by CAAHEP. Recertification is required every six years, either in the form of an exam or by keeping up a required number of points by attending conferences offered throughout the year. "Last month I went to a conference where we took gallbladders out of live pigs," John says. "It was really interesting. Going to conferences gives you points toward recertification and the conferences are a tax deduction." He laughs. "And it doesn't hurt that they're held in great places. Great warm places in the winter."

SCHOLARSHIPS AND GRANTS

Scholarships are available through the Foundation for Surgical Technology through the Association of Surgical Technologists (AST). Applicants must be students of programs accredited by CAAHEP. Selection is based on academic performance and financial need. Contact AST for more information (see "How Do I Learn More?").

Who Will Hire Me?

John received his training through the military in Texas. "That's how a lot of us were trained," he says. After completing his training, he was certified and worked as a surgical technologist in the military for a few years. Upon returning to Chicago, John had no trouble finding employment. "There are always openings for qualified surgical techs," he says.

About three quarters of surgical technologists work in hospitals, and students who go through hospital training programs are often hired by those hospitals after graduation. Community colleges that offer programs have placement centers and work with hospitals in the area, which like to hire technologists trained locally.

Within hospitals, surgical technologists may work in operating rooms, ambulatory areas, and central supply departments. Surgical technologists also work in the offices of physicians and dentists who perform outpatient surgical procedures. Others, known as private scrubs, are employed by surgeons who have special surgical teams that perform complex procedures such as liver transplants.

Where Can I Go from Here?

Advancement begins in the form of salary raises, but once a surgical technologist has acquired some experience, he or she can be employed in a number of diverse areas. "The training we get is really broad," John says. "It's a good thing, because you're able to adapt to different jobs from the start. And once you know what you're doing, there are a lot of possibilities." Experienced surgical technologists work as central service managers, surgery schedulers, and managers of materials such as instruments, equipment, and surgical supplies. Assistant operating room administrators order supplies and arrange work schedules. Assistant operating room supervisors direct the surgical technologists in the operating room.

For those who would like to get out of the operating room atmosphere, there are positions available in sales and management with companies that sell operating room equipment or supplies to hospitals. Some technologists find that they want to impart their knowledge and experience to others and become instructors in surgical technology training programs.

What Are the Salary Ranges?

The *Occupational Outlook Handbook* reports that surgical technologists had annual median earnings of $33,150 in 2003. Those in the lowest 10 percent made less than $23,290, while those in the highest 10 percent made more than $45,000.

Full-time employees are generally provided with a benefits package that includes health and life insurance.

What Is the Job Outlook?

According to the U.S. Department of Labor, job opportunities for surgical technologists are expected to grow faster than the average for all occupations. Competent surgical technologists are in great demand. Population growth, longevity, and more advanced medical procedures have contributed to a growing demand for surgical services and therefore surgical technologists. While general economic conditions could affect the growth of this field, it is probable that the trend will continue for years to come.

Due to the rising cost of health care, more surgery is being done on an out-patient basis. If this continues, there will be a great need for surgical technologists. But if more surgeries are performed in non-hospital settings, demand will drop because fewer technologists are hired in those settings.

Some hospitals are discussing the employment of staff members who will handle a wider range of tasks than surgical technologists are qualified to do. While this will limit the need for technologists, there is presently the issue of staff shortages involving nurses, and this works in the favor of surgical technologists, making it desirable to assign them more tasks. Technologists will also need to adapt to new developments in surgery, such as increased use of fiber optics and laser technology.

To be competitive for the best positions as surgical technologists, students should pursue advanced training in anatomy and physiology and aim for certification upon completion of training programs.

How Do I Learn More?

PROFESSIONAL ORGANIZATIONS

For career information and information about education and scholarships contact

Association of Surgical Technologists
7108-C South Alton Way
Englewood, CO 80112
800-637-7433
http://www.ast.org

For certification information contact

Liaison Council on Certification for the Surgical Technologist
128 South Tejon Street, Suite 301
Colorado Springs, CO 80903
719-328-0800
mail@lcc-st.org
http://www.lcc-st.org

BIBLIOGRAPHY

The following is a sampling of material relating to the professional concerns and development of surgical technologists:

Hinton, Debbie, and Tammy Allhoff. *Surgical Mayo Set-Ups*. Albany, N.Y.: Delmar Learning, 2002.

Price, Paul, and Teri Junge, eds. *Surgical Technology for the Surgical Technologist: A Positive Care Approach*. Albany, N.Y.: Delmar Learning, 2000.

Snyder, Katherine, and Chris Keegan. *Pharmacology for the Surgical Technologist*. Philadelphia: W. B. Saunders, 1999.

Wells, Maryann P., and Mary Bradley. *Pocket Guide to Surgical Instruments*. 2d ed. Philadelphia: W. B. Saunders, 1998.

THORACIC SURGEONS

Arthur waits in the surgeon's office. It is his first visit since he was released from the hospital after his coronary bypass surgery. When the doctor enters, she is looking at a lab report. "Your lab work looks great," she says. "How are you feeling?"

Arthur responds, "I haven't had much appetite and I'm not sleeping very well either. And I have a funny sensation in my chest sometimes, like a click or a thump."

"All of those things are perfectly normal after heart surgery," she reassures him. "It will take at least another month or two before you start feeling well again.

"Now, let's take a look at your incisions." The doctor sees no signs of infection or irritation and the wounds are healing as they should be. "I think we can get the nurse to take the staples out of your leg." Arthur had a bypass graft taken from his leg and was hoping that his staples would be removed.

"I'll also send someone in to arrange a rehab schedule for you," she says. Arthur has already been informed about cardiac rehabilitation. He will have to attend a series of one-hour sessions for several weeks that will help him gradually increase his physical activity, learn stress-management techniques, change his diet, and make other lifestyle changes. Arthur has a lot of work ahead of him, but he is determined to do whatever is necessary to be well. After enduring a heart attack and surgery, he knows he doesn't ever want to go through it again.

Definition
A surgeon who treats diseases and conditions of organs in the chest, including the heart, lungs, and esophagus.

Alternative Job Titles
Cardiothoracic surgeons
Cardiac surgeons

High School Subjects
Biology
Chemistry

Personal Skills
Helping/teaching
Technical/scientific

Salary Range
$150,000 to $182,690 to $350,000+

Educational Requirements
Bachelor's degree, medical degree, five-year general surgery residency, two- or three-year thoracic surgery residency, optional one- to two-year fellowships

Certification or Licensing
Required by all states

Outlook
About as fast as the average

DOT
070

GOE
14.02.01

NOC
3111

O*NET-SOC
29-1067.00

What Does a Thoracic Surgeon Do?

The thorax is the cavity within the human body in which the heart and lungs lie. *Thoracic surgeons* treat diseases, repair injuries, and correct deformities of the heart, lungs, and other organs in the chest cavity. They are trained to diagnose and surgically treat coronary artery disease, irregular heartbeats, abnormal heart valves, cancers of the lung and esophagus, and other conditions of the chest. Thoracic surgeons perform heart and lung transplants. They are concerned with pulmonary fibrosis, emphysema, cystic fibrosis, and other diseases of the lung.

A general thoracic surgeon is primarily concerned with diseases of the lungs, esophagus, and chest wall. Other surgeons operate on infants and children with congenital (birth) defects of the windpipe, esophagus, or heart. Thoracic surgeons who perform heart operations (coronary bypass, pacemaker insertion, heart valve replacement) are often called *cardiothoracic surgeons*.

Thoracic surgeons are skilled in state-of-the-art diagnostic procedures, including X rays, computed tomography (CT), and magnetic resonance imaging (MRI). They are trained in oncology and in the use of chemotherapy, radiation therapy, and other therapies used to treat thoracic diseases.

Patients with heart and lung disease are referred to thoracic surgeons when their primary care physicians believe that medication alone will not help and that surgery may be the best treatment for the condition. The thoracic surgeon reviews the patient's medical history and determines the best surgical procedure. The thoracic surgeon then discusses the case with the patient and other physicians, advising the patient of all the risks and benefits associated with the surgery.

The thoracic surgeon is responsible for working with a team of medical specialists and nurses to take the patient through the immediate evaluation prior to surgery, the final decision for surgery, and the recovery period following surgery. Usually, both the patient's physician and the thoracic surgeon see the patient in follow-up visits to make sure that the patient's recovery is progressing. Prior to surgery, nurses and surgical technologists prep the patient for surgery. The thoracic surgeon heads the operating team that includes the anesthesiologist, assistant surgeons, nurses, and technicians responsible for the heart-lung machine that is required in many operations. Following the surgery, nurses will care for the patient in an intensive care unit.

What Is It Like to Be a Thoracic Surgeon?

"The ability to have somebody trust you with their life, to stop their heart, to fix it, work with it, repair it, and then start it again—that's an incredible responsibility," says Dr. Edward D. Verrier, speaking about his work as a thoracic surgeon from his office at the University of Washington in Seattle, where he is chief of the division of cardiothoracic surgery. "There is something very unique about the heart," Ed says. "Some people believe it's the soul." Thoracic surgeons themselves are not immune to the wonder and awe that surrounds them and their work. Most, in fact, vividly recall the very moment they first experienced the life-giving power with which they are entrusted. Dr. Paul S. Levy, a cardiothoracic surgeon who now practices in Toledo, Ohio, will never forget his first encounter with a live heart during college. Students spent a semester focused on career development, working in and observing a profession of their choice.

Dr. Renee Hartz, chief of the division of cardiothoracic surgery at the University of Illinois' Chicago College of Medicine, says, "I spent four months working with five cardiothoracic surgeons in Arizona. To this very day, I remember it. I knew I wanted to go into cardiothoracic surgery when I was holding a beating heart in my hands. At that point, it was pure magic. I remember the day, I remember the patient. I was a junior resident in cardiac surgery and a young woman dying of a clot in her lungs was brought into the operating room. They were performing CPR on her as they wheeled her into the OR for pulmonary surgery. I saved her life. That was the day I decided to become a heart surgeon."

Just as unforgettable are the surgeon's experiences with patients that cannot be saved. "I remember a two-year-old dying on the table unexpectedly," Renee recalls. "It was very unsettling. I had seen a lot of children die when I was working in the emergency room, but for some reason this was different. I'd thought about going into pediatric cardiac surgery, but I knew then it wouldn't work. I couldn't, didn't, want to go through that on a daily basis."

These physicians are equally candid when sharing their reasons for entering medicine, in general. Renee says, "I'm not sure if I chose medicine or it chose me. I came from a very poor family in a small town where no one went to college. Even boys weren't counseled to go to college. Academics weren't emphasized. I only went to college because my friends were. I shocked myself by doing well."

"It's an evolutionary process, everyone has his own reasons," says Dr. Edward Verrier of his decision to enter the field of medicine. "All the altruistic reasons, of course, hold true. But also, I wanted to be successful. My father was an engineer. He built our house. But he didn't make a lot of money. I used to have to make a living and I had to caddy to earn money to help my father. And I caddied for successful people, a lot of whom were doctors. This profession gives you a good salary, a good security for your family. I very much wanted that security when I was growing up. And I wanted people to trust me and respect me," he says.

A typical case in which a cardiothoracic surgeon in private practice might see a patient is when the patient goes to the emergency room, complaining of chest pain. "A guy comes in with substernal chest pain to the ER," says Paul. "The ER calls his internist. With the cardiologist from the care unit, they determine he's got triple vessel coronary disease. They call us to come in and consult. They want to know, would he benefit from surgery?" Paul continues, "We'd look at the patient, talk to him, and if he's a good candidate for surgery, we explain the risk factors of surgery versus medical management of his condition. If he wants the surgery, we send him back to his internist to check him out, do blood work, see if he's in good enough health for surgery."

Thoracic surgeons in a university or teaching hospital see patients on a slightly different basis and their cases are used as the basis for instruction. For example, according to Paul, a typical patient in an urban teaching hospital might be a homeless man who's been referred to the attending physician. After an examination, it's determined that, in addition to having the risk factors for heart disease, the man is also a schizophrenic with vascular problems. The attending physician discusses the case with the resident or fellow. "Together, they review the results of the cardiac catheterization, which reveal single coronary disease; plus the guy's got an aneurysm in his arteries," says Dr. Levy. During surgery, they replace the ascending aorta and perform a bypass graft to the man's heart. Later, the thoracic surgeons provide postoperative care, and ready him for vascular surgery.

Lingo to Learn

Echocardiogram A sound wave picture showing the structure and functions of the heart.

Electrocardiograph (EKG) A machine that constantly monitors the heart's activity.

Stress test A test to measure the heart's performance during exercise. It provides more information than a resting EKG.

Heart catheterization A test in which a small tube is placed in the heart in order to take X rays, measure blood pressure within the heart, and to determine if there are any deformities or defects in the heart.

Heart-lung machine A device that maintains circulation during open heart surgery. Blood is diverted from the heart and lungs, oxygenated, and returned to the body.

Lobectomy The surgical removal of a section, or lobe, of a lung. When the entire lung is removed the procedure is called a **pneumonectomy.**

Do I Have What It Takes to Be a Thoracic Surgeon?

"You have to learn a lot about death and dying," Ed says. "It's very difficult to walk out to a mother and say, 'I'm sorry. I did all I could, but your child still died,'" he says. Paul agrees that the stakes are incredibly high, as are the pressure and responsibility. "There's no margin for mediocrity. When you get mediocre, people die."

Thoracic surgery is believed by most to be the most demanding surgical specialty. Physicians who enter this field will be challenged emotionally, physically, and intellectually. High levels of stress, long hours, and difficult, complex cases are among the drawbacks to working as a thoracic surgeon. Every case is a matter of life and death. While the surgical procedures are possible, they may not be successful. "You can do everything right and the patient dies, anyway. Cardiothoracic surgery is a contact sport; it can go badly very quickly," explains Paul. "You'll be going along and everything's perfect, and then all of a sudden, a suture breaks or a tie on a vessel comes off and you either lose the patient or have to start all over again."

Thoracic surgeons work long hours throughout their years of study, and these schedules can continue throughout their careers. Paul describes a typical year in thoracic residency: "You're on call all the time. We're talking about 100-hour weeks, easily." On those days that they have surgeries scheduled, they usually spend the entire day on their feet. Surgeries can take an hour or two, or they can last for much longer. "Sometimes, the pathologist takes 40 minutes trying to figure out whether or not the specimen is benign or malignant. Meanwhile, you've got this guy on the table with his chest opened up. It can be frustrating."

When it comes to their patients, thoracic surgeons are on call 24 hours a day. Like other physicians, they might be paged while eating dinner or watching a movie, or called while sleeping in the middle of the night. "You have to have a very understanding family," attests Ed.

Renee adds, "The work is labor-intensive. You have to want this very very badly, and you have to be able to focus—focus on a task and carry it to completion."

You have to want this very very badly, and you have to be able to focus—focus on a task and carry it to completion.

Thoracic surgeons, like all surgeons, must possess excellent manual dexterity skills and the ability to make and execute decisions promptly. "I'm an action-oriented person," Renee says, "decisive and quick. I tried to talk myself out of this profession and did a year of pediatric residency, but I loved surgery, so I went back to it. It suits me." Although all surgeries are planned, the degree of planning will differ according to the situation, depending upon whether the procedure is an emergency procedure. In every surgery, however, the surgeon faces the unexpected—a sudden drop in blood pressure, an inexplicable reaction to anesthesia, complications in the surgery, itself. Surgeons must be able to cope with these crises, and others, always mindful of maintaining their composure in stressful situations.

Another essential quality in surgeons is a genuine concern for people. Surgeons treat the individual with a surgical condition, not merely the surgical condition itself. Therefore, those who aspire to be thoracic surgeons must be able to deal compassionately with patients and their families, addressing any fears, questions, and needs they might have. A deep sense of responsibility should accompany a surgeon's compassion as well.

How Do I Become a Thoracic Surgeon?

EDUCATION

High School

You should prepare for a future in medicine by taking courses in biology, chemistry, physics, algebra, geometry, and trigonometry. Courses in computer science are a must, as well, since computers are changing the way medicine is taught and practiced. Since colleges, universities, and medical schools are looking for individuals with a well-rounded background, you should take English, history, literature, and psychology classes.

Postsecondary Training

For a career in thoracic surgery, you must first earn a bachelor's degree from an accredited four-year college or university. Courses that may help prepare students for medical school are math, biology, chemistry, anatomy, physiology, and physics, as well as courses in the humanities, such as English composition.

After receiving an undergraduate degree, you must apply to and be accepted by a medical school. Admission is competitive; applicants undergo an extensive admissions process that considers grade point averages, scores on the Medical College Admission Test, and recommendations from professors. Most premed students apply to several schools early in their senior year of college. Only about one-third of the applicants are accepted.

In order to earn an M.D. degree, you must complete four years of medical school. For the first two years of medical school, you attend lectures and classes and spend time in laboratories. Courses include anatomy, biochemistry, physiology, pharmacology, psychology, microbiology, pathology, medical ethics, and laws governing medicine. You learn to take patient histories, perform routine physical examinations, and recognize symptoms.

In your third and fourth years, you work in clinics and hospitals supervised by residents and physicians. You go through rotations, or brief periods of study in a particular area, such as internal medicine, obstetrics and gynecology, pediatrics, dermatology, psychiatry, and surgery. Rotations allow you to gain exposure to the many different fields within medicine and to learn firsthand the skills of diagnosing and treating patients.

Dr. Paul Levy realized right away that he didn't enjoy the rotations in medicine. "It was so frustrating to keep dealing with chronic noncompliers," he says, referring to people who are told they have to quit smoking, drinking, or eating poorly and to start exercising. "I couldn't fathom myself doing that day in and day out."

After graduating from medical school, physicians must pass a standard examination given by the

National Board of Medical Examiners. Most physicians complete an internship, usually one year in length. This helps graduates to decide on an area of specialization.

Following the internship, physicians begin a residency program. Physicians who wish to become thoracic surgeons must first complete a five-year residency in general surgery. Then they begin a two- or three-year residency in general thoracic surgery and cardiovascular surgery. The residency years are as filled with stress, pressure, and physical rigor as the previous four years of medical school, perhaps even more so as residents are given greater responsibilities than medical students. Residents often work 24-hour shifts, easily clocking in 80 hours or more per week. "You need a supportive environment to succeed," says Dr. Edward Verrier. "You need to have the physical and intellectual skills, but you also need the discipline to get through this."

CERTIFICATION OR LICENSING

Licensing is required in all states before any doctor can practice medicine. To qualify for certification by the American Board of Thoracic Surgery, a candidate must be certified in general surgery by the American Board of Surgery; have completed a residency in thoracic surgery at an approved academic medical center, and have successfully completed both the written and oral examinations given by the American Board of Thoracic Surgery. Certification in thoracic surgery is valid for 10 years, at which time the thoracic surgeon must apply for recertification. While certification is voluntary, it is highly recommended. Most hospitals will not grant privileges to a surgeon without board certification. HMOs and other insurance groups will not make referrals or payments without certification.

SCHOLARSHIPS AND GRANTS

Scholarships and grants are often available from individual institutions, state agencies, and special-interest organizations. Many students finance their medical education through the Armed Forces Health Professions Scholarship Program. Each branch of the military participates in this program, paying students' tuitions in exchange for military service. Contact your local recruiting office for more information on this program. The National Health Service Corps Scholarship Program (http://nhsc.bhpr.hrsa.gov) also provides money for students in return for service. Another source for financial aid, scholarship, and grant information is the Association of American Medical Colleges (http://www.aamc.org). Remember to request information early for eligibility, application requirements, and deadlines.

In-depth

Bypass Surgery

Coronary artery bypass grafting, or CABG (often pronounced "cabbage"), is the most commonly performed open heart surgery in the United States.

In the traditional CABG technique, the thoracic surgeon makes an incision down the front of the chest through the breastbone or sternum. The patient is connected to a heart-lung machine so that the heart can be stopped while the bypass is being performed.

All bypasses were originally performed using a vein from the leg to carry blood around the obstruction. The vein was attached at one end to the aorta and at the other end to the coronary artery beyond the blockage. In the 1970s and 1980s, thoracic surgeons discovered that they could use an artery from the inside of the chest wall instead of vein for the bypass grafts and that it stayed open longer than leg vein grafts. Today most CABG operations are performed using a combination of bypass grafts, including an artery from the chest and some vein from the leg.

Who Will Hire Me?

Many thoracic surgeons enter into private practice with a partner or a small group. Private practice is an attractive option for many thoracic surgeons as it provides a somewhat more stable routine. Patients will still need emergency care, but to some degree, the surgeon can aim for a more predictable schedule.

Many surgeons work at medical schools and in private hospitals. Ed and Renee, for example, practice in university hospitals so they can teach future generations of thoracic surgeons. "I've dedicated myself to teaching others about the responsibility of this work," says Ed.

Where Can I Go from Here?

The field is competitive, but thoracic surgeons advance in the time-honored ways in which all physicians and surgeons advance: by doing their jobs extremely well, working to create and maintain a solid reputation among both peers and patients, and building up their practices. Many surgeons in private practice form single- or multispecialty practice groups, which can lead to more referrals and greater income.

Thoracic surgeons who work as professors at universities and teaching hospitals can advance to become department heads or heads of hospitals. Heading a division of cardiothoracic surgery at a major medical institution is to reach the highest level.

What Are the Salary Ranges?

Because of the high skill level required, long hours, and high risks involved in the profession, surgeons earn some of the highest salaries of all occupations. According to he U.S. Department of Labor, the average annual salary for all surgeons in 2003 was $182,690. Thoracic surgeons can earn anywhere from $150,000 to more than $350,000 a year. Factors influencing individual incomes include the type and size of the practice, the number of hours worked per week, the geographic area, and the professional reputation of the surgeon.

What Is the Job Outlook?

The health care industry, in general, is among the fastest growing in the United States. Although managed health care policies may curtail some higher-risk procedures, patients will continue to need the special skills and expertise of thoracic surgeons. The U.S. Department of Labor reports that employment of physicians will grow at an average rate due to the expansion of health care industries and the growth of an aging population. It also says that the number of new physicians has leveled off and is likely to decrease over the next few years.

How Do I Learn More?

PROFESSIONAL ORGANIZATIONS

The following are organizations that provide information on the field of thoracic and cardiothoracic surgery:

American Association for Thoracic Surgery
900 Cummings Centre, Suite 221-U
Beverly, MA 01915
978-927-8330
http://www.aats.org

Society of Thoracic Surgeons
633 North Saint Clare Street, Suite 2320
Chicago, IL 60611
312-202-5800
http://www.sts.org

BIBLIOGRAPHY

The following is a sampling of materials relating to the professional concerns and development of thoracic surgeons:

Baumgartner, Fritz J. *Cardiothoracic Surgery.* 3d ed. Austin, Tex.: R. G. Landes Company, 2004.

Bohar, Robert M. *Manual of Perioperative Care in Cardiac Surgery.* 3d ed. Boston: Blackwell Science, Inc. 1999.

Shields, Thomas W., Joseph Locicero III, Ronald B. Ponn, and Valerie W. Rusch. *General Thoracic Surgery.* 6th ed. Philadelphia: Lippincott Williams & Wilkins, 2004.

Soltoski, Paulo R., Hratch Karamanoukian, and Tomas Salerno. *Cardiac Surgery Secrets.* 2d ed. Philadelphia: Hanley & Belfus, 2003.

TOXICOLOGISTS

A clue to the mystery is here somewhere, toxicologist Jim Bus is sure of it. He wanders through the neatly stacked cages in the animal lab and wonders what that clue is. For two years, he and his colleagues at Chemical Industry Institute of Toxicology have been exposing both male and female mice and rats to gasoline fumes to determine if they are harmful to living organisms. Throughout the study, the animals have demonstrated healthy behavior. When the research team began dissecting the animals for examination they were startled by what they found. All of the mice and all of the female rats had healthy organ tissue, but the male rats had developed kidney cancer. Suddenly the routine toxicology experiment had turned into a high-stakes puzzle. If gasoline causes cancer in living organisms, millions of people each day are putting themselves at risk at the gas pump.

Jim needs to determine how the gasoline fumes are causing cancer in the male rats and whether the same process could occur in human bodies. If it could, he would have to immediately alert the Environmental Protection Agency, the petroleum companies, and the public to the possible health threat. Measures would have to be developed to protect people from fumes at gas stations. The associated costs, in terms of both health care and new safety technology, would be staggering.

Jim opens a cage and draws out one of the remaining male rats. Gently stroking the animal's coarse fur, Jim considers several troubling questions. Why are the male rats getting sick when the mice and the female rats are not? Why are the rats able to live to their full expected lifespan despite the cancer? Is the kidney cancer somehow unique to male rats or does it indicate a potential health concern for humans?

After much research and hard work, Jim and his team are relieved to discover that the gas fumes causing cancer in the male rats do not have the same effect on humans.

Definition
Toxicologists determine the possible harmful effects, or toxicity, of substances on living organisms.

High School Subjects
Biology
Chemistry

Personal Skills
Helping/teaching
Technical/scientific

Salary Range
$20,000 to $100,000 to $200,000

Educational Requirements
Bachelor's degree, master's degree, doctorate

Certification or Licensing
Recommended (certification)

Outlook
Faster than the average

DOT
041

GOE
02.03.01

NOC
2121

O*NET-SOC
N/A

What Does a Toxicologist Do?

Toxicologists examine the way chemicals interact with living organisms. Their work enables us to use chemicals to improve the quality of our lives, without harming ourselves or our environment. Toxicologists are our protectors in a world that increasingly depends on manufactured chemicals to purify water, protect crops, cure diseases, and much more.

It is the job of *industrial and governmental toxicologists* to help protect the public and the environment from harmful chemicals and to make sure that beneficial chemicals are used in safe and appropriate ways. One way they do this is by assisting in the creation of regulations governing the production and use of chemicals.

Research toxicologists, many of whom work for universities or private research institutes, investigate the biochemical and cellular processes that take place in living organisms as a result of exposure to toxic substances.

Evaluating the safety of chemicals is a very complex process. Chemicals that are safe under some circumstances may be dangerous under others. In order to identify appropriate uses for chemicals, toxicologists must conduct extensive tests to determine if and how a chemical may harm living organisms, under what circumstances it might do so, and at what dosage. "In toxicology, we like to say that the dose makes the poison," says Jim. "Chlorine, for instance, can be dangerous in extremely high doses. The levels used to purify water, however, are not harmful." Thus, depending on the dose, a chemical may be beneficial or deadly.

Many of the tests toxicologists run are performed on laboratory animals. Toxicologists expose animals to a chemical by injecting it into their systems, by feeding it to them, or by surrounding them with fumes. To determine the dosage at which a chemical becomes harmful, toxicologists expose separate groups of animals to different amounts of the substance. The test results are measured by observing the animals' behaviors and by testing samples of their blood and tissue. At the end of a study, toxicologists usually dissect the animals to examine their organs for signs of damage or disease. To eliminate the possibility that something other than the chemical is causing the result, toxicologists also study one group of animals that is not exposed to the chemical.

"We are very careful to treat the animals in a humane manner," says Jim. "Whenever possible, we use in vitro, or test tube, studies, which do not involve animals. It is true, though, that toxicology experiments often cause disease in animals. We believe these tests are necessary because they enable us to prevent hazards to people. By testing animals," Jim explains, "science has been able to develop chemicals, medicines, and technologies that save lives."

Jim, who now works for Dow Chemical Company, is an industrial toxicologist. Before a company can commercially introduce a new chemical, industrial toxicologists must subject it to a barrage of tests to ensure that the chemical will not harm humans or the environment. If a chemical company wants to introduce a new insecticide, for example, industrial toxicologists must first conduct tests to see if the product harms animals when applied to their skin or when ingested. Environmental toxicologists conduct studies to measure the residue the insecticide leaves in soil and water and to determine whether the residue is harmful to fish or wildlife. The results of these tests are then carefully scrutinized by toxicologists who work for government agencies, such as the Food and Drug Administration and the Environmental Protection Agency. If the toxicologists at either of these agencies raise additional questions, the industrial toxicologist must run further studies.

"This is a very healthy process," says Jim. He explains, for example, that in the 1950s a chemical known as thalidomide was prescribed by doctors for some pregnant women to relieve anxiety and morning sickness. The results were disastrous. "Thalidomide caused birth defects in a large number of children. Thanks to toxicology, and to our system of checks and balances, the chance of a tragedy of that kind happening again are greatly reduced today. Toxicologists would discover a drug's potential to cause birth defects long before it could be approved for use."

Lingo to Learn

Benign Referring to a tumor, it means noncancerous.

Carcinogen A cancer-producing substance.

Control group A group in an experiment that is not exposed to a procedure or chemical that the rest of the group is.

Dissect To expose, through cutting, the internal organs of an animal for scientific examination.

In vitro From the Latin meaning "within glassware," referring to a biological process or experiment that takes place in laboratory equipment such as a test tube.

Malignant Tending to deteriorate or cause death. When referring to a cancer, it means highly invasive and quickly spreading.

Metabolism The combination of chemical processes that take place in a living organism resulting in growth, body functions, distribution of nutrients, etc.

Toxin A poison produced by a living organism such as a plant.

What Is It Like to Be a Toxicologist?

Jim describes his job in two words: terrifically exciting. "As a toxicologist," Jim says, "I can help ensure that chemicals are safely used to improve the quality of millions of lives. I can also have an impact on policies that protect the public."

In his work as an industrial toxicologist, Jim designs studies to test new chemical products for safety and regulatory compliance. These studies are typically conducted over a period of one to two years. Throughout this time, Jim supervises the toxicologists and laboratory technicians working on the study. These people implement the tests, observe the animals, and test the blood and tissue samples. Jim evaluates and interprets the results of the tests to determine how, and if, a product can be used safely. When an unexpected result occurs, Jim works with his research team to discover why that result occurred.

Once a study, or series of studies, has been completed, Jim presents the findings to the senior executives of Dow Chemical Company. These managers are extremely receptive to Jim's recommendations. "The last thing that this or any other chemical company wants to do is introduce a harmful product," Jim explains. "My job is to prevent that from happening. The company's management expects me to tell it the way I see it."

Because Dow Chemical Company does business all over the world, Jim also travels extensively to meet with regulatory agencies in other countries. "I've met with regulators in Russia, Japan, and many other countries to describe our testing procedures and to explain my evaluation of a product," says Jim. "These officials have a responsibility to make sure that we have thoroughly tested our products. Toxicology," he adds, "is not a huge discipline, but it is global in its impact."

In addition to meeting with foreign scientists, Jim occasionally must address the public. "Stories in the news may cause the public to feel inappropriate fear of certain chemicals. One special-interest group put out a story that use of chlorine is dangerous. They neglected to explain that the chlorine levels used to purify water are harmless. Tragically, a developing nation in South America was alarmed and stopped chlorinating their water. Many people subsequently died of water-borne diseases. I try to counter these scare tactics by informing the public about our exhaustive testing procedures and about the stringent governmental regulations we observe."

Jim also attends professional conferences and seminars. "Science," he observes, "is constantly changing. Continuing education is absolutely essential to someone in this field."

Because Jim works for a major chemical company, the focus of his research is determined by the products his employer manufactures. Toxicologists who work for colleges and universities are usually able to exert more control over their research. Some engage in basic research. Basic research does not provide any immediate commercial or public use, but it does contribute to our understanding of basic life processes. Others conduct applied research. Applied research is expected to yield direct social or commercial benefit. Research toxicologists may also develop new testing techniques or suggest new mathematical models to check the validity of their tests. In addition to conducting research, toxicologists who work for colleges or universities usually have administrative and teaching responsibilities.

Toxicologists who work for the federal government have widely varied responsibilities. Some are responsible for establishing and enforcing regulations pertaining to the manufacture, distribution, and use of chemicals. Others conduct research to assess risks to the public. One such toxicologist is Linda Birnbaum, the director of experimental toxicology for the Environmental Protection Agency. "Our department strives to assess the health consequences of living with the soup of chemicals we have in our world today. We ask, for example, how air pollution affects the immune system and other body functions." As the director of a large department, Linda is rarely able to pursue her own research. Instead, she designs and supervises major studies while managing the department and coordinating efforts with other government branches.

Do I Have What It Takes to Be a Toxicologist?

According to Jim Bus, toxicologists must be creative, intellectually curious, and insatiable readers. "I think it's important for people to realize that you don't have to be another Albert Einstein to be a successful scientist," he says. "I remember wondering if I would have enough good ideas to be a scientist. The truth is that you don't have to be a genius to come up with scientific ideas. You do have to read avidly, ask probing questions, and try to put things together."

Some toxicology studies may last up to two years, so a person who is considering toxicology as a profession must be persevering and patient. Extensive

To Be a Successful Toxicologist, You Should . . .

- be a responsible and detail-oriented worker
- be able to interact with a variety of people and communicate clearly
- enjoy problem solving
- have patience
- be able to perform experiments with animals
- enjoy continuous learning

studies also require meticulous record keeping, so toxicologists must be organized and disciplined. Jim also points out that many studies involve animal testing. "If a person would not be comfortable testing chemicals on animals," says Jim, "he or she should probably consider another field."

Studies in this field sometimes involve working with highly toxic chemicals. Toxicologists must be extremely responsible about taking every precaution to avoid exposing themselves or their colleagues to harmful substances. Because toxicologists usually work in research teams, strong interpersonal skills are also important. "Industrial toxicologists work closely with other scientists, with management, and with outside regulatory agencies," Jim explains. "You have to be able to communicate clearly about very complex issues."

How Do I Become a Toxicologist?

Students should be aware that there are a variety of ways to enter the toxicology profession. "There is no one straight and narrow path to becoming a toxicologist," Linda says. "Students do not have to decide in high school or even in college. I obtained a doctoral degree in molecular biology. I then completed postdoctoral fellowships in biochemistry and drug metabolism. While I was studying the way the metabolism reacts to foreign chemicals, I became interested in toxicology, so I pursued a third postdoctoral in toxicology."

EDUCATION

High School

Although no definite educational route to becoming a toxicologist exists, if you think you are interested in this career you need to begin by taking college preparatory classes in high school. Courses in science, such as biology, chemistry, and physics, as well as courses in math, such as algebra and geometry, are not only necessary but also allow you to discover the depth of your interest in these areas. English and speech classes provide you with the opportunity to improve your research and communication skills. Social studies or government courses give you an understanding of how society is structured, an understanding that will be necessary in your later career working with government agencies and government regulations. Finally, computer science classes are also beneficial, since much research and professional communication is done today using this technology.

Postsecondary Training

The next step on your educational path to becoming a toxicologist is to receive a bachelor's degree from an accredited college or university. Most students pursuing this career earn a degree in a science-related field, such as biology or chemistry. College course work for this field usually includes classes in chemistry, biology, physics, statistics, and calculus. English courses continue to be helpful, providing you with the opportunity to develop your research and writing skills.

An additional way to gain skills and test your interest in the field is through summer work in research laboratories. The Society of Toxicology provides information on summer internship programs. Although you can enter the profession at this point, there are an extremely limited number of jobs for people holding only a bachelor's degree and advancement is quite difficult.

Most students, after receiving a bachelor's degree, choose to go into graduate programs, either for a master's or a doctoral degree. Again, professional advancement with only a master's degree is extremely difficult. Most students either complete a doctoral (Ph.D.) program in toxicology or receive a Ph.D. in a related field, such as molecular biology, and then complete postdoctoral training in toxicology. This second method is the educational route that Linda took. Studies at the graduate level vary, depending on whether the student is receiving a doctorate in toxicology or a doctorate in a related field and then postdoctoral training in toxicology. Courses at this level, though, generally include pathology, biochemistry, epidemiology, molecular biology, and environmental toxicology. Doctoral degrees usually take four to five years to complete, and postdoctoral training usually takes two to three years.

CERTIFICATION OR LICENSING

Licensing is not required for this position. Certification is also not required, but it is recommended. Certification programs are available through the Academy of Toxicological Sciences and the American Board of Toxicology. The Academy of Toxicological Science bases its certification on the applicant's credentials, including published papers, research, and activities in the field of toxicology.

The American Board of Toxicology bases its certification on a 300-question examination. "The American Board of Toxicology exam offers a certification opportunity for industrial toxicologists who do not have as many opportunities to publish research papers as those employed by the government or by colleges and universities," says Jim. Toxicologists may apply to take this examination after practicing in the field for three to seven years.

SCHOLARSHIPS AND GRANTS

A number of federal agencies, including the National Institute of Environmental Health Sciences, the National Science Foundation, the Environmental Protection Agency, and the Armed Forces provide financial support to students pursuing graduate toxicology degrees. Ask your guidance counselors for information or contact the organizations listed under "How Do I Learn More?" at the end of this article.

Who Will Hire Me?

Toxicologists work in industry (particularly for chemical and pharmaceutical companies), in government agencies, and in academia. Unlikely as it seems, Jim's first experience with toxicology occurred on a golf course. "I was studying science in college but didn't know what I wanted to do with it," he recalls. "By chance, I ended up in a golf foursome with a man who worked for Upjohn as a toxicologist. He told me about his job and said that toxicology was a great field for someone who wanted to do exciting things with science. Twenty years later I ended up at Upjohn in a very similar position to his."

Throughout his career, Jim has been involved in performing toxicological research for industry, and he is in good company. Approximately 37 percent of all toxicologists work for chemical, pharmaceutical, and related industries. Industrial toxicologist positions involve product development, product safety evaluation, and regulatory compliance.

The majority of toxicologists, 47 percent, are employed by academic institutions. Most of the academic opportunities are in schools of medicine and public health at major universities, though smaller institutions have recently begun hiring toxicologists to teach toxicology within basic biology, chemistry, and engineering programs.

Another 13 percent of toxicologists are employed by the government. Though these positions have historically been limited to federal regulatory agencies, many states are now beginning to employ toxicologists as well. A growing number of toxicologists are also working as consultants or joining research foundations to conduct research on specific problems of industrial or public concern.

> **FYI**
>
> In 1984 one of the worst chemical industrial disasters in history occurred in Bhopal, India, when a pesticide factory leaked toxic gas, killing at least 4,000 people. In order to protect U.S. residents from such a chemical disaster, Congress passed the Emergency Planning and Community Right-to-Know Act in 1986 requiring industries to immediately report to local and state agencies the release of hazardous substances.

Where Can I Go from Here?

Toxicologists who have organizational and administrative skills as well as excellent scientific credentials, like Jim and Linda, will find many opportunities for advancement in their careers. For example, toxicologists who work for private industry may be promoted to head a research unit. As highly visible and influential members of the corporate organization, they may also be asked to join the executive management team. Toxicologists in colleges or universities may advance by being promoted to full professor and asked to head a department.

Managerial advancement, however, can have drawbacks for toxicologists who enjoy the challenges and rewards of research. Although those with managerial responsibilities usually receive higher pay, they also have administrative and budgeting responsibilities that can detract from the time one is able to devote to research.

What Are the Salary Ranges?

According to the Society of Toxicology, toxicologists with doctoral degrees earn starting salaries of $45,000 to $65,000. In general, positions in industry pay slightly better than positions in government or academia. Mid-range professionals with a Ph.D. and 10 years of experience can expect to earn $65,000 to $100,000 annually. Most executive positions in toxicology pay more than $100,000 per year, and some corporate executive toxicologists earn $200,000 or more. A toxicologist with a bachelor's degree typically receives a starting salary of $30,000. Those who have master's degrees can expect to begin at $35,000 to $40,000.

What Is the Job Outlook?

According to the Society of Toxicology, the demand for toxicologists has never been greater. In industry, agriculture, and health care, the world is becoming increasingly dependent on pharmaceuticals and chemicals to sustain its ever-increasing population. As the use of chemicals increases, so does the need for toxicologists who can develop, test, and regulate these substances.

Job opportunities for toxicologists should be most plentiful in large urban areas, near large hospitals, chemical manufacturers, and universities. Toxicologists with the most education, training, and experience will receive the best positions. Toxicologists with only a bachelor's degree may have difficulty finding a position. Those who have only a master's degree may find positions as laboratory researchers, but their chances for advancement are minimal. Those with a Ph.D. will fare best in the job market.

How Do I Learn More?

PROFESSIONAL ORGANIZATIONS

The following are organizations that provide information on toxicology careers:

American Board of Toxicology
PO Box 30054
Raleigh, NC 27622
919-841-5022
abtox@mindspring.com
http://www.abtox.org

American College of Toxicology
9650 Rockville Pike
Bethesda, MD 20814
301-634-7840
ekagan@actox.org
http://www.actox.org

National Science Foundation
4201 Wilson Boulevard
Arlington, VA 22230
703-292-5111
http://www.nsf.gov

Society of Toxicology
1821 Michael Faraday Drive, Suite 300
Reston, VA 20190
703-438-3115
http://www.toxicology.org

BIBLIOGRAPHY

The following is a sampling of materials relating to the professional concerns and development of toxicologists.

Derelanko, Michael J. *Toxicologist's Pocket Handbook*. Boca Raton, Fla.: CRC Press, 2000.

Goldfrank, Lewis R. *Goldfrank's Toxicologic Emergencies*. 7th ed. New York: McGraw-Hill, 2002.

Hayes, A. Wallace, ed. *Principles and Methods of Toxicology.* 4th ed. Philadelphia: Taylor & Francis, 2001.

Hodgson, Ernest, and Robert C. Smart. *Introduction to Biochemical Toxicology.* 3d ed. New York: John Wiley & Sons, 2001.

Massaro, Edward J. *Handbook of Human Toxicology.* Boca Raton, Fla.: CRC Press, 1997.

Olson, Kent R. *Poisoning & Drug Overdose.* 4th ed. New York: McGraw-Hill, 2003.

Timbrell, John A. *Introduction to Toxicology.* 3d ed. Philadelphia: Taylor & Francis, 2001.

Trestrail, John H. *Criminal Poisoning: Investigational Guide for Law Enforcement, Toxicologists, Forensic Scientists and Attorneys.* Totowa, N.J.: Humana Press, 2000.

TRANSPLANT COORDINATORS

The beeper goes off, waking Julie Petro, a transplant coordinator at a local hospital. She calls the organ procurement organization (OPO) where she works and learns of the death of a potential organ donor. The OPO gets over 100 calls a day. Every death in the state is called in and then evaluated for the possibility of organ transplant. In this case, a heart, lung, and kidneys may save the lives of some very sick people in the state or somewhere else in the country.

On her way to the hospital Julie prepares herself emotionally to meet with the parents of the young man who has just died. Though she recognizes the importance of procuring the organs, she also feels that the parents must be comfortable with whatever decision they come to. Not only will she talk to them about organ donation, but she will also stay with them, as long as needed, to help them through the difficult time.

Definition
Transplant coordinators plan transplant services, solicit organ donors, and assist medical staff in organ retrieval and transplantation.

High School Subjects
Biology
Psychology

Personal Skills
Helping/teaching
Technical/scientific

Salary Range
\$30,000 to \$51,020 to \$70,000

Educational Requirements
Bachelor's or associate's degree

Certification or Licensing
Voluntary

Outlook
Faster than the average

DOT
N/A

GOE
14.07.01

NOC
N/A

O*NET-SOC
N/A

What Does a Transplant Coordinator Do?

There are more than 75,000 people across the country waiting for an organ transplant. They may be waiting for a new heart, lung, liver, kidney, intestine, or pancreas. Tissues, such as corneas, heart valves, and skin, and bone can be donated as well.

In transplant centers (medical facilities where transplants are planned and performed), a number of professionals see to the needs of transplant recipients and the families of organ donors. A transplant center may be staffed by surgeons, nurses, operating room technicians, social workers, pathologists, psychologists, and transplant coordinators. A *transplant coordinator* is involved in practically every aspect of organ procurement (getting the organ from the donor) and transplantation; this involves working with medical records, scheduling surgeries, educating potential organ recipients, counseling donor families, and monitoring recipients' follow-up care.

Transplant centers have individual programs for specific organs. Many of them have programs for kidney transplants, heart transplants, and pancreas transplants. In addition to the centers, there are separate organizations such as organ procurement organizations and tissue typing laboratories that deal with specific aspects of organ transplantation. Organ procurement organizations, or OPOs, focus on procuring the organ from a donor. The OPOs were developed to serve as links between transplant centers and hospitals.

There are two types of transplant coordinators: procurement coordinators and clinical coordinators. *Procurement coordinators* help the families of organ donors deal with the death of a loved one as well as inform them of the organ donation process. *Clinical coordinators* educate recipients on how to best prepare for organ transplant and how to manage their health after surgery. Many coordinators, especially clinical coordinators, are registered nurses, but you are not required to have a nursing degree to work as a coordinator. Some medical background is important, however. Many transplant coordinators have degrees in biology, physiology, accounting, psychology, business administration, or public health.

For organs to become available, the donor patient must be declared brain dead, which means there is no brain function, no brain stem reflexes, no spontaneous movements, and the patient is no longer breathing on his or her own. Once this determination has been made by the physician, the procurement coordinator approaches the donor's family about organ donation. If the family gives their consent, the coordinator then collects medical information and tissue samples for analysis. The coordinator also calls the United Network for Organ Sharing (UNOS), a membership organization that includes every transplant program, organ procurement organization, and tissue typing laboratory in the United States. UNOS keeps a waiting list of people eligible for a transplant. This list is based solely on medical criteria, and there is a series of checks and balances to ensure this. A recipient must also match the donor's blood type and physical size.

UNOS attempts to match the organ with a recipient within the OPO's region. When no local match can be made, the coordinator makes arrangements for the organ to be delivered to another state. In either case, the procurement coordinator schedules an operating room for the removal of the organs and coordinates the surgery.

Once the organs have been removed and transported, a clinical transplant coordinator takes over. The clinical transplant coordinator is involved in preparing the recipient for the new organ. He or she arranges for the patient to be evaluated by transplant surgeons and arranges for tests and procedures, such as blood tests and stress tests. The coordinator also educates the patient about the transplant surgery, what to expect during the surgery and recovery process, and how to manage the lifetime regimen of medications. All of this preparation takes place before the patient is placed on the waiting list. Additional testing may be required periodically throughout the waiting period.

It is the clinical coordinator's job to see to the patient's needs before, during, and after the organ transplant. This involves admitting the patient, contacting the surgeon, arranging for an operating room, as well as contacting the anesthesiology department and the blood bank. After the transplant, the coordinator arranges outpatient housing, if necessary; reviews medication dosages and schedules; discusses side effects and signs of rejection or infection; and sets up a schedule of follow-up doctor's visits.

Another important aspect of the job of all transplant coordinators is educating the public about the importance of organ donation. Transplant coordinators speak to hospital and nursing school staffs and to the general public to encourage donation.

Lingo to Learn

Autotransplant A procedure in which an organ or tissue from one part of a patient's body is transplanted to another part of that patient's body.

Crossmatching A test of compatibility between the blood of a donor and prospective recipient.

Cyclosporine An immunosuppressant drug used to prevent the rejection of the transplanted organ.

Graft A transplanted tissue or organ.

Hepatic Pertaining to the liver.

Heterotransplants A procedure in which an organ or tissue from one species is transplanted into another species.

Homotransplants A procedure in which an organ or tissue is transplanted from one human to another.

Renal Pertaining to the kidney.

Tissue typing A blood test evaluating the match of tissues between the organ donor and the recipient.

What Is It Like to Be a Transplant Coordinator?

Julie Petro and Kathleen Ruping work for two different kinds of transplant centers. Julie is a procurement coordinator in Philadelphia and Kathleen is a clinical coordinator in Orlando.

Although Julie spends time at her desk with paperwork and writing letters to donor's families, she says, "Most of my time is not spent in the office; most of my time is spent in hospitals for procurement, or giving lectures." These lectures are to promote donor awareness among physicians, hospital administrators, and nurses.

Julie emphasizes the importance of counseling families of organ donors. She says, "People don't understand how much of this job has to do with the families. Half of our training is in bereavement issues. We're trying to help families, too, not just trying to help people get organs." Sometimes this involves staying in touch with the family long after the death of the organ donor, and she remains available to answer the family's questions. She never reveals the actual names of the organ recipients, but she does keep the donor families updated as to the recipients' health and progress, if they want to know.

After first talking to the family about donation and receiving the family's consent, Julie coordinates the organ donation. The patient, after being determined brain dead, stays on the ventilator so that blood and oxygen is still delivered to the organs. "I order the medications," Julie says, "the fluids, and all the tests necessary to determine if the organs can be transplanted." She then contacts UNOS for a list of patients in need of organs who match the donor's blood type and other requirements. If matches are found in the local area, Julie calls the physicians of the recipient patients to offer them the organs. She then contacts the surgeons.

"Once I've placed all the organs," Julie says, "I set up operating room times and take the patient there." Sometimes there are five or six surgeons in the operating room at the same time, one for each donated organ. "I'm in charge of the OR [operating room] . . . and of making sure they all do what they're supposed to do. I act as a liaison between the donor's family and the organ recipient. I make sure everything's done ethically and arrange for optimal organ care."

> I act as a liaison between the donor's family and the organ recipient. I make sure everything's done ethically and arrange for optimal organ care.

After surgery, a technician who specializes in organ restoration packages the organ. Sometimes an organ is placed on a commercial airline; the life of a kidney is 24 to 48 hours outside a patient's body but a heart should be transplanted within 4 hours. Julie also responds to calls from OPOs across the country; if a patient in her area is to receive an organ from another state, Julie will schedule a jet and, with a surgeon, fly out to get the organ.

Kathleen Ruping works with the recipients of organs, preparing them for transplant surgery. She evaluates blood work and visits patients. She offers support and teaches patients how the transplant process works and how to care for themselves post-transplant. She also promotes donor awareness. "Transplants save lives," she says. "We need more donors."

Kathleen usually arrives at the Translife clinic at 7:00 A.M. She starts her day by typing up blood labels for patients before the clinic opens at 8:00 A.M. "We have anywhere from two to 20 patients each day," she says. She draws blood from the patient, reviews medications, and discusses any problems that the patient may have. She then sends the blood to the lab.

At 9:30 A.M., Kathleen completes the lab work. She puts the completed work in charts for the physicians and then goes with the physician to visit the patients. By noon the clinic is closed and Kathleen returns to her desk to do paperwork. At this time she may interview new patients to see if they fit transplant criteria.

There are two different settings for Kathleen's work: the office and the hospital. "In the office," she says, "I'm evaluating patients, and I'm responsible for getting a patient to see a physician. Any testing is done through us." It is in the hospital where she does the physical evaluation of patients. "And if they have a new transplant," she says, "I teach them how to care for themselves."

Kathleen works more regular hours than Julie. Kathleen has a schedule of Monday through Friday, 7:00 to 3:30, and is on call every fifth weekend. Julie may work 50 to 70 hours a week.

Do I Have What It Takes to Be a Transplant Coordinator?

A transplant coordinator must pay close attention to many different details at once. Coordinators must be well-organized and efficient and also able to work quickly. The work isn't just careful planning and scheduling. Because coordinators work with families suffering the loss of a loved one or with sick patients needing an organ transplant, they must be caring and compassionate.

"You should be very detail-oriented," Julie Petro says, "but relaxed. You can't be stressed about everything. You're dealing with people's lives, so there's no room for mistakes." It's also important to maintain perspective. "If you're not dedicated to saving people's lives through transplant," she says, "you'll lose sight of what you're doing and why you're working so hard."

It's easy for Julie to keep a good perspective because she knows she's saving people's lives and helping families through difficult times. "I've been known to sit and talk with a family of a donor for six to seven hours to help them through things," she says. But this time commitment can also be frustrating. "You can be out all night, sleep for six hours, then your beeper goes off and you have to go back to work." This makes for a certain amount of unpredictability; Julie doesn't always know where she'll be going from day to day. "But it's nice to go to several different hospitals. You meet lots of people . . . CEOs, nurses, physicians."

A transplant coordinator must also be prepared to deal with death on a daily basis. "Every death in the area must be called into us," says Julie, "then we determine suitability. We may get a hundred calls a day."

Both Julie and Kathleen stress the importance of standing their ground with physicians. A procurement coordinator must make sure that orders are taken by the physicians, who may have gone on to deal with their living patients. "They stop focusing on the donor patient," Julie says, though many things must be done to keep the organs working until surgery.

Kathleen Ruping also must make demands for her patients who are to receive the organs. "I'm not afraid to get yelled at by doctors at two or three in the morning," she says. "I stand up for my patients. The best care is my concern." But the stresses of the job are made easier by the people she works with. "There are always other coordinators available," she says, "so I can bounce ideas off them."

Kathleen emphasizes the importance of good organization skills as well as compassion and intelligence. "I learn new things every day," she says. "I'm always amazed at what the body can do."

To Be a Successful Transplant Coordinator, You Should . . .

- be able to pay close attention to details
- have good communication skills
- be well-organized and efficient
- have a compassionate personality
- be able to work quickly and accurately
- be a persuasive speaker

How Do I Become a Transplant Coordinator?

Transplant coordinators come from a variety of backgrounds, though a medical background is most beneficial. Julie Petro received a bachelor's degree in nursing from the University of Delaware. She became familiar with transplants while working for four years in a children's hospital; she then worked for a year in Switzerland, helping a pediatric surgeon set up a hospital. Kathleen Ruping received her diploma in nursing from the Albany Medical Center, a teaching hospital. Neither Julie nor Kathleen is certified, but both plan to take the test in the coming months.

EDUCATION

High School

The courses that prepare you for a medical-based education are the most valuable. Science courses such as biology and chemistry are important, as are courses in psychology and sociology. You should also take math courses and courses in health and physical education.

If you live near a transplant center, there may be volunteer opportunities available at the center or in an outpatient care home for transplant recipients. Your local Red Cross may also need volunteers for promoting donor awareness.

Postsecondary Training

There is no specific educational track for transplant coordinators. One transplant coordinator may focus on financing and insurance, while another on education and

In-depth

History

Scientists have been researching human and animal organ transplantation since the 18th century. A technique for grafting human tissues was developed in 1875 by Jacques Reverdin, a Swiss surgeon. In 1905 Alexis Carrel, a French surgeon, developed a way to connect blood vessels that allowed a transplanted organ to function. That year also marked the first successful corneal transplant.

Greater research led to refinements in transplant technology and in 1954 the first successful human kidney transplant occurred in Boston.

The 1960s brought many successes in the field of organ transplants, including successful human liver and pancreas transplants. A headline-grabbing transplant occurred in 1967, when Dr. Christiaan Barnard, a South African surgeon, performed the world's first successful heart transplant in Cape Town, South Africa. His achievement became known throughout the world.

Despite these successes, many transplants eventually failed because of the body's immune system—its natural defense against foreign objects. The body of the organ recipient would eventually reject the new organ as a foreign object. This was especially true of transplants that involved complex tissues, such as hearts and kidneys. Early attempts at overriding the body's immune system, including high doses of radiation, had limited success.

Drugs that were designed to help the body accept transplanted organs were beginning to be developed in the 1960s. It was not until the early 1980s, however, with the introduction of cyclosporin, that a truly effective immunosuppressant drug was available. The new drug substantially improved the success rate of transplant surgeries. Also increasing the success rate was more precise tissue typing, or matching of donor and recipient tissues.

Though successful organ transplants have increased, some transplants still fail over time, despite modern drug treatments and closer matches of tissue. Research in this area continues to be done with the hope of continually increasing the rate of successful transplants.

awareness. Another coordinator may perform physical tests and evaluations, while another counsels grieving families. The more experience and education with health care and medicine you have, the better your job opportunities. Though a nursing degree isn't required of all coordinators, it does give you a good medical background. A bachelor's degree in one of the sciences, along with experience in a medical setting, will also open up job opportunities for you. Some people working as coordinators also have master's degrees in public health, or in business administration, and other coordinators hold doctorates in psychology or social work.

CERTIFICATION OR LICENSING

Certification, though not required, is available through the American Board of Transplant Coordinators. To qualify for certification an applicant must have already completed a year of full-time work as a coordinator.

There are two separate tests given: one for clinical transplant coordinators and one for procurement transplant coordinators. The test covers all organs and contains questions about analysis, treatment, and education of patients.

Who Will Hire Me?

A number of different institutions and organizations require transplant coordinators. In addition to the 261 transplant centers across the country, there are more than 50 independent organ procurement organizations and more than 50 independent tissue typing labs. These organizations and centers may be hospital-based, independent, or university-based.

Positions for transplant coordinators are advertised nationally in medical publications and on the Internet. The North American Transplant Coordinators Organization (NATCO) also offers job referral information.

Where Can I Go from Here?

Kathleen Ruping is very happy in her current position, though she would like to become more involved in the transplantation of organs other than kidneys. Julie Petro would be interested in moving into a clinical coordinator position. "Being on call is a little easier to deal with," she says. However, within the OPO where she works there is an internal clinical ladder. She could eventually move up into a senior coordinator position, which would involve less on-call duties and more internal education and mentoring. There are also different manager positions and positions that focus entirely on education.

A coordinator may also head committees and special programs within a transplant center or professional organization. Some may also pursue degrees while working as a coordinator, either to help them in their work or to move into another aspect of transplantation, such as surgery or hospital administration.

What Are the Salary Ranges?

Your educational background, experience, and responsibilities as a coordinator will determine your salary. Someone with a doctorate may be responsible for directing and developing a program. Someone with a master's degree may handle records or coordinate education and public awareness programs within the transplant center or may work as an instructor. These people may have a higher salary than those working at the clinical end.

Most transplant coordinators are registered nurses and according to the *Occupational Outlook Handbook,* the median annual salary for RNs is about $51,020. Nurse practitioners can earn $70,000 or more. Nurses working on the east and west coasts make more money than those in the Midwest. Social workers earned an average of about $40,000 in 2003. Though transplant centers and organ procurement agencies are nonprofit organizations, transplant coordinators receive very good health and retirement benefits.

> **FYI**
>
> There are 25 different organs and tissues in the human body that can be transplanted. Organs that can be donated after death include the heart, liver, kidneys, pancreas, lungs, bowel, and stomach. Living donors can also provide a kidney or part of a liver. Tissues that can be donated include corneas, sclera (white of the eye), middle ear, heart valves, veins, tendons, bones, skin, islet cells from the pancreas, and bone marrow.

What Is the Job Outlook?

The medical community must become even more dedicated to finding organ donors. The UNOS national patient waiting list contains thousands of people who have been evaluated and determined to be ready recipients for new organs. In 2004, UNOS reports that there were 27,025 transplant operations in the United States. As of April 2005, there were still 87,847 transplant candidates on the UNOS waiting list. As these numbers increase, so should the need for transplant coordinators.

Because there is still a shortage of donors, a number of organizations have been developed to promote organ donation, particularly among minorities. These education and public awareness programs are often run by transplant coordinators. It is hoped that more public awareness will have a significant effect on the number of donors and the number of lives saved each year through transplants.

Because the stress level can run high, transplant coordinators have a high burnout rate. Also, for a procurement coordinator, the hours can be long and irregular. On the average, procurement coordinators move on to other positions after only 18 months. This means continued job opportunities for those looking to work as coordinators.

How Do I Learn More?

PROFESSIONAL ORGANIZATIONS

The following are organizations that provide information on a career as a transplant coordinator and the certification process:

American Board of Transplant Coordinators
PO Box 15384
Lenexa, KS 66285
913-599-0198
http://www.abtc.net

North American Transplant Coordinators Organization
PO Box 15384
Lenexa, KS 66285
913-492-3600
http://www.natco1.org

The following organization provides information about organ donation and transplant operations:

United Network for Organ Sharing
PO Box 2484
Richmond, VA 23218
804-782-4800
http://www.unos.org

BIBLIOGRAPHY

The following is a sampling of materials relating to the professional concerns and development of transplant coordinators:

Caplan, Arthur L. and Daniel H. Coelho. *The Ethics of Organ Transplants: The Current Debate.* Amherst, N.Y.: Prometheus Books, 1999.

Ginns, Leo C., A. Benedict Cosimi, and Peter J. Morris, eds. *Transplantation.* Boston: Blackwell Science, Inc., 1999.

Nather, Aziz. *Advances in Tissue Banking: The Scientific Basis of Tissue Transplantation.* River Edge, N.J.: World Scientific Publishing Company, 2001.

Parr, Elizabeth, and Janet Mize. *Coping with an Organ Transplant: A Practical Guide to Understanding, Preparing for, and Living with an Organ Transplant.* New York: Penguin Putnam, 2001.

UROLOGISTS

Definition
A urologist is a physician who treats diseases of the genitourinary organs.

High School Subjects
Biology
Chemistry

Personal Skills
Helping/teaching
Technical/scientific

Salary Range
$160,000 to $285,356 to $375,000+

Educational Requirements
Medical degree

Certification or Licensing
Required by all states

Outlook
About as fast as the average

DOT
070

GOE
14.02.01

NOC
3111

O*NET-SOC
29-1069.99

"Everybody ready?" the urologist asks the members of his surgical team. He walks over and looks down at the patient, whose tiny body is lying on the operating table. She is turned on her side to give the surgeon access to her kidneys, which are growing outside her body.

Her name is Heidi Lynn and she's three days old. The urologist is about to move her kidneys back inside her body where they belong. He glances over his shoulder at the room where Heidi Lynn's parents watch anxiously. "Okay, Heidi girl, let's do it."

Several hours later, the parents look in on their daughter. Sutures line her delicate, pink skin where it's not covered by bandages, and tubes seem to spring from all over her tiny body. But her parents are smiling as they hold onto each other.

What Does a Urologist Do?

Urologists treat medical and surgical disorders of the adrenal gland and of the genitourinary system. They deal with diseases of both the male and female urinary tract and of the male reproductive organs.

Technically, urology is a surgical subspecialty, but because of the broad range of clinical problems they treat, urologists also have a working knowledge of internal medicine, pediatrics, gynecology, and other specialties.

Common medical disorders that urologists routinely treat include prostate cancer, testicular cancer, bladder cancer, stone disease, urinary tract infections, urinary incontinence, and impotence. Other, less common, disorders include kidney cancer, renal (kidney) disease, male infertility, genitourinary trauma, and sexually transmitted diseases (including AIDS).

The management and treatment of malignant diseases constitute much of the urologist's practice. Prostate cancer is the most common cancer in men and the second leading cause of cancer deaths in men. If detected early, prostate cancer is treatable, but once it has spread beyond the prostate, it is difficult to treat successfully.

Testicular cancer is the leading cause of cancer in young men between the ages of 15 and 34. Major advances in the treatment of this cancer, involving both surgery and chemotherapy, now make it the most curable of all cancers. Bladder cancer occurs most frequently in men age 70 and older, and treatment for it also has a high success rate.

Young and middle-aged adults are primarily affected by stone diseases, which represent the third leading cause of hospitalizations in the United States. Kidney stones, composed of a combination of calcium and either oxalate or phosphate, usually pass through the body with urine. Larger stones, however, can block the flow of urine or irritate the lining of the urinary system as they pass. What has become standard treatment today is called extracorporeal shock wave lithotripsy (ESWL). In ESWL, high-energy shock waves are used to pulverize the stones into small fragments that are carried from the body in the urine. This procedure has replaced invasive, open surgery as the preferred treatment for stone disease.

Lingo to Learn

Bladder A membranous sac that serves as a receptacle for fluid or gas, often used to describe the urinary bladder in humans.

Endoscope An instrument used to examine the interior of a hollow structure, such as the bladder.

Extracorporeal shock wave lithotripsy (ESWL) High-energy shock waves that pulverize kidney stones into small fragments so they can easily pass through the urinary system.

Kidneys A pair of organs that filter the blood, excreting the waste products of body metabolism in the form of urine.

Percutaneous Performed through the skin, such as the removal of tissues for a biopsy.

Ureter A duct that carries urine away from the kidney to the bladder.

Urologists also consult on spina bifida cases in children and multiple sclerosis cases in adults, as these diseases involve neuromuscular dysfunctions that affect the kidneys, bladder, and genitourinary system.

The scope of urology has broadened so much that the following are now considered subspecialties: pediatric urology, urologic oncology, and female urology.

What Is It Like to Be a Urologist?

"As a urologist, you're involved with people, instead of staying in a lab all the time," says Dr. William Kennedy. Dr. Kennedy, who happens to be a talented chef as well as a urologist, originally intended to go to cooking school. As he tells it, however, he was destined for other things. "My parents convinced me to go to college, which I didn't want to do. I ended up enjoying school, especially the science courses. At the end of college, I knew I wanted to do something fulfilling, and helping people regain their health was a good way to accomplish that."

William, a urologist and assistant professor at Lucile Packard Children's Hospital in Stanford, California, says he chose urology for a very specific reason. "I wanted a specialty where I could enjoy the continuity of care for all of my patients—from surgery to follow-up care and, in some cases, long-term postoperative care. And I liked the fact that I could be working with both adults and children, in both medicine and surgery."

One of the reasons medicine may have been in the back of his mind all along has to do with his brother. "He had a Ewing sarcoma, a tumor of the leg," explains William. "He was a patient for 10 years at Sloan-Kettering. I know my exposure to the doctors there had something to do with why I'm now in medicine. I saw the science being brought to the patient's bedside, and it was exciting and inspiring."

He describes his work in pediatric urology as covering a range of problems of the kidney, bladder, and the genitourinary system. "Pediatric urology deals with everything from simple infections to complicated cancers and reconstruction," explains William. "We treat cancer with medications or radiation, or we remove it."

"Reconstructive cases involve rebuilding. Children are often born with congenital abnormalities; their bladders are exposed to the outside skin, or there are blockages in the renal collecting system—the kidney's plumbing, so to speak."

Children can also have kidney stones, and a pediatric urologist uses sound waves to break the stones up. This process is the same as the one performed on adults, but special care must be given to the child with kidney stones.

The typical pediatric exam consists of an abdominal exam and a kidney exam, in which the urologist is feeling for lumps or bumps in the abdomen, pain or pressure when pressing on the bladder.

In treating children, urologists want to minimize radiation exposure, so they use more ultrasound than X rays in diagnostic procedures and treatments.

Do I Have What It Takes to Be a Urologist?

Urologists should like working with people and have a strong interest in promoting good health through preventive measures such as diet and exercise. "Medicine is 50 percent science and 50 percent people," says William. "You have to maintain an active interest in the things people do. It helps you relate."

> You have to maintain an active interest in the things people do. It helps you relate.

The urologist diagnoses and treats conditions of a very personal nature. Many patients are uncomfortable talking about problems relating to their kidneys, bladder, or genitourinary system. The urologist must show compassion and sensitivity to dispel the patient's fears and put him or her at ease.

Excellent communication skills are essential to patient-physician encounters. Urologists should be able to clearly articulate both the patient's problem and the recommended forms of treatment, including all of the options and their attendant risks and advantages.

Because of their frequent consultations with other physicians, urologists need to develop good working relationships with other medical specialists.

Urologists, like all surgeons, should be in good physical condition; they must remain steady and focused while standing for hours on their feet. Urologists who work in hospital trauma units should be prepared for the frenetic pace and tension of split-second decision making.

How Do I Become a Urologist?

EDUCATION

High School

If you are interested in becoming a urologist, take courses in biology, chemistry, physics, and mathematics. Courses in computer science are also recommended. Since colleges and medical schools are looking for individuals with well-rounded backgrounds, you should also take English, foreign languages, and history. Many colleges and universities that have medical schools offer special programs to high school seniors planning to attend medical school.

To Be a Successful Urologist, You Should . . .

- have good hand-eye coordination and manual dexterity
- be a good clinician
- be able to put patients at ease and comfortably discuss intimate areas of health
- enjoy helping and working with people
- be able to listen and communicate well

Postsecondary Training

In order to become a urologist, you must first graduate from an accredited four-year college or university. College courses that prepare students for medical school include math, biology, chemistry, anatomy, and physics, as well as courses in the humanities.

After receiving an undergraduate degree, you must then be accepted by one of the 141 medical schools in the United States. Most premed students apply to several schools early in their senior year of college. Admission is competitive; only about one-third of the applicants are accepted. Applicants must undergo a fairly extensive admissions process that considers grade point averages, scores on the Medical College Admission Test, and recommendations from professors.

In order to earn an M.D. degree, you must complete four years of medical school. For the first two years, you attend lectures and classes and spend time in laboratories.

Courses include anatomy, biochemistry, physiology, pharmacology, psychology, microbiology, pathology, and medical ethics. You learn to take patient histories and perform routine physical examinations.

In the third and fourth years, you work in clinics and hospitals. You go through what are known as rotations, or brief periods of study in a particular area, such as internal medicine, obstetrics and gynecology, pediatrics, dermatology, psychiatry, or surgery.

Rotations allow you to gain exposure to the many different fields of medicine and to learn first-hand the skills of diagnosing and treating patients. In fact, many physicians credit the rotation program for helping them choose their area or specialty. "I know I would never have thought about urology if not for the rotations. I really enjoyed my rotation in urology," William says.

Upon graduating from an accredited medical school, you must pass a standard examination given by the National Board of Medical Examiners. Physicians then complete an internship, usually one year in length, which helps graduates decide on an area of specialization.

Following the internship, physicians begin what is known as a residency. The surgical specialty of urology requires a five- or six-year residency in urology, of which the first two years are typically spent in general surgery, followed by three to four years of urology in an approved residency program.

Many urologic residency training programs are six years in length, with the final year spent in either research or additional clinical training, depending on the orientation of the program and the resident's focus. The residency years, without a doubt, are filled with stress, pressure, and physical labor. Residents often work 24-hour shifts, easily clocking in 80 hours or more per week.

CERTIFICATION OR LICENSING

At an early point in the residency period, all students are required to pass a medical licensing examination administered by the board of medical examiners in their state. The length of the residency depends on the specialty you choose.

Certification requires the successful completion of a qualifying written examination, which must be taken within three years of completing the residency in urology. The subsequent certifying examination, which consists of pathology, uroradiology, and a standardized oral examination, must be taken within five years of the qualifying examination. Certification by the American Board of Urology is for a 10-year period, with recertification required after that time.

UROLOGY SUBSPECIALTIES

The following urological sub-specialties are recognized by the American Urological Association:

- Pediatric urology
- Urologic oncology (cancer)
- Renal transplantation
- Male infertility
- Calculi (urinary tract stones)
- Female urology (urinary incontinence and pelvic outlet relaxation disorders)
- Neurourology (voiding disorders, urodynamic evaluation of patients, and erectile dysfunction or impotence)

SCHOLARSHIPS AND GRANTS

Scholarships and grants are often available from individual institutions, state agencies, and special-interest organizations. Many students finance their medical education through the Armed Forces Health Professions Scholarship Program. Each branch of the military participates in this program, paying students' tuitions in exchange for military service. Contact your local recruiting office for more information on this program. The National Health Service Corps Scholarship Program (http://nhsc.bhpr.hrsa.gov) also provides money for students in return for service. Another source for financial aid, scholarship, and grant information is the Association of American Medical Colleges (http://www.aamc.org). Remember to request information early for eligibility, application requirements, and deadlines.

Who Will Hire Me?

The vast majority of urologists enter into clinical practice after completing their residency program. However, fellowships exist in various subspecialties, including pediatrics, infertility, sexual dysfunction, oncology, transplantation, and others.

Academic medicine also offers opportunities. The American Urological Association (AUA) is fostering the development of AUA scholars, hoping to encourage residents to enter academic medicine.

What Are the Salary Ranges?

According to the Web site PhysiciansSearch.com, urologists earned annual average salaries of $285,356 in 2002. Salaries ranged from less than $180,000 to more than $375,000. The U.S. Department of Labor reports that general internists had average annual earnings of $160,000 in 2003. Factors that influence annual income include size and type of practice, hours worked per week, professional reputation of the individual, and the geographic location.

FYI

Bladder cancer is the fourth most common form of cancer in men and the ninth most common in women. Each year, there are more than 50,000 new cases of bladder cancer, accounting for 7 percent of all new cancers found in men and 2 percent in women. Nearly 10,000 Americans die each year of bladder cancer.

What Is the Job Outlook?

Employment prospects for physicians are expected to grow at an average rate over the next 10 years, according to the *Occupational Outlook Handbook.* There will probably be more jobs for primary care physicians such as general and family practitioners, general pediatricians, and internists, but a substantial number of jobs for specialists should be created in response to patient demand for specialty care. With the increasing population of the elderly, the need for qualified urologists will continue to be strong.

Unlike their predecessors, newly trained physicians face radically different choices of where and how to practice. New physicians are much less likely to enter solo practice and more likely to take salaried jobs in group medical practices, clinics, and health care networks.

How Do I Learn More?

PROFESSIONAL ORGANIZATIONS

The following are organizations that provide information on the career of urologist:

American Board of Urology
2216 Ivy Road, Suite 210
Charlottesville, VA 22903
804-979-0059
http://www.abu.org

American Medical Association
515 North State Street
Chicago, IL 60610
312-464-5000
http://www.ama-assn.org

American Urological Association Inc.
1000 Corporate Boulevard
Linthicum, MD 21090
866-746-4282
http://www.auanet.org

BIBLIOGRAPHY

The following is a sampling of materials relating to the professional concerns and development of urologists:

Blandy, John P. *Lecture Notes on Urology.* 5th ed. Boston: Blackwell Science, Inc., 1998.

Hanno, Philip M., Alan J. Wein, and S. Bruce Malcowicz. *Clinical Manual of Urology.* 3d ed. New York: McGraw-Hill, 2001

Murphy, William M. *Urological Pathology.* 2d ed. Philadelphia: W. B. Saunders, 1997.

Resnick Martin I., and Andrew C. Novick. *Urology Secrets.* 3d ed. Philadelphia: Williams & Wilkins, 2003.

Tanagho, Emil A., and Jack W. McAnich, eds. *Smith's General Urology.* 16th ed. New York: McGraw-Hill, 2003.

CHAPTER TITLES INDEXED BY THE *DICTIONARY OF OCCUPATIONAL TITLES (DOT)*

0/1: Professional, technical, and managerial occupations

CHAPTER TITLES INDEXED BY THE *GUIDE FOR OCCUPATIONAL EXPLORATION (GOE)*

CHAPTER TITLES INDEXED BY THE NATIONAL OCCUPATION CLASSIFICATION (NOC) SYSTEM

CHAPTER TITLES INDEXED BY OCCUPATIONAL INFORMATION NETWORK (O*NET)-STANDARD OCCUPATIONAL CLASSIFICATION (SOC) SYSTEM

JOB TITLE INDEX

Page numbers in **bold** indicate major treatment of a topic.

A

B

C

D

E

F

G

H

I

J

K

L

M

N

Q

R

S

T

U

V